READING PAUL WITH THE REFORMERS

Reading Paul with the Reformers

Reconciling Old and New Perspectives

Stephen J. Chester

WILLIAM B. EERDMANS PUBLISHING COMPANY

GRAND RAPIDS, MICHIGAN

Wm. B. Eerdmans Publishing Co.
2140 Oak Industrial Drive N.E., Grand Rapids, Michigan 49505
www.eerdmans.com

ISBN   978-0-8028-4836-9

26   25   24   23   22   21   20   19   18   17   3   4   5   6   7   8   9   10

Library of Congress Cataloging-in-Publication Data

Names: Chester, Stephen J., author.
Title: Reading Paul with the reformers : reconciling old and new perspectives /
    Stephen J. Chester.
Description: Grand Rapids : Eerdmans Publishing Co., 2017. |
    Includes bibliographical references and index.
Identifiers: LCCN 2017001984 | ISBN 9780802848369 (pbk. : alk. paper)
Subjects: LCSH: Bible. Epistles of Paul—Criticism, interpretation, etc.—
    History—16th century.
Classification: LCC BS2650.52 .C448 2017 | DDC 227/.0609—dc23
    LC record available at https://lccn.loc.gov/2017001984

To my parents, John and Ann Chester

Contents

Foreword

The last generation of Anglophone Pauline scholarship has suffered from a severe handicap. Several influential interpreters of Paul, although indebted to Protestant interpretation more than they realized, have rhetorically positioned themselves against "Lutheran" or "Reformation" exegesis of Paul on the basis of a paper-thin understanding of what they thought they opposed. In a discipline proud of its historical scholarship, this is a dispiriting phenomenon, and it has led to a swathe of misunderstandings, misinterpretations, and false antitheses. A counterblast from those committed to Reformation interpretations as the last word in Pauline exegesis has hardly helped, since it has reinforced the impression that one is either wholly "for" or wholly "against" Reformation readings of Paul, and that no third way, of receptive but critical dialogue, is either desirable or possible.

Up to this point, some Pauline scholars might have excused themselves by saying that one cannot know everything, and that the sheer volume of Reformation sources, not to mention the mountain of scholarship built upon them, was too great for any busy exegete to master. That excuse will hold no longer. In this remarkable book, the fruit of many years of reading and reflection, Stephen Chester has made a decisive intervention into Pauline scholarship that significantly alters the terrain. What is offered here is a well-informed but also accessible analysis of the Reformers' exegesis of Paul, carefully nuanced to indicate both what held them together in their break with medieval exegetical traditions and what distinguished them (specifically Luther, Melanchthon, and Calvin) from one another. More than that, as a Pauline exegete, Chester brings that wealth of knowledge into critical dialogue with the twists and turns of contemporary Pauline scholarship, shedding a flood of light in all directions. This is, in other words, an exemplary exercise in "reception history." By taking care properly to understand what the Reformers were trying to do, and through acute though not uncritical analysis of their achievements, Chester enables a dialogue between exegetes then and now, and between both bodies of exegesis and the original letters of Paul. In the process he reflects on what "reception" is about, and on the distinctive goals and methods of theological interpretation. The whole makes for a fascinating and compelling mix, from which readers of all kinds are bound to be hugely enriched.

The foundational layer of this book—to which students and scholars will return again and again—is the careful and finely nuanced reading of the Reformers themselves. With the impending five-hundredth anniversary, attention is everywhere focusing on what happened in the Reformation and why, but it is rare to find an analysis of Reformation interpretations of Paul (the exegetical heart of things) by a practicing exegete as deeply informed as Stephen Chester. After carefully setting out the common innovative "grammar" that structures their readings of Paul, Chester leads us through the exegesis of Luther, Melanchthon, and Calvin with a range, sympathy, clarity, depth, and theological understanding unparalleled in present-day scholarship. These chapters will go straight into the curriculum of required reading for any course on the history of interpretation of Paul. After they have read the primary texts themselves, students will find no better guide to these foundational interpreters of Paul, while seasoned interpreters will gain enormously from Chester's readings of the material and his engagement with contemporary scholarship. What he brings to the analysis is an eye trained to the task of exegesis, a dimension of the Reformers' work often overlooked by those who gravitate first to large theological themes. In the course of this analysis, Chester quietly but effectively banishes a range of common misunderstandings and misrepresentations. It here becomes clear that none of the Reformers understood a guilty conscience to be a prior requirement for conversion by grace; none of them took justification to involve a "fictional" righteousness; none understood this as a merely forensic imputation or an impersonal transfer. In none of them did human faith threaten or displace Christology, because in all of them (and especially in Luther and Calvin) justification by faith is effected only in and through union with Christ. Hours of futile disputes and reams of pages caricaturing the Reformers could have been avoided if Pauline scholars had known this material. From now on, if such caricatures persist, there will be a simple reply: "read Chester before you speak or write on this again."

At a second level, Chester skillfully brings his Reformation voices into dialogue with trends in Pauline scholarship post-Sanders, to hugely beneficial effect. The "New Perspective on Paul" is shown to be more dependent on the Reformers than it usually cares to admit, certain interpretative moves are found to be unnecessary intensifications of Reformation themes, and false antitheses (e.g., between justification by faith and participation in Christ) are shown to be easily avoided with the aid of the Reformers' exegesis. Chester is highly critical of some aspects of the Reformation tradition, especially its propensity to caricature Judaism, but he refuses a polarizing mentality, and finds much in Luther and Calvin that could help us through our current exegetical problems. In particular, his careful exposition of "union with Christ" as participation in a reality that remains in an important sense *external* to the believer is a significant contribution to current Pauline theology, and is just one example of how, by neglecting this seminal chapter in the history of interpretation, we have limited our resources and narrowed our options.

Chester is clear that the history of reception is a rich store of voices with which to converse on the interpretation of Paul, not an archive in which to find an ultimate, definitive reading. There are better and worse readings of Paul, some truer to the text and more historically plausible than others. But Chester makes clear in his opening chapter that there is no "holy grail" of a final, definitive interpretation, because any *interpretation* worthy of the name will be properly responsive to its own cultural and historical context—and that will keep changing for as long as Paul's letters are read. The Reformers were recontextualizing Paul for their own dramatic sixteenth-century situation, and who with any sympathy for literary interpretation, let alone theological hermeneutics, could fault them for doing so? Our contexts in the troubled and volatile years of the early twenty-first century are very different, and mere repetition of the Reformers will hardly meet all our current needs. But to neglect or disdain these gifts passed down by our hermeneutical forebears would be grossly irresponsible and willfully self-limiting. Chester here lays before us some of the most profound engagements with Paul ever undertaken, and we have cause to be truly grateful. His deep historical research will be honored and admired on all sides, and the rich materials he feeds back into the stream of theological interpretation will surely fertilize Pauline scholarship for many decades to come.

JOHN M. G. BARCLAY
Durham University
July 2016

Preface

This book has emerged over a long period. The very first work on it was undertaken in 2004 during a sabbatical from my faculty position at International Christian College, Glasgow. It is a source of much regret that the college itself no longer exists, but I am deeply grateful for my time there and for the colleagues with whom I first discussed the themes of the book, especially Marion Carson, Darrell Cosden, Derek Newton, and the late and much missed Ted Herbert. In 2006 I moved to North Park Theological Seminary, Chicago, and found a new home in which I have been supported and sustained by kind and generous colleagues and where it has been possible, alongside much else, to pursue this project to completion. I received a semester's sabbatical in 2011 (some of which was very happily spent at Tyndale House, Cambridge) and some further study time in 2013, which were crucial in allowing me to focus on research and writing for sustained periods. I owe particular thanks to my current and former colleagues at North Park in the biblical field (Jim Bruckner, Bob Hubbard, Paul Koptak, Max Lee, Jay Phelan, and especially Klyne Snodgrass) with whom at different times I have discussed the themes of this book and with whom I have shared in the work of teaching. Several teaching assistants at North Park have helped in different ways at various stages of the project, but special mention must go to Kyle Mecher, who has read and offered feedback on the final manuscript. If I succeed at all in communicating my argument clearly, it owes a great deal to Kyle's care and attention to detail.

I have presented papers using material from the book in several venues over the years and I am grateful to all those who asked questions and offered comments. In 2015 I had the opportunity to incorporate some of the main themes of this book into a class at North Park on the history of reception of Paul. I appreciate the engagement and insight of the students. I found particularly challenging working through Melanchthon's exegesis of Romans and reaching a clear perspective about the relationship between his characteristic positions and those of Luther. I would like to thank both Timothy Wengert and Olli-Pekka Vainio for their patience in answering my questions. I am similarly grateful to Jesse Couenhoven for his help in exploring Augustine's views on the nature of sin. The focus of research is also always sharpened by interaction with friends and colleagues and I am particularly grateful to John Barclay for several discussions of Luther and Calvin as interpreters of Paul. The stimulus provided to my research at several important points by John's own work on grace as a theme in Pauline theology will be apparent to readers. The chapter on Calvin was presented to the New Testament research seminar at the University of Durham and was strengthened as a result of the feedback received there. John Riches was a significant inspiration over many years and through his own writing and teaching stimulated my interest in the history of reception.

Michael Thomson at Eerdmans has believed in this project and good-naturedly encouraged me forwards even as it extended several years beyond our initial expectations. I am thankful for his patience. One of the main reasons for the lengthening timescale was that I became Academic Dean at North Park Theological Seminary at the start of 2012. The role brings many demands and it has remained enjoyable and sustainable because of the support of colleagues. I initially shared the Academic Dean's responsibilities with Brent Laytham and deeply valued this partnership with him. Later Dave Kersten became Dean of the Seminary and has now for several years been a continual source of wisdom and encouragement. Alex Macias and Deidre Robinson, who work in Seminary Academic Services, have shared in innumerable daily tasks. A highlight of each year at North Park is the *North Park Symposium on the Theological Interpretation of Scripture*, participation in which has done much to sharpen my own research questions. The event would not be possible without the work of Klyne Snodgrass and Guylla Brown. I have been blessed in my colleagues, both those named and the rest of the faculty and staff, and I would like to record my thanks to them all.

One of the convictions motivating the writing of this book is that attending to past interpreters can help us to interpret the Pauline texts for the mission of the church today. I have therefore always had ecclesial communities in my mind when writing, none more so than the two congregations to which I and my family have belonged during this research project. I am thankful for friendship and fellowship with all at Ruchazie Parish Church, Glasgow, and at Immanuel Evangelical Covenant Church, Chicago. Immanuel is a multi-ethnic congregation with many members who, like us, are immigrants to the United States. The life of the congregation has helped me to see as equally essential to the gospel both the overcoming in Christ of ethnic boundaries, creating a new family of God, and the only basis on which such a family can authentically exist, which is the incongruous grace of God in Christ that disregards all forms of human worthiness. My wife Betsy has borne with my working on this book for almost half the length of our marriage. I could not have completed it without her love and support or that of our sons, Iain and Mark. These years have seen them grow from childhood to adulthood and the privilege of being a parent through that process has prompted me to reflect how very much I owe to my own parents, John and Ann Chester, and to their care and guidance throughout my life. This book is dedicated to them with love.

Good Friday, 2016

Abbreviations

Unless otherwise stated, all other abbreviations follow *The SBL Handbook of Style: For Biblical Studies and Related Disciplines*, 2nd ed. (Atlanta: SBL Press, 2014).

Allen   *Opus Epistolarum Des. Erasmi Roterodami: Denuo Recognitum et Auctum*. Edited by Percy S. Allen. 12 vols. Oxford: Clarendon Press, 1906–1958.

ASD   *Opera Omnia Desiderii Erasmi Roterodami Recognita et Adnotatione Critica Instructa Notisque Illustrata*. Amsterdam: North Holland, 1969–.

CCSL   *Corpus Christianorum, Series Latina*. Turnhout: Brepols, 1953–.

CNTC   *Calvin's New Testament Commentaries*. Edited by David W. Torrance and Thomas F. Torrance. 12 vols. Grand Rapids: Eerdmans, 1959–1972.

CO   John Calvin. *Ioannis Calvini Opera Quae Supersunt Omnia*. Edited by Wilhelm Baum, Edward Cunitz, and Edward Reuss. 59 vols. Vols. 29–87 of the *Corpus Reformatorum*. Brunswick: C.A. Schwetschke and Sons, 1863–1900.

CR   Philip Melanchthon. *Philippi Melanthonis Opera Quae Supersunt Omnia*. Edited by Karl Bretschneider and Heinrich Bindseil. 28 vols. Vols. 1–28 of the *Corpus Reformatorum*. Halle: A. Schwetschke and Sons, 1834–1860.

CSEL   *Corpus Scriptorum Ecclesiasticorum Latinorum*. Vienna, 1866–.

CTS   Calvin Translation Society Edition of Calvin's Commentaries. 46 volumes. Edinburgh: Calvin Translation Society, 1843–1855.

CWE   *Collected Works of Erasmus*. Toronto: University of Toronto Press, 1974–.

HBW   *Heinrich Bullinger Werke: Dritte Abteilung: Theologische Schriften*. Zürich: Theologischer Verlag Zürich, 1983–.

Institutes   John Calvin. *Institutes of the Christian Religion*, 1559 edition. Translated by Ford L. Battles. Edited by John T. McNeill. 2 vols. Philadelphia: Westminster Press, 1960.

LB   Desiderius Erasmus. *Opera Omnia*. Edited by Jean Leclerc. 10 vols. Leiden: Brill, 1703–1706.

LW   *Luther's Works*. American Edition. 55 vols. original series; 9 vols. new series. St. Louis: Condordia, 1955–1986, 2010–.

MBWR/   *Melanchthons Briefwechsel: kritische und kommentierte*
MBWT   *Gesamtausgabe*. Edited by Heinz Scheible. Stuttgart-Bad Cannstatt: Frommann-Holzboog, 1977–. *R = Register* volumes; *T= Texte* volumes.

MSA   Philip Melanchthon. *Melanchthons Werke in Auswahl [Studiensausgabe]*. Edited by Robert Stupperich. 7 vols. Gütersloh: Gerd Mohn, 1951–1975.

OE   *Ioannis Calvini Opera Omnia*, Series II: *Opera Exegetica*. Edited by Helmut Feld. Geneva: Librairie Droz, 1992–.

PL   *Patrologiae Cursus Completus. Series Latina*. Edited by J. P. Migne. 221 vols. Paris: Petit-Montrouge, 1844–1864.

PLS   *Patrologiae Cursus Completus a J. P. Migne Editus. Series Latina. Supplementum*. Edited by Adalbert G. Hamman. 5 vols. Paris: Garnier, 1958–1974.

RCSNT   *Reformation Commentary on Scripture. New Testament*. Edited by Timothy F. George. Downers Grove: InterVarsity Press, 2011–.

SCG   Thomas Aquinas. *Summa contra Gentiles*. Translated and edited by Anton C. Pegis, James F. Anderson, Vernon J. Bourke, and Charles J. O'Neil. 4 vols. New York: Hanover House, 1955–1957.

ST   Thomas Aquinas. *Summa Theologiae*. Latin Text and English translation, introduction, notes, appendices, and glossaries. 60 vols. London: Eyre and Spottiswoode, 1962–1980.

WA   Martin Luther. *D. Martin Luthers Werke. Kritische Gesamtausgabe. Schriften*. 73 vols. Weimar: H. Böhlau, 1883–2009.

WA BR   Martin Luther. *D. Martin Luthers Werke. Kritische Gesamtausgabe. Briefwechsel.* 18 vols. Weimar: H. Böhlau, 1930–1985.

WA DB   Martin Luther. *D. Martin Luthers Werke. Kritische Gesamtausgabe. Die deutsche Bibel.* 15 vols. Weimar: H. Böhlau, 1906–1961.

WA TR   Martin Luther. *D. Martin Luthers Werke. Kritische Gesamtausgabe. Tischreden.* 6 vols. Weimar: H. Böhlau, 1912–1921.

Prologue

The argument of this book is straightforward: the Protestant Reformers of the sixteenth century have insights into the interpretation of the Pauline letters that can assist us as we attempt to interpret the same texts in and for contemporary contexts. This does not mean that they are right on every issue. It also does not mean that we may merely repeat what they said. We are interpreting for different times and to simply repristinate the exegesis of the Reformers would represent an unhelpful nostalgia that evades present challenges rather than meets them. To make effective use of the resources offered by the Reformers requires us instead to sift their exegetical conclusions critically and to bring them into conversation with our own questions and concerns, sharpening our own focus as we stage a dialog with them about interpretative issues. That this procedure would, until comparatively recently, have been controversial or unusual is profoundly odd and reflects the particular circumstances of Pauline studies in the western world over the last several decades. We existed for too long suspended between a postmodern skepticism that insists that all interpretations may be deconstructed, and that all claims to validity in interpretation are dubious, and the continued, but somewhat unreflective, practice of a historical criticism focused on the recovery of the original intention of the authors of biblical texts and on how those texts were understood by their first readers. Historical criticism is the better of these alternatives, for skepticism about the possibility of validity in interpretation is itself vulnerable to a skeptical evaluation. To interpret with validity is difficult and challenging. Nevertheless, we insist it is impossible because ultimately the only voices we can bear to hear speaking are our own. For all its weaknesses, historical criticism does at least genuinely *seek* to hear the other.

Nevertheless, the weaknesses of historical-critical interpretation of the Pauline texts are real enough and one of the most significant has been the tendency to ignore all but recent interpreters. We typically move between our contemporary horizon and the first-century horizon but pay little attention to the many generations of interpreters in between. This procedure is itself insufficiently historical. Interpretation is a self-involving task and the self is shaped by historical forces. The past is a foreign country, but it is imperialistic and aggressively colonizes the present. In relation to biblical interpretation one of the most significant historical influences upon us is the work of previous interpreters. Whether that influence takes the form of attraction or aversion it is impossible to escape. If we critically engage it, we may better understand ourselves as interpreters and so be better equipped to interpret the Pauline texts. If we ignore it and claim to evade it, then it will be unrecognized but no less powerful. For these reasons the emergence in the last few years within Pauline scholarship of a focus upon the history of reception is a hopeful development. Part I of this book, "Hermeneutics: The Sixteenth Century and the Twenty-First Century" (chapter 1) explores the implications of this development, seeking to explain what is involved in attempting to employ resources from past interpreters in the task of contemporary interpretation. Particular attention is paid to the relationship between the goals and methods of historical criticism and those of theological interpretation, and to the challenges posed by conflicts in interpretation. I argue that the goals of historical criticism and theological interpretation are different and that failure to recognize this leads to some persistent difficulties and confusions. Nevertheless, once such confusions concerning goals are resolved, the methods of historical criticism and the criterion of historical plausibility retain great significance within the practice of theological interpretation for the church. This argument is framed using the hermeneutical dimensions of the famous debate between Luther and Erasmus concerning the bondage and the freedom of the will. Already in the 1520s some of our most persistent and long-standing hermeneutical challenges were looming as the interpretative authority of the medieval church fractured under the force of Luther's critique. The disagreements between Luther and Erasmus about the nature of interpretation itself provide a pathway into discussion of our contemporary dilemmas in interpretation.

This hermeneutical relevance provides one of the reasons why an exploration of the Reformers' Pauline exegesis is particularly timely. It is not the only one, for there are other ways in which the Reformers are already embroiled in contemporary debates about Pauline interpretation. The publication in 1977 by E. P. Sanders of *Paul and Palestinian Judaism* inaugurated a new era in Pauline studies. This volume overturned trajectories in interpretation that many traced to the work of the Reformers. This revolution rapidly gained a label: the "New Perspective on Paul" (hereafter NPP). For several decades the Reformers were typically cast within NPP scholarship as misinterpreters of Paul. They were those ultimately responsible for the misrepresentation of Judaism as a crude religion of works-righteousness, for erroneous portrayals of Paul in his former life as a Pharisee struggling with inability to obey the law and a guilty conscience, and for a narrowly forensic understanding of Paul's teaching on justification that reduces it to a cold contractual legal fiction. They were the past to which present interpreters stood more or less self-consciously in contrast. Yet in the 1980s and 1990s few Pauline scholars read the exegesis of the Reformers or even the careful studies of it being published by outstanding historians such as Heiko A. Oberman, David Steinmetz, and their students. The Reformers served as the dark backdrop against which the insights of NPP scholarship shone all the more brilliantly. There was little interest in casting any light on the backdrop so as to ensure an accurate portrayal.

This was unfortunate, for the relationship between the Pauline exegesis of the Reformers and that of NPP scholarship was in reality rather more complex. The NPP did represent a significant and salutary step forward in the portrayal of Second Temple Judaism. The shadow of the Reformers' accusations of work-righteousness against the medieval church, and the analogy they drew between Paul's opponents and their own, had indeed helped to distort later scholarly accounts of Judaism. Yet while this issue was of central importance and marked genuine differences between the NPP and trajectories of interpretation derived from the Reformation, in other areas the contrasts assumed to exist were overdrawn. Neither in relation to the conscience nor in relation to justification by faith does the exegesis of the Reformers easily conform to its popular stereotypes. Indeed the evolution of scholarship itself should lead us to question sweeping contrasts between NPP scholarship and the exegesis of the Reformers. In the mid-twentieth century, interpretation of the thought of Martin Luther was dominated by existential accounts to which

3

justification, forensically understood, was of central significance. Subsequent trends have emphasized first the apocalyptic nature of Luther's thought (Oberman) and then the importance for Luther of union with Christ (the Finnish school). Are we really to suppose it to be coincidental that, broadly speaking, Pauline interpretation has followed similar trends over the same period (see 5.2)? Existential accounts of Pauline theology (Bultmann) were displaced by apocalyptic ones, but these too were then followed by a period of deep interest in participation in Christ which persists to the present. Thus, while it is true that the Reformers are far from the only figures in the history of reception that contemporary interpreters might critically engage with great benefit, there are reasons why the Reformers in particular demand our attention now. There are many other voices, representing diverse interpretative traditions, which also can provide us with significant resources as we attempt to interpret the Pauline texts for our own time, but the Reformers are already in the debate even if their contribution is frequently misunderstood and misrepresented within New Testament scholarship.

One of the main tasks of a study of the Reformers' Pauline exegesis is therefore simply to present for New Testament scholars and others an accurate picture of its central features. Part II and Part III of this book attempt this task of descriptive analysis. In doing so, attention is paid both to the unity and the diversity of the Reformers' Pauline exegesis. As R. Ward Holder points out, "there was not **one** 'Paul' in the sixteenth century, but several," but yet this is not a shapeless diversity, for "traditions of reading exist, and exercise hegemonic function over both academic and faith communities."[1] The Reformers do not speak with complete uniformity, yet they do together establish a new tradition of reading Paul that transforms the legacy of Pauline interpretation that they inherited from the patristic and medieval eras. Part II of this book, "Shared Convictions: The Reformers' New Pauline Exegetical Grammar" (chapters 2–4) investigates the key components of that new interpretative tradition. Whether in relation to the human plight apart from Christ (chapter 3, covering "sin," "the law," and "the conscience") or salvation in Christ (chapter 4, covering "works of the law," "grace," and "faith"), the Reformers make a number of key exegetical decisions that yield a soteriology standing in significant contrast to previous possibilities within the

1. R. Ward Holder, "Introduction," in *A Companion to Paul in the Reformation*, ed. R. Ward Holder (Leiden: Brill, 2009), 2, 10.

medieval tradition (chapter 2). This emphasis on the contrast between the Reformers' Pauline exegesis and that of their predecessors runs counter to recent trends in Reformation historiography where various aspects of continuity between the Reformers' theology and that of their medieval predecessors are emphasized. I argue that although helpful in several important ways, these historiographical trends underestimate the break represented by the Reformers' Pauline exegesis. This break is sufficiently sharp, and the Reformers sufficiently united in articulating exegetical positions over and against their Roman opponents, that the shared conclusions of their Pauline exegesis can aptly be characterized by analogy with the way the rules of grammar structure the use of a language. There can still be disagreements or differences of emphasis within the Reformers' Pauline interpretation. However, these differences take place inside the structure established by their shared exegetical grammar.

It is important to acknowledge that in making this argument I am using the label "the Reformers" in a particular way. It could legitimately be used to refer to all those who advocated for reform of the church in the sixteenth century, thus covering a much wider range of figures than I examine. For example, both Anabaptist theologians and Roman theologians seeking reform might then be included. However, my usage is shaped by the contemporary discussions of Pauline interpretation with which I am concerned. It is early Lutheran and early Reformed exegetes who established the trajectories of interpretation that are of continued significance in debates about the NPP, and it is with reference to them that I use the label "the Reformers." This particular focus on the Lutheran and Reformed traditions continues into Part III of the book, "Individual Perspectives: Luther, Melanchthon, and Calvin on Righteousness in Christ" (chapters 5–7). Here again, the figures selected for examination are chosen in part because of the subsequent influence exercised by their exegesis. They are also chosen as a counterpoint to the emphasis of Part II upon the unity of the Reformers' Pauline exegesis, for they exhibit important areas of diversity. Despite the extensive agreements between them on numerous exegetical issues, Luther (chapter 5), Melanchthon (chapter 6), and Calvin (chapter 7) offer distinctive perspectives on important aspects of justification by faith, especially its relationship with Paul's vocabulary of being "in Christ" and the remarkable associated imagery (e.g., being crucified with Christ) that the apostle uses to describe what this means. Luther makes union with Christ central to his account of justification in the Pauline texts whereas Melanchthon does not. Calvin preserves Luther's emphasis but wishes to distinguish justification from sanctification as twin aspects of union with Christ. In making this argument and then in later exploring similar themes in contemporary Pauline exegesis I do not distinguish between the phrase "union with Christ" and the phrase "participation in Christ." Both refer to the same broad category of vocabulary in the Pauline texts.

Only once an extensive descriptive analysis of the Reformers' Pauline exegesis has been accomplished, enabling accurate identification of patterns of similarity and difference between the Reformers' exegesis and that of contemporary Pauline scholarship, can the interpretative conclusions reached by the Reformers be brought into critical dialog with those reached by NPP interpreters. At this point the question of who is right in their Pauline exegesis emerges with full force and my pursuit of it contrasts with Holder, who comments that the question "has very little place in sensitive history."[2] The difference between historians of the sixteenth century who can restrict their concerns to who Paul was in and for that context and New Testament scholars who must interpret the Pauline texts in and for the twenty-first century here becomes clear. The latter cannot perform their task while bracketing the issue of who was right in their Pauline exegesis in the same way as the former. Unless we are to make what we will of the Pauline texts, disinterested in whether our interpretations and the life of the church reflect or distort the apostle's intentions, the question must be faced when interpreting for today. It should not be asked prematurely, as if the only interest past interpreters hold for us is the degree to which they anticipate our own exegetical conclusions or fail to do so. If we follow this rush to judgment, then we will learn little from the history of reception since our assumptions will never be subject to challenge. We will miss the opportunity to see exegetical issues from a different perspective and to return to our own exploration of the texts with an altered sense of the interpretative possibilities. Nevertheless, the question cannot be endlessly deferred and posing it is essential to any truly historical procedure. For the historian does not exist abstracted from the flow of history. Historians of Paul in the Reformation may not want to ask who in the sixteenth century was right in their interpretation of the Pauline texts, but the same historians would be failing in basic responsibilities if, for example, they failed to consider the influence upon them from previous interpretations of Luther's the-

2. Holder, "Introduction," 3.

ology. Their own perceptions of Luther's theology have been historically shaped and their pursuit of accurate interpretation of Luther demands that historians' own relationships to traditions in Luther interpretation be recognized, explored, and critically evaluated.[3] The historian of the sixteenth century does want to ask who has rightly understood Luther. Similarly, interpreters of the New Testament cannot avoid asking whether and how the Reformers are correct in their Pauline exegesis. This is true for New Testament scholars who conceive their interpretative goals as purely historical. It is also true for those who are theological interpreters and perceive careful historical evaluation of interpretative conclusions as a crucial step in accurately interpreting the Pauline texts for the mission of the church today.

Part IV of this book, "Contemporary Implications: The Reformers and the New Perspective on Paul" (chapters 8 and 9), therefore pursues at length a critical dialog between the Reformers' Pauline exegesis and that of prominent contemporary Pauline interpreters. Here I am particularly concerned with the ways in which the Reformers can provide us with exegetical insights that challenge contemporary positions. After a long period of rather uncritical positive reception of the Reformers' Pauline interpretation within Protestant scholarship, the advent of the NPP means that the Reformers today once again, as in their own sixteenth-century context, represent subversive voices calling into question dominant perspectives. Through this critical dialog several significant conclusions are reached:

1. The relationship between the Reformers' Pauline exegesis and contemporary Pauline scholarship cannot accurately be portrayed in straightforwardly antithetical terms. In some important respects, especially what Paul means by "sin" and "the flesh," dominant current perspectives concerning Pauline anthropology depend upon exegetical arguments made by the Reformers. In other areas, contemporary scholarship intensifies or perfects one aspect of the Reformers' Pauline exegesis at the expense of others. Divine initiative is emphasized at the expense of human response in some apocalyptic accounts of Pauline theology. N. T. Wright intensifies the Reformed theme of covenant at the expense of traditional accounts of justification.

3. See Christine Helmer and Bo Kristian Holm, eds., *Lutherrenaissance: Past and Present* (Göttingen: Vandenhoeck & Ruprecht, 2015).

2. Contemporary New Testament scholarship typically misinterprets the part played by the introspective conscience in the Reformers' Pauline exegesis. Misled by Krister Stendahl's historically unsubstantiated drawing of a straight line from "Augustine to Luther to Freud,"[4] New Testament scholarship often assumes that the Reformers typically regarded the preconversion Paul as struggling with inability to keep the law. This is not so, and Paul's phrase the "works of the law" is frequently identified by the Reformers not with such a struggle but with false confidence that the law is being fulfilled. There is considerable emphasis on the ultimate role played by the law in revealing sin, but this is not construed as an experiential sequence in which conviction of sin through the law will invariably precede repentance and faith.

3. The Reformers and NPP scholarship are genuinely in disagreement concerning what Paul means by the "works of the law." Here NPP interpreters are correct to argue that the term does not denote a general Jewish commitment to works-righteousness and the earning of salvation. The Reformers' Pauline exegesis is inadequate at this crucial point. However, NPP interpreters themselves err when they acknowledge the general reference of the phrase to a Jewish way of life characterized by nomistic observance but insist on interpreting all actual uses of it in the Pauline letters exclusively in terms of boundary markers separating Jews from Gentiles. This ignores the fact that for Paul the boundary between Jew and Gentile is also the boundary between holiness and sinfulness, with all credible temptation to magnify human ethical achievement lying on the Jewish side of the boundary. Paul is not always concerned with this when he contrasts the "works of the law" with justification by faith, but when he indicates that this is his focus Paul's statements may be taken at face value.

4. In relation to justification by faith the exegesis of Luther and Calvin offers significant resources to contemporary Pauline interpretation. Both hold together an emphatic insistence on the alien nature of the righteousness of Christ granted to the believer with an equally emphatic insistence that this alien righteousness is received always and only in union with Christ. That they do so enables them successfully to maintain as mutually reinforcing features of soteriology

4. Holder, "Introduction," 6.

8

both a focus on the complete sufficiency of divine grace in disregard of all notions of human worthiness and a focus on the transformation of believers and the central importance of the church.

5. Concern within contemporary Pauline scholarship to maintain divine initiative in salvation and to emphasize that believers participate in the faithfulness of Christ (subjective genitive translation of Paul's phrase πίστις Χριστοῦ in contrast to the objective genitive translation of "faith in Christ") has resulted in neglect of the theme of proclamation and inadequate accounts of human faith. There is a pressing need within contemporary scholarship for these important topics to be explored in ways which recognize that the proclamation of the gospel and belief in its message are no less divine actions for being performed through human beings. As divine actions they should be fully integrated with the apocalyptic and participatory aspects of Pauline theology.

6. Wright's covenantal account of justification—a divine verdict concerning membership of God's people—represents a significant misinterpretation. The available lexical evidence supports the traditional understanding that justification primarily concerns the way in which, through Christ, those who believe are forgiven and released from sin. The exegesis of Luther and Calvin is again here helpful, pointing us away from narrowly forensic accounts of how this is achieved. They rightly argue that believers receive the righteousness of Christ but do so only when united with Christ by faith. As faith grasps hold of Christ and receives his righteousness, then the church, the body of Christ in the world, is created.

7. The reconciliation of the most important insights of the Reformers and those of NPP scholarship is possible in exegetical practice. When a vital text such as Rom 4 is considered in light of both Reformation and contemporary scholarship, then elements often perceived as being in contrast and mutually exclusive emerge as compatible and mutually reinforcing. When rightly interpreted, this text includes a denial of the capacity of human deeds to justify. It also emphasizes the worldwide family of Abraham and characterizes justifying faith as participatory with the believer united with Christ and his righteousness.

These conclusions about the contemporary task of Pauline interpretation are the goal toward which the argument of the book is directed.

Different reading strategies are possible depending upon the primary interests of the reader. Those concerned largely with the sixteenth century and the account offered of the Reformers' Pauline exegesis may focus on Part II ("Shared Convictions: The Reformers' New Pauline Exegetical Grammar") and Part III ("Individual Perspectives: Luther, Melanchthon, and Calvin on Righteousness in Christ"). Those concerned with contemporary scholarship may focus on Part I ("Hermeneutics: The Sixteenth Century and the Twenty-First Century") and Part IV ("Contemporary Implications: The Reformers and the New Perspective on Paul"). Alternatively, those interested in tracing how the exegesis of particular terms in the Pauline texts influences descriptions of the human plight apart from Christ and descriptions of salvation in Christ may focus on Part II for discussion of the Reformers and on the first half of Part IV (chapter 8) for discussion of contemporary implications. Similarly, those interested particularly in the theme of justification by faith and its relationship to participation in Christ may focus on Part III and on the second half of Part IV (chapter 9). Yet, whatever the primary interest with which the book is approached, I hope that it will succeed in convincing readers that if we wish to be faithful interpreters for today we must pay more attention to the exegesis of previous eras.

PART I

HERMENEUTICS

The Sixteenth Century and the Twenty-First Century

1 The Hermeneutics of Reform

Erasmus, Luther, and Contemporary Theological Interpretation of Scripture

1.1. An Apparent or Real Quarrel?
Erasmus and Luther on Paul and Peter at Antioch

Disagreements about small features of the biblical texts sometimes indicate significant differences between exegetes concerning the whole nature of Scripture and the correct approach to its interpretation. Such an instance can be found in the early years of the Reformation. On April 18, 1524, Martin Luther wrote his last letter to Desiderius Erasmus. On the surface the letter was an attempt to maintain a civil relationship between the two men. In it Luther abandons his earlier hopes that Erasmus would join his cause against Rome and tries to forestall a public breach by accepting that the great humanist will stay neutral. He pledges himself not to attack Erasmus in print so long as Erasmus does not attack him. Yet, as one of Erasmus's modern editors notes, Luther "attempts to be polite and forbearing but is actually threatening and scornful."[1] The threatening effect is partly created by a pointed biblical allusion. Luther refers to Gal 2:11, where Paul reports that when Peter came to Antioch he "opposed him to his face." Luther warns Erasmus that if he publicly attacks evangelical teaching "necessity would then compel us to 'oppose you to your face.'"[2]

What is extraordinary about the allusion is that in the subsequent

---

1. *CWE* 76:lxvi.
2. *LW* 49: no. 144, 76–81 (78) = *WA* BR 3: no. 729, 268–71 (270, 20). The editors of *Luther's Works* and of the *Weimarer Ausgabe* both note the allusion to Gal 2:11.

public dispute between them, each man acted out his interpretation of Paul's statement. Following Jerome and the Greek Fathers, Erasmus held that Peter and Paul staged a prearranged quarrel for pedagogical purposes. He understood the Greek prepositional phrase, that Paul opposed Peter κατὰ πρόσωπον (literally "according to face"), to mean that the two opposed each other only in appearance. Their aim was to educate the church that the Mosaic food laws did not apply to Gentile believers. Luther disagreed, and held Augustine to be correct in asserting the quarrel to be real. The phrase κατὰ πρόσωπον is an idiom that here means not "in appearance" but "to his face," "in the open," or "before all."[3] The consequence of these contrasting interpretations was that Erasmus and Luther each saw his own behavior as an imitation of Paul at the same time as each found the other's behavior unacceptable and blameworthy. Actions mandated by Paul's example for one are reprehensible for the other when judged by that same example.

Erasmus had some general reasons for preferring Jerome's interpretation and for believing that Peter and Paul feigned disagreement in order to teach the church. This interpretation relieved any general Christian embarrassment at such apparent disharmony between the two most important leaders of the apostolic era and, in the early sixteenth century context, removed the potentially explosive implications of Paul having rebuked the sin of the man understood to have been the first Pope. Yet, of more immediate personal relevance for Erasmus, Gal 2:11 provides a biblical basis for engagement in similar practices of concealment. *Dissimulatio* (the disguising of an author's true thoughts) was a valid rhetorical technique if employed for a good purpose.[4] It is for Erasmus "neither reprehensible nor unethical, if only it leads the student toward being drawn into the truth."[5] It was also vitally necessary if Erasmus was to

3. There is no doubt that Luther and Augustine were correct about this. To my knowledge, all major modern commentaries simply assume their interpretation without discussion.

4. On the significance of Gal 2:11 in Erasmus's understanding of *dissimulatio*, see James D. Tracy, *Erasmus of the Low Countries* (Berkeley: University of California Press, 1996), 117–18. Paul's appeal to an unknown God in Acts 17:23 is also significant, as is Christ's dissimulation of his divinity in the gospels. See here James D. Tracy, "Erasmus among the Postmodernists," in *Erasmus' Vision of the Church,* ed. Hilmar M. Pabel (Kirksville, MO: Sixteenth Century Journal Publishers, 1995), 1–40 (esp. 9–12).

5. Manfred Hoffmann, *Rhetoric and Theology: The Hermeneutic of Erasmus* (Toronto: University of Toronto Press, 1994), 123.

survive in the dangerous political context in which he found himself in the mid-1520s.[6]

Back in 1516, when in a single year he had triumphantly published his *Novum Instrumentum* (Greek New Testament), the first part of his *Annotations* (critical notes on the New Testament text), and an edition of the letters of Jerome, Erasmus had felt that a new golden age was dawning.[7] There were critics who thought his work dangerous and who believed the work of theology should be based exclusively on the Latin Vulgate, the Bible translation that had served the western church for over one thousand years, but Erasmus was confident that his view would prevail. With typical humanist faith in the power of returning *ad fontes* (to the sources), he sought for the church a spiritual revival parallel to that hoped for in culture and learning through a return to the literature of ancient Greece and Rome. His biblical scholarship was an attempt to leap back over the accretions of medieval scholasticism to a way of theologizing and a manner of life that related Christian truth to personal spirituality. Although he never denounced monasticism or the rites and ceremonies of the church, Erasmus's focus was on a lay piety that combined faith in salvation with love of neighbor. He sought reform but "intended to rely on the gradual transformation of the spirits, attitudes, and behavior of his Christian readers, stimulated by the quiet voice of his writings and the preaching and works of his collaborators, high and low."[8]

The advent of Luther, who burst onto the European stage following the posting of his *Ninety-Five Theses* against the sale of indulgences in Wittenberg on October 31, 1517, was a disaster for Erasmus. The polar-

6. The extent to which Erasmus dissembled to survive can be seen in the uses to which he put Luther's letter. Erasmus complained to Melanchthon in a letter of September 6, 1524—the same month that *Freedom of the Will* was published—that Luther's letter in April 1524 had forced him publicly to criticize Luther. See CWE 10: no. 1496 (378, 20–379, 36) = Allen 5: no. 1496 (545, 17–31). Yet Luther's same letter was one of a number given to the Polish nobleman, Jan Laski, to show to the Polish king in order to prove that Erasmus and Luther were not allies.

7. See his letter from February 1517 to Wolfgang Capito: CWE 4: no. 541 (261–68) = Allen 2: no. 541 (487–92).

8. *CWE* 76:xxi. For an overview of the issues raised for contemporaries by Erasmus's biblical scholarship, especially his divergences from the Vulgate on the basis of the original languages, see Allan K. Jenkins and Patrick Preston, *Biblical Scholarship and the Church: A Sixteenth Century Crisis of Authority* (Aldershot: Ashgate, 2007), 3–80, and also Christine Christ-von Wedel, *Erasmus of Rotterdam: Advocate of a New Christianity* (Toronto: University of Toronto Press, 2013), 79–164.

ization of opinion caused by Luther's appearance undermined all hopes of quiet reform. Both Luther's supporters and opponents recognized that Erasmus's philological work on the New Testament provided a textual basis for some of Luther's views. Erasmus came under increasing pressure from both sides to clarify his own position. By the summer of 1522, nearly two years before Luther's final letter to him, Erasmus was being urged by the Emperor Charles V, by Henry VIII of England, and by Rome to write against Luther.[9] Erasmus's delay in decision, which irritated all sides, reflected his genuine dilemma. There is no evidence that Erasmus ever supported Luther's views on justification,[10] disagreeing with Luther's elimination of any causative role for good works in salvation. However, Erasmus did find attractive Luther's emphasis on faith as unconditional trust in God, and he had much private sympathy for many of Luther's criticisms of the institutional church. With considerable prescience given the religious wars that were to ravage Europe within a few decades, Erasmus also regarded the division itself as a disaster. Harmony was a spiritual goal and value.

Erasmus's way out of the dilemma, and his means of promoting concord, was to employ *dissimulatio*. In September 1524 Erasmus eventually did publish a work concerning Luther's views. In it, Erasmus implicitly invited Luther to join a pedagogical exercise similar to that in which he believed Paul and Peter to have engaged at Antioch. The tract *The Freedom of the Will* (*De libero arbitrio*) is subtle in both its form and its intentions. It was read by most, both at the time and subsequently, as an open attack on Luther, but there are indications that this was not Erasmus's perspective. The work considers whether the human will is

9. Erasmus had already moved from his native Low Countries, where Charles V ruled, to Basle in order to escape such pressure.

10. Luther seems to have understood this early. Therefore, he was always more realistic about what he could expect from Erasmus than Erasmus was about what he could expect from Luther. See Luther's letter to Georg Spalatin of October 19, 1516, *LW* 48: no. 9, 23–26 (24) = *WA* BR 1: no. 27, 69–72 (70, 4–16). Erasmus's position was essentially similar to that later adopted by reform-minded Roman theologians such as Gasparo Contarini and Girolamo Seripando in which the righteousness of Christ is imputed to those who believe, but the works performed by faith are not excluded from among the causes of justification. See Christ-von Wedel, *Erasmus of Rotterdam*, 145–53 (esp. 151). Indeed in discussing the faith of Abraham in Rom 4 Erasmus will speak of this faith as trust (*fiducia*) but insist that it was a work (*opus erat*) and that by it Abraham merited justification (*mereretur iusti titutlum*). See *CWE* 77:678–80 = *LB* X:1502E–1503A. The Reformers could never have interpreted Abraham's trust in God's promises in this way as a meritorious work.

free, classifying the question as among the *adiaphora* or "indifferent matters." Such adiaphora are important and require careful exploration, but contrary opinions are not worthy of condemnation. Further, the title continues *diatribe sive collatio* ("diatribe or comparison"), employing specific rhetorical terms with genre implications apparent only to humanist readers who understood them: "A *diatribē* is not an invective or harangue . . . a *diatribē* is more particularly a classical form of philosophical disputation."[11] Despite Luther's status as a condemned heretic, the genre belongs to deliberative rather than to judicial rhetoric. As for *collatio*, "according to Cicero's *De inventione*, a *collatio* is a subdivision of probability which depends on comparison . . . so it was that he had urged . . . the virtuosity of arguing on both sides of a question."[12] Again, the term suggests a genre less hostile than might be expected.

In harmony with this approach, Erasmus's investigation proceeds by means of careful comparison of those passages of Scripture that appear to imply the freedom of the will with those that appear to deny it. To be sure, his work of comparison leads Erasmus to a conclusion in favor of free will and contrary to Luther's views. Yet, Erasmus is inviting Luther to reply in kind, as a disputant and not an adversary. Erasmus will acknowledge that the largest part in salvation belongs to grace but will leave some room for free will and so stand on middle ground where there might be hope of conciliation.[13] Erasmus appears to oppose Luther. Yet if Luther replies in kind and with moderation, then together they will show Europe a better way to discuss theology than mutual denunciation and recrimination, creating middle ground where none currently exists. They will, Erasmus hopes, teach the church as Paul and Peter had done, appearing to disagree but for a higher purpose. Freedom of the will is "one among many disputed questions which Erasmus could have selected to illustrate the humanist issue of *Diatriba*: how to conduct and resolve the disputation of such questions which arise from literally conflicting texts of Scripture."[14]

Erasmus had hoped that *The Freedom of the Will* might encourage Luther to leave behind what Erasmus judged to be inflammatory dogma-

11. Marjorie O'Rourke Boyle, *Rhetoric and Reform: Erasmus' Civil Dispute with Luther* (Cambridge: Harvard University Press, 1983), 6.

12. Boyle, *Rhetoric and Reform*, 44. Boyle explores in convincing depth the influence of classical authors, especially Cicero, on Erasmus's concept of *dissimulatio*. However, she neglects the importance of the scriptural precedents such as Gal 2:11.

13. *CWE* 76:lxxxv.

14. Boyle, *Rhetoric and Reform*, 11.

tism for a more reasonable approach to settling theological differences. He was disappointed.[15] When Luther replied in December 1525 with *The Bondage of the Will* (*De servo arbitrio*), his text was not a polite *diatribē*. He does not proceed by comparison between apparently conflicting scriptural texts, and he does not treat the issue as among the *adiaphora*. Scripture is clear: the will is not free. The appropriate way to handle the issue is to assert the truth. Several dozen times he uses the term *causa* ("cause," "judicial process," or "lawsuit") to characterize the debate.[16] Whereas Erasmus chooses the genre of philosophical disputation, Luther rejects deliberative rhetoric in favor of juridical rhetoric, casting himself as the prosecutor of Christ's case. He is disgusted by Erasmus's slipperiness and the care taken "to be everywhere evasive and equivocal . . . you seek to assert nothing while appearing to assert something."[17] He rages against the priority given to concord over truth: "it does not matter to you what anyone believes anywhere, so long as the peace of the world is undisturbed."[18] And he condemns the rhetorical strategy employed: "I am trying to show you what frightful things a man is bound to babble if he undertakes to support a bad cause, and what it means to run counter to divine truth and divine Scripture when we put on an act to please others and play a part that is foreign to us against our conscience."[19] Erasmus's careful weighing of probabilities in search of the truth is rejected as contrary to the work of the Spirit, for "it is not doubts or mere opinions that he has written on our hearts, but assertions more sure and certain than life itself and all experience."[20]

That this was Luther's reaction is scarcely surprising given his interpretation of Gal 2:11 as indicating a genuine quarrel between Peter and Paul. Yet Erasmus felt injured and he produced a further two volumes against Luther (*Hyperaspistes I* published in February 1526 and

---

15. Erasmus's strategy may appear hopelessly impractical, but that he genuinely believed it could work is suggested by the fact that this was his second attempt at such a maneuver. In the autumn of 1520, after the papal bull against Luther, *Exsurge Domine,* reached the Low Countries, Erasmus collaborated in the production of *Concilium cujusdam,* an anonymous tract that suggested the bull to be a forgery and urged the Pope to remit the whole Luther issue to a committee of scholars.

16. Boyle, *Rhetoric and Reform,* 67.

17. *LW* 33:17 = *WA* 18:601, 33–35.

18. *LW* 33:23 = *WA* 18:605, 15–16.

19. *LW* 33:43–44 = *WA* 18:620, 14–17.

20. *LW* 33:24 = *WA* 18:605, 32–34.

Hyperaspistes II published in September 1527),[21] in which the Reformer's dogmatism is repeatedly attacked as unreasonable. This rejection, not just of Luther's conclusions but also of his style and tone, suggests that Erasmus had not grasped the full significance of Luther's earlier allusion to Gal 2:11 in his letter of April 1524. If Erasmus had done so, he would have realized that Luther could respond to the publication of *The Freedom of the Will* (*De libero arbitrio*) in no other way than to refuse to engage in *dissimulatio*.[22] For Luther was already in print disagreeing with Erasmus that Paul and Peter had employed *dissimulatio* in order to educate the church at Antioch. In his first *Commentary on Galatians* (1516–1517/1519), in a work otherwise sprinkled with positive references to Erasmus, Luther had rejected the views of Jerome and Erasmus on the verse.[23]

In following Augustine in insisting on a genuine public quarrel, Luther pictures Paul as courageously speaking up for the truth of the gospel. Even though he was the only one left to do so, Paul argued for freedom when it was being suggested that Jewish practices were also necessary for salvation rather than simply faith in Christ alone. Far from joining Peter in a charade designed to instruct, Paul was in deadly earnest. Luther's combative tone in *The Bondage of the Will*, and his insistence on assertion as a proper mode of theological discourse, is thus just as much an imitation of Paul as Erasmus's desire to instruct by disagreeing more in appearances than in reality. It also indicates the two men's completely different approach to the interpretation of Scripture in general. Their differences are just as much hermeneutical as they are focused on the theological issue of the freedom of the will. Their different interpretations of

21. See *CWE* 76:91–297 = *LB* X:1249–1336 and *CWE* 77 = *LB* X:1337–1536 respectively. *Hyperaspistes II* constitutes the whole of *CWE* 77.

22. Although a letter from Melanchthon to Erasmus in late September 1524 after the publication of *The Freedom of the Will* does report satisfaction at Erasmus's moderation and promises that Luther will reply in kind. See *CWE* 10: no. 1500 (392, 45–51) = Allen 5: no. 1500 (555, 42–48). Perhaps conscious of this, Luther begins *The Bondage of the Will* by referring to Erasmus's moderation and comparing *The Freedom of the Will* unfavorably to Melanchthon's theological textbook *Loci Communes*. See *LW* 33:16 = *WA* 18:601, 3–11. Melanchthon was later to have his own doubts about Luther's position on the freedom of the will.

23. *LW* 27:211–16 = *WA* 2:483, 32 – 487, 34. Many of Luther's "commentaries" have their origins in lecture series delivered at Wittenberg which were later published. Where they are cited, the first date given is that of the lecture series, the second date that of publication.

Gal 2:11 exemplify the two men's different understandings of the nature of Scripture and of appropriate interpretive strategies.[24]

1.2. Erasmus and Luther on Scripture and Interpretation

For Erasmus, the whole of Scripture is an act of divine accommodation. Just as Paul and Peter were not able to teach the truth directly because of the limitations of the believers at Antioch, so, in Scripture, God accommodates human limitations. Erasmus conceives reality in Platonic terms as divided between the intelligible world in which God dwells and the visible created world, and he regards human beings, as both body and soul, as participating in both worlds. Our sinfulness and rebellion against God drives apart these two aspects of human existence, and the effects of this can be clearly seen in human language. Rebellion against the divine word means that human words are divorced from their true meaning, and even Scripture is not exempt from this falling apart. There are the signs that are human words and the things that they imperfectly signify. There is the letter and there is the Spirit, and the interpreter needs a mediator to bridge the gulf between the two and so to translate the interpreter from the flesh to the Spirit.

Yet Scripture is unique among texts since it contains within itself the mediator that is needed. Just as the incarnate Christ was both fully divine and fully human, so is his presence in the words of Scripture. As Hoffman argues, in Erasmus's understanding, "Christ is at once symbolically present and really present in the sacred word, symbolically as to the human nature of the word and really in terms of the divine nature of the word."[25] The possibility of ascending from letter to Spirit therefore exists

---

24. Brian Cummings, *The Literary Culture of the Reformation: Grammar and Grace* (Oxford: Oxford University Press, 2002), 149: "The incapacity of Luther and Erasmus to agree about almost any matter of literary interpretation shows not how the debate was meaningless but that it was, fundamentally, about meaning."

25. Hoffmann, *Rhetoric and Theology*, 101. My description of Erasmus's hermeneutic relies on Hoffmann's book, esp. 95–133. Cummings, *The Literary Culture of the Reformation*, 105, notes that the presence of Christ in Scripture is powerfully asserted in *Paraclesis*, the preface to the general reader which Erasmus produced for the 1516 *Novum Instrumentum*: "Christ is our author; his authorship is present in his words; his presence guarantees truth; the truth is delivered in these words, written in scripture. Scripture presents a living and breathing Christ 'almost more effectively,' Erasmus breathtakingly declares, than when he dwelt among men."

with Scripture in a way as with no other text, and the vehicle of ascent is allegory. For Erasmus, the purpose of Scripture is to draw readers into the truth and so change them:

> The transition from the literal to the spiritual is made possible by accommodation of the divine Spirit to the letter, which in turn also effects by virtue of its power of persuasion the human transformation from the flesh to the Spirit. . . . Divine wisdom employs allegory to accommodate itself to the level of human comprehension. It lowers itself to the human condition. But then the Spirit also uses allegory to persuade human beings to rise to the truth.[26]

Allegory is the appropriate vehicle of ascent because language is more pleasant and attractive when it communicates indirectly, through similitudes, parables and allusions. Yet this does not mean that the letter of the scriptural text is to be despised. As Erasmus's philological scholarship and his immense labors with the New Testament text demonstrate, it remains crucial. The letter is the entry point from which the ascent to the spiritual takes place. There is no other basis from which to move to the higher meaning, and allegorical interpretation builds on historical sense rather than removing it. Hoffmann summarizes Erasmus's view of this process in the following way: "A word or a text reflects reality in a parabolic way."[27]

Luther's understanding of the nature of Scripture is difficult to summarize and categorize. He left no full-length treatise on the nature and interpretation of Scripture, and his many and varied statements in other

---

26. Hoffmann, *Rhetoric and Theology*, 106–7.

27. Hoffmann, *Rhetoric and Theology*, 76. The relationship between the historical and the allegorical does seem to have undergone some development in Erasmus's thought. In the *Enchiridion* (1503), Erasmus used a Neoplatonic account of Scripture as a vehicle to convey a practical lay piety, but puts little emphasis on salvation history or on the biblical languages. Jenkins and Preston, *Biblical Scholarship and the Church*, 33–52, emphasize that it is with his publication of Lorenzo Valla's annotations on the New Testament (*In Latinam Novi Testamenti Interpretationem Annotationes*) in 1505 that Erasmus becomes publicly committed to the interpretation of the biblical texts in their original languages. Christ-von Wedel, *Erasmus of Rotterdam*, 57–58, argues that Erasmus neglected salvation history in the *Enchiridion* but later developed a much more historical approach that placed greater emphasis on the humanity of Christ. Nevertheless it is acknowledged that this later Erasmus "continued to propound an internalized and intra-worldly piety and sought to contrast heaven and earth, divine and human things, spirit and flesh" (58).

works are occasionally in tension with each other. Discussion of his position has also tended to reflect a desire to claim his support in debates of later eras concerning biblical authority. Does he presuppose a doctrine of verbal inspiration or not? How does his commitment to the unity of Scripture cohere with his critical statements about certain biblical books?[28] Yet what is abundantly plain is Luther's commitment to the sufficiency of Scripture for faith and life, and the sense gained from him that "all Scripture must be read and interpreted from and toward Jesus Christ."[29] Luther does not insist that christological meaning must be found in every passage, but rather portrays Christ as the coordinating center of Scripture that grants it unity and coherence: "Take Christ out of the Scriptures, and what will you find left in them?"[30] Therefore, he naturally understands the nature of Scripture in relation to the incarnation, as when he states that "The Holy Scripture is the word of God written (as I might say) lettered and formed in letters, just as Christ is the eternal Word of God cloaked in human flesh."[31] As such, Scripture can be nothing other than an act of divine accommodation to human language.[32]

However, Scripture is an act of accommodation with a purpose, which is to communicate:

> For Christ has opened our minds so that we may understand the Scriptures (Luke 24:25), and the gospel is preached to the whole creation (Mark 16:15); "Their voice has gone out to all the earth" (Rom. 10:18), and "Whatever was written was written for our instruction" (Rom. 15:4); also, "All Scripture inspired by God is profitable for teaching" (2 Tim. 3:16).[33]

28. For a review of previous writings and a discussion of these issues, see Mark D. Thompson, *A Sure Ground on Which to Stand: The Relation of Authority and Interpretive Method in Luther's Approach to Scripture* (Carlisle: Paternoster Press, 2004), esp. chapters 2–4. See also Robert Kolb, *Martin Luther and the Enduring Word of God: The Wittenberg School and Its Scripture Centered Proclamation* (Grand Rapids: Baker, 2016), esp. chapters 2–4.

29. Bernhard Lohse, *Martin Luther's Theology: Its Historical and Systematic Development* (Edinburgh: T&T Clark, 1999), 195.

30. *LW* 33:26 = *WA* 18:606, 29.

31. *WA* 48:31, 4–8, quoted and translated in Thompson, *A Sure Ground*, 105. Thompson argues that the model of the prophets is also significant in Luther's view of the nature of Scripture (95–103).

32. On Luther's view of accommodation, see Thompson, *A Sure Ground*, 103–12.

33. *LW* 33:27 = *WA* 18:607, 4–7.

The word is a living proclamation addressed to human beings for their transformation. Therefore, Scripture effects what it promises. When the word of forgiveness is embraced in faith, it does not reflect a situation that already exists because human contrition has warranted divine forgiveness. Rather it establishes forgiveness, performing what it says as a free act of God.[34] In this effective word, Christ the Word, the very content of Scripture, gives himself and so there is no gulf to bridge between word and meaning, between sign and thing signified.

God may not have chosen to reveal all that God is in Scripture, but God truly is who God is revealed in Scripture to be. In contrast to Erasmus's construction of his understanding of Scripture around the distinction between words as signs and the meanings to which they point, for Luther "the linguistic sign is itself the reality."[35] The truth must be sought not behind but within the words. "For Luther, 'the human word itself' becomes 'bearer of the divine Spirit,' which, indeed, is 'actually wrapped in the swaddling cloth of the human word.'"[36] Allegory is not an essential tool for interpretation since there is no need for mediation between the letter and the Spirit.[37] In Scripture, God communicates openly and plainly and it is in order to do this that God has accommodated himself to human language in Scripture. For a preacher of the gospel like Paul in the situation in which he found himself when Peter came to Antioch, the only proper response is proclamation of the truth in defiance of all opposition. For it is in such proclamation that his hearers will encounter the God of the Word: "Luther is concerned with what the Word of God as 'Living Word' actually does when it invades our lives, our experience, our space."[38]

Not surprisingly, these different understandings of Scripture and its

---

34. Oswald Bayer, "Luther as an Interpreter of Holy Scripture," in *The Cambridge Companion to Martin Luther*, ed. Donald K. McKim (Cambridge: Cambridge University Press, 2003), 76, points out that it was in the context of early debates concerning the sacrament of penance (1518) that Luther first discovered his emphasis on the effective word.

35. Bayer, "Luther as Interpreter of Holy Scripture," 76. See at greater length Oswald Bayer, *Promissio: Geschichte der reformatischen Wende in Luthers Theologie*, 2nd ed. (Darmstadt: Wissenschaftliche Buchgesellschaft, 1989).

36. Lohse, *Martin Luther's Theology*, 191. Lohse is here quoting Peter Meinhold, *Luthers Sprachphilosophie* (Berlin: Lutherisches Verlagshaus, 1958), 56.

37. Thompson, *A Sure Ground*, 167-71, describes the diminishing significance of the letter/Spirit distinction in Luther's approach to interpreting Scripture.

38. Gerhard O. Forde, *The Captivation of the Will: Luther vs. Erasmus on Freedom and Bondage* (Grand Rapids: Eerdmans, 2005), 30.

interpretation, carrying with them different philosophies of language,[39] find expression in *The Freedom of the Will* and *The Bondage of the Will*. Erasmus begins by contending that the meaning of Scripture is not always plain. Its words do not straightforwardly reflect reality, and "there are some secret places into which God did not intend us to penetrate very far. . . . this is, presumably, to make us recognize the unsearchable majesty of divine wisdom, and the frailty of the human intellect."[40] Characteristically, Erasmus regards these obscurities as largely doctrinal in nature. In line with his emphasis on lay piety, absolutely clear are "the precepts for a good life."[41] It is issues such as the distinction between the persons of the Trinity, or the relationship between the divine and human natures in Christ, which are obscure.

They are also not for common ears. And in recognizing this, the prudent teacher is merely following apostolic example. "Paul knew the distinction between what is lawful and what is expedient: it is lawful to speak the truth; but it is not expedient to do so in front of anyone, at any time, in any way."[42] If he were convinced that a synod or council had erred in its interpretation of Scripture, it would be lawful for Erasmus to say so, but not wise, for the wicked would be granted the opportunity

---

39. The distinction maintained by Erasmus between word and meaning, between sign and thing signified, goes back to Augustine and remains central to contemporary hermeneutical debate. See Jean Grondin, *Introduction to Philosophical Hermeneutics* (New Haven: Yale University Press, 1994), ix–xi, 32–38. Speech-Act theory, another approach to language significant in contemporary hermeneutics, shares Luther's emphasis on the performative nature of language, and Bayer, "Luther as Interpreter of Scripture," 73–85, employs speech-act terminology several times in his account of Luther's views.

40. *CWE* 76:9 = *LB* IX:1216C. Cummings, *The Literary Culture of the Reformation*, 156: "Erasmus appears to construe a divide—perhaps a total divide—between areas of obscurity and areas of clarity in the scriptural text. Some areas are opaque to interpretation; others transparent. Erasmus gives no criteria as to how discrimination between the two areas is to be maintained, or how his eminently practical criticism may be learned."

41. *CWE* 76:10 = *LB* IX:1217B.

42. *CWE* 76:12 = *LB* IX:1217D–E. There is some irony in Erasmus arriving at this position since in his earlier correspondence with fellow humanist Guillaume Budé—conducted before Luther became a public figure—Erasmus had adopted a different position. See Daniel Ménager, "Erasmus, the Intellectuals, and the Reuchlin Affair," in *Biblical Humanism and Scholasticism in the Age of Erasmus*, ed. E. Rummel (Leiden: Brill, 2008), 43–45. It is Budé who employs Scripture (Prov 25:2) to defend writing in a way only accessible to the learned. See *CWE* 4: no. 493 (137–54, esp. 141, 139–43) = Allen 2: no. 493 (390–405, esp. 394, 131–34). Erasmus aims instead to be understood by the great majority to instruct and persuade. See *CWE* 4: no. 531 (238, 509–12) = Allen 2: no. 531 (471, 456–59).

to denigrate the authority of the Fathers. Instead, one should recognize the historically contingent nature of human perspectives on divine truth: "I would prefer to say that they felt their decision was correct for their own time, but that present needs suggest it should be repealed."[43] In the case of the freedom of the will, even were it true, it would not be wise publicly to advocate Luther's determinist position, since the multitude might conclude that indulging in sin is inevitable and give up any kind of struggle against it.

The presence of such obscurities in Scripture reveals the necessity in interpretation for the authority and tradition of the church. Erasmus acknowledges that Luther is formally correct to insist on the principle of *sola scriptura*. The authority of the Bible is greater than that of all human decisions, by whomever they are made. But for Erasmus, "the debate here is not about Scripture itself . . . the quarrel is over its meaning."[44] When obscurities in the text inevitably generate interpretative disagreement, it is wise to rely on "the judgments already made by very many learned and orthodox men, many saints and martyrs, many ancient and modern theologians, many universities, councils, bishops, and popes."[45] It will not do to invoke the Holy Spirit against tradition since, "What am I to do if many people assert different opinions, every one of them swearing that he has the Spirit?"[46] Rather, the Spirit should be identified with the consensus of tradition, and this identification makes incredible Luther's claim that the church has erred in its basic teaching about salvation. The Spirit of Christ cannot "have overlooked his church's error for more than thirteen hundred years, and have not found one of all those saintly people worthy of being inspired with what my opponents claim is the most important teaching of the gospel."[47] On an issue like the

---

43. *CWE* 76:12 = *LB* IX:1218E.

44. *CWE* 76:16 = *LB* IX:1219B.

45. *CWE* 76:16 = *LB* IX:1219A.

46. *CWE* 76:19 = *LB* IX:1220C. Cummings, *The Literary Culture of the Reformation*, 151, notes that "Erasmus establishes two broadly opposing theories for determining meaning: inspiration and consensus. He has to allow some credit to the possibility of inspiration. . . . But he is mainly hostile to the claim of inspiration, using the charge . . . that inspiration is equivalent to subjectivity, even solipsism. . . . Erasmus is therefore more attached to a second form of theory based on consensus, since it appears to have greater chance of objective status—indeed it seems of itself to form a verifying principle."

47. *CWE* 76:20 = *LB* IX:1220C–D. Christ-von Wedel, *Erasmus of Rotterdam*, 251–59, offers an interpretation of Erasmus that emphasizes his development of a new historical approach to the study of Scripture and the task of theology. Christ-von Wedel protests

freedom of the will, where some passages in Scripture seem to support the will's freedom and others to deny it, there can be no ultimate contradiction since all the texts are inspired by the same Spirit. One must trust the teaching of the church to resolve the issue, bow to the judgment that there are more and clearer texts in support of free will than for its denial, and accept that the true interpretation of these other texts lies in allegory. "It seems clear that in many places Holy Scripture is obscured by figures of speech, or seems at first sight to contradict itself, so that whether we like it or not we must depart from its literal meaning and guide our judgment by interpretation."[48]

In response, Luther denies Erasmus's premise that the meaning of Scripture is not always plain. Precisely because in Luther's view Scripture is God's living and transforming proclamation to men and women it must be clear, since otherwise God would have failed in God's intention for it. There are things in God that are unclear and meant to lie beyond the ability of human intellect to grasp, but Scripture communicates that of God which God has chosen to reveal. "If Scripture is obscure or ambiguous, what point was there in God's giving it to us?"[49] Luther designates those things necessary for salvation as especially clear but he also insists that his argument applies to the whole of Scripture and that no part of it is obscure. When readers experience texts as obscure or abstruse, this is either "because of our ignorance of their vocabulary and grammar"[50] or because of "the blindness or indolence of those who will not take the trouble to look at the very clearest truth."[51] The problem lies not in the nature of the text, but in the limits of its interpreters' linguistic knowledge and in their bondage to Satan. In the latter case, it is the truths of

---

against the failure of historical-critical scholarship of the Bible fully to acknowledge its debts to Erasmus and points to Erasmus's awareness of the part played by human fallibility in the transmission of the gospel message. These are valid points but Christ-von Wedel pays insufficient attention to the features of Erasmus's historical approach that differentiate it from later historical-critical scholarship. Erasmus does not understand his commitments to philology and to textual criticism to stand in contrast to allegorical interpretation but to provide its indispensable basis. Further, Erasmus's awareness of the historically-conditioned frailty of human beings as interpreters leads him not to reject tradition as a guide to interpretation but instead to emphasize the consensus of ecclesial tradition as the safest guide.

48. *CWE* 76:87–88 = *LB* IX:1248B–C.
49. *LW* 33:93–94 = *WA* 18:655, 25–26.
50. *LW* 33:25 = *WA* 18:606, 23.
51. *LW* 33:27 = *WA* 18:607, 10–11.

Scripture themselves that as God's revelation provide the cure for such sinfulness.

These truths, Luther demands, must therefore be taught openly in all times and places: "the things set forth in Scripture are of a kind intended for all, and must necessarily be broadcast and are thoroughly salutary."[52] Erasmus's distinction is therefore a false one between those things that are true and to be proclaimed and those things that are true but about which wisdom dictates silence before the multitude. Paul's own distinction between what is lawful and what is expedient in 1 Cor 6:12 does not speak of doctrine or of teaching the truth but instead of the use made of doctrine in justifying their behavior by "those who boasted of Christian freedom but were seeking their own ends and took no account of the hurt and offense given to the weak."[53] Erasmus twists the text in order to make it mean what he wants. The doctrinal questions that Erasmus alleges are obscure in Scripture are in fact quite clear, including the truth that the human will is not free.

At this point, Luther might be thought to be locked in something of a circular argument. The Scriptures clearly demonstrate that the human will apart from Christ is not free, and yet the very fact that the Scriptures are not clear to all is a product of the bondage of the human will.[54] The risk inherent in this argument is that one will judge whether interpretations are products of the Spirit or an expression of bondage to Satan simply by whether or not they agree with one's own. All interpreters speak out of human sinfulness except those who agree that what is clear in the text is precisely what Luther says it is. Erasmus was later to imply as much in *Hyperaspistes I* when he accused Luther of wanting to "impose on us the law that we believe whatever your interpretation is."[55] For Erasmus, Luther possesses a dangerous will to interpretative power and wants "to be the lord, not the steward, of Holy Scripture."[56] In *The*

---

52. *LW* 33:57 = *WA* 18:629, 20–21.

53. *LW* 33:56 = *WA* 18:628, 26–27. Erasmus will later admit this exegetical point but argue that Paul's statement naturally has a wider application than simply to behavioral issues. See *CWE* 76:171–73 = *LB* X:1280B-E.

54. I am indebted at this point, and in my discussion of Luther's distinction between internal and external perspicuity, to James McIntosh, *What Hermeneutical Issues Does the Doctrine of Perspicuity Raise: Can the Canonical Approach of B.S. Childs Assist in Answering Them?* (ThM diss, International Christian College, 2005), 7–15.

55. *CWE* 76:132 = *LB* X:1264A.

56. *CWE* 76:176 = *LB* X:1282B.

Bondage of the Will (De servo arbitrio), Luther attempts to anticipate such criticism by drawing a crucial distinction between two different ways in which Scripture is clear. There is both "internal perspicuity" and "external perspicuity." The internal clarity of which Luther speaks relates to the enlightenment given by the Spirit to each person concerning his or her own salvation. Without this work of the Spirit, "All men have a darkened heart, so that even if they can recite everything in Scripture, and know how to quote it, yet they apprehend and truly understand nothing of it."[57] It is only with the aid of the Holy Spirit that anyone can hear Scripture as God's transforming word to them.

About this internal clarity, Luther expects that Erasmus will agree. It is in regard to his concept of external clarity that they will disagree, for Luther insists that the clarity of Scripture is also publicly, that is externally, demonstrable:

> There is therefore another, an external judgment, whereby with the greatest certainty we judge the spirits and dogmas of all men, not only for ourselves, but also for others and for their salvation. This judgment belongs to the public ministry of the Word and to the outward office, and is chiefly the concern of leaders and preachers of the Word. . . . Thus we say that all spirits are to be tested in the presence of the Church and at the bar of Scripture.[58]

In making these judgments, the church will not resort to allegory unless the context of a passage, or the absurdity of the literal sense, forces it to do so. In keeping with God's intention that Scripture communicate his truth to men and women, the literal sense should determine interpretation: "We must everywhere stick to the simple, pure, and natural sense of the words that accords with the rules of grammar and the normal use of language as God has created it in man."[59] The rules of grammar thus provide a criterion that the church will use in assessing validity in interpretation, but it is nevertheless the church that will make the judgment.

Luther does not accept that he is replacing the authority of the

57. *LW* 33:28 = *WA* 18:609, 7-9.
58. *LW* 33:90-91 = *WA* 18:653, 22-28.
59. *LW* 33:162 = *WA* 18:700, 33-35. When Luther asserts the priority of the literal sense he does not necessarily mean by that what later historical-critical scholars were to mean. For Luther, the literal sense of Old Testament texts could include Christological or typological meanings.

church with that of an individual, namely his own. In fact, he insists, "it is impossible for the Church to err, even in the smallest article."[60] Erasmus's error is to identify the true church with the visible church when, in reality, the true church is often simply a remnant, as in the time of Elijah when only seven thousand refused to bow the knee to Baal (1 Kgs 19:18), or in the time when the Arian heretics dominated the public office of the church:

> Who knows but that the state of the Church of God throughout the whole course of the world from the beginning has always been such that some have been called the People and the saints of God who were not so, while others, a remnant in their midst, really were the People of the saints, but were never called so.[61]

In applying the test of external perspicuity to interpretations of Scripture, the question of the identity of the church is a vital one for Luther. The claim that the Scriptures are obscure or ambiguous has enabled the Papacy to claim false authority and to assert that "the spirit to interpret them must be sought from the Apostolic See of Rome. Nothing more pernicious could be said than this, for it has led ungodly men to set themselves above the Scriptures and to fabricate whatever they pleased."[62]

Erasmus and Luther thus present a fascinating comparison in their approaches to the nature of Scripture and its interpretation. Both regard Scripture as an act of divine accommodation to human language, both

---

60. *LW* 33:85 = *WA* 18:650, 3–4.

61. *LW* 33:86 = *WA* 18:650, 27–30.

62. *LW* 33:90 = *WA* 18:653, 4–8. Cummings, *The Literary Culture of the Reformation*, 38–44, somewhat misconstrues Luther on this point. Cummings takes Luther's strong emphasis on both the priesthood of all believers and on the literal interpretation of Scripture in *To the Christian Nobility of the German Nation* (1520) as an indication that Luther is asserting the authority of the individual to interpret: "The laity therefore had equal access to religious truth and independent authority to interpret" (41). Although his point is certainly based upon the priesthood of all believers, the priestly status of every believer is used by Luther not to establish the right of individuals to interpret autonomously but to set the interpretive authority of the church against that of the pope. See *LW* 44:135 = *WA* 6:412, 16–19: "Again, if the article, 'I believe in one holy Christian church,' is correct, then the pope cannot be the only one who is right. Otherwise we would have to confess, 'I believe in the pope at Rome.' This would reduce the Christian church to one man, and be nothing else than a devilish and hellish error." It is significant that Luther goes on to attack the sole right of the pope to call a council of the church.

emphasize that Scripture mediates Christ, and both believe that under the guidance of the Spirit the church ultimately will not err in interpretation. Yet their convictions about how this accommodation and mediation takes place, and how the Spirit guides the church, offer striking contrasts. Working within a Platonic framework, Erasmus is convinced that the presence of Christ within Scripture enables the reader to ascend by means of allegory from the literal to the spiritual. Textual criticism and philological scholarship are to be taken immensely seriously precisely because the letter of the text is the point of entry to a higher allegorical meaning. In places Scripture is obscure and it is wise to accept that this reflects divine intention and that some truths are not for public proclamation. In cases of obscurity it is also wise to attend to the tradition of the church and bow to the consensus of that tradition, since this provides guidance concerning the intentions of the Spirit. For his part, Luther emphasizes the transforming power and purpose of Scripture and the way in which human beings encounter God in its proclamation. The words of Scripture disclose Christ directly and so there is no gap to be bridged between the letter and the Spirit. Therefore, there is little need for allegory. Instead God communicates plainly through Scripture in order to enable human transformation. For the Scriptures to be obscure would defeat their purpose. The truths of Scripture are to be openly proclaimed and when difficulties in interpretation arise, they result from human sinfulness or from limited knowledge of the biblical languages. Close attention to grammar and normal linguistic usage provides guidance concerning the intentions of the Spirit. This does not displace the role of the church in interpretation, for the true church will interpret truly. Scripture is clear and if the visible church, especially the Papacy, errs in interpretation, this indicates that it is not the true church.

1.3. Erasmus, Luther, and the Goals of Contemporary Theological Interpretation

In describing and discussing the debate between Erasmus and Luther, we have had, as those providing historical descriptions usually do, an implicit present concern. How can their debate about the nature and interpretation of Scripture serve to illuminate contemporary discussions of biblical hermeneutics? In some respects, their debate does not seem very relevant to contemporary hermeneutical concerns. It seems unlikely that Erasmus's rather elitist insistence that some biblical truths should not be spoken before the multitude, or the priority that he grants in interpretation to allegory,[63] are due for imminent revival. Commitments that were plausible, even if contested, in the context of the era and his Platonic worldview no longer command credibility. Erasmus's comment that past decisions felt to have been correct for their own time can legitimately be revised in light of present needs could here be applied for his own rescue. However, other aspects of the debate between Luther and Erasmus appear highly relevant to contemporary concerns. For the issue that lies at the core of their argument, of where authority and validity in interpretation are to be located, is a familiar one for contemporary scholarship. Both men, despite radically different definitions of the church, ultimately locate that authority and validity in the church as the church is guided by the Holy Spirit. In this sense, they are both ecclesial interpreters. Although each man in his different way would warrant mention in any competent account of the precursors of historical-critical methods, they are united from a contemporary perspective precisely by the fact that they are ecclesial and not historical-critical interpreters.

It is widely perceived that the attempt of the last two centuries or more to replace the authority of the church in interpretation with impartial historical inquiry—conducted largely by means of the heroic efforts of individual scholars—has failed. This leads some to doubt the very possibility of validity in interpretation and generates a postmodern skepticism towards all acts of interpretation claiming such validity as implicit expressions of a will to power. For others, it has prompted a renewed interest in the interpretive authority of communities, among them the church. And it is here, along the rather indistinct and permeable border between theological interpretations and more traditional historical approaches, that the debate between Erasmus and Luther is of considerable interest. Some of Erasmus and Luther's shared emphases offer implicit support to contemporary advocates of church-orientated theological hermeneutics and their accompanying critique of historical-critical approaches. Yet such advocates have perhaps paid insufficient attention to the challenges that emerge from the disagreements between Luther and

63. This is not to deny a new appreciation for allegorical interpreters of the past understood within their own historical context. See, for example, Mark Edwards, *Origen Against Plato* (Aldershot: Ashgate, 2002), 123–58. Such appreciation is rather different, however, from contemporary writers practicing allegory in their own biblical interpretation, of which there is little evidence.

Erasmus about where to locate the interpretative authority of the church. We shall in turn consider both these shared emphases and disagreements and the implications of each.

Firstly, and most importantly, both Erasmus and Luther base their faith in the transformative power of Scripture on its incarnational nature. Christ is present in the text, for both he and it are the word of God. As such, he is the very content of Scripture. For Erasmus, he is that to which the text refers. For Luther he is the very reality within the words themselves. This is the focus of their interests as biblical interpreters, and it is central to our interest in them, since insistence on Christ as the content of Scripture has been revived in contemporary debates. Brevard S. Childs argues that "the goal of the interpretation of Christian Scriptures is to understand both Testaments as a witness to the self-same divine reality who is the God and Father of Jesus Christ."[64] Similarly, Angus Paddison defines Jesus Christ as "the subject matter of which Scripture speaks."[65] Christian revelation is God in Christ and he is therefore the only appropriate focus of interpretation. The purpose of the text is to disclose him, and it is the failure of historical-critical approaches to make this their central concern that indicates their inadequacy. Their basic failing is that they direct the attention of interpreters elsewhere:

> Biblical texts are read as sources whose origins define, control and limit any reference they have beyond their original context. . . . The search for the texts' *origins* drives . . . towards reconstructing the author's *intention*, best recovered through fixed attention to the text's original *context*.[66]

At a very general level, this historical-critical concern with origins links back to the reforming efforts of Erasmus and Luther. The humanist instinct to return *ad fontes* (to the sources) and the Protestant desire to sweep away elements in the tradition of the church that distort Scripture do reflect a concern with origins. Both men speak of and devote large parts of their lives to the study and use of the biblical languages in in-

64. Brevard S. Childs, "On Reclaiming the Bible for Christian Theology," in *Reclaiming the Bible for the Church*, ed. Carl E. Braaten and Robert W. Jenson (Grand Rapids: Eerdmans, 1995), 15.

65. Angus Paddison, *Theological Hermeneutics and 1 Thessalonians* (Cambridge: Cambridge University Press, 2005), 25.

66. Paddison, *Theological Hermeneutics*, 19.

terpretation. They certainly attempt to determine the meaning of words and sentences in their original linguistic contexts. However, at no point do these concerns harden into the typical outcome of historical-critical concern with origins, intentions, and contexts. For, although both Erasmus and Luther extensively discuss Paul as the author of those biblical texts most often relevant to their debates, *they do not reconstruct Paul's theology.* Their concern is not to understand Paul as such, but to understand what the Holy Spirit has said through Paul in his texts. They focus on the disclosure of Jesus Christ by these texts as part of the wider unified witness of Scripture.[67]

This distinction is vital, for the failure to observe it has produced widespread confusion about the proper goal of interpretation. Instead of a focus on the texts themselves in their disclosure of Christ, Paul's theology, reconstructed on the basis of historical criticism of his texts, becomes normative in place of the texts.[68] This problem can be illustrated by reference to the characteristically bold and stimulating recent contributions to the discussion of Paul's theology made by Douglas Campbell. In *The Quest for Paul's Gospel*, Campbell advocates a strategy for a campaign seeking Paul's gospel: "our overarching aim in this book—our quest—has been to find Paul's Gospel."[69] Rejecting models based around justification by faith or around salvation history, Campbell proposes instead what he terms PPME (pneumatologically participatory martyrological eschatology) as a coherent conceptual center in Paul's thought. He believes that this model will prove exegetically satisfactory in explaining the details of Paul's texts and fruitful in the life and mission of the church. With its assistance, we will be able to retrieve the soteriological center of Paul's thought and hence Paul's gospel: "we want the main event, his most important thoughts about God acting in Christ."[70] In his subsequent

67. As we shall discuss below, the Reformers do regard certain biblical texts, especially Romans, as interpretative keys that act as commentaries on the rest, determining the framework within which other texts are to be read. However, once again it is certain *texts* that are prioritized, not certain authors.

68. Ulrich Luz, *Studies in Matthew* (Grand Rapids: Eerdmans, 2005), 302, comments insightfully that "the belief that the *authors* of the texts, such as the apostles or the prophetic writer of the Johannine Revelation, were inspired by the Holy Spirit outlived the belief that the biblical *texts* themselves were inspired."

69. Douglas A. Campbell, *The Quest for Paul's Gospel: A Suggested Strategy* (London and New York: Continuum, 2005), 262.

70. Campbell, *The Quest for Paul's Gospel*, 19.

The Deliverance of God, Campbell does not simply provide an alternative model of Paul's gospel but also attempts to reread justification in Paul in a way consistent with this alternative model. However, the endpoint is similar in that the deployment of historical criticism again results in a fresh restatement of the gospel: "This book is an important step in the recovery of the authentic and orthodox Pauline gospel."[71] Paul's texts thus become sources from which his gospel is reconstructed and the resultant reconstruction of Paul's gospel governs the interpretation of Paul's texts.

The difficulty here is not the circularity of this procedure. For alternative competing models could be advanced and evaluated in relation to their ability satisfactorily to enable exegesis of Paul's texts. The difficulty lies rather in the transfer of authority, and hence of the goal of interpretation, from Paul's texts to Paul. It is now Paul's reconstructed theology or gospel that is the primary location where Christ is revealed, not the texts; it is now the goal of interpretation to understand Paul, not his texts. But Paul is not the word of God. It is instead his texts that are Scripture and hence authoritative for the church. *In the event that Romans, or any other of Paul's letters, could be shown to be an uncharacteristic or atypical expression of his theology, its authority for the church as a revelation of Christ would remain entirely undiminished.* This point can be made with particular clarity in relation to Romans, for, as Childs puts it, "regardless of Paul's intention, the letter to the Romans has been heard in a particular way in the subsequent development of the Pauline corpus."[72] However its contents are to be interpreted, Romans has been received as the fitting introduction to the rest of the Pauline letters, a status indicated by its position within the canon. The main event is thus not Paul's important thoughts as such, but rather what the Holy Spirit has said through Paul. The goal of theological interpretation of Scripture is to explicate that speaking of the Spirit.

To keep this goal clearly in focus is vital, since confusion between theological interpretation and historical interpretation has bedeviled Pauline studies. This confusion can also best be illustrated by reference to Romans. As Campbell notes in *The Quest for Paul's Gospel*, the three models of Paul's theology he explores correspond largely to the

---

71. Douglas A. Campbell, *The Deliverance of God: An Apocalyptic Rereading of Justification in Paul* (Grand Rapids: Eerdmans, 2009), 935.

72. Brevard S. Childs, *The Church's Guide for Reading Paul: The Canonical Shaping of the Pauline Corpus* (Grand Rapids: Eerdmans, 2008), 67.

soteriological priority granted to different argumentative units in Romans. Those finding the key to Paul's gospel in justification by faith appeal above all to chs. 1–4, those championing PPME to chs. 5–8, and those advocating salvation history to chs. 9–11. Typically interpreters seek to show that their favored argumentative unit is central to Paul and underlies the neighboring units.[73] Campbell himself takes a rather different route, fully developing in *The Deliverance of God* the argument that large parts of Rom 1:18–3:20 represent not Paul's own perspective but that of a teacher whom Paul is attempting to refute.[74] However, the resulting conclusion is similar: "only now is it possible to affirm coherently Paul's construal of 'sanctification,' which he seems to discuss with such profundity in Rom 5–8, elevating this material now to its rightful status. Paul's account of sanctification *is* the gospel."[75] Richard Longenecker reaches the same destination by a different route when he argues for the priority of Rom 5–8 on the basis that what Paul writes earlier in Rom 1–4 is what he shared with those to whom he wrote, being "based immediately on the confessions of the earliest Jewish believers in Jesus and ultimately on the fundamental structures and thought of Early Judaism."[76] It is when we reach chs. 5–8 that we reach what is quintessentially Pauline and what provides a statement of his gospel. This priority of chs. 5–8 "has great significance for our living as Christians, our proclamation of the gospel, and our contextualization of the essential Christian tradition."[77]

In both these instances, the need to demonstrate the priority of Rom 5–8 prompts a resort to misconceived historical arguments in order to sustain what is ultimately a theological preference. Campbell's novel proposal that Rom 1:18–3:20 largely does not represent Paul's own voice has immediately attracted criticism for its implausibility, whether because it is possible to indicate "points at which Paul's voice is present within this text in a way that it should not be according to Campell's re-

---

73. Campbell, *The Quest for Paul's Gospel*, 22–26.

74. This idea does also appear in Campbell, *The Quest for Paul's Gospel*, 233–61.

75. Campbell, *The Deliverance of God*, 934.

76. Richard N. Longenecker, *Introducing Romans: Critical Issues in Paul's Most Famous Letter* (Grand Rapids: Eerdmans, 2011), 366. This claim concerns 3:21–4:25 specifically, but Longenecker makes a very similar claim about 1:18–3:20 also (363). See now also, Richard N. Longenecker, *The Epistle to the Romans*, NIGTC (Grand Rapids: Eerdmans, 2016), 16–18, 538–47.

77. Longenecker, *Introducing Romans*, 376.

reading,"[78] or because of the lack of parallels in other ancient sources to "a thoroughgoing, extended use of speech-in-character in Rom 1:18–3:20," or because Campbell proposes "a flickering alternation between Paul's own thought and that of his opponent, and at each point this seems highly subjective."[79] In Longenecker's argument, the false assumption is made that what is of primary significance and authority in Paul's texts is what is unique to Paul in his historical context. For Longenecker and Campbell alike, it is only in Rom 5–8 that we hear with clarity Paul's own voice and it is in hearing Paul's own voice that we hear the gospel.

Yet if our goal is to understand what the Holy Spirit has said through Paul in his texts, then it does not necessarily follow that what he shares with those to whom he writes is of less significance than what is distinctive to Paul. Only if the historical figure of Paul possessed canonical authority could what is distinctive to him function as a criterion by which to assess the relative importance of different bodies of material within his letters. The problem is thus not merely that in the work of two such outstanding Pauline scholars the priority of Rom 5–8 is asserted using arguments that contradict each other. The obvious conflict between the position that Rom 1:18–3:20 reflects what Paul holds in common with those to whom he wrote (so Longenecker) and the position that large parts of it represent the position of a teacher whom Paul is attempting to refute (so Campbell) is merely symptomatic of a deeper issue.

This deeper issue is that there is little indication in the text of Romans as to which argumentative unit or units ought to be given priority in interpretation. Longenecker and Campbell's unconvincing historical arguments merely evade this difficulty. The Holy Spirit speaking through Paul has not communicated the priority of one or more argumentative units and so, although commonplace, for an ecclesial interpreter to build an interpretative strategy upon that priority is a false move. It results in theological preferences masquerading as historical arguments. We justify prioritizing one argumentative unit over the others on historical grounds but our primary reason is that we find it theologically appealing. This does not necessarily mean that our theological preferences are invalid or lack other good reasons, but it does mean that we are confusing

78. Barry Matlock, "Zeal for Paul but Not According to Knowledge: Douglas Campbell's War on 'Justification Theory,'" *JSNT* 34.2 (2011): 141.

79. Grant Macaskill, review of *The Deliverance of God*, by Douglas A. Campbell, *JSNT* 34.2 (2011): 159.

the goals of theological interpretation and historical interpretation. This confusion can be avoided only if we recognize that the goal of theological interpretation is not to understand Paul, but to understand what the Spirit has said through Paul in his texts as a revelation of Christ.

In making such a claim, it is almost as important to clarify what is not being said as it is to make the claim itself. My claim concerns the appropriate goal of different types of interpretation and is not a wholesale condemnation of historical interpretation and its methods. As we shall see, despite their different goals, the characteristic methods and procedures of theological interpretation and those of historical interpretation must overlap extensively in practice. The same tools can legitimately be used to perform different tasks. Further, attempts to reconstruct Paul's theology have their own rationale that makes sense in their own historical sphere. As one of the most influential figures in world history, it can be no less legitimate for the historian to want to understand Paul's thought than it can be to wish to understand that of Plato or of John Calvin or of a whole host of other major figures. Similarly, the assumption that there is a coherent center to Paul's thought that finds contingent expression in his various letters is entirely defensible. Although the authority of his letters for the church does not depend on them being characteristic expressions of his thought, it is perhaps unlikely that in dealing with issues in the life of the communities which he had striven to establish and serve, Paul would do anything other than bring his most important convictions to bear upon their difficulties and concerns. We may question whether the occasional nature and limited number of the texts available to us provide sufficient evidence on the basis of which to recover Paul's theology, but this doubt concerns whether the project is realizable, not whether it is legitimate in principle. My point is not that the project is wrong but that, even if achievable, its results can never be an authoritative guide to interpretation for the church. For in the church, authority lies with the Spirit-inspired texts in their disclosure of Christ, not with a reconstruction of the theology argued to have underlain those texts. Theological interpretation and historical interpretation each has its own validity, and the same scholar may with complete legitimacy engage in both at different times, but they are different from each other in their goals and should not be pursued as if those goals are the same.

1.4. Erasmus, Luther, and the Conflict of Interpretations

In drawing out the implications of the debate between Erasmus and Luther in relation to contemporary hermeneutics, it seems that so far we have favored Luther. Their joint relevance as ecclesial interpreters, for whom the content of Scripture is Christ, has been explored, but it is only Erasmus who has been critiqued in any detail. His view that some scriptural truths must not be spoken openly has been rejected. Although it has not been the focus of our discussion of the goals of theological and historical interpretation, Luther's understanding of Scripture as a divine communicative act undertaken for the purpose of disclosing Christ has been implicit. It is true of Scripture that, as James A. Nestingen summarizes Luther's understanding, "In the narratives, in the contradictions, in the hiddenness and obscurities that can be seen to mark all of God's dealings with sinful humanity in light of the cross, God in Christ is making himself known as the one at work in every moment."[80] Indeed, Erasmus's reliance on allegory as the vehicle by which the Spirit persuades human beings to rise to the truth through the doorway of the text could be criticized as a different version of the same mistake as that made by historical criticism. When allegory is relied upon, the locus of revelation and hence both the goal of interpretation and the site of authority, becomes somewhere other than the text itself, above, beyond, or behind it.

However, there are other aspects of the debate where Erasmus fares better. In his criticism of Luther's concept of the external clarity of Scripture, Erasmus successfully identified issues concerning conflict between interpretations that have proved problematic ever since. Luther's claim that his followers and not Rome constituted the one true church was undermined by Protestantism's enduring propensity to split precisely over issues of biblical interpretation. Already in *Hyperaspistes I* in 1526 Erasmus could pointedly ask, "If Holy Scripture is perfectly clear in all respects, where does this darkness among you come from, whence arise such fights to the death about the meaning of Scripture?"[81] Luther's claims about the church have been queried by the experience of the church. The teaching authority of the Catholic Church, on which

---

80. James A. Nestingen, "Introduction: Luther and Erasmus on the Bondage of the Will," in Gerhard O. Forde, *The Captivation of the Will: Luther vs. Erasmus on Freedom and Bondage*, ed. Steven D. Paulson (Grand Rapids: Eerdmans, 2005), 16.
    81. *CWE* 76:222 = *LB* X:1302D.

Erasmus ultimately relied to resolve interpretative disagreement, has proved irreplaceable. For in later centuries neither the substitution of the hermeneutical norms of various Protestant catechisms nor their own replacement by historical-critical methods have proved able to resolve disagreements.

Of enduring relevance also is Erasmus's sense that due weight in judging between interpretations ought to be given to the holy lives of previous interpreters whose views Luther rejects. He cannot be fully satisfied as an explanation for the existence of conflicts in interpretation with Luther's observation that even genuinely Spirit-filled interpreters can be wrong about some things without being wrong in everything. This may be true, but, once again, the subsequent endemic and enduring multiplication of interpretative disagreements within Protestantism tends to endorse Erasmus's view that the errors of readers are not sufficient to explain the apparent obscurity of parts of Scripture. The difficulty lies also in the texts themselves, not solely in human sinfulness. Erasmus is also incredulous at Luther's claim that, along with sinfulness, the existence of difficulties in interpretation can be attributed entirely to our limited knowledge of biblical languages: "if knowledge of grammar alone removes all obscurity from Sacred Scripture, how did it happen that St. Jerome, who knew all the languages, was so often at a loss?"[82] The texts are not always clear, and Erasmus's concern with how interpretative disagreements are to be resolved is as pressing today as it was in the sixteenth century. He identified this enduring problem in the historical moment in which it arose. If not by the Catholic Church, nor by the test of Protestant catechisms, nor by the assured results of historical scholarship, how are we to adjudicate between conflicting interpretations and to know what is a good reading of a text and what is a poor one?

While it is very unlikely that any complete solution lies to hand for a problem of almost five hundred years standing, it is certainly unnecessary at this point to yield to interpretative despair or to abandon faith in the capacity of the Spirit-inspired texts to reveal Christ. The debate between Erasmus and Luther does help us at least to establish a framework for interpretation. Firstly, while theological interpreters are correct

---

82. *CWE* 76:130 = *LB* X:1263C. Cummings, *The Literary Culture of the Reformation*, 29, comments on Montaigne's assessment of the impact of the Reformation on interpretation: "Luther has offered the ultimate linguistic fiction of a language without fiction, of words which really do render things. In the process he has apparently destroyed all confidence in any language which appears to do less."

to locate interpretive validity and authority in the church, simply to assert this is not sufficient. It is not enough to argue that, "In the face of fear of countless subjective readings, the presence of the church is a reminder that there is a specific community and tradition, normed by the Word, with the authority to determine the limits to particular interpretations."[83] The problem is precisely that within the church there is endemic disagreement in the exercise of this authority. If "the meaning of Scripture is historically generated within the life of the interpreting church,"[84] then the church has been too productive for its own good. The task of ecclesial interpreters is not to generate meaning within the life of the interpreting church, but rather to receive meaning there. Scripture has a perennial freshness; it is not an archaeological relic, but that freshness is known only as a gift: "Scripture is not an initial textual stage in divine revelation that is then completed by churchly activity. . . . The church does not illuminate Scripture but is illuminated by it and is wholly dependent upon Scripture to dispel its ignorance."[85]

It is at this point that the characteristic methods and procedures of historical criticism become a help rather than a hindrance to theological interpretation. The texts bear witness to the incarnation of Christ in a particular historical context and do so by means of human languages that are themselves subject to historical processes. These processes sometimes create challenges for the interpretation of texts in later eras and different locations. Luther's suspicion that what passes for obscurity in Scripture is often no more than the dislike of interpreters for what the text very clearly says may be well-founded, but this is not the only cause of debate about interpretation. Difficulties in interpretation are part of human processes of communication and should be understood within the divine accommodation of human language involved in the gift of Scripture. The Scriptures thus do not disclose Christ despite the historical processes to which the texts are subject but by means of them. The divine decision to work in this way, the triune God accommodating human realities, means that the exploration of these realities is necessary to Scripture's disclosure of its content, which is Christ. To locate authority in interpretation with the Spirit-inspired texts in their disclosure of Christ

83. Paddison, *Theological Hermeneutics*, 32.
84. Paddison, *Theological Hermeneutics*, 31.
85. John Webster, "Biblical Theology and the Clarity of Scripture," in *Out of Egypt: Biblical Theology and Biblical Interpretation*, ed. Craig R. Bartholomew, Mary Healy, Karl Möller, and Robin Parry (Carlisle: Paternoster; Grand Rapids: Eerdmans, 2004), 372.

does not require that we evade the challenge of historical reconstruction, but rather that we understand the role of historical reconstruction to be that of the servant of theological interpretation.[86] To explore the texts within the historical processes to which they are subject is not the goal of interpretation, and to suppose that it is the goal of interpretation causes endless confusion. Nevertheless, such exploration is necessary to assist theological interpretation towards its true goal.

There is thus great value for theological interpretation in exegesis to be subject to rigorous testing using the tools of historical criticism. In relation to Paul, this means we must recognize that answering some questions about Paul's communicative intentions on the basis of the evidence provided by the texts themselves is a precondition of their interpretation. We may not make the reconstruction of Paul's theology the goal of our interpretive activity, but it is necessary in some measure in order to serve the interpretation of his texts. The need for reconstruction also extends to gaining some sense of Paul's personality and approach to ministry, a discernment that will inevitably reflect the interpreter's own character to some degree.[87] This can be illustrated by the different interpretations of Paul's personality and approach to ministry involved in the disagreement between Erasmus and Luther over the interpretation of Gal 2:11. The contrast is instructive between the fearless proclaimer of the gospel that is Luther's Paul and the careful teacher accommodating the limitations of his pupils that is Erasmus's Paul. It is also difficult to imagine fruitful theological interpretation of Paul's letters that does not reconstruct the situations of the early Christian communities addressed in his letters. For example, which interpreter of Galatians can exegete the text without reconstructing the crisis that provoked its composition? Mirror-reading of Paul's texts is hazardous but unavoidable.[88]

For all these reasons, there is no justification for doing anything other than subjecting theological readings of Paul's texts to the most rigorous and critical historical examination. Theological interpreters will

---

86. In particular, it does not necessitate an ahistorical approach to the transmission of the texts themselves or an underestimation of the task of textual criticism.

87. A powerful and helpful reminder of this is provided by Margaret M. Mitchell, *The Heavenly Trumpet: John Chrysostom and the Art of Pauline Interpretation*, HUT 40 (Tübingen: Mohr Siebeck, 2000).

88. On mirror-reading, see John M. G. Barclay, "Mirror-Reading a Polemical Letter: Galatians as a Test Case," in *The Galatians Debate*, ed. Mark D. Nanos (Peabody, MA: Hendrickson, 2002), 367–82.

use historical arguments in exegesis. This does not guarantee interpretative agreement, and responsible historical argument may often seek to demonstrate merely that a preferred conclusion is more likely than the alternatives. Such use of historical arguments does, however, serve to define some limits to the interpretive discussion. For example, in the impassioned debates concerning what Paul means by the phrase "works of the law" (ἔργα νόμου) there have in the history of exegesis been only three broadly credible answers, and one of these may well be fatally wounded. Paul intends either to refer to human attempts to please God by our actions (so Luther), or to refer primarily to the social function of those aspects of the law that served as boundary markers for Jewish communities in their relationships with Gentiles (so James Dunn and other NPP interpreters). The view that Paul intends the ceremonial aspects of the law in contrast to those that might be termed ethical (so much of the medieval tradition) lacks historical justification. It may be possible to mediate between the first two positions in various ways, but not to appeal to the third. The theological interpreter will be no less deeply engaged in these debates than any historical critic since the outcome affects the manner in which the text discloses Christ and shapes the pattern made by the impact of that disclosure in particular cultural locations. Only through engagement in such debates can the building blocks be assembled for the interpretation of whole texts.

It is when the theological interpreter attempts to move to the wider interpretation of whole texts that the danger of substituting our reconstruction of Paul's theology for his texts arises. The reason for the particularly seductive nature of this temptation is explained by Paul Ricoeur:

> A text is more than a linear succession of sentences. It is a cumulative, holistic process. This specific structure of the text cannot be derived from that of the sentence. Therefore the kind of plurivocity which belongs to texts as texts is something more than the polysemy of individual words in ordinary language and the ambiguity of individual sentences. This plurivocity is typical of the text considered as a whole, open to several readings and several constructions.[89]

89. Paul Ricoeur, "The Model of the Text: Meaningful Action Considered as a Text," in *Hermeneutics and the Human Sciences: Essays on Language, Action and Interpretation*, ed. John B. Thompson (Cambridge: Cambridge University Press, 1981), 197-221.

Faced by the openness of our texts, we sometimes grasp to answer questions that are beyond historical reach. Unable to answer in anything other than highly provisional manner many of our questions about the theology of Paul the person, we make such provisional answers normative in our theological interpretation of Paul's texts, relegating one or other significant aspect of their content to subsidiary status. Our judgments about Paul's intention thus displace important aspects of the Holy Spirit's communicative activity. This is serious not because we have failed to reflect equally the significance of every part of Paul's texts in our interpretation. No single interpretation can direct its attention everywhere with equal focus. The problem is rather that in presenting historical reasons for prioritizing one or another aspect of the content of Paul's texts over the others, we have presented as normative our own theological preferences. By confusing the goal of theological interpretation, which is an understanding of the Holy Spirit's communication through Paul in his texts, with the goal of much historical interpretation, which is to reconstruct Paul's theology, we claim to have revealed Paul's gospel and seek to reshape the life and witness of the church on that authoritative basis. What we actually have is less sweeping, but for all that still potentially precious: a discernment, to be offered to the church for prayerful evaluation, of what the Spirit is saying to us through Paul's texts.

In offering such theological interpretations we should recognize that only historically plausible interpretations will be regarded as credible. The legions of implausible historical theses generated by the rewards granted to novelty in the building of scholarly careers can be safely discarded. However, we should also recognize that precisely because of their historical nature as ancient texts our knowledge of which is limited, it may be possible to provide several different accounts of what the Spirit is saying to us through Paul's texts that have more or less equal claims to historical plausibility. It is precisely this that accounts for our inability to reach a conclusion as to the center of Paul's theology. Justification by faith, participation in Christ, and salvation history all provide credible solutions to that debate. We may rightly insist that whichever one of the three is chosen as central, its formulation must be capable of including, and making sense of, those texts where the other two are dominant. It will not do to ignore texts where the other two are dominant or to interpret those texts in other terms. Nevertheless, there are no convincing historical criteria available to help us to judge which of the three is most central. The more fruitful path is to recognize this and thus to abandon our chimerical quest for Paul's theology. Instead we should offer more transparent theological explanations of why we find one of these concepts a more satisfactory center than the others around which to organize our interpretation of Paul's letters. Or, as I have suggested elsewhere, we may abandon the idea of a center constituted simply by a single theme, and instead identify and examine several important concepts as central, the significance of which lies in their inter-dependence and the way in which they are used by Paul to interpret each other.[90] Either way, theological lights will no longer need to be hidden under historical bushels, and explicitly theological concerns and concepts will find their place in the interpretive process in two principal ways.

First, the canon will play an important role. For as much as their reading of Scripture as a whole was profoundly shaped by their understanding of Paul, Erasmus and Luther were seeking an understanding of what the Spirit was saying through Scripture rather than through a single author. Thus, interpretations of Paul's texts must be plausible in the context of the reception of Scripture as a unified whole by the church. This is not to deny the existence of tensions within the canon. To harmonize prematurely the witness of various texts is to suppress the voice of the Spirit speaking through such tensions. And yet, the very existence of such tensions serves to enable a deeper unity precisely by placing constraints upon the interpretation of other canonical texts. For example, it will not do to pretend that Romans and Galatians on the one hand and the second chapter of James on the other teach the same thing about justification. They are different, and Paul is justly the louder canonical voice, but James decisively closes the door on crudely antinomian readings of Paul's texts just as Paul's texts serve to close the door on crudely Pelagian readings of the Sermon on the Mount.[91]

The canon, itself established through the work of the Spirit in the

90. Stephen J. Chester, *Conversion at Corinth: Perspectives on Conversion in Paul's Theology and the Corinthian Church* (London and New York: T&T Clark, 2003), 205-10.

91. The debate between Luther and Erasmus on the question of the clarity of Scripture proceeds without reflection on the difference made in interpretation by genre. As Anthony C. Thiselton, "Reception Theory, H.R. Jauss and the Formative Power of Scripture," *SJT* 65.3 (2012): 303, puts it, "'Open,' 'literary' or 'poetic' texts may lend themselves to multiple treatments far more readily than 'closed,' 'transmissive' or 'informational,' or 'engineering' texts." A discussion of biblical interpretation in general would need to pay more attention to this issue than I have done in an argument concerned specifically with interpretation within the single genre of the epistle.

church, thus serves to define some boundaries in interpretation as readers seek to listen to what the Spirit is saying to the church through the texts. "The preacher cannot be 'Jesusian' this week, then 'Jamesian' or 'Pauline' next Sunday,"[92] for there is only one Holy Spirit who speaks through the texts. Those scandalized by the imposition of the theological norm of the canon on texts that emerge from historically diverse expressions of early Christianity should themselves recall the historical fact that the canon is "the interpretative structure that the biblical text received from those who formed it and used it as sacred scripture."[93] As James McIntosh argues, "without the use of these texts as Scripture by the faith community, and the associated structuring of them as a unity, we would, arguably, not have these texts today."[94] In other words, historically it is only the twin convictions that the Spirit has granted unity to these texts and that the Spirit therefore speaks through these texts as a unified whole that generated the commitment necessary for the laborious work of copying. This copying, in turn, guaranteed their survival. The church and the canon are themselves historical preconditions for the very possibility of historical criticism.

In some ways, the criterion of canon will remain implicit in the rest of this study rather than being made explicit. As already noted, the Reformers were certainly not without their own picture of Paul, including his personality and characteristic concerns, but they did not produce interpretations of Paul's theology as such. They offered interpretations of particular Pauline texts, in which they often made significant use of other biblical texts, or made use of these texts in doctrinal works that also employed other scriptural resources.[95] In offering a discussion of how they interpreted Paul and its implications for contemporary interpretation, I am therefore operating within the genre conventions of

92. Luz, *Studies in Matthew*, 348. It must be recognized, however, that while such a sense of the unified voice of Scripture is indispensable, there is also more than one way in which that unified canonical voice may be heard by interpreters. To give merely one of the most obvious examples, a Lutheran canonical hermeneutic which organizes the relationship between the Testaments around the dialectic between law and gospel will be rather different from a Reformed canonical hermeneutic.

93. Brevard S. Childs, *Introduction to the Old Testament as Scripture* (London: SCM Press, 1979), 73.

94. McIntosh, *What Hermeneutical Issues Does the Doctrine of Perspicuity Raise?*, 39.

95. I believe that a study of their biblical intertextuality, for example of their use of John in the interpretation of Paul and vice versa, might enhance considerably our understanding of any of the major Reformers as biblical interpreters.

historical-critical scholarship rather than directly reflecting the more canonical ones of the sixteenth century. It is also the case that in drawing a distinction in relation to validity in interpretation between Paul's theology and the communicative action of the Holy Spirit through Paul's texts, I have left unaddressed the issue of which texts Paul is the author. For the Reformers there are thirteen letters unquestionably by Paul, but for historical-critical scholarship only seven are undisputed.[96] Nevertheless the Reformers' own convictions about the shape of the canon serve to mitigate these tensions. Just as for a recent canonical critic like Childs, so for the Reformers the letter to the Romans plays a special role. Luther states that "this epistle is really the chief part of the New Testament, and is truly the purest gospel."[97] Similarly, Calvin writes that "If we have gained a true understanding of this Epistle, we have an open door to all the most profound treasures of Scripture."[98] Galatians, in which similar themes appear, received passionate engagement from Luther and in the commentary of 1531/1535 resulted in his single most influential work of biblical interpretation.

Thus other biblical texts will typically be read and assessed by the Reformers in a way consistent with their key convictions about the central themes of Romans and Galatians. This is true for the other Pauline epistles. The Reformers may assume a single author of the entire thirteen Pauline epistles in a way that most contemporary scholarship does not, but in treating Romans and also Galatians as providing a key to the correct interpretation of the whole corpus, they foreground epistles accepted by historical-critical scholarship as coming from Paul himself. In this study the main focus is therefore on Romans and Galatians, but I do include where appropriate some material drawing upon the Reformers' interpretations of the now disputed epistles. I also sometimes use designations such as "Paul's texts" without either implying a commitment to the apostle's authorship of all the disputed epistles or conceding that the possibility of pseudonymous authorship in some instances compromises the canonical unity of the entire collection. The hermeneutical centrality of Romans and Galatians also holds true for the Reformers in relation to the rest of Scripture, as the quotations above from Luther and Calvin attest. In exploring

---

96. For the latest significant contribution to the very long-running debate within historical scholarship concerning Pauline authorship, see Douglas A. Campbell, *Framing Paul: An Epistolary Biography* (Grand Rapids: Eerdmans, 2014).

97. *LW* 35:365 = *WA* DB 7:3, 3–4.

98. *CNTC* 8:5 = *Argumentum in Epistolam ad Romanos* = *OE* 13:7, 11–12.

vital themes in the Reformers' interpretations of Paul's texts, I am therefore exploring what was for them the ground of the unity of the canon. In doing so, I am not assuming that to grant Romans canonical priority is the only procedure open to contemporary theological interpretation, but I am attempting to further our understanding of themes in Paul's letters that are essential in any discernment of the overall consistency of the canon.

Second, alongside the canon, current theological concerns also appropriately find a role in shaping the interpretation of Scripture. If the NPP is more consistent than many previous interpretations with theological respect for Judaism, community as a crucial goal of Christian faith, and respect for the cultures of others, these are strengths to which its advocates may legitimately appeal.[99] Such values do not remove or trump the requirement for historical plausibility, but neither should we pretend that they are unintentional consequences of objective historical investigation. These values form part of the motivation for (albeit often hidden) and partial explanations for the success of new interpretations of Paul. Those of us not persuaded by the NPP should be equally unafraid to highlight the value of theological themes and issues neglected in its advocates' readings of Paul's texts but placed in the foreground in our own. Nor should we seek to evade the challenge of demonstrating that our own interpretations are consistent with those values that the NPP has constructively embodied.

This is not to justify all forms of cultural relativism in interpretation. When we reconstruct the meaning of a text, we need to be reminded "that it is only a construction that we can offer, but that is not to say that some reconstructions are not (a lot) better than others."[100] There may be many theological interpretations of Paul's texts that owe little to the texts and owe more to contemporary values that are utterly inconsistent with what the texts themselves teach. Here the proper course is to reject such interpretations. It is just as plausible in principle that the Spirit should speak through Paul's texts in order to judge contemporary values and

---

99. See John M. G. Barclay, "Neither Jew nor Greek: Multiculturalism and the New Perspective on Paul," in *Ethnicity and the Bible*, ed. Mark G. Brett (Leiden: Brill, 1996), 197–214. Barclay comments about the NPP both that "few of its practitioners" seem conscious of these influences (199) and that interpretations of Paul "naturally (and properly) reflect the social and cultural questions dominant in the interpreters' environment" (197).

100. John K. Riches, "Why Write a Reception-Historical Commentary?," *JSNT* 29.3 (2007): 329.

mores as it is that the Spirit should use contemporary values and mores in order to alert the church to previously neglected emphases in Scripture. Either way, however, if Scripture is a living word through which the Spirit guides the church in the present, it is both unsurprising and appropriate that current theological criteria find a place in shaping and evaluating interpretation alongside historical criteria and in a manner appropriately disciplined by historical criteria.

The conflict of interpretations is thus best addressed by a mixed hermeneutic. The goal of hearing the Spirit speak through Paul in his texts is served by applying the triple criteria of historical plausibility, canonical consistency, and contemporary theological fruitfulness. Historical plausibility is foundational in the sense that the other two criteria can only fruitfully be applied once we already have a sense of credible possibilities in the interpretation of particular texts. Without the test of historical plausibility, the application of the other two criteria is in danger of becoming arbitrary. Nevertheless, the three belong together in the practice of theological interpretation. The identification of these criteria does not resolve the issues of validity and authority in interpretation, for their application certainly will not eliminate interpretive disagreement. They do, however, guide us away from both the false assumption that the texts can mean anything that interpreters say they do and the illusion that a final or definitive interpretation of a text is possible. In doing so, they define an arena for discussion in which judgment about interpretations can be pursued in, with, and for the church. Where theological interpretations fail to meet these criteria, and fall outside the boundaries of the arena, there may be occasion for Luther's favored interpretative mode of the assertion of truth in defense of the gospel. Sometimes to be for the church is necessarily to oppose the church, and then we may appropriately empathize with Luther's frustration at Erasmus's evasion of the institutional church's abuse of power in exercising its interpretative role, specifically Erasmus's refusal to recognize that his own scholarship had often served to expose this.[101] Contemporary theological interpretations

---

101. An otherwise sympathetic observer, Erika Rummel, *Erasmus* (London and New York: Continuum, 2004), 105, comments that Erasmus's desire to protect humanistic studies from the opprobrium adhering to the Reformers "involved him in the hopeless quest of separating philology from exegesis, which led him to adopt a willful blindness and to resort to implausible disclaimers." In other words, there were instances in which Erasmus refused to reject historically implausible interpretations even when his own work showed them to be so.

of Scripture often argue for a return to primarily communal modes of interpretation over against modes that are primarily individual. This is helpful in a variety of ways. Yet there can be no naïve assumption that communities of readers are inherently less likely to prove mistaken than individuals. Prophetic address to the erring people of God is after all prominent within Scripture itself.

More frequently, however, when competing interpretations can plausibly lay claim to serious consideration within the ongoing process of discernment of the Spirit's speaking through the texts, the civility favored by Erasmus will be the appropriate interpretive mode. Different Christian traditions and communities—chastened by the degree to which the events of the 1520s continue to overshadow the interpretation of Scripture—should regard the extension to each other of such civility as normal. The assumption, shared by both Erasmus and Luther, that the Spirit will ultimately lead the church into truth and that the church is therefore unable finally to err in matters of interpretation, is a divine promise that holds good only if human interpreters are shaped by that same Spirit, the first fruit of which is love (Gal 5:22). Erasmus's dismay at Luther's inability to recognize that his own interpretive judgments and those of the true church are not simply to be identified with each other continues to be salutary as we engage the task of interpretation for the contemporary world.

1.5. Erasmus, Luther, and Reception History

To some, it will appear that the defining of an arena for discussion in which judgments about interpretation in, with, and for the church can be pursued is an exercise in intellectual and spiritual damage limitation. They will regard it as the best that can be done in the face of the brokenness of the interpretative authority of the church initiated by the rupture of the Reformation. But in fact, this is not our situation and to understand why not, it is necessary to consider the historical location of interpreters. This factor in interpretation was at least acknowledged by Erasmus in his suggestion that it was possible for church councils to make decisions valid for their own time but now in need of revision. Historical location was completely overlooked by Luther, for whom "Paul was a contemporary. In Luther's mind there was no intellectual or human progress from Paul's day to his that would alter the theological task."[102] Yet progress lies in the eye of the beholder, and the relevance of historical location for interpretation comes less from intellectual or human progress than it does from the nature of divine revelation. Far from overlooking historical location, we should appreciate its importance for contemporary interpretation by attending to its theological significance. The Word became flesh at a time and place that is not our own, and that the Word did so "in accordance with the Scriptures," means that "for Christian theology, truth is textually mediated."[103] It is in the ancient texts, by means of their mediation, that we encounter Christ.

This textual mediation of truth should remove from us the temptation to believe that historical distance and differences between interpreters and the authors and first readers of biblical texts form an ugly ditch that must be overcome. "Distance in time is to be put to use and not—as historicism would have it—overcome, that is, abolished through a one-sided transplanting of the self into the spirit of the past."[104] The particular forms taken by the differences and the distance may partially be shaped by human sinfulness, but that there are differences, and that there is distance, is of itself no barrier to interpretation. The existence of historical differences and distance is divinely appointed. It is right to recognize that because the church now is united to the same grace of which the texts speak, there is also some continuity of interpretative location between the church now and the church then,[105] but it is a mistake to offer this as a counterweight to the existence of historical differences and distance as if their very existence were itself problematic.[106] For the Spirit chooses to speak now through texts written then. To treat this choice as problematic is to doubt divine wisdom.

102. Kenneth Hagen, *Luther's Approach to Scripture As Seen in His 'Commentaries' on Galatians* (Tübingen: Mohr Siebeck, 1993), 33.

103. Francis Watson, *Text and Truth: Redefining Biblical Theology* (Edinburgh: T&T Clark, 1997), 1.

104. Hans R. Jauss, *Question and Answer: Forms of Dialogic Understanding*, trans. Michael Hays (Minneapolis: University of Minnesota Press, 1989), 205. Jauss is here summarizing important aspects of Hans-Georg Gadamer, *Truth and Method,* 2nd ed. (New York: Crossroad, 1990), 297. Gadamer comments that temporal distance "is not a yawning abyss but is filled with the continuity of custom and tradition, in the light of which everything handed down presents itself to us."

105. Paddison, *Theological Hermeneutics*, 49.

106. John K. Riches, "Reception History as a Challenge to Biblical Theology," *JTI* 7.2 (2013): 185: "Truth is to be found as we live in this flux, not by leaping out of our historical skins."

The theological interpreter should instead regard the ministry and mission of the church spread through time and space as that which the biblical texts are inherently suited to enable. The task of the church is not to get back to the time and place in which the texts were composed but, empowered by the texts, to participate in the eschatological fulfillment of the ministry and mission given to it. The texts themselves testify that the interpretive process has an eschatological destination: "Go therefore and make disciples of all nations, baptizing them in the name of the Father and of the Son and of the Holy Spirit, and *teaching them to obey everything that I have commanded you. And remember, I am with you always, to the end of the age*" (Matt 28:19–20). As the church, straining towards the promise of eternity, endeavors to interpret and apply all that Christ has commanded through Scripture, Christ himself, the very content of Scripture, is no less present with the church of each successive generation than with the believers of those generations that produced the texts: "Have you believed because you have seen me? *Blessed are those who have not seen and yet have come to believe*" (John 20:29). Thus, while historical criticism plays a powerful role in exploring through the biblical texts the event of incarnation in a particular historical context, there is no necessary conflict between this and interpretation for the present. "Revelation as event and revelation as process, far from being mutually exclusive, are intrinsically bound together."[107]

To understand revelation in this way explains why it is a positive development to define an arena for discussion in which judgments about interpretation in, with, and for the church can be pursued. It is not merely a way of containing otherwise regrettable interpretative disagreements. For as the ministry and mission of the church, on the path to eschatological fulfillment, unfold across space and time, the same texts are able to nourish that work under very different historical conditions. Were it possible to produce definitive acts of interpretation, to succeed, for example, once and for all in a quest for Paul's gospel, his texts would immediately cease to provide such nourishment to succeeding generations of readers. In their different historical location the final word spoken yesterday would prove ineffective in revealing Christ today and tomorrow. A certain plurality in interpretation, which mirrors the diversity present within the very canon itself, is a crucial factor in the speaking of the Holy Spirit through the texts to every generation. Because the word lives, it is

---

107. Paddison, *Theological Hermeneutics*, 59. I am, of course, here pointing towards the significance of the church's performance of the texts in interpretation.

possible for new interpretations of texts to arise that satisfy the criteria of historical plausibility, canonical consistency, and contemporary theological fruitfulness. As they do so, they sustain the ministry and mission of the church in new historical contexts. Within the limits imposed by these three criteria, it is possible for there to be valid interpretations that meet the needs of an era but that are unable to do so as completely or satisfactorily in those of succeeding ones.

In making these points about temporality, I am clearly expressing in theological terms a parallel set of insights to those expressed in literary and philosophical terms within the field of reception history.[108] Building upon the work of Hans-Georg Gadamer and especially upon that of Gadamer's student, Hans Robert Jauss, reception theorists urge that attention be paid to the unfolding of the interpretation of texts within traditions across time:

> The possibility for diversity in understanding through time and across cultures is not evidence that we are never arriving at better

108. Recent attempts within Biblical Studies to characterize reception history as a field of scholarly activity seem less than fully successful, particularly in the inability of its proponents successfully to conceive its relationship to theology. See especially, Christopher Rowland and Jonathan Roberts, "Introduction," *JSNT* 33.2 (2010): 131-36: "The hermeneutical self-consciousness engendered by reception history makes the proprietorial academic and ecclesiastical claims over the biblical texts inadequate and the bracketing out of the particular context of the interpreting subject, whether religious or not, unsatisfactory. The goal of reception history is to develop an open-ended dialogic form of hermeneutics that is not alienated from human experience, and which enables exegesis to regain its interpretative self-consciousness" (here 133). The difficulty here is not the desire to include in reflection on the reception of biblical texts interpretations neither explicitly ecclesial nor theological. Similarly unproblematic is an emphasis on including in reception history the appropriation of biblical texts in literature and other media. What is problematic is the apparent assumption of the existence of some kind of necessary dichotomy between ecclesial interpretations and those that pay due attention to the particular context of the interpreting subject. In contrast, Nancy Klancher, "A Genealogy for Reception History," *Biblical Interpretation* 21.1 (2013): 99-129, provides several examples of interpreters from previous eras who display a "sophistication of cultural and institutional critique" (124-25). The only significant hermeneutical difference from the recent practice of reception history is that "The older exegeses embrace the 'applied' side of biblical interpretation understood as Christian edification, as 'a series of ecclesial messages' to be embodied, and not as a reader-oriented historical criticism, effective history, or the 'hermeneutics of consequences'" (125). Similarly, Thiselton, "Reception Theory, H.R. Jauss and the Formative Power of Scripture," 289-308, argues that "*Formation* is the key link between reception theory and the effects of Scripture" (289).

understandings of the subject-matter, or that our interpretations are not appropriate or correct. Instead, Gadamer's point is that when we understand, we will always understand differently, and this new understanding will contribute to the formation of future horizons of understanding. In this manner, Gadamer is able to find a middle position that explains the diversity in interpretations which can be true to the text and stand in relationship to each other (in their tradition) without being reduced to an anarchy of competing views.[109]

Within this process of tradition, the historical distance between the horizon of the author and first readers and the horizon of an interpreter in a subsequent era does not prevent understanding but enables it: "the possibility for productive understanding lies in the temporal distance between the horizons, which is not to be overcome but which allows the interpreter to see the foreignness of the text before the two horizons are fused."[110] Jauss is thus able to conceptualize "both how works influenced their readers; and how successive generations of readers influenced the understanding of texts and works."[111]

One of the ways in which Jauss elaborates on these ideas is to pay close attention to the nature of shifts in tradition. Continuity and innovation "are not opposing poles in Jauss's theory . . . the history of biblical interpretation consists of both tradition and innovation, archaeology and anticipation, and we need to preserve both sides of the coin."[112] Jauss conceptualizes this relationship between continuity and innovation by drawing upon Thomas Kuhn's theory of paradigm shifts in the natural sciences. Scientific research will be conducted in terms of the questions and answers conceivable within an existing paradigm unless and until a persistent anomaly forces an epistemological crisis and the formulation of a new paradigm. For Jauss, the interpretation of texts within a tradition operates in a similar manner. Paradigm shifts in the interpretation of texts may not be prompted by anomalies in empirical observation as in the natural sciences, but anomalies nevertheless arise in the sense that existing interpretations no longer answer the questions contemporary readers are

---

109. David P. Parris, *Reception Theory and Biblical Hermeneutics* (Eugene, OR: Wipf & Stock, 2009), 64.

110. Parris, *Reception Theory and Biblical Hermeneutics*, 150.

111. Thiselton, "Reception History, H. R. Jauss and the Formative Power of Scripture," 290–91.

112. Parris, *Reception Theory and Biblical Hermeneutics*, 173.

asking: "When a paradigm is no longer capable of explicating the text in a relevant manner then it is discarded in favor of one which is capable of answering these questions."[113] Such shifts are not without loose ends, and they rarely involve the wholesale abandonment of interpretive positions current within the previous paradigm. Instead some of these interpretive positions take their place within a revised overall framework alongside other newer elements. Further, even if a new paradigm can provide satisfactory answers to the questions that the old paradigm was unable to answer, it may in turn raise other problems. The task of interpretation is not fruitless but neither does it ever reach a final completion.

Gadamer's and Jauss's reflections on interpretation offer several obvious advantages for a project concerned with the Reformers' interpretation of Paul. For some of their major concerns are central to this project: consideration of the unfolding of the interpretation of Paul's texts across time, of the traditions formed by that interpretive activity, and of the nature of significant paradigm shifts within those traditions. The hermeneutical position outlined in this chapter reflects these concerns and frames the argument that follows in the rest of the book in the following ways:

1. It is not sufficient simply to investigate the Pauline interpretation of individual Reformers. Attention must also be given to the interpretive paradigm that preceded them and the manner in which together they succeeded in establishing an alternative paradigm. Only once the nature of the paradigm shift they achieved is understood can there then be a discussion of individual contributions and of significant differences between interpreters within the new paradigm.

2. The purpose of such a study of the Reformers is not to advocate the wholesale adoption of their Pauline interpretation. Our reading of Paul cannot simply reproduce that of the Reformers since our historical context is different from theirs. To attempt to reproduce their interpretations would only distort them since the same statements might well communicate in the twenty-first century meanings subtly different from those communicated in the sixteenth century.

---

113. Parris, *Reception Theory and Biblical Hermeneutics*, 184. Parris himself prefers to employ Alasdair MacIntyre's concept of a "core problematic" within literary paradigms, which he thinks fits with Jauss's theory even better than Jauss's own appropriation of Kuhn.

3. Rather than reproduction, the purpose of work in the history of reception is to put the insights of previous interpreters to work for present interpretative advantage. It does this by enabling critical reflection upon interpretation of the Pauline texts in our own historical context, both in terms of their content and of our reasons for preferring particular interpretative positions and approaches.

This third point is particularly crucial, and requires further elaboration in two ways. First, we should note that to use the work of interpreters from a previous era for present interpretative advantage is partly a matter of understanding the present for which we are interpreting. For all the differences between our own context and previous ones, here it must also be recognized that previous contexts have shaped our own. In reflecting on the Church Fathers, the Reformers, and on more recent predecessors in the last two centuries, Ulrich Luz reminds us that "The past is the horizon of our own situation . . . what they thought and how they lived is not simply past. It is *our* past and as such a space that determines and shapes us."[114] To explore and to clarify the past is particularly vital work in relation to the interpretation of Paul's texts by the Reformers since contemporary New Testament scholarship is acutely aware of their historical influence. The dominant Pauline scholarship of much of the twentieth century understood itself to stand to some degree in a Reformation tradition. That of the NPP understands itself significantly to reject this tradition, and this rejection is epitomized in Stendahl's now famous statement, "We all, in the West, and especially in the tradition of the Reformation cannot help reading Paul through the experience of persons like Luther or Calvin. And this is the chief reason for most of our misunderstandings of Paul."[115]

114. Luz, *Studies in Matthew*, 303-4. On this point, see also Riches, "Reception History as a Challenge to Biblical Theology," 178: "Powerful readings such as Luther's will have an effect on whole communities over a long period of time and will continue to influence the way people approach and understand them. Many will come to Galatians thinking that this is where Paul sets out his doctrine of justification by faith, that this is a—possibly *the*—key text for the understanding of Christian faith. This is to come to it within a horizon that is not just set by the boundaries imposed by a belief in the canonical status of the Christian Bible (though such a belief will indeed form part of that horizon), but by a particular understanding of the Christian faith and of the role of Galatians in supporting such an understanding."

115. Krister Stendahl, "Call Not Conversion," in *Paul among Jews and Gentiles* (Philadelphia: Fortress, 1976), 12. These words of Stendahl have been so influential that I have not hesitated to cite them several times. See also 122 n. 69 and 323 n. 6.

This status of the Reformers as the progenitors of erroneous trajectories of interpretation ensured that for several decades they received either little attention or only negative attention in serious scholarly work on Paul sympathetic to the NPP.[116] In recent years there are signs of a more informed approach among some, but also of continued misunderstanding or negative assessment.[117] The Reformers' influence on the present is acknowledged but is still too little understood. Insufficient attention is paid to significant differences of perspective between the Reformers or to the differences between them and the "Lutheran" scholarship of the modern era that is too easily assumed to reflect their central concerns accurately. When examined with care, the exegesis of the Reformers often fails to reflect the assumptions made about it when it is conceptualized simply as a negative foil to the insights of the NPP. As explained in the prologue, part of the purpose of this book is to provide a historically credible account of the Reformers' readings of Paul's texts so that the relationship between their readings and contemporary debates in Pauline scholarship might be better understood. The Reformers, especially but not only Luther, occupy such a central place in the history of Pauline interpretation that if we fail to understand what they say about Paul, then we fail properly to understand our own place in that history.

Second, the other, and even more important, aspect of putting previous interpretations to work for present interpretative advantage is to access the interpretive insights of the Reformers. In their readings, key contemporary assumptions about the most plausible interpretation of significant aspects of Paul's texts do not hold. As we enter into dialogue with them, we enter into an alternative world of interpretation that does not match our own and we are rescued from the temptation to take for granted the correctness of contemporary interpretations. They function to provoke and to challenge our own assumptions and dominant

116. The Reformers' exegesis accurately understood does inform the work of Stephen Westerholm, *Perspectives Old and New on Paul: The "Lutheran" Paul and His Critics* (Grand Rapids: Eerdmans, 2004), but this is unsurprising since Westerholm is the most prominent and sophisticated critic of the NPP.

117. For a more informed reception of the Reformers' exegesis in recent scholarship see, for example, Michael Bird, *The Saving Righteousness of God: Studies on Paul, Justification, and the New Perspective* (Eugene, OR: Wipf & Stock, 2007), and Grant Macaskill, *Union with Christ in the New Testament* (Oxford: Oxford University Press, 2013). For a negative assessment, see, for example, J. Albert Harrill, *Paul the Apostle: His Life and Legacy in Their Roman Context* (Cambridge: Cambridge University Press, 2012), 138-62.

contemporary interpretations.[118] Jauss comments in relation to works of literature that classic texts can be so successful in shaping the expectations of readers that their greatness and beauty becomes self-evident and somewhat anodyne, "so that it requires a special effort to read them 'against the grain' of the accustomed experience to catch sight of their artistic character once again."[119] Similarly with Paul's texts and their interpretation, the exegesis of another age can help us to read against the grain of accustomed experience: "the study of the reception history makes readers of biblical texts aware of the specificity and particularity of their own readings."[120] It may appear a little odd to some to speak of Reformation readings of Paul enabling us to read against the grain of accustomed experience. After all, one of the impacts of NPP readings was to overturn accustomed readings partially based on Reformation perspectives. However, Sanders's *Paul and Palestinian Judaism*—the work that initiated a dramatic change in dominant modes of interpreting Paul in the English-speaking world—was published in 1977, now a full forty years ago. The NPP cannot remain new forever, and for those who, like the present author, received their theological education after its advent, NPP interpretations provide the accustomed reading experience. Against that backdrop, serious consideration of the work of those sometimes alleged by NPP interpreters to lead us only into misunderstandings of Paul becomes a necessary intellectual exercise that allows us to evaluate again our own interpretative presuppositions.

To say this leads us back once more to Erasmus and Luther. In relation to their debate on the will, Erasmus finds it incredible that a dominant tradition of interpreting Scripture in a manner consistent with the existence of freedom of the will could be wrong (see 1.2). Luther's response is instructive. He confesses that he once thought the same but that he was compelled to a different view by "the pressure of my conscience and the evidence of facts."[121] Luther believes that he changed his view on the basis of the content of the texts. Nevertheless, he has already disputed Erasmus's claim that the whole Christian tradition supports him,

---

118. Thiselton, "Reception Theory, H.R. Jauss and the Formative Power of Scripture," 289–308 (esp. 297), regards this capacity to provoke and to challenge as one of the principal benefits of reception history.

119. Hans R. Jauss, *Towards an Aesthetic of Reception*, trans. Timothy Bahti (Brighton: Harvester Press, 1982), 26.

120. Luz, *Studies in Matthew*, 326.

121. *LW* 33:73 = *WA* 18:641, 8.

arguing that "Augustine, whom you overlook, is entirely with me."[122] In other words, Luther will not be bound by previous interpretations, but nor will he simply ignore them. Like Calvin and others within early Protestantism, his knowledge of the Fathers is extensive and his attitude is that of a critical reader who rejects what he finds to be illegitimate but will benefit from traditional readings when he can. He regards the Catholic Church of his own day as an aberration when judged by biblical criteria, but there is no evidence here of the later tendency in some Protestant circles to regard tradition as suspect just because it is tradition. As Bernhard Lohse points out, "Luther was also aware that the tradition has been preserved in the Roman church, from which evangelicals have received the true tradition."[123] Previous interpreters offer spiritual treasures and not only the lies of Satan. Intervening interpretations between the time of the New Testament and the present can be "stepping stones back to the text."[124]

It is this kind of relationship with previous interpretations that should be practiced now in relation to the Reformers' interpretations of Paul's texts. "Entering the horizon of history of tradition must not mean simply grateful acceptance of tradition. It must also mean, in the face of diverse traditions, making judgments, and that means saying yes or no."[125] This yes or no should not be spoken too hastily. A study that assessed prematurely or simplistically the contributions of interpreters of previous eras according to their success or failure in anticipating dominant contemporary perspectives could only fall into anachronism. For the Pauline interpretation of a previous era to be of benefit in the contemporary task of interpretation requires a serious attempt first to understand it on its own terms and in its own context. Yet if more is to be achieved than simply alerting us to the provisional nature of our own interpretations (they read Paul differently in the past and others will do so again in the future),

---

122. *LW* 33:72 = *WA* 18:640, 8–9.

123. Lohse, *Martin Luther's Theology*, 285. We have not yet, with the Reformers, reached a suspicion of tradition just because it is tradition as in the famous saying of Gadamer, *Truth and Method*, 270, that "the fundamental prejudice of the enlightenment is the prejudice against prejudice itself, which robs tradition of its power."

124. Tracy, "Erasmus among the Postmodernists," 7. In his famous account of his 'Reformation Discovery' of the true meaning of the righteousness of God in Rom 1:17, Luther records his pleasure in finding confirmation of his interpretation in Augustine's *The Spirit and the Letter*. See *LW* 34:337 = *WA* 54:186, 14–20.

125. Luz, *Studies in Matthew*, 327.

neither can judgments about validity be endlessly deferred if we are fully to recognize the historicity of the interpretive process itself. Precisely because interpretation unfolds in traditions to which contemporary interpreters are unavoidably connected, whether in approbation or aversion, and whether the connection is acknowledged or unrecognized, the question of what is of lasting value in previous interpretations is essential. For if the Reformers were entirely mistaken in their interpretations of Paul's texts, this book could be of interest only to historians of the sixteenth century. The decision to explore their work does reflect a conviction that a fresh consideration of their exegesis may help to correct errors in contemporary interpretation and challenge exegetical conclusions that are currently widely held. Our judgment of their exegesis may often be to conclude that they are correct. That does not mean, however, that they are always right and contemporary readings in the tradition of the NPP are always wrong. Nor does it mean that we can ignore the enormous differences in historical context between the sixteenth century and today. It means rather that as we attempt to interpret Paul's texts for today in ways that are historically credible, canonically consistent, and theologically fruitful, our stance towards the Reformers should be that of interlocutors engaging in a critical dialogue. We should be open to the possibility that they provide resources that help us in our own interpretative task. The remainder of this book is an exploration of those resources and of the directions in which they help to lead our Pauline interpretation. I will not only attempt accurately to analyze what the Reformers say within their own sixteenth-century context (parts II and III) but also with their help to consider exegesis for today (part IV) just as I have attempted to explore hermeneutics for today with the help of the debates between Erasmus and Luther about biblical interpretation (part I).

PART II

SHARED CONVICTIONS

The Reformers' New Pauline Exegetical Grammar

2 The Medieval Context of the Reformers

Pauline Exegesis and Soteriology

2.1. Continuity or Discontinuity?
The Reformers and Medieval Pauline Interpretation

The origins and causes of the European Reformation are varied and complex, and are certainly not to be restricted to the history of ideas in general or that of biblical interpretation in particular.[1] Yet given the very high potential personal cost of defying the power and authority of the church, it is also clear that events could only have turned out very differently without the profound conviction of the Reformers that the truth of the gospel was at stake. When one adds to this the issues of identity and self-understanding that arise for contemporary scholars, both Protestant and Roman Catholic, it is unsurprising that the exegesis of the Reformers has been subject to intensive study. Yet too often the focus of such study has remained at the level of the individuals involved. Luther's 1545 account of a "Reformation Discovery" in which his world was transformed by apprehending the true meaning of Paul's phrase "the righteousness of God" in Rom 1:17 has produced a preoccupation with identifying the moment and the content of this experience.[2] Although most Luther specialists now recognize that this retrospective account of events given more than twenty-five years later masks a more complex process of development in

---

1. For example, the invention of the printing press and Luther's clear-sighted exploitation of it were vital. See Andrew Pettegree, *Brand Luther: 1517, Printing, and the Making of the Reformation* (New York: Penguin, 2015).
2. *LW* 34:336–37 = *WA* 54:185, 12 – 186, 13.

understanding, his personal intellectual development is still the center of interest. Similarly, many studies of the ideas of other early Protestant figures begin with the question of the appropriation of Luther's theology before charting other influences and contextual factors contributing to the development of distinctive insights by their subjects.[3] All of this is important and of great value, but serves to push into the background something equally significant. Although there is considerable diversity in the theological positions reached by the Reformers, this diversity rests upon some shared exegetical convictions. There are foundational issues in the interpretation of Pauline texts where they very largely agree with each other and against more traditional alternatives. While they may disagree among themselves about other interpretive issues in the same texts, at this foundational level there is, with only a few and partial exceptions, a shared framework.

Such shared frameworks arise in the history of reception simply because of the persistence across time of the linguistic material of the Pauline texts. Paul's abiding obsession is with the person of Christ: "For to me, living is Christ and dying is gain" (Phil 1:21). Most great interpretations of his texts therefore unsurprisingly have Christology at their heart, and the Reformers provide no exception. In the third part of this book we will explore the distinctive christological foci of the three most influential exegetes of the Reformation era: Martin Luther, Philip Melanchthon, and John Calvin. However, such christological foci are expressed in relation to interpretive decisions about other foundational key terms or concepts in Paul. Whatever the historical and social context of the interpreter, reaching a perspective on the meaning of key terms like "sin," "the law," and "conscience" is an essential component of interpreting the witness of the texts concerning the human plight apart from Christ. Concerning salvation in Christ there is the same necessity for the meaning of terms such as the "works of the law," "grace," and "faith." The Reformers develop a powerful consensus about these terms and concepts and this sets limits to interpretations that can plausibly be proposed. Disagreements on

---

3. To give just one example, a major issue in recent scholarship on the theology of William Tyndale is the nature and extent of his debt to Luther and its relative importance compared to other influences. For discussion, see among others William A. Clebsch, *England's Early Protestants* (New Haven: Yale University Press, 1964), 137-204; Donald D. Smeeton, *Lollard Themes in the Reformation Theology of William Tyndale* (Kirksville, MO: Sixteenth Century Journal Publishers, 1994), 17-26; Carl R. Trueman, *Luther's Legacy: Salvation and the English Reformers* (Oxford: Clarendon, 1994), 83-120.

other points may abound, and they may be profoundly significant in their own right, but they take place within a shared framework. A helpful way to conceptualize this is by analogy with how language itself functions. The Reformers do not all say the same things as one another, but they do all speak the same language of Pauline theology.

Their language of Pauline theology is a new language, radically different from the language of Pauline theology spoken by their predecessors and sometimes unfathomable to those for whom that earlier language was native. The Reformers are able to speak this new language because in their shared exegetical conclusions they have developed a new grammar of Pauline theology. Just as grammatical rules and principles structure and enable the use of a language, so these exegetical conclusions about fundamental aspects of Paul's meaning provide structure for and enable the Reformers' new interpretations of Pauline texts.[4] To characterize the work of the Reformers in this way as a revolutionary upheaval that establishes a new exegetical grammar of Pauline theology, standing in sharp discontinuity with medieval Pauline interpretation, is to claim something significantly at odds with recent trends in Reformation historiography. For in the long debate stretching back over a century to Karl Holl and Adolf von Harnack (Luther's Reformation was the dawn of the modern age) and Ernst Troeltsch (the Reformation essentially continues the Middle Ages), the pendulum has swung to the side of continuity.[5] Volker Leppin, the author of a recent major biography of Luther,

---

4. I am here adopting and adapting a concept of Luther's own. He speaks of "a new and theological grammar" (*LW* 26:267 = *WA* 40:418, 24) which replaces a previous "moral grammar" (*LW* 26:268 = *WA* 40:419, 18) and which he applies to interpreting texts which might seem to speak of righteousness by works. In Luther's new grammar these texts speak of deeds of love as the fruit of faith that grows from justification rather than as in any way the basis on which justification is granted. For exposition see Sun-young Kim, *Luther on Faith and Love: Christ and the Law in the 1535 Galatians Commentary* (Minneapolis: Fortress, 2014), 180–84.

5. For a helpful brief overview of the debate, see Susan Schreiner, *Are You Alone Wise? The Search for Certainty in the Early Modern Era* (Oxford: Oxford University Press, 2011), 3–11. See also Gerhard Müller, "Luther's Transformation of Medieval Thought: Discontinuity and Continuity," in *The Oxford Handbook of Martin Luther's Theology*, ed. Robert Kolb, Irene Dingel, and L'ubomír Batka (Oxford: Oxford University Press, 2014), 105–14, and Leppin, "Luther's Transformation of Medieval Thought: Continuity and Discontinuity," 115–24. On Harnack and Holl, see Peter Grove, "Adolf von Harnack and Karl Holl on Luther at the Origins of Modernity," in *Lutherrenaissance*, ed. Christine Helmer and Bo Kristian Holm (Göttingen: Vandenhoeck & Ruprecht, 2015), 106–24.

sharply questions interpretations of Luther based upon "the idea of a radical disjunction between Luther's theology and the theology of the Middle Ages."[6] J. Todd Billings notes that in contrast to historiographies of rapid, dramatic change,

> scholars such as Heiko Oberman, David Steinmetz, and Richard Muller have posited accounts of Reformational theology that has areas of broad continuity between medieval Scholasticism, Reformation theology, and post-Reformation Scholasticism. There were changes, certainly, but the changes tended to be incremental and were often combined with areas of deep continuity.[7]

In many ways, this emphasis on continuity is extremely welcome. To write as did Karl Holl that "Luther stood 'in a conscious and deliberate contrast' to his time" both presupposes that it is possible to typify an age in contrast to Luther and implies a capacity on the part of Luther and the other Reformers to abstract themselves to a rather unlikely degree from their own historical and social contexts.[8] Their protests were directed not against an age as such but against specific ideas and practices that they regarded as unbiblical: "they strove for a *reformation* in the sense of the restoration of the original form of the true congregation of Jesus Christ— and in this respect a renewal of the contemporary Church: *renovatio* not *innovatio!*"[9] Whether the various attempts of the Reformers on this basis to change the world in which they lived amounted to a rejection of "their time" is itself a historical judgment that can only be reached through an evaluation of how continuity and discontinuity between the Reformers and their late medieval context relate to each other. Any judicious evaluation will recognize both continuity and discontinuity and seek to measure them against each other. Further, as Leppin himself points out,

6. Volker Leppin, "Martin Luther, Reconsidered for 2017," *LQ* 22 (2008): 375. See also Volker Leppin, *Martin Luther* (Darmstadt: Wissenschaftliche Buchgesellschaft, 2006).

7. J. Todd Billings, "The Catholic Calvin," *ProEccl* 20.2 (2011): 122.

8. Leppin, "Martin Luther Reconsidered for 2017," 375, quoting and translating Karl Holl, "Was verstand Luther unter Religion?" in *Gesammelte Aufsätze zur Kirchengeschichte. Bd. 1: Luther* (Tübingen: Mohr Siebeck, 1948), 108.

9. Berndt Hamm, "How Innovative Was the Reformation?," in *The Reformation of Faith in the Context of Late Medieval Theology and Piety: Essays by Berndt Hamm*, ed. Robert J. Bast (Leiden: Brill, 2004), 254.

it is often the case that "continuity and discontinuity lie conspicuously close to each other," and he acknowledges that to assert the significance of the late medieval context of Reformation theology is not to deny its novel aspects.[10]

It is thus clear that the judgments of recent historiography in favor of continuity have been made with considerable sophistication and in a nuanced manner. Nevertheless, such general judgments in favor of continuity find a challenge in the Reformers' Pauline exegesis. From the perspective of a New Testament scholar trained in Pauline exegesis, what stands out here is the rather massive scale of discontinuity. This does not necessitate a complete reversal of judgment so that sudden revolution becomes the only paradigm within which to understand the Reformation. It is possible still to recognize, as Berndt Hamm suggests, that "the Reformation owed its great success to the fact that it was not only a radical break but was also an amplification of changes which had already begun."[11] However, it is also necessary to recognize that the Reformation "abandons a wealth of medieval polarities in favor of a new kind of concentration on Bible and Gospel. Every kind of religious continuity is consequently directly surrounded and pervaded by aspects of change and qualitative leap."[12] The term "Reformation" is most appropriately applied to the complex of events it designates "when seen through the concept of a 'system crash' or paradigm shift."[13] It is precisely in examining the Reformers' Pauline exegesis that we are able to explore the crash site. Although worked out in dialog with patristic and medieval predecessors, the Reformers' new Pauline exegetical grammar differentiated them sharply from such predecessors and overturned widespread assumptions stretching back centuries about the meaning of key terms or concepts. Their undeniable frequent dependence on their predecessors

---

10. Leppin, "Martin Luther Reconsidered for 2017," 384.

11. Berndt Hamm, "The Place of the Reformation in the Second Christian Millennium," in *The Reformation of Faith in the Context of Late Medieval Theology and Piety: Essays by Berndt Hamm*, ed. Robert J. Bast (Leiden: Brill, 2004), 286.

12. Hamm, "How Innovative Was the Reformation?," 269–70. In the same chapter, Hamm develops a fourfold categorization of change at the Reformation in relation to the late medieval world with the aim of providing "an integrative working model for innovation which would lead out of the oscillation between continuous change and rapid transition" (258).

13. Berndt Hamm, "Justification by Faith Alone: A Profile of the Reformation Doctrine of Justification," in *The Early Luther: Stages in a Reformation Reorientation* (Grand Rapids: Eerdmans, 2014), 255 n. 55.

for particular exegetical points should not be allowed to obscure the fact that these continuities exist within a radically altered framework.[14]

Attention should therefore be paid to the development and content of the Reformers' new exegetical grammar. Its development was the work of many and cannot be reduced to one moment of discovery by Luther or restricted to his intellectual journey. Sometimes he adopted as vital the insights of others. And for grammar effectively to structure and enable the use of a language, it must be shared by all members of that language community. What is typical or endlessly repeated in early Protestant exegesis is only the more significant for its characteristic nature. Charting the fact that a particular exegetical conclusion is widely shared and expressed is therefore important. None of this is to dispute the genius of Luther. As Steinmetz puts it, throughout Luther's career "fresh ideas rose to greet him from the pages of the Bible."[15] His contribution to the new grammar is greater than that of any other single individual. The evolution of his exegetical ideas about Paul in the years up to 1521, when Luther made his famous stand at the Diet of Worms and subsequently spent months in isolation at the Wartburg, remains a key episode.[16] Yet Luther is such a consequential figure precisely because he was not ultimately an isolated one. He matters so much because the Reformers' new exegetical grammar of Pauline theology was widely adopted and endured for so long. Its endurance was so lengthy that today, approaching five centuries later, the greatest controversy in Pauline theology of recent decades has been the rejection by the majority of scholars of some

14. Gillian R. Evans, *The Language and Logic of the Bible: The Road to Reformation* (Cambridge: Cambridge University Press, 1985), 158–59, argues that the controversies of the sixteenth century mask continuing common assumptions about the nature and purpose of Scripture and its interpretation, but nevertheless notes that "Perhaps the essential difference between the sixteenth century view and that of the late medieval centuries is the bringing together again of speculative theology and exegesis, which had become separated for the purposes of study into two parallel tracks in the late twelfth century. After some practice Luther could use the Bible directly as a source-book for theological discussion, without reference to *Sentences* or *Summa.*"

15. David C. Steinmetz, "Preface to the Second Edition," in *Luther in Context*, 2nd ed. (Grand Rapids: Baker, 2002), ix.

16. Berndt Hamm, *The Early Luther: Stages in a Reformation Reorientation* (Grand Rapids: Eerdmans, 2014), 96 n. 105, seeks to lengthen the timeline, arguing that Luther's theology evolved in a multi-layered and gradual process stretching back to 1505, i.e., the quest for a single moment of breakthrough or even for a tight sequence of breakthroughs in the years 1515–1518 is misguided.

important elements of that exegetical grammar in favor of positions associated with the "New Perspective on Paul." A key aspect of Luther's achievement and that of the other Reformers lies in the creation of communities of interpreters employing a shared exegetical grammar.

As already implied, this makes indispensable an understanding of the interpretive context in which the Reformers' new grammar of Pauline theology arose. If we live at a moment in the history of Pauline interpretation when their exegetical grammar is in the process of replacement, or at least highly significant modification, then we will not truly understand what is at stake in our own time unless we understand what was at stake in the sixteenth century. In turn we will not understand what was at stake in the sixteenth century unless we also understand the medieval grammar of Pauline theology that the Reformers rejected and replaced. If we wish to avoid anachronism, we must explore that alternative grammar at least in outline.

2.2. Augustine

The only place to begin is in Hippo, for the influence of Augustine upon late medieval interpretation of Paul is endemic. It is also anything but straightforward. There are multiple ways in which the term "Augustinian" can be applied in relation to the period,[17] but this complexity exists precisely because of Augustine's success in establishing a Pauline exegetical grammar. Like the Reformers after them, medieval Pauline interpreters could say quite different things from each other and engage in profound interpretative conflicts. Yet they did so within a discourse structured and enabled by Augustine's Pauline exegesis. Despite the passing of a millennium or more, the boundaries of interpretative plausibility and acceptability were determined by compatibility with his insights into the soteriological significance of the same fundamental features of the Pauline texts as those confronted by the Reformers.

Augustine says that the righteousness of God in Rom 1:17 is "not that by which God is righteous, but that with which he clothes a human being (*induit hominem*) when he justifies a sinner (*iustificat impium*)."[18] In

---

17. David C. Steinmetz, *Luther and Staupitz: An Essay in the Intellectual Origins of the European Reformation* (Durham, NC: Duke University Press, 1980), 13–16, identifies at least five different senses in which the term "Augustinian" can be applied to late medieval theology.

18. Augustine, "The Spirit and the Letter," in *Answer to the Pelagians: The Works of*

this way Paul's statement about God's righteousness is clearly connected with his later assertion that God justifies the ungodly (Rom 4:5). However, the justifying of the ungodly is to *make* them righteous in substance and behavior: "What else, after all, does justified (Rom 3:24) mean but: made righteous (*iusti facti*) by the one, of course, who justifies sinners (Rom 4:5), so that from sinners they become righteous (*fiat iustus*)?"[19] This making righteous means that justification is not only something that happens at the outset of the Christian life but something that embraces its entirety and in which the Christian is to make progress. It is an event that begins a process. Paul's quotation of Hab 2:4, "The one who is righteous will live by faith" is interpreted with reference to the Christian life: "Having obtained this grace of faith, as a result of your faith you will be just, since *the just person lives from faith* (Rom 1:17), and you will gain God by living from faith. When you have gained God by living from faith, you will receive immortality and eternal life as your reward."[20] Here Augustine plainly means that faith is the source of good works: "Faith gives the proper foundation to our works; it gives them the proper orientation, and the good works which flow from faith are the steps by which we reach God."[21] In this understanding of Rom 1:17 human works can play no part in initial justification, but, once the gift of God's righteousness is received, works are vital if the Christian is to gain God and life eternal.

Thus, Augustine will adamantly insist that divine grace is only given its proper priority if it is recognized that "works do not precede justification," but he will also insist that works are profoundly significant since "justification precedes observance of the law."[22] The two belong together in sequence, for there is nobody who "can act justly (*operat iustitiam*)

St. Augustine I/23, trans. Roland J. Teske (New York: New City, 1997), 9.15 (158) = *CSEL* 60:155-229 (167, 7-8). On Augustine's understanding of justification see the exceptionally clear account in David F. Wright, "Justification in Augustine," in *Justification in Perspective: Historical Developments and Contemporary Challenges*, ed. Bruce L. McCormack (Grand Rapids: Baker, 2006), 55-72.

19. Augustine, "The Spirit and the Letter," 26.45 (178-79) = *CSEL* 60:155-229 (199, 10-12).

20. Augustine, *Homilies on the Gospel of John 1-40: The Works of St. Augustine III/12*, trans. Edmund P. Hill (New York: New City, 2009), 3.9 (75) = *PL* 35:1396-1405 (1400) in reference to John 1:16, "grace upon grace." For exposition see Stanislaus J. Grabowski, *The Church: An Introduction to the Theology of St. Augustine* (St. Louis: Herder, 1957), 325-28.

21. Grabowski, *The Church*, 327.

22. Augustine, "The Spirit and the Letter," 26.45 (178) = *CSEL* 60:155-229 (199, 5; 199, 10).

unless first justified (*iustificatus*)."[23] Human beings become doers of the law through grace and this grace is infused. Grace "is superadded to human nature. It is a divine aid bestowed upon the will so that it may fulfill the law and that it may live according to the doctrine revealed by God."[24] Given by God, grace is thus a healing reality resident in human beings. It is finally unclear whether for Augustine such grace is to be identified with the indwelling of the Holy Spirit or is understood as something distinct from, but closely associated with, the Spirit.[25] Either way, it is grace that enables human obedience and in so doing makes possible Augustine's famous paradox that "When God crowns our merits (*merita nostra*), he only crowns his own gifts (*munera sua*)."[26] Augustine seems to intend this paradox to remain as a paradox and not to be resolved. There is no merit without grace given by God, so merit in no sense constitutes a claim upon God. Perhaps for this reason Augustine "characteristically does not attribute justification to good works or to faith and good works."[27] Yet equally he could never say that justification is by faith *alone*. For in the act of justifying God gives back to human beings the capacity to will the good: "grace should be understood as the gift of what is most deeply our own: our own true will."[28] The works of the Christian genuinely belong to the Christian and therefore, although not a Pauline term, merit is for Augustine an appropriate concept to use in discussing Pauline texts that concern reward. Augustine can discuss the nature of justice according to Cicero's definition of "giving each what is due to them," since what is done or not done makes a real difference to reward. Yet this distributive concept of justice operates only within the wider framework of the justification of the ungodly as an act of divine healing directed towards "establishing the rectitude of the created order according to the divine intention."[29] It also

23. Ps 110:3. See Augustine, *Expositions of the Psalms 99–120: The Works of St. Augustine III/19*, trans. Maria Boulding (New York: New City, 2003), 288 = PL 37:1463–66 (1464).

24. Grabowski, *The Church*, 399.

25. For a discussion of the reasons for this see Lewis Ayres, "Augustine," in *The Blackwell Companion to Paul*, ed. Stephen Westerholm (Oxford: Wiley-Blackwell, 2011), 355. Ayres suggests that Augustine was aware that χάρις (grace) has a wide semantic range in Scripture and can sometimes denote divine favor.

26. Letter 194: 5.19. See Augustine, *Letters 156–210: The Works of St. Augustine II/3*, trans. Roland Teske (New York: New City, 2004), 296 = CSEL 57:176–214 (190, 14–15).

27. Wright, "Justification in Augustine," 65–66.

28. Ayres, "Augustine," 351.

29. Alister. E. McGrath, *Iustitia Dei: A History of the Christian Doctrine of Justification*, 3rd ed. (Cambridge: Cambridge University Press, 2005), 51.

operates within Augustine's understanding of predestination. Earlier in his career Augustine had held that God elects those whom God foreknows will choose faith in Christ, but consideration of Rom 9:10-13, where Paul speaks of God's choice of the younger Jacob over the older Esau, prompted a reevaluation.[30] Instead, divine grace is utterly gratuitous and beyond human discernment, as demonstrated by the conversion of Paul himself, overwhelmed by grace in the very act of persecuting believers.[31] The process of justification for the individual flows from God's electing decree so that "even faith is the result of God's grace."[32]

Given his understanding that to live by faith is to act justly as a consequence of having been justified, Augustine is unsurprisingly deeply influenced by Paul's statement in Gal 5:6 that what counts "is faith working through love." Here lies the agreement between Paul and the assertion that faith without works is dead (Jas 2:20). The person with only dead faith, which does not act but which merely assents to the truth of the gospel, is not justified. True faith that justifies is therefore closely associated with love and hope, and Augustine can also ascribe to love many of the characteristic powers and benefits of faith. Yet, unlike later medieval interpreters, Augustine does not define faith solely in terms of

---

30. See the second question in the first book of "Miscellany of Questions in Response to Simplician," in Augustine, *Responses to Miscellaneous Questions: The Works of St. Augustine I/12*, trans. Boniface Ramsey (New York: New City, 2008), 185-207 = *CCSL* 44:24-56. Much recent scholarship has followed Peter Brown in regarding the mid-390s as a crucial period in which intensive engagement with Paul's letters revolutionized Augustine's theology. This is now disputed by Carol Harrison, *Rethinking Augustine's Early Theology: A Case for Continuity* (Oxford: Oxford University Press, 2006). The issue at stake is whether Augustine's revised opinion about election marks a decisively new stage in his theological development or a return to what Augustine had in fact already believed before a temporary flirtation in the years 394-396 with a theology allowing a greater role in salvation for human choice. In arguing the latter Harrison seems to regard Augustine's theology of grace as self-evidently correct as a reading of Pauline texts.

31. Eugene TeSelle, "Exploring the Inner Conflict: Augustine's Sermons on Romans 7 and 8," in *Engaging Augustine on Romans*, ed. Daniel Patte and Eugene TeSelle, Romans through History and Cultures Series (Harrisburg, PA.: Trinity Press International, 2002), 111-12, and Paula Fredriksen, "Beyond the Body/Soul Dichotomy: Augustine on Paul against the Manichees and the Pelagians," *Recherches Augustiniennes* 23 (1988): 102-3, both suggest that the example of Paul's conversion was important for Augustine.

32. Philip Krey, Ian Christopher Levy, and Thomas F. Ryan, "Introduction," in *The Letter to the Romans: The Bible in Medieval Tradition*, ed. and trans. Ian Christopher Levy, Philip Krey, and Thomas F. Ryan (Grand Rapids: Eerdmans, 2013), 19.

cognitive content, or say that faith is itself inadequate to justify, or deny to faith the power to unite a person with Christ.[33] Faith acts, but the gift of faith is never given alone and is never unproductive: "What then does it mean, to believe in him? By believing to love (*amare*) him, by believing to cherish (*diligere*) him, to go to him by believing and be incorporated in his members."[34] Thus Augustine "does not understand the term 'faith' as merely an intellectual assent given under the inspiration of the will, but includes in it also the inner gift of God."[35] The renewal of life involved in justification by faith is therefore not to be understood apart from incorporation into the body of Christ. The deeds of those who are not Christians may be righteous before human beings, but they can never be righteous before God because they are not performed in Christ. The effects of grace "are inaugurated in the sacrament of baptism and consummated in the sacrament of the Eucharist."[36]

It is therefore only those in the church who exist in continuity with the right order granted to the universe by the creator. All others stand instead in essential relation to the disordered world marred by sin. Yet how had the effects of sin come about? In Augustine's context, the Manichees, a group to which he had himself belonged as a young man, taught a dualism that proposed not one creator but two separate sources of being, of light and of darkness. Against the Manichees, Augustine had to emphasize the derivative nature of sin, which exists not as an independent source of being but instead is parasitic upon the good creation of the one true God. Augustine would here stress the freedom of the human will as an explanation of the origin of sin. Thus, he can say of Gal 1:4—where Paul states that Christ died from our sins "to set us free from the present evil age"—that the present world is evil "because of the evil people who live in it, just as we say that a house is evil because of the evil people living in it."[37] Yet later in his career, in controversy with the Pelagians,

---

33. These are all errors made by McGrath, *Iustitia Dei*, 46 and highlighted by Wright, "Justification in Augustine," 66–68.

34. Augustine, *Homilies on the Gospel of John 1–40*, 29.6 (493) = *PL* 35:1628–32 (1631) in reference to John 6:29, "This is the work of God, that you believe in him whom he has sent."

35. Grabowski, *The Church*, 330.

36. Grabowski, *The Church*, 415.

37. Augustine, *Augustine's Commentary on Galatians: Introduction, Text, Translation, and Notes by Eric Plumer* (Oxford: Oxford University Press, 2003), 3.3 (129). This commentary dates from 394/395. Plumer includes with his translation on facing pages the Latin text from *CSEL* 84.

an emphasis on the freedom of the will presented obvious dangers. Here Augustine would stress the bondage to sin in which human beings live. It is not possible for human beings to delight in God and to do the good, "But so that we may love it, *the love of God* is poured out *in our hearts*, not by free choice which comes from ourselves, but *by the Holy Spirit who has been given to us* (Rom 5:5)."[38] To stress both the freedom of the will and bondage to sin without falling into contradiction required a carefully considered position worked out over several decades.[39]

Augustine achieves such a nuanced position by defining sin in terms of misdirected human affections and desires. It is a preference freely entered into for lesser goods, especially the self, as opposed to the highest good of all, which is God. Yet this exercise of freedom results in the bondage of the human will. Given over by God to its misdirected desires, the will is now "darkened in understanding and chilled in affection,"[40] and there is a disorder in the self that leaves the rational human mind perpetually swamped by cupidity invested with the compulsive force of habit. The human will is thus unable to choose the good, but not because of an external force restraining it. The good is unattainable rather because the will is no longer able truly to desire it. Commenting on what Paul says about desire (ἐπιθυμία) in Rom 7, Augustine says that "It's our debility, it's our vice. It won't be detached from us and exist somewhere else, but it will be cured and not exist anywhere at all."[41] The human plight thus consists in a profound sickness of the will. It is not quite clear whether for Augustine misdirected human desires, or concupiscence, are to be identified with inherited original sin itself or if they are more properly the punishment and penalty that result from that sin. Yet the role of concupiscence in the particular form of sexual desire in transmitting sin is clear (contrary to popular misinterpretation Augustine does not define concupiscence as sexual desire but rather thinks of sexual desire as one form of concupiscence), as is the practical impact of misdirected desires on the human capacity for right action. As we have already seen, one of the principal effects of grace is to restore to the human will its capacity to desire the good.

38. Augustine, "The Spirit and the Letter," 3.5 (152) = *CSEL* 60:155–229 (157, 22–24).

39. See William S. Babcock, "Augustine on Sin and Moral Agency," in *The Ethics of St. Augustine* (Atlanta: Scholars Press, 1991), 87–113.

40. Babcock, "Augustine on Sin and Moral Agency," 101.

41. Augustine, *Sermons 148–183: The Works of St. Augustine III/5*, trans. Edmund Hill (New York: New City, 1992), 151.3 (42) = *PL* 38:814–19 (816).

The prelude to this healing process is the revelation of humanity's plight provided by God's law.[42] An important text here is Gal 3:21-22 where Paul argues that righteousness would come through the law if a law had been given that could bring life, "but the Scripture has imprisoned all things under the power of sin, so that what was promised through faith in Jesus Christ might be given to those who believe." Augustine comments, "The law was not given, therefore, to take away sin, but to imprison all under sin. For the law showed that what the Jews, blinded by custom, could regard as righteousness was sin, so that having been humbled in this way they might recognize that their salvation does not rest in their own hands but *in the hand of a mediator*."[43] As he says elsewhere, "Prior to the Law we do not struggle, because not only do we lust and sin, but we even assent to sin. Under the Law we struggle but we are overcome. We admit that we do evil, and by that admission, that we do not really want to do it, but because we still lack grace we are overwhelmed."[44] The law tells human beings the truth but does not empower them to obey the truth. Therefore when Paul says that justification is not by works of the law, he is referring to the entire law in its inability to resist sin. Romans 3:20, with its reference to knowledge of sin through the law, and Rom 7:7, where Paul selects the commandment against desire as paradigmatic, rule out a reference simply to the ceremonial aspects of the law.[45]

The relationship of the Christian to the law is very different, however. Grace "pardons earlier sins and aids the struggling one, adds charity to justice and takes away fear. When this happens, even though certain fleshly desires fight against our spirit while we are in this life, to lead us into sin, nonetheless our spirit resists them because it is fixed in the grace and love of God."[46] Now it is possible to fulfill the law, and here Augustine does make use of a distinction between the moral and cere-

42. For a succinct summary of Augustine's views on the law see Krey, Levy, and Ryan, "Introduction," 30-32.

43. Augustine, *Augustine's Commentary on Galatians*, 25.9 (171) (Plumer's emphasis).

44. Paula Fredriksen Landes, *Augustine on Romans: Propositions from the Epistle to the Romans, Unfinished Commentary on the Epistle to the Romans* (Chico, CA: Scholars Press, 1982), 5-7 (Proposition 18) = *CSEL* 84:3, 3-7. This work is listed in the bibliography under Fredriksen.

45. Augustine, "The Spirit and the Letter," 8.14 (157-58) = *CSEL* 60:155-229 (166, 8-22).

46. Fredriksen Landes, *Augustine on Romans*, 5-7 (Proposition 18) = *CSEL* 84:7, 21-8, 1.

monial aspects of the law. At Gal 3:1–5, where Paul contrasts doing the works of the law with the ongoing work of the Spirit among the Galatians, Augustine comments that "it is impossible that the Apostle does not care whether a Christian is a murderer and an adulterer or chaste and innocent, in the same way that he does not care whether a man is circumcised or uncircumcised in the flesh."[47] The time of the sacraments of the Old Testament (circumcision, Sabbath observance, new moons, sacrifices, etc.) is past. Their "usefulness lies in what they signify,"[48] which implicitly is Christ and the sacraments of the church in which is available the grace necessary to fulfill the moral law. Yet as the Christian strives to fulfill the moral law, he or she is still tempted to sin. There are struggles between the spirit and the flesh, and "They will not cease save at the resurrection of the body."[49]

The issue therefore arises of the nature of this sin. How does sin under grace, where there has been a measure of healing and a restoration of the capacity to will good, differ from sin prior to grace, where the will is still in bondage? In answer to this question, Augustine develops an account of how the human will functions. Its textual locus is Rom 7:15–25 where Paul describes in some detail a personal struggle with sin. Whereas he had once taken this as a description of Paul's life before he met Christ, the older Augustine interprets it as a description of Paul's Christian life. In a series of sermons on Rom 7 and 8 preached in Carthage, probably in 419,[50] Augustine distinguishes between suggestion, inclination or desire, and consent. Sin is suggested to us "either through the senses or through our own free association of ideas."[51] This then arouses inappropriate and misdirected desires, to which people give consent and then act. What distinguishes the person of the Christian is that baptism deals with original sin and the guilt arising from concupiscence. Misdirected desires themselves remain, but guilt no longer

---

47. Augustine, *Augustine's Commentary on Galatians*, 19.4 (153).

48. Augustine, *Augustine's Commentary on Galatians*, 19.6 (153).

49. Fredriksen Landes, *Augustine on Romans*, 5–7 (Proposition 18) = *CSEL* 84:8, 9–10.

50. The question of date is complex. If 419 is not the correct date then 417 is the most likely alternative. See TeSelle, "Exploring the Inner Conflict: Augustine's Sermons on Romans 7 and 8," 114. For the sermons, see Augustine, *Sermons 148–83: Works of Saint Augustine III/5*, 151–56 (40–108) = PL 38:807–59 (except Sermon 154A, for which details of the Latin text can be found in note 54).

51. TeSelle, "Exploring the Inner Conflict," 118.

results for the Christian so long as these desires are not consented to and acted upon. Augustine is thoroughly ambiguous as to whether or not these misdirected desires that do not accrue guilt should nevertheless properly be termed sin,[52] but at a practical level he is very clear that the person of the Christian is a battlefield where there are two conflicting desires or inclinations. Grace and the work of the Spirit means that there is now genuine delight in the law of God where there was none before, and it is possible for the Christian to refuse to consent to or act upon sinful desires. Sin still threatens to disrupt the healthy hierarchies between soul and body, and between reason/the will and the other faculties of the soul, so that the lower parts refuse to obey the higher as they ought to do, but consent to sin no longer inevitably follows.[53] This is the personal experience of Paul who now summons Christians to the same fight. In this boxing bout between contrary desires, the conscience of the Christian is central:

> Christ is watching you fighting. The ring is your conscience, where two contestants are matched, mind and flesh. . . . A hard struggle; but the one who is watching you fighting can help you when you are in danger of losing. . . . And what does winning now mean for you? Not consenting to evil desires. Because you can't help having those evil desires, can you? But winning means not consenting to them.[54]

When these battles in the conscience of the Christian are won, grace increases and merit follows: "We have been justified; but this jus-

---

52. See Jesse Couenhoven, "St. Augustine's Doctrine of Original Sin," *AugStud* 36.2 (2005): 378-79.

53. Augustine reads many of the details of Rom 7:14-25 as concerning bodily desires as one of the principal expressions of misdirected human self-love. See Bernhard Blankenhorn, "Aquinas on Paul's Flesh/Spirit Anthropology in Romans," in *Reading Romans with St. Thomas Aquinas*, ed. Matthew Levering and Michael Dauphinais (Washington, DC: Catholic University of America Press, 2012), 1-38 (esp. 5-11): "The irony is that the late Augustine clearly leaves behind the anthropological dualism of his early period and simultaneously adopts an interpretation of the Pauline *sarx* as a reference to the ever-rebellious bodily passions of the Christian, though this meaning remains secondary to *sarx* as disordered self-love" (9).

54. Augustine, *Sermons 148-83: Works of Saint Augustine III/5*, 154A.3-4, 80-81 = *PLS* 2:667-70 (668). Although on the same text, this sermon is not actually from the Carthage series. Yet its content and imagery is entirely consistent with the Carthage sermons.

tice can grow, as we make progress."[55] When they are lost, then the goal of justice recedes: "Have we no justice at all? We certainly do have some. Let us be grateful for what we have, so that what we don't have may be added to it, and we don't lose what we do have."[56] In describing these losses, Augustine distinguishes, using a variety of terminology, between different levels of sin.[57] There are serious sins that separate those who commit them from God and, if there is not repentance, will result in loss of salvation. Yet there are also more minor sins that no one avoids in this life and that do not separate from God or lead to loss of salvation, in relation to which fasting, almsgiving, and prayer are efficacious. As the battle in the conscience rages, grace and justice are added to or depleted, restored or eroded. The changes involved are changes in being, in the substance of what the person is, as the Christian progresses on a journey towards God. In the imagery of a later age, the Christian is a pilgrim. Augustine understands Paul to be speaking of life "as a *via* for our transformation."[58]

2.3. Medieval Appropriations of Augustine's Pauline Exegetical Grammar

The world of medieval Pauline interpretation is rich and varied, but it exists within the exegetical grammar established by Augustine. It was widely assumed that justification encompasses the whole of the Christian life and involves the healing transformation of the person. Alongside this Augustinian heritage there was a new development in the life of the church that impacted all interpreters and constituted an additional shared element: penance. From the ninth century onwards the practice of private penance became widespread in Europe and the Fourth Lateran Council (1215) required all Christians to make confession at least once a year. The sacrament of penance came to play an important role in thinking about justification. The grace of baptism begins justification, but the

---

55. Augustine, *Sermons 148-83: Works of Saint Augustine III/5*, 158.5, 117 = PL 38:862-67 (864).

56. Augustine, *Sermons 148-83: Works of Saint Augustine III/5*, 158.5, 116 = PL 38:862-67 (864).

57. See Grabowski, *The Church*, 471-75.

58. Daphne Hampson, *Christian Contradictions: The Structures of Lutheran and Catholic Thought* (Cambridge: Cambridge University Press, 2001), 83.

merit of penance serves to counter the loss of grace and justice incurred by the sins of the baptized. The process of confession, an act of penance, and sacerdotal absolution restores justification.[59] From the medieval perspective, penance thus sits comfortably within the soteriological framework established on the basis of Augustine's exegetical grammar. It does not compromise divine initiative in salvation since nobody begins to be justified through penance. It is not the basis of God's initial gift of grace, but rather aids the Christian on the pathway of transformation by providing a mechanism through which setbacks are surmounted. This positioning of penance in relation to justification helps to explain how Luther's initial, fairly narrow breach with Rome over aspects of the doctrine of penance was not contained there and rapidly widened to encompass far broader soteriological issues.

Where differences arose between medieval interpreters in their appropriation of Augustine it was not in relation to the right understanding of sin, the law, and the conscience *as they impacted the Christian already engaged in the process of justification*. There could certainly be diverse discussions of the true nature of sin and the extent of the impact of original sin, but it was not disputed that the Christian should fulfill the law, that the conscience of the Christian is the site of a struggle with sinful desires in which grace is won or lost, or that there is a valid distinction between more serious mortal sins and less serious venial ones. In these areas, the only major exegetical departure from Augustine concerns the works of the law. A minority of commentators look back beyond Augustine to adopt the view of Ambrosiaster that the distinction between the moral and ceremonial law applies not only to the Christian who has already received initial justification, but also to initial justification itself. In his statements that justification is "not by the works of the law" Paul intends to rule out reliance in initial justification on Jewish ceremonies only, not also to make a statement about the irrelevance of good works.[60] On this view, Paul is not in his statements about works of the law actually addressing the question of the part played in justification by good works. For Augustine to affirm that initial justification is not by means of ceremonies is simply to leave

---

59. For a more detailed account, see McGrath, *Iustitia Dei*, 117–28.

60. David C. Fink, "Divided by Faith: The Protestant Doctrine of Justification and the Confessionalization of Biblical Exegesis" (PhD diss., Duke University Graduate School, 2010), 161–212.

open the questions of what part good works play and where that contribution should be located. It is not necessarily to break with Augustine's insistence that good works performed prior to the gift of faith do not justify, but simply to hold that this is not Paul's concern when using the formula "not by the works of the law."

The picture is rather more complicated in relation to the nature of justification itself. Here differences in detail among medieval interpreters in how they appropriated Augustine's exegetical grammar began to appear and were largely the consequence of a drive for precision that in the process generated new terminology. Just as unanswered questions may lie implicit in the statements of biblical writers, not least Paul himself, so too unanswered questions lay implicit in the exegetical grammar established by Augustine. To give but one example, we have seen that Augustine never clarified whether justifying grace was to be identified with the Holy Spirit, or regarded as something closely related to, but distinct from, the Spirit. This was widely discussed in the medieval period with divided opinions,[61] and the result was a terminological distinction between uncreated grace (*gratia increata*) and created grace (*gratia creata*). But if the grace infused in justification was not the uncreated grace of the Spirit but created grace, then what was that created grace? How was it to be understood and described? And how was grace infused within a person (*gratia gratum faciens*) to be distinguished from external divine aid (*gratia gratis data*)? Far from closing down theological debate or inhibiting innovation, Augustine's exegetical grammar did indeed structure and enable it. Yet, since its appropriation was also a process of elaboration, it remains very much a matter of perspective as to whether such elaboration was fully consonant with Augustine's vision or represents an adherence to its letter in defiance of its Pauline spirit. In order to get a sense of the range of positions possible within medieval Pauline interpretation, we will explore three different ways of appropriating Augustine's insights, all of which have been carefully considered in recent scholarship in relation to the development of Luther's thought. They are those of Thomas Aquinas, those of some nominalist theologians such as Gabriel Biel whose work formed an important component of Luther's theological education at the University of Erfut, and finally those of certain figures in the Augustinian

---

61. Peter Lombard, author of the *Sentences* (c. 1150), the basic theological textbook of the medieval period, argued for uncreated grace but the majority opinion of the subsequent centuries was against him.

order itself, most notably Johann Staupitz, Luther's superior and confessor in his early days as a monk.[62]

2.3.1. Thomas Aquinas

Thomas Aquinas's theological vision finds its primary expression in the great unfinished *Summa Theologiae*, which was written between 1265 and his death in 1274. Despite much uncertainty about precise dating, it is clear that intensive exegesis of the Pauline epistles and the reading of several of Augustine's anti-Pelagian writings either accompanied the writing of the *Summa* or preceded it in the early 1260s.[63] It is thus entirely natural that Thomas's profoundly creative and original theological vision incorporates Augustine's Pauline exegetical grammar, and he asserts that "the theme of the entire Pauline corpus is grace."[64] In that vision, Thomas gave fresh expression to the Platonic view, shared by Augustine, that created, contingent existence is a limited form of participation in the primary and absolute existence of God. The world was created for the manifestation of divine goodness outside of God and salvation is understood through the motif of return to God: "Now, all creatures, together and individually, return to their beginning insofar as they bear within themselves a resemblance to it in their very being and nature, which constitute for them a certain perfection."[65] For human

---

62. In selecting these three streams of medieval Pauline interpretation, I am not implying that they provide a complete or even sufficient description of the Reformers' intellectual context. In particular, I am not discounting the influence upon Luther of medieval mysticism in general or Johannes Tauler (c.1300–1361) more specifically. It is simply that, while Luther was to incorporate important motifs from mysticism into his Pauline exegesis, there does not emerge from medieval mysticism an exegetically based structure of Pauline soteriology. On the influence upon Luther of Tauler and of mysticism see Berndt Hamm, "How Mystical Was Luther's Faith" in *The Early Luther: Stages in a Reformation Reorientation* (Grand Rapids: Eerdmans, 2014), 190–232, and Leppin, "Luther's Roots in Monastic-Mystical Piety," 49–61.

63. Henri Bouillard, *Conversion et grâce chez S. Thomas d'Aquin, étude historique* (Paris: Aubier, 1944).

64. Levy, Krey, and Ryan, "Introduction," 42.

65. *SCG* II 46, n. 1230. The wording of this quotation is that of Jean-Pierre Torrell, *Saint Thomas Aquinas*, trans. Robert Royal, 2 vols. (Washington, DC: Catholic University of America Press: 2003), 2:56. For the Latin text alongside an English translation, see http://www.dhspriory.org/thomas/ContraGentiles.htm.

beings the highest aspect of their natural participation in the divine is the gift of an intelligent and free soul. Yet this gift of participatory being granted in creation is not on the same level as the gift of grace given in salvation, since grace provides a new mode of the presence of God in a person: "The gift of sanctifying grace perfects the rational creature, putting him in a state not only of freely using the created gift but also of *enjoying the divine person himself.*"[66] There is here a sense both that the return to God received in Christ is immensely higher than the participation available in nature and yet also of the indissoluble unity of the two: "Despite the differing levels of the gift of being and the gift of grace, Thomas finds no gap between them. It is the same God who takes the initiative in both kinds of gift in the unity of his plan of salvation for the world."[67]

This manner of relating the created and the divine in Aquinas has a number of consequences. One is the characteristic position that grace perfects rather than destroys nature. For human beings, this raises the issue of the relationship between natural existence and existence under grace. If grace is to perfect nature there can be no question of the form of the human body simply being separate from the soul. Instead, "the soul is the form of the body . . . the soul informs all aspects of our existence, not only our rational part but also our physical part."[68] Another consequence is that if the higher gift of grace involves the enjoyment of the divine person, then Aquinas will respond powerfully to Pauline texts expressing the notion of union with Christ. The justified person has entered a new mode of existence. A textual focus for all of this is provided by Aquinas's exegesis of Gal 2:19–20: "I have been crucified with Christ. It is no longer I who live, but it is Christ who lives in me. And the life I now live in the flesh I live by faith in the Son of God, who loved me and gave himself for me." Thomas's explanation of Paul's apparently contradictory assertions of not living (it is no longer I who live) and living (the life I now live) relies on his particular anthropology: "the soul of Paul was set between his body and God; the body, indeed, was vivified and moved by the soul of Paul, but his soul by Christ. Hence as to the life of the flesh, Paul himself lived and this is what he says, namely, *and that I live now in the flesh,* i.e., by the

66. *ST* 7:219 (Ia q. 43 a. 3 ad 1). The wording of this quotation is that of Torrell, *Saint Thomas Aquinas,* 2:97.

67. Torrell, *Saint Thomas Aquinas,* 2.60–61. Torrell provides a full exploration of Aquinas's view of salvation as a return to God, 2:53–100.

68. John K. Riches, *Galatians through the Centuries* (Oxford: Blackwell, 2007), 27.

life of the flesh; but as to his relation to God, Christ lived in Paul."[69] His explanation of what it means to be crucified with Christ is that it is "the strength to act well,"[70] to have affections and desires directed away from self and towards Christ and others. This is possible "because the love of Christ, which He showed to me in dying on the cross for me, brings it about that I am always nailed with him."[71]

This profound emphasis on union with Christ might be expected to incline Thomas towards the view that grace is to be identified with the Holy Spirit, i.e., as uncreated. In fact he takes the opposite view. His concern in doing so is to protect the proper distinction between God and sinful humanity: "In this life, the human person remains separated from God and is incapable of the direct vision of God. Rather, the individual is capable, through grace, only of acts that 'anticipate' in a way appropriate to human nature the final vision of and union with God."[72] Thus, the union of the Christian with Christ by the power of the Spirit in this life must be understood in such a way that the Christian is changed under the impact of the Spirit's action but the uncreated reality of the Spirit is not changed. The Spirit moves the rational soul of the justified to acts of charity, but in Thomas's view to say more than that would be to require a hypostatic union similar to that between divine and human wills in the incarnation. It would also be to rob human beings as creatures of their divinely granted freedom in manifesting divine goodness outside of God.[73] For all these reasons Thomas conceives of grace as created, a permeating quality in the human soul that enables the journey of the justified person back towards God. It is a transforming habit (*habitus*) of love, and while the justified person remains unable to avoid more minor venial sins, the

---

69. Aquinas, *Commentary on Saint Paul's Epistle to the Galatians by St. Thomas Aquinas*, trans. Fabian R. Larcher (Albany, NY: Magi, 1966), 63. For the Latin text alongside an English tranlation, see http://www.dhspriory.org/thomas/ssGalations.htm. See also Riches, *Galatians through the Centuries*, 118–21.

70. Aquinas, *Commentary on Saint Paul's Epistle to the Galatians*, 62. See n. 69 for details of the Latin text.

71. Aquinas, *Commentary on Saint Paul's Epistle to the Galatians*, 63. See n. 69 for details of the Latin text.

72. Joseph P. Wawrykow, *God's Grace and Human Action: 'Merit' in the Theology of Thomas Aquinas* (University of Notre Dame Press, 1995), 167. See also the classic study on grace in Aquinas's theology by Bernard Lonergan, *Grace and Freedom: Operative Grace in the Thought of St. Thomas Aquinas* (New York: Herder & Herder, 1971).

73. The logic of Aquinas's insistence on created grace is explained by Torrell, *Saint Thomas Aquinas*, 2:178–83.

fact that the rational soul as the form of the body is subordinate to God means that more damaging mortal sin can be avoided.[74]

This habitual grace forms only one of two principal parts in a complex analysis of grace in Thomas's mature theology. Habitual grace is gifted by God and then receives cooperation from the human beings involved as they progress in justice. However, habitual grace is first received as a part of initial justification. Only the justified have habitual grace (*gratia gratum faciens*), and in order for them to have it there must first be an exercise by God of what may be termed external or actual grace (*gratia gratis data*). Further, human beings are sufficiently fragile in relation to sin that even those who have habitual grace need to be moved by God to good acts. Actual grace continues to be required throughout the Christian life. There is here too cooperation with grace, since God conceives the end of a good deed, but human beings deliberate over and choose the means to the end and execute the act itself.[75] The result is that habitual grace does not become something quasi-independent from God who gave it, but functions within a framework of continuous divine sustenance. Aquinas perceives the justification of the individual to flow from the divine decree of predestination. It is here, enfolded within grace, that Thomas is happy to accept the prevalent motif within medieval concepts of justification that God will not deny grace to those who do what lies within them (*quod in se est*), i.e., their best. As Alister McGrath comments, in Thomas's hands the axiom effectively means "that God will not deny grace to those who do their best, in so far as they are moved by God to do this."[76]

Yet although the justification of the individual is enfolded in this way within grace, the concept of cooperation and Thomas's emphasis on the human creature as manifesting divine goodness leave considerable scope for notions of merit.[77] Thomas attempts to clarify Augustine's paradox that God crowns his own gifts. He recognizes that strict notions of merit make no sense before God, since no human action can correspond in worth to God's reward. However, God has ordained that in order to manifest God's goodness, certain actions are meritorious and establish a right in justice to a reward from God. Further, since the manifestation of divine goodness was the purpose of creation, this

---

74. On this point see McGrath, *Iustitia Dei*, 66.

75. Wawrykow, *God's Grace and Human Action*, 164–77. See also McGrath, *Iustitia Dei*, 135–38.

76. McGrath, *Iustitia Dei*, 111.

77. See especially Wawrykow, *God's Grace and Human Action*, 147–259.

ordaining of merit does not remain external to the structure of creation but is built into it. God graciously makes it part of the very nature of things that it is possible for God to be obligated to human beings. Aquinas speaks here to the distinction within medieval theology between merit on the part of the Christian that is congruous (*meritum de congruo*)—for God to grant a reward is appropriate, but the reward given exceeds what the person strictly deserves—and merit that is condign (*meritum de condigno*)—there is an objective correlation or match between the value of the meritorious actions concerned and the reward given, which is fully deserved.

There can be no possibility of even congruous merit in initial justification, but because God has ordained condign merit within the structure of creation it is possible for the person endowed with habitual grace to come to merit eternal life. God of course does merit condignly and since grace allows a person a degree of participation in the life of God, condign merit is possible for the Christian on the basis of adoption: "Insofar as the Holy Spirit makes us sons and daughters in the Son, our works truly deserve the inheritance that God gives us, namely our eternal sharing in his life."[78] Aquinas experiences some difficulty with Paul's statement at Rom 8:18 that the sufferings of the present are not worth comparison with the glory to be revealed to or in believers. The gap here between present reality and eschatological fulfillment seems too great if condign merit is indeed possible in the present. However, Aquinas argues that the sufferings of the present refer not to the whole condition of those adopted by God but specifically to the contribution that their free choice makes in the performing of actions.[79]

The role of faith within the process of justification is as the gift of beatifying knowledge. It is a foretaste of the knowledge of God that will be possessed in eternal life.[80] Since God is always true, there is an important sense in which this knowledge of faith is itself righteousness. When Abraham believes God in Rom 4, his acceptance of God's promises as true renders to God what is justly due to God. Thus, when God looks on the gift of faith that Abraham has received, God sees this faith as righ-

---

78. Matthew Levering, *Paul in the Summa Theologiae* (Washington, DC: Catholic University of America Press, 2014), 164. See 153–85 for discussion of Paul's influence upon Aquinas's treatment of grace in the *Summa*.

79. *ST* 30:207–9 (Ia-IIae q.114 a.3).

80. Torrell, *Saint Thomas Aquinas*, 2:322–26.

teousness, i.e., as what it actually is.[81] However, this initial knowledge of faith is only the first act of justice wrought in the Christian by the divine gift. In subsequent acts of justice love enables the knowledge of faith to be given concrete expression in deeds: "To will as one might is caused by charity, which perfects the will."[82] Aquinas expresses this conviction in his exegesis of Gal 5:6,[83] where Paul says that what counts is not circumcision or uncircumcision but "faith working through love." Following Peter Lombard,[84] Thomas takes the phrase "faith working through love" to refer specifically to "faith, not unformed, but the kind that worketh by charity: 'Faith without works is dead' (Jas. 2:26). For faith is a knowledge of the word of God 'That Christ may dwell by faith in your hearts' (Eph. 3:17)—which word is not perfectly possessed or perfectly known unless the love which it hopes for is possessed."[85]

There is a tension here between an inadequate factual knowledge and a personal knowledge in relationship that results in works of love, but Aquinas does not deal with this tension by refusing to categorize solely factual knowledge as faith, or arrive at a similar destination by terming it dead faith. Instead Aquinas refers to faith that is "unformed," clearly implying that only faith formed by love justifies and also raising the possibility of a faith that is in some sense truly faith but that is of lesser value and remains incomplete in relation to justification. Aquinas has here moved exegetically beyond Augustine's insistence that faith never comes alone and into a distinction between two kinds of faith: one formed by love and capable of the meritorious deeds that lead through the pilgrimage of the Christian life to the congruous meriting of salvation, the other lacking this formation and incapable of merit. It is the presence or absence of love that is crucial, for "When unformed faith becomes formed, it is not the faith itself that is changed, but the soul, the subject of faith; at one instant it has faith without charity, and at the next, faith with charity."[86]

---

81. See Marshall, "*Beatus vir*: Aquinas, Romans 4, and the Role of 'Reckoning' in Justification," 219–21.

82. *ST* 23:193 (IaIIae q.65 a.4).

83. See Riches, *Galatians through the Centuries*, 249–51, 258–9.

84. See John Van Engen, "Faith as a Concept of Order," in *Belief in History: Innovative Approaches to European and American Religion*, ed. Thomas A. Kselman (Notre Dame: University of Notre Dame Press, 1991), 31–36.

85. Aquinas, *Commentary on Saint Paul's Epistle to the Galatians*, 156. See note 69 for details of the Latin text.

86. *ST* 31:131 (IIaIIae q.65 a.4 ad.4). This statement is also highlighted by Sun-

This step may not have been perceived as of enormous significance by Aquinas himself but, as a result of the widespread adoption of such exegesis of the verse, Gal 5:6 was to become in the sixteenth century one of the battlefields between incompatible understandings of the meaning of the term "faith" in the Pauline texts.

2.3.2. *Nominalism and Gabriel Biel*

Aquinas's vision involved the conviction that all created beings participate in a limited way in the existence of God. If they did not do so, they would cease to exist. However, there is an alternative current within medieval theology that approaches the question of being very differently. In the late thirteenth and early fourteenth centuries, Duns Scotus and William of Ockham argued that being does not depend on participation in the divine. God certainly still creates by his divine word but God's will is a sufficient explanation for the existence of the creature: "That God wants something to be does not mean that he has to be present in it. . . . God's will can act from a distance to cause a being."[87] The power of God continuously sustains all beings in existence, but this gift is received from outside. God and humanity do not exist in a single hierarchical chain of being. The impetus behind this view is an emphasis on divine freedom. In arguing that existence depends on God's absolute will alone any possible implication that God acts in certain ways out of necessity is removed. God is not constrained by being implicated in a chain of being. Instead, that God behaves reliably in a particular way is mandated only by commitments that God has made. Promises freely entered into—caused by nothing external to God—are the only constraints upon divine behavior. It is therefore important to distinguish between the unlimited range of possibilities initially open to God in interacting with humanity and the self-imposed limitations involved in making promises that thereafter constrain divine actions. There is thus

---

young Kim, *Luther on Faith and Love: Christ and the Law in the 1535 Galatians Commentary* (Minneapolis: Fortress Press, 2014), 84.

87. Sammeli Juntunen, "Luther and Metaphysics: What Is the Structure of Being according to Luther?" in *Union with Christ: The New Finnish Interpretation of Luther*, ed. Carl E. Braaten and Robert W. Jenson (Grand Rapids: Eerdmans, 1998), 149. Scotus and Ockham disagree radically on many other issues, including significant aspects of justification, but here they are in agreement.

a distinction between God's absolute power (*de potentia absoluta*) and God's ordained power (*de potentia ordinata*).[88] God could have saved humanity in any manner God chose, but since divine promises have been made, God's ordained power is operative and a particular course of action will reliably follow.

In the hands of Ockham's theological descendants, above all those of Gabriel Biel, the most prominent German nominalist of the late fifteenth century and the first professor of theology at Tübingen, this approach yielded a distinctive account of Pauline teaching on salvation. It is often termed "Ockhamist," or "nominalist," but the terminology can be misleading unless handled with care. Ockham became most famous for his opposition to philosophical realism and his rejection of the existence of universals, and it is to this that the term "nominalism" formally refers. Ockham rejects the idea that there are universal categories lying behind specific instances of being. It is not true that people as individuals can only exist because humankind exists as a universal reality. Specific instances of being do not participate in universal realities and universals are in fact simply mental substitutes for real things. In rejecting an inherently participatory account of being, this philosophical position has obvious affinities with the process of thought that led to the distinction between the absolute and ordained powers of God. Yet it is perfectly possible within late medieval thought to be "nominalist" theologically without being so in this philosophical sense and vice versa. Further, like Aquinas's significantly different vision, the nominalist theological account of Pauline soteriology operates within an Augustinian exegetical grammar. Justification encompasses the whole of life as a pathway for the transformation of the Christian. The Christian who has received initial justification is for practical purposes in the same position as in Aquinas's understanding. In order to merit eternal life the Christian must cooperate with habitual grace in a progress towards justice. Profound disagreement comes not about what is in fact the case for the existing Christian, but over why it is the case. There are very different views in operation of divine freedom and its relationship to justification. For Aquinas, habitual grace justifies because that it should do so has been woven by the Creator into the nature of the creation. In the contrasting nominalist account, the emphasis on divine promise means that the biblical concept of covenant (*pactum*) is prominent. Habits of grace can indeed lead to condign merit

88. See McGrath, *Iustitia Dei*, 150–58.

before God, but there is nothing necessary in the connection between them and justification. The connection exists solely because God has covenanted that it should. That good works are meritorious is not built into the structure of creation but rests entirely upon divine fidelity to promises given.

By contrast, in relation to initial justification there are disagreements not only about why certain things are the case but also over what is in fact the case. Here the nominalists hold that human beings are able to prepare themselves for grace even in their fallen state. Although damaged by sin, human beings retain an inclination towards good. The human will is still able to choose the good despite the difficulty of doing so. If individuals do *quod in se est* ("what lies within them"), which is to humble themselves before God and to repent, God has committed on the basis of God's ordained power to give the gift of grace and to justify. This is not a matter of condign merit, by which eternal life is merited, but instead of congruous merit, by which the sinner receives habitual grace. The sinner has done something in no sense equal to the gift of grace, but because God has promised to respond to humility and repentance in this way it is appropriate and fitting that God should do so. Further, this capacity of the fallen human being congruously to merit the gift of habitual grace has complex consequences for predestination. From a human perspective it cannot be assumed that the recipient of habitual grace in initial justification will persevere and merit eternal life. Predestination cannot be verified until eternal life is actually awarded. Yet since perseverance depends upon cooperation with habitual grace received from God in response to a person's humility and repentance, it is inescapable that divine foreknowledge of how a person will behave is significant in predestination.

At this point, nominalists clearly depart from Augustine and have been perceived by many scholars as toppling over into semi-Pelagianism.[89] The force of this judgment is apparent at the exegetical level. When Biel's disciple Wendelin Steinbach, also a Tübingen theologian, comments on the faith of Abraham in Rom 4, his conclusions are, to say the least, less than convincing:

89. McGrath, *Iustitia Dei*, 158-76, makes sharp criticisms of Heiko A. Oberman's account of Biel's view of predestination in *The Harvest of Medieval Theology* (Cambridge: Harvard University Press, 1963), 185-216. Yet while McGrath makes some telling points he certainly cannot and does not dispute that foreknowledge is significant.

What we have here, in Steinbach's opinion, is a particularly outrageous example of Paul's peculiar *modus loquendi* or manner of speaking. When Paul says that Abraham is justified by faith and implies by this that Abraham is justified by faith alone, he is using a way of talking appropriate for catechumens who are not yet fully aware that faith alone (in the sense of unformed or acquired faith) cannot save. Only faith working by love saves. St. Paul knew that as well as St. James. What St. Paul is claiming (and we must be careful not to miss his point or be thrown off by his incautious phraseology) is that Abraham merited the first grace of justification by his good works, preeminently by the good work of believing God with his unformed faith.[90]

Yet despite such dubious construal of Paul's meaning, it is important to appreciate that nominalist theologians themselves felt not only that they had avoided Pelagianism but were explicitly concerned to do so. From their perspective, the radical disjunction between the feeble moral reality of human deeds and the high meritorious value accorded to them by God on the basis of God's covenanted promises ensured that the whole process was a matter of grace. The foreseen merits of the individual have significance only because God freely wills that they do so in an exercise of his ordained powers. Here it must be remembered that it was axiomatic for nominalists that the divine promises were themselves entirely uninfluenced by anything outside of God. It should also be noted that the divergence from Aquinas involved in these views was not widely recognized. Whether as a result of misreading of Aquinas's *Summa*, or as a result of reliance on his earlier commentary on Lombard's *Sentences* where he did countenance such a view, Aquinas was also understood to affirm that a sinner can merit initial justification congruously.[91] As we have seen, in his *Summa* Aquinas in reality explicitly denies this.

90. David C. Steinmetz, "Abraham and the Reformation," in *Luther in Context*, 2nd ed. (Grand Rapids: Baker, 2002), 36-38.

91. See John L. Farthing, *Thomas Aquinas and Gabriel Biel* (Durham, NC: Duke University Press, 1988), 150-80; David C. Steinmetz, "Luther Among the Anti-Thomists," in *Luther in Context*, 2nd ed. (Grand Rapids: Baker, 2002), 52-56; Heiko A. Oberman, "*Iustitia Christi* and *Iustitia Dei*: Luther and the Scholastic Doctrines of Justification," in *The Dawn of the Reformation: Essays in Late Medieval and Early Reformation Thought* (Edinburgh: T&T Clark, 1986), 208.

2.3.3. *Some Augustinian Theologians*

There is much scholarly literature that speaks of the existence of a school of theology in the early sixteenth century within the Augustinian order—typically termed the *schola Augustiniana moderna*—that may have exercised considerable influence upon the young Luther. However, recent studies have shown that there was significant diversity within Augustinian theology. Augustinian theologians teaching within universities were not necessarily typical of an order that stressed the fusion of ethics and learning in a practical piety. The influence of one late medieval Augustinian theologian upon another is difficult to disentangle from the impact made upon individuals by a direct reading of Augustine's texts.[92] Nevertheless, there are individuals within the Augustinian order in the early sixteenth century whose soteriological positions are of considerable interest because they stand at certain important points closer to the Reformers than do other Catholics. Despite this they were unwilling to join the Reformers. This was not simply out of horror at the tearing apart of the church, although this is undoubtedly significant, but also because they ultimately remained wedded to Augustine's Pauline exegetical grammar. They could not break with it as the Reformers did.

Due to his close personal association with Luther as the latter's superior in the Augustinian order, Johan Staupitz is the classic example of such an individual. Staupitz responded to the trauma of Luther's break with Rome by resigning in 1520 as Vicar-General of the order in Germany and subsequently became a Dominican abbot. Like the nominalists he laid considerable stress upon the humility and repentance of the sinner but utterly rejected their view that this constituted individuals doing *quod in se est* ("what lies within them") as an act of congruous merit in response to which God grants the grace of initial justification. Instead, humility and repentance are instilled in the sinner by God as a consequence of initial justification. They are the fruits of grace. Predestination is the cause of initial justification and here divine foreknowledge of faith plays no part, i.e., merit of any sort is excluded. The sinner indeed must do what lies within, but at this point what lies within is "to accuse oneself as a sinner, to abandon all hope of making oneself righteous before God by

---

92. See Eric L. Saak, *High Way to Heaven: The Augustinian Platform between Reform and Reformation, 1292-1524* (Leiden: Brill, 2002), 683-735.

one's own pious acts. Humility is not a virtue that the sinner offers to God in exchange for grace, but an embarrassed confession that the sinner has nothing whatever to exchange but his own sin. Goodness and dignity are found in God alone."[93]

If viewed in relation to initial justification only, there is nothing here very distant from the views of Aquinas. Yet when Staupitz discusses the subsequent Christian life, significant differences open up not only with the nominalists but with Thomas also. There is the same basic structure of the gift of grace with which the Christian cooperates to perform acts that are virtuous and meritorious, and there is the same deep conviction that in union with Christ the justified person has entered a new mode of existence. The difference is that this new existence is not understood primarily in terms of a created habit of grace:

> The Pauline doctrine is that sinners are made pleasing to God through election and then given the gift of love which makes their faith living and active. Staupitz does not use the metaphysical language of act and habit to describe this love, preferring rather to stress the bond of charity as a personal union of Christ with the Christian.[94]

Staupitz seems close here to simply regarding grace as uncreated rather than created.[95] Further, he has distinctive views as to the manner in which the works of the Christian are meritorious:

> Staupitz refuses, however, to allow the good works of the Christian to be regarded as merits of condignity, since only the works of Christ can claim to be merits in that sense. There is too great a disproportion between the inherent worth of the moral activity and the reward promised to such good deeds to permit anyone to think in terms of condign merit. Besides, the good works of the Christian are, in the last analysis, nothing more than the works of Christ in him.[96]

Again, Staupitz seems close to rejecting a classic medieval distinction between two types of merit just as he has come close to rejecting the

---

93. Steinmetz, *Luther and Staupitz*, 73.
94. Steinmetz, *Luther and Staupitz*, 106.
95. See McGrath, *Iustitia Dei*, 185.
96. Steinmetz, *Luther and Staupitz*, 107.

distinction between two types of grace. All Christian merit is congruous. More important, however, is the renewed emphasis on the sufferings of Christ. The disjunction between the actual worth of human deeds and the scale of the reward is not dealt with primarily by appeal to God's covenanted pledge to accept such deeds (the nominalist solution), nor primarily on the basis that despite this disjunction God has graciously built the possibility of condign merit into the structure of reality (Aquinas's position). The gap is bridged rather by the work of the cross: "The Christian is just with a righteousness given him by Christ, while Christ becomes a sinner through his assumption of the guilt and weakness of the Christian. . . . God . . . accepts even imperfect contrition when it is grounded in the sufferings of Christ."[97] The Christian may not be able to do all that the Christian ought to do, but for the shortfall the penitent Christian may rely on Christ: "only because we humans with our tiny feelings of love can climb onto the shoulders of Christ's giant love and great suffering, can our repentance—which by itself is so insufficient—become a repentance that nevertheless wipes out our sins. Diminutive human repentance can reach heaven on the shoulders of the giant Christ."[98] The issue is no longer how the Christian may be transformed into a person pleasing to God. Election means that the person in Christ already is pleasing to God. The issue rather is how the Christian may be changed so that God becomes truly pleasing to the Christian and the center of his or her affections and desires.

The powerful resonances between many of Staupitz's views and those later adopted by the Reformers should not blind us to the fact that his perspective remains wholly within Augustine's Pauline exegetical grammar. Staupitz does *not* regard the righteousness given to the Christian by Christ "as something extrinsic to the sinner, something imputed to him. The righteousness is intrinsic, something Christ effects in the Christian by his presence and activity."[99] This point can also be well made by reference to the career of Girolamo Cardinal Seripando, general of the Augustinian Order, who was both a highly competent exegete and papal legate to the Council of Trent. At the Council in 1546 he urged adoption of a view close to that of Staupitz, although by this

---

97. Steinmetz, *Luther and Staupitz*, 106-8.

98. Berndt Hamm, "Impending Doom and Imminent Grace: Luther's Early Years in the Cloister as the Beginning of his Reformation Reorientation," in *The Early Luther: Stages in Reformation Reorientation* (Grand Rapids: Eerdmans, 2014), 19.

99. Steinmetz, *Luther and Staupitz*, 106.

time its presentation and reception was influenced by the existence of the Reformers' alternative. Seripando and others advocated the idea of a *duplex iustitia* (double justice), arguing that righteousness of the Christian is both infused and imputed. The necessity for an extrinsic imputed element is based on Staupitz's point that, given the inherent lack of worth of his or her deeds, the Christian who has received initial justification must still rely on Christ's death for mercy. This position was rejected by a clear majority as suspiciously close to that of the Reformers, and Trent's decree on justification instead stressed the possibility that the person in Christ can fully satisfy the divine law and truly merit eternal life.[100] Yet, for all this, Seripando can say things in his Pauline exegesis that would excite the strong opposition of the Reformers. When he comments on the figure of Abraham in Rom 4, Seripando accepts that Paul's teaching excludes the view that good deeds performed prior to initial justification congruously merit the gift of grace. They are fleshly and do not justify. However, Seripando is equally clear that this exclusion does not apply to works performed by the Christian after the gift of grace has been received. Faith itself is a divine gift and is granted without any prior human merit, but if Abraham is justified by faith, "this faith is in turn consummated in works of charity. Faith must be living and active rather than idle and dead. Faith is related to works as a beginning to the end, as a foundation to the building erected upon it, as the root of a plant to the fruit which it finally bears."[101] Abraham's faith is formed by love and Augustine's understanding is preserved of the Christian life as a pathway of transformation along which progress is made as further grace is secured and justice increases.

100. Hampson, *Christian Contradictions*, 56-96. For an account of Seripando's advocacy at Trent and of the earlier discussions between Catholic and Protestant theologians at the Colloquy of Regensburg (1541), where Gasparo Contarini, whose opinions were close to those of Seripando, was an important figure on the Catholic side, see Anthony N. S. Lane, *Justification by Faith in Catholic-Protestant Dialogue: An Evangelical Assessment* (London and New York: T&T Clark, 2002), 45-85. Lane (58) feels that although similar in important ways it is not correct to characterize the article on justification agreed at Regensburg as teaching a *duplex iustitia*.

101. Steinmetz, "Abraham and the Reformation," 41-43.

2.4. The Impact on Luther and the Reaction of the Council of Trent

Our examination of selected medieval appropriations of Augustine's Pauline exegetical grammar thus reveals a clear overall pattern. They differ, and sometimes profoundly so, at points where they seek to explicate unanswered questions implicit in Augustine's thought. The drive for specificity in much altered historical contexts yields diversity. Yet this diversity is that of different structures erected on the same foundations. Disagreements take place within the framework of Augustine's Pauline exegetical grammar. Given this, what is an appropriate characterization of the relationship between these three medieval appropriations of Augustine's grammar and the Reformation revolution? They certainly provide a large part of the intellectual context of the Reformers' Pauline world. When Luther and others begin through their study of the Pauline texts to disagree with previously dominant positions, they naturally identify what they reject with the medieval tradition. Yet since it is Augustine's Pauline exegetical grammar that underlies all these medieval interpretations of Pauline soteriology, criticism of these appropriations of Augustine ultimately becomes criticism of Augustine's own interpretations. The Reformers eventually not only demolish the buildings of scholastic Pauline interpretation but also dig out the foundations.

As noted previously, the story of when and how they did so certainly does not concern only Martin Luther. He does not only exercise influence upon others but is himself influenced by contemporaries such as Erasmus and Melanchthon. Both these scholars were prominent humanists. While Luther did not himself receive a humanist education, Luther's revolution in Pauline exegesis is unimaginable without the impact of Renaissance humanism: "The Reformation 'scripture principle' belongs in this connection, with its mobilization of linguistic proficiency in Greek and Hebrew, rational textual criticism, academic education of ministers and the cultivation of literacy in the vernacular among the laity."[102] As part of a movement emphasizing a return to sources, humanists often approached biblical interpretation with "a philological approach, arguing on the basis of grammatical rules, etymology, and classical usage."[103] It

---

102. Hamm, "The Place of the Reformation in the Second Christian Millennium," 290.

103. Erika Rummel, *The Humanist-Scholastic Debate in the Renaissance and*

is unlikely that contemporaries would have found Luther's attack on the medieval tradition plausible had not humanism been so strongly present in the scholarly context.[104] Yet, Luther's own exegetical and theological development inevitably lies at the center of the story and research into it has generated considerable disagreement. Despite these debates, there are some things that may be said that are relatively uncontroversial. The lack of documentary evidence makes it difficult to discern the relative weight early in Luther's career of the somewhat contradictory influences of his nominalist education at Erfurt and his exposure to Staupitz. Indeed, it is not clear the degree to which his primarily pastoral relationship with Staupitz, which existed outside of a formal educational setting, would have exposed Luther to the detail of Staupitz's views on soteriology.[105] All that can be said is that while in his earliest works (his marginal comments on Augustine and on Lombard's *Sentences* from 1509–1510) Luther already seems doubtful about the role of created habits of grace in justification, his comments appear generally consistent with a nominalist perspective.[106] When Luther's theology later develops a more critical edge after his appointment as a professor at Wittenberg in 1512, it is against nominalism that he reacts with some ferocity. There is some disagreement as to whether his *First Lectures on the Psalms*, delivered in

---

Reformation (Cambridge: Harvard University Press, 1995), 12. Rummel argues that the revisionist tendency which regards the traditional picture of the rift between humanists and scholastics as enormously exaggerated is at least partially mistaken: "The conflict, which began in Italy as a literary debate, continued as interfaculty feuding at universities, where humanists and theologians were in competitive positions. Polarized by the Reformation, the parties turned feuds into dogmatic disputes. ... Their model was no longer familiar conversation elevated to a literary level, but the argumentation associated in classical handbooks with political and forensic oratory or with Aristotelian dialectic. ... A magisterial tone pervaded the writings of the scholastic theologians; invective was the weapon of choice in the humanist camp" (4–5).

104. For an overview of the impact of humanism on the university curriculum and its implications for study of Scripture, see Gillian R. Evans, *The Roots of the Reformation: Tradition, Emergence, and Rupture* (Downers Grove, IL: InterVarsity Press, 2012), 253–86.

105. On the difficulty of determining the detail of Staupitz's influence see Steinmetz, *Luther and Staupitz*, 27–34, 141–44. The whole argument of Hamm, *The Early Luther*, presupposes that the pastoral relationship between Staupitz and Luther would have been the means by which the theology of Staupitz was communicated clearly to Luther.

106. Alister E. McGrath, *Luther's Theology of the Cross: Martin Luther's Theological Breakthrough*, 2nd ed. (Oxford: Wiley-Blackwell, 2010), 111–15.

1513 but revised for publication in 1515-1516, represent an expression of nominalist soteriology or an incipient break with it,[107] but such a break is clearly apparent by the time of Luther's *Lectures on Romans* (1515-1516).

Since Luther's understanding of Aquinas was mediated through the nominalist misreading of Thomas, Luther will have perceived his attacks on nominalist soteriology as also impacting Aquinas.[108] He is at important points rejecting the whole medieval scholastic tradition as he understands it, but at this stage does so in the name of a more accurate appropriation of Augustine's Pauline exegetical grammar. In a letter of May 1517 Luther rejoices that "Our theology and St. Augustine are progressing well, and with God's help rule at our University. . . . It is amazing how the lectures on the *Sentences* are disdained."[109] Indeed, Luther—who, after all, as an Augustinian monk, was a member of an order that self-identified as true heirs of Augustine and true followers of his religion—remained always eager to claim Augustine's support.[110] Such respect for Augustine, and the fact that the Reformers used his exegesis at many points to correct what they regarded as the faults of later theologies, serves to obscure the sharpness of their break with Augustine's Pauline exegetical grammar. Yet the cracks show even in one of Luther's most laudatory later moments concerning Augustine. In his account of his "Reformation Discovery," Luther says that

> Later I read Augustine's *The Spirit and the Letter*, where contrary to hope I found that he, too, interpreted God's righteousness in a similar way, as the righteousness with which God clothes us when he justifies us. Although this was heretofore said imperfectly and he did

---

107. See the very different assessments reached by McGrath, *Luther's Theology of the Cross*, 115-20, and Steinmetz, *Luther and Staupitz*, 78-95. Hamm, "Impending Doom and Imminent Grace," 26-58, sees the *First Lectures on the Psalms* not only as breaking with nominalist soteriology but as the harvest of a reorientation that had already begun in the Erfurt cloister years earlier. The doubts expressed about created habits of grace in Luther's earlier writings are taken as evidence of this (46). Hamm also argues that the *First Lectures on the Psalms* mark a significant break with medieval concepts of faith (see 59-84).

108. Steinmetz, "Luther among the Anti-Thomists," 47-58.

109. *LW* 48: no 14, 41-42 (42) = *WA* BR 1: no. 41, 98-99 (99, 8-13).

110. The collective identity and ethos of the Augustinian Order is explored in detail by Saak, *High Way to Heaven*. In his final chapter (584-675) Saak explores the implications of the fact that despite excommunication by Rome in January 1521 Luther did not bring himself to put off the Augustinian habit until October 9, 1524.

not explain all things concerning imputation clearly, it nevertheless was pleasing that God's righteousness with which we are justified was taught.[111]

Luther can correctly claim that he and Augustine share a deep conviction that the righteousness of God in Rom 1:17 is a divine gift and not a divine attribute. Yet Augustine's expressing the divine gift of righteousness "imperfectly" and having failed to "explain all things concerning imputation clearly" in fact amounts to a radically different understanding of the nature of the gift. By 1545 honest acknowledgement of their differences thus prevents from being entirely successful Luther's claim that his exegesis represents a recovery of Augustine. The influence of Augustine is to be honored and respected where it grants insight into Scripture, but even the greatest patristic authorities have an authority subordinate to that of the Word itself.[112] Yet this does not necessarily mean that at the time it was apparent to the young Luther that he was engaged in breaking with Augustine's Pauline exegetical grammar. Nor does this easily become apparent to others, certainly not before the publication in November 1520 of the tract *The Freedom of a Christian* when a radically new theology appears in summary form for the first time.[113]

Luther's move away from Augustine is therefore a complex process and seems also not entirely self-conscious. In his comments on the nature of sin in Rom 7, Luther quotes Augustine approvingly, ac-

---

111. *LW* 34:337 = *WA* 54:186, 16-20.

112. Timothy J. Wengert, "Philip Melanchthon and Augustine of Hippo," in *Philip Melanchthon, Speaker of the Reformation: Wittenberg's Other Reformer* (Burlington, VT: Ashgate Variorum, 2010), 249-67, demonstrates a very similar attitude on the part of Melanchthon. "We drink from the streams of Augustine. Or, rather, we are led by him to the sources [*ad fontes*] that are purer than any writings of human beings" (254). See *MBWR* 7: no. 5890 = *CR* 7:651f. In a laudatory 1545 preface to an edition of "The Spirit and the Letter," Melanchthon also awkwardly notes the differences on justification between Augustine and the Wittenberg Reformers: "But elsewhere he often states that human beings are justified through grace when the Holy Spirit is given who enkindles love in our hearts. This explanation is not complete" (260). See *CR* 5:806.

113. Heiko A. Oberman, "Headwaters of the Reformation," in *The Dawn of the Reformation: Essays in Late Medieval and Early Reformation Thought* (Edinburgh: T&T Clark, 1986), 43-44: "For all those who could read either Latin or German, the *De libertate Christiana* presents without explicit polemics the platform of the new theology ranging from *iustificatio sola fide* to the priesthood of all believers and the distinction between law and gospel."

curately, and repeatedly.[114] He follows Augustine in refusing to grant sin an independent existence. It is a sickness or a wound that cannot exist separately apart from the human beings it disfigures. He also reproduces the distinction between experiencing inappropriate desires and consenting to them, identifying only the latter with sin in its fullest sense. It would be hard to disagree with the judgment that Luther's treatment of sin is here thoroughly "Augustinian." Yet Luther also emphasizes here that "Flesh and spirit are not higher and lower faculties in human nature; they are descriptions of the whole person considered in its different relationships. Flesh is not the body, but the whole person turned in upon itself and its irrepressible egoism and its radical alienation from God."[115] This is significant because although Augustine did identify Paul's term "flesh" (σάρξ) as encompassing the human will, which itself becomes fleshly, his comments on Rom 7 had affirmed what Luther is here concerned explicitly to deny, namely that inappropriate desires typically arise from the body as the lower faculty of human nature and that the mind as the higher faculty is to refuse to consent to them as they struggle against each other in the conscience of the Christian. In a passage where he intends to affirm Augustine, Luther also undermines an important aspect of how Augustine understands Paul to say that sin normally works.[116]

At the other end of the spectrum some departures from Augustine are so glaring that Luther must have understood them as such, as in the rejection of Augustine's understanding of grace as infused in the tract *Against Latomus* in 1521.[117] Luther now holds instead that grace is divine favor. If there is to be identified any single endpoint to Luther's process of breaking with Augustine's Pauline exegesis, this is the strongest candidate. The new Pauline exegetical grammar still has many points of detail to be elaborated and it still has to become truly the shared possession of communities of interpreters, but from this moment onwards it is impossible that Luther or any who follow after him can fit their understanding of salvation back into Augustine's framework. Thus Calvin can quite calmly, if also with due respect, dismiss Augustine's interpretation of Rom 3:21 and of the righteousness of God:

114. *LW* 25:336–43 = *WA* 56:348, 1–354, 26.

115. Steinmetz, *Luther and Staupitz*, 117.

116. This development of new ideas about sin by Luther is more fully described in the next chapter.

117. *LW* 32:227–30 = *WA* 8:106, 4–108, 18.

I am well aware that Augustine gives a different explanation. He considers that the righteousness of God is the grace of regeneration and this grace is free, he states, because God renews us, unworthy as we are, by His Spirit . . . But it is evident from the context that the apostle includes all works without exception, even those which the Lord produces in His own people . . . The two propositions, that man is justified by faith through the grace of Christ, and yet that he is justified by the works which proceed from spiritual regeneration, are held to be in the fullest agreement, because God freely renews us, and we also receive His gift by faith. But Paul suggests a very different principle, viz. that men's consciences will never be at peace until they rest on the mercy of God alone.[118]

There could scarcely be a more explicit rejection of Augustine's Pauline exegetical grammar with its notion that justification encompasses the entire Christian life as a pathway to transformation. Denied is the place that Augustine finds for human good works as a means to merit and growth in justice as a consequence of, and response to, God's gift of grace in initial justification. It is not the case that Christ in his righteousness enters into a person and, with their cooperation, produces a righteousness that is inherent to them. Instead the Reformers insist that however indispensable and profound the transformation wrought in a person, the righteousness of Christ upon which the believer relies remains external and is appropriated by faith. Human good works are not a means to merit before God, or to growth in justifying righteousness, since such righteousness is complete and full in Christ. It may be a matter of perspective as to whether or not this rejection is in fact truer to Augustine's principal theological concerns than many approving medieval appropriations of his Pauline exegesis. However, that it is a rejection is completely clear. While the Reformers passionately embrace Augustine's emphasis upon the priority of divine grace, they do so in ways that deny other crucial aspects of his interpretation of Paul. This renders utterly implausible the thesis that the division of the church might have been avoided had Luther only truly understood the theology of Aquinas and not been misled by his

---

118. *Comm. Rom* 3:21, *CNTC* 8:71 = *OE* 13:68, 17 – 69, 3. It is precisely on this central question of justification that there are indications in Luther's *Table Talk*, as recorded by Veit Dietrich, 1531–1533, of explicit recognition of his differences with Augustine. See no. 85 and no. 347 in *LW* 54:10, 49–50 = *WA TR* 1:32, 7 – 30; 140, 3-28.

teachers into viewing the medieval tradition largely through nominalist lenses. For, as we have seen, Aquinas works within Augustine's Pauline exegetical grammar. Even if Luther and others among the Reformers did not accurately understand Aquinas, their rejection of Augustine's Pauline exegetical grammar necessarily involved rejection of some of the basic presuppositions of Aquinas's theology.[119] While it remains crucial to historical understanding to trace points of continuity between the Reformers and their exegetical predecessors, the Reformation constitutes a moment of decisive rupture in the history of Pauline interpretation.

When it comes in 1546, the official Catholic response to the challenge posed by the Reformers demonstrates that its fundamental nature had been well understood. The Council of Trent's "Decree Concerning Justification" does not attempt to adjudicate between the different available opinions of the medieval era.[120] Indeed, the terminology of scholastic theology is avoided wherever possible. Instead the decree's language is thoroughly biblical in a forthright reassertion of Augustine's Pauline exegetical grammar. Thus, the question of whether grace is created or uncreated and the place of habits of grace in justification are left unaddressed, and so too is the legitimacy and use of the distinction between congruous and condign merit. The concern is rather to establish the boundaries of what may be considered Catholic. In doing so, the decree affirms the primacy of grace but holds that at all points in the process of justification it is the responsibility of Christians to cooperate with what has been divinely given so that justice may increase: "they, through the observance of the commandments of God and of the Church, faith cooperating with good works, increase in that justice received through the grace of Christ and are further justified."[121] Canon 24 specifically condemns any who deny that good works increase justice before God.[122] Canon 32 condemns those who deny that the good works of the justified are meritorious.[123] The understanding that justification is a lifelong pro-

119. Steinmetz, "Luther among the Anti-Thomists," 56–58.

120. For the text see H. J. Schroeder, trans., *Canons and Decrees of the Council of Trent: Original Text with English Translation* (St. Louis: Herder, 1941), 29–50 (Sixth Session). For commentary, see Hampson, *Christian Contradictions*, 56–96.

121. Schroeder, *Canons and Decrees of the Council of Trent*, 36 (Sixth Session, Chapter 10).

122. Schroeder, *Canons and Decrees of the Council of Trent*, 45 (Sixth Session, Canons).

123. Schroeder, *Canons and Decrees of the Council of Trent*, 46 (Sixth Session, Canons).

cess in which the Christian progresses in a journey towards God could not be more clearly stated. Unsurprisingly therefore, the faith that justifies is defined as faith formed by love: "For faith, unless hope and charity be added to it, neither unites man perfectly with Christ nor makes him a living member of His body."[124] The person in Christ is enabled by such formed faith to fulfill the law, and Christ is explicitly defined as a legislator and not only as a redeemer. Yet while the possibility of keeping the commandments is insisted upon, it is not inevitable that this will happen. The necessity of cooperation and a final divine judgment based upon where an individual has reached in the process of increasing justice means that assurance of salvation is an appalling presumption. The Christian can be certain that God will justify the elect but not that he or she numbers among them. No one contemplating his or her own sins and weaknesses may know for sure that the grace of God has been obtained.

As we have already seen, this reassertion of Augustine's views does not only rule out the exegetical conclusions of the Reformers, who have left behind Augustine's Pauline exegetical grammar. It also at points defines as un-catholic what would previously certainly have been regarded as being so. The emphasis on Christ as legislator and on the fulfillment of the law by Christians disallows aspects of the theology of those like Staupitz and Seripando who preferred to stress instead the Christian's continuing need for mercy. In effect their appropriation of Augustine is ruled out of bounds at some significant points because it is deemed dangerously close to slipping over into the emerging Protestant perspective. At the other end of the medieval spectrum, the implications of the decree for the nominalist view that sinners may congruously merit initial justification are far from clear. The importance of preparation for initial justification is asserted, but this preparation is understood as both a divine and a human work: "while God touches the heart of man through the illumination of the Holy Ghost, man himself neither does absolutely nothing while receiving that inspiration, since he can also reject it, nor yet is he able by his own free will and without the grace of God to move himself to justice in His sight."[125] What is said elsewhere makes it plain that it is certainly not possible condignly to merit initial justification. Trent

---

124. Schroeder, *Canons and Decrees of the Council of Trent*, 34 (Sixth Session, Chapter 7).

125. Schroeder, *Canons and Decrees of the Council of Trent*, 32 (Sixth Session, Chapter 5).

is plainly *not* Pelagian, but we are not told whether receiving and not rejecting the inspiration of the Holy Ghost should be considered a congruous merit. It seems likely that although the decree does not endorse this view it also does not exclude it. There were too many at the Council themselves committed to the position.[126]

In this sense Trent does not prioritize the Thomist or the nominalist or any other particular medieval soteriological tradition. Yet if we ask which of the three medieval traditions surveyed fits most comfortably without remainder within the framework of the decree on justification, even if the language employed is very different and even if no one is required to adopt it, the answer is undoubtedly that which stems from Aquinas. The Tridentine decree is not a Thomist document, but it does perhaps mark the start of the long historical process by which Aquinas was to ascend from being one important theologian among others to the declaration in an 1879 encyclical of Pope Leo XIII that Aquinas's theology is a definitive exposition of Catholic doctrine. In the long run, it was his appropriation of Augustine's Pauline exegetical grammar and the Reformers' very different Pauline exegetical grammar that were to prove the most compelling alternatives.[127] We now turn to an exploration of the alternative exegetical grammar of the Reformers.

---

126. On this point, see McGrath, *Iustitia Dei*, 344-57 (especially 347-48).

127. Marshall, "*Beatus vir*," 218: "Since the sixteenth century friend and foe alike have usually taken St. Thomas as the most important and convincing advocate of a transformational account of justification. He is thus more or less automatically aligned with one side of the post-Reformation debate about how to understand St. Paul's teaching on justification."

3 The Human Plight apart from Christ

Sin, the Law, and the Conscience

3.1. Sin

The Reformers' interpretation of Pauline statements about the human plight apart from Christ is intimately connected to their conception of salvation in Christ. If their ideas about salvation do not allow any place for meritorious human cooperation with divine grace, and instead attribute everything to reliance upon Christ and his righteousness, then it also makes sense that they should regard Pauline descriptions of the human plight apart from Christ as having rendered such meritorious human cooperation with grace simply impossible. In their understanding of sin, the law, and the conscience the Reformers hear Paul speak of a human condition so alienated from God and from divine intentions for humanity that only righteousness granted fully and completely in Christ apart from all considerations of merit can offer hope and ultimate victory.

The exegetical development of the distinctive features of the Reformers' account of humanity alienated from God began with Luther's recasting of traditional ideas about sin. This recasting was essentially complete early in the development of his Reformation theology.[1] In his *Lectures on Romans* (1515-1516) Luther rejects important aspects of what he regards as a distorted nominalist appropriation of Augustine's view

---

1. For helpful brief overviews of the development of Luther's views on sin see Lohse, *Martin Luther's Theology*, 45-47; 53-55; 70-72, and David C. Steinmetz, "Luther and Hubmaier on the Freedom of the Human Will," in *Luther in Context*, 2nd ed. (Grand Rapids: Baker, 2002), 63-67.

of sin. In key passages Augustine is referenced repeatedly and approvingly in support of Luther's own position. Yet, as we have already seen, whether Luther was conscious of it or not, in developing his view of sin through engagement with Pauline texts he not only reaffirmed Augustine but also went beyond him at vital points. This was ultimately to result in profoundly different views of the nature of sin in the Protestant and Roman Catholic traditions. As we have seen, Augustine had been less than clear about the formal relationship between the misdirected desires of concupiscence and original sin. Tatha Wiley suggests that "Augustine described *concupiscence* as the disordered desire that turns one away from God and *original sin* as an active culpable inclination of the will against God (*amor sui, cupiditas*). The nuance of meaning distinguishing the two realities is subtle, to say the least."[2] In the medieval period some regarded Augustine's intention as having been to distinguish between concupiscence and original sin; others understood that he had intended to identiy them with each other. Among the former many followed Anselm, who at the end of the eleventh century sought to clarify the nature of original sin by defining it as the privation of original justice. Original justice was a supernatural gift that before the fall enabled human nature to will what God wills. After the fall, human nature remained but this supernatural gift was now absent due to sin.

For Luther, to define original sin as a privation, as "a lack of a certain quality in the will,"[3] is far too passive a description to be faithful to Pauline statements about it. In his discussion of Rom 5:12 Luther insists that if original sin is a lack, it is "a total lack of uprightness and of the power of all the faculties both of body and soul and of the whole inner and outer man."[4] Yet more than even such an all-embracing privation, it is a positive inclination to evil, "nausea toward the good, a loathing of light and wisdom, and a delight in error and darkness."[5] Luther chooses to follow Peter Lombard's understanding of Augustine, in which original sin is concupiscence, but defines concupiscence much more radically than Lombard's identification of it with the sensuality of the body.[6] Orig-

2. Tatha Wiley, *Original Sin: Origins, Developments, Contemporary Meanings* (New York: Paulist, 2002), 96.

3. *LW* 25:299 = *WA* 56:312, 7.

4. *LW* 25:299 = *WA* 56:312, 9-10.

5. *LW* 25:299 = *WA* 56:312, 11-12.

6. Phillip W. Rosemann, *Peter Lombard* (Oxford: Oxford University Press, 2004), 114.

inal sin has for Luther the character of "a sick man whose mortal illness is not only the loss of health of one of his members, but it is, in addition to the lack of health in all his members, the weakness of all of his senses and powers, culminating even in his disdain for those things which are healthful and in his desire for those things which make him sick."[7] It is this sense of original sin as rampant misdirected desire that gives rise to Luther's new and famous description of sin as "the person turned in upon the self" (*homo incurvatus in se*).[8] It is important to appreciate that at one level Luther has genuinely returned to Augustine. Whether he in fact identifies concupiscence with original sin or not, Augustine considers original sin as something more than a privation. Yet at another level, Luther has gone beyond Augustine. The impact of sin is so severe that human nature is not so much simply seriously wounded as wholly corrupted:

> Hereditary sin or natural sin or personal sin is the truly chief sin. If this sin did not exist, there would also be no actual sin. This sin is not committed, as are all other sins; rather it *is*. It lives and commits all sins and is the real essential sin which does not sin for an hour or for a while; rather no matter where or how long a person lives, this sin is there also.[9]

Thus, for Luther, "the true nature of sin is to be found entirely in original sin and not in a mortal sin of *peccatum actuale* . . . the law declares every sin a mortal sin."[10] The implications of this radical view of sin become plain in Luther's exegesis of Rom 7:7-25, a text that in its entirety he takes to be discussing Paul's struggle with sin as a believer.[11]

---

7. *LW* 25:300 = *WA* 56:313, 6-10. Neither Augustine nor Lombard is explicitly mentioned here, but the editors of the English translation draw attention to the connection. See their n. 13 on the same page.

8. *LW* 25:345 = *WA* 56:356, 5-6. See also *LW* 25:291 = *WA* 56:304, 25-29.

9. *LW* 52:152 = *WA* 10.1.1:509, 1-4. This is from *Gospel for New Year's Day* (1521/22), one of a series of sermon guides designed to aid preachers published as the *Church Postil.*

10. L'ubomír Batka, "Luther's Teaching on Sin and Evil," in *The Oxford Handbook of Martin Luther's Theology*, ed. Robert Kolb, Irene Dingel, and L'ubomír Batka (Oxford: Oxford University Press, 2014), 238.

11. See *LW* 25:327 = *WA* 56:339, 5-7. "From this passage on to the end of the chapter the apostle is speaking in his own person and as a spiritual man and by no means merely in the person of a carnal man."

For whatever views previous interpreters held on original sin, they had agreed with Augustine and each other that, after baptism, concupiscence itself ceases to be truly sinful unless the misdirected desires involved are consented to by the will and acted upon. Concupiscence is now not sin itself but instead the tinder of sin (*fomes peccati*), a spark that can ignite sin but not in itself ultimately of great harm if handled with the necessary care. In contrast, for Luther, even in Paul's Christian life covetousness (Rom 7:7), the essence of misdirected desire, is sin. Not only has Luther identified the tinder of sin that is covetousness with original sin before baptism but he has now also asserted its continuance afterwards. Luther is still sufficiently attached to Augustine's account of how sin typically occurs to accept that God will not impute the guilt of desires to which assent is not given (and so in a particular restricted sense it is correct to say that we are not guilty), but nevertheless apart from such divine mercy "we ourselves are this weakness, therefore it is guilty and we are guilty until this weakness ceases and is cleansed."[12]

Luther recognizes, of course, that to speak of the believer as being this weakness, i.e., as a breathing walking mass of misdirected desire, is only part of the truth of Christian existence. Already he is developing a twofold account of what it is as a Christian to be both righteous and a sinner, and Luther responds powerfully and creatively to Paul's insistence that as regards the flesh he is in slavery to sin (Rom 7:14, 25). He does not accept that Paul here refers to a contest between different parts of a person in which sin disrupts the healthy hierarchies between soul and body. Similarly, Luther also rejects the idea that there is a conflict within the soul between reason (or the will) and other parts of the soul so that the lower parts refuse to obey the higher. Flesh is not to be identified primarily with the lower parts of the person. Paul's contrasts between the inner and the

---

12. *LW* 25:340 = *WA* 56:351, 14–15. Batka, "Luther's Teaching on Sin and Evil," 239, highlights Luther's interpretation of the Hebrew terms underlying Paul's quotation of Ps 32:1 in Rom 4:7 as also of particular significance in the identification of concupiscence as sin. The difficulties inherent in precisely describing Augustine's views are reflected in different perspectives on the relationship between his account of sin and that provided by Luther. Jairzinho Lopes Pereira, *Augustine of Hippo and Martin Luther on Original Sin and Justification of the Sinner* (Göttingen: Vandenhoeck and Ruprecht, 2012), argues for a much closer identification between Augustine's perspective and that of the young Luther than in much other recent scholarship, whereas Matt Jenson, *The Gravity of Sin: Augustine, Luther and Barth on homo incurvatus in se* (London and New York: T&T Clark, 2006), argues that Luther radicalizes Augustine's insights in important respects.

outer person and the mind and the bodily members (Rom 7:22-23) make it clear that sin has its characteristic sphere of operations, but the term "flesh" nevertheless does not refer primarily only to one part of a person:

> The apostle does not wish to be understood as saying that the flesh and the spirit are two separate entities, as it were, but one whole, just as a wound and the flesh are one. . . . The flesh is itself an infirmity or wound of the whole man who by grace is beginning to be healed in both mind and spirit. For who imagines that in a sick man there are these two opposing entities? For it is the same body which seeks health and yet is compelled to do those things which belong to its weakness.[13]

Luther notes carefully that, despite the distinction between the mind and the flesh, Paul does not at Rom 7:25 divide the self into two compartments but rather says that there are two different servitudes that are both characteristic of the self: "Note that one and the same man at the same time serves the law of God and the law of sin, at the same time is righteous and sins! For he does not say: 'My mind serves the law of God,' nor does he say: 'My flesh serves the law of sin,' but: 'I, the whole man, the same person, I serve a twofold servitude.'"[14] In Luther's view, the flesh is not part of a person but the entire person as he or she stands in opposition to God through sin. Here again there is both dependence on Augustine and a move beyond him. For while Augustine had insisted that flesh is not to be identified exclusively with bodily desires and is a disordering of the whole person, he had time and again described sexual desire as the characteristic expression of the flesh.[15] Even if sexual desire has profound psychological dimensions for Augustine, his account of what Paul means by "the flesh" lends itself to interpretation primarily in terms of desires arising in the body that lure the soul into complicity with sin. Luther's account of a twofold servitude moves into different territory.

In Luther's first *Commentary on Galatians* (1516-1517/1519), Paul's

---

13. *LW* 25:339-41 = *WA* 56:350, 22 - 352, 9.

14. *LW* 25:336 = *WA* 56:347, 2-6. The NRSV rather obscures Luther's point by using the English personal pronoun 'I' twice, once in respect to the mind and once in respect to the flesh. Paul's Greek uses the pronoun once emphatically at the outset (αὐτός ἐγὼ, "I myself") before describing the two aspects of the self's servitude.

15. On these points see Couenhoven, "St. Augustine's Doctrine of Original Sin," 372-76.

diverse list of the works of the flesh at Gal 5:19-21 prompts Luther to comment that "flesh is understood not only in the sense of lustful desires but as absolutely everything that is contrary to the spirit of grace . . . by flesh the whole man is meant . . . the inward and the outward man, or the new man and the old, are not distinguished according to the difference between soul and body but according to their dispositions."[16] Unsurprisingly, if in the flesh sin infects the whole person and if the flesh is not necessarily typified by sexual or other bodily desires, then there cannot be a "higher" religious life that corresponds to the higher parts or faculties of a person and is necessarily effective in battling sin. To restrain bodily desires through ascetic discipline cannot be identified with mastery over the flesh, for "the flesh" refers to the whole person and not merely to bodily desires. When Paul says that sin once lay dead apart from the law (Rom 7:8), Luther does not discount Augustine's opinion that he refers to childhood experience before both the attainment of reason and the breaking forth of sexual desire in adolescence. However, he prefers the view that Paul is speaking of those who burn with great zeal for the law but who are unable to recognize their own sin. Luther seems to have particularly in mind those who covet the religious life and feel that nothing else will please God, failing to see that God has called them to other things and that "whatever is coveted besides God, even if one covets it for the sake of God, becomes a sin."[17] To thus conceive the religious life as a potential expression of sin rather than the means of its cure was to challenge the church's prevailing practical assumptions about the Christian struggle with sin.

Despite the non-publication of Luther's *Lectures on Romans* (1515–1516) in the sixteenth century,[18] the exegetical positions he advocates there in relation to sin become the common property of early Protestant interpreters. The same Pauline texts appear repeatedly in defense of concupiscence as real sin in the life of the Christian and the flesh as "not a faculty but the *totus homo* in opposition and rebellion against God."[19]

---

16. *LW* 27:367 = *WA* 2:588, 26-32.

17. *LW* 25:337 = *WA* 56:348, 26-27.

18. Luther did not lecture on Romans again since Melanchthon took over this task upon his arrival at Wittenberg in 1518. Luther's manuscript and a single copy of it survived, the latter somewhat ironically in the Vatican Library, until rediscovered by Johannes Ficker with initial publication in 1908 and inclusion in the *Weimarer Ausgabe* of Luther's Works in 1938. For details see *LW* 25:ix-xiv.

19. David C. Steinmetz, "Calvin and Patristic Exegesis," in *Calvin in Context* (Oxford: Oxford University Press, 1995), 134.

There is, of course, appeal to Paul's use of the commandment against coveting in the argument of Rom 7 itself. Even though other Reformers do not join Luther in reading Rom 7:7-13 as Paul's reflections upon his life as a Christian, the nature of coveting here as the paradigmatic sin—in relation to which the law turned out to bring death—makes it difficult for them to accept that, even after baptism, it can ever be regarded as anything less than real sin.[20] The list of the works of the flesh in Gal 5:19-21, referred to above in relation to Luther's exegesis, is also cited frequently. Calvin notices the inclusion of both jealousy and envy and slyly turns a favorite scholastic authority against scholastic theology by observing that Aristotle "tells us that none but low and mean persons are envious, whereas he ascribes jealousy to lofty and heroic minds."[21] Calvin goes on to observe that "It should be observed that he (Paul) reckons heresies among the works of the flesh, for it shows clearly that the word flesh has a wider reference than sensuality, as the Sophists imagine. What produces heresies but ambition, which resides not in the lower senses but in the highest seat of the mind?"[22]

There is also repeated appeal to Rom 8:6-7, where Paul speaks twice of "the mind of the flesh" (τὸ φρόνημα τῆς σαρκὸς) that is unable to submit to God's law and contrasts it with "the mind of the Spirit" (τὸ φρόνημα τοῦ πνεύματος). It is difficult to read Paul here as contrasting the mind shaped by the Spirit with the mind overwhelmed by sensual desire since there is no real hint of a division between the higher and lower parts of a person. The contrast is instead between those "in the flesh" and those "in the Spirit" (8:9). The Reformers interpret this text as differentiating between the whole person lost in sin and the whole person in Christ. This had been obscured in previous translations and Calvin carefully makes the case for a revised understanding:

> Erasmus has 'affection' (*affectum*) for *cogitatio*, the Vulgate 'prudence' (*prudentiam*). Since, however, it is certain that Paul's τὸ φρόνημα is the same as that of Moses when he speaks of the imagi-

---

20. Heinrich Bullinger, "Sermon IV," in *Bullinger's Decades: The Third Decade*, ed. Thomas Harding, The Parker Society 8 (Cambridge: Cambridge University Press, 1851), 122 = HBW 3.1:312-20 (318, 333-35): "For although there be some which think that such motions, diseases, blemishes, and affections of the mind are no sins, yet God, by forbidding them in this law, doth flatly condemn them."

21. *Comm Gal* 5:19, CNTC 11:104 = OE 16:131, 26-27.

22. *Comm. Gal* 5:19, CNTC 11:104 = OE 16:132, 5-9.

nation (*figmentum*) of the heart (Gen. 6:5), and that this word includes all the feelings of the soul from the reason and understanding to the affections, it seems to me that 'mind' (*cogitatio*) is better suited to the passage.[23]

He elsewhere also draws attention to those Pauline texts that speak of the need for the mind to be renewed by the Spirit (Eph 4:23; Rom 12:2).[24] This emphasis on "mind" has dramatic consequences for the estimation of human deeds. Melanchthon writes in *Loci Communes* 1521 that since the mind of the flesh cannot submit to the law, "It follows, therefore, that all works of men, however praiseworthy they are externally, are actually corrupt and are sins worthy of death."[25] Heinrich Bullinger concludes a sermon in which he has cited Rom 8:6–8 with the reflection that "God requireth at the hands of those that worship him such kind of righteousness as is altogether sound and absolutely perfect, not in the outward deed alone, but also in the inward mind and settled purpose of the heart."[26] The component of action in human deeds may be genuinely good when assessed from a human perspective, but motivation matters and the flesh will ensure that it shares in corruption when assessed from the divine perspective.

Romans 8 is also significant for the degree to which it makes the Holy Spirit central to the discussion. It is the Spirit who makes it possible to fulfill the law and Melanchthon uses this to make a general point based on the pattern of Paul's argument in Romans.

> The apostle continually carries on his argument as follows: "The flesh could not fulfill the law; therefore there is need of the Spirit to fulfill it." If we should use the word "flesh" for only part of a man, how will Paul's argument stand? For it could be eluded in this way: "Even if the flesh could not keep the law, yet some better part of man could

---

23. *Comm. Rom* 8:6, *CNTC* 8:161 = *OE* 13:157, 26 – 158, 2. On the noetic dimensions of sin in Calvin's thought, see Barbara Pitkin, "Nothing but Concupiscence: Calvin's Understanding of Sin and the *Via Augustini*," *CTJ* 34 (1999): 347–69.

24. *Institutes* 2.1.9 (253) = *CO* 2:183–84.

25. *Loci Communes* is Melanchthon's influential theological textbook. For the 1521 version, which is the first edition, see Philip Melanchthon, "Loci Communes Theologici," in *Melanchthon and Bucer*, ed. Wilhelm Pauck (Philadelphia: Westminster Press, 1969), 3–152 (here 39) = *MSA* 2:3–163 (29:18–20); *CR* 21:81–228 (106).

26. Bullinger, "Sermon IV," 124 (in *The Third Decade*) = *HBW* 3.1:312–20 (320, 8–10).

have done so, and thus there would have been no need for the Spirit to fulfill the law."[27]

Since Paul makes it clear through the phrases "the Spirit of God" and "the Spirit of Christ" (8:9) that in view here is indeed the Holy Spirit, "it necessarily follows that you call 'flesh' whatever in us is foreign to the Holy Spirit."[28] Later in his *Commentary on Romans* (1540) Melanchthon will similarly insist that "*flesh* should be understood of whatever is in man without the Holy Spirit, namely, not only the desires of the senses, but also reason and will without the Holy Spirit."[29] Peter Martyr Vermigli will say succinctly that "whatsoeuer is in us besides the spirite and grace, is called fleshe."[30] Although flesh is not an external force and remains something in human beings, there is a powerful sense of the dilemma of humanity as not so much how to choose right actions but as how to be under the right lordship. Once the believer is justified under the lordship of Christ, then like a good tree he or she will naturally bear good fruit.

None of this means that all sense of a hierarchy within human personality is necessarily dismissed by every Reformer. For example, Calvin will acknowledge that a hierarchy is implied by the contrast between the inward person and the members in Rom 7:21-23: "The *inward man*, therefore, does not simply mean the soul, but the spiritual part of the soul which has been regenerated by God. *Members* means the other remaining part. As the soul is the more excellent and the body the inferior part of man, so the spirit is superior to the flesh."[31] Thus the soul is indeed higher than the body but, Calvin insists, this is not what Paul is saying here. Instead he is using the contrast between the two as a metaphor for a contrast between regenerate and unregenerate aspects of the soul. In the phrase "the body of death" in 7:24, "the word *body*

27. Melanchthon, "Loci Communes Theologici," 37 = *MSA* 2:27, 4-12; *CR* 21:104.

28. Melanchthon, "Loci Communes Theologici," 38 = *MSA* 2:28, 20-22; *CR* 21:105.

29. Philip Melanchthon, *Commentary on Romans*, trans. Fred Kramer (St. Louis: Concordia, 1992), 170 = *CR* 15:661-62. This is the second of three major commentaries on Romans by Melanchthon (1532, 1540, and 1556). Only the commentary of 1540 is available in English translation.

30. Peter Martyr Vermigli, *Most Learned and Fruitful Commentaries upon the Epistle of S. Paul to the Romanes*, trans. Sir Henry Billingsley (London: John Daye, 1568), 162a = *In Epistolam S. Pauli ad Romanos D. Petri Martyris Vermilii* (Basilae: Petrum Pernam, 1558), 225.

31. *Comm. Rom* 7:22, *CNTC* 8:153 = *OE* 13:149, 13-17.

means the same as *outward man* and *members* . . . in so far as his soul is degenerate, it may rightly be said to have changed into his body."[32] Sin means that the soul loses its reason. In Calvin's view Paul is not proposing that higher human faculties are overwhelmed by sensual desire but rather that the higher faculties are themselves so corrupted by sin that the hierarchy between soul and body is effectively abolished. Yet Paul also speaks of the mind as a slave to God's law (7:25). The term "mind" refers "not to the rational part of the soul honored by philosophers, but to that part which is illuminated by the Spirit of God, so that it may understand and will aright."[33] Once again, the meanings of all of Paul's other anthropological terms are determined by Calvin within what he takes to be the apostle's overarching dualism of the Spirit and the flesh. In the believer, the proper anthropological hierarchy is partially restored as the Spirit and the flesh struggle in the soul. Indeed, it is the presence of this struggle that is one of the main indications to Calvin and a majority of other early Protestant commentators that, despite its checkered history of interpretation, in Rom 7:14-25 Paul does indeed speak of life under grace and not life under the law. The unregenerate simply could not possess a "mind" with its affections rightly ordered enough for there to be such a struggle.[34]

It is also not the case that Augustine's account of how sin works in practice is entirely rejected. In the same sermon as he insists that a good outward action alone does not make a deed righteous, Bullinger is happy simply to reproduce Augustine's distinctions between suggestion, inclination or desire, and consent.[35] To consent to and act upon an evil desire

---

32. *Comm. Rom* 7:24, *CNTC* 8:154 = *OE* 13:150, 13-19. The notes in *The Geneva Bible: A Facsimile of the 1560 Edition* (Peabody, MA: Hendrickson, 2007), 72v, define "bodie" here as "This fleshlie lump of sinne and death." Augustine's influence is apparent here, for he too had argued that the soul has carnal desires which the higher spiritual part of the soul needed to resist. See Couenhoven, "Augustine's Doctrine of Original Sin," 374.

33. *Comm. Rom* 7:25, *CNTC* 8:155 = *OE* 13:151, 18-20.

34. See the discussion in David C. Steinmetz, "Calvin and the Divided Self of Romans 7," in *Calvin in Context* (Oxford: Oxford University Press, 1995), 110-21. In the medieval period the dominant trend was to follow the younger Augustine in treating these verses as concerning life under the law, but Thomas Aquinas was a notable exception. Steinmetz notes three sixteenth-century interpreters (two Protestant and one Catholic) who regard Rom 7:14-25 as concerning life under the law, but twelve interpreters (including four Catholics) who regard 7:14-25 as concerning life under grace.

35. Bullinger, "Sermon IV," 121-22 (in *The Third Decade*) = *HBW* 3.1:312-20 (318, 19-30).

is more serious than to refuse it. Similarly, Luther can say in relation to Gal 5:17 that the desires of the flesh do not endanger the salvation of Christians: "It is alright for them to be aware of it, provided they do not assent to it; it is alright for anger or sexual desire to be aroused in them, provided that they do not capitulate to it; it is alright for sin to stir them up, provided that they do not gratify it."[36] As we shall later explore further in relation to Luther himself (5.6), the difference is that this relaxed attitude is not because the desires involved do not count as real sin, but because the Reformers regard the godly as those both most aware of the conflict and of the true source of its resolution. Luther comments that "such people do not minimize sin; they emphasize it, because they know that it cannot be washed away by any satisfactions, works, or righteousness, but only by the death of Christ."[37]

What is at stake is not so much disagreement as to how sin works but disagreement over justification. In an Augustinian view of justification, acceptance by God depends in part on the renewal wrought within a person by the righteousness received through Christ. If concupiscence were sin in its full sense, there would be little hope for the growth of justifying righteousness. In the Reformers' view, although renewal will result, and although justification never exists without renewal, justification is not caused in any sense by what human beings do or become. Concupiscence can be real sin without threatening justification. It must be resisted, but acceptance by God depends upon the righteousness received through Christ that was already complete and perfect when it was given.

3.2. The Law

The Reformers' understanding of the law in Paul is complex, developed relatively slowly, and gave rise to controversy in the later history of Protestantism. Yet the center of their understanding is clear, appears in Luther's earliest Pauline exegesis, and is agreed upon by all. When Paul says that the law "brings knowledge of sin" (Rom 3:20) or that it was "added because of transgressions" (Gal 3:19), he means that the law reveals to human beings their sin. In his *Lectures on Romans* (1515-1516) Luther com-

36. LW 27:74 = WA 40.2:94, 13-15.
37. LW 27:75-76 = WA 40.2:95, 22-24.

ments on Rom 3:20 that when the law prompts a person to do the good in a way they would not otherwise have chosen, "then man understands how deeply sin and evil are rooted in him, which he would not have understood if he did not have the Law and had not attempted to work in accordance with it. . . . Hence, to say, 'Through the Law is the knowledge of sin' is the same as saying: 'Through the Law is the knowledge of sinners.'"[38] In his *Commentary on Galatians* (1516-1517/1519), Luther correlates Gal 3:19, where Paul says that the law was added because of transgressions, with Rom 5:20, where Paul says that sin came in order to increase the trespass. The excess of transgression serves a revelatory function: "The Law was laid down for the sake of transgression, in order that transgression might be and abound, and in order that thus man, having been brought to knowledge of himself through the Law, might seek the hand of a merciful God. Without the Law he is ignorant of his sin and considers himself sound."[39] The subsequent statements concerning imprisonment under the law until faith came and of the law as a "disciplinarian" or "guardian" (παιδαγωγός) until Christ came (3:23-24) are interpreted in a similar vein. The law may well restrain sin, but the point is not that in doing so it teaches delight in the good. Rather it frustrates the desire to sin and in that frustration shows human beings the truth that they are sinners. Similar pieces of exegesis from other Reformers could be documented almost endlessly. Calvin says of Rom 3:20 that "the law convinces us of sin and salvation"[40] and of Gal 3:24 that "the law, by displaying the righteousness of God, convinced them of their own unrighteousness . . . it gave them no rest until they were constrained to seek the grace of Christ."[41] Melanchthon comments on Paul's statement that "the power of sin is the law" (1 Cor 15:56) by saying that, "sin would not confound and terrify us unless it were shown to us by the law."[42] Bullinger brings together a medley of texts from Romans to show that "the proper office of Moses, and the principal use and effect of the law, is to show to man his sin and imperfection."[43]

In understanding the central purpose of the law as the revealing of the true position of humanity as sinners before God, the Reformers were

---

38. *LW* 25:240-41 = *WA* 56:253, 29 - 254, 15.

39. *LW* 27:269 = *WA* 2:522, 27-29.

40. *Comm. Rom* 3:20, *CNTC* 8:70 = *OE* 13:67, 27.

41. *Comm. Gal* 3:24, *CNTC* 11:66 = *OE* 16:85, 1-2, 10-11.

42. Melanchthon, "Loci Communes Theologici," 80 = *MSA* 2:78, 13-14; *CR* 21:151.

43. Bullinger, "Sermon VIII," 239 (in *The Third Decade*) = *HBW* 3.1.383-419 (385, 18-19).

repeating and emphasizing a theme already strongly present in Augustine. Where they went beyond his reflections was that they did not simply deal with the law on the basis of individual texts but began to articulate a formal distinction between different uses of the law: "Luther's treatment of the law under the concept of *usus* was clearly without precursors in all the tradition."[44] Luther had not employed the concept at all in the *Commentary on Galatians* (1516-1517/1519). It appears for the first time in a sermon on Gal 3:23-29 in the *Weihnachtspostille* (Christmas Sermons) for 1522,[45] and is frequent in the *Commentary on Galatians* (1531/1535).[46] The way in which Luther employs the concept does vary, but he typically speaks of a double or twofold use of the law (*duplex usus legis*). The second use is the principal or theological use discussed above, that of the revealing of sin. The first is a political or civic use. At Gal 3:19 Luther is clear that Paul is discussing the theological use of the law only, but the opportunity is taken nonetheless also to describe the civic use:

> God has ordained civic laws, indeed all laws, to restrain transgressions. Therefore every law was given to hinder sins. Does this mean that when the Law restrains sins, it justifies? Not at all. When I refrain from killing or from committing adultery or from stealing, or when I abstain from other sins, I do not do this voluntarily or from the love of virtue but because I am afraid of the sword and of the executioner. . . . Therefore restraint from sins is not righteousness but rather an indication of unrighteousness.[47]

The thought that the law exists not for the righteous but for the lawless and disobedient (1 Tim 1:9) may well be in the background here. Certainly, Melanchthon later refers to it in his *Commentary on Romans* (1540), both when he adds a locus on the effects of the law (Rom 5) and when he expounds Rom 3:20. As with Luther, Melanchthon accepts that Paul is not directly discussing the political use but he must comment on it

44. Lohse, *Martin Luther's Theology*, 270.

45. "New Year's Day," in *Luther's Epistle Sermons Vol 1: Advent and Christmas Season*, ed. John N. Lenker (Minneapolis: Luther Press, 1908), 267-310 (esp. 271-72) = WA 10.1.1:449-63 (esp. 454, 8 - 455, 23).

46. See Gerhard Ebeling, "On the Doctrine of the *Triplex Usus Legis* in the Theology of the Reformation," in *Word and Faith*, trans. J. W. Leitch (Philadelphia: Fortress, 1963), 69-72.

47. LW 26:308 = WA 40:479, 17-24.

to forestall the possible conclusion that the discipline involved in this use justifies.[48] The purpose of the civic or political use of the law is instead to save human society here and now from social chaos. As Calvin puts it, "this constrained and forced righteousness is necessary for the public community of men, for whose tranquility the Lord herein provided when he took care that not everything be tumultuously confounded."[49]

On these two uses of the law, it is very difficult to discern any significant differences among the Reformers.[50] This is not the case when we turn to two related topics. They are the hermeneutic of law and gospel developed by Luther, and the concept of a third use of the law, which became important in the Reformed tradition. Luther's hermeneutic is a departure from the dominant medieval tradition "which had understood the two terms as a description of two phases of salvation history, with the gospel of Christ replacing the law which foreshadowed it."[51] Instead Luther came to understand that Old and New Testament each contain both law and gospel, with law "as that word of God which sets forth the Creator's demand for human performance" and gospel as "the promise of God which recreates sinners as God's children and restores the loving, trusting relationship between them and their Lord."[52] Yet here too he is not without precedent in Augustine, who comments on Gal 6:2— with its insistence that the law of Christ is fulfilled by believers in the bearing of each other's burdens—that "The same scripture and the same commandment, then, is called the Old Testament when it weighs down slaves panting for earthly goods, and the New Testament when it lifts up free people ardent for eternal goods."[53] Augustine had also declined to interpret 2 Cor 3:6, with its reference to the killing letter and the life-giving Spirit, primarily as a distinction between the literal and figurative senses of texts. Instead he took Paul to mean that "the letter of the law,

---

48. Melanchthon, *Commentary on Romans*, 98, 140-43 = *CR* 15:585 and *CR* 15:631-34.

49. *Institutes* 2.7.10 (359) = *CO* 2:260.

50. Calvin does reverse the order from that found in Luther and Melanchthon. Calvin terms the theological use the first use and the civic or political use the second use. See I. John Hesselink, *Calvin's Concept of the Law* (Allison Park, PA.: Pickwick, 1992), 238-39 (esp. n. 95).

51. Robert Kolb, *Martin Luther: Confessor of the Faith* (Oxford: Oxford University Press, 2009), 50-51.

52. Kolb, *Martin Luther*, 51.

53. Augustine, *Augustine's Commentary on Galatians*, 58.3 (227).

which teaches that we should not sin, kills, if the life-giving Spirit is not present."[54]

The difference between Augustine and Luther is that the latter did not simply use this distinction in relation to individual texts, but articulated it as a formal principle of biblical interpretation to be generally applied. It appears as such a principle for the first time in a sermon from Advent 1522, prompted by Jesus's answer to John the Baptist's enquiry about his messianic identity that in Jesus's ministry the poor have good news preached to them (Matt 11:5):

> Therefore, hold to this distinction, and no matter what books you have before you, be they of the Old or of the New Testament, read them with a discrimination so as to observe that when promises are made in a book, it is a Gospel-book; when commandments are given, it is a law-book. But because in the New Testament the promises are found so abundantly, and in the Old Testament so many laws, the former is called the Gospel, and the latter the Book of the Law.[55]

There is thus a clear unity to God's word. Both Testaments contain both law and gospel, albeit not in equal proportions, and Luther holds both that the Old points towards the New and that the New discloses the true sense of the Old.[56] However, this is no longer solely a matter of different eras of salvation history but also of the dual pattern of the ministry of God's word (2 Cor 3:7–11).

One issue not resolved by Luther's new hermeneutic, nor through the concepts of the theological and civic uses of the law, is that of the part played by the law in the life of the Christian. Luther could distinguish between the Decalogue and other aspects of the Mosaic Law that were only ever intended to be local and ethnic in their application and insist in relation to the latter that Christ is the end of the law (Rom 10:4). Yet once it was clear that such laws were not binding on Christians Luther could also make positive use of them as recommendations for Christian behavior in catechesis. In an attempt to bring greater clarity, Melanchthon did something that Luther never did, which was to propose a third use of the law in

---

54. Augustine, "The Spirit and the Letter," 5.8 (154) = CSEL 60:155–229 (160, 12–13).

55. "Third Sunday in Advent," in *Luther's Church Postil Vol 1: Gospels: Advent, Christmas, and Epiphany Sermons*, ed. John N. Lenker (Minneapolis: Lutherans in all Lands, 1905), 87–113 (esp. 96–103) = WA 10.1.2:147–70 (155, 21 – 159, 4).

56. Lohse, *Martin Luther's Theology*, 191–93.

which it is understood as binding for Christian conduct. This appeared in substance in the *1535 Loci Communes* but was not expressed using the term "third use" until the 1543 edition.[57] Melanchthon comments that "the law must be preached to the regenerate to teach them certain works in which God wills that we practice obedience . . . the divine ordinance remains that those who have been justified are to be obedient to God."[58] Unsurprisingly, Melanchthon's concept provoked anxiety over the consistency of such statements with the insistence that obedience to the law is not a cause of justification. The situation was ultimately clarified for Lutheranism by Article 6 of the *Formula of Concord* (1577), which accepts the third use of the law but conceives of the law as applying to the believer only in so far as the believer is still unregenerate. The law restrains the sin of the believer and reveals the sin of the believer, so acting as a spur to ever-closer union with Christ, but obedience, understood positively as something willingly rendered on the basis of renewal, remains the province of the Spirit.[59]

This account of the place of the law in the Christian life was insufficiently positive for Calvin, who insisted on understanding the law in the context of the grace of God's covenant with Abraham. The law retains an abiding validity as the expression of God's will for human behavior and instructs believers as to the content of this divine will and encourages them to persevere in pursuing righteousness.[60] Nevertheless, in terms of the uses of the law, Calvin certainly also accepts a sharp distinction between the law as a threatening word and the promises of the gospel. When expounding Paul's texts, Calvin recognizes a dual pattern in the ministry of God's word, and he interprets the killing letter and the life-giving Spirit in 2 Cor 3:6 explicitly as a contrast between law and gospel:

---

57. Ebeling, "On the Doctrine of the *Triplex Usus Legis* in the Theology of the Reformation," 65-69. Although all accept that Luther did not use the term or formally propose a "third use" of the law, some Luther interpreters argue that the substance of the concept is present in his work. See, for example, Paul Althaus, *The Theology of Martin Luther* (Philadelphia: Fortress, 1966), 273. For a comparison of the contrasting views, see Kim, *Luther on Faith and Love*, 255-59.

58. Philip Melanchthon, *Loci Communes 1543*, trans. J.A.O. Preus (St. Louis: Concordia, 1992), 74 = CR 21:601-1106 (719). This is the third major edition of *Loci Communes*. The second edition of 1535 has never been translated into English.

59. *The Book of Concord: The Confessions of the Evangelical Lutheran Church*, ed. Robert Kolb and Timothy J. Wengert (Minneapolis: Fortress Press, 2000), 502-3.

60. For an overview, see Günther H. Haas, "Ethics and Church Discipline," in *The Calvin Handbook*, ed. Herman J. Selderhuis (Grand Rapids: Eerdmans, 2009), 332-44 (esp. 335-40).

"it is the function of the Law to show us the disease without offering any hope of a cure, and it is the function of the Gospel to provide a remedy for those in despair."[61] Exegetically, there is no difference here with Luther. Calvin copes with the tension between Paul's statements connecting the law with sin and condemnation and his own conviction of its gracious nature by pointing out that Paul tells the truth about the law but is not concerned in individual statements to say everything about its nature. At Gal 3:19 Calvin finds only the theological use of the law but comments that "The law has many uses, but Paul confines himself to one which serves his present purpose ... this definition of the use of the law is not complete and those who acknowledge nothing else in the law are wrong."[62] At Rom 8:15, where Paul contrasts a spirit of bondage with that of adoption, Calvin sees a contrast between law and gospel but also says that "Although the covenant of grace is contained in the law, yet Paul removes it from there. In opposing the Gospel to the law he regards only what was peculiar to the law itself, viz. command and prohibition, and the restraining of transgressors by the threat of death. He assigns to the law its own quality, by which it differs from the Gospel."[63]

In Calvin's perspective, Paul's concern in such contrasts is with what distinguishes the law from the rest of Scripture and what may be uniquely said of law. The law abstracted from the promises of the covenant "is the bare law (*nuda lex*),"[64] but a full account also requires attention to the law in the context of covenant promises. If understood in this context of covenant promises, the law is itself transformed. In his righteousness Christ fulfills all of the law's requirements, and that righteousness is received in faith by believers. Therefore, while the law may still exhort and chide the Christian, it can no longer have the character of a curse: "it may no longer condemn and destroy their consciences by frightening and confounding them. ... What Paul says of the curse unquestionably applies not to the ordinance itself but solely to its force to bind the conscience."[65]

---

61. *Comm. 2 Cor 3:6*, CNTC 10:45 = OE 15:58, 2–3. There may be a difference in tone, with Calvin more characteristically describing the role of the law in revealing to human beings their own unrighteousness as the holding up of a mirror to sin as compared to Luther's characteristic descriptions of the law killing and battering in order to reveal unrighteousness, but there is no difference in function.

62. *Comm. Gal 3:19*, CNTC 11:61 = OE 16:77, 13–14.

63. *Comm. Rom 8:15*, CNTC 8:168–69 = OE 13:165, 8–12.

64. Hesselink, *Calvin's Concept of the Law*, 91.

65. *Institutes* 2.7.14–15 (362–63) = CO 2:263.

Freed from its role as a curse, in the life of believers "through Christ the teaching of the law remains inviolable; by teaching, admonishing, reproving, and correcting, it forms us and prepares us for every good work [cf. II Tim. 3:16-17]."[66] The law is now a positive guide for those aiming to live life participating in Christ to the glory of God: "The law is not God, but points to God: What kind of God wants humans to behave in this way? What does God like and not like, want or not want? Precisely as a reflection of the will of God, the law points to where God might be and what God might be doing and indicates the scope and intent of God's activities."[67] By such means is Calvin able to correlate Pauline statements about the law's abrogation (e.g., Rom 7:6) with Christ's teaching that he did not come to abolish the law (Matt 5:17-18).[68] Calvin's position is different from that of Lutheranism, but the substance of the difference does not relate to Pauline exegesis. The divergence concerns more how shared exegetical understandings of Pauline texts were to be related to other aspects of Scripture. Yet the disagreement is important in its own right. In subsequent generations, the distinction between the role of the law in the Christian life as restricted to revealing and restraining the sin of the believer (Lutheranism) or as a more general positive guide to obedience (the Reformed tradition) was to mark a principal difference in identity between the two confessional communities.

3.3. Conscience

Few aspects of the Reformers' Pauline exegesis are less well understood at a popular level than the manner in which their convictions about sin and the law make an impact upon their understanding of the conscience. It is often assumed that Luther's own struggles with guilt and despair (*Anfechtungen*), which led him to abandon hope that individuals can do *quod in se est* ("what lies within them," i.e., their best) and prompted his discov-

---

66. *Institutes* 2.7.14 (363) = *CO* 2:263.

67. Merwyn S. Johnson, "Calvin's Third Use of the Law and Its Problems," in *Calviniana: Ideas and Influence of Jean Calvin*, ed. Robert V. Schnucker (Kirksville, MO.: Sixteenth Century Journal Publishers, 1988), 46. For an overview of Calvin's approach to issues of law and gospel, see Michael S. Horton, "Calvin and the Law-Gospel Hermeneutic," *Pro Eccl* 6.1 (1997): 27-42.

68. Calvin alludes to both these texts in the discussion in *Institutes* 2.7.14 = *CO* 2:263.

ery of a different soteriology, also led him to misread Paul. As Stendahl famously argued, Luther was struggling with a guilty conscience and Paul was not: "We all, in the West, and especially in the tradition of the Reformation, cannot help reading Paul through the experience of persons like Luther or Calvin. And this is the chief reason for most of our misunderstandings of Paul."[69] Further, the assumption that the Reformers understood the preconversion Paul, the passionate Pharisee, to have struggled with a guilty conscience leads to the conclusion that they believed such struggles with guilt to be typical of Judaism. This conclusion then appears to find further confirmation in their heavy emphasis on the theological use of the law to bring conviction of sin. If this is the principal function of the law, then the Reformers must suppose guilt to be characteristic of a religion in which law observance plays a central role.

The historical reality is quite otherwise. There is little evidence in either the Reformers' exegesis or their other writings of a concern with the law bringing conviction of sin *as an experience*. Its experiential contours and any associated feelings of guilt are of little concern compared to the fact that it does convict and therefore turns those impacted by it towards faith in Christ. Their interest is not psychological, and the principal backwards projection of cultural values involved in the debate is not that of the Reformers onto Paul but of twentieth- and twenty-first century scholars onto the Reformers. Of more significance exegetically is the typical treatment of Phil 3:6 where Paul claims that as a Pharisee he had been blameless (ἄμεμπτος) as regards righteousness under the law. This text is used widely in recent exegesis to disprove the notion that as a Jew Paul struggled with a guilty conscience due to an inability to obey the law.

---

69. Stendahl, "Call Not Conversion," 12. These words of Stendahl have been so influential that I have not hesitated to cite them several times. See also 55 n. 115 and 323 n. 6. See also Stendahl, "Paul and the Introspective Conscience of the West," 78–96. Stendahl's charges are later echoed by both E. P. Sanders and James Dunn. See especially, E. P. Sanders, *Paul* (Oxford: OUP, 1991), 49, and James D. G. Dunn and Alan M. Suggate, *The Justice of God: A Fresh Look at the Old Doctrine of Justification by Faith* (Carlisle: Paternoster, 1993), 13. In James D. G. Dunn, "The Justice of God: A Renewed Perspective on Justification by Faith," *JTS* 43.1 (1992): 1–22, he is a little more cautious, speaking indirectly of the "negative influence of Luther's conversion" resulting from "the reflection backwards of Luther's experience on to Paul" (2–3). Nevertheless, the unwary reader would certainly be left with the impression that Luther himself was guilty of such backward reflection of his experience on to Paul. For a refutation of these charges specifically in relation to Luther, see Stephen J. Chester, "Paul and the Introspective Conscience of Martin Luther," *BibInt* 14.5 (2006): 508–36.

In fact *the Reformers read in precisely the same way*. Of course, they were not focused in historical-critical fashion on the question of the nature of Second Temple Judaism. Their concerns are explicitly Christian and theological, but the implications of what they do say are nevertheless clear. In his *Commentary on Galatians* (1531/1535), Luther expounds Gal 1:13–14 by means of Phil 3:5–6. Paul's words imply that if even he, with all his reasons for confidence in the flesh, had to be justified by faith, the Galatians would be foolish to trust those urging circumcision but whose record with regard to the righteousness of the law was less impressive than Paul's own. Going on to discuss Gal 1:15–17, where Paul recounts God's grace in calling him to be an apostle, Luther places an exposition in Paul's own mouth:

> It is as though he were saying: "I did not deserve this; for I was zealous for the Law of God, but without judgment. In fact, my foolish and wicked zeal so blinded me that, with the permission of God, I fell into even more abominable and outrageous sins. I persecuted the church of God; I was an enemy of Christ. . . . But the abundant grace of God, who calls and shows mercy, pardoned and forgave all those blasphemies. And in place of these horrible sins of mine, which I then regarded as a service most pleasing to God, He gave me His grace and called me to be an apostle."[70]

In similar vein, when preaching on Gal 1:11–14, Calvin argues that Paul's persecution of the church "does not mean that he did not strive to live in all holiness and perfection for he shone as a mirror of great integrity. Indeed, he refers to himself as 'blameless' ('*irreprehensible*,' Phil 3:6), and not without good cause. Rather, he is saying that he was blind enough to consider himself justified in God's sight simply because there was no spot in him which men could reproach him for."[71] Similar themes appear when in the last months of his life, in early 1546, Luther preaches on Paul's conversion in Acts 9. Paul's sins were grave but they were committed in the sincere belief that he was doing God's will and he responded obediently when shown his error by Christ on the Damascus road. In contrast, the pope, cardinals, and monks of Luther's day are

70. *LW* 26:69 = *WA* 40:136, 24 – 137, 16.
71. John Calvin, *Sermons on the Epistle to the Galatians*, trans. Kathy Childress (Edinburgh: Banner of Truth, 1997), 71–72 = *CO* 50:333 (Sermon 5). Tyndale (1526) had more paraphrased than translated ἄμεμπτος at Phil 3:6 with "I was soche a won as no man coulde complayne on."

worse since they know that they are doing wrong but refuse to change even when their errors are pointed out to them:

> But Paul was not like this. He had no delight or desire to deceive or make monkeys of the people, as the pope and cardinals, and monks do; rather, he was an upright, learned Israelite and Pharisee who proceeded with true zeal for the Law and his native land, as he himself boasts in Philippians 3 [:4, 6]: "If anyone else thinks he has reason to boast in the flesh, I have more," etc.; "as to zeal, a persecutor of the Church." [He] wanted to keep the people in their former way of life ... he was concerned for his native land and was zealous for it, thinking and supposing that they were being led astray through the teaching about Christ. Thus he thought he was doing right and pleasing God.[72]

Paul's preconversion life is thus a kind of paradigm of the Reformers' view of sin. His major sins are not the consequence of bodily desire but in fact stem from his deepest religious impulses and devotion. Sin infects his higher faculties as well as his lower ones. As such, his sin springs also from his commitment to the law and demonstrates the inability of the law to justify. It is this that explains the otherwise shocking manner in which Paul speaks of the law. Vermigli will ask of Phil 3:6, "If we could obtain righteousness by this means, should such profitable things be counted as losses, such precious and holy things as vile, and matters acceptable and pleasing to God as dung?"[73] As an obedient Jew the preconversion Paul does have a different kind of righteousness, but it corresponds for the Reformers only to the civic or political use of the law. As Calvin comments on Phil 3:6,

> I say that there is a twofold righteousness of the law. The one is spiritual—perfect love to God and our neighbors: it is contained in doctrine, and never existed in the life of any man. The other is literal—such as appears in the view of men, while nevertheless, hypocrisy reigns in the heart, and there is in the sight of God nothing but

---

72. *LW* 58:370-84 (378) = *WA* 51:135-48 (142, 25-40). Note also the assessment of this sermon offered by Bruce Corley, "Interpreting Paul's Conversion—Then and Now," in *The Road from Damascus: The Impact of Paul's Conversion on His Life, Thought, and Ministry*, ed. Richard N. Longenecker (Grand Rapids: Eerdmans, 1997), 10.

73. *RCSNT* XI:75.

iniquity. Thus the law has two references; the one to God, the other to men. Paul, then, was in the judgment of men holy and free from all blame. A rare praise and almost unique. But let us see how much he cared for it.[74]

The distinction drawn here between the hypothetical spiritual and the actual literal forms taken by righteousness clearly parallels that made by Luther in the summary of the argument of the letter with which he begins the *Commentary on Galatians* (1531/1535) and by which he structures his interpretation. There is an earthly, active righteousness of the law that produces good works but is not righteousness in the sight of God and does not justify, and there is a heavenly, passive righteousness that is not performed but is received by faith and creates a new person.[75] The preconversion Paul has the earthly, active righteousness of the law but lacks heavenly, passive righteousness: "For if there were any grounds for boasting in the righteousness of the law, I would have more grounds for boasting than anyone else."[76]

As someone confusing justifying righteousness and righteousness of the law, the preconversion Paul is, from the Reformers' perspective, typical of Judaism. This can be seen in their treatment of Paul's famous phrase the "works of the law" (ἔργα νόμου), which is *not* identified with the theological use of the law in revealing sin. In his *Lectures on Romans* (1515–1516), Luther says that the works of the law are not those that drive one to repentance, but are rather those that "are regarded in themselves as being sufficient for righteousness and salvation."[77] These doers of the works of the law are not guilt-racked sinners, but those who

> work in such a way that they think they are fulfilling the Law and thus are righteous, even though they neither desire grace nor realize and hate the fact that they are sinners; because they have worked according to the outward form of the Law, they do not dispose themselves to seek righteousness, but rather boast as if through these works it were already in their possession.[78]

74. *Comm. Phil* 3:6, *CNTC* 11:271 = *OE* 16:351, 28 - 352, 5.
75. *LW* 26:4–12 = *WA* 40:41, 15 - 51, 34.
76. *LW* 26:69 = *WA* 40:135, 23–24.
77. *LW* 25:241 = *WA* 56:254, 19–22.
78. *LW* 25:241 = *WA* 56:255, 8–11.

This idea receives one of its most striking expressions in the interpretation of Rom 7:9 where Paul says that he was once alive apart from the law but that, when the commandment came, sin revived and he died. This bringing of death is identified with the theological use of law to reveal sin, but the time when he was alive apart from the law is identified with his career as a law-observant Pharisee. As Calvin puts it, "he was satisfied with the outward mask (*larva*) of righteousness. He refers, therefore, to the law as absent because, although it was before his eyes, it did not impress on him a serious sense of the judgment of the Lord. Thus the eyes of hypocrites are covered with a veil which prevents them from seeing how much is demanded of us by the precept which forbids us to covet."[79] That Paul speaks of blind zeal for the law as life apart from law is a position also adopted in various forms in early Protestant commentaries by Oecolampadius, Melanchthon, Bullinger, Brenz, Ochino, and Alesius.[80]

The confusion in Judaism between the righteousness of the law and justifying righteousness arises because, as Calvin implies in the above quotation, it is impossible to obey the law fully. As we have seen in the Reformers' account of sin, its infection of soul and mind means that even where external deeds are good, the motivations of the heart will be imperfect. The classic text here is Gal 3:10, where Paul asserts that those who "rely on the works of the law" (ἐξ ἔργων νόμου εἰσίν) are under a curse since Deut 27:26 pronounces as cursed those who do not obey "all the things written in the book of the law." As we shall see when considering the phrase "the works of the law" in its own right (4.1), the Reformers take the word "all" (πᾶς) to indicate that Paul's reference is to the moral as well as to the ceremonial law. However, Paul's words imply that anyone who did obey in every respect would be justified. The Reformers infer that, since those who rely on the works of the law are cursed, such obedience must be impossible. In the *Commentary on Galatians* (1531/1535) Luther argues that "the statement of Moses, 'Cursed be everyone who does not abide by all things, etc.' is not contrary to Paul's declaration that all who rely on works of the Law are under a curse. For Moses demands a doer who keeps the Law perfectly. But where are we to find such a one? Nowhere."[81] Vermigli employs Gal 3:10

---

79. *Comm. Rom* 7:9, *CNTC* 8:144 = *OE* 13:140, 30–34.

80. See Mark Elliott, "Romans 7 in the Reformation Century," in *Reformation Readings of Romans*, ed. Kathy Ehrensperger and R. Ward Holder (New York: T&T Clark, 2008), 171–88.

81. *LW* 26:260 = *WA* 40:408, 22–25.

as one of a medley of Pauline texts designed to refute the charge of "our adversaries" that "we contemptuously weaken the law of God and make it useless when we assert that it cannot be observed by men in their natural strength."[82] At the level of political or civil righteousness obedience is possible, but not at the level of justifying righteousness. As Bullinger expresses it in preaching, "God's commandments require the whole man, and a very heavenly (*plane divinam*) kind of perfectness; which whosoever performeth not, he is accursed and condemned by the law. Now no man doth fulfill that righteousness; therefore we are all accursed by the law. But this curse is taken away, and most absolute righteousness is freely bestowed on us, through Christ Jesus."[83] Not surprisingly it makes little sense in such a view to treat conscience simply as the ethical organ or ethical part of a person within a wider anthropological structure. The conscience is not that part of a person that renders reliable judgment upon whether a person's actions are right or wrong. Rather the validity or invalidity of the judgments made by the conscience is indicative of the whole person's standing before God.[84]

In the case of the person seeking to be justified by works, the judgments of conscience are erroneous and confused. The conscience considers as righteous the person whose status before God is in reality that of sinner. Yet, for the Reformers, this is only one of various possible relationships between the law and the consciences of individuals. As Luther outlines these relationships in his *Prefaces to the Old Testament* (1523), there is indeed the upright person, who confuses justification with civic righteousness and attempts to fulfill the law in his or her own strength. Yet there is also the blatant sinner willfully disregarding the law, and there is also the sinner in the process of being driven to Christ by the realization that the law demands impossible things.[85] Even in the last instance, where people correctly perceive their true position before God, to stay there permanently

---

82. Peter Martyr Vermigli, *Predestination and Justification: Two Theological Loci*, trans. and ed. Frank. A. James III, The Peter Martyr Library 8 (Kirksville, MO: Sixteenth Century Essays and Studies, 2003), 128 = *In Epistolam S. Pauli ad Romanos D. Petri Martyris Vermilii*, 534. The two *loci* are included by Vermigli in his *Commentary on Romans* but are here translated separately.

83. Bullinger, "Sermon VIII," 253 (in *The Third Decade*) = HBW 3.1:383-419 (393, 12-16).

84. See Bernhard Lohse, "Conscience and Authority in Luther," in *Luther and the Dawn of the Modern Era: Papers for the Fourth International Congress for Luther Research*, ed. Heiko A. Oberman (Leiden: Brill, 1974), 158-83 (esp. 160-68).

85. *LW* 35:245-56 = *WA* DB 8:27, 3-24.

would be to fall into the sin of blasphemous despair of God's mercy. Further, this theological use of the law is a matter not simply of conscience but of revelation. In none of these three attitudes towards the law is the human conscience ultimately an appropriate and reliable guide to the human situation, and given the Reformers' perspective on sin this is scarcely surprising. Only those who are in Christ have the beginnings of a healthy conscience: "Thus he is a true doer of the Law who receives the Holy Spirit through faith in Christ and then begins to love God and to do good to his neighbor. Hence 'to do' includes faith at the same time. Faith takes the doer himself and makes him into a tree, and his deeds become fruit . . . there must be a doer before deeds, not deeds before the doer."[86] As Bernhard Lohse puts it, "Luther identified a good conscience with faith. . . . Luther understands a good conscience to be the proper confidence in God."[87]

Yet even believers live their earthly lives caught up in the conflict between the Spirit and the flesh. On the one hand, it is perfectly possible that there will be good works produced, inspired by the Holy Spirit, in which it is proper to rejoice, and for which to give thanks. In so far as they stem from a renewed heart and pure motives, they are a consequence and expression of true righteousness. On the other hand, awareness of the continued presence of the flesh will prevent the Christian from imagining that very much reliance can be placed on a clear conscience. As even good works can be ultimately self-serving, a lack of awareness of sin does not mean that there is none. Paul tells the Corinthians, "I am not aware of anything against myself, but I am not thereby justified. It is the Lord who judges me" (1 Cor 4:4). However, this text functions for Luther not merely as proof that a self-approving conscience can be legitimate, but also as evidence that such self-approval may not always be reliable. Commenting on 1 Tim 3:2, with its requirement for a bishop to be above reproach, Luther uses the verse to suggest that there is a difference between human and divine estimations of righteousness. "Paul writes: I am conscious of no evil (cf. 1 Cor 4:4). Let the Our Father stand: 'Forgive us.' Before God no-one is above reproach, but before men the bishop is to be so, that he may not be a fornicator, an adulterer. . . ."[88] There thus remains the possibility of sinning with a clear conscience. When Paul writes at Rom 14:23 that those who eat meat despite doubts about its propriety are condemned since "what does

---

86. *LW* 26:255–56 = *WA* 40:401, 30 – 402, 21.
87. Lohse, "Conscience and Authority in Luther," 164.
88. *LW* 28:284 = *WA* 26:51, 14–16. Luther lectured on 1 Timothy in 1527–1528.

not proceed from faith is sin," Vermigli is reluctant to identify faith with conscience in any simple or straightforward way: "If I were to grant that in this passage faith means conscience, I suppose we should also add that the conscience should not be believed unless it is instructed by the word of God. For there are many who have such a superstitious conscience that, whether they obey it or not, they sin most severely."[89]

To identify the Reformers as heroes of the conscience, advocating adherence to it as a straight path to true experience of God, is therefore a distortion. For, as is apparent from the revelatory nature of the theological use of the law, even repentance is not a human work but a divine gift: "Real preparation for grace is not the preparation sinners make through their contrition and confession but the preparation God has made by his election, calling, and gifts. Contrition is the fruit of grace not its presupposition."[90] The conscience itself is quite unable to move a person towards God and is thereby condemned and moved to the margins, not made central. As Luther himself puts it, "This is the reason why our theology is certain: it snatches us away from ourselves and places us outside ourselves, so that we do not depend on our own strength, conscience, experience, person, or works but depend on that which is outside ourselves, that is, on the promise and truth of God, which cannot deceive."[91] Thus the conviction of sin brought by the law is a matter of revelation, not of attentiveness by the individual to the promptings of conscience. The drama of justification is about God's truth breaking in from outside, not about human beings finding truth by listening to an inner voice.[92] Recognizing this, Oberman emphasizes something of Luther that is no less true of the other Reformers: it is an error to read Luther in a way that makes crucial

> the Protestant citadel, the "better self," the conscience, which thus becomes the site of the Last Judgment, where the believer, con-

---

89. Peter Martyr Vermigli, *Predestination and Justification*, 106 = *In Epistolam S. Pauli ad Romanos D. Petri Martyris Vermilii*, 525.

90. David C. Steinmetz, "Luther against Luther," in *Luther in Context*, 2nd ed. (Grand Rapids: Baker, 2002), 10.

91. *LW* 26:387 = *WA* 40.1:589,25-28. See 5.6 for this quotation's implications for Luther's view of alien righteousness.

92. On the history and problems of interpreting Luther as a champion of inward religious experience, see Jörg Lauster, "Luther—Apostle of Freedom? Liberal Protestant Interpretations of Luther," in *Lutherrenaissance Past and Present*, ed. Christine Helmer and Bo Kristian Holm (Göttingen: Vandenhoeck & Ruprecht, 2015), 127-43.

fronted with the Laws of God, acknowledges that he is a sinner and declares himself at the same time to be righteous by virtue of Christ's sacrifice.... It is precisely this conventional, conscience-orientated morality that man's innermost self struggles to fulfill, and that Luther, to the horror of all well-meaning, decent Christians, undermined.[93]

That all this is perfectly clear from the Reformers' exegesis does not mean that there are no loose ends in their thought concerning conscience. In particular, attempts to locate the conviction of sin brought by the law in its theological use caused controversy among early Protestants. Conviction of sin and subsequent repentance are both divine gifts, but should they be understood as a preparation for conversion or as its consequence? In other words, is the order of experience law first and then gospel or is the kind of self-knowledge involved in the recognition of sin only possible as a consequence of apprehending the gospel by faith? These questions arose in Luther's personal circle through Johannes Agricola, a student and supporter who appealed to some of the statements of the young Luther in order to argue that the gospel terminates the law: "a believer is converted, justified and instructed through the proclamation of the gospel of Christ. The continuing divine demand of the law—even of ecclesiastical regulations—was no longer of interest in this context."[94] In Agricola's view the demand of the law and its revealing of sin can only be truly understood from the standpoint of faith where the believer has in fact already been delivered from them. He expressed these opinions in the context of a disagreement with Melanchthon, which flared up in 1527, when Agricola objected to statements about repentance made by Melanchthon in articles for use in a visitation of Saxony churches, and then later in a disagreement more directly with Luther himself in the late 1530s.[95]

The contrast with Melanchthon can be illustrated by Melanchthon's comments on Rom 7:7-13, which he relates to Paul's conversion. The

---

93. Heiko A. Oberman, *Luther: Man between God and the Devil* (New York: Image, 1992), 155. See also 129, 226, 319-20.

94. Martin Brecht, *Martin Luther: The Preservation of the Church 1532-1546*, trans. James L. Schaaf (Minneapolis: Fortress, 1993), 156.

95. For a detailed account of events in 1527 see Timothy J. Wengert, *Law and Gospel: Philip Melanchthon's Debate with John Agricola of Eisleben over Poenitentia* (Grand Rapids: Baker, 1997). For the controversy of the late 1530s see Brecht, *Martin Luther: The Preservation of the Church 1532-1546*, 156-71, and Lohse, *Martin Luther's Theology*, 178-84.

statement that apart from the law sin is dead (7:8) means that "when I was a carnally secure Pharisee, I thought that I was satisfying the Law, that I was righteous."[96] However, the statement that sin revived when the commandment came and produced death (7:9-10) refers to the law causing anxiety in "those who are oppressed by fears and torments . . . if Paul had not heard the voice of the Gospel, he also would have perished in such terrors."[97] Although he does not spell it out, Melanchthon appears to imply a period of preparation for conversion in which Paul struggled with inability to keep the law. It is the intervening step for Paul between the robust conscience, mentioned in Phil 3:6, and faith in Christ. Melanchthon does not explain how this idea relates to the accounts offered of Paul's conversion in Acts, which are more naturally read as narratives of sudden grace. Moreover, the idea that Paul endured a preconversion struggle with a guilty conscience does not appear at all prominently in Protestant exegesis until the rise of historical-critical scholarship in the nineteenth century. Yet Melanchthon's exegesis here illustrates very well his construal of the order of salvation "in successive stages consisting of the law, the gospel, and the necessary renewal of the Holy Spirit."[98] With this he provides a partial exception to the Reformers' lack of focus on the experiential contours of justification. For Melanchthon there is a sense in which "experience actually made theology,"[99] since the move from fear to comfort is what happens to believers in the transition from law to gospel.

Luther's various statements on the issues involved clearly place him closer to Melanchthon than to Agricola, with whom his friendship had ended by 1540. However, he is less wedded to a chronological or experiential sequence than Melanchthon. Luther thought out his position within the framework of his law/gospel hermeneutic. Luther insists with Melanchthon that "those who teach and understand the Law correctly are the ones who lead the people to a realization of their sins and alarm them with the Law, and then comfort and cheer the dejected and terrified with the Gospel."[100] There is a need for the preaching of the law before

---

96. Melanchthon, *Commentary on Romans*, 157 = CR 15:648.

97. Melanchthon, *Commentary on Romans*, 157 = CR 15:648. See also Melanchthon, "Loci Communes Theologici," 79-80 = MSA 2:76, 24 - 78, 4; CR 21:149-51.

98. Lohse, *Martin Luther's Theology*, 179.

99. Timothy J. Wengert, *Defending Faith: Lutheran Responses to Andreas Osiander's Doctrine of Justification, 1551-1559* (Tübingen: Mohr Siebeck, 2012), 350.

100. LW 22:146 = WA 46:664, 20-23. Luther is here commenting on John 1:17:

the preaching of the gospel, but knowledge of sin alone can evoke only a repentance that ultimately leads to despair. True repentance does indeed require faith and therefore repentance cannot simply belong with the preaching of the law as a prelude to the preaching of the gospel: "Repentance includes both law and gospel."[101] Thus we should not be misled by the fact that Luther's "oft-repeated statements that one can only become a Christian and a theologian through experience (that is, only by going through *Anfechtung*) are famous."[102] These statements are often divorced by interpreters from their context, in which the experience to which Luther refers is the very specific one of despairing of any possibility of ascending to God through one's own powers or efforts. As such, it is almost a kind of negative experience or "anti-experience" that demonstrates the futility before God of reliance on any other kinds of human experience. Luther's guilty conscience is only guilty in the very specific form of the shattering realization that behavior that is highly commendable from a human perspective is nevertheless tainted by sin and does not justify before God. Far from pointing to inwardness and higher forms of religious experience as the solution to human unrighteousness, such "anti-experience" redirects the focus of the repentant sinner outwards towards reliance on Christ and his justifying righteousness.

The issues involved in the Antinomian Controversy did not arise with the same force in the early history of the Reformed movement as in Lutheranism. Calvin nowhere deals systematically with the relationship between the theological use of the law, the gospel, and repentance. He is less insistent on the preaching of law before gospel than Luther, but Calvin's position on repentance is very similar to that of Luther. He distinguishes between two kinds of fear and two kinds of repentance. The fear of God and repentance that come from the theological use of the law will by themselves lead only to hell. It is only when they are followed by the fear of God and repentance that come from the gospel that they are productive: "the beginning of repentance is a sense of God's mercy, that is, when men are persuaded that God is ready to grant pardon, they then begin to gather courage to repent; otherwise perverseness will ever increase in them; how much soever their sin may frighten them, they

---

"For the law was given through Moses; grace and truth came through Jesus Christ" in a sermon preached in October 1535 at the height of the Antinomian Controversy.

101. WA 39.1:414, 11–12.

102. Hamm, "Impending Doom and Imminent Grace," 32.

will yet never return to the Lord."[103] Statements such as these make it clear that for the Reformers the role of the guilty conscience in conversion is always qualified. Its significance cannot be denied in the light of their very heavy emphasis on the knowledge of sin that comes through the law, but it is ultimately of very little value in and of itself without the assurance that comes from the gospel and God's promises.

Nevertheless, the irony remains that having marginalized and condemned the conscience by stressing its incapacity to know sin apart from revelation through the law, the Reformers' exegesis leaves open the possibility that some might make experience of the conscience's incompetence an essential aspect of conversion.[104] That is, there is a danger of the reintroduction of the introspective conscience in a different form from that typical of theologies and spiritualities in the medieval tradition. Despite the fact that the Reformers were focused on the *objective* fact of sin revealed by the law, and on the fear that resulted, as moving the sinner towards Christ, in several different strands of later Protestantism others used the same emphasis on the theological use of the law to make a *subjective* experience of guilt of central importance in preparation for conversion.[105] However, this preparatory experience of guilt was *not* understood to apply to Paul and his conversion, and such an application did not occur prior to the rise of historical-critical exegesis in the nineteenth century. Before historical criticism developed the idea of a psychological struggle for the preconversion Paul with inability to obey the law, the closest that Protestant interpretation came to asserting that Paul experienced guilt was to identify the coming of the law (Rom 7:9) and the conviction of sin with the moment of his conversion itself on the Damascus Road.[106] There remained considerable emphasis on the sud-

---

103. *Comm. Hos 6:1, Commentaries on the Twelve Minor Prophets Vol. 1: Hosea*, trans. John Owen (Edinburgh: Calvin Translation Society, 1846), 215 = CO 42:463. See the extensive discussion in Hesselink, *Calvin's Concept of the Law*, 217-38.

104. For discussion of issues of conscience in relation to conversion in Protestantism, see Stephen J. Chester, "Romans 7 and Conversion in the Protestant Tradition," *ExAud* 25 (2009): 135-71.

105. Kim, *Luther on Faith and Love*, 118 comments that "as far as the east is from the west, so far is Luther's faith from a merely subjective, personal, and psychological fervor or confidence."

106. See Bruce C. Hindmarsh, *The Evangelical Conversion Narrative: Spiritual Autobiography in Early Modern England* (Oxford: Oxford University Press, 2005), 143, for an account of a 1741 sermon by George Whitefield in which Paul's vision on the Damascus Road was his awakening of conscience. In this and other examples it is not

den and exceptional nature of Paul's conversion. Yet, being exceptional, it could coexist, especially in the Puritan and Pietist traditions, with the assumption that for most others an experience of true contrition and appropriate self-loathing would be the gateway through which subsequent peace and assurance might be entered.

A similar loose end is also characteristic of the Reformers' treatment of the place of conscience in the Christian life. They eliminate any role for good works as a basis of justification and loudly proclaim that the only foundation of assurance of salvation is faith in Christ. However, since they also insist that good works will nevertheless inevitably follow from justification, the presence of good works can function as one of its confirmations. The conscience will recognize that the struggle between the Spirit and the flesh means that such works are inevitably imperfect, but their presence can be a confirmation of assurance. The Reformers' focus is not on this but on the liberation from fear brought by the gospel proclamation of the forgiveness of all sins, including such residual ones. It is essential not to rely on the self and its experiences and feelings, but instead to rely on Scripture and its promises. Luther is prepared to enumerate the external signs of grace that believers can observe in their lives, but only after he has established a scriptural and theological basis that has nothing to do with the self and its experiences. Luther first comments of Gal 4:6 that "God has also sent the Spirit of His Son into our hearts, as Paul says here. Now Christ is completely certain that in His Spirit He is pleasing to God. Since we have the same Spirit of Christ, we, too, should be certain that we are in a state of grace, on account of Him who is certain."[107] Yet this containing and limiting of a confir-

---

clear on what basis a vision of the risen Christ is to be identified with the convicting work of the law.

107. LW 26:378-79 = WA 40:577, 20-23. Schreiner, *Are You Alone Wise?* argues that the culture of the sixteenth century was pervaded by a search for certainty and by anxiety about certainty. An important aspect of this is anxiety over demonic deception and, after tracing Luther's concern with the issue, Schreiner concludes that "Luther's ultimate criterion for 'testing the spirits' became the experience of certitude itself" (303). However, the texts cited to demonstrate this claim in fact reveal that Luther's ultimate criterion is Scripture. Schreiner is careful at various points to avoid projecting contemporary ideas about the self and subjectivity back onto the sixteenth century (see 209-12, 258-59), but the term "experience" is used so indiscriminately and without definition that this attempt is not entirely successful. While it is profoundly helpful to place the Reformers' concern with certainty alongside that of others in the same era, the differences between their estimation of the kind of "experience" that matters (re-

matory role for good works might in other contexts be less effective. In later periods, particularly in those strands of the Reformed tradition in which the doctrine of predestination became central, believers anxiously examined their works for signs of proof of their election. Again, the Reformers' marginalization and condemnation of the conscience ironically gave rise to a reintroduction of the introspective conscience.[108] Yet it is abundantly clear that this was something they could not have foreseen and certainly did not intend.

3.4. Summary

Luther and the other Reformers return to Augustine in defining original sin not merely as a privation of good but as an active inclination of the will against God. However, they go beyond Augustine by refusing to identify concupiscence primarily with the desires of the body. Sin does not only disrupt healthy hierarchies between mind and body and between reason (or the will) and other parts of the soul. Sin also captures the higher faculties and therefore Paul's term "flesh" denotes not primarily the lower parts of the person but the entire person as he or she stands in opposition to God through sin. This means that even when, estimated in terms of action alone, a human deed appears to be good, the flesh will ensure that the motivation for the deed shares in corruption. It also follows that concupiscence continues to be truly sinful in the Christian life even when the desires involved are not translated into action. The Spirit struggles against the flesh and the renewal that results is genuine, but sin also remains a reality until death. Justification is not threatened since it no longer partially depends on a growth in righteousness resulting from good works but is instead given completely in the gift of Christ's righteousness.

Unsurprisingly given sin's capture of the rational faculties of human

---

sponding in faith to the promises of Scripture, if need be in defiance of all other "experience") and those made by others in their context are somewhat obscured. The examples drawn by Schreiner from within Catholicism and from among the radical Reformers betray a greater concern for what a contemporary reader might term "inwardness" or "introspection" than do the magisterial Reformers, for whom all such "experience" is subsidiary to the Word.

108. For discussion of this issue in the theology of Luther and Calvin, see Randall Zachman, *The Assurance of Faith: Conscience in the Theology of Martin Luther and John Calvin* (Louisville: Westminster John Knox, 2005).

beings, conviction of sin and self-understanding as a sinner is not a matter of natural perception but of revelation. The instrument of revelation is the law. It demonstrates to people their sin and drives them to seek the grace of Christ. This principal or theological use of the law must be kept distinct from its political or civic use. The latter refers to the law's role in human society in restraining sinful actions and ensuring harmony. This use is valuable in its own place but must not be confused with justifying righteousness. To be restrained by law and fear of punishment is not the same thing as a pure heart and mind. Differences do emerge among the Reformers, and ultimately between early Lutheranism and the early Reformed tradition, over the application of a hermeneutic of law and gospel and the place of the law in the Christian life. However, these significant differences operate not so much at an exegetical level in Pauline texts, where there is agreement, but at a canonical level in terms of how shared exegetical conclusions here are related to other parts of Scripture.

In describing the theological use of the law, the Reformers are concerned with the fact of the conviction of sin and not primarily with its psychological dimensions as an experience. They do not portray the preconversion Paul as struggling with a guilty conscience or assume such struggles to be typical of Judaism. Rather, Paul's preconversion life paradigmatically illustrates the Reformers' view of sin. His persecution of the church sprang not from bodily desires but from his commitment to the law and as such demonstrates the inability of the law to justify. He had a righteousness that corresponds only to the political or civic use of the law. Similarly, Paul's phrase "the works of the law" is identified not with guilt-racked sinners but with those falsely convinced that they are fulfilling the law and are righteous before God. Their confused consciences do not recognize that the law is impossible to obey fully and that they stand in desperate need of Christ as a mediator. The conscience cannot move a person towards God and is therefore marginalized in favor of the revelation of sin through the theological use of the law. Yet even this is ultimately of very little value in and of itself without the assurance that comes from the gospel and God's promises. Even in the Christian life there remains the possibility of sinning with a clear conscience. Some of the heirs of the Reformers would later make a subjective experience of guilt of central importance in preparing for conversion or much more strongly emphasize the function of an appropriate quantity and quality of good works as a confirmation of election, but these developments were unforeseen and unintended.

Therefore, in each one of these key dimensions of the human plight apart from Christ, the Reformers made departures from Augustine's Pauline exegetical grammar. Augustine's insight that the purpose of the law is to reveal sin was significantly extended by the Reformers' introduction of the formal concept of uses of the law, and Augustine's already profound sense of human bondage to sin was deepened further. No longer is the human problem primarily the inability to want to do the good but also the inability of the conscience reliably to identify the good. Through consistent application of the conclusion that Paul's term "flesh" applies to the whole human being in opposition to God, Augustine's sense that the fallen human will is darkened in understanding was given a new intensity.

4 Salvation in Christ

The Works of the Law, Grace, and Faith

4.1. Not by the Works of the Law

The Reformers' conceptions of salvation in Christ are less uniform than their understanding of the human plight apart from Christ. There are significant differences of emphasis among them, especially in the way in which they understand justification by faith and relate it to another major theme in the Pauline letters, namely the concept of "participation in Christ" or "union with Christ."[1] Some of these differences will be explored in the next section of this book, which focuses on individual contributions (Part III "Individual Perspectives: Luther, Melanchthon, and Calvin on Righteousness in Christ"). Yet despite such differences in soteriology there remains a shared exegetical foundation that clearly differentiates the Reformers from their opponents. There are key concepts concerning salvation in Christ where they do speak with a common voice, their exegesis both shaping and being shaped by their conviction that to allow any place in salvation for meritorious human cooperation with divine grace was to undermine Paul's teaching. In particular, there are shared convictions about the interpretation of the phrase "works of the law," and the interpretation of the terms "grace" and "faith."

The Pauline letters frequently state that salvation is not by works and, in several key texts in Romans and Galatians, the works that do not

---

1. The phrase "in Christ" is used over 50 times in the seven undisputed letters of Paul alone, in addition to which stand more complex images of being "joined to" or "united with" or "conformed to" Christ.

save are specified as "works of the law" (ἔργα νόμου). The greatest concentration of these phrases comes in Gal 2:16: "yet we know that a person is justified not by works of the law but through faith in Jesus Christ, so that we might be justified by faith in Christ, and not by doing the works of the law, because no one will be justified by the works of the law."[2] In their interpretation of the phrase "works of the law" the Reformers speak with one voice. They insist that by the "works of the law" Paul intends the whole law, including its ethical aspects, and not merely ceremonies. This was a crucial point and at times it can feel as if this difference of exegetical opinion encapsulates a straightforward confessional divide between the Reformers and their opponents, with the divide impacting even translation. As early as 1525 William Tyndale's *New Testament* excludes interpretation of the phrase in terms of ceremonies alone by rendering it into English as the "dedes of the lawe."[3] Later in the century, the *Rhemes New Testament* (1582)—the first ever English edition of the texts sanctioned by Rome—includes a marginal note to Gal 2:16 insisting that "when justification is attributed to faith, the workes of charitie be not excluded, but the workes of Moyses law: that is, the ceremonies, sacrifices and sacraments thereof principally."[4]

Yet things are not as simple as a contrast between an early Protestant interpretation of the "works of the law" as denoting the whole law and a Catholic interpretation of them as ceremonies.[5] As we have already seen (2.3), both positions were represented in medieval exegesis and both were understood as consistent with a causal role in justification for works

2. As well as the three uses here in Gal 2:16, the phrase also appears in Rom 3:20, 27, 28; Gal 3:2, 5, 10.

3. Luther A. Weigle, ed., *The New Testament Octapla: Eight English Versions of the New Testament in the Tyndale-King James Tradition* (New York: T. Nelson, 1962), 1058. Tyndale used this wording again in the 1535 edition of his New Testament. He was followed by the *Great Bible* (1540) and the *Bishops' Bible* (1568) but not by the *Geneva Bible* (1560) or by the *King James Version* (1611), the two most influential Protestant English translations. Ironically, some scholars now argue on the basis of a parallel phrase in the Dead Sea Scrolls (especially 4QMMT) that "deeds of the law" is the best English translation. See Karl P. Donfried, "Justification and Last Judgment in Paul—Twenty Five Years Later," in *Paul, Thessalonica and Early Christianity* (Grand Rapids: Eerdmans, 2002), 279–92.

4. *The Rhemes New Testament* (Rhemes: John Fogny, 1582), 499.

5. In a previous article I come unfortunately close to portraying the exegetical issue as forming a straightforwardly confessional divide. See Stephen J. Chester, "When the Old Was New: Reformation Perspectives on Gal 2:16," *ExpTim* 119.7 (2008): 322–24.

performed subsequent to the gift of grace in baptism and enabled by this gift. The young Luther himself in his *Lectures on Romans* (1515–1516) takes the use of the phrase in Rom 3:28 to refer to the whole law but is careful to specify that the works concerned belong to those who regard such works "as the reason for their justification, and by the performance of which they consider themselves righteous."[6] Paul is not excluding the works of grace and faith humbly performed by those who seek after righteousness and for whom the Christian life is a pathway to it. His target is rather those who arrogantly think themselves already to possess righteousness. It is only once Luther and other Reformers reject human cooperation with grace in justification that the difference between the two positions becomes contentious. For if the phrase "works of the law" refers to the whole law, then debate may follow as to whether Paul intends, like the Reformers, to exclude human works from justification entirely or simply to exclude those performed prior to faith. However, if ceremonies are intended, then any general exclusion of works from justification becomes implausible. The insistence that Paul means the whole law is therefore not a sufficient basis for the Reformers' rejection of a causal role for works in justification, but it is essential to that rejection. Sixteenth-century interpreters of Paul could agree with the Reformers about the meaning of the phrase "works of the law" and still disagree with them over justification and salvation, but they could not embrace the Reformers' teaching on justification and salvation while rejecting their understanding of the "works of the law."[7]

By the time of his first *Commentary on Galatians* (1516–1517/1519), Luther teaches that works result from righteousness rather than lead to it and that "he who wants to be saved must despair altogether of all strength, works, and laws."[8] He draws this conclusion from an asser-

---

6. *LW* 25:252 = *WA* 56:264, 27–28.

7. A partial exception here is Martin Bucer. See Edwin Tait, "The Law and Its Works in Martin Bucer's 1536 Romans Commentary," in *Reformation Readings of Romans*, ed. Kathy Ehrensperger and R. Ward Holder (New York: T&T Clark, 2008), 62: "Bucer interprets the 'works of the law' mentioned in Rom 3:20 as the ceremonies of the OT law. In this he takes his stand with the bulk of the patristic tradition and with contemporary Catholics over against Augustine in the early church and contemporary evangelicals such as Melanchthon. But he does not regard this as a restriction of Paul's critique of the law—rather, Bucer argues that Paul is focusing on the ceremonial law because this was the part of the law in which his opponents were trusting.... The 'works of the law' in question (the ceremonial *mitzvoh*) cannot justify *because* the whole law cannot justify."

8. *LW* 27:223 = *WA* 2:492, 8–9.

tion that the "works of the law" means the whole law. If even the Ten Commandments do not justify, then no law can do so. Luther also draws attention to what he regards as the implausibility of a division within the divine law. The apostle cannot be arguing that ceremonies are now obsolete as regards justification but that the ethical aspects of the law remain involved in justification since, "Just as the ceremonial law was good and holy at that time, so it is good and holy now; for it was instituted by God Himself."[9] A similar point is made again in the later *Commentary on Galatians* (1531/1535), where Luther comments that "the ceremonial law was as much the divine law as the moral laws were. Thus circumcision, the institution of the priesthood, the service of worship, and the rituals were commanded by God as much as the Decalog was."[10] If all parts of the law are equally worthy in their own nature, then one part cannot have been removed from a role in justification while another remains relevant. In his *Commentary on Galatians* (1548), John Calvin also refuses to find anything inherently wrong with the Jewish practices of Paul's opponents: "The use of ceremonies for edification was free so long as believers were not deprived of their liberty. . . . Paul was worried not so much about ceremonies being observed as that the confidence and glory of salvation should be transferred to works."[11] The same basic point is made even more forcefully by Peter Martyr Vermigli when lecturing at Oxford in the early 1550s: "Is it not good and laudable conduct to worship God with certain fixed rites which he has commanded?"[12]

These arguments serve the exegetical point of their authors: Paul's target is the whole law in its inability to justify. His concern in Gal 2 is not with ceremonies as such but with the mistaken notion that law ob-

---

9. *LW* 27:223 = *WA* 2:492, 15–16.

10. *LW* 26:138 = *WA* 40.1:242, 18–20. As early as 1524 Melanchthon protested in a letter to Cardinal Campeggio against the misunderstanding of Luther's theology as an assault on ceremonies. Luther is instead focused on the difference between divine and human righteousness and his critique of ceremonies concerns their confusion with justifying righteousness: "It is truly impious to think that the whole power of religion depends only upon either the condemnation or the observation of ceremonies." See *MBWT* 2: no. 324 (135, 29–31), quoted in Timothy J. Wengert, "Philip Melanchthon's Last Word to Cardinal Lorenzo Campeggio," in *Philip Melanchthon: Theologian in Classroom, Confession, and Controversy*, ed. Robert Kolb, Irene Dingel, and L'ubomír Batka (Göttingen: Vandenhoeck and Ruprecht, 2012), 80.

11. *Comm. Gal* 2:14, 15, *CNTC* 11:36, 39 = *OE* 16:46, 33 – 47, 2; 50, 5–7.

12. Peter Martyr Vermigli, *Predestination and Justification*, 118 = *In Epistolam S. Pauli ad Romanos D. Petri Martyris Vermilii* (Basilae: Petrum Pernam, 1558), 530.

servance contributes anything to justification. The wider consequence is that those rites of the Roman Catholic Church repudiated by the Reformers cannot be rejected simply because they are ceremonies. They can only be rejected on the grounds that, in contrast to the true sacraments of Baptism and the Lord's Supper, God did not institute them and they are the fruits of mere human invention. Calvin drives the point home when he comments that Paul's opponents "at least were able to say that they were not introducing their own ideas or traditions. . . . The Papists, however, have no such foundation, for all their rituals have arisen according to the will of men."[13]

This more positive attitude towards ceremonies understood as divinely instituted stands in contrast to the position adopted by Erasmus, who, in making the argument for a different kind of reform from within the Roman church, did adopt a more generally negative attitude towards ceremonies. Again and again, Erasmus's interpretation of Galatians contrasted faith not with the observance of the whole law but with that of ceremonies: "If they perceive that these ceremonies are being observed by the chief apostles, those who are somewhat superstitious will conclude that without these ceremonies the faith of the gospel is not enough for attaining salvation."[14] As we have seen (1.1), for Erasmus the dispute at Antioch in Gal 2:11–14 does not reflect actual disagreement between Paul and Peter about salvation, but merely a pious pretense at law observance by Peter out of a desire not to offend Jewish sensibilities.[15] The issue is not that the Galatians fail to understand that the law is unable to justify and that all human works are fallen and inadequate before God. Rather, they fail to appreciate that the time of the transitory law has passed now that Christ has come: "the Jews, because of a certain human tendency, desire to force their own rites upon everyone, clearly in order under this

---

13. Calvin, *Sermons on Galatians*, 115 = CO 50:368 (Sermon 8). Even among those Reformers most anxious to root out ceremonies from Protestant worship it is their lack of biblical warrant rather than a contrast between them and true inward piety that is the basis for their rejection. See Jane Dawson, *John Knox* (New Haven and London: Yale University Press, 2015), 90–108.

14. *CWE* 42:104 = *LB* 7:949C.

15. The idea that Peter, understood as the first pope, could have been in serious theological error is one naturally resisted by sixteenth-century Roman Catholic interpreters. In his *Annotations*, Erasmus devotes the bulk of his comments on Gal 2 to this issue. See *Erasmus' Annotations on the New Testament: Galatians to the Apocalypse*, ed. Anne Reeve and M. A. Screech (Leiden: Brill, 1993), 571–75.

pretext to enhance their own importance. For each one wishes that the things which he himself has taught should appear outstanding."[16] Paul challenges this clinging to the obsolete, motivated by cultural chauvinism, in the name of "a universal salvation without the aid of circumcision."[17]

As much as his interpretation of Gal 2:16 contrasted with those favored by the Reformers, Erasmus's position also bristled with danger from a traditional perspective. Since it is clear that slavery to human ceremonies in general is an error and not only to those of the Mosaic law,[18] then it must have been obvious to Erasmus's readers that this could potentially be turned against the Catholic church and its ceremonies: "Erasmus' representations of Paul's historical situation . . . as one dominated by a coterie of Judaizers determined to shackle Christians with regulations and stifle them with ceremonies, invite cogent analogies with ecclesiastical life in the sixteenth century."[19] There are considerable ironies here, for by insisting that the phrase "works of the law" refers to the whole law, the Reformers denied themselves any general criticism of ceremonies despite its obvious utility for their own critique of the sacramental system. Conversely, even while insisting that the phrase "works of the law" refers to ceremonies, and in the process distancing himself from the Reformers' soteriology, Erasmus can also use that interpretation implicitly to criticize the sacramental system of the church in the name of true inner piety. There thus can be no simple identification of the Reformers' views on the "works of the law" with hostility to ceremonies. What was principally at stake in their passionate debates with opponents about the meaning of the phrase "works of the law" was the issue of cooperation with divine grace as a cause of justification.

There is also then the further irony that this positive assessment of Jewish ceremonies as divinely approved in nature is partly what leads the Reformers to pay little attention in their exegesis of Galatians 2 to issues of Jewish practice. If Paul intends by the phrase "works of

16. *CWE* 42:99 = *LB* 7:945F.

17. *CWE* 42:102 = *LB* 7:948A.

18. Rummel, *Erasmus*, 39, comments that he regarded piety, among other things, as "an internal quality and independent of the external observance of rites."

19. Robert D. Sider, "Historical Imagination and the Representation of Paul in Erasmus' Paraphrases on the Pauline Epistles," in *Holy Scripture Speaks: The Production and Reception of Erasmus' Paraphrases on the New Testament*, ed. Hilmar M. Pabel and Mark Vessey (Toronto: University of Toronto Press, 2002), 100.

the law" to denote not ceremonies but rather all that the law requires and to eliminate law observance entirely as a cause of justification, then the focus of his argument cannot be Jew/Gentile relationships in the church at Antioch. In his first *Commentary on Galatians* (1516–1517/1519) Luther had given these relationships some weight, reserving his comments on the theology of justification for 2:16 and expounding 2:11–13 largely in terms of the misguided imposition of Jewish customs on Gentile believers.[20] It is not quite clear whether Luther then believed that Peter's fault was to go back on a decision to eat food forbidden by the law, or simply to eat food approved by the law with Gentiles present or in some sense in a Gentile manner. Yet, by the time of his later *Commentary on Galatians* (1531/1535), Luther argues that Peter had eaten forbidden food, and that from the outset the debate concerned not the customs of different ethnic groups but the contrast between law and gospel.[21] Calvin shows himself conscious of the shift between discussing Jew/Gentile relationships in the church and the principle of justification, but takes the discernment of the relationship between the two to be essential to Paul's argument:

> Many will be thinking, What! The issue at stake is the ceremonial law. Why, then, does Paul throw himself right into the middle of the battle by raising issues such as righteousness, man's salvation and the forgiveness of sins? . . . Well, to speak even of one of the ceremonies of the law involves discussing the role and function of the law. . . . He (Paul) not only gave his attention to what the Jews believed concerning eating pork . . . he considered why they believed such things. They claimed that the observance of the law was vital to salvation, and this was a yoke upon the conscience that Paul found intolerable.[22]

Again, the contrast with Erasmus is clear. What is primary is not Jew/Gentile relationships in the Antioch church, or any Jewish desire to

---

20. *LW* 27:213 = *WA* 2:485, 1–29. Luther uses phrases like "segregating himself from the food of the Gentiles," "reverting to Jewish practices," eating "in Jewish or Gentile fashion."

21. *LW* 26:106–22 = *WA* 40.1:191, 29 – 217, 25.

22. Calvin, *Sermons on Galatians*, 162–64 = *CO* 50:407–8 (Sermon 11). In the introduction to his commentary Calvin cites Acts 15 as another example of a dispute occasioned by ceremonies provoking a wider discussion of the principles of salvation in Christ. See *Comm. Gal Dec.*, *CNTC* 11:3–7 (6–7) = *OE* 16:5, 3 – 9, 39 (9, 6–22).

impose their customs upon others, but a theological question involving the whole law and therefore the basis of human relationships with God.

In arguing for this emphasis, Calvin employs what is initially a somewhat surprising argument. Paul's focus must be on the whole law and its inability to justify since "context" shows that this is what is meant. Yet context, the fact that Gal 2:16 is prompted by Paul's recounting of the dispute at Antioch over eating practices, might be thought one of the strongest arguments for the opposite view. How can Calvin claim context in his own support? Calvin's point is that "almost everything Paul adds relates to the moral rather than the ceremonial law."[23] Context for Calvin is not the circumstances of the dispute at Antioch but the rest of Paul's argument in Galatians, an argument that appears to offer general contrasts between the law and faith. For while Paul does come "at length to the specific question of ceremonies,"[24] by which Calvin presumably refers to the renewed discussion of circumcision from 5:2 onwards, the other things that Paul says about the law do not relate to ceremonies alone. Thus, the rest of Galatians is viewed as an unpacking of the thesis statement of 2:16. As the introductory notes to Gal 2 in *The Geneva Bible* (1560) were to claim, Gal 2:16 is "the principal scope" of the letter, the term "scope" indicating the aim, intent, or central purpose of the text.[25] If the scope concerns ceremonies, then the subsequent argument of the text should reflect this. Its failure to do so was one of the main indications for early Protestant interpreters that they were correct to understand the phrase the "works of the law" in terms of the inability of the law in its entirety to justify.

Of particular importance in enabling this inference to be drawn from the nature of the rest of Paul's argument in the letter was Gal 3:10, with its assertion that all those who rely on the works of the law are under a curse. For, as Deut 27:26 states, "Cursed is everyone who does not observe and obey all the things written in the book of the law." *The Rhemes New Testament* insists that Paul understands the curse to apply only to "such as commit great and damnable crimes, and so by grevous and

---

23. *Comm. Gal* 2:15, *CNTC* 11:38 = *OE* 16:49, 4–5.

24. *Comm Gal* 2:15, *CNTC* 11:39 = *OE* 16:50, 16–17.

25. *The Geneva Bible*, 87v. This translation was produced by English exiles in Geneva during the reign of Queen Mary but subsequent editions were printed in England. On the term "scope" see Gerald T. Sheppard, "Between Reformation and Modern Commentary: The Perception of the Scope of Biblical Books," in William Perkins, *A Commentary on Galatians*, ed. Gerald T. Sheppard (New York: Pilgrim Press, 1989), xlviii–lxxvii.

mortal transgressions wholly break God's precepts."[26] Those who commit minor sins are not cursed and so again there was a distinction made within the law. For Erasmus, the point was that "the law does not depend on faith but on the observance of prescribed ceremonies."[27] Protestant interpreters, however, emphasized the use of the word "all" so that everyone who does not perfectly perform the whole law falls under the curse. Perfect obedience would justify, but there are none who are perfectly obedient and so all are under the curse (see 3.3). As Calvin argues, "Notice these words very carefully, they do not say 'Cursed is the one who has rejected the law and has altogether disobeyed it,' but rather, cursed is he who fails to observe every jot and tittle of it."[28] The consequence that the works of law must include both ceremonial and moral aspects is forcefully expressed from the pulpit by Heinrich Bullinger in a sermon preached around the year 1550:

> Now unless we do by the deeds of the law understand the morals, as well as the ceremonials, I do not see how his proof can hang to that which went before. For he saith expressly, "In all the things which are written in the book of the law to do them." Now who knoweth not that the ceremonials were not written alone, but that the morals were written also?[29]

This specific argument about Gal 3:10 is often then strengthened by the drawing in of other texts where Paul seems to make or imply a general contrast between the law and faith. In discussing 3:18, with its opposition between inheritance by law and inheritance by promise, Calvin writes that Paul "asserts that salvation by the law and by the promise are contraries. Who will dare to expound this only of ceremonies

---

26. *The Rhemes New Testament*, 503.

27. *CWE* 42:110 = *LB* 7:953E. Interestingly, Erasmus seems very conscious of the problem of the word "all." His response is not to deny that "all" means "all" but to deny that perfect observance of the law would grant righteousness before God. Precisely because the works of the law are ceremonies, perfect observance of them would merely grant righteousness before men and freedom from the fear of punishment by civil authorities in this life.

28. Calvin, *Sermons on Galatians*, 264 = *CO* 50:494 (Sermon 17). He here calls for support on Jas 2:20, "For whoever keeps the whole law but fails in one point has become accountable for all of it."

29. Bullinger, "Sermon VIII," 248 (in *The Third Decade*) = *HBW* 3.1:383–419 (390, 10–13).

when Paul comprehends under it whatever opposes the free promise?"[30] Calvin's logic asserts that if the term "law" is used in such a contrast without verbal qualification and without indication that anything other than the law as a whole is in view, then similar contrasts using the phrase "works of the law" are unlikely to refer to the ceremonial parts of the law alone. Other relevant Pauline texts can be drawn in, and Calvin here makes reference to the parallel antithesis between inheritance by law and promise in Rom 4:14. However, any general contrast between law and faith can be used to make a similar point and Protestant interpreters constructed medleys of texts that served to demonstrate that Paul's polemic is not against ceremonies alone. Vermigli concluded his survey with Gal 3:10, but he had already employed texts from each of the first six chapters of Romans, and several other Pauline letters, providing along the way a more substantial discussion of Rom 7:7 and 11:6.[31] Along with all other early Protestant interpreters he was convinced that Paul intends universal antitheses between the entire law and faith, not restricted ones between ceremonies and faith. To say that justification is not by works of the law is to say that meritorious human deeds do not number among its causes.[32]

---

30. *Comm. Gal* 3:18, *CNTC* 11:59 = *OE* 16:76, 4–6.

31. Peter Martyr Vermigli, *Predestination and Justification*, 115–19 = *In Epistolam S. Pauli ad Romanos D. Petri Martyris Vermilii*, 529–31.

32. Brian Lugioyo, *Martin Bucer's Doctrine of Justification: Reformation Theology and Early Modern Irenicism* (Oxford: Oxford University Press, 2011), 37–102, suggests that Bucer again provides a partial exception among early Protestant commentators on this point. He conceives justification both as declarative and effective, and the latter embraces the works of the believer. Such works are a secondary efficient cause of justification enfolded within the primary cause of God's electing grace: "the works of a believer are accepted by God as worthy of merit not because they are so in themselves but because, first, God has decreed them to be such and, second, they are his very works in the believer" (95). Bucer thus remains much closer to Augustine's exegetical grammar than do the other Reformers, but he nevertheless breaks in significant ways with medieval appropriations of Augustine. Bucer has no place for habits of grace, ascribing the works of the believer to the activity of the Holy Spirit. He also insists that God's rewards always remain fundamentally disproportionate to the reality of the believer's works. They are rewarded because God has covenanted to do so. Thus all Christian merit is congruous and condign merit is simply impossible. This is not a theory of double justification in the sense that grace and works are understood both to be formal causes of justification, but works are allowed a place as a secondary cause that itself stems from grace.

4.2. Grace

Alongside their rejection of any role for human deeds as an efficient cause of justification, the Reformers' Pauline exegesis is also marked by a rejection of the concept of infused grace. Rather than something infused into human beings, given by God gradually to change them, grace (χάρις) is understood as a disposition in God determining God's actions towards people of faith. Grace is God's favor (*favor*) or mercy (*misericordia*) and, as such, a shorthand for the divine desire to forgive sins on the basis of Christ's saving sacrifice. At Rom 5:2, where Paul speaks of the grace in which he and the Roman believers stand, Melanchthon comments that the word here really means "gratuitous mercy—the remission of sins and imputation of righteousness."[33] At Col 1:2 where "grace" is used as a greeting, Melanchthon says that "Grace means simply the forgiveness of sins, or God's favour."[34] Hundreds of similar comments could be collected from a wide variety of early Protestant interpreters. There is also a clear impact on translation. In 1525, Tyndale uses "favour" to translate χάρις six times, especially at crucial points in Rom 4 and 5.[35] Such favor is understood as free (*gratis*), which the Reformers take to mean that the causes of God's gracious disposition do not in any respect lie outside of God with meritorious human deeds.

This does not mean that all occurrences of "grace" are forced into a linguistic straitjacket. The same interpreters are very much aware of the wide semantic range of the term. Bullinger even draws his congregation's attention to this by including a brief survey of alternative meanings in a sermon:

> The word "grace" is diversely used in the holy scriptures, even as it is in profane writings also. For in the Bible it signifieth thanksgiving, and also a benefit, and alms; as 2 Cor viii. Moreover, it signifieth praise and recompence, as in that place where the apostle saith: 'If, when ye do well, ye are afflicted, and yet do bear it; that is praiseworthy before God.' It doth also signify faculty and licence; as when we

33. Melanchthon, *Commentary on Romans*, 124 = CR 15:613.

34. Philip Melanchthon, *Paul's Letter to the Colossians*, trans. D. C. Parker (Sheffield: Almond Press, 1989), 31–32 = MSA 4:213, 32–33.

35. Rom 4:4, 16; 5:2, 15, 17; 11:6. In 1534 Tyndale replaces "favour" with "grace" in all instances except Rom 4:4 and 4:16. *The Great Bible* (1539) 1540 also uses "favour" at 4:4 and 4:16, while *The Geneva Bible* (1560) uses it at 4:4 alone.

say, that one hath gotten grace to teach and execute an office. For the apostle saith that he received grace; and immediately, to expound his own meaning, he addeth, to execute the office of an apostle. Moreover the gifts of God are called grace, because they are given gratis, and freely bestowed without looking for of any recompense.[36]

Only after this does Bullinger go on to discuss justifying grace as divine favor or mercy. Calvin notes that "the grace of God" in 1 Cor 1:4 refers clearly to the spiritual gifts the Corinthian believers have received: "For the word grace means here, not the favour of God, but, by metonymy, the gifts which he freely lavishes upon men."[37] He also refuses to construe the reference at Rom 6:14 to being not under law but under grace as narrowly concerning divine favor, taking it to include not only justification but also "the sanctification of the Spirit, by whom He (God) forms us anew to good works."[38]

Yet alongside such recognition of diversity in meaning stands a passionate insistence that in key texts relating to justification, Paul uses the term "grace" to refer to gratuitous divine favor. The textual basis for this is above all Rom 3:24, where Paul says that all who believe are justified by God's grace "freely" (δωρεάν, the accusative form of δωρεά, another Greek noun meaning "gift," but here used as an adverb and translated by the Vulgate as *gratis*). It is this qualification or further defining of grace that the Reformers find significant in ruling out human cooperation with grace in justification. In his treatment of grace in the 1543 edition of *Loci Communes*, Melanchthon comments that "This exclusive particle means that reconciliation is given for the sake of the Son of God, the Mediator, and not because of our worthiness, not because of our merits, not because of our virtues or deeds."[39] A decade later,

---

36. Heinrich Bullinger, "Sermon I," in *Bullinger's Decades: The Fourth Decade*, ed. Thomas Harding, The Parker Society 9 (Cambridge: Cambridge University Press, 1851), 6–7 = HBW 3.1: 491–522 (494, 19-26). The texts alluded to but not named here are 1 Pet. 2:20 and Rom 1:5.

37. *Comm. 1 Cor 1:4*, CNTC 9, 21 = CO 49:310.

38. *Comm. Rom 6:14*, CNTC 8, 131 = OE 13:127, 15–16. See similarly, Peter Martyr Vermigli, *Most Learned and Fruitful Commentaries upon the Epistle of S. Paul to the Romanes*, 152a-b = *In Epistolam S. Pauli ad Romanos D. Petri Martyris Vermilii*, 211: "Grace, as touching this place, signifieth two things: first, the forgeuenes of sinnes by imputing of righteousness through Christ: secondlye the gifts of the holy ghost, and the renuing of our strengths."

39. Philip Melanchthon, *Loci Communes (1543)*, 92 = CR 21:753.

Martin Chemnitz provides a brief philological analysis of the adverb and suggests that it appears in Rom 3:24 precisely in order to counter alternative possible definitions of "grace." He points to the Septuagint version of Gen 39:4, where "The text says of Joseph: 'He found grace in the sight of Potiphar.' But there is the added note 'because he was a prosperous man,' that is, on account of the eminent gifts which he noticed in Joseph he loved him and made him great."[40] Potiphar's grace, he argues, was based on qualities possessed by the recipient. Therefore, it is the addition of "freely" that shows that in Rom 3:23 Paul is *not* thinking of this kind of usage of grace but instead intends something entirely gratuitous.

In a context where infused grace and cooperation with it was central to traditional soteriology, and in which the sacramental system of the church was one of the principal means by which such grace was mediated, there could scarcely be a more incendiary exegetical conclusion. It also represents a fundamental rupture in the history of reception. Despite all the subsidiary issues on which the opinions of the Reformers constituted a recovery of Augustine, here they broke decisively with him. The origins of this break lie in surprising places. Although Erasmus would not have supported the Reformers' conclusions about grace, they originate in his careful philological work on the term. In the *Annotations* published to accompany his 1516 edition of the Greek New Testament, Erasmus noted at Rom 1:5 ("we have received grace and apostleship") that "grace" can have various meanings including "sometimes 'favour,' for example, 'you have found *gratiam* [favour] with God.'"[41] This reference to Luke 1:30 and the annunciation to Mary is significant since the *Annotations* to Luke 1:28 argue that the Vulgate translation of the term of address "favored one" or "beloved" (κεχαριτωμένη) as "full of grace" (*gratia plena*) was in error.[42] Erasmus found himself under fierce attack from the future Archbishop of York, Edward Lee, and subsequently defended his translation, diffusing the threat it posed to Marian devotion by insisting that it did not undermine the belief that Mary was "full of grace" since "what is the grace that fills pious people if not the love

---

40. Martin Chemnitz, *Examination of the Council of Trent Vol. 1*, trans. Fred Kramer (St. Louis: Concordia, 1971), 496.

41. *CWE* 56:19 = Desiderius Erasmus, *Annotations on the New Testament: Acts, Romans, I and II Corinthians: Facsimile of the Final Latin Text with All Earlier Variants*, ed. Anne Reeve and M. A. Screech (Leiden: Brill, 1990), 338.

42. *ASD* VI-5:458–59 (368–404). No English translation yet exists of the *Annotations* on Luke.

with which God embraces them and through which he draws them to himself."[43]

While this defense suggests that Erasmus's intention was not to attack the traditional view of grace, he could not control how his readers interpreted his work. He also left further hostages to fortune in his *Annotations* on Rom 5:16 and 5:20. In the first he notes that the Vulgate erred in translating Paul's reference to "gift" (χάρισμα) as *gratia* (grace) and not as *donum* (gift) "unless we suppose that 'gift' and 'grace' are entirely the same."[44] He also makes the same criticism at other places in the Pauline texts. In the second, Erasmus approves the Vulgate's choice of *gratia* for χάρις but again distinguishes "grace" from "gift."[45] Erasmus appears to think of these as translation issues rather than theological ones. In his *Paraphrases* of the New Testament he employs a wide range of terms for χάρισμα, including *favor Dei* (the favor of God).[46] But others were to regard the distinction between "gift" and "grace" as theologically crucial. These included Philip Melanchthon, whose opinion on grace changed rapidly under the impact of Erasmus's work. Both Erasmus's understanding that grace can denote divine favor and his distinction between grace and gift influenced Melanchthon when he began to deliver a lecture series on Romans at Wittenberg in May 1520 and had the new 1519 second edition of Erasmus's New Testament (Greek text, Latin translation, and annotations) printed for his students.[47] In his earlier lectures on Matthew, begun in the autumn of 1519 and by the spring of 1520 only recently com-

---

43. *CWE* 72:136 = *ASD* IX-4:124-25 (466-88). For a full account of the debate see Erika Rummel, *Erasmus' Annotations on the New Testament: From Philologist to Theologian* (Toronto: University of Toronto Press, 1986), 167-71.

44. *CWE* 56:170 = Erasmus, *Annotations on the New Testament: Acts – Romans – I and II Corinthians*, 375.

45. *CWE* 56:172 = Erasmus, *Annotations on the New Testament: Acts – Romans – I and II Corinthians*, 375.

46. Robert D. Sider, "Χάρις and Derivatives in the Biblical Scholarship of Erasmus," in *Diakonia: Essays in Honor of Robert T. Meyer*, ed. Thomas Halton and Joseph P. Williman (Washington, DC: Catholic University of America Press, 1986), 259.

47. I rely here and in what follows on the careful documentation of the likely sequence of events in Melanchthon's changing understanding of grace provided by Rolf Schäfer, "Melanchthon's Interpretation of Romans 5.15: His Departure from the Augustinian Concept of Grace Compared to Luther's," in *Philip Melanchthon (1497-1560) and the Commentary*, ed. Timothy J. Wengert and M. Patrick Graham (Sheffield: Academic Press, 1997), 79-104. Even if the dating of Melanchthon's shift to mid-1520 is not correct, there is clear evidence that it had taken place by February 1521 when grace as favor appears in one of his polemical tracts (83).

pleted, Melanchthon had expressed a traditional view of grace. Yet in his new lecture series Melanchthon argues for grace as favor and employs as evidence for that understanding the distinction between grace and gift. The traditional view of grace makes grace into a gift, but Melanchthon articulates what was to become the usual Protestant view of justifying grace. Although closely connected, grace and gift are not the same. Grace motivates divine gift and assuredly leads to gift, but is not itself the gift and, unlike gift, remains as something in God and not in human beings.

In making this distinction between grace and gift, Melanchthon was to appeal repeatedly to Rom 5:15 where Paul speaks of "the grace of God and the free gift in the grace of the one man, Jesus Christ." Despite his comments on 5:16 and 5:20 Erasmus's *Annotations* say nothing concerning this verse. However, once he had distinguished grace and gift in the very same context, it is not surprising that Melanchthon's attention should focus on it. The first 1521 edition of his theology textbook *Loci Communes* states simply that "Paul in Rom 5:15 distinguishes 'grace' from the 'gift of grace'. . . . He calls grace the favor of God in which he embraced Christ and because of Christ, all the saints. Therefore, because he favors, God cannot help pouring out his gifts on those on whom he has had mercy."[48] Melanchthon will continue to refer to the verse in all subsequent editions of the textbook and to propose this interpretation in all editions of his *Commentary on Romans*. As a humanist scholar concerned with analysis of the rhetorical structure of the letter, Melanchthon found the distinction between gift and grace in Romans all the more compelling.[49] He regarded 5:12–8:39 as a distinct section within Romans. Whereas Paul had previously set down propositions (e.g., Rom 3:9, 3:20, 3:22) and argued against their opposites, he now provides analysis of the terms that have been crucial to his propositions.[50] The very purpose of Rom 5:12–8:39 is therefore not to argue directly against opposite positions

---

48. Philip Melanchthon, "Loci Communes Theologici," in *Melanchthon and Bucer*, 87-88 = MSA 2:86, 29 - 87, 5; CR 21:158.

49. On Melanchthon's approach to commentary on ancient texts see John R. Schneider, "The Hermeneutics of Commentary: Origins of Melanchthon's Integration of Rhetoric into Dialectic," in *Philip Melanchthon (1497-1560) and the Commentary*, 20-47, and Manfred Hoffmann, "Rhetoric and Dialectic in Erasmus's and Melanchthon's Interpretation of John's Gospel," in *Philip Melanchthon (1497-1560) and the Commentary*, 48-78. Melanchthon's rhetorical approach to interpreting Romans is discussed at more length later (see 6.1).

50. Melanchthon, *Commentary on Romans*, 131-32 = CR 15:621-22.

but to analyze the terms "sin," "law," and "grace." If in 5:15 Paul speaks both of "grace" and of "the gift in the grace," this cannot be redundancy for the sake of emphasis but must represent a significant distinction: "Here it does not have to do with a piece of rhetoric, in which a reader or listener is to be convinced and in which pathos, ornament and figures of speech can surpass logical precision. On the contrary, the matter is depicted briefly and precisely, in scientific terms."[51]

This kind of approach to biblical interpretation in which rhetorical analysis is highly emphasized was not that of Luther, who had not received a humanist education. Nevertheless he moved to adopt both the general definition of grace as favor and Melanchthon's emphasis on the distinction between grace and gift at Rom 5:15. In 1515–1516 Luther had specifically identified grace and gift: "But 'the grace of God' and 'the gift' are the same thing, namely the very righteousness which is freely given to us through Christ."[52] In the *Commentary on Galatians* (1516–1517/1519), despite his new understanding that works are not part of the basis of righteousness, Luther's comment on Gal 3:7 reveals an explicit rejection of the understanding of grace as favor: "For just as God loves in very fact, not in word only, so, too, He is favorably disposed with the thing that is present, not only with the word."[53] God's favor is here explicitly something present in the believer and not solely a disposition in God. Yet in his tract *Against Latomus*, written at the Wartburg in 1521, Luther makes explicit use of Rom 5:15 and the distinction between grace and gift:

> A righteous and faithful man doubtless has both the grace and the gift. Grace makes him wholly pleasing so that his person is wholly accepted, and there is no place for wrath in him anymore, but the gift heals from sin and from all his corruption of body and soul. . . . Everything is forgiven through grace, but as yet not everything is healed through the gift. The gift has been infused. The leaven has been added to the mixture. It works so as to purge away the sin for which a person has already been forgiven, and to drive out the evil guest for whose expulsion permission has been given.[54]

51. Schäfer, "Melanchthon's Interpretation of Rom 5:15," 96.
52. *LW* 25:306 = *WA* 56:318, 28–29.
53. *LW* 27:252 = *WA* 2:511, 20–21.
54. *LW* 32:229 = *WA* 8:107, 13–24.

It is easy but erroneous to read Luther as here aligning grace with justification by faith and the gift with subsequent renewal. However, he has already defined the gift as "faith in Christ,"[55] and is able therefore to say that "A person neither pleases, nor has grace, except on account of the gift which labors in this way to cleanse from sin."[56] God graciously justifies because a person has faith but such justifying faith is itself identified with the gift. Grace and gift are mutually conditioning rather than sequential and, despite Luther's elimination of meritorious works as one of its efficient causes, justification is not confined solely to grace as opposed to gift.[57] Thus, as always, Luther is a creative theologian. He takes Melanchthon's exegesis and uses it in his own way. Melanchthon understood the gift in Rom 5:15 as the Holy Spirit, and this difference concerning gift will prove significant when we explore their individual perspectives on justification and participation in Christ (see 6.7). Luther did not use the new definition of grace to separate justification and renewal in the way that became typical in later Protestant interpretations. Nevertheless, Luther had made a decisive shift in his understanding of grace by 1521. The flow of influence was from Erasmus to Melanchthon to Luther. Throughout the remainder of the sixteenth century and long afterwards, Rom 5:15 and its distinction between grace and gift were cited by Protestant interpreters as evidence against understanding grace as infused and for understanding grace as favor.[58] For Luther, it even

55. *LW* 32:228 = *WA* 8:106, 25-26.

56. *LW* 32:229 = *WA* 8:107, 33-35.

57. For a full discussion of the relationship between Luther's view of justification and his interpretation of this verse see Simo Peura, "Christ as Favor and Gift: The Challenge of Luther's Understanding of Justification," in *Union with Christ: The New Finnish Interpretation of Luther*, ed. Carl E. Braaten and Robert W. Jenson (Grand Rapids: Eerdmans, 1998), 42-69. Ragnar Skottene, *Grace and Gift: An Analysis of a Central Motif in Martin Luther's 'Rationis Latomianae Confutatio'* (Frankfurt: Peter Lang, 2008), 131: "The intimate relationship between *gratia* and *donum upwards* in relation to God as well as *downwards* in confrontation with sin confirms the organic connection between imputative (forensic) and effective (recreating) justification in Luther's theology." Skottene, 103, also points out that despite the simultaneity and mutuality of grace and gift, it is grace that has the conceptual priority for Luther because the gift comes to human beings rooted in the grace of Christ: "Faith has nothing in itself, but everything outside itself—in God's grace." Luther and Melanchthon's perspectives on this issue in Rom 5:15 will be further explored later (6.7).

58. Calvin and Peter Martyr Vermigli provide examples from the early Reformed tradition. For Calvin see *Comm. Rom* 5:15, *CNTC* 8:115 = *OE* 13:112, 10-19 and for Vermigli see *Most Learned and Fruitful Commentaries upon the Epistle of S. Paul to the Romanes*, 115b = *In Epistolam S. Pauli ad Romanos D. Petri Martyris Vermilii*, 158-59. At the very end

became a benediction with which to end a letter: "May the grace and the gift be with you."[59]

4.3. Faith

If the new view of grace proposed by the Reformers was perhaps the most fundamental of their departures from traditional interpretations, of no less overall significance was their perspective on faith. They argue that in many Pauline texts concerning justification the Greek noun "faith" (πίστις) bears the sense of "trust" (*fiducia*) in response to God's promises. In trusting divine promises sinners must accept that they come before God empty-handed and that their hope is based entirely upon the gifts of God that can only come to them from outside the self. In this sense, faith is primarily receptive. However, it is not passively receptive. Faith is *active* and impacts every aspect of a person's existence. As Luther famously defined faith in the *Preface to Romans* (1522) of his German Bible: "It kills the old Adam and makes us altogether different men, in heart and spirit and mind and powers; and brings with it the Holy Spirit. O it is a living, busy, active, mighty thing, this faith."[60] By contrast, in medieval interpretation the necessity for faith to be formed by love in order to justify was based upon an understanding of *fides*, the usual Latin translation of πίστις, as denoting primarily intellectual assent to the truth of the gospel. It seemed obvious to medieval interpreters that intellectual assent alone does not justify a person. If faith then consists of such consent, it needs the shaping and forming power of love to be alive and to justify. But once faith was defined by early Protestant exegetes as trusting and active, the restriction of the sense of the term to intellectual assent disappeared and with it the necessity for faith to be formed by love.[61] As Melanchthon expresses it:

> Obviously, when Paul says, "since we are justified through faith, we have peace with God" [Rom 5:1], he speaks of a faith which brings

---

of the sixteenth century, Perkins, *Galatians*, 7 still relies upon on Rom 5:15 to sustain a distinction between grace and gift.

59. *LW* 49: no. 202, 264-67 (267) = *WA* BR 5: no. 1527, 236-37 (237, 19-20). The letter is to Nicholas Hausmann, pastor at Zwickau, and probably dates from early February 1530.

60. *LW* 35:370 = *WA* DB 7:11, 7-10.

61. For exploration of the exegetical basis of the concept of faith formed by love in Gal 5:6, see the discussion of Aquinas (2.3.1).

comfort and peace to the heart. This peace is not just knowledge, for the devils know, and it causes them to tremble and flee from Christ; they are certain that God will punish them.[62]

Thus the Reformers and their opponents agree that Jas 2:19 ("Even the demons believe—and shudder") shows that a knowledge of the historical truth of the gospel does not save. But whereas this leads one side to the conclusion that faith must be formed by love, it leads the other side to the conclusion that faith is not to be understood simply in terms of historical knowledge.[63]

Nevertheless, as with the word "grace," the Reformers were well aware of the wide semantic range of the term. They did not wish to deny the significance of knowledge of the events of incarnation and redemption, but rather to deny that this was all that Paul intended by the term "faith." Melanchthon understood faith as including trust and knowledge, stating that "Faith embraces both trust in the mercy of God and knowledge of the historical events, that is, it looks to Christ, of whom it is necessary to know that He is the Son of the eternal God, crucified for us, raised again etc."[64] Although on this topic the Reformers seem initially to have influenced Erasmus rather than the other way around, here again, his philological work provided the ammunition for opinions that he would not entirely endorse. He comments on the phrase "from faith to faith" in Rom 1:17:

> But sacred literature frequently uses these words loosely, for it often uses *fides* [faith] for *fiducia* [trust] in God almost in the sense of hope; sometimes for the belief or conviction by which we assent to the things handed down to us about God—by which even the demons believe. Sometimes the word *faith* [*fides*] embraces all these meanings: that assent to the truth both of the historical record and

62. Philip Melanchthon, *Melanchthon on Christian Doctrine*, trans. Clyde L. Manschreck (New York: Oxford University Press, 1965), 158 = CR 22:330. This is the 1555 German edition of *Loci Communes*.

63. Yet again, a partial exception here is Bucer, whose insistence that mental convictions determine affections and actions leads him to deny the meaningfulness of these distinctions between different aspects of faith. Right knowledge will lead to right actions; faith will lead to deeds of love. See Lugioyo, *Martin Bucer's Doctrine of Justification*, 87–90.

64. Melanchthon, *Loci Communes (1543)*, 87 = CR 21:743.

of the promises, and the *trust* [*fiducia*] that arises from his omnipotent goodness, not without the hope, that is, the expectation, of the promises.[65]

The tone of Erasmus's comment is careful and even-handed. Yet, his refusal to restrict the meaning of the term "faith" to knowledge of the historical events of the gospel makes it difficult to hear his exposition as a ringing endorsement of the necessity for faith to be formed by love in order to justify.[66] Indeed, it is precisely such a sense of the variety of meanings of πίστις ("faith") that the Reformers will sometimes use to defend their position. When opponents appealed to 1 Cor 13:2—where Paul derides faith that can move mountains but that is without love as nothing—the Reformers repeatedly insist that the faith discussed here is not justifying faith.[67]

---

65. *CWE* 56:43-44 = Erasmus, *Annotations on the New Testament: Acts - Romans - I and II Corinthians*, 345. Erasmus added the entirety of this comment to his *Annotations* for the first time in 1527 several years after Luther etc. had begun to advocate trust as a primary component of faith. Greta Grace Kroeker, *Erasmus in the Footsteps of Paul: A Pauline Theologian* (Toronto: University of Toronto Press, 2011), argues that careful attention to changes made to later editions of his *Annotations* and his *Paraphrases* indicates that, after the end of his public controversy with Luther in 1527, Erasmus became less concerned with his *Philosophia Christi*. Under the influence of Paul's texts and their patristic interpretation, Erasmus developed a theology centered on issues of grace and justification. While acknowledging that significant differences remained, Kroeker argues that the older Erasmus was a Pauline interpreter whose concerns were much closer to those of Luther and Melanchthon than earlier in his career. On the whole the evidence presented supports a deeper engagement by the older Erasmus with the exegesis of the Fathers rather than an embrace of reforming positions incompatible with Erasmus's continuing commitment to the Catholic Church. However, Erasmus does seem to make faith more central to his interpretation of Romans and to understand it more frequently as trust (*fiducia*). See, for example, not only this extensive annotation on Rom 1:17 (109-14), but also the addition of the phrase *ac fiduciam* (and trust) to the 1532 paraphrase of Rom 3:22 (102-5).

66. Numerous texts deal with the objection raised by Catholic opponents that to reject faith formed by love was shockingly to undercut any need for holiness of life. Again and again it is insisted that although justification is by faith alone, genuine faith will inevitably express itself in works. For a discussion see James R. Payton Jr., *Getting the Reformation Wrong: Correcting Some Misunderstandings* (Downers Grove, IL: InterVarsity Press, 2010), 116-31.

67. For example, see Bullinger, "Sermon IX," 334 (in *The Third Decade*)= *HBW* 3.1: 419-50 (437, 20-23) "That faith doth not comprehend Christ wholly, but only the power in shewing of miracles: and therefore it may be sometime in an unjust man and an hypo-

The foremost biblical example of justifying faith as trust in God's promises is, of course, that of Abraham, as presented by Paul in Gal 3 and Rom 4. Luther's comments on Abraham's faith in his *Lectures on Romans* (1515-1516) and his *Commentary on Galatians* (1516-1517/1519) are curiously flat, doing little more than establishing that Abraham was indeed a true example of faith. Even in *The Freedom of a Christian* (September 1520), a text in which a rich and multi-faceted concept of faith bursts forth,[68] Abraham's faith plays a restricted, albeit significant role. In believing God's promises Abraham considers and confesses God to be truthful and in so doing gives God the worship that is God's due. Faith justifies because in accepting God's promises it acknowledges and honors God as God. Faith lets God be God. Paul's statement in Rom 4:20 that Abraham "grew strong in his faith as he gave glory to God" was one of the biblical bases upon which this emphasis found an enduring place in early Protestant exegesis. Calvin is typical of many when he makes this aspect of faith paradigmatic of true worship:

> no greater honour can be given to God than by sealing His truth by our faith. On the other hand, no greater insult can be shown to Him than by rejecting the grace which He offers us, or by detracting from the authority of His Word. For this reason the main thing in the worship of God is to embrace His promises with obedience. True religion begins with faith.[69]

---

crite; as it was in Judas Iscariot, to whom the faith of miracles profited nothing, because he was without justifying faith, which faith is never without, but itself engendereth, charity."

68. This tract certainly seemed to Melanchthon to be the most significant and accessible summary of Luther's teaching on faith from the early stages of the Reformation since a little over a year later in December 1521 he directs readers of the first edition of his *Loci Communes* to *The Freedom of a Christian* for further instruction on the nature of faith. See Melanchthon, "Loci Communes Theologici," 93 = *MSA* 2:94, 13-15; *CR* 21:164. Berndt Hamm, "Why did 'Faith' become for Luther the Central Concept of the Christian Life?," in *The Reformation of Faith in the Context of Late Medieval Theology and Piety*, ed. Robert J. Bast (Leiden: Brill, 2004), 153-78, argues that a significant break with medieval conceptions of faith can already be found in Luther's *First Lectures on the Psalms* (1513-1515). However, Hamm does not dispute that Luther subsequently developed his view of faith much further and this can be seen particularly clearly if one compares the references to faith in his *Commentary on Galatians* (1516-1517/1519) with those in his *Commentary on Galatians* (1531/1535).

69. *Comm. Rom* 4:20, *CNTC* 8:99 = *OE* 13:96, 23-28.

Yet this emphasis on acknowledging and honoring God by believing God's promises does not stand alone for long, either in Luther's own writings or in those of others. Paul's insistence that Abraham was justified while uncircumcised (Rom 4:10) prompts Luther to argue in his *Preface to Romans* (1522) that "if the work of circumcision contributed nothing to his righteousness, though God had commanded it and it was a good work of obedience, then surely no other good work will contribute anything to righteousness."[70] Paul's argument is thus construed not merely as chronological—i.e., Abraham was justified before he was circumcised, which might arguably leave open the possibility of a contribution from subsequent works—but also as qualitative—i.e., if such a preeminent work as circumcision does not justify, then no other works whatsoever can contribute to justification.[71] More significantly still, the incredible nature of the divine promise of a son is emphasized. Abraham received what was not possible humanly speaking. He walked by faith and not by sight (2 Cor 5:7):

> Abraham is justified not because he believes this or that promise of God but because he stands ready to believe *any* promise of God, no matter how violently it may contradict the judgments of his own prudential reason and common sense. Abraham's faith is not so much an act (e.g., believing that Sarah will become pregnant in spite of her advanced years) as a disposition (e.g., believing that whatever God promises, however startling, he is able to perform).[72]

This emphasis on faith as believing in defiance of reason or common sense demonstrates that faith trusts however discouraging its circumstances. When commenting on Gen 15:6 in the late 1530s Luther noted that, "In this passage no mention is made of any preparation for grace, of any faith formed through works, or of any preceding disposition. This, however, is mentioned: Abraham was in the midst of sins, doubts, and fears, and was exceedingly troubled in spirit."[73] And as Calvin was

---

70. *LW* 35:374 = *WA* DB 7:16, 7–10.

71. Paul's Greek actually speaks of Abraham "being in circumcision" or "being in uncircumcision" with his justification occurring when in a state of uncircumcision, i.e., Luther's qualitative point is more exegetically defensible than most English translations might suggest.

72. Steinmetz, "Abraham and the Reformation," 41.

73. *LW* 3:20–21 = *WA* 42:563, 13–16.

to say, again of Rom 4:20, "Our circumstances are all in opposition to the promises of God. . . . What then are we to do? We must close our eyes, disregard ourselves and all things connected with us, so that nothing may hinder or prevent us from believing that God is true."[74] The first consequence of this commitment to trusting reception of divine promises in the face of experiences that appear to contradict these promises is an emphasis on the certainty of faith or assurance. Sin and death may lead people to doubt salvation, but faith says that those who believe are justified and that God is not wrathful but benevolent in attitude towards them. This stands in sharp contrast to the insistence of the Reformers' opponents that it is only possible to be certain that God will justify the elect but not possible to be certain whether one numbers among them. The Reformers argue that the basic issue is whether the promises of God contained in Scripture are reliable. They do not understand how Paul's assertions that the Spirit enables believers as children of God and heirs of a divine inheritance to cry "Abba! Father!" (Rom 8:15-17; Gal 4:6-7) can be consistent with uncertainty about justification: "For whoever doubts the grace of God toward him this way must necessarily doubt the promises of God and therefore the will of God, as well as the birth, suffering, death, and resurrection of Christ. There is no greater blasphemy against God than to deny the promises of God and God Himself, Christ, etc."[75]

In relation to assurance, discussion by the Reformers of Abraham's example often draws on Rom 4 with reference to Heb 11:1.[76] The text in Hebrews says that "Faith is the *hypostasis* of things hoped for, the conviction of things not seen." Historical-critical commentators still debate the correct translation and interpretation of the noun ὑπόστασις (*hypostasis*), and the Reformers also are not unified about this, offering variously "substance" (*substantia*), "possession" (*possessio*), and "assurance/

74. *Comm. Rom 4:20, CNTC* 8:99 = *OE* 13:96, 11-18.

75. *LW* 26:385 = *WA* 40:587, 11-15. For a full discussion of the Reformers' interpretations of these texts, see Schreiner, *Are You Alone Wise?*, 37-77. In this quotation Luther has so welded together faith as trust in God's promises and faith as assent to the historical truth of the gospel that to doubt the promises is also to doubt the historical truth.

76. It should be remembered that in the sixteenth century the Pauline authorship of Hebrews was seriously debated. The trend is towards recognition that Paul did not write the letter, but perfectly serious biblical interpreters could hold the opinion that he did. For example, although rejected by Calvin, Paul's authorship was accepted by Bullinger and, although they changed their minds, Luther and Erasmus both at one stage accepted it.

confidence" (*fiducia*).[77] Nevertheless, even if *substantia* or *possessio* are preferred, these terms are interpreted in a manner that emphasizes their relationship to certain trust in divine promises.[78] The rest of Heb 11 is ripe with examples of faith in promises not yet fulfilled. The noun ὑπόστασις is interpreted by the Reformers in relation to them. The contemporary relevance in the sixteenth century of this strong emphasis on trust and assurance for the Reformers and their followers is clear. Those who stake all on the truth of the evangelical gospel in defiance of the power and prestige of the Catholic Church trust as Abraham trusted.

Nevertheless, coordinating between texts to produce coherence and consistency in teaching could be complex. In his 1521 *Loci Communes* Melanchthon uses texts from Romans to insist that "Nothing, therefore, of our own works, however good they may seem or be, constitutes our righteousness. But FAITH alone in the mercy and grace of God in Christ Jesus is our RIGHTEOUSNESS."[79] Faith is trust in the promise of this gracious mercy and the first example that Melanchthon gives of such faith follows Heb 11:17-19 in pointing to the faith involved in Abraham's willingness to sacrifice Isaac: "What, then, did Abraham believe? Did he believe only in the existence of God? No! He believed also in the promise of God, and later he showed this faith in a singular way when he was on the verge of sacrificing his son. He did not have a doubt that God would

77. Individuals could also change their mind about this. Barbara Pitkin, *What Pure Eyes Could See: Calvin's Doctrine of Faith in Its Exegetical Context* (Oxford: Oxford University Press, 1999), 76-77, notes that after careful discussion of *hypostasis* as *substantia* in his 1549 *Hebrews* commentary, in the 1550 *Institutes* Calvin proposes *fiducia* as a translation. Melanchthon is a consistent advocate of "assurance/confidence" and he influences Luther in that direction despite Luther's earlier choice of *possessio* in his 1516-1517 lectures. See Kenneth Hagen, *A Theology of Testament in the Young Luther: The Lectures on Hebrews* (Leiden: E. J. Brill, 1974), 83-87.

78. See, for example, Martin Bucer, *The Common Places of Martin Bucer*, trans. D. F. Wright (Abingdon, Berkshire: Sutton Courtenay Press, 1971), 172: "Faith is rightly called the *hypostasis*, that is, the substance or reality, of things hoped for, and the certain intimation, as it were, of things that otherwise the human mind cannot comprehend. Once we are convinced by faith, with every doubt fully dispelled, of the reality of these true and eternal benefits in which stands our entire happiness, we will inevitably place our whole trust in the only God." Wright here translates a locus from the preface of Bucer's *Commentary on Romans* (1536). There are no modern critical editions of the commentary. See *Martin Bucer (1491-1551): Bibliographie*, ed. H. Pils, S. Ruderer, and P. Schaffrodt (Gütersloh: Gütersloher Verlag, 2005), no. 76 and no. 223 for details of the 16th-century Latin editions.

79. Melanchthon, "Loci Communes Theologici," 89 = *MSA* 2:88, 16-19; *CR* 21:159.

give him posterity even though this son died."[80] This example of the near sacrifice of Isaac may be effective as an argument against the concept of faith formed by love. Abraham's faith is not simply intellectual assent to the truth of God's existence but from the outset trusts God in relation to the deepest of the patriarch's human concerns. Melanchthon's comment is certainly also effective in dispelling the false notion that the Reformers held a passive notion of faith that deemphasized human actions, for it is Abraham's trust in God that almost propels him into otherwise unthinkable actions. Finally, Melanchthon's comment also fits well with Luther's statement about faith in the *Preface to Romans* (1522) that "It is impossible for it not to be doing good works incessantly. It does not ask whether good works are to be done, but before the question is asked, it has already done them and is constantly doing them."[81] Yet Melanchthon's interpretation also leaves certain hostages to fortune, especially given the use made by Jas 2:21 of the same episode. For it does not obviously contradict, and might even be held to support, the view that while justifying faith is essentially trust, there remains a causal role for subsequent works in justification precisely when actions express trust (a view that approximates, for example, to that of Erasmus).

It is notable that in the editions of *Loci Communes* from 1543 and 1555 the discussions of faith no longer employ the example of Abraham's willingness to sacrifice Isaac. In the *Apology of the Augsburg Confession* from 1530 it is specifically denied that Abraham was prepared to sacrifice Isaac "with the idea that this work was the payment and atoning sacrifice on account of which he would be regarded as righteous."[82] Melanchthon addresses the issue of Abraham's willingness to sacrifice Isaac at greater length in his *Commentary on Romans* (1540), denying that it contributed to his justification:

> Although a work by a believer has its praise, is necessary obedience, and becomes righteousness, it nevertheless does not possess worth

80. Melanchthon, "Loci Communes Theologici," 94 = *MSA* 2:94, 22–27; *CR* 21:164–65. Melanchthon returns to the sacrifice of Isaac several times in this *locus*. See 101–3.

81. *LW* 35:370 = *WA* DB 7:10, 10–12.

82. "Apology of the Augsburg Confession," in *The Book of Concord*, par. 209–10. Melanchthon was the author of the "Apology," but drew on the comments of colleagues. This translation is based on the octavo edition of September 1531, the revised version which Melanchthon himself preferred over the initial quarto edition of April/May 1531. *CR* 27:419–646 provides the Latin text of the quarto edition, and for this reason subsequent citations of the "Apology" are to the translation only.

so that a person may have remission of sins on account of the work itself and be righteous, that is, accepted to eternal life before God. It is necessary that a person first have forgiveness of sins and justification. Afterward, the obedience which has been begun is found pleasing, and is worship of God.[83]

This embodies what was to become the principal Protestant method of relating faith and works. Works are essential and their absence demonstrates the absence of justification, but they nevertheless are not an efficient cause of justification. As Luther puts it in the *Preface to Romans* (1522), although works do not justify, "good works emerge from faith itself ... it is impossible to separate works from faith, quite as impossible as to separate heat and light from fire."[84] Elsewhere he uses organic images, emphasizing works as the fruit of faith and ubiquitously quoting Matt 7:17, "every good tree bears good fruit." And, as Melanchthon's statement that a believer's work becomes righteousness suggests, the Reformers feel no need to deny that when using the noun δικαιοσύνη (righteousness) Paul often refers not to justifying righteousness granted apart from works but instead to the obedient behavior that emerges from justification. When in Rom 6:19 Paul urges his readers to present "your members as slaves to righteousness for sanctification," Calvin comments that "you should wholly forget sin and turn your whole heart to righteousness, into the service of which you have been brought."[85] At Phil 1:11, with its prayer that the readers be filled with "the fruits of righteousness," Calvin says bluntly that Paul desires "them to be fertile in good works, to the glory of God."[86] Luther insists that when Paul speaks of "the hope of righteousness" at Gal 5:6 it is an eschatological reference to the hope of future freedom from the sin that during their earthly lives clings to the flesh of those who have already been justified. In speaking of "faith working through love," Paul is therefore not indicating the need for faith to be formed by love in order to justify. Instead "he attributes the working itself to faith rather than to love. ... He makes love the tool through which faith works."[87]

Thus it is quite clear that for the Reformers, however much works might be inseparable from faith, justification is by faith *alone*. This can be

83. Melanchthon, *Commentary on Romans*, 109 = CR 15:598.
84. *LW* 35:369–71 = *WA* DB 7:7, 22 – 11, 23.
85. *Comm. Rom* 6:19, CNTC 8:133 = OE 13:129, 30–32.
86. *Comm. Phil* 1:11, CNTC 11:233 = OE 16:302, 32–33.
87. *LW* 27:29 = *WA* 40.2:36, 8–14.

seen clearly in comments on the contrast between faith and the "works of the law" in Gal 2:16. For Luther and for Calvin, the point is simply that Paul's use of an antithesis excludes any cooperation between faith and works in justification. "We have to ascribe either nothing or everything to faith or to works."[88] Others later added a grammatical argument. The particle ἐὰν μή usually translated "but" in the first part of the verse (NRSV: "a person is not justified by works of the law *but* through faith in Jesus Christ") can mean "except" in Greek and might yield the sense that no one can be justified by such works unless they are allied to faith in Christ. But this seems unlikely given the rest of the verse and Paul's statements about the works of the law elsewhere. Protestant commentators argued for the stronger contrast. Martin Chemnitz was not unusual in producing a list of other biblical examples where the particle excludes the preceding clause or clauses of the sentence. He concluded that "These are the exclusive particles commonly employed by Paul. We cannot express these more briefly and fittingly in our languages than through the little word *sola* ('only,' 'alone')."[89]

Despite this extensive common ground in understanding faith on the basis of the Pauline texts, some differences of emphasis do emerge. The Reformers' insistence on faith as trust (*fiducia*) in God's promises provides a powerful existential element in their Pauline interpretation. Yet, without rejecting this element, both Bucer and Calvin develop understandings of faith that emphasize the knowledge of God. If Melanchthon and Luther can insist that faith is not solely historical knowledge, they can insist that it is not solely trust. Bucer provides a preface on faith in his *Commentary on Romans* (1536) in which faith begins with knowledge of God's existence and God's providence. It is not possible to have faith without knowing what or who to have faith in, and so assent (*assensus*) to God's own testimony of his existence and care for creation is the first step. A further level of knowledge comes through assent to the gospel message about Christ, which Bucer identifies with certain persuasion (*persuasio*).[90] Only then does trust in God result, which expresses itself

88. *Comm. Gal* 2:16, CNTC 11:40 = OE 16:51, 18–19. See also LW 26:137 = WA 40.1:239, 12 – 242, 14.

89. Chemnitz, *Examination of the Council of Trent* vol. 1, 584.

90. Note also the similarity of Peter Martyr Vermigli, *Most Learned and Fruitful Commentaries upon the Epistle of S. Paul to the Romanes*, 62b = *In Epistolam S. Pauli ad Romanos D. Petri Martyris Vermilii*, 81: "Now it is meete to tell what fayth (*fides*) is: faith therefore is an assent (*assensus*), and that a firm assent to the words of God, obteyned

in love, and it does so on the basis of knowledge: "For a man's affections and conduct are determined in their entirety by his mental convictions."[91] As he considers faith to include trust as its highest element but not to be reducible to trust, Bucer is unsurprisingly content to translate πίστις ("faith") as *fides*.

So too is Calvin, for whom *fides* denotes both the objective content of faith and the subjective act of believing. His famous definition of faith in the *Institutes* makes trust in God's promises central but not all-encompassing: "Now we shall possess a right definition of faith if we say that faith is a firm and certain knowledge of the divine benevolence towards us, which, founded on the truth of the free promise in Christ, is both revealed to our minds and sealed on our hearts through the Holy Spirit."[92] Here trust is a very important aspect of faith as knowledge (*cognitio*), but faith is not simply equated with trust. As Barbara Pitkin demonstrates in a careful and detailed study, space is created here for understanding faith not only in relation to God's saving activity but also in relation to God's creative and providential activity.[93] Holding this understanding that faith relates to the whole of the Christian life, Calvin can insist that "faith lays hold of regeneration just as much as forgiveness of sins in Christ."[94] What remains clear, however, is that for all the Reformers the character of faith as trust stands at the forefront in relation to key Pauline texts on justification.

More significant differences occur among the Reformers in relation to the christological focus of faith, although these differences arise in the context of agreement upon some fundamental issues. All agree that it is not some human quality inherent to faith that means that it justifies.[95] In

---

not by reason or by naturall demonstration, but by the authority of the speaker, and by the power of the holy ghost."

91. Bucer, *The Common Places of Martin Bucer*, 177. The entirety of the preface on faith is here provided in English translation. For exposition of Bucer's argument, see Lugioyo, *Martin Bucer's Doctrine of Justification*, 80-90. It should be noted that the pattern of similarities and differences between Bucer and Calvin is itself subtle. Both highlight a cognitive element but one doubts that Calvin would agree that a person's affections and conduct are entirely determined by mental convictions.

92. *Institutes* 3.2.7 (551) = CO 2:403.

93. Pitkin, *What Pure Eyes Could See*, esp. 9-40 ("From Fiducia to Cognitio").

94. *Comm. 1 Cor* 1:30, CNTC 9:46 = CO 49:331.

95. The insistence that faith does not justify because of any human quality inherent to it still leaves some tension between statements and images that develop this recognition by minimizing the greatness of faith and those that develop it by magnifying

1536 Bucer approvingly comments about Romans that "Philip Melanchthon in his highly erudite and devout *Commentary* on this Epistle rightly condemns those who want to make 'We are justified by faith' mean, 'Faith is the source or cause that produces other virtues for whose sake we are pronounced righteous,' or 'Faith itself is in us a virtue, deserving of God's approval.'"[96] In late 1530 Melanchthon had expressed a very similar sentiment in more positive mode in the *Apology of the Augsburg Confession*: "faith is the very righteousness by which we are reckoned righteous before God, not because it is a work that is worthy in and of itself, but because it receives the promise by which God has pledged that on account of Christ he desires to be gracious to those who believe in him."[97] The *Belgic Confession of Faith* of 1561, written by Guy de Bray, is at pains to stress that "We do not mean that faith itself justifies us, for it is only an instrument with which we embrace Christ our Righteousness. But Jesus Christ, imputing to us all his merits, and so many holy works, which he hath done for us and in our stead, is our Righteousness."[98] The *Second Helvetic Confession* of 1566, composed by Bullinger, states that "because faith receives Christ our righteousness and attributes everything to the grace of God in Christ, on that account justification is attributed to faith, chiefly because of Christ and not therefore because it is our work."[99] And Luther asserts, most strikingly of all, in his *Commentary on Galatians* (1531/1535): "Faith takes hold of Christ and has him present, enclosing him as the ring encloses the gem. And whoever is found having this faith in the Christ who is grasped in the heart, him God accounts as righteous."[100]

Thus faith justifies because it receives Christ and his saving benefits. If faith is described as itself a kind of righteousness, as in the quo-

---

faith as a divine gift. On this tension in the context of the Osiander controversy in the 1550s, see 9.6.

96. Bucer, *The Common Places of Martin Bucer*, 164.

97. "Apology of the Augsburg Confession," par. 86.

98. *The Creeds of Christendom Vol. III: The Evangelical Protestant Creeds*, ed. Philip Schaff, 6th ed. (Grand Rapids: Baker, 1931), 408. This edition gives both an English translation and the French text.

99. *Reformed Confessions of the Sixteenth Century*, ed. Arthur C. Cochrane (Louisville: Westminster John Knox, 2003), 256 = *The Creeds of Christendom Vol. III*, 267.

100. *LW* 26:132 = *WA* 40:233, 16-19. Ian D. K. Siggins, *Martin Luther's Doctrine of Christ* (New Haven: Yale University Press, 1970), 147, comments, "Luther loves to illustrate the character of faith by the figure of an empty container. Faith is merely a husk, but Christ is the kernel. It is a purse or coffer for the eternal treasure, an empty vessel, a poor little monstrance or pyx for gems of infinite worth."

tation above from the *Apology of the Augsburg Confession*, it is named as such solely on the grounds of this reception. Over and over again it is stressed that Christ is righteousness and that justifying righteousness is something imputed to those who are of faith. Here Luther may speak for all, again from his *Commentary on Galatians* (1531/1535), this time commenting on the faith of Abraham (3:6):

> Christ protects me under the shadow of His wings and spreads over me the wide heaven of the forgiveness of sins, under which I live in safety. This prevents God from seeing the sins that still cling to my flesh. My flesh distrusts God, is angry with Him, does not rejoice in Him, etc. But God overlooks these sins, and in His sight they are as though they were not sins. This is accomplished by imputation on account of the faith by which I begin to take hold of Christ; and on His account God reckons imperfect righteousness as perfect righteousness and sin as not sin, even though it really is sin.[101]

There is some variety, however, in how the imputation of which Luther speaks is understood to take place. In Melanchthon's account of justification, he characteristically, although not exclusively, expresses this in relational terms, stressing that the superabundant righteousness of Christ's life and sacrificial death is set against the wrath of God against sin and brings forgiveness for those who have faith in Christ. Here Christ's righteousness is effective on behalf of the believer, with the Father justifying sinners because this righteousness pleads for them before Him. Others, including Luther, characteristically, although not exclusively, argue that faith unites the believer with Christ and that in the context of this union the righteousness of Christ is given directly to the believer.

Either way, such assertions convey a powerful sense of the sufficiency of Christ's saving work and the corresponding redundancy of works in justification. There is unanimity among the Reformers in viewing justification as requiring a looking away from the self and outside of the self to Christ alone. The righteousness reckoned to believers in justification is always an alien righteousness that is not the believer's own. It does not stem in any degree from the believer's works.[102] It is

---

101. *LW* 26:231-32 = *WA* 40:367, 13-21.

102. On the alien nature of the righteousness received through faith, See Berndt Hamm, "What Was the Reformation Doctrine of Justification?" in *The Reformation of*

the reception by faith of this righteousness from outside that brings those who believe into right standing before God. Justification by faith always has this christological focus for the Reformers and, in exegetical terms, it is significant that they find such a focus in Rom 3:21–31, prior to the discussion of the faith of Abraham in Rom 4. Calvin's comments on Rom 3:22 are instructive in this respect:

> Faith is therefore said to justify, because it is the instrument by which we receive Christ, in whom righteousness is communicated to us. When we are made partakers of Christ, we are not only ourselves righteous, but our works also are counted righteous in the sight of God, because any imperfections in them are obliterated by the blood of Christ. The promises, which were conditional, are fulfilled to us also by the same grace, since God rewards our works as perfect, inasmuch as their defects are covered by free pardon.[103]

Faith as trust in God's promises cannot be abstracted from its christological basis. Such faith (*fiducia*) is always trust in Christ's saving work, as indeed Rom 4:23–25 makes clear. Here Abraham's faith is preceded by discussion of faith in Christ and it prefigures the faith of those "who believe in him who raised Jesus our Lord from the dead, who was handed over to death for our trespasses and was raised for our justification."

As a result of this christological focus, the Reformers' understanding of faith reflects a profound awareness of the ecclesial context of justification. If Protestant interpreters in the post-Enlightenment era come to provide rather individualistic accounts of Paul's soteriology, this is not true of the Reformers. Since faith justifies because it trusts God's promises and appropriates Christ and his saving benefits, then justification by faith cannot be understood other than in the context of the church as Christ's body. And once justification is understood in an ecclesial context, then it is also related to the sacraments. Luther notes of Christ that we "rely upon his righteousness, life, and blessedness. And through the interchange of his blessings and our misfortunes, we become one loaf, one bread, one body, one drink, and have all things in common. O this is a great sacrament, says St. Paul, that Christ and the church are one

---

Faith in the Context of Late Medieval Theology and Piety, ed. Robert J. Bast (Leiden: Brill, 2004), 179–216.

103. *Comm. Rom* 3:22, CNTC 8:73 = OE 13:71, 1–8.

flesh and bone."[104] Calvin will insist against Erasmus and the Vulgate in discussion of the phrase "into the fellowship (κοινωνία) of his son Jesus Christ" in 1 Cor 1:9 that the translation *communionem* and not either *consortium* (partnership) or *societatem* (society) best expresses the saving significance of union with Christ: "For the whole purpose of the Gospel is that Christ be made ours, and that we be ingrafted into His body. But when the Father gives Him to us as a possession, He also imparts Himself to us in Christ, and because of this we really come to share in every blessing."[105] When Paul asks of the cup of blessing "is it not a communion (κοινωνία) in the blood of Christ?" (1 Cor 10:16), Calvin relates this explicitly sacramental statement to the same soteriological concepts: "κοινωνία or communion of the blood is the alliance (*societatem*) which we have with the blood of Christ when He ingrafts all of us into His body, so that He may live in us, and we in Him."[106] To receive Christ in justification by faith is necessarily also to become one body with all believers and for this communion with Christ and his church to be expressed through baptism and the Lord's Supper.

4.4. Summary

The Reformers never tire of asserting that by his insistence that justification is not by the "works of the law" Paul intends to remove the whole law from the sphere of justification and not simply to say that ceremonies do not justify. Further, this exclusion of works from justification applies not only to those performed prior to faith but also to those performed by the baptized. As rites commanded by God for worship, ceremonies cannot be relegated to a subsidiary or less enduring position within the law. If they are excluded from among the effficient causes of justification, then so too are the law's ethical commands. Perfect obedience to the law would justify but this is impossible for fallen human beings. Hope for

---

104. *LW* 35:58 = *WA* 2:748, 16–20. The editor of the English translation notes that Luther perhaps thinks here of Eph. 5:32 where the Vulgate gives *sacramentum* ("sacrament") for μυστήριον ("mystery"). The tract from which the quotation comes is *The Blessed Sacrament of the Holy and True Body of Christ, and the Brotherhoods* (1519).

105. *Comm. 1 Cor 1:9, CNTC* 9:24 = *CO* 49:313.

106. *Comm. 1 Cor 10:16, CNTC* 9:216 = *CO* 49:464. Thus Calvin is prepared to use the more general term *societatem* to explain Paul's meaning but only once the alliance involved has been specifically defined in terms of κοινωνία/communion and ingrafting.

their salvation is not merely founded upon divine mercy or inconceivable apart from such mercy but consists wholly and exclusively in this mercy.

If this is so, then the understanding of grace as infused, which for previous interpreters from Augustine onwards made possible the meritorious good works of the baptized, is redundant. In key Pauline texts concerning justification, grace denotes a divine disposition, the favor or mercy that is God's desire to forgive sins on the basis of Christ's saving sacrifice. As such, grace is gratuitous and depends not at all on human actions since it remains unconditioned by anything outside of God. Grace is the indispensable basis of the divine gift that makes obedient human actions possible, but it is not itself to be identified with this gift. Such obedience is in this life partial, but grace sustains the Christian precisely because it remains external and total. That which is in the believer is not justifying grace, but faith, the means by which Christ and his saving benefits are received. This justifying faith includes for the Reformers historical and doctrinal knowledge of Christ's person and work but it is always most fundamentally a disposition of trust in God's promises, as exemplified in the Pauline letters by the biblical example of Abraham. As trust in divine promises, faith does not need to be formed by love in order to be alive. It is inherently active and alive or it is not faith. Yet faith justifies not because it leads to good works or is itself meritorious but because it looks away from self and to Christ, receiving an alien righteousness that comes to the believer from outside. It is through faith and only through faith that this alien righteousness may be received, and it is in this sense that the Reformers claim that justification is by faith alone. The trust involved in faith is trust in Christ's saving work and so faith is always focused on Christ. Precisely because faith always has this christological focus, the church as the body of Christ is always the context of justification, and, properly used, the sacraments of baptism and the Lord's Supper are always an expression of the justifying faith that receives Christ.

These changes in the exegesis of key terms describing salvation in Christ mark a decisive rejection of the medieval Pauline exegetical grammar. Along with changes in the exegesis of key terms describing the human plight apart from Christ, the exclusion of any and all works from among the causes of justification, the insistence that grace is divine favor and not something infused into those who believe, and the replacement of faith formed by love with faith as trusting reception of Christ and his benefits, together provide the basis of the Reformers' new Pauline exegetical grammar. Their Pauline exegetical grammar rejects as a basis for justification the lifelong pilgrimage of the Christian towards righteousness and instead insists that transformation rests upon the divine provision of a perfect righteousness, already complete and full, that is given to the believer from outside through Christ. Yet, despite the general agreement that justification involves the receiving of an alien righteousness provided through Christ, it is in their various expressions of the christological focus of justifying faith that significant differences between the Reformers emerge. Unanimity is left behind when we move beyond general assertions into more detailed discussion of the nature of the imagery of justification, of how alien righteousness is received through Christ, of what exactly is involved in imputation, and of how the imagery of justification relates to Paul's language of union with Christ. Despite the development of a powerful shared Pauline exegetical grammar, it is through the Reformers' different expressions of the christological focus of justifying faith that contrasting exegetical and theological emphases emerge. It is also in such differences that there emerge distinct possible trajectories of appropriation of the Reformers' Pauline exegesis in the contemporary world. For these reasons exploration of the Reformers' Pauline exegesis cannot remain solely concerned with the shared conclusions that made up their new Pauline exegetical grammar. It is necessary also to explore the contributions made by key individuals.

PART III

INDIVIDUAL PERSPECTIVES

Luther, Melanchthon, and Calvin on Righteousness in Christ

5 Alien Righteousness in Christ

The Integration of Justification by Faith and
Union with Christ in Martin Luther's Pauline Exegesis

5.1. Luther's Account of Justification in Its Early Protestant Context

As we have seen, there is a relentless external emphasis in early Protestant accounts of justification. God encounters people in justification only outside of themselves and the righteousness received remains an alien righteousness. The task of identifying such shared features of early Protestant accounts of justification has been undertaken with some thoroughness by Berndt Hamm, who in doing so seeks to answer the question, "what links the Wittenberg Reformation of Luther and Melanchthon, the Reformation of Zwingli in Zurich and Calvin's Geneva-based Reformation in their opposition to medieval Catholic doctrine and the reforming Catholicism of the sixteenth century?"[1] Hamm provides several answers to this question, but within them the theme of the extrinsic nature of justification and the alien nature of the righteousness granted to the believer through Christ is prominent. Justification is "unconditional" in the sense that acceptance by God is not in any way caused by works performed by the believer either prior to faith or subsequent to faith. The concept of merit is utterly rejected as inappropriate to Pauline exegesis and the righteousness granted to the believer in justification is and remains wholly and entirely that of Christ. The sinner is accepted into holiness, and holiness is the correlate of acceptance, but holiness forms

---

1. Hamm, "What Was the Reformation Doctrine of Justification?," 179. See also Hamm, "Justification by Faith Alone," 233-57.

no part of its basis before God. There is a strong sense of the complete and perfect nature of the salvation granted to the believer: "In place of the two-way medieval Catholic path of gradual cooperation between God and humanity that leads to salvation, there entered the new theme that God alone is effective."[2]

If this is true, then grace cannot be a quality in the believer. Instead, grace "is nothing but God himself in his mercy, the grace of God, God giving himself in community with the sinner."[3] As such, grace is prior to any and all believing activity on the part of a person and therefore becomes the basis of assurance. The believer stands in the grace of God so that there is an "eschatological final validity of justification. Through the acceptance of the sinner, his entering into the righteousness of Christ, something final has taken place."[4] All of this is received by faith alone, and this faith is bound to the biblical word of God. Only in this trustworthy word that is given by God and that takes sinners outside of themselves into total reliance on divine promises can faith have validity. However much it is the case that justification truly speaks to the deepest inner needs of sinners, "people do not find the gracious God when they find themselves and God in their innermost being. Instead, God encounters people outside of themselves as the unconditionally loving one."[5] This strong emphasis upon alien righteousness is rooted in the work of Martin Luther. Yet it is important to see that, although a vital part of Luther's account of justification, Luther's contribution is not restricted to this extrinsic emphasis or reducible to it. In particular, Luther typically explains alien righteousness in relation to union with Christ and in relation to the apocalyptic themes of his theology. In the integration of these elements and especially in the way Luther expresses the christological nature of alien righteousness there emerges the distinctive nature of his Pauline exegesis. For all that they share a new Pauline exegetical grammar, and for all that each of them emphasizes the alien nature of the righteousness received by believers, Luther, Melanchthon, and Calvin each hear Paul differently in this important respect. Melanchthon and Calvin are profoundly influenced by Luther but do not simply reproduce his exegetical conclusions. The exploration of Luther's exegesis is therefore the first

---

2. Hamm, "Justification by Faith Alone," 257.
3. Hamm, "What Was the Reformation Doctrine of Justification?," 193.
4. Hamm, "What Was the Reformation Doctrine of Justification?," 198.
5. Hamm, "Justification by Faith Alone," 252.

step in understanding the relationship between their interpretations of Paul and the different ways in which they express the christological focus of justification by faith.

5.2. Interpreting Luther Interpreting Paul

Luther is an elusive thinker, whom scholarship finds difficult to pin down. He returns to the same themes and ideas again and again in his vast corpus of work, but rarely for the sake of producing tightly defined doctrines. He produces tracts for the times and expositions of Scripture, but not systematic theology.[6] As a result, his characteristic ideas and themes appear not for their own sake but in the service of other goals. Luther is more concerned to counter the arguments of his critics, or to communicate clearly the meaning of the biblical authors, than he is with achieving consistency in the use of his intellectual resources. This is not necessarily to allege that Luther contradicts himself, although his ideas certainly develop during the course of a turbulent career spanning several decades. Rather, it is to acknowledge that his thought is as sprawling as it is fertile. Luther's thought resembles the complexity and variety of a great Gothic cathedral, not the clean lines of a modernist building. There may be genuine coherence and unity, but the structure could scarcely be described as uniform or regular.[7]

It is therefore potentially misleading to discuss Luther's "view" or "understanding" or "doctrine" of justification by faith or, indeed, union with Christ, as if they constituted single, easily definable entities.[8] In his exegesis Luther provides different explanations of them as he is prompted by the demands of the text and of debate. His theology of justification can be particularly difficult to pin down. Concern with it permeates his writings, Luther perceiving it as relevant to virtually every other theological issue. Luther is spoken to powerfully about justification not only by texts

6. For a discussion of the problems this presents to Luther's interpreters, see Bernhard Lohse, *Martin Luther's Theology*, 3-10.

7. I am here applying to Luther a metaphor current in New Testament studies. See Gerd Theissen, *A Theory of Primitive Christian Religion* (London: SCM, 1999), 17-18, 306-7, who uses the metaphor of a semiotic cathedral in relation to early Christianity.

8. Siggins, *Martin Luther's Doctrine of Christ*, 144-45, comments that "Luther rarely deals with justification as a separate locus, yet in another sense he deals with it constantly by speaking always of Christ, who is our righteousness."

where Paul directly addresses that theme but also by texts with a different focus. This pervasiveness of the theme of justification in Luther's Pauline exegesis leads Luther to employ together explanations of justification that were to become distinct from each other in later eras. In turn this makes difficult a systematic analysis of justification in Luther's Pauline exegesis and therefore, in what follows, the focus is on his dominant or typical patterns of explanation.

The identification of what constitutes such typical or dominant patterns is a matter of controversy. Contrary to the images of Luther often prevalent within contemporary New Testament scholarship, his contribution is not reducible to a rather "thin" forensic account of justification or to his radical rejection of all works righteousness. In fact, since the end of the Second World War, trends and new developments in the interpretation of Luther have been broadly analogous to trends and new developments in the interpretation of Paul. Developments in each field have both reflected contemporary intellectual currents and generated vigorous debate. In the interpretation of Paul, previously dominant existential accounts have been succeeded by ones focusing on apocalyptic categories and/or on union with Christ. Meanwhile, Luther has successively been interpreted primarily within existential categories (the dominant longstanding tradition within German Luther scholarship),[9] or as an apocalyptic thinker (so the late Heiko Oberman and many of his students),[10] or most recently as one centrally concerned with participation in Christ (Finnish Luther scholarship).[11] Finally, again as in the interpretation of Paul, some have sought to incorporate the insights of the other major approaches within their own paradigm. From within the German tradition Oswald Bayer portrays Luther primarily as a theologian of God's performative word that accomplishes what it declares. Bayer begins with a discussion of Luther's apocalyptic mode of thinking and he also pays considerable attention to union with Christ.[12]

The strong resemblance between these patterns of development in the interpretation of Paul and of Luther should lead New Testament scholars to pause for reflection. Without downplaying the significance

9. See, for example, Oswald Bayer, *Martin Luther's Theology: A Contemporary Interpretation* (Grand Rapids: Eerdmans, 2008).

10. Oberman, *Luther*.

11. Tuomo Mannermaa, *Christ Present in Faith: Luther's View of Justification* (Minneapolis: Fortress, 2005).

12. Bayer, *Martin Luther's Theology*, 1-12, 214-38.

of the NPP, and especially its revised account of Second Temple Judaism, wariness is necessary as regards contrasts with Luther that are too simple or sweeping. Particularly in relation to the theme of justification, something more complex may be happening than the replacement of an inadequate interpretation of Paul's texts based upon traditions derived from Luther with superior ones freed from that inheritance. The apocalyptic Luther or the Luther focused on union with Christ may have more to offer contemporary Pauline scholars as a dialog partner than is usually supposed. As will be explored (see 8 and 9) in more detail in later chapters, contemporary interpretations of Paul may be exegetically indebted to Luther and to other Reformers in ways currently unacknowledged. In particular the relationship within Luther's exegesis between justification by faith and his participatory and apocalyptic motifs holds promise in terms of relevance to contemporary discussions of Paul.

5.3. The Human Plight: Luther's Apocalyptic Anthropology

In relation to soteriology, appreciation of the apocalyptic nature of Luther's appropriation of Paul is foundational to an accurate understanding of what he teaches about justification by faith and the manner in which justifying faith establishes union with Christ. For justification and union with Christ function within an apocalyptic dualism that configures the gulf between those who are being saved and those who are perishing in absolute terms.[13] There is no way to understand their positive value for Luther if we do not first understand the human plight in contrast to which they stand. Description of this plight is therefore the indispensable backdrop to discussion of these themes in Luther's Pauline exegesis. We have already seen many features of this plight when discussing the Reformers' shared convictions concerning sin, shared convictions of which Luther was the single most significant originator (3.1). Most significantly, there is the severe and total impact of sin upon human nature encapsulated in Luther's description of sin as "the person turned in upon the self" (*homo*

13. Oberman, *Luther*, 12, writes that in Luther's theology, "where God is at work—in man and in human history—the Devil, the spirit of negation, is never far away." The term "apocalyptic" as applied to Luther denotes his conviction that this struggle is a central aspect of reality and that the defeat of evil and the provision of salvation are possible only though divine intervention in Christ. Human beings are either aligned with God through faith in Christ or, even if unwittingly, they serve the devil.

incurvatus in se).[14] The fallen human being has no resources to apply to salvation but is in bondage to the self, in love with sin, and incapable of loving God.

Having reached this view, it is scarcely surprising that Luther rejected the nominalist soteriology (see 2.3.2) in which he had been schooled as a young theologian.[15] In this soteriology initial acts of repentance are within the power of fallen human beings and fulfill their part of a divine covenant (*pactum*) with humanity. If individuals do *quod in se est* ("what lies within them"), God will justify despite the feeble nature of such repentance. Luther's difficulty is that, given his view of sin, he simply does not believe that even the limited required level of repentance is possible for anyone. Repentance is not a human possibility that provides a gateway to justification and to union with Christ. Rather, it is a divine gift that truly exists only within these realities. For Luther, if the nominalist position were accurately to describe how God justifies, it would be nothing other than an announcement of universal damnation.[16] However, Luther's rejections go further. His views also contradict other perspectives within medieval Pauline interpretation, such as that of Thomas Aquinas (see 2.3.1), or that of some theologians within the Augustinian order (see 2.3.3), who did not share the nominalist optimism about the capacity of fallen human beings to repent. On these views, initial repentance is a gift from God, and human beings then cooperate with divine grace in a process of renewal. Christ in his righteousness enters into individuals and, with their cooperation, produces a righteousness that is inherent to them such that they can eventually stand before God on the basis of their own merits.[17] Such merits can only ever be gained when rooted in the grace of God (i.e., medieval soteriology is not Pelagian), but they are truly a person's own.

---

14. *LW* 25:345 = *WA* 56:356, 5-6. See also *LW* 25:291 = *WA* 56:304, 25-29.

15. An overview of nominalist soteriology was provided earlier (2.3.2).

16. The young Luther initially connected the requirement for individuals to do *quod in se est* with the humility of faith. Yet while this emphasis can be seen in the *Lectures on Romans* (1515-1516), it has been left behind by 1519-1520. Luther insists on divine unilateralism, but the nominalist theology of justification defines covenant as a bilateral agreement. See McGrath, *Luther's Theology of the Cross*, 127-200.

17. Oberman, "*Iustitia Christi* and *Iustitia Dei*," 119-20: "According to this tradition the 'iustitia Christi' is granted in justification to the sinner as gratia or caritas. But the 'iustitia Dei' is not granted together with or attached to the 'iustitia Christi.' . . . The 'iustitia Dei' is the standard according to which the degree of appropriation and the effects of the 'iustitia Christi' are measured and will be measured in the Last Judgment."

Luther's rejection of this cooperative framework of the pilgrim's progress towards righteousness occurs partly because he comes, along with Melanchthon, to view grace not as infused but instead as divine favor (see 4.2). Grace is the divine disposition of mercy rather than something in humans with which they cooperate, and this disrupts the medieval paradigm in very significant ways. This rejection occurs because of Luther's apocalyptic dualism. Salvation from the total and complete nature of the human bondage to sin requires a righteousness that is equally total and complete. For this reason, Luther rejects not only the view that repentance is an efficient cause of justification but also the view that subsequent works are justifying. All works without exception, before or after baptism, are excluded from any part in securing justification. In their place stands complete reliance on the person of Christ, his saving work, and the reception of his perfect righteousness through faith; a faith that unites believers with their Savior.

One of Luther's most compelling expressions of this complete reliance on Christ comes in his *Commentary on Galatians* (1531/1535). Luther comments on Paul's assertion that having been crucified with Christ he no longer lives but Christ in him (Gal 2:19–20). Luther identifies this union with Christ not with the gradual healing of the self but with its death. By "it is no longer I who live," Paul means "not in my own person or substance."[18] Anyone who could live in his or her own person or substance in such a way as truly to exhibit faith formed by love, something that in Luther's view is merely hypothetical and impossible in reality, would in any case not be saved. Such a person "would have only a historical faith about Christ, something that even the devil and all the wicked have (James 2.19)."[19] Instead, the self must be crucified with Christ. Far from being gradually changed into the likeness of Christ through cooperation with infused grace, the Christian must leave behind his or her own life for that of Christ:

> Christian righteousness is, namely, that righteousness by which Christ lives in us, not the righteousness that is in our own person. Therefore when it is necessary to discuss Christian righteousness, the person must be completely rejected. For if I pay attention to the person or speak of the person, then, whether intentionally or unin-

18. *LW* 26:166 = *WA* 40:282, 16.
19. *LW* 26:168 = *WA* 40:285, 22–23.

tentionally on my part, the person becomes a doer of works who is subject to the Law. But here Christ and my conscience must become one body, so that nothing remains in my sight but Christ, crucified and risen. . . . By paying attention to myself . . . I lose sight of Christ, who alone is my righteousness and life.[20]

Luther rams the point home again, cautioning that "when it comes to justification, therefore, if you divide Christ's person from your own, you are in the Law; you remain in it and live in yourself, which means that you are dead in the sight of God and damned by the law."[21] For Paul to continue to live as Paul would be death for him, but to die and for Christ to live in him is life. The old person and the new creation, the self under sin and the individual in Christ, are opposite possibilities. To think at all of meritorious human cooperation in reaching the goal of righteousness is a delusion. Union with Christ and the receiving of his justifying righteousness cannot be reduced to an aspect of this transition, even if it is the aspect on which the whole transition depends and which makes possible human merit. Rather, for Luther the person of Christ encompasses the whole of salvation. For this reason, to be united with Christ is simply to be identified with salvation just as justification by faith in Christ is simply to be identified with salvation. One cannot in Luther's view be partially united with Christ or partially righteous.

Yet, of course, Luther knows well that believers continue to sin.

20. *LW* 26:166 = *WA* 40:282, 17-28. Considerable emphasis is placed on Luther's interpretation of this verse by Wilfried Joest, *Ontologie der Person bei Luther* (Göttingen: Vandenhoeck and Ruprecht, 1967), 365-86. My own position is close to that of Joest, who argues that Luther's teaching on justification has both forensic and effective aspects so that the righteousness of the believer remains alien throughout life and yet involves the beginning of a new life: "daß 'unsere' Gerechtigkeit auf der ganzen Linie ein Leben aus aliena *bleibt* und das *dennoch* von einem Anfangen neuen Lebens und konkreter Werk des Glaubens gesprochen werden kann - wie Luther dies ja tut" (376). In an extensive review of Joest's book, Jared Wicks, "Luther on the Person before God," *TS* 30.2 (1969): 289-311, remarks that "At the center of Luther's thought, we could conclude, there is ultimately a deadly serious appropriation of Gal 2:20, 'It is no longer I who live, but Christ who lives in me,' which Luther takes with stark and awful literalness" (296). Reception of Joest's work has developed over time. Wicks hails it as a break with existential interpretations of Luther (294), but Dennis Bielfeldt, "Response to Sammeli Juntunen," in *Union with Christ: The New Finnish Interpretation of Luther*, ed. Carl E. Braaten and Robert W. Jenson (Grand Rapids: Eerdmans, 1998), 161-62, regards it as an expression of such interpretations.

21. *LW* 26:168 = *WA* 40:285, 15-17.

He holds that the Christian experiences two different and competing servitudes in one person that pull in different directions: the service of God and the service of sin. Just as in Christ the believer is completely righteous, so he interprets "the flesh" that wars against the Spirit (Gal 5:16–17) as the whole person lost in sin in contrast to this whole person in Christ (see 3.1). Paul's term is not to be interpreted in relation to a dichotomy between body and soul in which the fleshly desires of the body refuse to submit to the soul. The solution is therefore not for the believer gradually to become righteous by cooperating with grace in order to subdue such desires. Since "the flesh" refers to the whole person lost in sin and not simply to bodily desires, victory over "the flesh" cannot be achieved through ascetic discipline. Rather, the conflict between "the flesh" and the Spirit is to be understood in the context of Luther's apocalyptic anthropology. The believer faces constant strife between two modes of existence occupying the same body. When the believer lives out of union with Christ (living the Christ-life, not the life of the self), the Christian is then truly and wholly righteous because Christ is truly and wholly righteous. But when faith falters, and the Christian lives from the self (living the life of the self and not the Christ-life), the Christian is then truly and wholly a sinner. Whereas the person apart from Christ, whatever he or she perceives to be the case, in fact has only the possibility of enslavement to sin, the believer also has the possibility of obedience to Christ. As the notion of a twofold competing servitude makes clear, the Christian daily dwells victoriously in Christ and under his lordship or falls back defeated into captivity to sin. When the devil accuses believers of sin and attempts to deceive them into doubting divine mercy, "We have nothing to strengthen and sustain us against these great and unbearable cries except the bare Word, which sets Christ forth as the Victor over sin, death, and every evil."[22] The Christian lives on an apocalyptic battlefield.

5.4. Christ Present in Faith: Justification and Union with Christ

It is within this apocalyptic dualism of Christian existence that Luther's famous assertion that the believer is "simultaneously justified and a sinner" (*simul iustus et peccator*) is to be understood. Contrary to popular misinterpretation, this slogan is not a shorthand summary of an exclu-

---

22. *LW* 26:380 = *WA* 40.1:580, 15–17.

sively forensic account of justification that grants to the believer a merely fictional righteousness.[23] According to this misconceived but widespread account of Luther's views, God acquits the believer because, cloaked in Christ's righteousness, he or she appears in God's sight as a righteous person even while remaining largely in fact a sinner. Further, while justification brings eternal security, in this life the believer is at best stalled early in a process of transformation that will never move more than marginally forwards. To be sure, on occasion Luther does express himself in ways that, viewed in isolation, could be taken to support this caricature. For example, when commenting on Gal 3:6 ("Abraham believed God and it was reckoned to him as righteousness"), Luther suggests that its application to the believer is that God reckons "imperfect faith as perfect righteousness for the sake of Christ."[24] This reckoning works in the following way:

> We live under the curtain of the flesh of Christ (Heb 10:20). He is our "pillar of cloud by day and pillar of fire by night" (Ex 13:21), to keep God from seeing our sin. And although we see it and feel remorse of conscience, still we keep running back to Christ, our Mediator and Propitiator, through whom we reach completion and are saved. In Him is everything; in Him we have everything; and He supplies everything in us. On His account God overlooks all sins and wants them to be covered as though they were not sins. He says: "Because you believe in My Son, even though you have sins, they shall be forgiven, until you are completely absolved from them by death."[25]

Although explicitly forensic imagery is not used here (Luther rarely does so), the explanation of justification that he offers can be forced into accounts that regard it exclusively as a divine declaration of acquittal. To understand Luther's intentions fully, however, requires careful attention to what he means by believing in God's Son and the manner in which he integrates the themes of justification and union with Christ. In the same context Luther has already spoken of imputation as happening "on account of the faith by which I begin to take hold of Christ."[26] It is in such accounts of faith that it becomes clear that Luther intends something

23. Thus, for example, Sanders, *Paul*, 49, misleadingly speaks of Luther's erroneous emphasis on "fictional, imputed righteousness."
24. *LW* 26:231 = *WA* 40:366, 29–30.
25. *LW* 26:232 = *WA* 40:367, 22 – 368, 2.
26. *LW* 26:232 = *WA* 40:367, 18–19.

very different by the term "imputation" than a fictional righteousness. For Luther's rich understanding of faith possesses several dimensions. Each time Paul uses this one word, it carries multiple connotations for Luther. We have already noted when discussing the shared convictions of the Reformers about the meaning of the term "faith" (see 4.3) that it plays a relatively restricted role in Luther's first *Commentary on Galatians* (1516–1517/1519). However, if one reads through the later *Commentary on Galatians* (1531/1535) alongside this earlier exposition, it is clear that Luther's concept of faith has been transformed. Indeed, this transformation is perhaps the most significant development in Luther's interpretation of Galatians. In contrast to its marginal significance in the earlier commentary, the nature of faith is a major topic by 1535.

When commenting on Paul's use of Gen 15:6 in Gal 3:6 and the words "Abraham believed God," Luther understands faith as trust in God's promises. Abraham believed against reason that God would keep his promise that the aged Sarah would have a son. Similarly, the Christian is called upon to embrace "the foolishness of the cross" (1 Cor 1:18-25), and so "faith slaughters reason and kills the beast that the whole world and all the creatures cannot kill."[27] However, this is not all. In thus believing God's promises, faith acknowledges God for who God is. It regards God as "truthful, wise, righteous, merciful, and almighty . . . as the author and donor of every good."[28] God has been given God's rightful place by God's creatures, God's glory has been affirmed, and so "faith justifies because it renders to God what is due him; whoever does this is righteous."[29] Further, by this giving to God of God's glory, faith "consummates the deity; and, if I may put it this way, it is the creator of the deity, not in the substance of God but in us."[30] Luther goes so far as to compare faith, in its relationship with works, to the divinity of Christ in relation to his humanity:

> Let faith always be the divinity of works, diffused throughout the works in the same way that the divinity is throughout the humanity of Christ. Anyone who touches the heat in the heated iron touches the iron; and whoever has touched the skin of Christ has actually

27. *LW* 26:228 = *WA* 40:362, 15–16.
28. *LW* 26:227 = *WA* 40:360, 22–23.
29. *LW* 26:227 = *WA* 40:361, 12–13.
30. *LW* 26:227 = *WA* 40:360, 24–25.

touched God. Therefore faith is the "do-all" (*fac totum*) in works, if I may use this expression. Thus Abraham is called faithful because faith is diffused throughout all of Abraham. When I look at Abraham doing works, therefore, I see nothing of the physical Abraham or of the Abraham who does works, but only Abraham the believer.[31]

However, Luther does not merely discern the relationship between faith and the person of Christ as analogical. In his previous comments on Gal 2:15–16, where Paul asserts that justification is by faith in Christ and not by works of the law, Luther emphasizes that Christ himself is present in faith. "Faith justifies because it takes hold of and possesses this treasure, the present Christ . . . the Christ who is grasped by faith and who lives in the heart is the true Christian righteousness."[32] In an important passage, Luther uses another image:

> Here it is to be noted that these three things are joined together: faith, Christ, and acceptance or imputation. Faith takes hold of Christ and has him present, enclosing him as the ring encloses the gem. And whoever is found having this faith in the Christ who is grasped in the heart, him God accounts as righteous.[33]

Thus, faith takes hold of Christ and has him present. Because the righteous one is present in faith, imputation is possible. When Luther says, "Christian righteousness consists in two things, namely, faith in the heart and the imputation of God,"[34] it is important to recognize that faith itself is to be identified with union with Christ. Luther makes clear, again in his comments on Gal 3:6, that it is faith's capacity to grasp hold of Christ that is vital to its justifying nature: "to take hold of the Son and to believe in him with the heart as the gift of God causes God to reckon that faith, however imperfect it may be, as perfect righteousness."[35] Christ himself is the gift received by the believer. It is therefore clear that imputation of Christ's righteousness to the believer is not defined over and against, or even in indifference to, union with Christ. Rather, imputation

31. *LW* 26:266 = *WA* 40:417, 15–21.
32. *LW* 26:130 = *WA* 40:229, 22–29.
33. *LW* 26:132 = *WA* 40:233, 16–19.
34. *LW* 26:229 = *WA* 40:364, 11–12.
35. *LW* 26:234 = *WA* 40:371, 18–21.

itself involves union with Christ. God imputes because the Christian believes, but the faith of the Christian is itself a divine gift in which Christ is present.[36]

Further, it is this presence of Christ in the faith of the believer that creates the possibility of living the life of Christ. The Christian is only able to engage in the apocalyptic struggle between opposing modes of existence and live as righteous because his or her life has been invaded by Christ, and the self has been crucified with Christ, in order that there might be a new creation. Obedience results from justification and not vice versa. Works "should be done as fruits of righteousness, not in order to bring righteousness into being. Having been made righteous, we must do them; but it is not the other way around: that when we are unrighteous, we become righteous by doing them. The tree produces fruit; the fruit does not produce the tree."[37] To describe the believer as simultaneously justified and a sinner is not for Luther a pessimistic estimation of the possibilities of the Christian life but instead a battle cry. It summons those liberated from the previous certainty of defeat to the struggle to live in union with Christ and therefore within Christ's victory over sin, death, and the devil.

5.5. Receiving Christ's Righteousness

It is, of course, axiomatic for Luther that this victory is Christ's victory and that the believer receives it and lives in it but contributes nothing to it from his or her own resources and works. In union with Christ the believer is not so much empowered to live another life but inserted into the life of a victorious other. Set free from all and any reliance on a self that is doomed to defeat, the Christian seeks not to cooperate with divine grace in order to come to merit justification but rather relies solely on the righteousness of Christ granted to those united with him by faith.

---

36. Indeed, Luther is explicit that Christ is more than the object of faith. See *LW* 26:129 = *WA* 40:228, 31 – 229, 15: "It takes hold of Christ in such a way that Christ is the object of faith, or rather not the object but, so to speak, the One who is present in faith itself." In a contemporary context the term "imputation" is usually associated only with exclusively forensic accounts of justification that do not involve union with Christ. The meaning of the term has changed. It is therefore vital not to project this contemporary usage anachronistically back onto Luther.

37. *LW* 26:169 = *WA* 40:287, 20-23.

This reliance on Christ alone is partly a matter of freedom from anxiety about salvation. The Christian need not fear that his or her continuing sins result in a loss of grace that calls justification into question. Such sins are blotted out by the righteousness of Christ. Yet Luther's assertion of reliance on Christ alone does not simply serve the cause of personal serenity. For anyone who receives Christ's righteousness can join battle against the flesh with gusto, ultimate victory secure.[38] There is not only assurance of salvation but also assurance that the relationship between being justified and a sinner is asymmetrical: "righteousness is supreme and sin is a servant."[39] For Luther, confident engagement in the struggle of the Christian life stems from his certainty that the Christ grasped hold of by faith is for us righteousness from God and that to be united with Christ by faith is therefore to receive this infinite righteousness. It is thus clear that when Luther speaks of imputation he is not speaking of a righteousness that is transferred from Christ to the believer apart from Christ's person, but instead of a righteousness that is received by the believer because in being united with Christ the believer is joined with the one who personifies righteousness.

It is therefore a serious misunderstanding to think that Luther's rejection of works as in any sense a contributory effective cause of justification stands in contrast to a bare declaration of acquittal. Rather, it stands in contrast to his particular account of union with Christ. Those united with Christ rely exclusively on sharing in the person and deeds of Christ. Because of this exclusive reliance on Christ, Luther utterly rejects concepts of justification based in part on the merits of what a person becomes. He perceives any element of self-reliance, even in cooperation with grace, as contradictory to the believer's union with Christ. Human beings need to live not a new, improved version of their existing life but instead as new creations to live the life of Christ. The justification of the individual is therefore an apocalyptic event that participates in and relies upon God's larger apocalyptic intervention in Christ for the redemp-

---

38. There is thus a temporal aspect to *simul iustus et peccator*. On the one hand sin will cling to the flesh of the Christian throughout earthly life, the conflict between the flesh and the Spirit ceasing only with death. On the other, God's act of justification determines the whole of existence such that the Christian lives now from the future on the basis of promise and hope. See Hampson, *Christian Contradictions*, 27, and Eberhard Jüngel, *Justification: The Heart of the Christian Faith* (Edinburgh: T&T Clark, 2001), 218-19.

39. *LW* 27:74 = *WA* 40.2:93, 21.

tion of the world. God's act of justification for the individual Christian is rooted in God's wider action in the world. It depends on incarnation,[40] and flows from the life, death, and resurrection of Jesus. This can be seen clearly in Luther's frequent assertions that between Christ and the believer there is a "joyous exchange" in which, having taken upon himself the sins of the world, Christ gives to the believer his righteousness.[41] What is ours becomes his, while what is his becomes ours. In the *Commentary on Galatians* (1531/1535), this is expressed particularly clearly in Luther's lengthy comments on Gal 3:13, "Christ redeemed us from the curse of the law by becoming a curse for us." Luther rages against those, especially Jerome, who are nervous at the apparent impiety of the idea that Christ was cursed by God. Instead, Luther thinks it absolutely necessary to emphasize that, although innocent in his own person, Christ became "the greatest thief, murderer, adulterer, robber, desecrator, blasphemer etc., there has ever been anywhere in the world."[42] If he is not, then his righteousness cannot become the Christian's righteousness, and salvation is lost. As it is, having taken on himself the sins of the world, Christ is able to give to the believer his righteousness. "By this fortunate exchange with us He took upon Himself our sinful person and granted us His innocent and victorious Person."[43]

Luther links this exchange with Christ's emptying of himself (Phil 2:7), a text that he also used to express the same idea years previously in an important sermon entitled *Two Kinds of Righteousness* (preached

40. For a helpful general discussion of this relationship, see George Yule, "Luther's Understanding of Justification by Grace Alone in Terms of Catholic Christology," in *Luther: Theologian for Catholics and Protestants*, ed. George Yule (Edinburgh: T&T Clark, 1985), 87-112.

41. The understanding that justification is effected through joyous exchange is vital to a proper appreciation of the exegetical basis of imputation. Luther reads all texts that contain the idea of exchange (e.g., Rom 8:3; Gal 3:13; Phil 2:5-11) as supporting the view that Christ's righteousness is given to believers. Taking the idea from the Fathers, especially Athanasius and Augustine, Luther concentrates on righteousness as it provides the answer to sin and is prominent in Paul's vocabulary. However, he does also include other properties of Christ in the exchange. As Siggins, *Luther's Doctrine of Christ*, 156, suggests, "if Christ is our righteousness, and justification is by faith alone, so he is our holiness, and sanctification is by faith alone."

42. *LW* 26:277 = *WA* 40:433, 27-28. Unsurprisingly, Luther uses Gal 3:3 and 2 Cor 5:21 to expound the idea of joyous exchange in his *Lectures on Deuteronomy* (1523-1525) when commenting on 27:26. See *LW* 9:215-16 = *WA* 14:699, 18 - 700, 18.

43. *LW* 26:284 = *WA* 40:443, 23-24.

late 1518/early 1519). Because of Christ's willingness to empty himself by taking upon himself all sins, the believer "can with confidence boast in Christ and say: 'Mine are Christ's living, doing and speaking, his suffering and dying, mine as much as if I had lived, done, spoken, suffered and died as he did.'"[44] It is not merely that Christ accomplishes something on the believer's behalf but rather that the believer shares in what Christ does. Luther inserts "the believer directly into the history of Christ."[45] We can see once again that the exchange is not an exchange of detachable qualities between those who have sin as a component of their identities and someone who has righteousness as a component of his identity. Rather it is an exchange of persons between those whose existence is currently constituted by enslavement to sin and the one who personifies righteousness. It is the same Christ, the incarnate son of God, human and divine, who fought and conquered sin and death in his person, who exchanges his righteousness with the believer's sinfulness, who is present in the believer's faith, and whose life the believer now lives.

5.6. Living an Alien Life

As we have already seen, a similar pattern of thought is prompted by Paul's statement that he has been crucified with Christ and that he no longer lives but Christ in him (Gal 2:19–20). Luther emphasizes that the righteousness received by the believer is not the believer's own but is instead that of Christ. It remains an alien righteousness even in relation to the justified person. Further, the faith in which Christ is present is received through the preaching of the Word.[46] There is a consistent pattern in that just as the believer receives an alien righteousness, so God's transforming Word of promise always comes from outside. Reflecting on Paul's statement that the Spirit cries "Abba! Father!" in the hearts of believers (Gal 4:6), Luther comments:

44. *LW* 31:297 = *WA* 2:145, 16–18.

45. Marc Lienhard, *Luther: Witness to Jesus Christ: Stages and Themes of the Reformer's Christology* (Minneapolis: Augsburg, 1982), 273, referring to Karin Bornkamm, *Luthers Auslegungen des Galaterbriefs von 1519 bis 1531—Ein Vergleich* (Berlin: Walter de Gruyter, 1963), 166–67.

46. On the role of the preaching of the Word in justification, see Robert Kolb, *Martin Luther and the Enduring Word of God: The Wittenberg School and Its Scripture-Centered Proclamation* (Grand Rapids: Baker, 2016), 54–65.

This is the reason why our theology is so certain: it snatches us away from ourselves and places us outside ourselves, so that we do not depend on our own strength, conscience, experience, person, or works but depend on that which is outside ourselves, that is, on the promise and truth of God, which cannot deceive.[47]

This locating of the person of the believer outside of the self is crucial. That the righteousness granted to the believer remains alien does not result in it being a fictional righteousness because, Luther teaches, united with Christ the believer lives an alien life:

I am not living as Paul now, for Paul is dead. Who then is living? "The Christian." Paul, living in himself, is utterly dead through the Law but living in Christ, or rather with Christ living in him, he lives an alien life. Christ is speaking, acting, and performing all actions in him; these belong not to the Paul-life, but to the Christ-life. . . . "By my own life I am not living, for if I were, the Law would have dominion over me and hold me captive. To keep it from holding me, I am dead to it by another Law. And this death acquires an alien life for me, namely, the life of Christ, which is not inborn in me but is granted to me in faith through Christ."[48]

The Christian has Christ's righteousness through union with him, but that union does not work on the basis of the improvement or transformation of the existing self of the Christian. It works rather on the basis of the leaving behind and abandonment of that self. As one contemporary Lutheran theologian expresses it, "faith as self-forgetfulness is the most intensive form of certainty of God."[49] Only outside of the self and in Christ can the believer receive new life.

To speak of union with Christ as involving a changed or renewed life is therefore potentially misleading. It is simply not radical enough to capture Luther's sense that union with Christ involves the recreation of the person. If we are to speak of a restoration or healing of the self in this regard, then it cannot take place through improvement via cooperation

---

47. *LW* 26:387 = *WA* 40.1:589, 25-28. See 3.3 for this quotation's implications for Luther's view of the conscience.

48. *LW* 26:170 = *WA* 40:287, 30 – 288, 2.

49. Jüngel, *Justification*, 243.

with grace but only on the basis that the Christian has to come out of him- or herself in order to come to him- or herself. In his sense that faith "places us outside ourselves,"[50] Luther is repeating an idea that had long been central to his theology, for in 1520, in his famous tract *The Freedom of the Christian*, Luther had written that "a Christian lives not in himself, but in Christ and his neighbor. Otherwise he is not a Christian."[51] This soteriological necessity to live an alien life means that

> There is no linear progress from being a sinner to being justified. It is not that that which is given in creation is transformed through grace. It is only through a discontinuity, through repentance and failure, that in response to the good news of the gospel the human being can come to gain a sense of himself through trusting not in himself but in God.[52]

Luther knows well that this radical discontinuity between a person's own life and his or her life in Christ is open to an obvious objection. To the charge that Paul still appears as Paul with no apparent change, Luther in fact affirms that Paul still indeed appears as Paul to the casual observer. He uses physical things such as food and clothing just like any other human being. However, this is only "a mask of life,"[53] for although Paul lives in the flesh, it is not on the basis of his own self. Before his conversion, Paul spoke blasphemy, but after it words of faith. Before, Paul spoke, but after, Christ speaks. The voice and tongue were the same in each case, but the words came from an entirely different source. Luther himself cannot teach, preach, write, pray, or give thanks except by using the physical instruments of the flesh, but "these activities do not come from the flesh and do not originate there; they are given and revealed divinely from heaven."[54] This alien and spiritual life cannot be perceived by the unspiritual person, who does not recognize its true source. The unspiritual person remains ignorant of the fact that "This life is not the

---

50. See *LW* 26:387 = *WA* 40:589, 26.

51. *LW* 31:371 = *WA* 7:69, 12-13.

52. Hampson, *Christian Contradictions*, 101. For Luther, salvation does reinstate what creation was intended to be so that we relate to God in the manner first intended (hence my use of the term "recreation" above). The radical discontinuity stems from the fact that through sin what was intended for creation was so grievously and entirely lost (35).

53. *LW* 26:170 = *WA* 40:288, 25.

54. *LW* 26:171 = *WA* 40:289, 25-27.

life of the flesh, although it is a life in the flesh; but it is the life of Christ, the Son of God, whom the Christian possesses by faith."[55]

5.7. Faith and Good Works

Perhaps unsurprisingly, if the believer lives the alien life of Christ, then good works inevitably follow. Context is everything here. Whereas Luther never tires of asserting that justification is not by works of the law and that human works cannot merit anything before God, he also places considerable emphasis on the works that flow from justifying faith in which Christ is present. Both these emphases can be seen together in Luther's famous introduction to the argument of the epistle in his *Commentary on Galatians* (1531/1535). Luther distinguishes between active and passive righteousness. Righteousness by faith is not the active righteousness by which people strive to do what lies within them (*quod in se est*) but instead passive righteousness "which we do not perform but receive, which we do not have but accept."[56] The active righteousness that does not justify, which Luther can also term civic or political righteousness, comprises every other kind of righteousness, including obedience to the Mosaic Law. It is to be highly valued in its rightful sphere but appalling consequences follow from any confusion between the two kinds of righteousness. In 1532, when commenting on Ps 51:16, a verse that expresses Yahweh's refusal to delight in animal sacrifices, Luther asserts that

> Political righteousness is a very delightful and good thing for its purpose, that there might be peace and mutual association among men. But if you want to be righteous before God because you are a good citizen, a chaste spouse, or an honest merchant, you make a most delightful thing into an abomination which God cannot stand.[57]

---

55. *LW* 26:172 = *WA* 40:290, 30–31. Oberman, "Iustitia Christi and Iustitia Dei," 120–25, finds significant the vocabulary used here by Luther. Justifying righteousness is different understood as *possessio* than as *proprietas*. The former term denotes legal occupancy and enjoyment of something, the latter ownership proper. As it is *possessio*, "the righteousness granted is not one's property but one's possession" (121). Hampson, *Christian Contradictions*, 24, draws an analogy with a library book. Once it is borrowed from the library I have it legitimately in my possession, but I am not its owner.

56. *LW* 26:6 = *WA* 40:43, 15–16.

57. *LW* 12:400 = *WA* 40.2:455, 39 – 456, 1. On political or civic righteousness, see

This is another apocalyptic dualism, with political or active righteousness a possibility for fallen human beings but passive righteousness possible only through faith in Christ. Nevertheless, this dualism too often is interpreted exclusively in relation to the activity or passivity involved, with the conscience of the believer as its sole arena. Luther's focus is not on the contrast between activity or passivity *per se*, as if to be active is a human disposition that angers God and to be passive a human disposition that secures God's favor.[58] Rather, Luther also applies the dualism to the radical discontinuity between the believer's own life and life in Christ: "Christian righteousness applies to the new man, the righteousness of the Law applies to the old man, who is born of flesh and blood."[59] He is also explicit that "We set forth two worlds, as it were, one of them heavenly and the other earthly. Into these we place these two kinds of righteousness, which are distinct and separated from each other."[60] That righteousness by faith exists in the context of these sharp contrasts between active and passive, old and new, earthly and heavenly, means that when the believer is united with Christ by faith, he or she is empowered actively to live an alien life for the sake of the world: "When I have this righteousness within me, I descend from heaven like the rain that makes the earth fertile. That is, I come forth into another kingdom, and I perform good works whenever the opportunity arises."[61] As Luther will express the same idea in his *Preface to the New Testament (1522)*:

> Faith, however, is a divine work in us which changes us and makes us to be born anew of God ... It kills the old Adam and makes us altogether different men, in heart and spirit and mind and powers; and it brings with it the Holy Spirit. O it is a living, busy, active, mighty thing, this faith. It is impossible for it not to be doing good works incessantly. It does not ask whether good works are to be done, but before the question is asked, it has already done them, and is con-

---

also *LW* 12:363–64 = *WA* 40.2:402, 26 – 404, 24; *LW* 17:63 = *WA* 31.2:309, 31 – 310, 4; *LW* 25:86 = *WA* 56:96, 12–13; *LW* 25:410–11 = *WA* 56:418, 22 – 419, 18.

58. That the active nature of the concept of faith appears throughout the commentary, and especially in the discussion of Gal 5:6, shows that in using the term "passive righteousness" Luther is pointing to the nature of grace as *favor* and to the nature of true righteousness as sheer gift, not to the gift of faith as itself essentially passive.

59. *LW* 26:7 = *WA* 40:45, 27–28.

60. *LW* 26:8 = *WA* 40:46, 19–21.

61. *LW* 26:11 = *WA* 40:51, 21–23.

stantly doing them. Whoever does not so such works, however, is an unbeliever[62]

It is therefore apparent that while righteousness is passive (nothing a human being can do will kill the Old Adam, but only an act of God), justifying faith in which Christ is present is inherently active (it is the act of God that makes us entirely different people). What must be avoided is any suggestion that the active nature of faith represents a contribution of the believer to justification. Rather, the faith of the believer is itself divine provision for helpless humanity. When faith is expressed in human actions, these actions are genuinely those of the believer, but the believer only exists in union with Christ. Otherwise, apart from Christ, there is a fallen human person but there is no believer. It is this total dependence upon divine favor and upon the gift of Christ that Luther seeks to capture with the motif of passive righteousness. As the designation of faith as a divine *work* suggests, Luther is not motivated by any abstract general hostility to working but rather by what he regards as the complete confusion surrounding justification in his contemporary context. That, aside from righteousness by faith, Luther does not accord any general valuation to working or not working is clear in his comment that "Whatever there is in us besides Him (Christ)—whether it be intellect or will, activity or passivity etc.—is flesh not Spirit."[63] What matters as regards human conduct is not any particular quality as a disposition but rather whether the person is united with Christ. Then good works will inevitably result. Luther thus will celebrate good works but only when they are placed in their proper apocalyptic context of Christian righteousness as new creation. This new creation is sustained in being only by the total sufficiency of the alien righteousness of Christ, which is effective in the day by day struggle of the believer to live obediently. Even when the flesh temporarily gains the upper hand in its struggle with the Spirit (Gal 5:17), its apparent triumph ultimately serves the ends of righteousness, for it drives the believer back to reliance on Christ:

> For when his flesh impels him to sin, he is aroused and incited to seek forgiveness of sins through Christ and to embrace the righteousness

---

62. *LW* 35:370 = *WA* DB 7:11, 6–13. The *Preface to the New Testament* was originally written in 1522, but the version presented in *LW* 35 is that found in the Bible of 1546. See 4.3 for discussion of the conviction of the active nature of faith among the Reformers in general.

63. *LW* 27:25 = *WA* 40.2:30, 20–21.

of faith, which he would otherwise not have regarded as so important or yearned for with such intensity. . . . Through such an opportunity a Christian becomes a skillful artisan and a wonderful creator, who can make joy out of sadness, comfort out of terror, righteousness out of sin, and life out of death, when he restrains his flesh for this purpose, brings it into submission, and subjects it to the Spirit.[64]

The Christian lives in the shadow of sin and death, but is able to snatch victory from their clutches by transforming them into their own opposites through righteousness by faith. Confronted by a struggle between two modes of existence, the believer is enabled to create joy, comfort, righteousness, and life—rather than sadness, terror, sin, and death—by the daily appropriation of the presence of Christ in justifying faith. The crucial question of Christian existence is therefore whether or not the Christian will live by faith each day and hence in Christ and hence as righteous. There is a sense in which the Christian can grow in this faith and make progress in it. Luther makes reference to this.[65] It is possible to learn to trust more fully. However, precisely because, as with justification itself, the nature of this progress depends on the appropriation of Christ in faith, such progress in faith is also a return to the beginning. For this reason, progress in faith can never cohere into a stable internal quality of the Christian's own, since faith concerns the relationship of the believer with Christ: "For just as Christ came once physically, according to time, abrogating the entire Law, abolishing sin, and destroying death and hell, so He comes to us spiritually without interruption and continually smothers and kills those things in us."[66] To have trusted God today and to have lived the life of Christ still leaves open the question of what will be the case tomorrow. In this daily struggle the human propensity to sin by turning from Christ to self remains, for "to the extent that I look back to myself and my sin I am miserable

---

64. *LW* 27:74 = *WA* 40.2:93, 24 – 94, 11.

65. See, for example, *LW* 35:370 = *WA* DB 7:11, 6–15; *LW* 31:299 = *WA* 2:146, 29–35; *LW* 31:358 = *WA* 7:59, 24 – 60, 9. See also Joest, *Ontologie der Person bei Luther*, 382, who says that it is only extrinsically in Christ that "our spiritual life has its permanence and continuity" ("hat unser geistliches Leben seinen Bestand und seine Kontinuität").

66. *LW* 26:350 = *WA* 40:537, 31-34. Jonathan D. Trigg, *Baptism in the Theology of Martin Luther* (Leiden: Brill, 2001), 171, comments that "the image that most fully represents Luther's understanding of the Christian life is that of a spiral. . . . A continual return to the start is not the opposite of progress for Luther; it is the very essence of it."

and the greatest of sinners."[67] Victory requires the believer to constantly take hold of Christ in faith anew.

5.8. Faith and Love

That righteousness by faith is for Luther an apocalyptic concept is also vital to understanding the way in which he expresses the relationship between faith and love. Apart from faith in Christ, the love of God and neighbor that pleases heaven is not a possibility for human beings. The good works that express such love flow from justifying faith and not vice versa. Even when Luther uses the imagery of marriage to explain justification, he is clear that love exists before marriage only on the divine side of the relationship. For the believer, love results from being united with Christ. He comments on Gal 2:16 that the faith that unites a person with Christ the savior "justifies without love and before love. . . . By faith we are in Him, and He is in us (John 6:56). The Bridegroom, Christ, must be alone with His bride in His private chamber, and all the family and household must be shunted away. But later on, when the Bridegroom opens the door and comes out, then let the servants return to take care of them and serve them food and drink. Then let works and love begin."[68] Works and love are not the consummation of the believer's union with Christ but are instead a new possibility opened up only because in justifying faith that consummation has taken place.[69]

It is for this reason that Luther utterly rejects the doctrine of faith formed by love (*fides caritate formata*).[70] He will not accept that this is

---

67. *WA* 39.1:508, 5-7. This translation, from *The Third Disputation against the Antinomians* (1538), is given in Jüngel, *Justification*, 216.

68. *LW* 26:137-38 = *WA* 40:240, 16 - 241, 16.

69. It is precisely this apocalyptic context of Luther's use of marital imagery for justification, with its insistence that the believer's love flows from union with Christ rather than constituting part of its basis, that goes unrecognized by Michael Waldstein, "The Trinitarian, Spousal, and Ecclesial Logic of Justification," in *Reading Romans with St. Thomas Aquinas*, ed. Matthew Levering and Michael Dauphinais (Washington, DC: Catholic University of America Press, 2012), 274-87. Waldstein sees Luther's use of marital imagery for justification as inconsistent with his rejection of faith formed by love, arguing that such marital imagery ought to imply a role for love in justification: "Does not the primary meaning of spousal love lie precisely in taking hold of the beloved?" (284).

70. On this issue, see Kim, *Luther on Faith and Love*, esp. 63-116.

what Paul intends when he says that "in Christ Jesus neither circumcision nor uncircumcision counts for anything; the only thing that counts is faith working through love" (Gal 5:6). As we have already seen (2.3.1 and 3.3), when confronted by the need to coordinate the statements of James that faith without works is dead (2:17) and that even the demons believe and tremble (2:19) with Paul's statements in Gal 5:6, medieval interpreters did not categorize factual knowledge of God as something other than faith or term such knowledge dead faith. Instead, they developed a distinction between two different kinds of faith: formed and unformed. From Peter Lombard in the twelfth century onwards, unformed faith was understood as a cognitive acceptance of the facts of the gospel which does not of itself justify. It is "a 'quality of mind' (*qualitas mentis*) but one that remains 'unformed' because it lacks the shaping effect of love or charity."[71] This unformed faith soon became identified with what is received in the sacrament of baptism and the transition to a formed faith was identified with the sacrament of penance: "Forming faith meant persuading people to put the faith into practice by way of charity or penance, and restraining or absolving them from mortal sin."[72] On this view it is only faith formed by love that can justify since it is only faith so formed that can cooperate with grace in producing the good works necessary for the believer eventually to merit heaven.

For his part, Luther finds it monstrous that his opponents teach that unformed faith is at once both a divine gift and yet not able to justify since it requires formation by love: "Who could stand for the teaching that faith, the gift of God that is infused in the heart by the Holy Spirit, can coexist with mortal sin . . . to believe this way about infused faith is to admit openly that they understand nothing about faith."[73] He also appeals to what he regards as the basic sense of Paul's words: "Paul does not make faith unformed here, as though it were a shapeless chaos without the power to be or to do anything; but he attributes the working itself to faith rather than to love. . . . He does not say 'Love is effective.' No, he says: 'Faith is effective.' He does not say: 'Love works.' No, he says: Faith works.' He makes love the tool

---

71. John Van Engen, "Faith as a Concept of Order in Medieval Christendom," 33. See 31–36 for a fuller account of the distinction between unformed and formed faith.

72. Van Engen, "Faith as a Concept of Order in Medieval Christendom," 35.

73. *LW* 27:28 = *WA* 40.2:35, 14–19.

through which faith works."[74] Although Luther does not say so, these points clearly rely on taking the participle ἐνεργουμένη ("working") as middle rather than passive. If passive it could be taken as saying that faith "is made effective through love." Yet, while some patristic writers do take the participle as passive, the Latin of the Vulgate itself and the majority of commentators in all eras take it as middle.[75] Luther's argument is that when the participle is so taken as middle in voice, Paul's words do not easily speak of faith as something passive or unformed but as something active and working.

Luther thus considers it essential to hold that faith works or it is not faith. It is faith that justifies and unites with Christ and leads to love, not love that justifies and unites with Christ and leads to faith. At this point, the centrality of union with Christ in Luther's understanding of justification again comes into sharp relief, for he makes his point about the right ordering of the relationship between faith and love by reference to the presence of Christ in faith. In Luther's exposition of Gal 2:15-16 this presence is compared to the mysterious presence of God in the darkness on Mt. Sinai or in the Holy of Holies in the temple. Luther contrasts this divine presence with scholastic explanations of faith formed by love that employed the image of a blank wall (bare faith) to which living color (love) must be added in order to make it visible. Sinners are not saved through faith formed by love but through faith that unites with Christ:

> This rejection of the metaphor of the "visible wall" in favor of that of an "invisible cloud" is bound up with Luther's insistence that "formal righteousness" does not have to do with a formal quality that is added to a power, but rather with the union of two "persons." More concretely stated, it has to do with the distinction between the person of the sinner (who is outwardly visible) and the person of the Savior (who cannot be seen).[76]

On this view faith lives as faith, without the necessity of being formed by love, because present in faith is the living person of Christ.

---

74. *LW* 27:29 = *WA* 40.2:36, 8-14. See 4.3 for this quotation's implications for the view of the relationship between faith and works among the Reformers in general.

75. Riches, *Galatians through the Centuries*, 262.

76. Mark Seifrid, "Paul, Luther, and Justification in Gal 2:15-21," *WTJ* 65 (2003): 223.

Luther expresses this in terms of a direct contrast: "just as the sophists say that love forms and trains faith, so we say that it is Christ who forms and trains faith or who is the form of faith."[77]

As Luther reads Paul, there is thus no place for human love that justifies: "we must not attribute the power of justifying to a 'form' that makes a man pleasing to God; we must attribute it to faith, which takes hold of Christ the Savior Himself and possesses Him in the heart."[78] Luther's apocalyptic dualism here leads him sharply to distinguish faith and love in an attempt to order their relationship correctly, for confusion between the two can only obscure in deluded and dangerous ways the necessity of new creation. Luther simply finds it incredible that the power to love is accessible to human beings in any way other than through the presence of Christ in faith: "Only after this faith in Christ has correctly established the right relationship of human beings toward God and made them children of God can Luther now cautiously say that Christ in faith enables them to love God rightly out of a pure heart."[79] There is a fundamental discontinuity between existence before faith and justified existence in Christ through faith. Nevertheless, the relationship between faith and love matters profoundly for Luther. While faith and love must be distinguished, it is equally important that they are not separated. For if faith justifies and unites with Christ and thereby makes a new creation, then love must follow: "love is the incarnation and fruit of faith."[80] The cliché that faith alone justifies but that justifying faith is never alone is true to Luther's thought. The believer who produces no works of love is not a believer. If Christ is present in faith, then he will grant what was lacking, the power to love. So too, on the contrary, if love is absent, then the faith in which Christ is present does not exist and a person is not justified.

Thus, the love given by Christ "must be done."[81] It is only genuine if it is active, but this imperative to action arises from the spontaneity of new creation and overflows from the presence of Christ in the faith that defines the being of the believer. Unsurprisingly, Luther's favorite way of expressing what he takes as a right ordering of the relationship between faith and love is the horticultural image of a tree and its fruits:

77. *LW* 26:130 = *WA* 40:229, 27–28.
78. *LW* 26:137 = *WA* 40:240, 14–16.
79. Kim, *Luther on Faith and Love*, 99.
80. Kim, *Luther on Faith and Love*, 64.
81. Kim, *Luther on Faith and Love*, 165.

"To do" includes faith at the same time. Faith takes the doer himself and makes him into a tree, and his deeds become fruit. First there must be a tree, then the fruit. For apples do not make a tree, but a tree makes apples. So faith first makes the person, who afterwards performs works.[82]

The method by which such fruit-bearing trees are cultivated is the ministry of the Word, in which God is the primary agent. Luther comments on "the hearing of faith" (Gal 3:5) that "when a preacher preaches in such a way that the Word is not frustrated in producing fruit but is efficacious on the hearers, that is, when faith, hope, love, patience etc. follow—then God supplies the Spirit and performs powerful deeds in the hearers."[83] Such effective preaching produces believers who "have become generous, chaste, gentle, patient, and loving."[84] The result of dependence on the creative power of the Word is that the believer lives the alien life of Christ, a life exemplified by love.

5.9. The Finnish School and Their Opponents

We have now seen that despite the sprawling nature of Luther's Pauline exegesis and the challenges it poses in identifying and discussing dominant or typical patterns of explanation, there is a remarkable underlying integration of justification by faith, union with Christ, and apocalyptic themes. Further, there is also a strong relationship with Luther's theology of the Word. This coheres with the integrative pattern in that just as the believer receives an alien righteousness and must live an alien life, so God's transforming Word of promise always comes from outside. Yet, perhaps inevitably, given the successive trends in the interpretation of Luther over recent decades (existential, apocalyptic, and participatory), disputes remain within Luther scholarship concerning the detailed shape of such integration. Indeed, the greatest current controversy in the interpretation of Luther stems precisely from an attempt to understand one major element of his thought through its relationship to another. The

---

82. *LW* 26:255 = *WA* 40:402, 13–17. On Luther's use of this image, see Kim, *Luther on Faith and Love*, 198–201.
83. *LW* 26:220 = *WA* 40.1:351, 36 – 352, 13.
84. *LW* 26:220 = *WA* 40.1:352, 27–28.

Finnish school argues that union with Christ is crucial to Luther's expla-nations of justification. While the account I have offered of justification in Luther's Pauline exegesis certainly does not depend on every aspect of the Finnish interpretation proving correct, this central claim is vital. It is therefore important for my own argument to explore the work of the Finnish school and to demonstrate its basic validity, but also to identify any limitations or areas marked by a lack of clarity.

Emphasizing the presence of Christ in faith, and working in the context of ecumenical exchanges between Lutheranism and Russian Orthodoxy, the Finns regard Luther's explanations of justification as fruitful in dialogue with Orthodox notions of salvation as *theosis* or "di-vinization."[85] As Tuomo Mannermaa, the patriarch of the Finnish school, expresses it, "because faith means a real union with Christ, and because in Christ the Logos is of the same essence as God the Father, therefore the believer's participation in the essence of God is also real."[86] This idea of the believer's participation in the essence of God has proved particu-larly controversial because "the idea of Christ's presence is 'real-ontic,' not just a subjective experience or God's 'effect' on the believer,"[87] as German Luther interpretation has typically held. Within that German tradition Oswald Bayer is happy to speak of the believer participating in God's nature, but such participation takes place exclusively through divine promise and God's nature is defined primarily in terms of com-municative being.[88] For the Finns and those sympathetic to their claims, such interpretation strays too close to the view that reality is linguistically constituted and foists later post-Enlightenment categories back onto Lu-ther.[89] While agreeing that Luther moves beyond medieval understand-

85. As accessible entry-points to the work of the Finnish school, see *Union with Christ: The New Finnish Interpretation of Luther*, ed. Carl E. Braaten and Robert W. Jenson (Grand Rapids: Eerdmans, 1998), and Mannermaa, *Christ Present in Faith*.

86. Mannermaa, *Christ Present in Faith*, 19.

87. Veli-Matti Kärkkäinen, "Deification View," in *Justification: Five Views*, ed. James K. Beilby and Paul R. Eddy (Downers Grove, IL: InterVarsity Press, 2011), 225.

88. Bayer, *Martin Luther's Theology*, 341: "If God is understood as Word, then the Trinity is to be comprehended as dialogue: God, within himself, is communication, relationship, a relational 'three-ness.'"

89. Oswald Bayer, "The Being of Christ in Faith," *LQ* 10.2 (1996): 135-50, does make clear that he is not completely comfortable with contemporary ontology and that Luther points the way beyond both it and older conceptions towards a distinctive con-cept of being: "theology can only be critically related to both ancient substance meta-physics and to the metaphysics of modern subjectivity because both of them cannot

ings of being based exclusively on the concept of substance,[90] they insist that talk of God is not to be understood entirely in relationship to human experience: "Although Luther emphasizes the relation of the objects of faith to their existential appropriation . . . he obviously assumes an objectivity to God and language referring to God."[91]

At this point the whole debate has clearly moved into the realm of ontology (the category of philosophy concerned with the nature of being). Typical German interpretation regards Luther as pointing the way forward to a relational ontology radically distinct from medieval patterns of thought, whereas the Finnish school regards this as anachronistic.[92] The mere exegete is perhaps entitled to feel that such philosophical questions belong to those of a higher pay grade and also that there is, in any case, something unsatisfactory about this debate. This is partly because the whole debate has proceeded without a clear definition of what is meant by the term *theosis* or "divinization."[93] However, it is also because Lu-

---

permit a concept of existence grounded in an ex-centric and permanently foreign being" (145).

90. See Olli-Pekka Vainio, *Justification and Participation in Christ: The Development of the Lutheran Doctrine of Justification from Luther to the Formula of Concord (1580)* (Leiden: Brill, 2008), 12 n. 36. The Finns wish to insist that substance and relations are both relevant categories for the discussion of God's being.

91. Dennis Bielfeldt, "Luther's Late Trinitarian Disputations," in *The Substance of the Faith: Luther's Doctrinal Theology for Today*, ed. Dennis Bielfeldt, Mickey L. Mattox, and Paul R. Hinlicky (Minneapolis: Fortress, 2008), 64–65.

92. The debate has become so significant that a recent major introduction to Luther's theology includes two chapters on Luther's view of justification, one written from the Finnish perspective and the other offering a more forensic account. See Risto Saarinen, "Justification by Faith: The View of the Mannermaa School," in *The Oxford Handbook of Martin Luther's Theology*, ed. Robert Kolb, Irene Dingel, and L'ubomír Batka. (Oxford: Oxford University Press, 2014), 254–63, and Mark Mattes, "Luther on Justification as Forensic and Effective," in *The Oxford Handbook of Martin Luther's Theology*, ed. Robert Kolb, Irene Dingel, and L'ubomír Batka (Oxford: Oxford University Press, 2014), 264–73.

93. I am not equipped properly to assess the claims made by the Finns about Luther and *theosis*, which would require both a careful analysis of Orthodox concepts of *theosis* and a careful comparison of them with Luther. I am not aware of studies by either the Finns or their opponents providing this. Luther does occasionally use the term *theosis* and his Christology is deeply indebted to the Alexandrian Church Fathers, for whom *theosis* certainly was a central concern. Writing before the Finns, Lienhard, *Witness to Jesus Christ*, 54, 386–87, twice mentions the possible significance of the theme of divinization for Luther on the basis of his familiarity with patristic writings. It seems likely that further study will reveal that there are certain senses in which the term can

ther was not himself primarily concerned to pursue the ontological implications of union with Christ. The Finns' affirmation that the union of the believer with Christ in justification is "real-ontic" does not take us very far forward in exegetical terms, especially since Luther "wrote little about such questions as 'What is the ontological structure of the world?'"[94] He was focused rather upon biblical categories and terminology and therefore upon where union with Christ fits within his reflections upon Scripture and upon salvation. The work of both the Finnish school and its critics has somewhat neglected this, and, in particular, said far too little about how Luther relates union with Christ to the apocalyptic themes of Paul's theology.

Yet the whole debate cannot be ignored. Although the relationship between ontological claims and concepts of justification is complex, the Finnish account necessarily implies significant differences between Luther himself and subsequent Lutheran traditions concerning justification. For in emphasizing the presence of Christ in faith, the Finns have stressed the effective aspects of justification in which the believer is not only declared to be righteous before God but is also transformed. This in turn raises the issue of how the works of the believer relate to justification. The Finns certainly do not intend to suggest that for Luther such works are an efficient cause of justification, but on their view works are very definitely for Luther a constitutive part of justification. Justification itself encompasses renewal because the presence of the risen and crucified Christ in faith is the righteousness granted to the believer. Olli-Pekka Vainio argues that Luther's use of the term "form" (*forma*) in relation to the presence of Christ in faith should be understood as a specific and creative variant on the Aristotelian view of knowledge in which "the form of the object of knowledge is transferred into the knower."[95] When the believer apprehends Christ in faith, he becomes the "new will" of the sinner and "Christ himself is both object of faith and subject of faith."[96] On the Finnish view, in the person of Christ present in faith God's grace (*favor*) as the forgiveness of sins exists in inseparable unity with the gift (*donum*) of renewal.[97]

---

legitimately be applied to Luther but that his concept of *theosis* is different in very significant ways from those found in the Orthodox tradition.

94. Sammeli Juntunen, "Luther and Metaphysics," 129.

95. Vainio, *Justification and Participation in Christ*, 31.

96. Vainio, *Justification and Participation in Christ*, 33.

97. Vainio, *Justification and Participation in Christ*, 9: "German scholarship has

However, critics of the Finnish account of justification dispute this interpretation of Luther's statements. While many would accept that faith unites the believer with Christ, and that within this union Christ communicates himself to the believer, this communication is a different aspect of union with Christ from justification itself. Justification is by contrast conceived exclusively in forensic terms as a declaratory "word-event," in which it is the divine speech-act of acquittal that alone creates a new reality for the believer: "Only on account of this truly objective foundation of imputation as forgiveness for Jesus' sake is the gift (*donum*) of the present Christ preached and so given."[98] If this view is correct, then the *Formula of Concord* (1577), a key document within the Lutheran confessional tradition, may express Luther's own intentions when it insists

> that neither renewal, sanctification, virtues, nor good works are to be viewed or presented *tanquam forma aut pars aut causa iustificationis* (that is, as our righteousness before God or as a part or a cause of our righteousness). They are also not to be mixed into the article of justification under any other pretense, pretext, or terminology. Instead, the righteousness of faith consists alone in the forgiveness of sins by sheer grace, because of Christ's merit alone.[99]

Here there certainly remain significant moral consequences of justification. God's word is powerfully creative and the believer is a new creation. Transformation is affirmed, but renewal is not to be identified with forensic justification itself (renewal is not only excluded as a cause of justification but also as a part of justification in any sense) and to do so is to merge what Luther intended to remain inseparable but clearly distinct. The *Formula* insists that salvation involves the indwelling of God

---

taken the change involved in justification seriously but has not interpreted the change from the viewpoint of christological union; *unio cum Christo* is an existential, not christological, category. The change is understood as an external causal influence."

98. Mattes, "Luther on Justification as Forensic and Effective," 268. Such criticisms of the Finnish school are more substantive than the often repeated suggestion that they distort Luther's position by relying too heavily on his early texts. Long before the rise of the Finnish school it was noted by Joest, *Ontologie der Person bei Luther*, 368, that union with Christ is a "Grundmotiv in Luthers Denken" and that "Wir finden es in frühen und späteren Schriften."

99. "The Solid Declaration, Article III: Righteousness," in *The Book of Concord*, 562–73 (par. 39).

in the believer but also that "this indwelling of God is not the righteous-ness of faith, which St. Paul treats. . . . Rather, this indwelling is a result of the righteousness of faith which precedes it."[100] The consequences of the *Formula's* position for interpreting those occasions when Luther and Paul use the vocabulary of participation in relation to justification are clear. Whatever Paul's participatory language means, it cannot have been understood by Luther in the way claimed by Mannermaa as denot-ing that justification involves the believer's participation in the essence of God. While Mannermaa certainly does not wish to emphasize such participation in isolation from the objective nature of Christ's atoning sacrifice, but to hold the two together, he cannot separate them in the manner of the *Formula*.

5.10. The Finnish School and Alien Righteousness

In relation to this debate, the Finns often significantly neglect the apoca-lyptic themes of Luther's Pauline exegesis. In particular, they frequently pay far too little attention to the alien nature of the righteousness of Christ received by the believer and the alien nature of the life that the believer must now live. In doing so, they miss an opportunity to nuance their own position and to demonstrate its essential validity. For Luther's insistence that the alien righteousness of Christ remains alien to believ-ers throughout their lives might be held to challenge the claims made by the Finnish school about the significance of union with Christ for justifi-cation. If justification encompasses renewal, then can the righteousness received by believers remain truly alien and avoid becoming the believ-ers' own righteousness? Luther so clearly teaches that the righteousness of the believer remains alien that the validity of the Finnish interpreta-tion can only be maintained if it is shown to be consistent with the alien nature of righteousness. In exploring this question it is helpful to examine the most famous of all Luther's contributions to Pauline interpretation.

In the *Preface* to the 1545 Latin edition of his writings, Luther re-

---

100. "The Solid Declaration, Article III: Righteousness," par. 54. Olli-Pekka Vainio, "Luther and Theosis: A Response to the Critics of Finnish Luther Research," *Pro Eccl* 24.4 (2015): 471, attempts to minimize the gap by arguing that the *Formula* is here dealing only with inchoate ethical renewal and not commenting directly on union with Christ in justification. While this is true, comment on the former does seem to have implications for the latter.

called that a breakthrough in his understanding of the phrase "the righteousness of God" (Rom 1:17) was crucial in the development of his Reformation theology. Having formerly understood the phrase to be a subjective genitive in the Greek, Luther came to read it as an objective genitive.[101] No longer was the righteousness of God a reference to God's just nature, that is, to God's distributive justice, whereby he judges each person according to what they deserve on the basis of their actions. Instead it is the righteousness given to the believer, "the passive righteousness with which a merciful God justifies us by faith."[102] As Luther had put it almost 30 years earlier in his *Lectures on Romans* (1515-1516), "by the righteousness of God (δικαιοσύνη θεοῦ) we must not understand the righteousness by which He is righteous in Himself (subjective genitive) but the righteousness by which we are made righteous by God (objective genitive)."[103] If the righteousness of God revealed in the gospel is thus not God's own righteousness (that by which God is righteous in God's self), then this seems to contradict Mannermaa's emphasis that through union with Christ in faith the believer participates in the essence of God. Indeed, Luther's insistence on understanding the phrase as an objective genitive might seem more consistent with accounts of justification that explain the alien nature of the righteousness received by the believer exclusively in relation to a declaratory word-event rather than in relation to union with Christ.

Yet context matters. Luther is specifically concerned in his interpretation of Rom 1:17 to break with medieval traditions in which the righteousness of Christ is granted to the believer as grace or love, and the believer then cooperates to make progress towards the righteousness of God.[104] This is Luther's primary concern rather than any attempt to establish that God's own righteousness and the righteousness received by

---

101. For Luther's reflections on the grammatical issues involved in construing such genitive phrases and on the difficulties of translating them into Latin, see *LW* 7:250-53 = *WA* 44:485, 25 - 486, 38.

102. *LW* 34:337 = *WA* 54:186, 7.

103. *LW* 25:151 = *WA* 56:172, 3-5 (my insertions). See also on Rom 3:21: *LW* 25:30, n. 20 = *WA* 56:36, 11-23; and see on Rom 3:5: *LW* 25:200-201 = *WA* 56:215, 16-20.

104. Heiko A. Oberman, "Iustitia Christi and Iustitia Dei," 120, points out that in contrast to such medieval traditions which separate the righteousness of Christ and the righteousness of God, "One can summarize, therefore, Luther's discovery in the following sentence: *the heart of the Gospel is that the iustitia Christi and the iustitia Dei coincide and are granted simultaneously*" (his emphasis).

the believer are not to be identified with each other. This can be seen in Luther's treatment of references to "the righteousness of God" in other contexts. Paul may at Rom 1:17 refer specifically to the righteousness by which believers are made righteous, but this does not exclude other legitimate interpretations of the phrase "the righteousness of God." In his exposition of Rom 3:7, where Luther interprets Paul's mention of God's truthfulness with reference to righteousness, he acknowledges ways in which it is biblical to assert that God is indeed righteous in God's own nature before again insisting that this formal divine righteousness is not Paul's meaning in the text under discussion.[105] At Rom 3:26, Paul says that the salvation provided by God in Christ has the purpose of displaying God's righteousness so as to prove "at the present time that He himself is righteous and that he justifies the one who has faith in Jesus." Luther argues that the righteousness displayed is indeed again that by which God justifies human beings, but this serves to prove that "He himself is righteous," which Luther glosses as "that He may be known by His nature as the only God."[106] It also serves to prove that God justifies the person of faith, such that Luther can say, "God is called righteous by the apostle because He justifies or makes us righteous."[107] And so, "the remission of sins proves that He is righteous and that He is able to justify."[108]

In relation to God's justifying activity demonstrating God's righteousness in this way, Eberhard Jüngel comments that "God's own being righteous shows itself in the fact that he makes (the one who believes on Jesus) righteous . . . God *is* righteous because of the fact that he *calls* us righteous."[109] The righteous nature of God is known to men and women only because God has engaged with humankind.[110] In this engagement,

---

105. *LW* 25:204-6 = *WA* 56:220, 1 - 221, 19.

106. *LW* 25:33 = *WA* 56:38, 12 - 39, 1.

107. *LW* 25:249 = *WA* 56:262, 19-20.

108. *LW* 25:249 = *WA* 56:262, 6-7.

109. Jüngel, *Justification*, 76–77 (the emphasis is his). Mark C. Mattes, *The Role of Justification in Contemporary Theology* (Grand Rapids: Eerdmans, 2004), 51, criticizes Jüngel on the basis that in his theology "God's being-for-self and being-for-us are identical." This is not quite what Jüngel says, who emphasizes not the identity but the complete consistency and compatibility of the two.

110. On Luther's epistemology in relation to the divine, see Hampson, *Christian Contradictions*, 21–22. Hampson quotes Walter von Loewenich, *Wahrheit und Bekenntnis im Glauben Luthers: Dargestellt im Anschluss an Luthers grossen Katechismus* (Wiesbaden: F. Steiner, 1974), 16: "Luther's theology does not begin with a general doctrine of God, with God's aseity, or the immanent trinity, only then afterwards to turn to what this God

he has shown that he is righteous not because he distributes justice according to deserts, but because he practices grace. The point for Luther is not to deny that the phrase "the righteousness of God" means God's being righteous in God's self, but rather to insist that this subjective genitive sense is true *for us* only on the basis of the objective genitive sense. Only in the righteousness that he gives to the Christian may God be known to human beings by his nature. Luther himself clarifies this when commenting on Ps 5:8 ("Lead me, O Lord, in your righteousness because of my enemies"). He rehearses the argument, with reference to several texts in Romans, that God's righteousness is not that with which he himself is just and condemns the wicked, but that with which he justifies those who believe. However, he goes on to state that it is not to be rejected in every respect that God's righteousness is "that righteousness by which God himself is righteous, so that through *one and the same* righteousness God and we may be righteous—just as God through *one and the same* word creates and we are what he himself is, so that we may be in him and his being (*esse*) may be our being (*esse*)."[111]

Thus, in the final analysis, Luther does identify God's own righteousness with the righteousness of Christ given to the believer through faith.[112] Luther's opposition to speculative theology and his insistence that what may be known about the divine nature is revealed in the emptying and self-giving of Christ forbids the interpretation of this identification by employing notions of ascent from humanness to God-likeness. If there are notions of *theosis* in Luther's thought, it is not to this that it refers. Luther does not mean by sharing in God's being that believers leave behind their humanity, but paradoxically that such sharing involves leaving behind their fallen self-justifying drive to be like God. If one focuses on this idolatrous human desire to be like God, then justification

---

in his abstract nature means for me. To Luther that would represent the speculation of the theology of glory. . . . When Luther speaks of God, he speaks of that God who has turned towards humankind and directed them."

111. *WA* 5:144, 19–22. The English translation provided comes from Jüngel, *Justification*, 77. The emphasis is his but the insertions of the Latin text mine. An older English translation is available. See *Select Works of Martin Luther Vol. 3*, trans. Henry Cole (London: Simpkin and Marshall, 1826), 211. The lecture comes from the period 1519–1521.

112. Vainio, "Luther and Theosis: A Response to the Critics of Finnish Luther Research," 474: "the righteousness of God that makes us righteous is simply the righteousness of Christ that he possesses as a human-divine person in which we participate through our consubstantial human nature."

by faith shows in contrast what it is to abandon such self-deception and to become truly human.[113] However, if one focuses on the theology of the cross, in which God's love works new creation "in the midst of nothingness and evil"[114] and in which God gratuitously loves unlovable sinners who have no lovable attributes that might call forth God's love, then believers do share in the being of God that is there revealed. They share this being in the specific sense that the presence of Christ in justifying faith makes it possible for them to give themselves in love of neighbor in a parallel way to that in which Christ gave himself for them.[115]

As Mannermaa himself admits, *theosis* understood in this way constitutes "a particular kind of divinization."[116] It is so particular in its nature, and reflects such a deliberate rejection by Luther of any identification of participation in the essence of God with the exaltation or ascent of the believer that one wonders if the term *theosis* or "divinization" is a helpful description of it. Nevertheless, the fact that in receiving the righteousness of Christ the believer is receiving God's own righteousness means that if we return to the 1545 *Preface* with this in mind, then Luther's account begins to take on a different accent. Luther writes that having understood the righteousness of God as the righteousness given to the believer, he "ran through the Scriptures from memory. I also found in other terms an analogy, as, the work of God, that is, what God does in us, the power of God, with which he makes us strong, the wisdom of God, with which he makes us wise, the strength of God, the salvation of God, the glory of God."[117] As Mannermaa argues, all of these properties are primarily to be understood as given by God, but, in giving them, God gives in a cruciform manner that which God is in God's self.[118]

Mannermaa cautions that this is not to be understood as collapsing

113. Thus in a different context Jüngel appeals to Luther's exposition of the same Psalm 5 to establish that justification results in humans becoming human. See Eberhard Jüngel, *The Freedom of a Christian: Luther's Significance for Contemporary Theology* (Minneapolis: Augsburg, 1988), 19–27.

114. Tuomo Mannermaa, *Two Kinds of Love: Martin Luther's Religious World* (Minneapolis: Fortress, 2010), 59.

115. On this theme of believers becoming Christs to their neighbors, see Kim, *Luther on Faith and Love*, 189–95.

116. Mannermaa, *Two Kinds of Love*, 64.

117. *LW* 34:337 = *WA* 54:186, 10–13.

118. Tuomo Mannermaa, "Why Is Luther So Fascinating?," in *Union with Christ: The New Finnish Interpretation of Luther*, ed. Carl E. Braaten and Robert W. Jenson (Grand Rapids: Eerdmans, 1998), 16–17, makes this point forcefully.

the distinction between God as Creator and the believer as creature. For even as he claims that the participation of believers in Christ (the Word) amounts to participation in the essence of God, Mannermaa notes that this does not for Luther mean that the substance of believers changes into the substance of the Word.[119] Yet what is the distinction that seems to be implied here between essence and substance? Opponents of the Finnish school are rightly entitled to feel that here there is a need for significant clarification of terms such as "being," "essence," and "substance." For example, Robert Kolb alleges that the Finnish approach

> ignores the nature of the "union" of bride and bridegroom that Luther employed so frequently (in which the two participants in the union do not become "one essence" but retain their distinctiveness), and his understanding of the preposition "in" when Luther uses the Hebraic concept of two distinct entities being "in" each (that is, in a close association which does not merge them but brings them together in intimate relationship).[120]

119. Mannermaa, *Two Kinds of Love*, 64, quotes *WA* 1:28, 39-41 where Luther both affirms that because believers are united with the Word by faith they can properly be said to be the Word and denies that this involves their substance changing into that of the Word.

120. Kolb, *Martin Luther: Confessor of the Faith*, 128. Kolb is not here directly defending continuity between Luther and *The Book of Concord* and elsewhere is explicitly concerned to explore the evolving nature of early Lutheran theology. See Robert Kolb, "'Not without the Satisfaction of God's Righteousness.' The Atonement and the Generation Gap between Luther and His Students," in *Archive for Reformation History Special Volume: The Reformation in Germany and Europe: Interpretation and Issues*, ed. Hans Rudolf Guggisberg, Gottfried G. Krodel, and Hans Füglister (Heidelberg: Gütersloher Verlaghaus, 1993), 136-56. In his criticism of the Finns, Kolb follows Klaus Schwarzwäller, "Verantwortung des Glaubens: Freiheit und Liebe nach der Dekalogauslegung Martin Luthers," in *Freiheit als Liebe bei Martin Luther/Freedom as Love in Martin Luther*, ed. Dennis B. Bielfeldt and Klaus Schwarzwäller (Frankfurt: Peter Lang, 1995), 146-48. Schwarzwäller (147) argues that the Finns confuse linguistic levels in Luther ("Sprachliche erkenne ich eine Verwechslung der Ebenen") and treat concise images such as joyous exchange as metaphors and translate them into ontological statements (und übersetzt sie in Seinsaussagen"). The problem, of course, is that as a theologian Luther is committed to capturing reality through his interpretation of biblical texts. He spins remarkable image after remarkable image in his attempt to grasp the meaning of Paul's own remarkable imagery. It therefore seems most unlikely that Luther operates with a clear distinction of linguistic levels in the way that Schwarzwäller suggests. Whatever Luther's ontological presuppositions, they will be expressed through such images.

For Kolb, Luther's understanding of participation in Christ conceives it as an intimate relationship but one in which the two parties remain unmerged and distinct. Different kinds of union entail different kinds of unity and what is meant by the believer participating in Christ is to be understood in different terms from those provided by the Finnish school.[121] To the extent that terms like "one essence" and "real-ontic" are under-defined in the work of Finnish scholars, Kolb's criticisms are very much on target.

Nevertheless, the point of marital imagery in the context of justification for Luther is scarcely that it presents a limit guarding against overestimates of what is involved in the presence of Christ in faith. While Luther is appropriately conscious of the mystery of the manner of Christ's presence in the faith, marital imagery provides him with the only human bond capable of conveying not just close relationship but actual oneness. Kolb's picture of the union of Christ and the believer as one in which the two parties are in a close relationship but remain distinct and unmerged struggles to do justice to Luther's repeated insistence on their oneness: they are as "one person" and as "one body" and "faith couples Christ and me more intimately than a husband is coupled to his wife."[122] How this "oneness" is to be understood certainly requires exploration. If "merge" means that two formerly distinct entities cease to exist, having combined so as to become a new third entity, then Kolb is correct that this is not what Luther intends. Some account of mutual indwelling is needed that can be distinguished from merging. Yet if "oneness" is not for Luther becoming "one essence" in which distinctiveness is lost, it is also not merely a "close association," even if that association is intimate. As Kolb's reliance on a particular construal of the preposition "in" suggests, his position depends on taking Luther to mean less than he appears to say.[123]

121. See Carl R. Trueman, "Is the Finnish Line a New Beginning? A Critical Assessment of the Reading of Luther Offered by the Helsinki Circle," *WJT* 65 (2003): 235: "the meaning of 'union with Christ' is not a universal given. Marriage union, legal union, ontological union—these all offer models of understanding the idea that may well differ in significant ways."

122. *LW* 26:168 = *WA* 40:284, 25-26; 285, 25; 286, 16-17. Of course it is Paul who insists that sexual union involves becoming one body just as the believer becomes one spirit with the Lord (1 Cor 6:16-17). The text is instructive in relation to the discussion of Luther's use of marital imagery in that in this passage Paul seems disturbed precisely by the fact that the believer and the prostitute who have sexual relations do not in his view remain distinct entities.

123. Mannermaa, *Christ Present in Faith*, 21-22, quotes from a sermon in which

Perhaps unsurprisingly given that the issue at stake is the manner in which the believer participates in Christ, it is Christology that may provide a way forward here. Vainio comments that "The parties to this conjunction participate in each other's attributes without changing or losing their own essence. . . . The relation between Christ and the believer must be examined according to the rules of Christology."[124] In classical Christology the two natures of Christ are not confused and remain distinct but do so in one person without division or separation. There is still significant work to be done in exploring this analogy if the Finnish school is to clarify its account of justification in Luther. Yet, despite the need for greater precision in some of the claims made, the assertion from the Finnish school about the effective nature of justification does not stand in any inherent contradiction to the alien nature of the righteousness received by the believer. The motif of the presence of Christ in faith holds these two together. So long as for Luther (1) union with Christ through faith does not result in a confusion of the essence of Christ and of the believer, but (2) does require a sharing by the believer in Christ's attributes, then (3) the righteousness of Christ received by the believer can both remain alien and be effective in renewal (the living of an alien life). Indeed, on this account the third point is an appropriate outworking of the first two points. Believers live an alien life because they share in Christ's attributes, especially his righteousness, without any confusion of essence.[125] This conclusion has two major consequences. The first is

---

Luther discerns Paul's "Hebrew manner of speaking" to indicate that God fills believers so that "everything that He is and everything He can do (*war er ist und vermag*) might be in us in all its fullness, and work powerfully." See *WA* 17.1:438, 14-28. In contrast, Kim, *Luther on Faith and Love*, 262, feels that Luther's recognition of Paul's use of Hebraism clearly tells against the Finnish position. This is not so obvious in relation to recent explorations of Christology in New Testament scholarship. Richard Bauckham, *Jesus and the God of Israel* (Grand Rapids: Eerdmans, 2008), x, seeks a way beyond standard distinctions between ontic and functional Christology into what he terms a "Christology of divine identity," consistent with Old Testament and Jewish understanding of God, in which "the so-called divine functions which Jesus exercises are intrinsic to who God is."

124. Vainio, *Justification and Participation in Christ*, 35. Like Trueman, "The Finnish Line," 239, Bielfeldt, "Response to S. Juntunen," 165, worries that the Finns' claims imply that for Luther the finite human being participates in the substance of the infinite. This leads Bielfeldt to propose a more precise definition of participation drawing from the doctrine of the Trinity the image of *perichoresis*: "It is not that the infinite can be predicated of the substance of the finite, but rather that the infinite is present in, permeating the substance of the finite in a nonaccidental way."

125. J. Todd Billings, "The Contemporary Reception of Luther and Calvin's Doc-

that while Luther and the *Formula of Concord* are in obvious agreement in dismissing the view that the works of the believer contribute to justification, it is far from clear that Luther separates justification and renewal in the manner of the *Formula*. The Finnish view that for Luther justification encompasses renewal is plausible. The second is that the apocalyptic and participatory strands in recent Luther interpretation can and should be thoughtfully integrated.

5.11. Conclusions and Implications: United with the Victor

For all the ways that Luther's influence, whether positive or by aversion, looms over the subsequent history of Pauline interpretation, his contribution is not well understood, especially among New Testament scholars. While it is recognized that he breaks with accounts of justification in which human works are meritorious, his alternative proposal is often misrepresented. In particular, it is not recognized that in his exegesis of what Paul means by righteousness by faith Luther integrates union with Christ with the apocalyptic themes of Paul's theology.[126] Dominated by the devil in their fallen plight, it is only when human beings are relocated outside of themselves in Christ and so receive his righteousness that salvation is possible. Exploring this integration leads to conclusions that serve to dispel some common misapprehensions about Luther's Pauline exegesis. Contrary to suggestions otherwise:

---

trine of Union with Christ: Mapping a Biblical, Catholic, and Reformational Motif," in *Calvin and Luther: The Continuing Relationship*, ed. R. Ward Holder (Göttingen: Vandenhoeck & Ruprecht, 2013), 165–82, therefore misses the point when he asserts against Mannermaa that "the *Formula of Concord's* refusal to *ground* the declarative act of justification in an ontological indwelling is actually in strong continuity both with Luther and other early Reformational theologians" (168, his emphasis). The debate does not concern whether for Luther justification is grounded in divine indwelling (it is not) but rather whether the only way to avoid grounding justification in divine indwelling is to deny that justification encompasses renewal. On an appropriately nuanced version of the Finnish view this is not a necessary step and one that Luther did not take. For Luther, justification necessarily encompasses renewal because it is grounded in Christ's alien righteousness.

126. These themes are also integrated with Luther's theology of the Word. The faith in which Christ is present is received through the preaching of the Word, and, just as the believer receives an alien righteousness and must live an alien life, so God's transforming Word of promise always comes from outside.

1. Luther does not offer an account of Paul's soteriology in which making justification by faith central implies neglect of Christology. That Christ's presence within faith is central to what Luther understands Paul to mean by faith makes it impossible for Luther to construe justification and union with Christ as contrasting categories. To be justified requires union with Christ, since it is only in being united with him that his righteousness is received, and to be united with Christ requires justification since it is in justifying faith that Christ is present.

2. Luther does not divorce justification from the story of Jesus Christ. Atonement is vital to justification, but justifying faith does not appeal to the merit of Christ's death separately from Christ's presence in such faith itself. Instead, the two are identified with each other, for the Christ present in faith is the same Christ who lived as a human being and in his crucifixion and resurrection overcame sin and death. Further, the gift of Christ's righteousness never becomes the property of the believer but always remains alien: "Christ is, of course, a reality *pro nobis* ('for us') and *in nobis* ('in us'), but he is also and remains *extra nos* ('outside of us')."[127] Christology is not absorbed into anthropology.

3. Luther does not establish a contractual view of justification. Faith does not justify because it is the appropriate response to God's grace and is the right kind of religious disposition to fulfill the human side of a contract between God and humanity. Instead, faith justifies because it grasps hold of Christ and unites the believer with Christ.

4. When he speaks of imputed righteousness, Luther does not mean fictional righteousness. The charge is simply erroneous.[128] If faith justifies because it grasps hold of Christ and unites the believer with him so that his righteousness is received, then it is simply impossible to Luther that such faith will not produce works. The righteousness received is not the believer's own and remains alien, but it is not fictional since through Christ's presence in faith the believer must live an alien life. If the insights of the Finnish school are correct, this also means that while Luther is extremely concerned to

127. Lienhard, *Luther: Witness to Jesus Christ*, 392.
128. Hampson, *Christian Contradictions*, 122: "It is of course a complete farce to say that according to Luther God leaves man corrupt!"

insist that works are not an efficient cause of justification, he does not separate them from justification so that they are understood exclusively as a consequence of justification but retains them within his account of justification itself.

It is important to acknowledge that in no sense for Luther is this kind of integration a step back towards scholastic ideas of meritorious human cooperation with divine grace. Just as the righteousness of Christ received by the believer is an alien righteousness, so the life that the believer now lives in union with Christ is an alien life. In Gal 2:19b–20, with its statement that Christ and not the believer now lives within the person who has been crucified with Christ, Luther finds a key exegetical resource for the consistent expression of this perspective. The ironies of the history of reception of this important aspect of Luther's appropriation of Paul are apparent in McGrath's comment that

> By arguing that grace and faith are given in Christ, Luther is able to assert at one and the same time that the righteousness of believers is, and will remain, extrinsic to them, while Christ is nonetheless really present within believers, effecting their renovation and regeneration. ... The reinterpretation of grace as an absolute external quality, and faith as a partial internal one, permits Luther to maintain what is otherwise clearly a contradiction within his theology of justification—his simultaneous insistence upon the external nature of the righteousness of Christ, and upon the real presence of Christ in the believer.[129]

Luther would here surely recognize a basically accurate summary of central parts of his theology of justification but nevertheless be indignant at the implication that there is an inherent structural contradiction that he somehow manages to bridge. The external nature of the righteousness of Christ and the presence of Christ in the believer are not opposite poles, for external righteousness is granted only in union with Christ by faith and that union only occurs when the self is crucified with Christ and the believer begins to live the alien life of Christ. The righteousness received by the believer, the divine Word that evokes faith in which Christ is present, and the life now lived are all alien. The polarity of Luther's concern is that between the old self dead in sin and captive

129. McGrath, *Iustitia Dei*, 229.

to the devil, and the believer as new creation. The self must die. To say otherwise is from Luther's perspective is to set aside the grace of God.[130] Commenting on Gal 2:16 and its assertions that justification is by faith and not by works of the law, Luther says of the believer:

> For to the extent that he is a Christian, he is above the Law and sin, because in his heart he has Christ, the Lord of the Law, as a ring has a gem. Therefore when the Law accuses and sin troubles, he looks to Christ; and when he has taken hold of Him by faith, he has present with him the Victor over the Law, sin, death, and the devil—the Victor whose rule over all these prevents them from harming him.[131]

In union with Christ through faith, by having Christ "as a ring has a gem," the justified believer shares in Christ's victory.

---

130. The distinctive nature of Luther's perspective can be illustrated by comparing it to an influential contemporary account of the same verses. Miroslav Volf, *Exclusion and Embrace: A Theological Exploration of Identity, Otherness, and Reconciliation* (Nashville: Abingdon, 1996), 69–71, uses Gal 2:19b-20 to dispute philosopher Richard Rorty's concept of the self. Volf's context and concerns are thus hugely different from Luther's, and so too is his reading of the text: "Paul clearly has in view a continued life of that same self after its 'crucifixion.' . . . For if Christ 'lives *in* me,' as Paul says, then *I* must have a center that is distinct from 'Christ the center.' . . . By the process of decentering the self did not lose a center of its own, but received a new center that both transformed and reinforced the old one. Recentering entails no self-obliterating denial of the self that dissolves the self in Christ" (his emphasis).

131. *LW* 26:134 = *WA* 40:235, 21–25.

6 Relational Righteousness

Justification on Account of Christ in
Philip Melanchthon's Pauline Exegesis

6.1. Melanchthon in the Shadow of Luther

Philip Melanchthon has the misfortune often to be labelled as the originator of much that is deemed unsatisfactory by contemporary scholars in later Protestant accounts of justification. His emphasis on the forensic nature of the imagery of justification in the Pauline letters is perceived to lead to accounts in which the righteousness received by the believer is a cold legal fiction and any emphasis on ethical transformation muted. In such assessments, Melanchthon is often ironically cast both as Luther's closest colleague and supporter at Wittenberg and as the individual most responsible for misdirecting Luther's legacy. Yet Melanchthon was a very considerable Pauline exegete in his own right. Further, his role in relation to Luther is not always that of a disciple. While the overall influence of Luther upon his younger colleague is not to be doubted, in some important exegetical matters, such as the nature of "grace," it was Melanchthon who exercised influence over Luther.[1] In order to understand both the similarities and the significant differences between Melanchthon's Pauline interpretation and that of Luther it is necessary first to explore Melanchthon's exegesis in its own right. In particular it is important to understand how Melanchthon sustained and developed Luther's emphasis on the alien nature of the righteousness received by the believer. Melanchthon did this through the stress he laid on the importance of rhetoric for exegesis and through his strongly relational account

1. See 4.2.

218

of justification. Only once the contours of Melanchthon's own Pauline exegesis have been appropriately mapped in this way is it then possible to see how these aspects of Melanchthon's exegesis also served to open up vital differences from Luther, particularly in Melanchthon's manner of expressing the christological focus of alien righteousness.

6.2. Melanchthon's Rhetorical Approach to Interpreting Romans

As we have seen (4.2), it is upon his exegesis of Romans that Melanchthon's reputation as a Pauline interpreter chiefly rests. There is also no doubt concerning the significance for that exegesis of the rhetorical tools provided by Melanchthon's humanist education or about the impact that his rhetorically-informed approach to exegesis made upon his sixteenth-century contemporaries:

> Melanchthon combined his humanist training in the analysis of ancient texts with a single-minded conviction regarding the central point of Romans. As a result, he produced a commentary that to contemporary readers, who were also steeped in humanism's rhetorical techniques, would have sounded like the Apostle Paul's own voice commenting from the first century on the sixteenth century's most critical theological debates. For these readers Melanchthon's method rendered the exegete and exegetical tradition nearly invisible by inviting them to consider Paul's dialectic and rhetoric in the light of the very rules for argument and speech being taught by Melanchthon in Wittenberg's classrooms.[2]

His *Annotations* (1522) on the text of Romans, first published without his consent on the basis of notes taken in his lectures, were followed in 1529/1530 by a *Dispositio* of Romans, an analysis of the rhetorical structure or outline of Paul's letter.[3] Then came the *Commentary on Ro-*

2. Timothy J. Wengert, "Philip Melanchthon's 1522 Annotations on Romans and the Lutheran Origins of Rhetorical Criticism," in *Biblical Interpretation in the Era of the Reformation*, ed. Richard A. Muller and John L. Thompson (Grand Rapids: Eerdmans, 1996), 118.

3. Melanchthon first published a partial disposition in 1529 and then a fuller version in 1530. For the latter see *CR* 15:441-92. It is not available in English.

mans (1532) followed by revised versions in 1540 and 1556.[4] As the above quotation indicates, the content of Melanchthon's exegesis of Romans cannot be abstracted from his method. Melanchthon's humanist training provided him with the tools of his exegetical craft. Before he published anything on Paul's letters, Melanchthon was already the author of a Greek grammar and of textbooks on rhetoric (the arts of discourse used by speakers to inform or persuade audiences) and dialectics (the resolution of disagreement through rational argument). Against the backdrop of the use of Aristotelian dialectics as the characteristic form of debate in later medieval scholasticism, typically scorned by humanists for what they perceived as its sterile and quibbling use of tightly structured logical arguments, Melanchthon offered an alternative account of dialectics that integrated it with rhetoric. He read Aristotle primarily as a rhetorician and in so doing rendered dialectics usable again within a humanist approach to biblical interpretation centered on the grammatical analysis of texts.[5] The result is that Melanchthon pays close attention to Paul's rhetoric but begins with a concern for the correct definition of terms or topics (*loci*) which provide the underlying structure of a text. Only when questions are asked that allow such *loci* to be correctly defined is it possible then to see how Paul's argument is organized and so properly to understand its urgent message about salvation.[6] In particular it is necessary by means of correct definition to identify the *scopus* (the main thing Paul had in mind in his argument) and also the *status caussae* (the summary

4. For the 1532 commentary, see *MSA* 5:25–371. For the 1540 commentary see *CR* 15:493–796. It is available in English as Melanchthon, *Commentary on Romans*. For the 1556 commentary see *CR* 15:797–1052. For a succinct overview of Melanchthon's exegesis of Romans, see Robert Kolb, "Philipp Melanchthon's Reading of Romans," in *Reformation Readings of Paul*, ed. Michael Allen and Jonathan A. Linebaugh (Downers Grove, IL: InterVarsity Press, 2015), 73–96.

5. For a full account, see John R. Schneider, "The Hermeneutics of Commentary: Origins of Melanchthon's Integration of Dialectic into Rhetoric," in *Philip Melanchthon (1497–1560) and the Commentary*, ed. T. J. Wengert and M. Patrick Graham (Sheffield: Academic Press, 1997), 20–47.

6. Melanchthon's work on the *Dispositio* of Romans was to be crucial to his later commentaries on the letter. Rolf Schäfer, "Melanchthons Hermeneutik im Römerbrief-Kommentar von 1532," *ZTK* 60 (1963): 216–35, argues that "In the commentary of 1532 Melanchthon used the schema of 1529/30, with some changes in the details, as a framework for the detailed interpretation of Romans" (220, my translation). Schäfer goes on to discuss in depth the structure of Paul's argument in Romans as Melanchthon perceives it. See also Carl Joachim Classen, *Rhetorical Criticism of the New Testament* (Tübingen: Mohr Siebeck, 2000), 144–60.

statement or proposition that sums up this main concern and "to which all proofs and arguments are referred").[7]

Accordingly, in Romans the *status* is introduced in 1:16–17, where, in speaking of the righteousness of God, Paul provides "a summary of the Gospel, which is the purpose of the whole disputation which follows . . . when he mentions the righteousness of God, he embraces all the benefits of Christ."[8] This summary is then expounded at greater length in 3:21–26, where there is "the principal proposition which . . . contains the real and chief statement of the Gospel."[9] The central matter of the letter and of the gospel is justification by faith apart from the works of the law. Melanchthon thus perceives that Luther's central theological preoccupation is the same as Paul's central theological preoccupation in Romans and grounds this assertion in the rhetoric of the letter: "The very course of Paul's argument brings about this meaning which I give. The meaning must be taken from the apostolic speech itself, not another imagined sense invented against the proper sense of the speech."[10] Almost five centuries of familiarity with Protestant interpretations of Romans that follow Melanchthon in regarding these particular texts as key to discerning the message of the entire letter should not blind us to his originality in his own context. Melanchthon's own words powerfully express this originality for us:

> There are two parts to the epistle. The first contains a long disputation. In the latter there are precepts about morals. Many people judge that only the latter about morals is now worthy to be read, and they read it like a poem of Hesiod or Phocylides. They think it contains only quarrels regarding Jewish ceremonies about which nobody now fights. But one ought to think otherwise. The first part contains an examination (*disputationem*) which is most necessary for every age and for the entire church. It contains the foremost and enduring topics of Christian doctrine, distinguishes the Gospel from the Law and from philosophy, shows the benefits of Christ, the gratuitous remission of sins, liberation from eternal death, the imputation of righteousness, the gift of the Holy Spirit, and eternal life. It proclaims these great things; it does not quarrel only about ceremonies.[11]

7. Wengert, "Lutheran Origins of Rhetorical Criticism," 128–29.
8. Melanchthon, *Commentary on Romans*, 70 = *CR* 15:558.
9. Melanchthon, *Commentary on Romans*, 98 = *CR* 15:586.
10. Melanchthon, *Commentary on Romans*, 11 = *CR* 15:495.
11. Melanchthon, *Commentary on Romans*, 11 = *CR* 15:495.

Melanchthon here reacts against what he perceives as a prevalent approach, of which Erasmus was the most prominent contemporary representative, which prioritizes the ethical material contained in Rom 12-15 and even there too often fails to perceive any contemporary relevance. Instead, Melanchthon gives priority to Rom 1-11 and sustains this conclusion on the basis of Paul's type of speech. In his 1532 commentary, Melanchthon "began his exposition of Rom 12 by stating that Paul's judicial kind of speech was concluded and that, as a kind of appendix, Paul now switched to the *genus suasorium* (a kind of deliberative speech)."[12] It is therefore Rom 1-11 that contains Paul's *disputatio*, expresses the heart of the Christian gospel, and has vital contemporary relevance. This conclusion is sustained by rhetorical analysis, which is essential to the correct interpretation of the letter since Melanchthon holds that Paul masterfully integrates rhetoric and dialectics in precisely the manner to which Melanchthon himself aspired: "Paul knew exactly how to prosecute a good argument and how to write an effective speech. The Epistle to the Romans was the work of someone who knew both how to speak *and* how to think."[13]

Unsurprisingly, this view of Romans as a rhetorically sophisticated and deliberate summary of the gospel in turn led Melanchthon to regard the letter as "the *scopus* of the Scripture."[14] It was the gateway to true interpretation of Paul's other letters and of the rest of the Bible. Thus, for example, Melanchthon will insist of Colossians that

> Here therefore is the argument and *status* of this letter—the nature of the Gospel. The apostles offered to the world what one might call a new teaching, which he here defines. His definition is not brief. On the contrary, he fully distinguishes between Christian righteousness and the human righteousness that is gathered by our industry and by our strength, whether from the commands of men or from the Mosaic Law (that is, the Decalogue).[15]

---

12. Timothy J. Wengert, "The Rhetorical Paul: Philip Melanchthon's Interpretation of the Pauline Epistles," in *A Companion to Paul in the Reformation*, ed. R. Ward Holder (Leiden: Brill, 2009), 151-52.

13. Wengert, "The Rhetorical Paul," 134 (his emphasis).

14. Timothy J. Wengert, *Human Freedom, Christian Righteousness: Philip Melanchthon's Exegetical Dispute with Erasmus of Rotterdam* (Oxford: Oxford University Press, 1998), 58.

15. Melanchthon, *Paul's Letter to the Colossians*, 29 = *MSA* 4:211, 26-31. The same paragraph is also quoted in Wengert, *Human Freedom, Christian Righteousness*, 52-53.

Paul's central concerns in this letter reflect those of Romans. What Melanchthon terms "Christian righteousness," i.e., justification by faith alone, is the *status caussae* here also. As Rom 1:16–17 and 3:21–26 provide the hermeneutical key with which to unlock the argument of Romans, so Romans provides the hermeneutical key with which to approach other parts of Scripture. For Melanchthon this is neither an arbitrary decision nor one based solely on theological discernment. It rests also on rhetorical analysis.

This deep commitment to employing rhetoric in order to understand Paul also influenced the form in which Melanchthon presented his interpretations of Romans. His commentaries on the epistle do not immediately enter into exegesis of Rom 1 but begin with extensive definitions of the key terms and topics of Paul's letter such as sin, justification, grace, faith, works of the law, etc. This is a direct consequence of Melanchthon's view that the correct definition of such *loci* is essential to identifying the *scopus* and *status caussae* of a text. It also reflects something of Paul's own method since Melanchthon believes that the apostle himself provides definitions of terms for his readers. From Rom 1:16 to 5:11, Paul develops his argument, bringing forth and defending various propositions that clarify the essence of the gospel, reaching a climax in Rom 5:1–11, where the peace with God obtained through justification by faith offers spiritual comfort to the reader. However, at Rom 5:12 he begins "as it were, a new book,"[16] in which the argument is no longer developed. Like the first "book" of Romans, this "new book" reaches a climax, this time in 8:12–39 where new obedience is discussed and the comfort of the everlasting love of God is offered to the reader. Prior to this, from 5:12 until 8:11, Paul first provides extended and careful definitions of the terms that have been vital to his earlier argument: "sin," "law," and "grace." Just as it is necessary in medical education for the unlearned to be taught "how veins, nerves, and arteries differ,"[17] so it is necessary for Paul to define his terms. Proper understanding of the nature of sin, law, and grace is as vital to grasping Paul's gospel as understanding the nature of veins, nerves, and arteries is to sound medicine. This careful differentiation of the terms "brings much light to the earlier propositions because definitions and causes are the source of all kinds of transactions."[18]

16. Melanchthon, *Commentary on Romans*, 132 = CR 15:622.
17. Melanchthon, *Commentary on Romans*, 132 = CR 15:622.
18. Melanchthon, *Commentary on Romans*, 132 = CR 15:622.

Equipped with such careful definitions, Melanchthon is able to comment on the text of Romans according to Paul's own intentions. Well-constructed definitions allow him to distinguish between what is central and what is more peripheral in Paul's argument. If a text is not relevant to the main point that Paul was trying to make, Melanchthon does not treat that particular text. Since Paul was attempting to grant his readers a clear grasp of the gospel, this too is the commentator's main task and complete comprehensiveness is of less significance. At the same time, his careful definitions also provide Melanchthon with powerful tools by means of which to relate different parts of Scripture to each other. The same *loci* crop up again and again in different parts of the Bible. His readers can find that in the midst of a comment on a single text Melanchthon plunges them into "a world filled with definitions, final causes or effects, syllogisms and, above all else, explanations of other texts of the Bible."[19] From Melanchthon's perspective these are not digressions but integral parts of his task as a commentator in explaining the gospel. They also frequently enable him to bring the message of the text to bear on contemporary theological debates.

Finally, his insistence on the definition of terms opens up for Melanchthon a new approach to teaching theology. The first edition of his widely influential textbook, *Loci Communes* (1521, "The Commonplaces"), replaces the categories of Lombard's *Sentences*, the standard medieval textbook, with categories organized according to Paul's topics in Romans. For if Romans provides a summary of the gospel and a hermeneutical key to the rest of Scripture, then a textbook that follows its topics approaches the practice of theology in a manner in tune with Scripture itself. Subsequent editions of *Loci Communes* were to stick less closely to the structure of the argument of Romans than the 1521 edition, but Melanchthon's overall approach remained similar. The close relationship between Melanchthon's exegesis of Paul and his vision for teaching theology ensured that *Loci Communes* makes many similar exegetical points to those found in his commentaries on Romans.[20]

19. Wengert, "The Rhetorical Paul," 137. See especially 131–41 on Melanchthon's methods of interpretation.

20. Major editions of *Loci Communes* (there were innumerable minor ones) were published in 1521, 1535, and 1543 (all in Latin), and in 1555 (in German). For the 1521 text ("Loci Communes Theologici") see *Melanchthon and Bucer*, ed. Wilhelm Pauck = *MSA* 2:3–163; *CR* 21:81–228. The 1535 edition has never been translated into English. See *CR*

6.3. The Drama of Law and Gospel in Melanchthon's Interpretation of Romans

Melanchthon uses his rhetorical analysis of Romans to bring into focus what he regards as Paul's deepest theological convictions. In particular, he hears Paul speak of the relationship between God and human beings within a soteriological drama to which the categories of law and gospel are central. Justification by faith understood in forensic terms is prominent, but it is only within this wider drama that forensic justification makes sense and it is therefore important to begin an account of the content of Melanchthon's interpretation of Romans not with a detailed discussion of Paul's use of the verb δικαιόω ("justify") but with the overall drama of law and gospel. For Melanchthon, this drama begins with the human plight apart from Christ, and in understanding that plight he is completely committed to the common account widely shared among early Protestant interpreters (see 3.4). In Melanchthon's view, philosophy and reason do reveal a civil righteousness of disciplined and upright deeds that is possible for fallen human beings. However, the law of God "demands not merely outward works, but perfect obedience. Therefore it is easily understood that no one is able to be righteous before God, that is, accepted because of outward discipline, as Paul clearly says: 'By the works of the Law no flesh shall be justified' [Rom 3:20]. This statement takes away the praise of righteousness not only from ceremonies, but also from moral works, and speaks about the entire discipline."[21]

Human beings are utterly incapable of contributing to their own salvation through meritorious obedience and this is what Paul intends to communicate when he denies that justification is by works of the law. In failing to appreciate this and restricting the reference of the phrase "works of the law" to ceremonies only, the great error committed by the Reformers' Catholic opponents confused a civil righteousness with the righteousness that justifies before God: "they imagine that righteousness in the sight of God or what the law of God demands is nothing else than the discipline with which philosophy is satisfied."[22] Melanchthon interprets in relation to this confusion Paul's statement in Rom 2:1 that those

---

2:331–560. For the 1543 text see Melanchthon, *Loci Communes 1543* = CR 21:601–1106. For the 1555 text see *Melanchthon on Christian Doctrine* = CR 22:61–636.

21. Melanchthon, *Commentary on Romans*, 15 = CR 15:500.

22. Melanchthon, *Commentary on Romans*, 12 = CR 15:496.

who judge others for the sins previously described in 1:18–32 themselves do the same things. The one who judges another is "whoever possesses civil morals and condemns only those who are beholden to manifest turpitude, and does not condemn himself but thinks he is just because of his morals." Such an individual may not commit the same sinful actions outwardly, but does so "with the inner impulses of the mind."[23] Such gross confusion is only further evidence of human captivity to sin, and there are only disputes about the nature of this captivity because "people do not see the uncleanness of the heart, namely these sins: doubt about God; lack of the fear of God, trust, and love; and harboring dreadful impulses against the Law of God. They do not see these vices, much less the fact that they are sins. Therefore the ungodly imagine that original sin is nothing."[24]

It is noteworthy that the unrecognized sins that Melanchthon here names as constituting the sinfulness of those who falsely consider themselves righteous focus on their attitude towards God. For it is as a restoration of relationship with God that Melanchthon principally understands the salvation available through Christ. From the very moment that human beings fell, God responded not only with judgment but also with gracious promises of salvation:

> When Adam had fallen and was accused, he could think nothing except what the Law showed—that he would perish because he had not obeyed God. But God comes forward, and although he subjects the human race to death of the body and other ills, he nevertheless sets forth a consolation: he promises liberation from sin and death, and the restoration of the human race. He says that it would come to pass that the seed of the woman would crush the head of the serpent [Gen. 3:15]. When this had been said, the Son of God moved the heart of Adam and poured new light and life into him.[25]

The law judges and condemns human failure to obey God's commandments, but the gospel promise of gratuitous forgiveness and new life dogs its footsteps. Already Adam, the father of humanity, was righteous through faith; already in its opening narratives Scripture is to be

---

23. Melanchthon, *Commentary on Romans*, 86 = CR 15:575.
24. Melanchthon, *Commentary on Romans*, 133 = CR 15:623.
25. Melanchthon, *Commentary on Romans*, 23 = CR 15:508.

interpreted according to Luther's hermeneutic of law and gospel. The knowledge of sin convicts and brings terror, but Paul's purpose is not to leave his readers simply with a right understanding of their bondage. Instead, it is that they should transition from law to the comfort of the gospel, the hermeneutic of law and gospel itself becoming a lived experience. As Wengert comments,

> on several occasions in his exposition of Romans, Melanchthon used and relied upon the examples of Adam and David (as Paul had used the example of Abraham in Romans 4), because they showed that justification by faith alone was not a matter of some "cold, lifeless concept of the soul" but had to strike fear into a person's heart and provide true comfort. Here, in Adam fleeing the Garden of Eden and David being caught by Nathan in his murderous affair with Bathsheba, one saw clearly, from Melanchthon's perspective, what actually happened to believers as they moved from law to gospel. It was precisely this experience of grace (Adam hearing the proto-Evangelium of Genesis 3:15 and David receiving God's forgiveness in Psalm 51) that defied reason and, effectively, broke the very syllogism on which human existence after the fall was based.[26]

All of Paul's rhetorical and dialectical skill in constructing Romans was bent towards the pastoral purpose of delivering this experience of the truth of the gospel to his readers.

At the heart of this experience of the gospel lies justification by faith alone. From Melanchthon's perspective, any attempt to rely on human works and their merits is to step away from the gospel and back towards the misguided attempt to be saved through law. It is only by complete reliance through faith on Christ's saving work that justification is possible. Here the insistence that Paul's use of the verb δικαιόω ("justify") is a piece of forensic imagery, with which Melanchthon's name is indelibly associated, is indeed important. However, Paul's purpose in using a legal metaphor is most clearly understood for Melanchthon within the category of relationship:

> This word "relational" (Latin: *relative*), which Melanchthon consistently used after 1531, is a more accurate description of his intention

---

26. Wengert, *Defending Faith*, 350.

than the standard term, forensic. When Melanchthon compared justification to what happens *in foro* (in a court of law) to a guilty person who is pronounced not guilty, he did so to explain Paul's Hebraism and to explain the relational aspect of such righteousness-producing faith.[27]

As we have already noted, it is Rom 3:21–26 that Melanchthon regards as the *status caussae* or principal proposition of the letter and on which his comments give us the clearest insight into his understanding of justification. When Paul speaks of Christ's death as a redeeming sacrifice in 3:24–25 Melanchthon comments that, "The world does not see the greatness of the wrath of God against sin, and says that sin is an unimportant thing. But here let us learn that the wrath is so great that no sacrificial victim could placate God, save only the death of his Son."[28] In his crucifixion, Christ is the propitiator whose obedient sacrifice is effective where all efforts to rely on works and their merit are doomed to failure: "For we are righteous, that is, accepted by God, not on account of our perfection but through mercy on account of Christ, as long as we take hold of it and set it against the wrath of God."[29] Melanchthon will sometimes say that the righteousness received by the believer is the righteousness of Christ, but his phrasing in this quotation that believers are justified "on account of (*propter*) Christ" (alternatively translated "because of/for the sake of Christ") is far more characteristic. He does not argue that Christ is present in faith and hence, united with him by faith, the believer receives Christ's righteousness. Nor does he characteristically argue that Christ's righteousness is in some sense transferred to the believer. Melanchthon seems content to say that Christ is and remains the mediator whose death pleads the believer's case before the Father.

Commenting on the nature of faith in Rom 3:25, Melanchthon attacks what he regards as the disastrously restricted mediating role granted to

27. Wengert, "The Rhetorical Paul," 155 n. 92. That it is the relational structure of justification that is primary for Melanchthon and not the forensic image can be seen in the "Apology of the Augsburg Confession," in *The Book of Concord*, par. 305–6 where he actually contrasts forensic imagery with his own understanding of justification: "Justification here means to be regarded as righteous. However, God does not regard a person as righteous in the way that a court or philosophy does (that is, because of the righteousness of one's own works, which is rightly placed in the will)."

28. Melanchthon, *Commentary on Romans*, 100 = CR 15:588.

29. "Apology of the Augsburg Confession," par. 227.

Christ by his Catholic adversaries, "as when the head of a family, angry with a servant, is placated by some friend. There the friend procures access to the master for the servant. Thereafter he has no business there, but the servant pleases because of his own service. They give to Christ only this, that He merited this beginning and chance for us to merit."[30] In contrast, wiser interpreters know that "Christ always remains the mediator. . . . We ought not to oppose our virtues to the judgment of God, but Christ, the sacrificial victim and propitiator."[31] It is Christ and his saving work on the cross who turns away divine judgment against sin and who continuously secures access to the Father for believers. It is this relational dynamic that Melanchthon again and again emphasizes in his accounts of justification. It helps him to clarify exactly what he understands Paul to mean by faith as trust (*fiducia*), distinct from the infusion of virtue-producing grace characteristic of medieval understandings of justification. For having first noted that to say "we are justified by faith" is correlative to saying "we are pleasing to God through mercy," i.e., they are alternative ways of expressing the same truth, Melanchthon then continues:

> Although I fully agree that faith and trust are qualities, they nevertheless become, like the names of the other desires, relational, as love behaves itself in a way relative to that which we love, fear to the object which is feared, and trust to its object on which it rests . . . it is necessary that mention be made of faith because it is necessary that there be some impulse by which we accept the gift and apply it to ourselves. . . . This impulse of faith in our minds is not an idle cogitation, but it wrestles with the terrors of sin and death.[32]

On this account faith has a strong cognitive dimension, for it is an impulse of the mind. Yet this cognitive element is not primarily a question of knowledge but of desire. Melanchthon will go on to speak of the devil's attempts to break weak minds so that there is either contempt of God or despair, but also to emphasize that faith "fights lest it lose God, lest it be torn away from God. . . . God is seen in his Word, and when the mind looks upon the Word, its faith is strengthened."[33] Given life by its

---

30. Melanchthon, *Commentary on Romans*, 101 = CR 15:589.
31. Melanchthon, *Commentary on Romans*, 101 = CR 15:589.
32. Melanchthon, *Commentary on Romans*, 29 = CR 15:514.
33. Melanchthon, *Commentary on Romans*, 30 = CR 15:516.

encounter with God's word, faith justifies "because it takes hold of the mercy."[34] The *Apology of the Augsburg Confession* expresses things similarly when it says that "faith is the very righteousness by which we are reckoned righteous before God, not because it is a work that is worthy in and of itself, but because it receives the promise by which God has pledged that on account of Christ he desires to be gracious to those who believe in him."[35] Faith is so important from Melanchthon's perspective because through Christ, the mediator, it brings and keeps human beings in relationship with God. It is reliance upon this relationship secured by justification that he opposes to the emphasis of his opponents upon an infused righteousness. The alien righteousness upon which believers rely is the righteousness of Christ, who intercedes for them before the Father with complete sufficiency.

6.4. Forensic Imagery in Melanchthon's Interpretation of Romans

Having explored the relational nature of Melanchthon's interpretation of justification in Romans, it is then possible to understand the part played by its specifically forensic nature (i.e., with the verb δικαιόω identified as an image drawn from the law court) without caricaturing Melanchthon's account as fictional. Melanchthon famously highlights the forensic nature of justification in his definition of the term. He has previously used such a definition in *Loci Communes* (1535) and introduces it into one of his commentaries on Romans for the first time in 1540, where it is already coordinated with his relational perspective:

> According to the Hebrew usage of the term, to justify is to pronounce or to consider as just, as is said in Hebrew: "The Roman people justified Scipio when he was accused by the tribunes," that is, absolved him or pronounced him just. Thus we know for certain that in these disputations of Paul justification signifies the remission of sins and acceptance to eternal life, as the fourth chapter of Romans testifies in a sufficiently clear manner, where it defines justification as the forgiveness of sins. Therefore when we say we are justified by faith

34. Melanchthon, *Commentary on Romans*, 57 = CR 15:545.
35. "Apology of the Augsburg Confession," par. 86.

it is the same thing as saying that we are accounted just by God on account of (*propter*) Christ when we believe.... It signifies the imputation of *iustitia*, or acceptance. And *iustus* is in this way understood relationally (*relative*) as acceptance to eternal life.[36]

The historical reference here is to the Roman general Scipio Africanus (236–183 BCE), victor over Hannibal in the Second Punic War at the battle of Zama in 202 BCE. When later accused in the mid-180s BCE of having taken a bribe from the Seleucid King Antiochus III, Scipio did not deign to defend himself against the charges but to popular acclaim on the anniversary of Zama simply reminded the court of his victory on behalf of Rome. He then left the court to go to offer sacrifices of thanksgiving to the gods, followed by virtually all present, leaving the tribunes with no defendant and no trial. It is odd that Melanchthon should write as if the Roman people pronounced Scipio innocent in Hebrew. What he appears to mean, given that the accounts of Scipio's trial in our Latin and Greek sources do not actually speak of his acquittal as a justification,[37] is that the Hebrew verb in the Old Testament equivalent to the Greek δικαιόω ("justify") is a forensic term. If one were to speak about Scipio's acquittal in Hebrew then one would speak of him as having been justified by the people. Melanchthon writes in a less confusing way in the *Loci Communes* (1535) and *Loci Communes* (1543), but in those places he also uses the example of Scipio to illustrate a Hebrew expression.[38] The episode clearly

---

36. Melanchthon, *Commentary on Romans*, 25 = CR 15:510–11 (my insertions). Stephen Strehle, *The Catholic Roots of the Protestant Gospel* (Leiden: Brill, 1995), 66–68, argues that Melanchthon is here crucially influenced by Erasmus, who had argued in his *Annotations on Romans* that the Vulgate's rendering of λογίζομαι in Rom 4:3 using *reputare* (to consider) is incorrect and that *imputare* (to count to one's credit) should be preferred. See CWE 56:107–8 = *Annotations on the New Testament: Acts, Romans, I and II Corinthians*, 359. "To impute" is then defined using *acceptilatio*, a concept that refers to a debt not paid but by agreement deemed as such. While this definition of imputation in terms of acceptation certainly is helpful for Melanchthon, I doubt that Erasmus's work is quite the influence upon him at this point that Strehle suggests. The Vulgate does once translate λογίζομαι using *accepto ferre* and twice using *imputare* (compared to four uses of *reputare*), so Erasmus is not making a previously unimaginable equation between the terms, and Melanchthon himself does not use this grammatical analysis to argue for the validity of his account of justification.

37. Ironically there is, however, some support provided for another significant aspect of Melanchthon's Pauline interpretation. Polybius, *The Histories* 23.14.2, says that Scipio gained "the affection of the people and the confidence (πίστις) of the senate."

38. See CR 21:421 (*Loci Communes*, 1535), and *Loci Communes* (1543), 86 = CR 21:742.

appeals strongly to Melanchthon. This may partly be due to Scipio's idealized status within the humanist tradition. Petrarch had conceived Scipio as a "living symbol of what history and philosophy teach regarding what man should strive to be."[39] To use an individual outstanding in civic righteousness as a primary illustration of how sinners are justified before God would certainly seem to serve Melanchthon's theological purposes. More important are the parallels presented by the details of the episode to his relational understanding of justification. Scipio is pronounced righteous by the Roman people not because he disproves the charges against him but because they set against the charges the overwhelming virtue of his service to Rome, without which, had he not defeated the Carthaginians, a Roman court in which to put him on trial would not even exist. Similarly, the believer does not disprove his or her sinfulness but in God's court there is set against this charge the overwhelmingly greater work of Christ as a propitiating sacrifice.[40]

Melanchthon's use of the example of Scipio's trial to illustrate justification drew an early response from the Catholic scholar Johannes Gropper, who in 1540 was to attend the Diet of Augsburg in the entourage of the Archbishop of Cologne. In his *Enchiridion Christianae Institutionis* (1538), Gropper argues that Scipio was wrongly accused and therefore truly innocent, whereas "the reconciled sinner is more to be compared with one who has suffered a sentence and then been restored, than to one who has been absolved in a court."[41] The reconciliation involves not just

39. Aldo Bernado, *Petrarch, Scipio, and the "Africa": The Birth of Humanism's Dream* (Baltimore: Johns Hopkins, 1962), 10. Also to be noted is Augustine's identification of Rome's ingratitude to Scipio with the tipping point in the decline of Rome's morals. See Augustine, *The City of God against the Pagans*, trans. Robert W. Dyson (Cambridge: Cambridge University Press, 1998), 3.21 (129–31) = *CSEL* 40.1: 147–49.

40. Timothy Wengert, "Philip Melanchthon and John Calvin against Andreas Osiander: Coming to Terms with Forensic Justification," in *Calvin and Luther: The Continuing Relationship*, ed. R. Ward Holder (Göttingen: Vandenhoeck & Ruprecht, 2013), 63–68, comments that when using the term *relatio* with regard to justification, Melanchthon "was thinking of the technical usage in law: a retorting or rejecting of a charge, that is, turning a charge back on the accuser. In this case, however, Melanchthon inverted the meaning. Here not the accused, but the accuser (God) overturned the accusation with the *beneficia Christi*" (68).

41. Gropper's work receives extensive discussion in Lugioyo, *Martin Bucer's Doctrine of Justification*, 103–33 (here 126). The *Enchiridion* has never appeared in English. The translation provided here is that of Lugioyo. See also the analysis offered by Reinhard Braunisch, *Die Theologie der Rechtfertigung im "Enchiridion" (1538) des Johannes Gropper* (Münster: Aschendorffsche Westfalen, 1974), 361–69. Braunisch notes Grop-

the setting aside of the sentence but the reform of the prisoner who, as in Augustine's understanding of justification, is not simply declared righteous but actually made righteous. The charge that forensic justification constitutes a legal fiction is thus leveled against Melanchthon almost immediately. Unsurprisingly, Melanchthon seems to regard all such charges as misguided. In fact, in his final *Commentary on Romans*, published in 1556, Melanchthon even makes a similar charge in the opposite direction. He suggests that to conceive justification either as the infusion of a divine *habitus* of love or even more directly as divine indwelling is not to propose real change in the believer since "when water is poured into a jug there is no change in the jug."[42] What Melanchthon is presumably driving at with this comparison is the partial nature of the transformation of the believer in this life claimed by his opponents. Sin persists and if salvation depends on such partial transformation then there can be no assurance of salvation for the believer.

For Melanchthon, infusion is the fiction and not his own understanding of justification, in which the total obedience of Christ as mediator grants complete righteousness to the believer. Christ's sacrifice is the ever-present reality that is set against and overwhelms sin in the divine courtroom. As Wengert puts it, Melanchthon was "not simply talking about a mental construct, a fictive judicial 'as if,' but an actual turn of events before God's judgment seat. Thus, the actual sinner, oppressed by sin (that is, under the law), heard the judge speak a completely unexpected word of grace . . . for Melanchthon everything changed because of this divine pronouncement of judgment (law) and forgiveness (gospel)."[43] The divine declaration of acquittal that constitutes justifi-

---

per's argument that Scipio's "was a normal acquittal, as is typically done in a criminal case for lack of evidence or proven innocence" (362, my translation). From a contemporary perspective Scipio's failure actually to deny the charges against him inevitably appears suspect, but Gropper's position is less odd once one realizes that humanist tradition had indeed regarded Scipio as innocent in fact. Martin Chemnitz, *Loci Theologici Vol. II*, trans. Jacob A. O. Preus (St. Louis: Concordia, 1989), 476–80, notes Gropper's criticism of "the *Scipio* of Philipp" (476) but does not further defend the example, choosing instead to provide an extensive biblical word-study. The two volumes of the *Loci Theologici* appeared posthumously in 1591 and 1594 (Chemnitz died in 1588). In 1596 the perceived Erasmian tendencies of Gropper led to the inclusion of the *Enchiridion* on the *Index of Forbidden Books*.

42. CR 15:912-13. The translation is that of Wengert, *Defending Faith*, 339.

43. Wengert, *Defending Faith*, 341. In this same volume (330–51) Wengert provides extensive discussion of Melanchthon's remarks on justification in the 1556 commentary.

cation is an effective word, in which divine speech accomplishes what it pronounces. It is, as contemporary Melanchthon scholarship has often termed it, a "word-event" (*Wortgeschehen*) that is the gateway to new life.[44] The divine word of acquittal fulfills the divine word of promise on account of the offering of Christ, the word of God, which is testified to in the Scriptures that are also the word of God. As Melanchthon says when commenting on Rom 10:8 ("The Word is near, in your mouth"): "God is found nowhere outside of his Word, or without his Word; he wants to be known through it. By means of this instrument he wants to work."[45]

Thus, Melanchthon believes that by means of God's word new life is brought to the believer, and the gift of the Holy Spirit is an essential aspect of this vivification: "Yes, the Son of God, the eternal Word of the eternal Father, imparts comfort to us through the external word in our hearts, and thus gives his Holy Spirit. Athanasius says, 'The Holy Spirit is thus in men by means of the word.'"[46] This emphasis on new life through the word is crucial, for Melanchthon is insistent that alongside justification the believer receives renewal. Even as he introduces the example of Scipio to illustrate the forensic nature of the verb "to justify," Melanchthon insists that "one must know that in the forgiveness of sins there is given at the same time (*simul*) the Holy Spirit. . . . Thus the gift of the Holy Spirit is connected with justification, which begins not only one virtue—faith—but also others: fear and love of God, love of the truth, chastity, patience, justice toward the neighbor, as I shall say later about works."[47] Commenting on Rom 5:15, he will write that grace overcomes sin "doubly, by imputation and by its effect. It overcomes by imputation, because God accounts those who lay hold of grace to be righteous, although in fact they still have the remnants of sin. Thereafter, it also overcomes it in effect, because in them, although they are weak, there are new impulses which resist sin."[48] Melanchthon characteristically attributes this renewal and the capacity to produce good works to the work of the Holy

44. See especially Martin Greschat, *Melanchthon neben Luther: Studien zur Gestalt der Rechtfertigungslehre zwischen 1528 und 1537* (Wittenberg: Luther-Verlag, 1965), 83, who speaks of the "central significance" ("zentrale Bedeutung") which the "word-event" occupies in the theological thought of the Reformer.

45. Melanchthon, *Commentary on Romans*, 198 = CR 15:691.

46. *Melanchthon on Christian Doctrine*, 201 = CR 22:447. Melanchthon is referring to Athanasius, *Defense Against the Arians* 3.25:24-25 (NPNF² 4:406-7).

47. Melanchthon, *Commentary on Romans*, 25 = CR 15:511.

48. Melanchthon, *Commentary on Romans*, 136-37 = CR 15:627.

Spirit in the believer.[49] The Spirit is the crucial difference between the outward good works of merely civil righteousness and good works that come from inner renewal and are truly pleasing to God:

> Although human diligence can provide outward discipline to some extent, nevertheless spiritual impulses cannot be brought about without the Holy Spirit. Therefore, when hearts are raised up by faith, the Holy Spirit is given in order that he may kindle a new light in the minds and excite pious impulses which are in agreement with the Law of God, according to the saying of Paul: "In order that we may receive the promise of the Spirit through faith" [Gal 3:14].[50]

Melanchthon thus takes great care in his exegesis of Romans to provide an overall account of salvation that includes the ethical renewal of the believer. Justification is a forensic declaration and renewal is a distinct phase consequent upon justification, but renewal is made prominent. A failure to stress renewal would have provided his opponents with an opportunity to charge him with antinomianism.

6.5. Chronological Development in Melanchthon's Interpretation of Justification in Romans

This careful articulation by Melanchthon of the relationship between different aspects of soteriology took several decades to achieve. Melanchthon's interpretative coordination between the forgiveness of sins in justification and the renewal of the believer through the work of the Holy Spirit developed over time. He had not always carefully distinguished between justification and renewal by the Spirit as distinct realities that are also connected. In the 1520s Melanchthon appears content to make clear that the good works of renewal are not in any sense a cause of justification or a source of merit but nevertheless to

49. This emphasis continued throughout Melanchthon's career. See the comments of Robert Kolb, "Melanchthon's Doctrinal Last Will and Testament: The 'Responsiones ad articulos Bavaricae inquisitionis' as His Final Confession of Faith," in *Philip Melanchthon: Theologian in Classroom, Confession, and Controversy*, ed. Irene Dingel, Robert Kolb, Nicole Kuropka, and Timothy J. Wengert (Göttingen: Vandenhoeck and Ruprecht, 2012), 141-60 (esp. 147-49).
50. Melanchthon, *Commentary on Romans*, 37 = CR 15:523.

speak as if such good works of renewal are in some sense included in what is meant by justification. In *Loci Communes* (1521), justification "is described as participation in Christ's righteousness while it is actualized in the new affects that are evoked by the Spirit and renewed according to the Law of God."[51] Faith is itself a gift evoked by the Holy Spirit and "this faith in the good-will of God permeates the whole life, all works, all physical and spiritual trials." It is therefore quite clear that this faith is active and performs works. While it is plain that the works of faith are not meritorious, what is conspicuously not said is that such works of faith are to be sharply distinguished from justification. No clear boundary is delineated. This situation persists throughout the 1520s. In the *Apology of the Augsburg Confession* (1531) Melanchthon states that "we have demonstrated fully enough both from the testimonies of Scripture and from arguments derived from the Scripture that by faith alone we are justified, that is, out of unrighteous people we are made righteous or are regenerated."[52] Melanchthon has earlier glossed a similar statement about regeneration by saying that "faith alone makes a righteous person out of an unrighteous one, that is, alone receives the forgiveness of sins."[53] He could therefore here simply be using the term "regeneration" not to refer to the good works that result from justification but rather to the Holy Spirit's gift of faith, the rebirth that enables a person to desire and receive the promise of forgiveness of sins through Christ.[54] Yet even if this is Melanchthon's intention, interpretation is not easy and the reader can be forgiven for confusion.

However, at the time of the *Apology* Melanchthon was in the process of developing a much clearer boundary between justification and the works produced through the renewal by the Holy Spirit that accompanies justification.[55] In a letter of May 12, 1531, he responds to a now lost enquiry from Johannes Brenz by highlighting the danger of the view that faith is the foundation and root (*radix*) of good works and that an individ-

---

51. Vainio, *Justification and Participation in Christ*, 63-93, provides an account that distinguishes three phases in Melanchthon's development of his views on justification.

52. "Apology of the Augsburg Confession," par. 117.

53. "Apology of the Augsburg Confession," par. 72.

54. Vainio, *Justification and Participation in Christ*, 74, formalizes this distinction between two dimensions of regeneration: "One who has been justified and who has received the promise of forgiveness of sins is also made capable of good works and love (*renovatio₁*). The active love (*renovatio₂*), however, does not justify, only faith does."

55. For a full account of this process, see Wengert, *Law and Gospel*, 179-85.

ual is justified on the grounds of fulfilling the law through the agency of the Holy Spirit.[56] Melanchthon says that "we are justified by faith alone, not because it is the root, as you write, but because it apprehends Christ, on account of which we are accepted"[57] and that this acceptance is "not on account of the gift of the Holy Spirit in us."[58] This distinction between justification as acceptance and renewal by the Spirit is then reflected in the *Commentary on Romans* (1532) where Melanchthon will state bluntly that "Although it is necessary that the new movements will occur in those who are reconciled, justification does not, however, mean having new virtues. It is understood as a matter of relation (*relative*), which refers to God's will of those who are approved and accepted by God."[59] The traditional term "imputation" by which justification is described is to be identified with acceptance by God in a way that excludes the renewal that brings new virtues. Imputation does not have an effective aspect: "Melanchthon henceforth holds exclusively to imputation, with which acceptation is equated."[60] As Melanchthon will express it in the *Commentary on Romans* (1540): "We must include these things when we dispute about justification: remission of sins and imputation of righteousness— that is, acceptance—joined to which is the gift of the Holy Spirit and acceptance to life eternal."[61] Melanchthon insists that justification is always accompanied by renewal through the Holy Spirit. However, he also insists that it is not itself to be identified with or included in justification. Renewal by the Holy Spirit is still an essential part of what Melanchthon understands to be Paul's soteriology, but it is a different, albeit closely related, aspect of salvation from justification.

Yet even this position, although stable, was not Melanchthon's fi-

---

56. *MBWT* 5: no. 1151 (104–13) = *CR* 2:501–3.

57. *MBWT* 5: no. 1151 (109, 15–17) = *CR* 2:501: "sola fide sumus iusti, non quia sit radix, ut tu scribis, sed quia apprehendit Christum, propter quem sumus accepti . . ." (my translation).

58. *MBWT* 5: no. 1151 (41–42) = *CR* 2:502: "non propter dona Spiritus sancti in nobis" (my translation).

59. *MSA* 5:39, 12–16. The translation is that of Vainio, *Justification and Participation in Christ*, 77.

60. Robert Stupperich, "Die Rechtfertigungslehre bei Luther und Melanchthon 1530–1536," in *Luther and Melanchthon in the History and Theology of the Reformation*, ed. V. Vajta (Philadelphia: Muhlenberg Press, 1961), 83: "Melanchthon hält sich nunmehr ausschließlich an die imputatio, mit der die acceptatio gleichgesetzt wird" (my translation).

61. Melanchthon, *Commentary on Romans*, 100 = *CR* 15:588.

nal word on justification. Later in Melanchthon's career, after Luther's death, he became involved in the Osiander controversy that gripped the Lutheran movement in the 1550s. Andreas Osiander, who had been a key figure in the adoption of the Reformation in Nuremberg in the 1520s, and who later became professor at the new Königsberg University, claimed that Melanchthon and others were distorting Luther's teaching. Osiander wrote that:

> They teach [doctrines] colder than ice, that we are accounted righteous only on account of the remission of sins, and not also on account of the righteousness of Christ dwelling in us by faith. God is not indeed so unjust as to regard him as righteous in whom there is really nothing of true righteousness.[62]

Thus, Osiander's basic complaint is that union with Christ in faith is being neglected in Melanchthon's construal of justification. For Osiander, it is not that faith is a human virtue or *habitus*, but rather that imputation must be defined so as to include the presence of Christ. If it does not, then Luther's position is abandoned and justification by faith is indeed "something created, which is theologically unacceptable. In that case, from Osiander's perspective, righteousness would be a created righteousness (*creatürliches gerechtigkeit*), i.e., habitus."[63] It is therefore the presence of Christ's divine nature in the believer (which Osiander termed "essential righteousness") that justifies and is the main event of salvation, not his obedience and death on the cross. The crucifixion is the moment when Christ's sacrifice takes away divine wrath and brings forgiveness, but this simply serves to make possible the believer's subsequent union with Christ by faith. Unsurprisingly, Osiander's severing of Christ's person from his work received a universally negative reaction. Further, Osiander's critique of what he saw as fictional accounts of justification generated the suspicion that he was allowing works once again to play a part in justification. Although this may have been the very opposite of his intention, it did not help that "he insisted throughout the debate

---

62. The translation is from Reinhold Seeberg, *Textbook of the History of Doctrines*, trans. Charles E. Hay (Philadelphia: Lutheran Publication Society, 1905), 370 = Andreas Osiander, *Gesamtausgabe*, ed. Gerhard Müller and Gottfried Seebaß, 10 vols. (Gütersloh: Gütersloher Verlagshaus, 1975-1997), 9:444, 7-9.

63. Vainio, *Justification and Participation in Christ*, 99. See 95-108 for Vainio's overview of Osiander's teaching.

on a single definition of *iustitia* (*Gerechtigkeit*) as 'that which moves us to do the right.'"[64]

Melanchthon vigorously rejected Osiander's accusation that he had abandoned Luther's teaching and maintained the validity of his own account of justification. In his *Commentary on Romans* (1556), Melanchthon begins his comments on Rom 3:21 by alleging that "Osiander understands the righteousness of God to be God dwelling in the reborn person and moving that one to do righteous things. So, by this approach [*res*] itself he teaches that a human being is righteous by renewal [*novitas*] and works."[65] For Melanchthon, if Osiander's teaching is accepted, then the comfort of the gospel promise is lost since the believer is left dependent for salvation upon the uncertainties of his or her own works. Melanchthon in contrast still wants to maintain that imputation is relational and is to be understood in terms of the forgiveness of sins and divine acceptance. Yet Melanchthon is clearly sensitive to the charge that his theology neglects the truth that God dwells in the believer and he is even more emphatic in his later works that he too embraces this. In *Loci Communes* (1555), when discussing "faith" and the peace with God that results from justification, Melanchthon writes:

> It is not untrue to say that the Lord Christ effects this peace, or that the Holy Spirit does. God is present in this comfort. He is active, however, through the external word, and kindles faith in the heart. But these are all together—the external word, contemplation of the external words in us, and the Son of God, who works through the external word, manifests the eternal father, speaks comfort to the heart, and gives the Holy Spirit, which produces love and joy in God.[66]

Without conceding the distinction between justification and renewal, Melanchthon here clearly wishes to emphasize that this distinction does not diminish the soteriological significance of the presence of

---

64. Wengert, *Defending Faith*, 78. He quotes from Osiander, *Gesamtausgabe*, 10:163, 23. There are those who regard Osiander as generally and unfairly misunderstood. See, for example, Anna Briskina, "An Orthodox View of Finnish Luther Research," in *LQ* 22.1 (2008): 16–39. Yet even if this were proven to be true, it remains the case that Osiander as I have presented him above is how he was understood by his contemporaries.

65. *CR*15:855. The translation is that of Wengert, *Defending Faith*, 338.

66. *Melanchthon on Christian Doctrine*, 158–59 = *CR* 22:330.

God in the believer. In his comments on justification itself, Melanchthon will insist on imputed righteousness but also speak of the eschatological righteousness to which Paul refers in Gal 5:5 ("the hope of righteousness"), when in eternity "God himself is in the saved, and makes them like himself, so that they are entirely pure, without sin."[67] This is anticipated in the life of the believer here and now:

> The Holy Spirit is a living divine motion in us, producing in us that which is akin to God. . . . Thus there is a spark of new obedience in those who are converted to God; but the faith that *for the sake of the Lord Christ* we have forgiveness of sins, and are pleasing to God, must always precede, and this faith must be grounded on the *obedience of the Lord Christ*, God and man. When this comfort is in the heart, then we are the dwelling place of God and obedience is begun.[68]

In such statements, clear anti-Osiandrian sentiments are leavened with recognition of the truth of divine indwelling. It is also in this context that Melanchthon will again speak not only of justification as "on account of/because of/for the sake of" Christ but also, as he had in *Loci Communes* (1521), as the imputation of the righteousness of Christ (*die Gerechtigkeit des herrn Christi*).[69] Whether this recognition that believers receive the imputed righteousness of Christ amounts to a further significant development in Melanchthon's own teaching on justification is a matter of dispute. Wengert says of Melanchthon in the 1550s that "Christ's presence in the justified was a result of the work of the Holy Spirit and followed from justification."[70] In contrast Vainio's opinion is that "justification is both imputation and donation of the Spirit. The qualitative change caused by the Spirit, however, is not righteousness *coram Deo*."[71] Whichever is correct, it is at least clear both that justification and renewal cannot be divorced for Melanchthon, but are received together, and that they are not the same thing and are to be distinguished. He says of justification and *sanctification* [*Heiligung*] that "these two words are clear and distinct."[72]

67. *Melanchthon on Christian Doctrine*, 158–59 = CR 22:332.
68. *Melanchthon on Christian Doctrine*, 162 = CR 22:334.
69. *Melanchthon on Christian Doctrine*, 155–56, 161 = CR 22:327, 333.
70. Wengert, *Defending Faith*, 319.
71. Vainio, *Justification and Participation in Christ*, 91.
72. *Melanchthon on Christian Doctrine*, 163 = CR 22:334.

6.6. Melanchthon and Luther on Justification: Contrast or Continuity?

Despite Melanchthon's emphasis on the salvific significance of divine indwelling, his careful distinguishing from justification of the renewal brought by this indwelling ensured that, in relation to justification itself, his legacy would subsequently be identified with exclusively forensic accounts. As we noted at the beginning of this chapter, it is precisely for this reason that Melanchthon has often been held responsible for the alleged errors of later forensic accounts of justification within various strands of Protestant Orthodoxy. Yet whatever the rights and wrongs of such debates, another critique has dogged Melanchthon and his reputation. It forms a prologue to these debates. Even during Luther's lifetime some read Melanchthon's account of justification as departing in various significant ways from Luther's teaching. Conrad Cordatus, preacher at Niemegk, made this complaint in the 1530s in response to a lecture he heard delivered at Wittenberg. The lecture was delivered by Melanchthon's student Caspar Cruciger, but Cruciger based his remarks on Melanchthon's notes and was perceived as presenting Melanchthon's views.[73] As we have already seen, Osiander later made a similar charge in the 1550s. The charge of discontinuity arose again in early twentieth century scholarship in the work of Karl Holl, who alleged that Luther's original insight into the inner, transforming righteousness received by faith alone is distorted by Melanchthon's legal metaphor of forensic justification.[74]

In contemporary discussion this question of the relationship between Luther's and Melanchthon's accounts of justification is intimately related to more general debates about the interpretation of Luther. If the account of Luther offered in the last chapter is correct, in which his emphasis on the presence of Christ in faith distinguishes Luther's understanding of justification from the *Formula of Concord*, then there must be significant differences between Luther and Melanchthon on justification (see 5.9 and 5.10). For Melanchthon's concern to distinguish all notions

---

73. For the chronology of this dispute, see Wengert, *Law and Gospel*, 206-10.

74. See Timothy J. Wengert, "Melanchthon and Luther / Luther and Melanchthon," in *Philip Melanchthon, Speaker of the Reformation*, ed. Timothy J. Wengert (Burlington, VT: Ashgate Variorum, 2010), 55. Wengert refers to Karl Holl, "Die Rechtfertigungslehre in Luthers Vorlesung über den Römerbrief mit besonderer Rücksicht auf die Frage der Heilsgewißheit," in *Gesammelte Aufsätze zur Kirchengeschichte Bd. 1: Luther* (Tübingen: Mohr Siebeck, 1948), 111-54 (esp. 124-29).

of divine indwelling from justification by faith clearly anticipates the *Formula* on this issue. His statements also fit comfortably with the views of those in our contemporary context "who define Luther's theology by the Word event."[75] However, because Melanchthon's consistency with the *Formula* in these important respects is not at issue, there are also converse possibilities. If it can be demonstrated that there are no significant differences between Luther and Melanchthon on justification, then accounts of Luther that differentiate his teaching on justification from that of the *Formula* are called into question. Given the central importance of the *Formula* for the Lutheran tradition, discussion of the relationship between Luther's and Melanchthon's accounts of justification also involves discussion of continuity or discontinuity between the Lutheran tradition and its founding figure.

That there is a confessional tradition at stake in contemporary discussion of the relationship between Luther's and Melanchthon's accounts of justification has not always served the interests of clarity. In his otherwise immensely erudite and helpful *Defending the Faith*, a monograph on the Osiander controversy, Timothy Wengert—who believes that Melanchthon accurately represented Luther's views on justification—associates with Osiander's position both Karl Holl and the Finnish school of Luther interpretation (and even the NPP). Wengert asks concerning the Osiander controversy, "How can one argue that Luther was such a brilliant teacher if nearly all of his closest students completely misunderstood his teaching on justification by faith and if the only person to understand his position never sat in his classroom and was universally vilified by the very students who did?"[76] The implication is that if Osiander can be shown to have misinterpreted Luther, then Holl and the Finnish school must also have done so in contrast to Melanchthon's accurate grasp of his colleague's intentions. The difficulty with this argument is that representatives of the Finnish school do not identify their own interpretations of Luther with those of either Osiander or Holl. Vainio is clear that Osiander's understanding of justification in terms of the indwelling of Christ's divine nature is not that of Luther.[77] Tuomo Mannermaa, the patriarch of the Finnish school, devotes a monograph to Luther's understanding of divine love and demonstrates that it begins from *rejection* of the view

---

75. Wengert, *Defending Faith*, 316.
76. Wengert, *Defending Faith*, 3.
77. Vainio, *Justification and Participation in Christ*, 95-107 (esp. 98-99).

that "God always loves that which is something, whereas 'what is not,' or what is nothing, cannot be the object of God's love in any other way but in relation to something that already is; it, or they, can be loved as potentialities for something and, thus, as 'being something.'"[78] Instead, Mannermaa holds that Luther conceives divine love as finding nothing lovable, either actual or potential, in sinners but instead as creating that which is lovable to it. This is plainly incompatible with Holl's sanative interpretation of justification in Luther in which "God's present justification of sinners is based upon his anticipation of their final sanctification, in that the present justification of humans takes place on the basis of this foreseen future righteousness."[79] It is thus perfectly possible to hold that there are significant differences between Luther and Melanchthon while also holding that Osiander and Holl misunderstand Luther. The differences between Luther's and Melanchthon's accounts of justification are real but the scope of these differences is not as great as those between Luther and either Osiander or Holl.

What is lacking in the current debate is comparison between the exegesis of Luther and Melanchton in its historical context. The Reformers are first and foremost biblical interpreters who ground their theology in their exegesis. Their goal is fidelity to Scripture. If there are significant differences between them in understanding justification, these should emerge first and foremost as they interpret texts. What results if their comments on the same texts in the Pauline letters are considered side by side? Whatever emerges, it is necessary to heed the fact that Luther and Melanchthon never broke with each other over justification or even engaged in public disagreement. Further, given their shared struggle with the existing church, the reading public of the sixteenth century will naturally have assumed that what they read from the pen of one of the two Wittenberg colleagues reflected also the opinions of the other. It is simply not credible that either regarded the position of the other as standing in contradiction to his own. We have already noted the existence of a basic consensus concerning justification among early Protestant interpreters in which there are a number of defining characteristics, especially insistence upon the alien nature of the righteousness received by the believer.[80] Yet non-contradictory differences can exist

---

78. Mannermaa, *Two Kinds of Love*, 19.
79. McGrath, *Iustitia Dei*, 225.
80. See Hamm, "What Was the Reformation Doctrine of Justification"?, 179–216.

within broader frameworks of agreement. Contradiction is only one possible form of significant difference. Heinz Scheible assumes significant differences in theology between Luther and Melanchthon but then asks the following question about Luther: "Why did he not jump all over Melanchthon as he did his Roman Catholic opponents, the prince of humanists, Erasmus, or even his own student John Agricola?" Scheible's answer is that Luther displays "the ability to put up with the individuality of a colleague with whom he felt in basic agreement. The added conviction that he needed him may have assisted Luther in being able to do this."[81] If there are significant differences, they will exist within this kind of basic agreement.

It is not as easy to make comparisons between the Pauline exegesis of Luther and Melanchthon as might be imagined. With the exception of Luther's *Lectures on Romans* (1515-1516), delivered before Melanchthon joined the Wittenberg faculty,[82] Luther taught Galatians and Melanchthon taught Romans. However, it is possible to gather from various texts their comments on the same verses in Paul. In what follows I will compare their comments on important texts in which Paul employs the phrase "the righteousness of God" (especially 2 Cor 5:21), paying particular attention to differences in their interpretation of the christological basis of justification. I will also return to Rom 5:15 and the relationship between grace and gift, demonstrating that their different treatments of gift are also determined by their different christological approaches to justification. Luther's comments are gathered from various sources, but those from Melanchthon are predominantly from his *Commentary on Romans* (1540).

6.7. Exegetical Comparison: Melanchthon and Luther on Justification in Key Pauline Texts

The agreements between Luther and Melanchthon in how they understand Paul's important phrase "the righteousness of God" (Rom 1:17; 3:5, 21-26; 2 Cor 5:21) are extensive. As we have already seen (5.8), Luther

---

81. Heinz Scheible, "Luther and Melanchthon," *LQ* 4.3 (1990): 317-39 (esp. 335, 337-38).

82. On Melanchthon's early life and his crucial first years at Wittenberg up until 1524, see Gregory B. Graybill, *The Honeycomb Scroll: Philipp Melanchthon at the Dawn of the Reformation* (Minneapolis: Fortress, 2015).

formally agrees with Augustine that in Rom 1:17 "by the righteousness of God (δικαιοσύνη θεοῦ) we must not understand the righteousness by which He is righteous in Himself (subjective genitive) but the righteousness by which we are made righteous by God (objective genitive)."[83] However, Luther gives the righteousness granted by God an entirely different sense and refuses to understand it as an initial gratuitous gift of grace and love with which the believer must then cooperate in good works in order to gain God and eternal life. Luther argues instead that the righteousness given to the believer is complete and full in Christ and that as such it excludes any reliance upon human works. It is a passive righteousness received by faith alone. All of this is understood and accepted by Melanchthon and is implicit in his own comment on Rom 1:17: "in the Gospel there is revealed the righteousness of God, that is, acceptance by which God is now certainly propitious toward you, forgives your sins, and accounts you righteous."[84] Similarly both decline to understand Paul's quotations from Hab 2:4, "the righteous shall live by faith" (Rom 1:17; Gal 3:11), as meaning that the Christian will live a life characterized by faith in such a manner as ultimately to merit eternal life. Instead, they understand it to mean that faith in God's promise of salvation is the gateway to life. Thus, Luther claims that Paul understands the prophet as referring to "a true and certain faith that has no doubts about God, or the divine promises or the forgiveness of sins through Christ. Then we can remain safe and secure in Christ, the object of faith, and keep before our eyes the suffering and blood of the Mediator and all his blessings."[85] Similarly, Melanchthon will say that the verse teaches "that we shall be just not when we look to the Law, not when we set out virtues and deeds before God, but when we declare that God is propitious to us by faith, that is, by confidence in mercy, that he hears us, wants to save us, and that we expect salvation."[86] Both Reformers assert that faith means trust and confidence in a faithful God.

Luther and Melanchthon are also close in their comments on Rom 3:25–26 where Paul states that God provided Christ's atoning sacrifice in order to demonstrate his righteousness and that he justifies the person who has faith in Jesus. Twice Melanchthon says that Paul's references here to God's righteousness denote a divine declaration that God is the

---

83. *LW* 25:151 = *WA* 56:172, 3–5 (my insertions). See also on Rom 3:21: *LW* 25:30 n. 20 = *WA* 56:36, 11–23; and see on Rom 3:5: *LW* 25:200–201 = *WA* 56:215, 16–20.

84. Melanchthon, *Commentary on Romans*, 70 = *CR* 15:558.

85. *LW* 26:270 = *WA* 40:423, 24–28.

86. Melanchthon, *Commentary on Romans*, 71 = *CR* 15:559.

one who justifies: "God would declare that he himself is the one who justifies."[87] As Luther expresses it, "God, through the remission of sins which we have committed in the past, shows that He is the justifier of all."[88] Further, both allow that God's justifying activity demonstrates something about his character. There is a reference here to the righteousness by which God is righteous in God's self, a righteousness that is exhibited in the justification of sinners. Luther is the more explicit on this point, saying that "the remission of sins proves that He is righteous *and* that He is able to justify,"[89] but Melanchthon too will say that "God reveals his righteousness, that is, that he himself is the one who will justify in the way He promised in the promises."[90] God's own righteousness is here shown in God's fidelity to God's promises.

We thus reach the entirely unsurprising conclusion that both Luther and Melanchthon believed that when Paul spoke of the righteousness of God he referred primarily to the righteousness with which God justifies, but that both nevertheless recognized as theologically significant the truth that God is righteous as a facet of divine nature. Yet what is not clear is whether Melanchthon connects these two legitimate ways to speak of the righteousness of God as closely as does Luther. Is it true in quite the same way for Melanchthon as for Luther that the righteousness with which God justifies and the righteousness with which God is righteous in God's self are one and the same righteousness? Does Melanchthon evidence in his exegesis Luther's sense that in granting the gift of righteousness to the believer God gives that which God is in God's self?[91] Here it is instructive to compare comments from each of them on 2 Cor 5:21, both of which are made in contexts where the definition of justification is under discussion and in which they use this verse to help establish the meanings they propose. To Melanchthon, when Paul speaks of believers becoming the righteousness of God in Christ this means that they are accepted by God through imputation:

> But the righteousness about which the Gospel specifically speaks signifies relationally, the imputation of righteousness, that is, gratuitous acceptance to eternal life, although joined to it is the gift of the Holy

87. Melanchthon, *Commentary on Romans*, 101 = CR 15:589.
88. LW 25:249 = WA 56:262, 4–6.
89. LW 25:249 = WA 56:262, 6–7.
90. Melanchthon, *Commentary on Romans*, 101 = CR 15:589.
91. We have already explored this aspect of Luther's understanding of justification (5.8).

Spirit. So when you hear the word *justified*, you should think about the Hebrew phrase which signifies "to be accounted or pronounced righteous," or that the accused person is absolved. And *righteous* signifies "accepted by God to eternal life." 2 Cor 5[:21]: "He made him to be sin for us who knew no sin, so that in him we might become the righteousness of God," that is, Christ was made guilty for us so that we might become accepted because of him. This is the simple grammatical and true explanation of the words.[92]

Melanchthon of course does here refer to God's giving of God's self. He emphasizes the gift of the Holy Spirit. Yet he is very clear that this is not included in justification but is instead joined to it. As important as the gift of the Holy Spirit is, it is not this to which the phrase "the righteousness of God" refers.

That Luther reads the same verse in a significantly different way can be seen in the postscript he added to a letter Melanchthon wrote to Brenz in May 1531 (see 6.5), correcting Brenz's view of justification. Interpreters have read the postscript in conflicting ways, either as an endorsement of Melanchthon's account of justification or as a significant correction of it. However, such general judgments are less helpful in identifying similarities and differences than is attending to Luther's specific use of Paul's text:

And I am accustomed, my Brenz, for the sake of understanding it better, to think of it in these terms: as if there is no quality in my heart that might be called "faith" or "love," but in that place I put Jesus Christ and say, "This is my righteousness; he is the quality and (as they say) formal righteousness," so that I may in this way set myself free and disentangle myself from considering the law and works—even from considering that objective Christ, who is understood as teacher or giver. But I want him to be the gift and teaching in himself, so that I may have all things in him. Thus Christ says, "I am the way, the truth, and the life;" he does not say I give you the way, truth, and life, as if Christ stood outside of me and worked such things in me. He ought to be, dwell, live, speak in me, not through me or into me etc. 2 Cor 6 [, 16], so that we would be the righteousness of God in him, not in love or the gifts that follow.[93]

---

92. Melanchthon, *Commentary on Romans*, 56 = CR 15:543.
93. *WA BR* 6: no. 1818, 98–101 (100, 49–101, 59) = *MBWT* 5: no. 1151, 104–13 (112,

Clearly Luther here wishes to support Melanchthon in denying that qualities worked by the Holy Spirit as a consequence of faith are justifying. But it is equally clear that Luther identifies becoming "the righteousness of God in him" with Christ being, dwelling, living, and speaking in the believer. The analogy with John 14:6 in which Luther explicitly denies that Christ stands outside of him is particularly telling, as is the fact that Christ himself is specifically named as the divine gift. In giving Christ, God gives in justification that which God is in God's self. Indeed, Luther's manner of expression demands the presence of Christ in faith for his teaching to remain coherent. For if it is denied that faith is a quality or virtue in the heart, and if it is said that Christ himself is the quality, then, if one wishes to continue to speak of justification by faith (and Luther certainly does wish to do so), Christ must be present in justifying faith. Luther here expresses very similar ideas about justification to those we found in his exegesis of Gal 2:20, where he distinguishes the righteousness by which Christ lives in the believer from the righteousness that is in the believer's own person.[94] United with Christ by faith, the believer lives not his or her own life but that of Christ, such that while the believer genuinely has righteousness, it can never properly be termed his or her own or used as a claim of merit.

Luther's postscript simply does not express the idea of becoming the righteousness of God in Christ in the same terms as Melanchthon's description of it as being accepted by God on account of Christ's sacrifice. At the same time, it is also true that the very act of both writing about justification in the same letter shows that Melanchthon and Luther did not consider their two accounts to be contradictory. One could also argue that Melanchthon's relational account of justification itself here expresses what he implicitly understands by union with Christ. His exegetical response is to take Paul's "in him" as meaning "because of him" and to say that "it signifies relationally." Yet Melanchthon himself does not here make this equation explicit or then use any of Paul's vocabulary

---

51–113, 62) = *CR* 2: 501–3. The translation is that of Wengert, "Melanchthon and Luther / Luther and Melanchthon," 69. Versification did not appear in editions of the New Testament before the 1550s, so the specific verse reference is the work of editors. However, Luther does appear to intend to tie together the thought of 2 Cor 6:16: "I will live in them and walk among them" with that of 2 Cor 5:21 in which Christ was made sin "so that in him we might become the righteousness of God."

94. We should note the chronological proximity of this letter in May 1531 to Luther's lectures on Gal 2, delivered between July 24 and August 21, 1531.

of union with Christ in relation to 2 Cor 5:21. He does not *argue* for the equating of his relational language with Paul's vocabulary of union, and he reserves all discussion of divine indwelling for the Holy Spirit's work of renewal consequent upon justification. Exegetically it remains the case that Luther finds union with Christ central to Paul's meaning in 2 Cor 5:21 whereas Melanchthon does not.[95]

Luther's interpretation of this verse is also significant as one of a number in which he employs the motif of "joyous exchange," in which Christ becomes what we are (sinners) in order that we might become what he is (righteous). Thus, when commenting on Gal 3:13, which states that "Christ became a curse for us," Luther draws 2 Cor 5:21 into the discussion:

> Thus he calls Him "sin" in 2 Cor 5:21 when he says: "For our sake God made him to be sin who knew no sin." Although these statements could correctly be expounded by saying that Christ became a "curse," that is, a sacrifice for the curse, or "sin," that is, a sacrifice for sin; nevertheless, it is more pleasing if the precise meaning of the terms is preserved for the sake of greater emphasis (*si servetur propria significato vocum, propter maiorem Emphasin*). For when a sinner really comes to knowledge of himself, he feels himself to be a sinner not only concretely or adjectivally but abstractly and substantively. That is, he seems to himself to be not only miserable but misery itself; not only a sinner, and an accursed one, but sin and the curse itself. Thus in Latin, when we want a strong way to say that someone is a criminal, we call him a "crime." It is something awful to bear sin, the wrath of God, the curse, and death. Therefore a man who feels these things in earnest really becomes sin, death, and the curse itself.[96]

95. Wengert, *Defending Faith*, 69, comments on Luther's postscript that "the central point for Luther was not that justification was an ontological joining of Luther to Christ but precisely the opposite: In place of a quality or virtue in the soul, Luther pronounced an absolution and union with Christ to himself: I *put* Jesus Christ and *say*." Wengert rightly notes Luther's language of union with Christ but his association of the phrase "ontological joining" with "a quality or virtue in the soul" illegitimately serves to eliminate the possibility that Luther articulates union with Christ in a third sense that cannot fairly be identified either with faith as a quality in the soul or with Melanchthon's relational perspective on justification. Luther's position is of course undoubtedly closer to that of Melanchthon than it is to that of scholasticism, but it is still different in significant ways.

96. LW 26:288 = WA 40:448, 29 – 449, 19.

Thus, while Luther can accept the explanation of Christ being made sin as Christ being made a sacrifice for sin, it also matters to him to insist that significance be accorded to Paul's choice of nouns in Gal 3:13 and 2 Cor 5:21 (κατάρα, ἁμαρτία), and their literal sense ("precise meaning"). He can then explain atonement in terms of a duel within the person of Christ in which sin and death are annihilated as they confront divine righteousness and life. In contrast, when commenting on Rom 8:3, where Paul says that God condemned sin in the flesh by sending his Son in the likeness of sinful flesh, Melanchthon brings together the same texts without making the same points:

> He says that Christ was made sin, or the sacrifice for sin. For here in "on account of sin," the word sin after the Hebraic manner signifies the sacrificial victim for sin, that is, the penalty or satisfaction for sin, or as the Latins say, the propitiatory sacrifice, and the Greeks κάθαρμα (that which is thrown away in cleansing). It means the same thing as in the words *curse* and *anathema*, which signify things destined for satisfaction, for placating the wrath of God. Thus Isaiah [53:10] says of Christ: "Because he will make his soul sin," that is, a sacrifice for sin. For this reason Paul so often inculcates, as in 2 Cor 5 [:21]: "Him who did not know sin he made sin for us," that is, he was made the sacrificial victim who should bear the punishment of sin and make satisfaction for our sins. And to the Galatians [3:13] he says likewise that Christ was made a curse, that is, a propitiatory sacrifice, bearing the curse and wrath of God against sin.[97]

Melanchthon is happy to regard Paul's nouns as figures of speech indicating that Christ was a sacrificial victim, but to Luther it is necessary to insist that Christ was not simply a sacrifice for sin but actually became sin and a curse. The primary reason for this difference is *not* contradictory theologies of atonement. Despite Gustav Aulén's famous use of passages from Luther like the ones dealing with 2 Cor 5:21 to set Luther's teaching on atonement against Latin theological traditions in which the fundamental concepts are satisfaction and merit,[98] there is no evidence that Luther

---

97. Melanchthon, *Commentary on Romans*, 165 = CR 15:657.

98. Gustav Aulén, *Christus Victor: An Historical Study of the Three Main Types of the Idea of the Atonement* (London: SPCK, 1931), 117–38. Aulén blames Melanchthon for returning to "the Latin type" (140).

would have perceived the conflict. In response to other texts he has no difficulty in expressing atonement in terms similar to Melanchthon:

> It was not possible to overcome God's wrath, judgment, conscience, hell, death, and all evil things, and indeed to gain all benefits, unless God's righteousness received satisfaction, sin was given its due reward, and death was overcome by justice. Accordingly, St. Paul generally refers to the suffering and blood of Christ when he proclaims the grace of God in him, in order to indicate that all the benefits that are given to us through Christ, are granted only because of his ineffable merit and the price he paid.[99]

The significance of the difference is rather that particular texts (Gal 3:13; 2 Cor 5:21; Rom 8:3, 13) prompt a different exegetical response from Luther than they do from Melanchthon. Luther finds in them the motif of exchange, and so when discussing these texts expresses both atonement and justification in terms compatible with that motif, whereas Melanchthon does not. Agreement elsewhere shows that this is not in Luther and Melanchthon's own context a doctrinal contradiction, but neither will it do to underplay the difference. Luther simply and importantly finds in Paul a wider range of ways of expressing these key aspects of the gospel than does Melanchthon.

When discussing justification, Luther plays out the motif of "joyous exchange" in terms of union with Christ. His comments on Gal 3:14 where Paul discusses the blessing of Abraham coming to the Gentiles, provide an example of this:

> Through the curse, sin, and death of Christ we are blessed, that is, justified and made alive. So long as sin, death, and the curse remain in us, sin damns us, death kills us, and the curse curses us; but when these things are transferred to Christ, what is ours becomes His and what is His becomes ours. Let us learn, therefore, in every temptation to transfer sin, death, the curse, and all the evils that oppress us from

99. *LW* 52:280 = *WA* 10.1.1, 555–728. Luther is here in the *Church Postil* (1521–1522) providing a sermon guide for the Feast of Epiphany and commenting on the sacrificial significance of the wise men's gifts of gold, frankincense, and myrrh in Matt 2:11. It is perhaps worth noting, in relation to the debates of later centuries concerning atonement, that despite Luther's deep concern with divine anger and judgment, he does not here speak directly of the satisfying of divine wrath but of the satisfying of divine righteousness.

ourselves to Christ, and, on the other hand, to transfer righteousness, life, and blessing from Him to us.[100]

That Luther has already expounded Gal 2:20 in terms of union with Christ removes all temptation to the error of assuming that he intends to speak of a transfer in which qualities are passed from Christ to the believer: "'Christ,' he says, 'is fixed and cemented to me and abides in me. The life that I now live, He lives in me. In this way, therefore, Christ and I are one.'"[101] Luther means rather that righteousness, life, and blessing are received by the believer because he or she is united with Christ by faith. Luther must insist that Christ literally became sin and a curse if the reality of Christ's righteousness in the person of the believer, received in union with Christ, is to be matched by, and grounded upon, the preceding reality of the sins of the world in the person of the savior. Once such a pattern of exchange is found in Paul's texts, it is impossible to expound justification solely in a relational paradigm within which the vocabulary of union with Christ is not employed.

Thus, the pattern of exegetical differences between Luther and Melanchthon in interpreting the phrase "the righteousness of God" revolves around union with Christ. This significant difference appears also in their exegesis of Rom 5:15, where it is easier to compare their comments directly with each other. We have already seen (4.2) the development of their interpretations of this verse where Paul speaks of "the grace of God and the free gift in the grace of the one man Jesus Christ."[102] Prompted by Erasmus's observations on the meaning of χάρις (*gratia*/grace), first Melanchthon and then Luther argue that, in key texts concerning justification, Paul uses the word to speak not of infused grace but of divine favor. In doing so, they provide one of the key components of a new Pauline exegetical grammar within early Protestantism. However, their understanding of the term δωρεά (*donum*/gift) in this verse is quite different from each other. Luther interprets the gift not only as the Holy Spirit but also in strongly christological terms, and this christological dimension he connects to justification. In contrast, as early as *Loci Communes* (1521) Melanchthon identifies the gift with the Holy Spirit given as a consequence of grace. In his *Commentary on Romans* (1540) Melanchthon clarifies this further in relation to the persons of the Trinity:

---

100. *LW* 26:292 = *WA* 40:454, 29 – 455, 10.

101. *LW* 26:167 = *WA* 40:283, 30-32.

102. On this verse, see Schäfer, "Melanchthon's Interpretation of Romans 5:15," 79-104, and Peura, "Christ as Favor and Gift," 42-69.

Grace signifies gratuitous acceptance because of Christ, that is, gratuitous remission of sins, and gratuitous imputation of righteousness because of Christ. The gift through grace signifies the giving of the Holy Spirit and eternal life . . . the conscience declares that we are righteous, that is, accepted, because of Christ. It does not look to our own worthiness, but to the Word or promise, and according to that it speaks about the will of God toward us, and thus apprehends Christ, the mediator. When this happens the Holy Spirit is given and new impulses come into being in us.[103]

The gift is therefore distinguished from imputed righteousness and is identified with the consequent renewal of the believer wrought by the Holy Spirit. Things are quite different in Luther, where "the gift in the grace of one man" is identified with faith in Christ. This identification, with which Luther begins his treatment of the text in *Against Latomus* (1521), is crucial to understanding what follows, in which grace and gift are portrayed as mutually conditioning, i.e., gift as a consequence of grace and grace as a consequence of gift. Grace has conceptual priority in the sense that the gift "is given to us through the grace of Christ, because he alone among all men is beloved and accepted and has a kind and gentle God so that he might merit for this gift and even this grace."[104] The divine intention to act graciously in Christ for sinners comes before all things, and so "the grace of God is not contingent upon a gift of righteousness already received."[105] However, gift can also be spoken of as having priority for the believer, for justifying faith is a gift and it is only through such faith that the believer enters into divine favor. Thus, it is true that "Everything is forgiven through grace, but as yet not everything is healed through the gift,"[106] and it is also true that "A person neither pleases, nor has grace, except on account of the gift which labors in this way to cleanse from sin."[107]

---

103. Melanchthon, *Commentary on Romans*, 137–38 = CR 15:627–28.

104. *LW* 32:228 = *WA* 8:106, 26–28.

105. Mark Seifrid, "The Text of Romans and the Theology of Melanchthon: The Preceptor of the Germans and the Apostle to the Gentiles," in *Reformation Readings of Paul*, ed. Michael Allen and Jonathan A. Linebaugh (Downers Grove, IL: InterVarsity Press, 2015), 114. A similar point is made by Risto Saarinen, "Finnish Luther Studies: A Story and a Program," in *Engaging Luther: A (New) Theological Assessment*, ed. Olli-Pekka Vainio (Eugene, OR: Wipf & Stock, 2010), 1–26 (esp. 17–18) and by Skottene, *Grace and Gift*, 73–76.

106. *LW* 32:229 = *WA* 8:107, 21.

107. *LW* 32:229 = *WA* 8:107, 34–35.

Luther plainly does *not* mean that justification is to be understood as granted partly on the basis of the works of the believer: "For what sin is there where God is favorable and wills not to know any sin, and where he wholly accepts and sanctifies the whole man? However, as you see, this must not be attributed to our purity, but solely to the grace of a favorable God."[108] What he means rather is that since he holds Christ to be present in the gift of justifying faith, there is a sense in which the gift is a prerequisite for grace (the gift of faith results in the believer being accepted into God's favor) just as there is also a different sense in which grace is a prerequisite for the gift. He therefore simply cannot make parallel exegetical moves to Melanchthon and identify Christ and justification primarily with grace and the gift primarily with the Holy Spirit and with renewal that is consequent upon justification. Luther instead associates Christ and the Spirit as gift, writing in his *Preface to Romans* that grace is God's favor, "by which he is disposed to pour Christ and the Holy Spirit with his gifts into us."[109] Even in his later years, Luther maintains this interpretation of Paul's statements. In July 1542, at the licentiate examination of Heinrich Schmedenstede, Luther comments that "Paul embraces two parts in justification, according to Rom 5[:15–17], grace and the free gift."[110]

---

108. *LW* 32:229 = *WA* 8:107.

109. *WA* DB 7.9: 10–14. Peura, "Christ as Favor and Gift," 43 n. 3, provides this translation and critiques *LW* 35:369 where the sentence is erroneously translated in such a way as to separate Christ and the Holy Spirit: "by which he is disposed to give us Christ and to pour into us the Holy Spirit with his gifts." Mark Mattes, review of *Justification and Participation in Christ: The Development of the Lutheran Doctrine of Justification from Luther to the Formula of Concord*, by Olli-Pekka Vainio, *LQ* 23 (2009): 114–17, is thus only partially correct when he criticizes the Finnish perspective on the grounds that "*favor* is construed as objective while *donum* is somehow subjective. . . . God's *favor* is not a possession or essence of God's own but *is* precisely the *gift*, applied to the unrighteous while and as they are unrighteous. . . . *God's favor and gift are not distinguished as object and subject; they are both objective and external to the sinner*" (117, his emphasis). The Finns do insufficiently emphasize that the gift means living an alien life and that the subjective aspect of the grace/gift duality can only be understood in terms of this objectivity. However, in Mattes' comments the objective and the subjective are being posed as alternatives in a way that Luther does not (as illustrated by the pouring of Christ and the Spirit into the believer) while it is asserted that grace is the gift when Luther in fact distinguishes the two. Skottene, *Grace and Gift*, 171–85, explores the part played by the Holy Spirit in Luther's understanding of grace and gift, arguing that through the preaching of the gospel "the ministry of the Holy Spirit is to impart grace and gift" (171).

110. *LW* 34:320 = *WA* 39.2: 202, 28–29. Luther may also have noted that in Rom 5:17

Luther and Melanchthon are completely united against interpretations of Paul's words that make justification a question of the believer's cooperation with divine grace in order ultimately to come to merit God and eternal life. They also both have a strong sense that Paul teaches the union of the believer with God. However, Melanchthon identifies this union primarily with the work of the Holy Spirit consequent upon justification whereas Luther identifies it primarily with the presence of Christ in faith and as an intrinsic part of justification.

6.8. Justification and Good Works: The Dialog at Pastor Bugenhagen's House

Differences in expressing the truth of justification by faith were to surface again in direct discussion between Luther and Melanchthon at a potential point of crisis in the life of the Wittenberg faculty. In late 1536, in a dialog concerning justification and good works that took place at the home of Johann Bugenhagen, a faculty colleague and pastor of the Wittenberg city church, Melanchthon posed questions in writing to Luther that he in turn answered in writing. This discussion took place in the context of the Cordatus controversy. As already noted (see 6.6), Conrad Cordatus made a formal complaint about what he regarded as the false teaching contained in a lecture given on July 24, 1536, by Caspar Cruciger, a student of Melanchthon. As Cruciger based his lecture on Melanchthon's notes, the accusation was essentially also an accusation against Melanchthon.[111] The essence of the controversy concerns the part played by repentance or contrition in justification.

In defending himself against the allegation that he taught justification by works, Cruciger continued to argue that contrition in the person justified is necessary as an indispensable cause (*causa sine qua non*) of justification. This Cordatus perceived as a significant departure from Luther's teaching, who had always insisted—especially against Erasmus in *The Bondage of the Will* (1525)—that contrition is a divine gift. Clearly much depends here on the exact sense of *causa sine qua non*. Both Luther

---

Paul goes on to associate righteousness directly with the free gift: "the abundance of grace and the free gift of righteousness."

111. For a clear chronological account of the complex series of letters and meetings generated by this dispute see Wengert, *Law and Gospel*, 206–10.

and Bugenhagen were publicly to present the dispute as a dispute over the definition of words.

Yet the charge of a departure from Luther's teaching was sensitive and potentially embarrassing because this was indeed an area in which Melanchthon had developed distinctive views. He worried that Luther's rigorous insistence on the bondage of the unregenerate human will might deter people from even trying to obey or to believe. From Melanchthon's perspective, afflicted sinners had to know that the gospel promise is universal and that they could struggle against the weakness of the will if they were sustained by the Word and the work of the Spirit.[112] In *Loci Communes* (1535) he had written that in justification "three causes are conjoined: the Word, the Holy Spirit and the will, not really as a passive thing [*otiosam*], but fighting its weakness."[113] Similarly, in *Loci Communes* (1543) he was to write that the third cause of good works is "the human will which assents to and does not contend against the Word of God."[114]

It is not quite clear here what kind of "cause" the human will is being said to be,[115] but for our purposes the significance of Melanch-

112. Notger Slencza, "Luther's Anthropology" in *The Oxford Handbook of Martin Luther's Theology*, ed. Robert Kolb, Irene Dingel, and L'ubomír Batka (Oxford: Oxford University Press, 2014), 230, describes the aspect of Luther's teaching that concerned Melanchthon: "The one who wills does not govern his will. The will thus does not face the alternative of sin and grace but rather—without distracting from its character as a will—is determined by it without recourse, inevitably. Being bound by sin means being a sinner freely, but without the capability to govern this direction of will. . . . Sin is an inevitable act of freedom." Thus, on Luther's view, the will is not coerced but because of its bondage nevertheless inevitably desires sin. At a metaphysical level Luther also argues that it follows from the omniscience of God and the immutability of the divine will that everything that happens does so necessarily, a position that inevitably leads to the denial of human free will in any traditional sense. Theodor Dieter, "Luther as Late Medieval Theologian," in *The Oxford Handbook of Martin Luther's Theology*, ed. Robert Kolb, Irene Dingel, and L'ubomír Batka (Oxford: Oxford University Press, 2014), 42, comments that this metaphysical argument "is in principle different from his theological argument referring to the doctrine of grace except that both meet in the denial of the freedom of the will."

113. *CR* 21:376. The translation is that of Wengert, *Human Freedom, Christian Righteousness*, 143-44. In 139-48 he discusses the details of the evolution of Melanchthon's position on this issue. See also Robert Kolb, *Bound Choice, Election, and Wittenberg Theological Method* (Grand Rapids: Eerdmans, 2005), 67-102, and Gregory B. Graybill, *Evangelical Free Will: Philipp Melanchthon's Doctrinal Journey on the Origins of Faith* (Oxford: Oxford University Press, 2010), 199-223.

114. *Loci Communes (1543)*, 43 = *CR* 21:658.

115. Kolb, *Bound Choice*, 93, points out that in Aristotelian analysis "the material

thon's development on this issue lies in its timing. It took place in the early 1530s, in the same period as he was also developing his views on justification. As Wengert argues, the two sets of changes appear to be connected:

> Three forces—Melanchthon's insistence on forensic justification, his quest for clear, nonspeculative definition in theology, and his conviction that all theology served to comfort the individual conscience—converged to create something new in his thought. By 1531 Melanchthon was already insisting on expressing the doctrine of justification in exclusively forensic terms. For him this insistence implied a greater field of play for the law and human activity in all other areas of his theology, so long as one excluded them from justification.[116]

These connections are important in understanding the strategy adopted by Melanchthon in the dialog at Bugenhagen's house.[117] For he

---

'cause' or element described or defined the object upon which the effective element—the actual cause responsible for the object—worked to produce the phenomenon." The degree to which Melanchthon is ascribing an active role to the human will could therefore still be limited. Note also the dangers of misinterpretation discussed in Wengert, "Philip Melanchthon and the Origins of the 'Three Causes' of Conversion," 183-208.

116. Wengert, *Human Freedom, Christian Righteousness*, 146. Seifrid, "The Text of Romans and the Theology of Melanchthon," 107-20, also sees these connections, arguing that once Melanchthon has granted even a restricted role in justification to human choice he must make justification exclusively forensic and deny that it involves a change in the human being if he is to preserve the truth that God justifies the ungodly. Consequently union with Christ is not emphasized in relation to justification since such union involves a change in the human being. This seems to me a correct assessment with the following reservations: (1) Calvin will demonstrate that it is possible to integrate an exclusively forensic account of justification with a strong emphasis on union with Christ, and (2) Seifrid's characterization of Melanchthon's account of justification as anthropological as opposed to christological is not entirely just. It is not that Melanchthon neglects the place of Christology in justification as such but rather that his christological focus falls exclusively on Christ's role as mediator.

117. This discussion is not included in the major English translations of Luther's *Works*. However, an obscure translation can be found in the anonymous "Cordatus' Controversy with Melanchthon," *Theological Quarterly* 11.4 (1907): 193-207. It appears in the *Corpus Reformatorum* in a supplementary volume: Philip Melanchthon, *Philippi Melanchthonis Epistolae, Iudicia, Consilia, Testimonia Aliorumque ad eum Epistolae quae in Corpore Reformatorum Desiderantur*, ed. Heinrich E. Bindseil (Halle: Gustav Schwetske, 1874), 344-48. See also *WA* TR 6:148, 29 - 153, 15 (German text) and *WA* BR 12: no. 4259a, 191-96 (Latin text). Analysis is offered in Greschat, *Melanchthon neben Luther*, 230-42,

did not so much attempt to defend himself as to imply that Luther's way of formulating justification was no more immune to misunderstanding than his own. Accused of opening the door to justification by works by allowing that the contrition of the sinner could be termed a cause of justification, Melanchthon asks Luther questions implying that Luther's failure to adopt an exclusively forensic view of justification poses the same dangers. Melanchthon begins by introducing Augustine into the discussion. He assumes that Luther did not intend to follow Augustine's account of justification in which there is an initial gratuitous gift of grace and love with which the believer must then cooperate in good works in order to gain God and eternal life. However, Melanchthon suggests, Luther's failure to exclude works from what is included in justification raises the possibility of falling back into Augustine's view: "You grant a two-fold righteousness, and also that both are necessary in the sight of God, namely, the righteousness of faith and that other, of a good conscience, in which faith supplies what is lacking in regard to the Law. What else is this than saying that a person is not justified by faith alone?"[118] Melanchthon will press Luther repeatedly on this issue: "It seems that one is righteous not by God's mercy alone. For you teach yourself that the righteousness of works is necessary, and that, in the sight of God. And Paul is acceptable both as a believer and as a doer; if he were not a doer, he would not be acceptable. Hence, our own righteousness is, at least, a kind of partial cause (*aliqua partialis causa*)."[119]

While Luther certainly also wishes to reject the errors that Melanchthon rejects in his account of Augustine's teaching on justification, he is less certain than Melanchthon that this fully represents Augustine's position. He sees Augustine as closer to the evangelical position than does Melanchthon. Luther also refuses to give any ground on the main points that Melanchthon raises. On the one hand, he will not accept that justification includes good works as a cause: "I hold that a righteous person becomes, is, and remains righteous, or a righteous person, simply by mercy alone. For this righteousness is perfect; it is set

---

and in Mark Seifrid, "Luther, Melanchthon, and Paul on the Question of Imputation," in *Justification: What's at Stake in the Current Debates?*, ed. Mark Husbands and Daniel J. Treier (Downers Grove, IL: InterVarsity Press, 2004), 137–52.

118. "Cordatus' Controversy with Melanchthon," 198 = *Philippi Melanchthonis Epistolae*, 345.

119. "Cordatus' Controversy with Melanchthon," 199 = *Philippi Melanchthonis Epistolae*, 346.

up against God's wrath, death, and sin, and swallows up all these, and renders a person absolutely (*simpliciter*) holy and innocent, just as if, in reality, there were no sin in him."[120] Yet on the other hand, neither will Luther accept that to uphold this truth requires an exclusively relational account of justification in which the renewal manifested in good works is consequent upon justification rather than constitutive of it. He will not answer Melanchthon's question about works as a partial cause of justification using the same terminology but instead admits and defines his belief that the righteousness of works is necessary:

> It is necessary, however, not by a legal necessity, or one of compulsion, but by a gratuitous necessity, or one of consequence, or an unalterable condition. As the sun shines by necessity, if it is a sun, and yet does not shine by demand, but by its nature and its unalterable will, so to speak, because it was created for the purpose that it should shine so a person created righteous performs new works by an unalterable necessity, not by legal compulsion. For to the righteous no law is given. Further, we are created, says Paul, unto good works . . . it is impossible to be a believer and not a doer.[121]

Luther returns to this point of the nature of the believer again and again: "believers are new creatures, new trees; accordingly, the aforementioned demands of the law do not apply to them, *e.g., faith must do good works*, just as it is not proper to say: *the sun must shine, a good tree must produce good fruit, 3 + 7 must equal 10*. For the sun shines *de facto*, a good tree is fruitful *de facto*, 3 + 7 equal 10 *de facto*."[122] Because faith works or it is not faith, so works cannot be excluded from discussion of justification by faith. "Faith is a work of promise, or a gift of the Holy Spirit . . . necessary, in order that the Law be fulfilled, but it is not obtained by the Law and its works."[123] Melanchthon was apparently unconvinced by the necessity of unalterable condition. In *Loci Communes* (1543) he discusses

---

120. "Cordatus' Controversy with Melanchthon," 198 = *Philippi Melanchthonis Epistolae*, 345.
121. "Cordatus' Controversy with Melanchthon," 199 = *Philippi Melanchthonis Epistolae*, 346.
122. "Cordatus' Controversy with Melanchthon," 202 = *Philippi Melanchthonis Epistolae*, 348.
123. "Cordatus' Controversy with Melanchthon," 201 = *Philippi Melanchthonis Epistolae*, 348.

the reasons why good works are to be done. Various kinds of necessity are identified, but gratuitous necessity is not included and first and foremost he places what he terms the necessity of command: "For although it is one thing to speak of compulsion, yet there does remain in force the eternal ordering of the immutable God that the creature shall render obedience to the will of God. This immutable ordering is the necessity of command and the necessity of debt, as Paul says in Rom 8:6, 'We are under obligation to God, not to the flesh.'"[124]

Thus, there emerged from the discussion at Bugenhagen's house very different senses of the relationship between justification by faith and the good works performed by believers, and also of how this is to be articulated without lapsing into works righteousness. For Melanchthon, it is essential that works are done if faith is to be retained "because the Holy Spirit is driven out and grieved when we permit sins against conscience."[125] Therefore faith can never be without works, but he does not speak like Luther as if to be active in works is constitutive of faith. For Melanchthon, it is only if justification on account of Christ and renewal by the Holy Spirit are distinguished that the danger of righteousness by works can be avoided, but for Luther the same danger is posed more seriously by separating the gratuitous necessity of good works from justification:

> It is, therefore, an unhappy distinction to divide a person (as far as he is a believer) into beginning, middle, and end. Accordingly, a person's works shine because they are rays of his faith, and are accepted because of his faith, not vice versa. Otherwise, in the matter of justification, the works which follow faith would be more excellent, and thus, faith would be justifying faith only in the beginning, afterwards it would step aside and cease and would leave the distinction (of justifying a person) to works, and become void and defunct.[126]

Although this dialog lacks any direct discussion of the person of Christ in justification, what it reveals is of a piece with what we found in our exploration of differences in exegesis between Luther and Melanchthon. If, as Luther teaches, Christ is present in justifying faith and the

124. *Loci Communes (1543)*, 103 = CR 21:775.
125. *Loci Communes (1543)*, 103 = CR 21:775.
126. "Cordatus' Controversy with Melanchthon," 200 = *Philippi Melanchthonis Epistolae*, 347.

believer must live not his or her own life but the life of Christ, then such justification must pertain to the whole of the Christian life. If it does so, then it must also encompass, but not be obtained by, works of righteousness.[127] Melanchthon's relational account of justification differs significantly precisely because it does not rely on the presence of Christ in faith.

6.9. Conclusions

The fundamental theological agreements between Melanchthon and Luther are extensive. They agree about the nature of sin and grace and therefore are united in rejecting the idea that faith is a quality or virtue by which a person cooperates in his or her own justification. They agree that the righteousness received by the believer is an alien righteousness and that acceptance by God is based not on any aspects of a person's deeds but is grounded in God. They agree that this righteousness is received by faith alone when the believer trusts in the divine promises communicated in Scripture. They agree that the alien nature of this righteousness is vital in granting to the believer assurance of salvation since, despite the continued presence of sin in the believer's life, a final eschatological word has been pronounced in justification. They agree that union with the divine is a vital aspect of soteriology. They agree that faith is never without works. It is important to enumerate these agreements, simply the most important among many, to place their differences into context. When two biblical theologians agree so extensively in a situation of extreme conflict such as the early Reformation, remaining differences are less likely to be interpreted as contradictions. However, such differences may still be significant in their own right and may become more significant still in the history of reception as their statements are subsequently interpreted according to the demands and concerns of later contexts.

In the case of Melanchthon and Luther, setting interpretations of Pauline texts from the two alongside each other allows us to see that they understand important christological dimensions of justification differently. For Luther, Christ is present in faith. Justification encompasses the

127. Vainio, "Luther and Theosis," 459-74, argues that for Luther this distinction is entirely consistent with his insistence on the presence of Christ in faith: "the basis for the imputation of Christ's righteousness is not the inchoate renewal caused by Christ's indwelling but Christ's own righteousness, which is given in faith to the believer" (470).

renewal of the believer expressed in works. For Melanchthon, justification means acceptance on account of Christ's sacrificial death. The renewal of the believer expressed in works is consequent upon justification rather than part of it. In relation to several key texts, Paul's vocabulary of union with Christ receives a direct exegetical response from Luther whereas Melanchthon makes no direct response to this vocabulary.[128] Luther finds in these texts God's giving of God's self in justification and the motif of the joyous exchange between the sinner and the incarnate Christ. Luther can respond to other Pauline texts in ways that are much closer to Melanchthon, but he nevertheless finds in Paul a wider range of ways to express the truth of justification than does Melanchthon. I am therefore unable wholly to agree with Martin Greschat when he concludes that from around 1531 "Luther approaches in his explanations more and more the Melanchthonian form of the doctrine of justification."[129] There may be important respects in which this is true, but as a general conclusion it ignores the significant exegetical differences between them.

How are we to evaluate Melanchthon as an interpreter of Paul in light of these differences? Certainly it should be clear that some accusations typically leveled against him are unjust. His relational account of justification amounts to a great deal more than simply the forensic metaphor. Despite Osiander's protests, the fact that this relational account of justification is tied so strongly to the terror of the consciences of sinners and the comfort brought to them by the gospel promise means that it is no cold legal fiction. From Melanchthon's perspective it is no fiction, but, even if it is held to be so, it cannot fairly be termed cold. If it constitutes a legal fiction, it is at least a hot one. Rather than icy

---

128. This point is missed by Billings, "The Contemporary Reception of Luther and Calvin's Doctrine of Union with Christ." Billings regards Luther, Melanchthon, and Calvin as standing in essential continuity with each other in asserting the forensic nature of justification and believes that various recent proposals concerning the part played by union with Christ in the theology of Luther and Calvin erroneously call this continuity into question. Union with Christ is significant for Luther and Calvin but is inherited from Scripture and the Augustinian tradition: "Because Luther and Calvin are concerned to comment upon the language of Scripture, it is necessarily the case that they use language of union with Christ, participation in Christ, justification, and divine indwelling" (174). That Melanchthon largely fails to use language of union with Christ or participation with Christ in his exegesis of Romans illustrates that this is not in fact necessarily the case.

129. Greschat, *Melanchthon neben Luther*, 84: "Luther nähert sich in seinen Erläuterungen mehr und mehr der melanchthonischen Gestalt der Rechtfertigungslehre" (my translation).

detachment, the danger is more that Melanchthon's influence will help to create an invariable expectation about the subjectivity of conversion with terror over sin and judgment as an essential emotional prelude to true faith. Further, even if a clear distinction between justification as a once for all external act and renewal as a lifelong process deteriorated into an unhealthy separation between the two in later Protestantism, this development still lay in the future. Melanchthon is clear that, although distinct, justification and renewal always belong together in the experience of the believer. Renewal he identifies strongly with the indwelling of the Holy Spirit. It is also the case that his understanding of justification is in one sense thoroughly Christocentric, with immense emphasis on the role of Christ as mediator.

Yet at the exegetical level with which we are primarily concerned, there remains Melanchthon's perplexing failure to respond to Paul's language of participation in Christ. One could argue that his relational paradigm for justification implies that union with Christ takes place precisely at a relational level in the conscience of the believer. When Paul talks of being in Christ, this is simply a figure of speech by which the apostle expresses the truth that Christ is with and for us.[130] However, although this is a way of exegetically appropriating Melanchthon, it is not an argument he makes. In his *Commentary on Romans* (1540) he gives us an interpretation of the epistle that, as distinct from his frequent discussion of the work of the Spirit within the believer, offers no direct response to Paul's vocabulary of participation in Christ. One could also explain this by pointing to Melanchthon's understanding of his task as a commentator, which was not to provide a comprehensive treatment of the text but rather to identify Paul's main points and grant to his readers a clear grasp of the gospel. Yet viewed from the perspective of reception history, a treatment of Paul's main points that does not include participation in Christ is at the least an eccentric one.[131] If Melanchthon gives us Paul,

---

130. See texts such as Melanchthon, *Commentary on Romans*, 38 = CR 15:524. "Christ was present with Jacob, and blessed him, and strengthened him with the Holy Spirit; he was present with Daniel, and indeed conversed with him. Therefore he governs in this way, that he is present with his members, strengthens them with his Spirit, and protects them against the wiles and onslaughts of the devil."

131. It is striking in this respect that Melanchthon also does not seem to recognize the significance of this theme in patristic sources. H. Ashley Hall, *Philip Melanchthon and the Cappadocians: A Reception of Greek Patristic Sources in the Sixteenth Century* (Göttingen: Vandenhoeck and Ruprecht, 2014), mounts an effective argument for the

it is a version abridged in significant ways. To say this is not to make an entirely retrospective judgment, for we know of at least one sixteenth-century reader who felt similarly and made union with Christ central to his own interpretation and theology. In the dedication of his *Commentary on Romans* (1540), John Calvin expresses admiration for Melanchthon's learning and it is probable that Calvin consulted Melanchthon's works quite extensively: "although it cannot be proved directly, it is highly likely that he wrote his commentary with Melanchthon's works open in front of him."[132] Calvin nevertheless does not hesitate to critique Melanchthon's method, observing that while discussing the main points Melanchthon has passed over many others that require attention: "Melanchthon's use of common places, or *loci*, so influential for Calvin's 1539 *Institutes*, is not, in his view, appropriate to biblical commentary because such groupings of theological topics can lead to the neglect of parts of Scripture. This was a violation of the humanist principle of reading the whole text."[133] Melanchthon neither commented on the whole text nor recognized union with Christ as central to Paul's message. Calvin would do both.

---

significance of Melanchthon's use of Cappadocian works, but union with Christ appears nowhere in the discussion.

132. Bruce Gordon, *Calvin* (New Haven: Yale University Press, 2009), 109. For the Dedication to Simon Grynaeus, see *CNTC* 8:1–4 = *OE* 13:3–6. Calvin's own commentary was first published in 1540, so as well as other less directly relevant works by Melanchthon he could have had available to him Melanchthon's *Commentary on Romans* (1532) and *Loci Communes* (1521/1535).

133. Gordon, *Calvin*, 105.

7 Righteousness and Reciprocity

Justification and the Works of the Believer
in John Calvin's Pauline Exegesis

7.1. Calvin as Pauline Interpreter in the Context of Luther and Melanchthon

There is no doubt that the Pauline letters are the most important biblical resource for Calvin's soteriology.[1] He draws on them with results that both resemble Luther and Melanchthon and differentiate his reading of Paul from theirs. Like Luther but unlike Melanchthon, Calvin integrates union with Christ and his understanding of justification by faith. Like Melanchthon but unlike Luther, Calvin nevertheless distinguishes clearly between justification and sanctification and makes extensive use of forensic imagery to describe the former. Like both Luther and Melanchthon, Calvin strives to clarify the relationship between justification and the good works of the believer. Unlike either, Calvin seeks to find a way not only to value such works but also to stand with the medieval tradition in regarding them as a pathway of transformation along which the goal of steady growth in sanctity throughout the Christian life is sought. Calvin rejects any place for notions of human merit in salvation and yet also offers a strong account of reciprocal human response to divine initiative. In doing so he achieves a synthesis that incorporates the widest possible range

---

1. Barbara Pitkin, "John Calvin and the Interpretation of the Bible," in *The Medieval through the Reformation Periods*, vol. 2 of *A History of Biblical Interpretation*, ed. Alan J. Hauser and Duane F. Watson (Grand Rapids: Eerdmans, 2009), 341-71: "he was fundamentally a Pauline theologian" (357). See also Alexandre Ganoczy, "Calvin als paulinischer Theologe: Ein Forschungsansatz zur Hermeneutik Calvins," in *Calvinus Theologus*, ed. Wilhelm H. Neuser (Neukirchen-Vluyn: Neukirchener, 1976), 39-69.

of Pauline texts and themes. Crucial to Calvin's synthesis is the manner in which he understands Paul's statements about union with Christ and his employment of this theme as a central soteriological concept.[2] Only when Calvin's reflections on union with Christ are understood is it possible fruitfully to explore his affirmation of human works in response to the grace of God. This chapter will first examine in some detail Calvin's handling of union with Christ before turning to consider his use of Pauline texts to describe the role of human reciprocity in salvation.

7.2. Union with Christ (1): Justification

In Calvin's exegesis of Paul's texts, it becomes clear that the theme of union with Christ is in fact closely connected with his rejection of any part for human merit in soteriology. The drive for merit is for Calvin an expression of a destructive desire for escape from divine dependency, whereas union with Christ contains the possibility of human flourishing in communion with God: "It is fallen humanity which sees itself as essentially independent of God—claiming that it has power 'in itself' rather than 'in' or 'united to' God. . . . Humanity at its fullness is humanity united to God."[3]

Thus, for Calvin, union with Christ is essential if human beings are to receive the benefits available through Christ's saving work. At the very outset of Book Three of the *Institutes* ("The Way in Which We Receive the Grace of Christ"), Calvin makes an explicit statement that apart from union with Christ there is no salvation: "First, we must understand that as long as Christ remains outside of us, and we are separated from him, all that he has suffered and done us for the salvation of the human race remains useless and of no value to us. . . . [A]ll that he possesses is nothing to us until we grow into one body with him."[4] Calvin is also extremely

2. In the aftermath of extensive and inconclusive attempts within Calvin scholarship to identify the central dogma in his theology, Mark A. Garcia, *Life in Christ: Union with Christ and Twofold Grace in Calvin's Theology* (Eugene, OR: Wipf & Stock, 2008), 18, is rightly wary of claiming this role for union with Christ. However, he does claim that, as distinct from Calvin's theology as a whole, "the doctrine of union with Christ does appear to stand as a singularly determinative idea in Calvin's *soteriology*" (his emphasis).

3. J. Todd Billings, *Calvin, Participation, and the Gift: The Activity of Believers in Union with Christ* (Oxford: Oxford University Press, 2007), 44–45.

4. *Institutes* 3.1.1 (537) = *CO* 2:393. This does not mean that Calvin's vision is fo-

clear about the agency through which that union is achieved: "The Holy Spirit is the bond by which Christ effectually unites us to himself."[5] Human faith is vital, but such faith "is the principal work of the Holy Spirit."[6] Calvin makes this point exegetically in his discussion of 1 Cor 6:11, where Paul says that the Corinthians were washed, sanctified, and justified "in the name of the Lord Jesus Christ and in the Spirit of our God." Everything is obtained from Christ, "But Christ Himself, with all His blessings, is communicated to us by the Spirit. For we receive Christ by faith; and it is by faith that his benefits (*gratiae*) are applied to us. The author of faith is the Spirit."[7] Whatever aspects of salvation Calvin identifies will involve union with Christ and whatever aspects of salvation Calvin identifies will be realized through the agency of the Spirit. It is this agency and not infused habits of grace that provides the bond between God and redeemed humanity. In offering such an explanation of this bond, Calvin provides a shift away from "a more Platonic view (based on an ontological similarity between divine and human) to the person of the Holy Spirit . . . anchoring human participation only in God himself, beginning with the self-gift of God to us in the person of the Spirit."[8]

Calvin identifies two principal saving benefits received in union with Christ by the agency of the Spirit, a *duplex gratia* or double grace, the first of which is justification and the second of which is regeneration or sanctification.[9] It is at this point that potential for considerable confusion arises, for Calvin clearly defines justification in forensic terms. Twenty-first-century readers, accustomed to thinking of forensic and participatory categories as opposites, often find difficulty in conceptualizing forensic justification as an aspect of union with Christ even if they themselves belong to the Reformed tradition. For example, Bruce McCormack finds inconsistency in Calvin's thought here, suggesting that union with Christ

---

cused narrowly on the salvation of the individual. Susan E. Schreiner, *The Theater of His Glory: Nature and Natural Order in the Thought of John Calvin* (Grand Rapids: Baker, 1991), 112: "Also on the basis of Rom 8:20, Calvin maintained that the renovation of nature would follow that of the head of creation, namely, the human being."

5. *Institutes* 3.1.1 (538) = *CO* 2:394.

6. *Institutes* 3.1.4 (541) = *CO* 2:396.

7. *Comm. 1 Cor* 6:11, *CNTC* 9:127 = *CO* 49:395. This commentary was first published in 1546.

8. Julie Canlis, *Calvin's Ladder: A Spiritual Theology of Ascent and Ascension* (Grand Rapids: Eerdmans, 2010), 98.

9. For a concise overview of Calvin's concept of the *duplex gratia* see Paul Helm, *Calvin at the Centre* (Oxford: Oxford University Press, 2010), 196-226.

is difficult to distinguish conceptually from regeneration and that by making union the basis of justification Calvin also unintentionally makes regeneration the basis of justification. McCormack finds it problematic that Calvin speaks both of sanctifying regeneration through union with Christ as a logical consequence of justification and of justifying faith itself as a gift received through union with Christ. Calvin's insistence that the two are chronologically simultaneous is helpful. However, since to be united with Christ is the very nature of regeneration, McCormack worries that to base the gift of faith on union with Christ is also to base justification on regeneration: "For where regeneration is made—even if only logically—to be the root of justification, there the work of God 'in us' is, once again, (and now on the soil of the Reformation!) made to be the ground of the divine forgiveness of sins."[10]

This objection to Calvin's procedure is in part simply anachronistic. Calvin appears to make regeneration the root of justification only if one shares the frequent later assumption that forensic justification inherently has less to do with union with Christ than sanctification. Further, the objection also proceeds as if Calvin has overlooked a flaw in the structure of his own thought, failing to appreciate the consequences of rooting both the gift of faith and sanctifying regeneration in union with Christ. However, Calvin's exegesis suggests that he sees clearly the relationships he has established but simply does not regard them as problematic. In his comments on Rom 5:15 ("the grace of God and the free gift in the grace of the one man, Jesus Christ, abounded for the many"), Calvin insists that grace is in God and is God's unmerited love for us. Grace is not infused but remains external to the believer. Instead, it is the "effect of grace that is in us."[11] This gift in the grace of Christ is "the fruit of this mercy which has come to us, viz. the reconciliation by which we have obtained life and salvation. It is also righteousness, newness of life, and every other similar blessing."[12] This logical prioritizing of grace, along with the denial that it is an infused quality, removes all danger of merit and allows Calvin without anxiety to associate not only newness of life with the gift but also reconciliation and righteousness.

10. Bruce McCormack, "What's at Stake in Current Debates over Justification? The Crisis of Protestantism in the West," in *Justification: What's at Stake in the Current Debates?*, ed. Mark Husbands and Daniel J. Treier (Downers Grove, IL: InterVarsity Press, 2004), 102.

11. *Comm. Rom* 5:15, *CNTC* 8:115 = *OE* 13:112, 18–19.

12. *Comm. Rom* 5:15, *CNTC* 8:115 = *OE* 13:112, 13–16.

Thus, justifying faith and sanctifying regeneration can both be rooted in union with Christ without implying that the former results from the latter because both depend on grace. Indeed, Calvin bases his denial of infusion on the contrast between it and union with Christ, who is made by the Father "the fountain out of whose fullness all may draw."[13] Justification is a work of God for us that is received always and only in union with Christ. We shall see that there is for Calvin a logical dependence of sanctification on justification, but both are grounded in union with Christ. Justification cannot be logically prior to union with Christ itself since the gift of faith that unites those who receive it with Christ is logically prior both to the divine declaration of righteousness and to sanctifying regeneration: In Calvin's soteriology, "the Spirit grants the faith to receive Christ for justification and for sanctification, but, analogous to God's performative utterance in creation, it is the forensic verdict ("Let there be!") that evokes the inner renewal that yields the fruit of the Spirit ("Let the earth bring forth . . .")."[14] For Calvin forensic justification is no less a participatory concept than sanctification. In his exegesis, forensic justification is understood christologically as an aspect of union with Christ.[15]

As these comments on Rom 5:15 illustrate, it is indeed in his *Romans* commentary that Calvin's christological account of forensic justification can be seen most clearly. In his summary of the argument of the epistle, Calvin identifies justification as its main subject, suggests that this is dealt with in Rom 1–5, and further suggests that Paul turns to discuss sanctification at the start of chapter 6. What Calvin does not do is to identify union with Christ primarily with the discussion of sanctification in chapter 6 onwards. In fact, union with Christ is prominent at crucial points in his exegesis of chapters 1–5 as well.[16] A particularly clear example of forensic

13. *Comm. Rom* 5:15, *CNTC* 8:115 = *OE* 13: 112, 20–21.

14. Michael S. Horton, "Calvin's Theology of Union with Christ and the Double Grace: Modern Reception and Contemporary Possibilities," in *Calvin's Theology and Its Reception: Disputes, Developments, and New Possibilities*, ed. J. Todd Billings and I. John Hesselink (Louisville: Westminster John Knox, 2012), 91. McCormack, "What's at Stake in Current Debates over Justification?," 106–10, does actually propose as a "thought experiment" that faith should be considered as the logical consequence of the divine verdict rather than as its presupposition. The problem of course is that such a move is exegetically unsustainable.

15. McGrath, *Iustitia Dei*, 253–57, expounds this point succinctly, clearly, and accurately.

16. Charles Raith II, *Aquinas and Calvin on Romans: God's Justification and our Par-*

justification understood in terms of union with Christ occurs in relation to Rom 3:22, where Paul speaks of the revelation of "the righteousness of God through faith in Jesus Christ for all who believe" (δικαιοσύνη δὲ θεοῦ διὰ πίστεως Ἰησοῦ Χριστοῦ εἰς πάντας τοὺς πιστεύοντας).[17] Calvin takes this righteousness to be that which is found in Christ and is received by faith. However, Paul terms it the righteousness of God, making it clear for Calvin that God is its author and that it flows from God. Its first cause is therefore "the tribunal of God."[18] Since before that court only perfect obedience to God's law is reckoned as righteousness, no human being possesses righteousness in him or herself. Only Christ can render human beings just through the granting to them of his righteousness. However, Calvin will go on to explain further and clarify what he means by this forensic account of justification:

> When, therefore, we are justified, the efficient cause is the mercy of God, Christ is the substance (*materia*) of our justification, and the Word, with faith, the instrument. Faith is therefore said to justify, because it is the instrument by which we receive Christ, in whom righteousness is communicated to us. When we are made partakers of Christ (*facti sumus Christi participes*), we are not only ourselves righteous, but our works also are counted righteous in the sight of God, because any imperfections in them are obliterated by the blood of Christ.[19]

For all the emphasis here on the instrumental role of faith, it is important to note that Calvin does not say that it is the instrument by

---

ticipation (Oxford: Oxford University Press, 2014), 5, appears to miss this point, writing of Rom 6 "that we wait until this chapter of Romans—in which, for Calvin, Paul turns from addressing justification to addressing sanctification—before we begin to see robust signs of participation." However, it becomes apparent in the subsequent discussion that Raith recognizes the part played by union with Christ in Calvin's interpretation of Rom 1–5 (see, for example, 42–43) but disqualifies it from being considered participatory because what counts as participatory is to be measured by conformity to the exegesis of Aquinas. It is one thing to compare Calvin's account of participation in Christ to that of Aquinas and to prefer that of Aquinas (such judgments are an inherent part of the task of interpretation), but quite another to confuse such theological judgments with historical description.

17. See Garcia, *Life in Christ*, 113–19, for a fuller discussion of Calvin's comments on Rom 3:21–26.

18. *Comm. Rom* 3:22, CNTC 8:73 = OE 13:70, 33.

19. *Comm. Rom* 3:22, CNTC 8:73 = OE 13:70, 39 – 71, 5.

which righteousness is received. Instead, he says that it is the instrument by which *Christ* is received, and that righteousness is communicated in him. While Calvin is quite clear that it is the righteousness of Christ that justifies, he refuses to sever righteousness as a benefit of Christ from Christ's person. It is only in union with Christ that a man or woman can receive his righteousness. The point is further hammered home in Calvin's comment on Rom 3:24, where Paul describes justification as being by God's grace a gift: "The meaning is that since there is nothing left for men in themselves but to perish, having been smitten by the just judgment of God, they are therefore freely justified by His mercy, for Christ comes to the aid of their wretchedness, and communicates Himself to believers, so that they find in Him alone all those things of which they are in want."[20] From such statements it is clear that Calvin conceived justification by faith in terms of union with Christ from the very outset of his exegetical career. His *Commentary on Romans* was his very first biblical commentary, published in 1540. Though it was significantly revised for the 1551 and 1556 editions, the material quoted here from 3:21–26 comes from the first edition.

With this understanding in place, Calvin can go on to exegete Rom 4 in terms of Abraham's faith and its exclusion of merit. Here Calvin will not directly discuss union with Christ, but his prior work in establishing that forensic justification is to be conceived in terms of union means that he can give full weight to Paul's emphasis on human faith *without* compromising the christological basis on which justification rests. Calvin's famous definition of faith in the *Institutes* is that faith is "a firm and certain knowledge of God's benevolence toward us, founded upon the truth of the freely given promise in Christ, both revealed to our minds and sealed upon our hearts through the Holy Spirit."[21] This definition of faith as knowledge appears in the 1539 edition (see 4.3) and marks a development since the first 1536 *Institutes* where Calvin tends to discuss faith as *fiducia* (trust). This shift will make possible further developments in Calvin's later exegetical works on other parts of Scripture, where Calvin will not only focus on justifying faith but also on the life of faith, not only on saving faith but also on providential faith, not only on knowing God's redeeming activity through faith but also his activity as creator. Faith for Calvin is not only relevant to justification but also to sanctification.

---

20. *Comm. Rom* 3:24, CNTC 8:74 = OE 13:72, 12–15.
21. *Institutes* 3.2.7 (551) = CO 2:403.

Yet it clearly remains the case that "*fiducia* is a characteristic of faith as knowledge,"[22] and that the knowledge of which faith consists is not so much comprehension as assurance (*certitudo*). As we might expect, Calvin expounds Abraham's faith in terms of saving faith that trusts firmly in God's promises and rescues human beings from the despair of their encounter with a divine law they cannot fulfill. This understanding of faith is expressed in Calvin's comments on Rom 4:14, where Paul says that if it is those who are of the law who are the heirs of Abraham's inheritance, then "faith is null and the promise is void." He writes, "The apostle tells us that faith perishes if our soul does not rest securely in the goodness of God. Faith is therefore not the mere acknowledgement of God or of His truth, nor is it even the simple persuasion that there is a God, and that His Word is truth, but it is the sure knowledge of divine mercy which is conceived from the Gospel, and brings peace of conscience in the presence of God and repose."[23]

That this peace of conscience in God's presence is anchored christologically becomes clear when Calvin follows Paul back into direct discussion of Christ's saving work in 4:24-25.[24] Precisely because he has earlier defined forensic justification in terms of union with Christ, Calvin experiences little difficulty with Paul's thought that Christ was "raised for our justification" (4:25). He resists any notion that this phrase refers to "newness of life,"[25] i.e., sanctification, and insists that Paul is speaking of imputed justification, but comments of Christ that "He is said to have been raised for our justification, because He fully restored life to us by His resurrection."[26] In what sense this full restoration of life stems from imputed justification can be seen by looking both backwards and forwards to Calvin's comments on other texts in Romans that relate righ-

---

22. Pitkin, *What Pure Eyes Could See*, 30. My short discussion here of Calvin's understanding of faith draws upon Pitkin's work.

23. *Comm. Rom* 4:14, *CNTC* 8:93 = *OE* 13:90, 5-10.

24. Here I find myself in rare disagreement with Garcia, *Life in Christ*, 131-33, who argues that in his comments on these verses Calvin correlates the death and resurrection of Christ with the *duplex gratia* of justification and sanctification as elsewhere he correlates them with the distinction within sanctification between mortification and vivification (see below). However, Calvin discusses here not the two parts of our salvation, but the two parts of the cause of our salvation (*salutis causam*), i.e., Christ's death and Christ's resurrection. He certainly relates the death of Christ to sanctification in Rom 6, but here throughout 4:24-25 he is discussing justification. See *CNTC* 8:102 = *OE* 13:99, 17-18.

25. *Comm. Rom* 4:25, *CNTC* 8:103 = *OE* 13:100, 90.

26. *Comm. Rom* 4:25, *CNTC* 8:103 = *OE* 13:100, 18-20.

teousness and life. In dealing with Paul's quotation in 1:17 of Hab 2:5, "the righteous shall live by faith," Calvin says that the ungodly may have the illusion of life but destruction awaits and "the faith of the righteous alone brings everlasting life."[27] He also argues that "The verb in the future tense designates the undivided perpetuity of the life of which he is speaking, as though he had said, 'It shall not continue for a moment, but shall endure forever.'"[28] Thus the life granted by imputed justification in 4:25 is eternal life received through divine forgiveness of sins. This becomes even clearer at Rom 5:18, where Christ's righteous act "leads to justification and life for all" (εἰς πάντας ἀνθρώπους εἰς δικαίωσιν ζωῆς). Calvin says that "In my judgment *justification of life* means absolution, which restores life to us, or is 'life-giving.' Our hope of salvation is God's being propitious toward us, and we cannot be accepted by him unless we are righteous. Life therefore has its origin in justification."[29] It is the risen Christ who was "exalted into the kingdom of life, so that He might freely give His people righteousness and life."[30]

Calvin's chain of thought about justification is therefore clear. Sin brings death and death is the human destiny apart from Christ because divine judgment will ultimately fall upon all who are not righteous. Acceptance by God depends upon being righteous and therefore so too does life. Works cannot lead to this righteousness and life, which can only be received in Christ by means of faith because Christ is the one who has defeated sin and death. The risen Christ, "having been received into the glory of heaven, reconciled God to us by His intercession."[31] Thus precisely because Paul's texts do not allow him to, Calvin does not understand justification exclusively in relation to the cross. However, this does not modify his conviction that justification is centrally concerned with reconciliation and forgiveness of sins, but instead he shows how he relates these to the gift of eternal life. Righteousness is not an independent commodity available to believers as a result of Christ's sacrificial death but instead a personal attribute of the Christ who died and rose again, which can be received only through union with him. Many of the different

---

27. *Comm. Rom* 1:17, *CNTC* 8:29 = *OE* 13:28, 34–35.

28. *Comm. Rom* 1:17, *CNTC* 8:28 = *OE* 13:28, 30–32.

29. *Comm. Rom* 5:18, *CNTC* 8:118 = *OE* 13:114, 34–37. Calvin's "justification of life" and the NRSV's "justification and life" reflect different ways of understanding Paul's genitive construction.

30. *Comm. Rom* 4:25, *CNTC* 8:103 = *OE* 13:100, 21–22.

31. *Comm. Rom* 4:25, *CNTC* 8:102 = *OE* 13:100, 6–7.

elements of this pattern of thought can be seen in Calvin's comment on Rom 5:17 where Paul says that through Christ the free gift of righteousness will "exercise dominion in life." Calvin says,

> We are not accounted righteous because we have righteousness within us, but because we possess Christ Himself with all His blessings, given to us by the Father's bounty. The gift of righteousness, therefore, does not signify a quality with which God endows us, for this is a misinterpretation, but is the free imputation of righteousness. The apostle is expounding his interpretation of the word *grace*. . . . In order, however, that we may participate in the grace of Christ, we must be ingrafted into Him by faith. . . . [W]e attain fellowship (*consortium*) with Him by faith.[32]

In this quotation it is striking that Calvin has no hesitation in using the noun "imputation" in the context of participation in Christ. Indeed, the application of atonement only makes sense for Calvin in this context. When Paul discusses life in relation to justification for Calvin, it is always life in an eternal, eschatological sense and not life in the sense of renewal or fullness of life here and now. It is, however, nonetheless life in union with Christ.

7.3. Union with Christ (2): Sanctification

The fear that participatory righteousness in Christ as Calvin describes it runs the risk of rooting justification in regeneration is not the only possible concern about this concept. It is also possible on the other flank to worry that if such participatory righteousness in Christ is not an infused quality Calvin may court the danger of proposing a fiction in which in reality little changes in the life of the believer. Calvin addresses this danger with vigor at Rom 6:1, where Paul raises and dismisses the suggestion that we should sin in order that grace might abound: "Throughout this chapter the apostle maintains that those who imagine that Christ bestows free justification upon us without imparting newness of life shamefully rend Christ asunder."[33] As Calvin reads Romans, Paul is embarking on discussion of

---

32. *Comm. Rom* 5:17, *CNTC* 8:117 = *OE* 13:113, 34 – 114, 10.
33. *Comm. Rom* 6:1, *CNTC* 8:121 = *OE* 13:117, 7 – 10.

regeneration or sanctification, the second principal benefit received in union with Christ. While Calvin will insist that justification and sanctification are distinct, he will also strongly maintain that they are inseparable: "we are justified for this very purpose, that we may afterwards worship God in purity of life."[34] Not surprisingly, Calvin will therefore insist that dying and rising with Christ in baptism in Rom 6:2-4 is not a washing alone and that newness of life is not simply an imitation of Christ. Paul is speaking again of union with Christ, and the thought that union with Christ in a death like his will lead to a future sharing in a resurrection like his (Rom 6:5) prompts Calvin to borrow from later in the letter (Rom 11:17-24) Paul's own horticultural imagery of ingrafting. Calvin uses it to explain the meaning of being united with Christ's death. Ingrafting signifies "the secret union (*arcanam coniunctionem*) by which we grow together with Him, in such a way that He revives us by His Spirit, and transfers His power to us. Therefore, as the graft has the same life or death as the tree into which it is ingrafted, so it is reasonable that we should be as much partakers of the life as of the death of Christ."[35] However, there is also a difference between this secret union and the details of horticulture:

> In the grafting of trees the graft draws its nourishment from the root, but retains its own natural quality in the fruit which is eaten. In spiritual ingrafting, however, we not only derive the strength and sap of the life which flows from Christ, but we also pass from our own nature into His. The apostle desired to point quite simply to the efficacy of the death of Christ, which manifested itself in putting to death our flesh, and also the efficacy of His resurrection in renewing within us the better nature of the Spirit.[36]

In his final sentence here Calvin identifies what he takes to be Paul's two emphases in discussing sanctification, first the putting to death of the flesh, or its mortification, and second, the granting of the better nature of the Spirit, or vivification.[37]

34. *Comm. Rom* 6:2, *CNTC* 8:122 = *OE* 13:118, 7-8.
35. *Comm. Rom* 6:5, *CNTC* 8:123-24 = *OE* 13:120, 13-17.
36. *Comm. Rom* 6:5, *CNTC* 8:124 = *OE* 13:121, 7-13.
37. For discussion of the twofold nature of sanctification in Rom 6 in particular, see Garcia, *Life in Christ*, 125-33. For discussion of it in Calvin's theology in general, see Ronald S. Wallace, *Calvin's Doctrine of the Christian Life* (Edinburgh: Oliver & Boyd, 1959), 41-100.

Mortification involves for Calvin the putting to death of the self that existed before faith. When Paul speaks of putting to death the body of sin through crucifixion with Christ (Rom 6:6), Calvin comments that "man, when left to his own nature, is a mass of sin."[38] Everything must change through the rooting out of sinful desires. This Calvin conceives as a possibility now open that was previously closed. Paul's comment in 6:7 that "whoever has died is justified from sin"[39] is interpreted both according to this context and as a forensic image: "*Justified* means freed or reclaimed from bondage. Just as the prisoner who is absolved by the sentence of the judge is freed from the bond of his accusation, so death, by releasing us from this life, sets us free from all its responsibilities."[40] Thus the person who has been justified can be effective in struggling against sin, although this will require a continual struggle that will endure for the whole of a person's earthly life. Calvin paraphrases Paul in the following way:

> If you are a Christian, you must show in yourself a sign of your communion in the death of Christ (*communionis cum morte Christi*), and the fruit of this is that your flesh will be crucified together with all its desires. Do not assume, however, that this communion is not a real one if you find traces of the flesh still existing in you. But you are continually to study to increase your communion in the death of Christ, until you arrive at the goal.[41]

However, this emphasis on the crucifying of sinful desires is not the whole of mortification for Calvin. Mortification also involves sharing in Christ's sufferings. This is discussed in his comments on Rom 8:29,

---

38. *Comm. Rom* 6:6, CNTC 8:125 = OE 13:121, 24–27.

39. This is my own translation. Most English translations employ the phrases "set free from sin" or "liberated from sin." While this seems to make sense in the context, the Greek verb used is δικαιόω (justify). For further discussion of the translation of Rom 6:7, see 9.5. Calvin's comment seems to take the phrase as stressing the inter-connected nature of justification and dying to sin, and not as suggesting that a person is justified because they have died to sin. This would call into question the distinction between forensic justification and sanctification that Calvin carefully maintains. Calvin avoids this challenge by similar means in his interpretation of Rom 8:2, "For the law of the Spirit of life in Christ Jesus has set you free from the law of sin and of death." See *Comm. Rom* 8:2, CNTC 8:157 = OE 13:153, 4–5: "Paul is not here assigning the reason, but merely specifying the manner, in which we are delivered from guilt."

40. *Comm. Rom* 6:7, CNTC 8:125 = OE 13:121, 8–11.

41. *Comm. Rom* 6:7, CNTC 8:126 = OE 13:122, 17–22.

where the thought of God's glorification of the elect causes Calvin to comment that "the afflictions of believers, which cause their present humiliation, are intended solely that they may obtain the glory of the kingdom of heaven and reach the glory of the resurrection of Christ, with whom they are now glorified."[42] Calvin comments about these sufferings at much greater length in his *Commentary on 2 Corinthians*, where Paul's description in 4:11 of always being given up to death for Jesus' sake is labeled as "external mortification" in contrast to the "internal mortification" of putting to death the desires of the flesh described in Rom 6. This "external mortification" means that "the elect have participation in the Son of God so that all their miseries that are in their own nature curses are made helpful for their salvation."[43] If Paul reports being continually harassed and exposed to danger, then Calvin presumably has no difficulty in seeing the apostle's words as directly applicable to the persecution, exile, and martyrdoms experienced by early Protestant communities. Sanctification is for Calvin not only an internal struggle with sin but also a bearing of the cross in the public arena by declaring for the evangelical faith and faithfully accepting the consequences. The mention once again of participation in Christ in this comment reminds the reader that it is not an imitation of Christ, but an aspect of union with him, a reflection of the pattern of his death and resurrection.[44]

The other aspect of sanctification, which is vivification, is to share in Christ's resurrection. In one respect this has a fundamentally eschatological orientation, since the believer awaits bodily resurrection beyond this life and experiences in greater measure here and now the mortification of sharing in Christ's death. Yet since the believer is in Christ and the risen Christ is in glory in heaven, then when Paul speaks of the believer's glorification in Rom 8:30 in the past tense (in Greek the aorist is used: ἐδόξασεν), Calvin says that "Although glorification has as yet been exhibited only in our Head, yet, because we now perceive in Him the inheritance of eternal life, His glory brings to us such assurance of our own glory, that our hope may justly be compared to a present possession."[45]

---

42. *Comm. Rom* 8:29, *CNTC* 8:182 = *OE* 13:178, 35 – 179, 2.

43. *Comm. 2 Cor* 4:10, *CNTC* 10:60 = *CO* 50:55. This commentary was published in French in 1547 with the first Latin edition in 1548. Some revisions were made for further editions in 1551 and 1556.

44. Garcia, *Life in Christ*, 140–43, helpfully terms this patterning of the believer's experience after that of Christ as a "replication principle."

45. *Comm. Rom* 8:30, *CNTC* 8:182 = *OE* 13:178, 24–28.

The present troubles of believers deform this glory before the world, "yet before God and the angels it always shines in perfection."[46] In another respect, vivification is the positive counterpart of mortification. It is the good works of the believer enabled by the Holy Spirit. Here the liberation of the believer's conscience is vital, for Calvin says in relation to Paul's instruction in Rom 12:1 to present the body as a living sacrifice that "a godly mind is not formed to obey God by precepts or sanctions so much as by a serious meditation upon the divine goodness towards itself."[47] The law will still provide guidance for living, but the assurance of salvation in Christ means that its accusation against the conscience is gone. The Spirit has been given "to bring our minds to a state of tranquility, and to stir us up to call on God with confidence and freedom."[48] We can say "Abba Father" (Rom 8:15) because the Spirit of adoption has replaced a covenant of law with a covenant of grace. Love of neighbor is the fulfilling of the law (Rom 13:8), "for true love to men flows only from the love of God, and is the evidence and effect of this love."[49] When describing the fruit of the Spirit in his *Commentary on Galatians* (1548), Calvin comments that "all virtues, all good and well regulated affections, proceed from the Spirit, that is, from the grace of God, and the renewed nature which we have from Christ. . . . In the sight of God nothing is pure but what proceeds from the fountain of all purity."[50] For Calvin the whole of the believer's life is a daily journey toward sanctification through the power of the Spirit in union with Christ.

7.4. Union with Christ (3): 1 Corinthians 1:30 as an Exegetical Center

As we have now seen, Calvin with equal emphasis expounds both forensic justification and sanctification as aspects of union with Christ. Further exegetical confirmation of this can be found in a disagreement with Eras-

---

46. *Comm. Rom* 8:30, *CNTC* 8:182 = *OE* 13:178, 33–34.
47. *Comm. Rom* 12:1, *CNTC* 8:263 = *OE* 13:255, 29–31.
48. *Comm. Rom* 8:15, *CNTC* 8:167–78 = *OE* 13:164, 8–9.
49. *Comm. Rom* 13:8, *CNTC* 8:285 = *OE* 13:276, 28–29.
50. *Comm. Gal* 5:22, *CNTC* 11:105 = *OE* 16:133, 10 – 134, 4. This commentary was first published in 1548 in one volume with those on Ephesians, Philippians, and Colossians. They were lightly revised for a new edition in 1551 and thoroughly revised for an edition of 1556.

mus as to the best translation of the Greek preposition ἐν. At Rom 6:11 Paul instructs readers to consider themselves dead to sin and alive to God ἐν Χριστῷ Ἰησοῦ, and Erasmus, in his 1519 edition, and all subsequent editions, of the New Testament, translates this with the instrumental *per Christum* ("by" or "through" Christ). Calvin by contrast insists on retaining the Vulgate's *in Christo Iesu* ("in Christ Jesus") because it "communicates more clearly the union-engrafting idea that Paul intends."[51] Here, of course, Calvin regards Paul as discussing sanctification. Calvin also departs from Erasmus in precisely parallel fashion at 2 Cor 5:21, insisting that we do not become the righteousness of God "by" or "through" Christ but "in" Christ. Here Calvin says that he retains the preposition *in* because this is in line with Paul's intended meaning that "we are judged in relation to Christ's righteousness, which we have put on by faith, that it may become our own."[52] Calvin thinks that Paul is discussing forensic justification in this verse, not sanctification, but he insists on maintaining Paul's participatory logic in exactly the same way.

While Calvin's equal emphasis on union with Christ in relation to both justification and sanctification is clear, how the relationship between these two main elements of salvation works is not quite so apparent from the *Commentary on Romans* alone. He will say at 8:2 that sanctification and justification are "at the same time," thus removing any temptation to read them as chronological stages in an *ordo salutis* (order of salvation).[53] We have also already seen Calvin say in his exposition of 6:1 that to separate justification and sanctification is to rend Christ asunder (see 7.3), thus suggesting that further explanation will focus on the person of Christ. Yet both these statements are revisions made for the 1556 edition of the commentary, which had already been revised once before in 1551. It is far from clear that in the first 1540 edition such explanations are offered at all.[54] It

51. Garcia, *Life in Christ*, 127. See *Comm. Rom* 6:11, CNTC 8:128 = OE 13:124, 27-29.

52. *Comm. 2 Cor 5:21*, CNTC 10:81-82 = CO 50:74.

53. Whether there is a logical or causal ordering of the relationship between different aspects of salvation in Calvin's thought is a related but different question. See Richard A. Muller, *Calvin and the Reformed Tradition: On the Work of Christ and the Order of Salvation* (Grand Rapids: Baker, 2012), 202-43.

54. I have not undertaken a thorough comparison between the ways in which union with Christ is expressed in the three editions of the *Romans* commentary. Such a study by a Calvin specialist, especially if widened to include comparison between union with Christ in the 1536 *Institutes* and the 1539 *Institutes*, might shed considerable light on a crucial stage of development in Calvin's soteriology.

is then only clear that sanctification cannot be conceived apart from justification, since the latter grants the cloak of Christ's righteousness that provides believers, who still sometimes lose their struggle with vestigial sin, with assurance that the incomplete nature of their sanctification in this life does not lead to their rejection by God.

The reason for this earlier comparative lack of explanation is that Calvin's exegetical resources for providing one lie outside Romans. In April 1538 his first spell in ministry in Geneva came to an abrupt end when his supporters fared poorly in municipal elections. He found refuge in Strasbourg until 1541. This period was crucial in his theological development as he worked simultaneously on his *Romans* commentary and on the first major revision of his *Institutes* (Latin 1539 / French translation 1541).[55] Here in the revised *Institutes* Calvin employs for the first time in fully developed form his favorite means of explaining the relationship between justification and sanctification in union with Christ. He relies upon 1 Cor 1:30,[56] where it is said that Christ Jesus "became for us wisdom

55. On this period in Calvin's life, see Bruce Gordon, *Calvin* (New Haven: Yale University Press, 2009), 82-102, and Herman J. Selderhuis, *John Calvin: A Pilgrim's Life* (Downers Grove, IL: InterVarsity Press, 2009), 85-109. The *Romans* commentary was probably based on lectures previously given in Geneva in the period 1536-1538. See T. H. L. Parker and D. C. Parker, "Introduction," *OE* 13:11-73 (esp. 11-15). The *Institutes* had first been published in 1536 as a shorter catechetical work. In the 1539 edition it is for the first time a handbook, largely for ministers, of the whole Christian religion. Richard Muller, *The Unaccommodated Calvin: Studies in the Foundation of a Theological Tradition* (Oxford: Oxford University Press, 2000), 101-36, helpfully discusses the symbiotic relationship in context and method between the *Institutes* and Calvin's biblical commentaries: "The commentaries frequently shed light on the meaning of a passage in the *Institutes*, sometimes offer indications of why topics are augmented in certain ways in the *Institutes*; sometimes, when topics have been explained in the *Institutes* prior to the examination of a related text, the commentaries explicitly refer the readers to extended discussions in the *Institutes*" (108). As we have seen (see 6.2), Melanchthon had moved away from the traditional phrase-by-phrase exegesis of texts, instead organizing his *Commentary on Romans* around theological *loci* according to his determination of the rhetorical structure of the letter. Bucer did both in one massive volume. In his commentary, Calvin provided phrase-by-phrase exegesis but made extensive use of rhetorical analysis, and reserved his *loci* for the *Institutes*, which related not just to Romans but the whole of Scripture. On Calvin's methodology, see also T. H. L. Parker and D. C. Parker, "Introduction," *OE* 13:11-73 (esp. 51-55).

56. Mark Garcia rightly emphasizes the importance of this text for Calvin. See Garcia, *Life in Christ*, 219-25, and Mark Garcia, "Imputation and the Christology of Union with Christ: Calvin, Osiander, and the Contemporary Quest for a Reformed Model," *WTJ* 68 (2006): 219-51. Garcia, *Life in Christ*, 219-21, also helpfully draws at-

from God, and righteousness and sanctification and redemption." The importance of Calvin's comment in indicating how he integrates justification and sanctification on the basis of this text warrants a full citation:

> For from where does it come that we are justified by faith? It is because by faith we grasp Christ's righteousness which alone reconciles us to God. Now we cannot grasp this righteousness without also having sanctification. For when it is said that Christ is given to us for redemption, wisdom, and righteousness, it is likewise added that He is given to us for sanctification [1 Cor 1:30]. From that it follows that Christ does not justify anyone whom He does not at the same time sanctify. For these benefits are joined together by a perpetual tie; when He illumines us with His wisdom, He ransoms us; when He ransoms us, He justifies us; when He justifies us, He sanctifies us. But because it is now only a question of righteousness and sanctification, let us stop with these two. So although they must be distinguished, nevertheless Christ contains both inseparably. Do we want to receive righteousness in Christ? We must first possess Christ. Now we cannot possess Him without being participants in His sanctification, since He cannot be torn in pieces. Since, I say, the Lord Jesus never gives anyone the enjoyment of His benefits except in giving Himself, He gives both of them together and never one without the other. From that it is clear how true the sentence is: that we are not justified without works, although it is not by works, since participation in Christ, in which our righteousness consists, contains our sanctification no less.[57]

tention to statements in Calvin's catechism of 1537/1538 and in his *Response to Sadoleto* of 1539 that use 1 Cor 1:30 to stress the inseparability of justification and sanctification, but the first of these does not really stress union with Christ's person in order to do so. It is in the latter text, which is again from the Strasbourg period, that we seem to see a significant development in this regard.

57. John Calvin, *Institutes of the Christian Religion: 1541 French Edition, The First English Version*, trans. Elsie A. McKee (Grand Rapids: Eerdmans, 2009), 356 = CO 4:303-4. This is an English translation of the 1541 French translation of the 1539 Latin version. However, the French translation was undertaken by Calvin himself. Neither the Latin or French versions of this edition have previously appeared in English. The verse reference in brackets in the middle of the quotation is the work of the modern editor, not of Calvin (verse divisions did not make their first appearance until the 1550s), but quite obviously reflects a correct identification of the text Calvin is discussing. On the issue of subtle distortions of Calvin's intention through the addition of a modern critical apparatus, see Muller, *The Unaccommodated Calvin*, 140-48. However,

Here Calvin clearly focuses on the person of Christ and on the unity of his person. Since Christ is a living person, his saving benefits cannot be detached from his person and can only be received in union with him. For the same reason, these saving benefits cannot be separated from each other. They are received together in him or not at all. As should already be clear, this quotation makes it extremely plain that in his frequent use of the noun *imputatio* ("imputation") Calvin simply cannot mean that righteousness is first given to the believer as a preliminary forensic step that then makes union with Christ possible. He does not mean that righteousness is given to the believer as a quality abstracted from Christ's person, initially passed on to the believer independent of any other of Christ's properties. Instead, Paul's forensic imagery functions for Calvin within the wider context of participation in Christ, and Calvin states that it is necessary first to possess Christ in order to receive his righteousness. His logical order of reasoning can thus sometimes be opposite from that in later popular Protestant concepts of imputation where forensic justification is the gateway to union with Christ.[58] The divine verdict that constitutes justification is indeed for Calvin essential to union with Christ, but it is so as one of the principal components of that union and not as its prelude. Calvin will carefully maintain the distinction between justification and sanctification. Justification is a forensic declaration, and not an infusion of righteousness. It is in that sense a work of God for us and not a work of God in us. Yet Calvin is equally keen to maintain that it is only received integrated within the wider union with Christ that he sees as indicated by 1 Cor 1:30 and similar texts.

Further aspects of the integrative function served by 1 Cor 1:30 in Calvin's soteriology can be found in his later *Commentary on 1 Corin-*

McKee is duly careful to indicate to readers where she has inserted verse references. See *Institutes* 3.16.1 (798) = CO 2:586 for the same passage in the Battles translation of the 1559 edition. Note that here the editors have added an unconvincing second verse reference linking Calvin's statement that Christ cannot be torn into pieces specifically to 1 Cor 1:13. However, while there certainly is a reference to dividing Christ in Paul's text, it is in the context of baptism, not that of the receipt of righteousness and sanctification.

58. Calvin can do the opposite and speak as though justification is logically prior to union. See *Institutes* 3.11.21 = CO 2:550-51: "Thus, him whom he receives into union with himself the Lord is said to justify, because he cannot receive him into grace nor join him to himself unless he turns him from a sinner into a righteous man." It is not that Calvin must speak in one order or the other, but rather that he can do either because justification and sanctification are simultaneously received.

thians (1546). Here he repeats and personalizes his statement in the *Institutes* that justification and sanctification are inseparable since Christ cannot be torn into pieces: "if anyone tries to separate them he is, in a sense, tearing Christ to pieces."[59] He also responds directly to the accusation that the preaching of justification by faith alone leaves people with no motivation for good works. A person cannot be justified in Christ "unless at the same time he lays hold of Him for sanctification; in other words he must be born anew by His Spirit to blamelessness and purity of life."[60] If there can be no justification without sanctification, then there can also be no faith without works even though justification is not by works. Finally, and most importantly, the meaning of faith is itself explored more deeply and broadly, not only as justifying faith but for the whole of the Christian life:

> Faith lays hold of regeneration just as much as forgiveness of sins in Christ. . . . [S]ince there is scarcely another passage in Scripture which gives a clearer description of all the offices of Christ, it can also give us the best understanding of the force and nature of faith. For, since Christ is the proper object of faith, everyone who knows what benefits Christ gives to us, also learns what faith is.[61]

Thus faith belongs not only in the discussion of justification, but also in that of sanctification. Indeed, Calvin's words appear to imply that a proper understanding of faith requires attention to the other benefits that Christ brings and not only to justification and sanctification.

This positioning by Calvin of faith in relation to all of Christ's saving benefits also has significant exegetical implications. It means that Calvin does not feel the need to insist that all of Paul's uses of the term have the same meaning.[62] In 1 Cor 13 Calvin's opponents seize

---

59. *Comm. 1 Cor* 1:30, *CNTC* 9:46 = *CO* 49:331. Garcia, *Life in Christ*, 228-41, provides an extended discussion of Calvin's use of this metaphor, charting an increased use on through the 1550s. He also describes discussion of this text in the commentary as providing, outside the *Institutes*, "the most concise articulation of Calvin's soteriology" (238).

60. *Comm. 1 Cor* 1:30, *CNTC* 9:46 = *CO* 49:331.

61. *Comm. 1 Cor* 1:30, *CNTC* 9:46-47 = *CO* 49:331-32.

62. For more general discussion of the capacity of several of the Reformers to recognize that the same term may have different nuances of meaning depending upon context, see 4.2 and 4.3.

upon Paul's subordination of faith to love in order to argue their position that in order for faith to save, it must be formed by love. Calvin simply agrees that love is greater, asserts that faith's power to justify is not a matter of the merit of faith, and suggests that faith here is not to be identified solely with justifying faith. Instead, he says in relation to 13:13 that faith has "a wider range of meaning than in earlier instances of its use. . . . We now understand what is meant by faith in this verse, viz. the knowledge of God and His will . . . faith understood in its fullness, and in its proper sense."[63] Similar flexibility can be seen in relation to other key terms in Paul's soteriology. Where context demands a different meaning, Calvin does not have to force Paul's words always to have a meaning at odds with the interpretation of his opponents. Another example of this appears in his comments on grace. He will often insist that it denotes the favor of God as distinct from the gifts that God gives, but not always. Paul gives thanks in 1 Cor 1:5 that the Corinthian believers have been enriched in Christ in every way. Here Calvin makes explicit what is implicit in his characterization of justification and sanctification as a *duplex gratia* ("double grace"). He comments that grace can be a general term embracing all kinds of blessing. It means here "not the favour of God, but, by metonymy, the gifts which He freely lavishes upon men."[64]

Most strikingly of all, Calvin can do the same thing with the vocabulary of righteousness. Paul speaks explicitly in Rom 6:19 of presenting "your members as slaves to righteousness for sanctification." Calvin comments: "you should wholly forget sin and turn your whole heart to righteousness, into the service of which you have been brought."[65] The noun δικαιοσύνη ("righteousness") speaks plainly here of the obedience required in sanctification and Calvin will also interpret it in relation to sanctification in many other contexts. At Phil 1:11, with its prayer that the readers be filled with "the fruits of righteousness," Calvin says bluntly that Paul desires "them to be fertile in good works, to the glory of God,"[66] and immediately goes on to defend the consistency with his teaching on justification of identifying together in this way the meaning of the term "righteousness" and good works. At Eph 5:9, Calvin characterizes righ-

---

63. *Comm. 1 Cor* 13:13, *CNTC* 9:282–83 = *CO* 49:515.
64. *Comm. 1 Cor* 1:5, *CNTC* 9:21 = *CO* 49:310.
65. *Comm. Rom* 6:19, *CNTC* 8:133 = *OE* 13:129, 30–32.
66. *Comm. Phil.* 1:11, *CNTC* 11:233 = *OE* 16:302, 32–33. See note 50 above for details of publication.

teousness as a fruit of obedience.[67] Calvin will also reconcile with his own soteriology awkward uses of the verb δικαιόω ("justify") by other biblical writers through arguing that they really speak of sanctification. The same word means different things for different writers. Thus at Jas 2:21 Calvin says of justification that "to Paul, the word denotes our free imputation of righteousness before the judgment seat of God, to James, the demonstration of righteousness from its effects, in the sight of men; which we may deduce from the preceding words, *Shew me thy faith, etc.*"[68] At Ps 106:31, where Phinehas's zeal is said to have been credited to him as righteousness, Calvin says that such imputation occurred "in the same way as God imputes the works of the faithful to them for righteousness."[69] As God accepts believers' works of sanctification as righteous because their imperfections are covered by Christ's righteousness, so God also accepted Phinehas's zeal. Calvin is even happy in this sense to speak of works righteousness in a positive sense so long as it is understood to depend upon faith and free justification.[70] Calvin is completely committed in all instances to interpreting the vocabulary of righteousness in ways that are consistent with his understanding of justification, but he does not insist that this vocabulary always and only expresses such an understanding.

These examples show us a second significant way in which union with Christ is integrative for Calvin. We have already seen that his focus on the person of Christ allows Calvin to characterize justification and sanctification as distinct but inseparable in his soteriology. Here we see that it also allows him to hold together in an exegetical synthesis texts that otherwise might appear to stand in tension with each other. Finally, it also makes it possible for Calvin to change his mind about individual

---

67. *Comm. Eph.* 5:9, *CNTC* 11:200 = *OE* 16:259, 2–4. See note 50 above for details of publication.

68. *Comm. Jas.* 2:21, *CNTC* 3:285 = *CO* 55:406. This commentary was first published in 1550.

69. *CTS* 6.4:233 = *CO* 32:128.

70. *Institutes* 3.17.9 = *CO* 2:597. See also Steven R. Coxhead, "John Calvin's Subordinate Doctrine of Justification by Works," in *WTJ* 71 (2009): 1–19. Anthony N. S. Lane, "Twofold Righteousness: A Key to the Doctrine of Justification? Reflections on Article 5 of the Regensburg Colloquy," in *Justification: What's at Stake in Current Debates?*, ed. Mark Husbands and Daniel J. Treier (Downers Grove, IL: InterVarsity Press, 2004), 205–24 (esp. 215–17), argues that it is his comfort with this kind of language that enabled Calvin to react positively to the proposal of double justification that emerged from Regensburg in contrast to Luther's outright rejection.

texts without altering the overall framework within which he works. In his *Commentary on Galatians* from 1548, Calvin interprets 2:20, with its statement that "It is no longer I who live, but it is Christ who lives in me" as concerning the believer's justifying participation in Christ's righteousness.[71] Calvin does countenance the idea that a reference to the work of the Holy Spirit in sanctification might also be intended here, and finds it an unobjectionable interpretation, but he prefers to read 2:20 as concerning justification by faith. However, by 1557–1558 when he preaches on this text, Calvin has modified his interpretation so as definitely to include both justification and sanctification. He expresses this shift using one of his favorite metaphors. The work of the Spirit in sanctification and the remission of sins in justification "are inseparably joined together, just as the brightness of the sun cannot be separated from its heat." Nevertheless, although the sun is hot and shines at the same time, "the brilliance of the sun is not the same as its heat."[72] As we have seen, both this commentary and this sermon date from many years after Calvin had reached the position that justification and sanctification are distinct but inseparable aspects of union with Christ. The integrative power of Calvin's exegesis of 1 Corinthians 1:30 is such that he can change his mind even about a text as significant as Galatians 2:20 without any wider impact on his soteriology.

7.5. Union with Christ (4): The Spirit and Christ's Humanity

Alongside these exegetical consequences, Calvin's positioning of faith in relation to all the saving benefits of Christ and hence to the whole of salvation also has significant theological implications. It was to become of great importance in his critique of Osiander and the latter's insistence on justification as the receipt of an "essential righteousness," in which justification is secured by the specific presence of the divine nature of Christ in the believer.[73] Finding himself under suspicion from Lutheran sources as dangerously close to Osiander, Calvin is determined in the 1559 *Institutes* emphatically to distinguish his teaching on union with Christ from "essential righteousness" and to reassert the significance

---

71. *Comm. Gal* 2:20, *CNTC* 11:43–44 = *OE* 16:55, 22–24.
72. Calvin, *Sermons on Galatians*, 198–99 = *CO* 50, 438 (Sermon 13).
73. See 6.6 for further details on Osiander's theology.

for justification of Christ's incarnate obedience unto death. Here again, 1 Corinthians 1:30 is a significant text, for it had also been important to Osiander. Anxious to avoid making justification a legal fiction, Osiander had used the verse to deny the propriety of a sharp distinction between justification and sanctification. He and Calvin agree that the text treats both justification and sanctification as aspects of union with Christ and therefore indicates their simultaneity. However, Calvin will not have it that simultaneity implies a lack of clear distinction: "Scripture, even though it joins them, still lists them separately. . . . For Paul's statement is not redundant: that Christ was given to us for our righteousness and sanctification [1 Cor 1:30]."[74]

Further, Calvin insists that the granting of the righteousness of Christ to the believer in justification is conceivable only on the basis of Christ's incarnate role as mediator. Calvin asserts that "we are justified in Christ, in so far as he was made an atoning sacrifice for us, something that does not comport with his divine nature (*quod a divina eius natura abhorret*)."[75] How, he asks, can it be said at 1 Corinthians 1:30 that Christ was made righteousness for us according to a divine nature when he already shared divine righteousness with the Father and the Spirit? Paul's statement is "surely peculiar to the person of the Mediator, which, even though it contains in it the divine nature, still has its own proper designation by which the Mediator is distinguished from the Father and the Spirit."[76] Christ carried out his saving acts according to his human nature, taking on the form of a servant and justifying believers through his obedience to the cross. Calvin says, "From this we conclude that in his flesh, righteousness has been manifested to us."[77] Calvin is not here simply pitting an emphasis on Christ's human nature as vital to justification against Osiander's insistence on Christ's divine nature as essential to justification. Calvin is quite clear that Christ's divinity is essential to his saving work, and will elsewhere defend the doctrine of the communication of properties between Christ's divine and human natures as essential if he is to be the mediator between God and hu-

---

74. *Institutes* 3.11.6 (732) = CO 2:537. The apparatus of chapter and verse is original, being included in the margin of the 1559 Latin text.

75. *Institutes* 3.11.9 (736) = CO 2:540.

76. *Institutes* 3.11.8 (734) = CO 2:539. The Battles translation here includes the apparatus of chapter and verse where it is absent from the margin of the 1559 text but there seems little doubt that 1 Cor 1:30 remains here the principal text in Calvin's mind.

77. *Institutes* 3.11.9 (735) = CO 2:541.

manity.[78] Nevertheless, Christ's human nature is vital to justification on Calvin's view since believers

> are not simply united to a divine nature that is righteous because it is divine or even united to a second Adam who lived a righteous life and hypothetically could have died a natural death. Rather, the righteousness of Jesus Christ is the righteousness of the cross—the mystery of the cross connected to the "wondrous exchange" language which is so closely related to imputation—in which the sin of sinners is imputed upon Christ, and the righteousness of Christ is imputed to sinners.[79]

From Calvin's perspective, Osiander also overlooks a crucial pneumatological point: "Now it is easy for us to resolve all his difficulties. For we hold ourselves to be united with Christ by the secret power of his Spirit."[80] It is this role for the Spirit as the bond of the believer's union with Christ that defines the nature of that union. Calvin agrees with Osiander that "we are one with Christ."[81] He even agrees that, if appropriately defined, "the righteousness of which Christ makes us partakers with himself is the eternal righteousness of the eternal God."[82] Yet this is completely different for Calvin from what he regards as Osiander's insistence that "Christ's essence is mixed with our own" or that there is "a mixture of substances by which God—transfusing himself into us, as it were—makes us part of himself."[83] Calvin thus rejects the vocabulary of substance in favor of the bond of the Spirit, and this allows Calvin to maintain a strong doctrine of union with Christ without compromising what he regards as a proper distinction between Creator and creature.

78. In June 1560 Calvin and the other ministers of Geneva wrote to Francesco Stancaro (1501-1574), professor of Hebrew at Königsberg, rejecting Stancaro's view that Christ's divinity played no part in his role as mediator. In order to make their case the Genevan pastors employ the communication of properties. See Joseph Tylanda, "Christ the Mediator: Calvin versus Stancaro," in *Articles on Calvin and Calvinism*, ed. Richard C. Gamble, 14 vols. (New York: Garland, 1992), 5:161-72.

79. J. Todd Billings, "Union with Christ and the Double Grace: Calvin's Theology and Its Early Reception," in *Calvin's Theology and Its Reception*, ed. J. Todd Billings and I. John Hesselink (Louisville: Westminster John Knox, 2012), 61.

80. *Institutes* 3.11.5 (730) = *CO* 2:536.

81. *Institutes* 3.11.5 (730) = *CO* 2:536.

82. *Institutes* 3.11.9 (736) = *CO* 2:540.

83. *Institutes* 3.11.5 (730-31) = *CO* 2:536.

The believer and Christ are one, but this does not involve sameness. Instead, their unity is the "bringing together of two 'unlikes' in a relationship of mutual indwelling."[84]

Here Calvin draws a distinction between mutual indwelling and a sharing of substance or of essence that he had not previously made with consistency. For, while insisting on the role of the Spirit in union with Christ, he had previously spoken directly of the sharing of Christ's substance.[85] There is no doubt that, when attacking Osiander, Calvin is forced by polemical necessity to to reconsider his vocabulary, but the reconsideration helps him to distinguish even more clearly his own understanding of participation in Christ from those that expressed it in terms of infusion.[86] It also allows him to emphasize union with Christ in

84. Canlis, *Calvin's Ladder*, 142.

85. *Comm. Eph.* 5:30, *CNTC* 11:208 = *OE* 16:272 (*substantiae eius communicare et hac communicatione nos coalescere in unum corpus*). This is pointed out by Andrew J. Ollerton, "*Quasi Deificari*: Deification in the Theology of John Calvin," *WJT* 73 (2011): 248-49. In arguing that Calvin does teach deification or *theosis*, Ollerton rather overlooks the new care taken in handling the vocabulary of substance in Calvin's attacks on Osiander. Ollerton's article is part of an evolving debate on the issue. See also Carl Mosser, "The Greatest Possible Blessing: Calvin and Deification," *SJT* 55.1 (2002): 36-57; Jonathan Slater, "Salvation as Participation in the Humanity of the Mediator: A Reply to Carl Mosser," *SJT* 58.1 (2005): 39-58; Yang-ho Lee, "Calvin on Deification: A Reply to Carl Mosser and Jonathan Slater," *SJT* 63.3 (2010): 272-84. Calvin's focus on union with Christ seems to offer considerable possibilities for dialogue between his soteriology and those of the Orthodox churches, but his dispute with Osiander also seems to set certain limits. Calvin, *Institutes* 3.11.10 (737-38) = *CO* 2:541, treats the promise of 2 Peter 1:4 that believers will become partakers of the divine nature as wholly eschatological: "As if we now were what the gospel promises that we shall be at the final coming of Christ." Billings, *Calvin, Participation, and the Gift*, 54, considers that we may legitimately speak of *theosis* in Calvin, but only if it is recognized that believers are incorporated into the Triune life of God "while remaining creatures." Note also the judgment of Horton, "Calvin's Theology of Union with Christ and the Double Grace," 93 that Calvin's "account provides ample space for an exclusively forensic justification *and* transformative renewal—even a form of deification."

86. François Wendel, *Calvin: Origins and Development of His Religious Thought* (Grand Rapids: Baker, 1997), 236 suggests that Calvin "did not perceive the danger, or at least imprudence of certain formulations until he had read some of Osiander's writings which appeared in 1550 or 1551." In a letter of August 8, 1555, to Peter Martyr Vermigli, Calvin contrasts his own emphasis on the Spirit with views of union with Christ that involve "gross notions of any mixture of substance; for it is sufficient to me, while the Body of Christ dwells in celestial glory, that life flows from Him to us in the same manner as the root transmits sap to the branches." See George C. Gorham, *Gleanings of a Few Scattered Ears* (London: Bell and Daldy, 1857), 350 = *CO* 15:722-25 (Letter 2266). This can be con-

a manner entirely consistent with the alien nature of the righteousness of Christ received by the believer. As Julie Canlis expresses it, Calvin is "extrospective" rather than "introspective," for "while Osiander was preoccupied with whether the individual subject was really righteous, Calvin no longer looked to the bounds of the person to define truth about the person. The new 'Reformation ontology' did not begin with the human being as a substance prior to all community, but it began with the truth of the person-in-Christ."[87]

This beginning with the truth of the person in Christ is crucial for understanding how Calvin conceives the works of the believer performed in response to God's gracious saving initiative in Christ. For part of the gracious character of this initiative is its participatory and mediated nature in which, in the person of Christ, the saving work itself is already human as well as divine. Philip Butin articulates the part played by the Spirit in orchestrating this human and divine dynamic:

> The Holy Spirit is the Spirit of Christ, who is the epitome of humanity and the authentic embodiment of the divine image. This Spirit actualized and empowered the incarnate Christ to fulfill genuine humanity. This same Spirit unites believers by faith to that same Christ; authenticating in turn their humanity; not over against God, but rather by incorporation into the divine life.[88]

This takes us back to the opening statements of Book III of the 1559 *Institutes* with which we began our discussion of union with Christ in Calvin's Pauline exegesis. The Trinitarian context of the union between divinity and humanity received by faith is asserted using a medley of Pauline quotations:

> To share with us what he has received from the Father, he had to become ours and to dwell within us. For this reason, he is called "our

---

trasted with an earlier statement in *Comm. Rom* 6:5, *CNTC* 8:124 = *OE* 13:121, 8–10. Here Calvin says that "In spiritual ingrafting, however, we not only derive the strength and sap of the life which flows from Christ, but we also pass from our own nature into His."

87. Canlis, *Calvin's Ladder*, 146. Canlis (139–47) provides extensive and illuminating commentary on the dispute with Osiander.

88. Philip W. Butin, *Revelation, Redemption, and Response: Calvin's Trinitarian Understanding of the Divine-Human Relationship* (Oxford: Oxford University Press, 1995), 93.

Head" [Eph. 4:15], and "the first-born among many brethren" [Rom 8:29]. We also, in turn, are said to be "engrafted into him" [Rom 11:17], and to "put on Christ" [Gal 3:27]; for as I have said, all that he possesses is nothing to us until we grow into one body with him. It is true that we obtain this by faith. Yet since we see that not all indiscriminately embrace that communion with Christ which is offered through the gospel, reason itself teaches us to climb higher and to examine into the secret energy of the Spirit, by which we come to enjoy Christ and all his benefits.[89]

Christ, the second person of the Trinity, does not benefit humanity while remaining apart from humanity but only by becoming ours and, dwelling within us, shares what he has received from the Father. The dynamic of this sharing is the Spirit who "empowers, enables, and authenticates faithful human response to the grace that God the Father offers humanity, through the renewal of the divine image in Christ."[90] In responding in faith to the saving divine initiative, believers are reciprocating God's actions for them but can only do so when united with Christ because it is only in Christ that authentic humanity is to be found. For Calvin, there can be no separate human response to an exclusively divine initiative because in the incarnate Christ this divine initiative, and indeed the divine nature, is expressed in perfect humanity. The divine saving work is already itself, in the person of Christ, a human response.

7.6. A Conflict of Errors: Recent Criticism of Calvin's Characterization of Human Response

That human response to divine initiative finds its place only in union with the incarnate Christ who died and rose again implies that whatever is said by Calvin concerning the works of believers can accurately be interpreted only in this context. Human reciprocity participates in the responsiveness of the Son to the Father through the power of the Spirit. This has not been clearly grasped in several recent highly critical assessments that focus upon Calvin's characterization of the relationship

---

89. *Institutes* 3.1.1 (537) = CO 2:293. The chapter and verse references for all the Pauline quotations do appear in the margin of the 1559 text.

90. Butin, *Revelation, Redemption, and Response,* 93.

between divine and human agency. At one extreme, in a work of intellectual history, Steven Ozment asks the question, "Were Calvinists really Protestants?"[91] Ozment argues that Calvin emphasized human works sufficiently to jeopardize the principle of justification by faith alone. By allowing that his or her own good works might confirm to the believer the indwelling of the Holy Spirit and divine election, Calvin and the Genevan church compromised Luther's relentless focus on faith in God's promises. They "once again made good works and moral behavior the center of religious life and reintroduced religious anxiety over them."[92]

At the opposite extreme, in the work of Radical Orthodox theologians, most notably that of John Milbank on the theology of gift, Calvin is held to give too little weight to human reciprocity in response to divine gift. The problem with Calvin is that "his notion of salvation as gift is unilateral, as exemplified in the doctrines of imputation and, by extension, predestination. As such, the human is left passive, and the divine model for giving is one-sided rather than reciprocal."[93] While Calvin rightly emphasizes participation in Christ, he does so in a manner incompatible with the Radical Orthodox synthesis of Augustinian and Thomistic notions of reciprocity. Milbank comments that "the idea of justification as imputation, although muted in Calvin, is still not acceptable. . . . We must indeed receive, as Aquinas taught, an infused *habitus* of *iustitia*. . . . [F]aith in God must be already, and indeed must be primordially, the love of God. So the infused habit of justice is also, from the outset, an infused habit of charity."[94] Calvin's forensic emphasis is held effectively to undermine his own commitment to participation in Christ and to risk substituting trust and hope for love as the central Christian theme, some-

---

91. Steven Ozment, *The Age of Reform 1250–1550: An Intellectual and Religious History of Late Medieval and Reformation Europe* (New Haven: Yale University Press, 1980), 372–80.

92. Ozment, *Age of Reform*, 379.

93. J. Todd Billings, *Calvin, Participation, and the Gift*, 12.

94. John Milbank, "Alternative Protestantisms," in *Radical Orthodoxy and the Reformed Tradition: Creation, Covenant, and Participation*, ed. J. K. Smith and J. H. Olthuis (Grand Rapids: Baker, 2005), 32–33. Radical Orthodoxy is passionately concerned to deny the autonomy of the secular and to insist that all of reality depends for its existence upon participation in the divine. Calvin does not address this theme directly but does say that as originally created "man was blessed, not because of his own good actions, but by participation in God" (*Institutes* 2.2.1 = CO 2:186). However, Calvin's deep sense of the disfigurement wrought upon human beings by sin seems to imply that such participation is lost in the Fall, propelling his theology in a more apocalyptic and Pauline trajectory.

thing Milbank regards as in many ways "the *gravest imaginable* heresy."[95] Calvin's concept of union with Christ is of the wrong kind.

In between these two extremes, New Testament scholar Campbell finds Calvin not so much one-sided as grotesquely inconsistent. At times Calvin's texts betray support for a theory of justification that Campbell finds to be individualist, conditional, and contractual, but then Calvin's "commitments to depravity, to election, and to Christian regeneration by the Spirit" run entirely in the opposite direction. Calvin's emphasis on the regeneration of humanity by the Spirit represents an alternative soteriological principle to his account of justification. For Campbell, the more one emphasizes divine initiative, the less room there is for human reciprocity and vice versa, and Calvin ineffectually and confusedly refuses the choice.[96]

In a very different kind of study, social historian Natalie Zemon Davis includes criticism of Calvin in her exploration of gift-giving in sixteenth-century France. Zemon Davis traces the social consequences of Calvin's soteriology, pointing out that his emphasis on the gratuity of God's gift entailed the sweeping away not only of traditional theological understandings but also of a host of traditional social practices predicated on reciprocal gift-giving. There is gain in this, for Calvin encourages gratitude for the divine gift, expressed as love of neighbor in similarly gratuitous giving to others. The public welfare system in Geneva expands impressively under his guidance. Yet there is also a loss:

> Calvin's theology refused to conceive of human solidarity in terms of any measured reciprocity. . . . He talks only of the obligation to give to the limits of one's faculties and without regard to the inevitably disappointing merits of others. . . . All Christians have a mutual obligation to each other in Calvin's theological vision, but he does not build it into a patterned structure, a rhythm of giving and receiving. Humans are left free and uncharted with their gifts.[97]

---

95. Milbank, "Alternative Protestantisms," 33.

96. Campbell, *The Deliverance of God*, 276.

97. Natalie Zemon Davis, *The Gift in Sixteenth Century France* (Madison: University of Wisconsin Press, 2000), 119–20. The issue of reciprocity had arisen much earlier in Luther scholarship, with Karl Holl and others lauding what was regarded as Luther's conceptualization of justification as 'pure gift' free from entanglement with notions of reciprocity. For a critique of this interpretation of justification in Luther, see Bo Kristian Holm, "Resources and Dead Ends of the German *Lutherrenaissance*: Karl

There is, suggests Zemon Davis, a lack of instruction on how legitimately to receive.

Thus, depending upon his critic, Calvin puts too much soteriological emphasis on human works, or too little, or alternately emphasizes each in an inconsistent manner, or emphasizes them in a way that cannot produce a sustainable social pattern by which to give expression to human solidarity. Calvin's soteriology is clearly being understood in different, rarely compatible, ways by different critics. The question of how Calvin actually understood the relationship between divine initiative and human reciprocity is therefore a significant one. Calvin's characterization of human reciprocity in fact has a profoundly christological basis, built upon the union of the believer with Christ. It is not possible accurately to understand the anthropological implications of this characterization without paying attention to union with Christ. One of the reasons for recent conflicting critical accounts of the relationship between divine initiative and human reciprocity in Calvin's soteriology and Pauline exegesis is that such attention has not been paid. Calvin's comments about reciprocity are read in isolation from their basis in union with Christ. Even when Calvin does not directly mention union with Christ it is necessary to remember that in discussing reciprocity in Calvin we are simply observing where the anthropological apple falls from the christological tree.[98] What Calvin says about reciprocity will express and be consistent with his soteriological principle that to be united with Christ is the only way in which to receive and respond to any of the benefits of his saving work.

7.7. Doing but not Meriting

The first area in which heeding the participatory context of Calvin's remarks about human reciprocity can bring greater clarity to their interpre-

---

Holl and the Problems of Gift, Sociality, and Anti-Eudaemonism," in *Lutherrenaissance Past and Present*, ed. Christine Helmer and Bo Kristian Holm (Göttingen: Vandenhoeck & Ruprecht, 2015), 127–43.

98. I am here borrowing an image from Canlis, *Calvin's Ladder*, 143, who sees Osiander's emphasis on "essential righteousness" received by the believer as resulting from a failure to appreciate Jesus' obedience as an expression of God's righteousness: "As usual, the anthropological apple does not fall far from the christological tree."

tation is in his discussion of faith and works. Here Philippians 2:12b–13 is a crucial text. Paul tells the Philippian believers to "work out your own salvation with fear and trembling; for it is God who is at work in you, enabling you both to will and to work for his good pleasure." The injunction to work in relation to salvation might be thought to raise difficulties for Calvin's insistence on justification by faith alone. Yet rather than a challenge to his soteriology, Calvin finds here an important confirmation of it, especially in Paul's subsequent explanation of how God is at work in believers. For in verse 13 Paul attributes both the Philippians' willing and working to divine enabling. In his *Commentary on Philippians* (1548, revised for later editions in 1551 and 1558) Calvin comments that "This is the true artillery for destroying all haughtiness; this is the sword for killing all pride, when we hear that we are utterly nothing, and can do nothing, except through the grace of God alone."[99] He goes on to attack his opponents for assigning to human free-will a separate power by which it can cooperate with the initial gift of divine grace. Calvin regards this as inconsistent with Paul's statement attributing to God the Philippians' desire to do what is good. They indeed will the good, but only when that will is granted by the Holy Spirit. The unwary reader could erroneously conclude that Calvin understands Paul's words to imply that the working involved in salvation only appears to be human and in reality is exclusively divine.

However, in his earlier polemical work, *On the Bondage and the Liberation of the Will* (1543), Calvin had offered a fuller explanation of his views on this crucial verse. This explanation clarifies considerably the intention of his subsequent statements in the *Commentary on Philippians*. For Calvin, the crucial impact of the power of sin upon humanity lies in our bondage to sin. We can exercise our will, but our bondage lies in the perennial inclination of that will to evil. Human beings are not forced to sin, but necessarily always choose to do so. As Calvin explains,

> We allow that man has choice and that it is self-determined, so that if he does anything evil, it should be imputed to him and to his own voluntary choosing. We do away with coercion and force, because this contradicts the nature of will and cannot coexist with it. We deny that choice is free, because through man's innate wickedness it is of necessity driven to what is evil and cannot seek anything but evil.

99. *Comm. Phil.* 2:13, CNTC 11:253–54 = OE 16:330, 1–3.

And from this it is possible to deduce what a great difference there is between necessity and coercion. For we do not say that man is dragged unwillingly into sinning, but that because his will is corrupt he is held captive under the yoke of sin and therefore of necessity wills in an evil way. For where there is bondage, there is necessity. But it makes a great difference whether the bondage is voluntary or coerced. We locate the necessity to sin precisely in corruption of the will, from which it follows that it is self-determined.[100]

On this view of unredeemed humanity, sin is simultaneously entirely unavoidable and entirely our own choice. Our problem is precisely that we will what is wrong. Unsurprisingly, Calvin also goes on to argue that believers' good works are genuinely their own in that they must will them in order to do them, but at the same time entirely due to the work of the Spirit. He says of God, "so that he may have willing servants who follow of their own accord he creates a new heart in them and renews a right spirit in their inner nature."[101] All this, Calvin argues, "is comprehended by Paul in a single statement when he teaches that there is one God who effects in us both to will and to do according to his good pleasure."[102] To use a contemporary image, human beings obey only because of a heart transplant performed by the divine surgeon. Twenty-first-century readers, accustomed to define freedom in relation to concepts such as autonomy and independence, may understandably feel that such externally determined freedom to will the good is not truly free at all. Calvin would surely respond that as creatures made according to divine purpose, human beings are free only when able to fulfill that purpose. He asserts that the soteriology of his opponents erroneously divides responsibility for good works between God and believers, conceiving of a human free-will

---

100. Calvin, *On the Bondage and the Liberation of the Will: A Defense of the Orthodox Doctrine of Human Choice against Pighius*, ed. A. N. S. Lane, trans. G. I. Davies (Grand Rapids: Baker, 1996), 69 = CO 6:280 (Book 2). The Dutch theologian Albert Pighius published a polemic against Calvin's views on grace and free-will in August 1542. Calvin replied in February 1543, but the debate went no further due to Pighius's intervening death in December 1542. The 1996 translation is unfortunately the very first into English. The debate revolved around the correct interpretation of Augustine, with Pighius labeling Calvin a Manichee and Calvin labeling Pighius a Pelagian. On this point Calvin was posthumously vindicated when in the early seventeenth century Rome placed part of Pighius's work on the *Index of Forbidden Books*.

101. *Bondage and Liberation of the Will*, 193 = CO 6:367 (Book 5).
102. *Bondage and Liberation of the Will*, 175 = CO 6:353 (Book 5).

"which can turn by its own movement, and have a peculiar and separate capacity, by which it can cooperate with the grace of God."[103] Calvin instead insists that believers' good works are wholly due to God and, precisely as such, are also simultaneously wholly and truly their own. It is true to Calvin's position to say that such good works are "enclosed, intended, and enabled within the divine act of salvation."[104] In a comment on Rom 9:16, where Paul says of election, "So it depends not on human will or exertion, but on God who shows mercy," Calvin sums up what he regards as the correct attitude for human beings to adopt by alluding to Phil 2:12: "We are, therefore, to learn to ask and hope for all things from Him, and to ascribe all things to Him, while wholeheartedly pursuing our salvation with fear and trembling."[105]

It is thus clear that Calvin's soteriology does not rest on a contrast between the saving deeds of God and the passive believing of humans. Since, like their faith, believers' good works are also wholly the product of the Spirit's agency, human believing and human doing are not oppositional categories for Calvin.[106] Rather than contrasting faith and deeds, Calvin pits faith against merit. This, and not the exclusion of human actions from soteriological significance, is what Calvin takes to be the point of Paul's contrast between faith and works. Calvin wishes to stress the positive value of good works, while also insisting vehemently that since such works are divinely given they do not merit anything before God. In Rom 4:4-5 Paul famously speaks of the justification of the ungodly, contrasting the person who works and whose reward therefore cannot be based on grace with the person who does not work and whose faith is therefore credited as righteousness. Calvin's principal concern in interpreting the text is to distinguish between working and meriting:

103. *Comm. Phil.* 2:13, *CNTC* 11:254 = *OE* 16:330, 16–18. Billings, *Calvin, Participation, and the Gift*, 40–48, also argues that Calvin's objection is to the divided nature of Pighius's understanding of the relationship between divine and human agency, in which one or other, but not both simultaneously, are operative at different stages in the soteriological process. For an overview of Calvin's position on this issue explored in the philosophical category of compatibilism rather than in exegetical terms, see Paul Helm, *Calvin at the Centre*, 227–72.

104. Francis Watson, "New Directions in Pauline Theology," *Early Christianity* 1.1 (2010): 13.

105. *Comm. Rom* 9:16, *CNTC* 8:205 = *OE* 13:201, 5–7.

106. Butin, *Revelation, Redemption, and Response*, 92: "There is a Trinitarian dynamic to human faithfulness that prevents any polar opposition of divine and human action. The human pole is not erased; rather, it is affirmed in the Trinitarian enablement that God provides for it."

By "him that worketh" Paul does not mean the man who is given to good works, a pursuit which ought to be zealously followed by all the children of God, but the one who merits something by his own achievements. Similarly, by "him that worketh not" he means the one who is due nothing by the merit of his works. He does not want believers to be indolent, but merely forbids their being mercenary-minded by demanding something from God as their due.[107]

This aversion to the idea that anything could be due to human creatures from God also appears strongly in Calvin's interpretation of a text that we have already seen him link to Phil 2:13. In Rom 9:14–18, Paul deals with the possible charge of divine unfairness in the election of Jacob and not Esau prior to either brother having done anything good or bad. Calvin insists on interpreting the passage in terms of the predestination of individuals, the reasons for which in divine wisdom are beyond human understanding. Calvin comments that this teaching, which he understands as that of Paul, "might appear to be lacking in warmth (*frigida esse*),"[108] but the complete exclusion of all external causes in the divine decision also excludes all emphasis on merit. He says of 9:16 that

> Paul deduces from this statement the incontrovertible conclusion that our election is to be attributed neither to our diligence, zeal, nor efforts, but is to be ascribed entirely to the counsel of God. Let no one think that those who are elected are chosen because they are deserving, or because they have in any way won for themselves the favor of God, or even because they possessed a grain of worthiness by which God might be moved to act.[109]

Calvin is also clear that the attempt to rely in any way on merits can only be disastrous since they cannot save: "The constancy of our election is wholly comprehended in the purpose of God alone. Merits are of no

---

107. *Comm. Rom* 4:4, *CNTC* 8:84 = *OE* 13:81, 29–34.

108. *Comm. Rom* 9:16, *CNTC* 8:204 = *OE* 13:199, 37.

109. *Comm. Rom* 9:16, *CNTC* 8:205 = *OE* 13:200, 23–28. Despite the firm popular association of Calvin's name with the doctrine of double predestination, his views on this subject were not unchanging and underwent significant development across his career. For an overview, see Wilhelm H. Neuser, "Predestination," in *The Calvin Handbook*, ed. Herman J. Selderhuis (Grand Rapids: Eerdmans, 2009), 312–23.

avail here, for they issue only in death. Worthiness is disregarded, for there is none, but the goodness of God reigns alone."[110]

Aversion to merit appears once more in relation to Eph 2:10: "For we are what he has made us, created in Christ Jesus for good works, which God prepared beforehand to be our way of life." In this text the good works of believers are emphasized in a context where grace and faith have just been characterized as saving in contrast to works: Calvin's comments focus on the verb "prepare beforehand" (προετοιμάζω), which he perceives as incompatible with notions of merit: "Now, if the grace of God forestalled us, all ground of boasting has been taken away."[111] Calvin also insists that the idea of divine workmanship in the new creation of the believer in Christ encompasses the whole of the human being, including the will to do the good. Calvin again comments on the same verse, this time more extensively, in a later sermon, preached in 1558:

> There is the kind of host who is not only pleased to be charitable to a man, but who, carrying further his superabundance, after he has found him both bed and board, will say to him, "Take here something with which to pay; in order that it may not seem to you that my charitable dealing has made you contemptible, I will receive payment for it at your hand; but yet it shall come from my own purse." Now shall he to whom such generosity has been displayed go and say that he has paid his host well? But with what money? Even with the same money that was put into his hand. Thus the case stands with those who put forward their good works to say that God has not saved them freely, but that they themselves were a help towards it.[112]

There is much that could be commented on in this striking piece of imagery, which is surely deliberately unrealistic in terms of social practice. Yet what is of most significance is the fundamental idea that it is fitting and appropriate that the guest pay the host but that, since the resources to do so come from the host himself, this payment can never be construed as meritorious. The guest cannot justly claim to have paid the host well. Neither can human beings claim to have paid God by means of

---

110. *Comm. Rom* 9:11, *CNTC* 8:201 = *OE* 13:196, 36–40.

111. *Comm. Eph.* 2:10, *CNTC* 11:147 = *OE* 16:187, 13–14.

112. John Calvin, *Sermons on the Epistle to the Ephesians* (Edinburgh: Banner of Truth, 1973), 166 = *CO* 51: 383–84 (Sermon 11).

good works since the works themselves have been given freely by God. For Calvin, working belongs with believing in salvation, but the works concerned can never merit anything before God or act as an efficient cause of that salvation. Union with Christ is not directly discussed in this context, but everything Calvin does say coheres with the idea that human response to divine initiative takes place in union with Christ. This union is itself wholly gifted and soteriologically complete, i.e., salvation is Christ and Christ is salvation. Therefore human beings cannot act to reciprocate God as a discrete step or moment in their relationship with God, but only from within God's own saving initiative as they are united with Christ. From Calvin's perspective the notion of merit in relation to working is therefore redundant.[113] In arguing that Calvin places too much or too little soteriological emphasis upon human works, or is inconsistent about them, his contemporary critics therefore miss his point entirely. It is the soteriological location of human works, not the degree of their importance, which is the vital issue for Calvin. If such works are disastrously identified as a means to merit before God and to growth in justifying righteousness, then it is impossible to expend too much energy warning that they cannot justify. Yet if such works are appropriately located as a means of sanctification in union with Christ and apart from all notions of merit, then it is equally impossible to exaggerate their positive significance.

7.8. Unmerited Rewards

Such emphasis on the soteriological significance of works rightly located can be seen in the importance Calvin attaches to practical holiness. Having eliminated the value of good works as a meritorious response to the gift of salvation, Calvin is free to assert their value as a pathway of trans-

---

113. Raith, *Aquinas and Calvin on Romans*, 58, regards this rejection of merit by Calvin as incompatible with any truly participatory relationship with Christ's own justice: "the works produced by the justified are not fully righteous and worthy of a reward. For Calvin, then, we cannot say that the believer is taken up into his or her own justification; rather the believer grasps Christ through faith and Christ's justice 'clothes' the believer. The believer, however, is still condemnable *in se* even if accepted by God *in Christo*. Clearly the work of Christ *for* and *to* the believer takes precedence over the work of Christ *in* and *through* the believer." Doubtless Calvin would be puzzled as to why his insistence that the work of Christ for and to the believer results in the works of the believer performed in and through Christ should be considered less participatory than Raith's formulation.

formation. To be sure, believers remain imperfect. In union with Christ these imperfections are covered by his righteousness, but the Christian life is once again, as in the medieval tradition, a journey towards fuller sanctification. The Christian should make steady progress in sanctity. This perspective allows Calvin to give full weight to texts in which Paul stresses the obligation of believers to grow in obedience. When at 2 Cor 7:1 Paul says that he and his readers should "cleanse ourselves . . . making holiness perfect in the fear of God," Calvin comments: "It is of the very nature of God's promises that they summon us to sanctification, just as if God had inserted an implied condition."[114] At Phil 3:10, where Paul expresses the wish to share in Christ's sufferings in order to attain the resurrection from the dead, Calvin says bluntly: "Let everyone, therefore, who has become through faith a partaker of all Christ's benefits, acknowledge that a condition is presented to him—that his whole life be conformed to His death."[115] And at Rom 6:22 where freedom from sin and enslavement to God results in sanctification and eternal life, Calvin holds that "this, unless we are immeasurably stupid, ought to create in our minds a hatred and horror of sin, and a love of and a desire for righteousness."[116] The exegetical examples could be multiplied but the point remains the same: good works are a requirement for salvation.

Of course, it is true for Calvin that here God gives what God commands. The renewed will that enables such good works is the work of the Holy Spirit. Since this is the case, the works involved are not meritorious. Yet because the will is not bypassed but is indeed renewed in this way, these works are also fully those of the believer and therefore the exercise of the believer's will is essential to them. The only explanation there could be for blatant disregard for holiness is that a person is not genuinely a believer and has not truly been justified and renewed. Thus, although the believer's good works are not meritorious and are not a cause of justification, they are essential to salvation. Nor, as the quotations above show, are they simply organic, with good trees automatically producing good fruit. Calvin takes their nature as a condition of salvation with the utmost seriousness, even if it is a condition that the true believer will satisfy. This has consequences for the nature of covenant as an important theological category in Calvin's work. If we ask whether Calvin conceives

---

114. *Comm. 2 Cor* 7:1, *CNTC* 10:93 = *CO* 50:83.
115. *Comm. Phil* 3:10, *CNTC* 11:276 = *OE* 16:357, 13–15.
116. *Comm. Rom* 6:22, *CNTC* 8:136 = *OE* 13:132, 15–17.

of the covenant as unilateral or bilateral, the answer is both. As Calvin himself puts it, "in all covenants of his mercy the Lord requires of his servants in return uprightness and sanctity of life. . . . [N]onetheless the covenant is at the outset drawn up as a free agreement, and perpetually remains such."[117] From one perspective it is unilateral in that there is no aspect of covenant that is not in its entirety the work of God, yet from another it is bilateral since in justification Christ's sinless humanity is vital and in sanctification so too are the works of the believer.[118]

A more fruitful way of approaching the category of covenant is to ask about the other imagery with which Calvin associates it. How does he characterize what it means for God's attitude towards believers? Here Calvin emphasizes that God's stance towards believers' works is that of a loving father rather than that of a strict judge.[119] The very first title given to the Holy Spirit in the *Institutes* is "the spirit of adoption because he is the witness to us of the free benevolence of God with which God the Father has embraced us in his beloved only-begotten Son to become a Father to us."[120] We should note here the very strong connection with Calvin's definition of faith, which speaks of faith as "a firm and certain knowledge of God's benevolence toward us."[121] Central to faith is the conviction of God's desire to have us as his children in Christ with all this entails. This emphasis on adoption and on God's affectionate and fatherly attitude towards believers is vital to Calvin in at least two important ways.[122]

---

117. *Institutes* 3.17.5 (808) = CO 2:594.

118. On covenant in Calvin, see Peter Lillback, *The Binding of God: Calvin's Role in the Development of Covenant Theology* (Grand Rapids: Baker, 2001). Through abundant citation Lillback proves conclusively wrong those who regard covenant as unimportant in Calvin's theology. However, this is not the same as demonstrating that covenant was a central category in Calvin's theology, nor as demonstrating Lillback's further claim that Calvin's concept of covenant stands in essential continuity with subsequent Reformed theologians for whom it was central. This would require a comparison of the characterization of covenant and the weight assigned to it in the overall patterns of thought of the different theologians concerned.

119. Lillback, *The Binding of God*, 196 n. 10, provides an extensive list of texts in support of this claim.

120. *Institutes* 3.1.3 (540) = CO 2:395.

121. *Institutes* 3.2.7 (551) = CO 2:403.

122. For a fuller consideration of adoption as a theological theme in the Reformed tradition, see Tim J. R. Trumper, "The Theological History of Adoption I: An Account," *Scottish Bulletin of Evangelical Theology* 20.1 (2002): 4–28; Tim J. R. Trumper, "The Theological History of Adoption II: A Rationale," *Scottish Bulletin of Evangelical Theology* 20.2 (2002):

First, it mitigates any possible challenge to assurance posed by his emphasis on good works as a condition of salvation. The foundation of assurance for Calvin is the saving work of Christ, his righteousness covering over the sinfulness that remains even in the good works of believers who are serious about holiness. Yet Calvin is willing to allow that the experience of the Christian life has a part to play in confirming this assurance, speaking of "the grace of good works, which shows that the Spirit of adoption has been given to us [cf. Rom 8:15]."[123] Given this, one might expect the question to arise of exactly how serious is serious enough when it comes to holiness. How much is needed to confirm that the Spirit has been given and that the believer numbers among the elect?[124] In fact, this question does not seem to arise for Calvin, who is always willing to emphasize that the evangelicals enjoy assurance whereas their Catholic opponents do not. The principal reason it does not arise is Calvin's conviction of divine benevolence towards believers.[125] Second, the strength of his emphasis on this point helps Calvin to meet a difficult exegetical challenge. What of texts that speak of rewards for believers? Do these texts not demonstrate that good works must in some sense be meritorious? Even if God is always rewarding God's own gifts, must not the concept of reward include an assessment of the merits of the use made of the gift?

To meet this challenge Calvin must find a way to accommodate rewards for believers within his own soteriology but do so without reintroducing merit. He accomplishes this by placing God's reception of the works of believers and the granting of rewards specifically in the context of God's fatherly affection. Here rewards can be acknowledged but without merit as their basis. How this functions from Calvin's perspective is illustrated by a striking piece of imagery contained in a sermon on Gal 2:17–20 preached in 1557/1558:

177–202; and Tim J. R. Trumper, "A Fresh Exposition of Adoption I: An Outline," *Scottish Bulletin of Evangelical Theology* 23.1 (2005): 60–80; Tim J. R. Trumper, "A Fresh Exposition of Adoption II: Implications," *Scottish Bulletin of Evangelical Theology* 23.2 (2005): 194–215.

123. *Institutes* 3.14.18 (785) = CO 2:577.

124. Zachman, *The Assurance of Faith*, argues that this is a point of instability in Calvin's theology that made possible subsequent crises of assurance for later generations in the Reformed tradition. This may be correct, but it is still necessary to ask why there is no evidence that Calvin himself experienced this difficulty.

125. Schreiner, *The Theater of His Glory*, 122: "For Calvin, the need for salvation does not leave believers analyzing their own condition; justification by faith and predestination release their energies and direct them outward to the world."

Picture a child who is seeking to obey his father: when his father asks him to do something, he will accept what the child does, even though the child may not understand what he is doing. The child may even break something in the process, and yet the father will not fret about the broken object when he sees his child's affection and willingness to obey. But if a man hires a servant, he will expect him to perform his task perfectly. Why? Because he is going to receive wages, and, therefore, he cannot afford to ruin what has been committed to his hands. If the task is not done well, the master will not be content with it. Our Lord, speaking of the days of gospel grace, says that he will accept our service, just as a father accepts the obedience of his child, even if all that is done is of no value. That is to say, he does not accept it because it is perfect, for it is not, but he bears with us out of his abundant mercy. He shows himself to be so bountiful and kind to us by accepting what we do as if it were fully pleasing to him, although there is no inherent merit or worth in our works at all. Thus, we can have the freedom and the courage to serve God; we can know that God will bless all that we do for him because whatever is wrong with our offerings is washed away in the blood of the Lord Jesus Christ.[126]

The believer is to have confidence that the very attempt to be obedient will be favorably received by God, and is also to know that if God rewards what has been done it will be because the attempt has been made and not because of the intrinsic worth of what has been achieved. The works are loved not because of the qualities possessed by the works but because the believer is loved as a child of God. In medieval soteriologies that emphasized God's reward for individuals who do *quod in se est* (what lies within them), God already graciously accorded human works a value in the economy of grace beyond their inherent worth. However, in such soteriologies, God still operated in a judicial mode. Even if works were assigned a value greater than their actual worth, their value was still measured by relative achievement. But in Calvin's view God has moved out of a judicial mode and into a fatherly one. On this point, Brian Gerrish says of Calvin's theology, "If God casts aside his judicial person for us, that is only because justice has been done by another. Nevertheless, there really is a sense in which the legal language of justification by faith 'self-destructs': the point of the doctrine is to move us out of the world

126. John Calvin, *Sermons on Galatians*, 202 = *CO* 50:441 (Sermon 13).

of legal relationships into the world of family relationships."[127] In one way, Gerrish is entirely wrong here. The idea that his legal language of justification self-destructs would horrify Calvin and is a blatant anachronism. As we can see from the above quotation, where the blood of Christ washes away the imperfections of the believer's works, justification is for Calvin an abiding and sustaining presupposition of God's fatherly kindness.[128] Yet Gerrish is right that for Calvin justification has served to move the believer into the world of family relationships.[129]

It is therefore no surprise to find Calvin elsewhere drawing on texts that allow him to translate promises of reward into familial language. All merits are Christ's and all rewards are an inheritance. Calvin appeals to Col 3:24, where slaves are encouraged to obey their earthly masters and to expect a reward from God if they do so, but the promised reward consists "of the inheritance" (τῆς κληρονομίας).[130] And although Calvin does not say so in his sermon, the image of a father valuing his child's attempt at obedience far beyond any achievement involved is noteworthy in another way. It asserts a real distance between God and humanity in that even our best attempts at goodness appear in God's sight like the faltering efforts of a young child. Yet at the same time it leaves room for human reciprocity. The distance involved does not mean that the relationship runs only in one direction. In the child's affection and willingness to obey, the father receives exactly what he most desires. Calvin says in the *Institutes*, "God's children are pleasing and lovable to him, since he sees in them the marks and features of his own countenance. For we have elsewhere taught that regeneration is a renewal of the divine

127. Brian Gerrish, *Grace and Gratitude: The Eucharistic Theology of John Calvin* (Minneapolis: Fortress, 1993), 60–61.

128. Horton, "Calvin's Theology of Union with Christ and the Double Grace," 93: "We are not looking away from justification when we consider union with Christ. . . . This does not mean that every gift of this union is forensic, but rather that the entire line of the *ordo salutis* is forensically charged."

129. Adoption is not a third grace to be set alongside justification and sanctification. As Billings, "Union with Christ and the Double Grace: Calvin's Theology and its Early Reception," 67 comments, it is rather "a prominent biblical and theological image used to speak about the double grace of union with Christ." Adoption is not an alternative to an emphasis on justification but like union with Christ instead encompasses both justification and sanctification. Canlis, *Calvin's Ladder*, 130–39, argues that adoption enables Calvin to explain with greater precision what he means by union with Christ.

130. *Institutes* 3.18.2 (822) = *CO* 2:604.

image in us."[131] Far from eliminating human reciprocity to the divine gift in good works and thus constructing a soteriology that is unilateral, Calvin's interpretation of the Pauline texts includes and encourages such reciprocity. At Phil 1:29 Paul remarks that God has given his readers the privilege not only of believing in Christ but also of suffering for him. Calvin comments: "I do not deny, indeed, that God rewards the right use of His gifts of grace by bestowing grace more largely upon us, provided only that you do not place merit . . . in opposition to His free liberality and the merit of Christ."[132] Contrary to Calvin's contemporary critics, his soteriology is radical not in eliminating reciprocity, or in reintroducing it in a way that could lead back to justification by works, or in treating reciprocity in an inconsistent way, but rather in relocating it away from notions of cooperation with divine grace and placing it instead in relation to union with Christ, in whom believers become children of God. Merit is irrelevant simply because it is not the basis of a healthy relationship between parent and child.[133]

7.9. Ecclesial and Social Reciprocity

Yet if contemporary critiques of Calvin's treatment of reciprocity often rest upon theological misconceptions, what of Zemon Davis's rather different concern with social patterns of reciprocity? Calvin's soteriology is bound up with the creation of a new ecclesial community in Geneva and so inevitably has consequences for social practices of reciprocity, even if the connections are complex. An appraisal of the rituals of the church, especially the Lord's Supper, which enacts theological belief as social practice, begins to illuminate these connections. In Calvin's case, as with all the Reformers, his understanding of the Lord's Supper is closely correlated with his most important soteriological concerns.[134] It is unsurprising to find that union with Christ in the power of the Spirit is central to

---

131. *Institutes* 3.17.5 (807) = CO 2:593.

132. *Comm. Phil.* 1:29, CNTC 11:243 = OE 16:315, 33 – 316, 3.

133. Gerrish, *Grace and Gratitude*, 90: "The theme of adoption, the new birth, the transition from 'children of wrath' to 'children of grace,' takes us to the heart of the Reformers' protest against the prevailing gospel of the day."

134. In post-Enlightenment academic contexts it is possible to discuss soteriology in Protestantism without including the sacraments. In the sixteenth century such a procedure would have appeared incredible, since the Mass and the Lord's Supper were

Calvin's understanding of the Lord's Supper. While Christ's saving work is complete and unrepeatable, the sanctification of the believer is subject to both growth and impediments. Therefore, the appropriation of Christ's work needs to be continuous. In the Lord's Supper the empowering gift of the life-giving risen Christ is given repeatedly and is received by faith in the divine promise. Christ's body and blood is made present not by any alteration to the substance of the bread and the wine but by the agency of the Spirit. Thus, here it seems we have one-way movement from God to humanity, something apparently confirmed by Calvin's swingeing attacks on the Mass as something offered to God: "There is as much difference between this sacrifice and the sacrament of the Supper as there is between giving and receiving."[135]

Is this really a gift flowing from God to human beings with no return? Certainly, if there is a sacrifice made to God it is a sacrifice of praise and gratitude in which service to others is central. Zemon Davis characterizes it in this way: "The gift flow thus is downward from the Lord and outward from us. Can we visualize it as a child receiving an inheritance in gratitude and then passing it on to his or her own children?"[136] Yet things are also more complicated than they appear, for such an account fails to reckon with the emphasis in Calvin's soteriology on Christ's humanity. This emphasis is inevitably reflected in Calvin's understanding of the Lord's Supper: "In the Eucharist the church has to do with the whole Christ—indeed, in a special sense with his body and blood. For it was in his humanity that he won redemption."[137] The gift itself is not simply one made from divinity to humanity since Christ himself as both giver and gift is fully human. Neither is the expression of gratitude to God by the believer through service of others conceived as a set of interactions between three separate parties since the believer is united with Christ and acts in Christ. The idea of gift certainly has an important place here, but again it is subsumed within the more important concept of union. Commenting on Paul's thought in 1 Cor 10:16–17 that the cup and the bread are a sharing in the blood and body of Christ and that therefore "we who are many are one body, for we all partake of the one bread," Calvin says,

locations in which basic soteriological disagreements were experienced in practice by ordinary Christians.

135. *Institutes* 4.18.7 (1435) = CO 2:1056.

136. Zemon Davis, *The Gift*, 118.

137. Gerrish, *Grace and Gratitude*, 135–39, outlines six principles of Calvin's Eucharistic theology of which this is the second (136).

We shall benefit very much from the sacrament if this thought is impressed and engraved upon our minds: that none of the brethren can be injured, despised, rejected, abused, or in any way offended by us, without at the same time, injuring, despising, and abusing Christ by the wrongs we do; that we cannot disagree with our brethren without disagreeing with Christ; that we cannot love Christ without loving him in the brethren.[138]

Service to others who are united with Christ is service to God in Christ and thus is a return to God in a way more direct than a disposition of gratitude, as important as such a disposition is for Calvin. He interprets Deut 16:16, with its instruction not to come empty-handed before God in worship, as now implying a command to give alms, and so also implicitly regards such alms-giving as giving to God. Indeed, the collection of alms was not conducted separately from the worship of God but was a regular feature of worship services among the Reformed.[139] Finally, the importance Calvin placed upon both Christ's priesthood and that of all believers should be taken into account. In the Supper, as in life, believers offer themselves to God. As Gerrish puts it:

Calvin does not say here that by our prayers we offer Christ, but rather that he is our intercessor, our high priest who opens an access for us, and even the altar on which we lay our gifts. He it is who made us a kingdom of priests to the father (Rev. 1:6). The eucharistic sacrifice thus arises out of the two parts of Christ's priestly office. For we have no access to God except by the sacrificial death of Christ in our place; in this sense, the dignity of the priesthood fits him alone. And yet he is also our eternal intercessor who shares the dignity of the priesthood with us: we are priests in him, offering ourselves and all that is ours to him.[140]

138. *Institutes* 4.17.38 (1415) = CO 2:1041.

139. Elsie Anne McKee, *John Calvin on the Diaconate and Liturgical Almsgiving* (Geneva: Droz, 1984), 53–58, 63–65. Ironically, Geneva in Calvin's lifetime was one of the places where this did not happen as alternative practical arrangements already existed. However, Calvin seems to have employed such collections during his short pastorate in Strasbourg (1538–41) and they were introduced in Geneva after his death.

140. Gerrish, *Grace and Gratitude*, 155–56. The claim of Zemon Davis, *The Gift*, 114 n. 30, that her interpretation of Calvin's theology and that of Gerrish "converge on the whole" is true only on the whole.

In interpreting Calvin's theology of the Supper, as in his soteriology, we should heed the following pattern: the theme of union defines the context for a discussion of gift and not vice versa. And when the theme of gift is placed in relation to that of union, then more room appears in Calvin for ideas of human reciprocity than if gift is made the central focus.

If we move outwards from the Lord's Supper into other social interactions, then we find a similar pattern. In thinking about the poor, Calvin and the other Reformers swept away previous notions of almsgiving as meritorious in which the poor provided an opportunity for the rich to be saved. Notions of giving to the poor and what the rich might expect to receive for it were therefore recast. Still, reciprocity did not cease to flow but merely flowed through different channels. Paul's comment at 2 Cor 8:9 that, although rich, Christ became poor for the sake of the Corinthians in order that they might become rich, prompts Calvin to argue that "Thus He sanctified poverty in His own person, so that believers should no longer shrink from it, and by His poverty He has enriched us so that we should not find it hard to take from our abundance what we may expend on behalf of our brethren."[141] The giving of alms therefore has a christological basis and approaches to the act of giving not consistent with it are unacceptable: "For you may see some who wish to seem very liberal and yet bestow nothing that they do not make reprehensible with a proud countenance or even insolent words. And in this tragic and unhappy age it has come to this pass, that most men give their alms contemptuously."[142]

It is only if they are moved with compassion for the poor that God will hear the prayers of the rich when their own time of affliction comes. Giving must be undertaken recognizing that those who receive alms are brothers and sisters in Christ. Calvin is critical of those rich persons who wish to lead lives separate from the poor without contact with them apart from the roles occupied by the poor as servants. There must instead be personal relationship and communication in the church. As Bonnie Pattison writes:

> Fellowship will only happen if the rich agree to associate with the poor and truly live in community with them. Ultimately community

141. *Comm.* 2 Cor 8:9, *CNTC* 10:111 = *CO* 50:99.
142. *Institutes* 3.7.7 (697) = *CO* 2:511.

is only possible if the rich and the poor see their relationship to one another as being part of their relationship to Christ. If the rich give to the poor as giving to the Lord, and if the poor receive as if they received from the Lord able to recognize "that it is for my [Christ's] name's sake that he is nourished," then God will be honored.[143]

Yet again we find that the fundamental reality is union in Christ and that patterns of giving and reciprocity find their place within it. The rich give to the poor what they have received from God, but recognize that in doing so they are also giving back to God, while the poor receive from the rich but recognize that the gifts involved are also from God and give back to God through gratitude and praise.[144]

What is certainly true in this general question of almsgiving, however, is that the reciprocity is not measured. If God has given to the rich in an unlimited way in Christ, there is no easily defined limit to their obligation to the poor. However, in other contexts, both theological and highly practical, Calvin does seem to be at ease with the concept of a debt that can be measured and discharged. At Rom 15:27, where Paul stresses the responsibility of the Gentile believers to offer material support to the Jerusalem church because in the gospel the Gentiles now share in the spiritual blessings of the Jews, the use of the verb λειτουργῆσαι ("to minister") prompts Calvin to think of the general responsibility of believers to minister to the poor. When they do so they offer to God a sweet-smelling sacrifice. Yet Calvin immediately checks himself with the observation that "In this passage, however, Paul was referring strictly to the mutual right of compensation."[145] There seems to be a specific debt that the Gentile believers can repay and the Jewish believers are right to expect to be so honored. In a tragic personal example, Calvin dedicates his *Commentary on 2 Thessalonians* to Benedict Textor, his wife's doctor. Calvin tells Textor that in Idelette's final illness, "you did everything that you could to help her as far as diligence, effort, and application were concerned. Since, further, you do not allow me to make you any other

143. Bonnie L. Pattison, *Poverty in the Theology of John Calvin* (Eugene, OR: Wipf & Stock, 2006), 342.

144. Calvin also appreciates the importance of almsgiving in relation to ecclesiology more generally. For a thorough survey of his exegesis of Pauline texts relating to the diaconate as an office of benevolence see McKee, *John Calvin on the Diaconate and Liturgical Almsgiving*, 91–268.

145. *Comm. Rom* 15:27, CNTC 8:316 = OE 13:306, 24.

payment, I have wanted to inscribe your name on this Commentary, so that there may be some proof on my part of the good wishes which I bear towards you."[146] The doctor makes a unilateral gift of his services but Calvin feels compelled to reciprocate with a payment of public honor and gratitude. Far from dispensing with reciprocity, Calvin here insists upon it.

Such examples of reciprocity certainly do not mean that Calvin's soteriology did not lead to a significant recasting of patterns of giving and receiving in Genevan society. It seems overwhelmingly likely that it did. Nor do such examples demonstrate that there was not a new uncertainty in measuring reciprocity. It may well be the case that along with new social forms there was a lack of definition as to when it was legitimate to receive and what constituted a proper level of reciprocity in return for gifts. Yet what they do show is that Calvin did not approach the social arena with an abstract principle of unilateralism in human social relations. There were circumstances in which it was legitimate to expect to receive back in a way that saw discharged the obligation of another party to return an earlier gift, and this is entirely unsurprising given the strength of Calvin's ideas concerning the obligation of believers to pursue holiness.[147] Whatever the unintended social consequences, Calvin's soteriology is not centrally concerned with a new principle of giving and receiving, whether between human beings or between them and God. His problem with medieval soteriologies is not that they have tried to give back to God but that in meritorious deeds they have given back to God the wrong things. It is wrong to try to measure the human response to God in this way not because there is something inherently wrong about measuring obligations in general but because in Calvin's view only perfect obedience beyond our means could possibly satisfy the debt. God instead graciously makes us children through adopting us in union with Christ, and within this union the pattern of giving and receiving follows its own specific logic and consequences. For Calvin, receiving from God and giving to God are not to be understood by analogy with general hu-

---

146. *Comm. 2 Thess*, CNTC 8:385 = CO 13:598. This commentary was first published in 1551. Idelette died in 1549.

147. See John M. G. Barclay, *Paul and the Gift* (Grand Rapids: Eerdmans, 2015), 130: "Calvin's theology of the superabundant and incongruous grace of God results not in the idealization of unilateral giving, but in the circulation of human gifts in the bonds of social due, and this as part of the human return to God of the obedience and righteousness that echo God's good-and-just government of the cosmos."

man patterns of gift and reciprocity but by analogy with the patterns that exist between parent and child.

7.10. Conclusions and Implications: Union at the Center

We have now explored several central elements of Calvin's soteriology, which he carefully integrates, that can be summarized as follows:

1. Faith unites believers with Christ. It is in Christ—as twin aspects of union with him—that believers receive justification and sanctification, which as saving benefits of his person can only be received together.
2. The humanity of Christ as mediator forbids any simple contrasts between divine giving and human reciprocity. Precisely because they are united with Christ, the response of believers to the divine gift of salvation is enfolded within, as well as enabled by, the divine initiative itself.
3. Human faith is the work of the Holy Spirit, but in making this gift the Spirit does not by-pass the human will but instead engages and liberates it. We may therefore speak of what believers do as fully their own actions and simultaneously fully the works of the Spirit. Whatever their importance in other terms, these works are not meritorious and can only be construed as such with disastrous consequences.
4. Justification is a forensic declaration of the forgiveness of sins in Christ in which the works of the believer play no part, but in sanctification these works are central. It is a condition of salvation that believers strive for holiness, but God as a loving Father values their attempts at obedience more than their achievements. The continued sin of believers has been dealt with in justification.
5. Whether in the Eucharistic worship of the church or in the impact of Calvin's soteriology on social practices more widely, we find a radical redirection of patterns of human reciprocity but not their absence or exclusion on principle.

These conclusions stand in sharp contrast with those of critics who question the appropriateness of Calvin's account of divine and human agency. Such critics discern weaknesses in Calvin's soteriology as a consequence of an inadequate account of the relationship between divine initiative and human response in salvation. As is perhaps suggested by the failure of his critics to agree about the nature of the inadequacy of this account, Calvin's treatment of divine initiative and human response is in fact coherent and clear. Why, then, do Calvin's critics fail to appreciate this? The distortions in their interpretations stem, at least in part, from their decision to focus on the theme of divine initiative and human response. To approach Calvin's soteriology with this as the framing issue through which it is explored is already to distort his thought. For Calvin does not himself place this issue at the heart of his soteriology.[148] He simply does not categorize the important elements of his soteriology as representing either divine agency or human agency as if more of one is necessarily less of the other. Neither does he posit unilateralism or bilateralism in divine-human relationships as a structuring principle. Instead, Calvin is much more concerned with what happens when divine and human agencies become one in Christ by the power of the Spirit. His focus is on this union with Christ. As in the conclusions above, reciprocity within such a relationship of union will still remain important. It will remain important just as giving and receiving do so in familial relationships such as those between parents and children or between wives and husbands. Yet compared to other kinds of social relationships, giving and receiving look very different in specifically familial relationships, where a narrow focus on giving and receiving could only be an indicator of ill health. Patterns of reciprocity in Calvin's soteriology will find their place only contained within, and not separately from, the more fundamental reality of union with Christ. This reality structures his patterns of reciprocity rather than vice versa.

Union with Christ thus sits at the center of Calvin's soteriology. Far from being one-sided or lacking in balance, his soteriology is better described as a synthesis. It is a synthesis constructed on the basis of biblical texts, in which the Pauline letters occupy a position of central importance. It is also a synthesis that is textually inclusive. Calvin's soteriology does not resonate powerfully with some Pauline texts and themes, only to leave others largely out of account. In accordance with his presuppositi-

---

148. Billings, *Calvin, Participation, and the Gift*, 186-90: "The concept of 'gift' which tends toward the two options of being 'unilateral' or 'bilateral,' 'passively' or 'actively' received, is simply not adequate to express the biblical and theological complexity of Calvin's thought" (190).

tions about the nature of Scripture and of the canon, Calvin expects the biblical texts to present a unified vision and strives for unity himself in his theological interpretation of these texts. He does not regard them as the kind of texts where some things turn out to be unimportant or marginal. Everything must be included. Gerrish comments that although Calvin was not systematic in a modern sense of deducing everything from a first principle, "He looked assiduously for the interconnections between doctrines, the way they hang together (their *Zusammenhang*)."[149] Unsurprisingly, both the strengths and the weaknesses of Calvin's Pauline interpretation arise from this synthetic approach. The different elements and themes of Pauline theology are genuinely brought into relationship with each other, but the rather precise balance that is achieved will sometimes seem rather too neat and tidy to twenty-first-century interpreters given the occasional nature of Paul's letters. The price of including everything may be that sometimes the inclusion seems a little forced.

As regards strengths, due attention must be paid to Calvin's exegetical and theological debts to Luther. Calvin does not share the strength of Luther's concern with the hiddenness of God and emphasizes in a way that Luther does not that creation is a manifestation of divine glory.[150] Yet despite this significant difference, Calvin fully maintains Luther's apocalyptic dualism as it relates to the human plight apart from Christ. Creation serves to reveal God, but only to those who in Christ are able to see it through the spectacles of Scripture.[151] The discontinuity between the fallen self apart from Christ and the self in Christ through faith by the power of the Spirit is profound. There is nothing in the former that can lead to or prepare for the latter, and conversion is a work of God alone. Unsurprisingly, Calvin shares Luther's emphasis on the alien nature of the righteousness received by the believer. And just as Luther treats alien righteousness in relation to union with Christ, so too does Calvin.

---

149. Gerrish, *Grace and Gratitude*, 15–16.

150. On the hiddenness of God as a theme in Luther's thought, see Steven Paulson, "Luther's Doctrine of God," in *The Oxford Handbook of Martin Luther's Theology*, ed. Robert Kolb, Irene Dingel, and L'ubomír Batka (Oxford: Oxford University Press, 2014), 187–200.

151. See Eberhard Busch, "God and Humanity," and Susan E. Schreiner, "Creation and Providence," in *The Calvin Handbook*, ed. Herman J. Selderhuis (Grand Rapids: Eerdmans, 2009), 224–35 and 267–75 respectively. See also I. John Hesselink, "The Revelation of God in Creation and Scripture," in *Calvin's Theology and Its Reception*, ed. J. Todd Billings and I. John Hesselink (Louisville: Westminster John Knox, 2012), 3–24.

It never occurs to Calvin to interpret justification by faith in isolation from Christology, or to present justification as in opposition to union with Christ. Nor does it ever occur to Calvin to detach the faith of the believer from the story of Jesus Christ. Calvin's sense of the importance of the righteousness of Christ in his human nature, which is demonstrated by his earthly obedience, is too strong to permit this. These criticisms, often made of later Protestant interpretations of Paul and erroneously projected back onto the Reformers, simply do not apply. It is true that the central theme of union with Christ is expressed in different, less traditional ontological terms than in other Christian traditions, but it is no less central for that.[152] Further, Luther's protest against merit, with his profound sense of the complete sufficiency of the grace of God for salvation, is powerfully sustained. Despite very significant differences as to the canonical and hermeneutical significance of the law, Calvin maintains Luther's insistence that in key Pauline texts the law functions soteriologically to reveal to human beings their own unrighteousness and incapacity to obey God, demonstrating their need for Christ (see 3.2). Calvin is also at one with Luther in his interpretation of Paul's insistence that justification is not by the "works of the law," hearing it not merely as a rejection of any role in causing justification for works performed prior to faith but also as a rejection of any such role for the works of the baptized (see 4.1).

Yet in other respects, Calvin stands out as different from Luther. Whether as the result of deliberate reflection or otherwise, Calvin differs by incorporating some of Melanchthon's characteristic concerns into his own soteriological synthesis. Melanchthon's emphasis on the forensic nature of justification reappears in Calvin, as does the sense that the obedience offered to God by the believer does not simply arise spontaneously as the consequence of justification but also fully retains the character of an obligation. One of the most striking features of Calvin's synthesis is that these emphases are given considerable weight but not at the expense of Luther's emphasis on union with Christ. Rather than making justification by faith the central category in his theology into which everything else must fit, Calvin instead pairs it with sanctification as twin aspects of union with Christ. This seems closer exegetically to the Pauline texts, where participatory language is ubiquitous but the

---

152. Canlis, *Calvin's Ladder*, 13: "These relationships are qualitatively different from Platonic schemes of 'participation' in that they are characterized by intimacy and differentiation, not consubstantiality."

vocabulary of justification, for all its undoubted significance, is not. The establishment of sanctification as a distinct focus, distinguishable from justification even if never separable from it, also offers some exegetical advantages. For example, Paul does sometimes phrase imperatives in strongly conditional terms and Calvin's willingness to treat them fully as obligations reflects Paul's language. Calvin does not deny Luther's important observation that good trees will organically bear good fruit, but he does decisively move beyond it. Alongside the insistence that they are not meritorious, human good works are given a positive value as a source of divine pleasure in a way that makes it difficult to fall into the error of regarding the very attempt to obey God as a corrupt attempt to establish one's own righteousness.

Yet, perhaps inevitably, potential weaknesses in Calvin's Pauline interpretation are connected to its strengths or are even consequences of them. The formula that the twin saving benefits of justification and sanctification are distinct but inseparable in Christ masks the fact that Calvin ultimately makes a very sharp distinction between them. The twin benefits must be received at the same time, for Christ cannot be divided, but justification represents an exclusively forensic movement whereas renewal is allocated entirely to sanctification. As we have seen, Calvin is entirely capable of recognizing that Paul can use the vocabulary of righteousness in relation to sanctification. He does not have to force texts to speak unnaturally, but the very fact that Paul can use vocabulary ostensibly belonging to one category in relation to another illustrates how closely intertwined in Paul's texts are what Calvin defines as justification and what he defines as sanctification. This makes it necessary at least to raise the question of how stable in exegetical terms is the sharpness of the distinction between justification and sanctification.

As we have seen, this is decidedly not a credible objection with regard to Luther's Pauline interpretation, where there is scarcely any distinction made between justification and sanctification. Luther's pairing of an alien righteousness with the necessity for the believer to live an alien life produces a very distinctive non-linear vision of the Christian life in which Christ is appropriated on a daily basis in faith and any progress in faith is also a return to baptism and to the beginning of that life. Righteousness is not a quality that increases gradually over time so that it becomes a quality inherent to the believer, but always remains a matter of living in someone external. With Calvin by contrast, precisely as lived in union with Christ, human life once again is a *via* or pathway for the transformation of the believer. Calvin's view is more linear, and while he will emphasize in various ways that the righteousness received in justification is and remains alien, he will not emphasize this in relation to sanctification. In this respect Calvin reinstates something of significance in medieval accounts of salvation in Paul. Even as he empties good works of merit, Calvin does make progress in them central to his vision of the Christian life. In turn, this connects with his assertion of the continued role of the law in offering guidance for the Christian. Whether this constitutes an interpretative gain and a proper holding together of the indicative and imperative in Paul, or a backwards step and a potential domestication of the radical edge of Pauline theology, is itself a matter for significant debate. So too is the question of whether the sharpness of Calvin's distinction between justification and sanctification is the only appropriate way of maintaining together both Calvin's insistence upon the alien nature of the righteousness granted to the believer and Calvin's insistence upon the nature of works as obligations leading to progress in the Christian life and to growth in holiness.

Finally, as is perhaps inevitable with such a comprehensive and subtle synthesis, Calvin is vulnerable to the distortion of his soteriology by subsequent interpreters, both admirers and critics alike. If Calvin's careful rooting of justification and sanctification in union with Christ's person is neglected, then they can be turned into successive chronological stages in an *ordo salutis* ("order of salvation") with the accompanying risk of reducing justification to a legal fiction. And if the strength of Calvin's emphasis on adoption and God's fatherly attitude towards believers is diluted and sanctification as well as justification is treated in largely legal terms, then there is the immediate danger of introspective anxiety over election. It ceases to be a source of assurance and becomes instead one of anxiety, with believers worrying over how much they must do to satisfy divine requirements and so demonstrate their election. These distortions represent fundamental misunderstandings of Calvin's intentions, but their prevalence in some subsequent contexts demonstrates that Calvin's soteriological synthesis is delicate. If some of its parts are twisted a little out of their proper shape the stress on the entire structure can rapidly become extreme.

Yet, for today's interpreters, working in the aftermath of twentieth-century attempts to discern the center of Paul's theology, proper attention to such weaknesses and vulnerabilities should not be allowed to obscure the important resources that Calvin has to offer to contemporary Pauline interpretation. For the very act of producing an exegetically inclusive soteriological synthesis, whatever its potential risks, is superior to the modern procedure of attempting to identify the component parts of Paul's theology and order them hierarchically according to importance.[153] Calvin does not play off against each other justification by faith and union with Christ as fundamentally different tracks or categories in Paul's thought, one of which must emphasized at the expense of the other. Instead, union with Christ functions as an integrating center in Calvin's soteriology that serves to highlight the significance of justification rather than diminishing it. In their different ways both Calvin and Luther integrate these twin emphases in Pauline theology, not by finding a means to hold together what would more naturally belong apart, but because for each of them the plight of fallen humanity requires an alien righteousness that can only be found in the person of Christ and so can only be received when united with him by faith.

153. On this point, see Chester, *Conversion at Corinth*, 205-10.

PART IV

CONTEMPORARY IMPLICATIONS

The Reformers and the New Perspective on Paul

8 Mapping Complexity

A Revised Account of the Relationship between
Reformation Exegesis and the "New Perspective on Paul"

8.1. The Reformers and the Rhetoric of "The New Perspective"

In their different eras the Reformers' Pauline exegesis and the "New Perspective on Paul" (NPP) shifted the way in which the letters of Paul were interpreted. Each challenged dominant perspectives. However, is this similarity between the two superficial or substantial? Is the scale and type of change that followed the publication in 1977 by Sanders of *Paul and Palestinian Judaism* of the same magnitude as that which the Reformers' inaugurated? In part II of this book, I argued that the metaphor of grammatical structure can usefully be applied to the Reformers' Pauline exegesis. They reached a consensus about the meaning of key Pauline terms in which their conclusions stood over and against those of their medieval predecessors, and their Pauline exegetical grammar then served to structure subsequent debates in Pauline interpretation within the Protestant tradition. How does the phenomenon of the NPP compare to this exegetical grammar? Has it in a similar manner provided a structuring framework or paradigm for subsequent debates? In fact, the unity of the NPP operates across a much narrower front. In the crucial question of the nature of Second Temple Judaism and Paul's relationship to it, the impact of the NPP has run very deep. It is no longer possible to portray Judaism credibly as a legalistic religion devoid of grace oriented towards the earning of salvation.

Yet outside of this central area, the commitments shared by NPP interpreters are neither as extensive nor as cohesive as those developed by the Reformers. The metaphor of an exegetical grammar therefore seems less apt. The label NPP continues to be used even as it has become ever clearer that what has resulted is not a monolithic single viewpoint but rather a variety of newer perspectives. Nevertheless, despite all the differences between them, many of these newer perspectives are perceived to belong at least to the same constellation of interpretations of Paul.[1] While it may provide a less complete framework than the Reformers' exegetical grammar, the label NPP does denote some genuinely shared characteristics. One of these characteristics is that those interpreters to whose work the label NPP might today appropriately be applied share a conviction that the older trajectories of interpretation, derived ultimately from the Protestant Reformers, are significantly in error. Despite their own disagreements, the characterization of such interpreters as standing together in contrast to previous Protestant tradition helps to grant continued vitality to the otherwise misleadingly unitary label of the NPP.

This status of the Reformers as the progenitors of erroneous trajectories of interpretation ensured that for several decades they received either little attention or only negative attention in serious scholarly work on Paul among those sympathetic to the NPP.[2] This straightforwardly negative approach continues among scholars wholly committed to the NPP. Thus, although not by any means a major theme, nearly all references to the Reformers or to Reformation interpretation in Wright's recent *Paul and the Faithfulness of God* set what he understands to be their significance in contrast to his own conclusions.[3] A different approach—perhaps best represented by Barclay's *Paul and the Gift*—attempts to move beyond the NPP in a way that both reaffirms some basic insights of NPP scholarship and yet also pays careful and sympathetic attention to the history of reception, including the work of the Reformers. Barclay writes that "the reading of Paul offered in this book may be interpreted either as a recontextualization of the Augustinian-Lutheran tradition, returning the dynamic of the incongruity of grace to its original mission environment . . . or as a reconfiguration of the 'new perspective,' placing its best historical and

---

1. Kent L. Yinger, *The New Perspective on Paul* (Eugene: Wipf & Stock, 2011), 27–38, provides a chapter entitled "The NPP Spreads and Mutates: Varied Forms of the NPP."

2. The Reformers' exegesis accurately understood does inform the work of Westerholm, *Perspectives Old and New on Paul*, but this is unsurprising since Westerholm is the most prominent and sophisticated longstanding critic of the NPP.

3. See, for example, N. T. Wright, *Paul and the Faithfulness of God*, 2 vols. (Minneapolis: Fortress, 2013), 1:24, 1:42, 1:67, 1:114, 1:141, 2:385, 2:461, 2:514, 2:737.

exegetical insights within the frame of Paul's theology of grace."[4] Barclay is one of a number of scholars now acknowledging a more complex relationship between Reformation exegesis and contemporary exegesis than straightforward rejection of the Reformers' conclusions.[5] Yet such significant reengagement with the exegetical legacy of the Reformers only makes more pressing the issue of the validity of the Reformers' exegetical conclusions. Several broad criticisms of the Reformers, crucial to the development of the NPP, remain widespread across contemporary scholarship. These criticisms fall into three broad areas:

1. The introspective conscience. Writing some years before the advent of the NPP, Stendahl is widely acknowledged as its crucial forerunner. In his classic article "Paul and the Introspective Conscience of the West" and in other pieces, Stendahl argues that Paul had a robust conscience before he became an apostle. He did not struggle with guilt as a result of his inability to keep the law and he did not formulate his understanding of justification by faith as an answer to such a guilty conscience. These errors in interpretation stem from the Reformation. Stendahl writes that "The Pauline awareness of sin has been interpreted in light of Luther's struggles with his conscience,"[6] and, as if to remove any doubt as to the seriousness of what is at stake, "We all, in the West, and especially in the tradition of the Reformation, cannot help reading Paul through the experience of persons like Luther and Calvin. And this is the chief reason for most of our misunderstandings of Paul."[7]

2. The "works of the law" ($ἔργα νόμου$) and the nature of Judaism. If Paul's vehement denials that justification is by "works of the

4. Barclay, *Paul and the Gift*, 573. A third significant kind of approach, consideration of which lies beyond the scope of this study, is sometimes labelled the "radical new perspective or perspectives." Here the NPP is criticized not because the NPP rejects trajectories of interpretation stemming from the Reformation but because it remains too close to them. See Mark D. Nanos and Magnus Zetterholm, eds., *Paul within Judaism: Restoring the First Century Context to the Apostle* (Minneapolis: Fortress, 2015).

5. For a more informed reception of the Reformers' exegesis in recent scholarship see, for example, Michael Bird, *The Saving Righteousness of God: Studies on Paul, Justification, and the New Perspective* (Eugene, OR: Wipf & Stock, 2007) and Grant Macaskill, *Union with Christ in the New Testament* (Oxford: Oxford University Press, 2013).

6. Stendahl, "Call Not Conversion," 12.

7. Stendahl, "Call Not Conversion," 12. These words of Stendahl have been so influential that I have not hesitated to cite them several times. See also 55 n. 115 and 122 n. 69.

law" are not to be understood as a reaction to a losing struggle to obey the law, how are they to be interpreted? Here Sanders's construal of Second Temple Judaism as a religion of grace and James Dunn's alternative proposal as to what Paul intends by the phrase the "works of the law" are both important. If, as Sanders argued, Judaism did not teach salvation via good works that earned divine approval, with what is justification by faith contrasted by Paul? For Dunn, the contrast is with "an ethnocentric identification of righteousness with Jewish identity."[8] The phrase the "works of the law" encompasses all that the law requires but denotes especially those practices that serve as key Jewish identity markers and which maintain the separation of the Jews from the nations: circumcision, food laws, and Sabbath observance. By reading the phrase as a rejection of works-righteousness the Reformers erroneously project back onto Paul the controversies of their own place and time: "Martin Luther understood Paul's reaction against Judaism in the light of his own reaction against medieval Catholicism. The degeneracy of a Catholicism that offered forgiveness of sins by the buying of indulgences mirrored for Luther the degeneracy of a Judaism that taught justification by works."[9]

3. Justification by faith. While there is certainly no one single understanding of justification within NPP scholarship, there are dominant trends in which justification is interpreted either in terms of the inclusion of the Gentiles in God's people or in terms of participation in Christ or some combination of the two. Wright comments on the strangeness for those holding a traditional Protestant understanding of justification (based on Luther and the Westminster

8. James D. G. Dunn, *The Theology of Paul the Apostle* (Edinburgh: T&T Clark, 1998), 366.

9. James D. G. Dunn, "New Perspective View," in *Justification: Five Views*, ed. James K. Beilby and Paul R. Eddy (Downers Grove, IL: InterVarsity Press, 2011), 179–80. Dunn can also write more appreciatively of the contribution of the Reformation to the interpretation of Paul. See James D. G. Dunn, "The New Perspective: Whence, What and Whither?" in *The New Perspective on Paul*, rev. ed. (Grand Rapids: Eerdmans, 2005), 18–23. Yet here also the central point of contention remains the difference between understanding Paul's rejection of the "works of the law" in terms of legalism or ethnocentrism. For a catena of texts from recent Pauline scholarship ascribing to the Reformers a misreading of the nature of Judaism, see Aaron O'Kelley, *Did the Reformers Misread Paul? A Historical-Theological Critique of the New Perspective* (Milton Keynes: Paternoster, 2014), 11–18.

Confession) of "the emphasis I have put on Israel, on the covenant with Abraham and the fulfillment of that covenant in Jesus the Messiah, and on the covenant membership which God's people enjoy because they are 'in the Messiah' and wearing his own badge of *pistis*."[10] For Campbell, Luther is the wildly inconsistent originator of an individualist, conditional, and contractual account of justification that the Reformer himself often contradicts. In contrast, Campbell emphasizes justification as God's deliverance of human beings from their enslavement to sin and construes faith (commenting on Rom 9:27–10:21) as "a *marker* of salvation . . . it is a marker of participation in the faithful and resurrected Christ, which thereby implicitly *guarantees* for the believer a future participation in the resurrection that Christ has already achieved."[11] The Reformers thus serve as the foil to different contemporary accounts of justification that are often themselves contrasting in various ways.

In terms of the nature of Paul's own theology, the most central of these areas of critique is justification by faith, precisely because its discussion relates so closely to that of salvation history and of participation in Christ. There may not be a single unifying center to Paul's theology but there are several central themes that the apostle uses to interpret each other. Justification numbers among them.[12] For this reason justification will be discussed in a separate chapter. Yet, in terms of rendering plausible the NPP and rendering alternative perspectives implausible, the most central of the three areas of critique is not justification but the "works of the law" and the nature of Judaism. That this is indeed central can be illustrated by the question of forerunners of the NPP. While Stendahl may be the most influential of such forerunners upon the formation of the NPP itself, he is neither the only nor even the earliest scholar who could be regarded as such. From the early twentieth century the work of William Wrede and Albert Schweitzer could also be cited. However, their views were decidedly those of a minority until Sanders's reevaluation of Second Temple Judaism made it appear unlikely that Paul's critique of the "works of the law" was a rejection of works-righteousness. It is this reinterpretation of Judaism that then renders plausible radically new di-

---

10. Wright, *Paul and the Faithfulness of God*, 1129.
11. Campbell, *The Deliverance of God*, 817.
12. Chester, *Conversion at Corinth*, 51–58, 205–10.

rections in the interpretation of Paul. In particular, it appears to validate Stendahl's critique concerning the introspective conscience. If Judaism emphasized grace, then Stendahl must have been correct to dismiss the idea that Paul struggled with a guilty conscience before his Damascus Road experience and to associate such an erroneous supposition of a guilty conscience with interpretations of Paul that identify the "works of the law" with Jewish works-righteousness. It is these two areas of critique that will be considered in the current chapter.

It should at once be acknowledged that there are serious issues here. It would be surprising if sixteenth-century interpreters were able to offer accounts of Second Temple Judaism fully credible in terms of historical criticism. Yet before engaging the historical issues directly we should pause to note the rhetorical function that the Reformers have fulfilled in NPP scholarship. They are accused, either explicitly or implicitly, of offering a false analogy between the soteriology of medieval Catholicism and that of Second Temple Judaism, and in doing so of arming themselves with a powerful but illegitimate rhetorical weapon: they are to be identified with Paul and his gospel; their opponents are to be identified with Jewish works-righteousness. However, NPP scholars also armed themselves with a powerful rhetorical weapon by contrasting their own positions with those of the Reformers: *they were to be identified with responsible historical interpretation of Paul and of Second Temple Judaism and any who rejected their conclusions with the regressive and discredited interpretations of the Reformers.* This casting of the Reformers as Paul's misinterpreters-in-chief masked a more complex reality that is now being acknowledged by those paying serious attention to the history of reception. Contemporary scholarship, whether produced from within the NPP or offered by those seeking to move beyond the NPP, *simultaneously* offers various credible challenges to interpretive positions widespread among the Reformers *and* continues to be influenced by the exegetical conclusions of the Reformers. This dependence is sometimes fully recognized but also sometimes unacknowledged or only partly acknowledged. In some instances, the dependence involves restating positions advocated by the Reformers in contemporary form. In other instances, this dependence involves the heightening or intensification of some parts of the Reformers' Pauline exegetical grammar at the expense of some of its other elements.[13] Given this situation a disentanglement of the various

13. The problem is akin to that identified by John K. Riches, "Book of the Month:

elements is essential. *Instances of dependence upon the exegetical conclusions of the Reformers and the intensification of some aspects of their Pauline exegesis at the expense of others must be distinguished from each other. They must also be distinguished from more straightforward differences of opinion in which the positions of the Reformers accurately understood and those of the majority of contemporary interpreters do indeed stand in conflict.*

Where such genuine differences occur, judgments about who is right and who is wrong are inevitable and, while these judgments will vary according to who is making them, it is unlikely that any truly critical assessment could find the views of the Reformers to be correct at all points. For as we have seen, there are important differences among the Reformers. They may provide a Pauline exegetical grammar that constitutes a tighter constellation of readings of Paul than recent NPP scholarship, but theirs is nevertheless not a monolithic perspective. There are points at which for some of them to be judged correct would be for others of them to be judged wrong. Even more importantly, the enormous differences in context between the sixteenth and the twenty-first centuries mean that our own interpretations of Pauline texts cannot simply reproduce those of a previous era. The purpose of engagement with the Reformers' work, just as with the work of figures from other eras of the history of reception, ought not primarily to be to allocate praise or blame for the degree to which their conclusions either anticipate our own or fail to do so. This is simply to patronize figures of the past for the presumption of failing to reflect the present. The purpose is rather to construct a critical conversation that enables us to read the Reformers' exegesis in a discriminating manner, reaching different conclusions from them where necessary but also taking advantage of the considerable resources they have to offer for our own efforts to interpret Paul in contemporary contexts. The first step in constructing such a critical conversation is to identify areas in which dependence upon exegetical positions advocated by the Reformers continues undiminished.

Commenting on Romans in Its Original Context," *ExpTim* 119.1 (2007): 29, when reviewing Robert Jewett's *Commentary on Romans*: "Jewett seems to buy in so enthusiastically to the school of thought which imagines that truly historical readings of the biblical books can be achieved only if we divest ourselves of traditional church understandings. Where those of strong Christian beliefs are concerned such an act of self-mutilation usually results in their readings being unconsciously guided by their (only partially discarded after all) theological prejudices (Gadamer)."

8.2. Continued Dependence: Pauline Anthropology

The continued influence of exegetical positions developed by the Reformers upon contemporary interpreters is seen nowhere more clearly than in the treatment of Paul's anthropology, especially his use of the term "the flesh" (σάρξ) and its relationship to "sin" (ἁμαρτία). As we have seen, the Reformers strongly insist that "the flesh" refers not to part of a human being but to the whole person as he or she stands in opposition to God through sin. "The flesh" does not represent the lower component of anthropological hierarchies either within the soul or between the soul and the body. As Melanchthon sharply formulates it, "*flesh* should be understood of whatever is in man without the Holy Spirit."[14] It is striking that disagreements in recent scholarship about what Paul means by "the flesh" often take place *within* this fundamental understanding developed by the Reformers, an understanding that seems uncontroversial to many contemporary scholars but was not so in the sixteenth century. The Reformers' understanding of "flesh" signaled a rejection of the interpretation of many medieval exegetes. In his influential 1988 monograph *Obeying the Truth*, Barclay rejects Rudolf Bultmann's previously dominant treatment of the term. Bultmann had argued that "*sarx* can mean *the whole sphere of that which is earthly or 'natural,'*" and that a man's "nature is determined by the sphere within which he moves, the sphere which marks out the horizon or the possibilities of what he does and experiences."[15] Bultmann goes on to define living according to the flesh in a way that reflects his commitments both to existential philosophy and to a Reformation critique of works-righteousness. As regards the former, Barclay criticizes Bultmann for his particular stress on "the flesh" as that which is visible or outward and for his exclusive focus on the individual: "'Flesh' and 'Spirit' are defined in terms of the individual's self-understanding, his authentic or perverted relationship to himself and the possibilities that are (or are not) open to him."[16] As regards the latter, Barclay critiques

---

14. Melanchthon, *Romans*, 170 = CR 15:661-62.

15. Rudolf Bultmann, *Theology of the New Testament*, 2 vols. (London: SCM, 1952), 1.234-35.

16. John M. G. Barclay, *Obeying the Truth: Paul's Ethics in Galatians* (Edinburgh: T&T Clark, 1988), 197-98. Without retreating from his earlier criticisms, Barclay has now offered an evaluation of Bultmann's anthropology that pays more attention to what he considers to be its strengths. See John M. G. Barclay, "Humanity under Faith," in *Beyond Bultmann: Reckoning a New Testament Theology*, ed. Bruce W. Longenecker and

Bultmann for typifying fleshly behavior in terms of Jewish boasting in law-observance: "the self-reliant attitude of the man who puts his trust in his own strength and in that which is controllable by him."[17]

Barclay goes on to locate his own understanding of "the flesh" within an apocalyptic dualism in which living according to the flesh is characteristic of human existence under the present evil age in contrast to the new age inaugurated by the death and resurrection of Jesus. "The flesh" is "what is merely human, in contrast to the divine activity displayed on the cross and in the gift of the Spirit."[18] Paul includes the Jewish tradition to which he had formerly been devoted within the realm of what is merely human, but he makes this radical move because the Jewish tradition now belongs on the previous side of the turn of the ages rather than because of any critique of works-righteousness as such. Yet while Barclay can critically note that "Bultmann's interpretation drew on the Augustinian and Lutheran emphasis on man's sinful self-reliance (*cor incurvatum in se*),"[19] he also correctly notes the implication of his own position that "Paul is not concerned here with a 'fleshly' part of each individual (his physical being or his 'lower nature') but with the influence of an 'era' and its human traditions and assumptions."[20] This can be compared to Luther's assertion that "by flesh the whole man is meant. . . . [T]he inward and the outward man, or the new man and the old, are not distinguished according to the difference between soul and body but according to their dispositions."[21]

There are some important differences in what these two statements affirm the nature of "the flesh" to be, notably between Luther's emphasis on the flesh as the total disposition of the unredeemed person and Barclay's broader focus on an era and its traditions (although a contrast between Paul's gospel and human traditions and assumptions is scarcely

---

Mikeal C. Parsons (Waco: Baylor University Press, 2014), 79–100. However, Barclay has also continued to assert and elaborate the interpretation of "the flesh" offered in *Obeying the Truth*. See Barclay, *Paul and the Gift*, 426–27: "'the flesh' represents the environment of all human agency untransformed by the Spirit. . . . [E]verything is either beholden to God-in-Christ or beholden to human tradition (1:10–11), either 'new creation' or *passé* cosmos (6:14–15), either Spirit or flesh (3:3)."

17. Bultmann, *Theology of the New Testament*, 1.240.
18. Barclay, *Obeying the Truth*, 206.
19. Barclay, *Obeying the Truth*, 195.
20. Barclay, *Obeying the Truth*, 213.
21. *LW* 27:367 = *WA* 2:588, 26–32.

antithetical to Luther). However, the two are identical in what they deny. Even as Barclay parts company with the particular way in which Bultmann developed and intensified the Reformers' attitude towards works, his own alternative proposal ultimately relies on the Reformers' rejection of anthropological hierarchy as the appropriate context within which to understand Paul's statements about "the flesh." Similarly, Wright asserts that Paul's anthropological terms "sometimes appear to designate different 'parts' of a human being, but, as many have pointed out, it is better to see them as each encoding a particular way of looking at the human being *as a whole* but *from one particular angle*."[22] The significant point is not that there are no differences in detail between the positions of these contemporary scholars and those of the Reformers, but rather that a commonplace conclusion in contemporary scholarship (note Wright's phrase "as many have pointed out") is an expression of the same exegetical conclusions as those reached by the Reformers.

In developing his interpretation of "the flesh," Barclay was influenced by the work of Ernst Käsemann, who also had placed Paul's use of such terms in an apocalyptic context.[23] Käsemann too reacted against Bultmann's emphasis on the self-reliant individual. Instead, Käsemann emphasized the cosmic dimensions of Paul's pitting of the flesh against the Spirit. For Käsemann these terms denote in relation to the human being "that reality, which, as the power either of the heavenly or the earthly, determines him from outside, takes possession of him and thereby decides into which of the two dualistically opposed spheres he is to be integrated."[24] In making this assertion, Käsemann built on work undertaken from the nineteenth century onwards in which historical-critical scholars

> increasingly saw the need to interpret Paul's letters in the light of contemporary beliefs about the nature of evil and God's plans for overcoming it contained in the apocalyptic literature of the turn of the era.... In such writings the world is frequently portrayed as under the sway of demonic powers which can be broken only by divine

22. Wright, *Paul and the Faithfulness of God*, 491.

23. Barclay, *Obeying the Truth*, 205, is quite explicit in acknowledging Käsemann's contribution: "Here Käsemann's insight is of fundamental importance." See also Barclay's discussion of Käsemann in *Paul and the Gift*, 140-46.

24. Ernst Käsemann, "On the Subject of Primitive Christian Apocalyptic," in *New Testament Questions of Today* (London: SCM, 1969), 136.

intervention, often culminating in some final cosmic battle, preceded by a time of great suffering.[25]

On this view Christ is God's invasion of the present evil age in order to liberate humanity and to bring new creation, with the cross as an act of cosmic warfare. The bondage from which Christ liberates human beings is so all-encompassing that even their acts of piety are no more than aspects of this bondage.

Here it is very clear that Käsemann and those, like Barclay, who have followed after him are saying something significantly different from the Reformers, who did not have the same access to the apocalyptic literature of Second Temple Judaism. The Reformers do not understand the terms "sin" and "the flesh" as themselves denoting external forces. Rather, they understand them as forces in human beings. Nevertheless, the Reformers do understand the corruption and human failure involved in sin as total, as extending even to piety, and they do regard the condition of the human being as one of captivity. Luther at least goes even further and does not hesitate to speak of the present age as evil (Gal 1:4) because "whatever is in this age is subject to the evil of the devil, who rules the entire world."[26] It is his sense of the profound nature of this evil that decisively separates Luther's theology from those who hold that in salvation what is given in creation is transformed through grace. For Luther, what was given in creation has been so wholly lost through sin that what is necessary is the radically new beginning from outside that is granted through union with Christ and the receipt of his alien righteousness. It is this that has led to recent interpretations of Luther, especially those of Oberman and his students, which are often themselves termed "apocalyptic."[27]

For all the differences, which are many, between the apocalyptic patterns of thought in Luther and Käsemann (who as a Lutheran theologian was scarcely unfamiliar with Luther), the latter is inconceivable without the former. This point can be brought into sharp relief by comparing Luther's willingness to speak of the reign of the devil with the patristic interpretations of Gal 1:4 (Christ "gave himself for our sins to

---

25. John K. Riches, *Galatians through the Centuries* (Oxford: Blackwell, 2008), 81.

26. *LW* 26:39 = *WA* 40.1:94, 16-17.

27. Oberman, *Luther*. Oberman's biography elegantly encapsulates an apocalyptic approach to interpreting Luther.

set us free from the present evil age") that were followed by the medieval western church. Forged in the context of dualist heresies positing two creators, these interpretations avoid any hint that nature is evil and insist that the present age is evil because it is populated by people who choose to commit evil actions. Augustine comments that "The present world is understood to be evil because of the evil people who live in it, just as we also say that a house is evil because of the evil people who live in it."[28] In contrast, Luther's thoroughgoing insistence on humanity's bondage to sin and the reign of the devil establishes new trajectories in the history of interpretation.[29] Thus while in recent discussion of Paul's anthropology there is a sharp rejection of Bultmann's particular way of appropriating Reformation insights, some of the most prominent alternative proposals rely just as heavily on exegetical positions first developed by the Reformers. However significant the other differences between the Reformers' exegesis and that of dominant voices within contemporary scholarship, here the Reformers' influence continues whether it is always fully recognized or not. The near universal acknowledgment of the significance of apocalyptic thought for interpreting Paul is not something that in itself sets contemporary scholarship in any obvious opposition to the exegesis of the Reformers with regard to the apostle's theological anthropology.[30]

8.3. Intensification: "Apocalyptic" Interpretations of Paul

Yet while at this general level the acknowledgment that Paul is an apocalyptic thinker is widely shared within contemporary scholarship, there is a particular construal of Paul's apocalyptic thought that is more controversial. It is increasingly labelled as the "apocalyptic" interpretation

28. Augustine, *Augustine's Commentary on Galatians*, 3.3 (129). For further discussion of Augustine's comment on Gal 1:4 in his own context, see above 2.2.

29. On the history of reception of Gal 1:4, see the excellent treatment by Riches, *Galatians through the Centuries*, 77-82, on which I depend here. Calvin is more reluctant to speak in cosmological terms of the rule of the devil, but his sense of humanity's captivity to sin is equally strong.

30. An exception to the acceptance of apocalyptic thought as important for understanding Paul can be found in the work of Stanley Stowers and his students. See Stanley Stowers, *A Rereading of Romans: Justice, Jews, and Gentiles* (New Haven: Yale University Press, 1994); and Emma Wasserman, *The Death of the Soul in Romans 7: Sin, Death, and the Law in Light of Hellenistic Moral Psychology*, WUNT 2.256 (Tübingen: Mohr Siebeck, 2008).

of Paul in contrast to others that locate Paul's apocalyptic thought as a prominent element within a theology better termed "covenantal" as a characterization of its essential nature.[31] J. L. Martyn, one of the most prominent among recent "apocalyptic" interpreters of Paul, writes that in Paul's view "religion is the polar opposite of God's apocalyptic act in Christ. It is patriarchal (i.e., human) tradition. . . . [R]eligion is the human being's superstitious effort to come to know and to influence God, rather than faith that is elicited by God's invasive grace and that is active in love of neighbor."[32] Unsurprisingly Martyn holds that it is a misunderstanding of Paul's gospel to imagine that the Gentiles are now being called into a covenantal people that has persisted generation after generation through the centuries from Abraham onwards: "Paul says that the blessing of Abraham has *come* to the Gentiles (*genêtai eis*), not that the Gentiles have been granted the possibility of entering the blessed family of Abraham. . . . [T]he gospel is about the divine invasion of the cosmos (theology), not about human movement into blessedness (religion)."[33] To be sure, Martyn will agree that it is in a church containing both Jews and Gentiles that God is now enacting through Christ the covenant made with Abraham, but it makes little sense to speak of this invasive act of new creation that cuts across all that has gone before as covenantal in any conventional sense or as a climactic episode within an unfolding story.

Similarly, Martyn takes Paul's disputed genitive phrase πίστις Ἰησοῦ Χριστοῦ (which can be translated either as an objective genitive: "faith in Christ," or as a subjective genitive: "faithfulness of Christ") to refer to Christ's faithful obedience, thereby removing any possibility of misconstruing justifying faith as a human possibility: "God has set things right without laying down a prior condition of any sort. God's rectifying act,

---

31. See, for example, Wright, *Paul and the Faithfulness of God*, 40: apocalyptic "still denotes, at its heart, something which Paul really does seem to have made central." Yet while happy to acknowledge in this way that apocalyptic themes are genuinely significant for Paul, Wright later comments (1038) that it and the term "salvation history" are "two inadequate half-broken signposts to a larger, richer reality than either had imagined. That is the reality which, I have suggested, is better described with (mutually defining) words such as 'messianic' and 'covenantal.'" On these different ways of interpreting the significance of apocalyptic themes in Paul's thought see now Ben C. Blackwell, John K. Goodrich, and Jason Maston, "Paul and the Apocalyptic Imagination: An Introduction," in *Paul and the Apocalyptic Imagination*, ed. Ben C. Blackwell, John K. Goodrich, and Jason Maston (Minneapolis: Fortress, 2016), 3–21.

32. J. L. Martyn, *Galatians*, AB 33A (New York: Doubleday, 1997), 37 n. 67.

33. Martyn, *Galatians*, 349 (his emphasis) commenting on Gal 3:14.

that is to say, is no more God's response to human faith in Christ than it is God's response to human observance of the law. God's rectification is not God's response at all. It is the *first* move; it is God's initiative, carried out by him in Christ's faithful death."[34] The importance of the works performed by the believer may be emphasized but very much as a participation in the saving and liberating divine initiative. Paul speaks of a series of apocalyptic antinomies or contrasts previously characteristic of the fundamental structures of the cosmos but now abolished in the death of Christ, prominent among them the contrast between circumcision and uncircumcision.[35] Martyn pays no direct attention to the exegesis of the Reformers, but it is not difficult to discern a reflection (via the theology of Karl Barth) of their own critique of human religiosity and their own emphasis on the soteriological priority of divine initiative.[36] Yet this element has become so highly developed as to limit what can be said on the basis of Paul's texts concerning the Reformers' equally emphatic emphasis on the active nature of human faith and its crucial role in appropriating Christ and his saving benefits. It is one thing to insist with the Reformers on the gifted nature of human faith but quite another so to fear any compromise of divine initiative as to be left unable to say very much concerning the nature of the gift.[37] The very intensification of one motif or interpretative element leads to the diminution of another out of a sense of the paramount importance of preserving the former in its purest possible form. Here is an example of what Barclay, drawing on the work of the literary critic Kenneth Burke, terms the "perfecting" of a concept. It is pushed to "an end of the line extreme, developing its meaning to the maximum, exploiting the concept to its fullest possible extent . . . much like we might speak of a terrible concatenation of events as a 'perfect storm' or a complex and extremely inconvenient obstacle as a 'perfect nuisance.'"[38]

---

34. Martyn, *Galatians*, 271 (his emphasis) commenting on Gal 2:16.

35. J. L. Martyn, "Apocalyptic Antinomies," in *Theological Issues in the Letters of Paul* (Edinburgh: T&T Clark, 1997), 111-24.

36. Barclay, *Paul and the Gift*, 147-50, traces the influence upon Martyn of both Barth and Käsemann.

37. Martyn, *Galatians*, 275-77, does not ignore human faith or deny its importance, but is left with little to say about faith *exegetically* except to deny its human origin.

38. John M. G. Barclay, "Pure Grace? Paul's Distinctive Jewish Theology of Gift," *ST* 68.1 (2014): 5. For a fuller discussion of "perfecting" a concept, see Barclay, *Paul and the Gift*, 66-78.

An even stronger example of this *intensification* of divine initiative by an "apocalyptic" interpreter of Paul can be found in the work of Douglas Campbell, who rejects a model of Paul's soteriology that he terms "Justification Theory" in favor of his own emphasis on the liberating divine initiative in Christ that breaks human bondage to sin.[39] Campbell says of "Justification Theory" that "The conditionality of this model of salvation involves a sustained focus on the individual. . . . The system is thus highly anthropocentric, and tension is largely unavoidable when it is juxtaposed with a system that emphasizes divine initiative over against human choice and couples that with a liberative and transformational view of salvation."[40] Campbell does pay considerable attention to the Reformers in his work, but remains puzzled by their failure entirely to fit the pattern of his own strong contrasts between conditional and unconditional salvation, between prospective epistemology (prior human awareness of sin prompts repentance and faith) and retrospective epistemology (the divine gift of faith reveals the depth of human bondage to sin), and between individualist and corporate emphases. Here it is the first member of each pair that represents a catastrophic misinterpretation of Paul, while the second member of each pair represents according to Campbell a healthy pathway in the interpretation of Paul. Among the Reformers only Melanchthon is consistent, and misguidedly so, appearing on the wrong side of each of Campbell's contrasts.[41] From Campbell's perspective Luther is the ultimate source of each of these errors, having heard Paul speak of God's response to human failure to obey God's commands in terms of a more generous offer of salvation in which the punishment due to sinners is redirected onto Christ in his death and the more manageable condition of faith (an act of belief) replaces for each individual the requirement for complete obedience. However, Luther is also contradictory, undoing his own interpretation of Paul through his strong emphasis on human depravity and bondage to sin.[42] Similarly, Calvin falls into the same errors but fails to notice that his own "com-

---

39. Barclay, *Paul and the Gift*, 171-73, suggests that Campbell is unique in insisting on all six of the possible perfections of the concept of grace he identifies.

40. Campbell, *The Deliverance of God*, 4.

41. Campbell, *The Deliverance of God*, 258-60.

42. Campbell, *The Deliverance of God*, 250-58, 264-70. For a defense of Luther's consistency in response to Campbell, see Graham Tomlin, "Luther and the Deliverance of God," in *Beyond Old and New Perspectives on Paul: Reflections on the Work of Douglas Campbell*, ed. Chris Tilling (Eugene: Wipf & Stock, 2014), 23-33.

mitments to depravity, to election, and to Christian regeneration by the Spirit" stand in severe tension with them.[43]

As one reviewer comments, "Campbell's own research is trying to tell him something here, but he refuses to listen."[44] What is happening is not that Luther and Calvin are reading Paul in a grossly inconsistent manner. Instead they simply do not read Paul in the conditional, prospective, and individualistic manner that Campbell suggests. Indeed, in many respects their insistence on faith as gift and on grace in opposition to works is intended to oppose many of the soteriological emphases to which Campbell objects. He simply misunderstands important elements of their exegesis of Paul's texts because his intensification or perfection of divine initiative in salvation leaves him unable to hear any other notes at all in Paul, and in the Reformers' exegesis of Paul, as anything other than its contradiction. All elements in Paul and his interpreters thought to entail the risk of such contradiction must be eliminated. Hence Campbell produces the negative construct of "Justification Theory," a theory for which he is hard pressed to name any recent advocates.[45] Yet, this theory usefully personifies all the theological dangers of any compromise of divine initiative in salvation. In order to eliminate elements in Paul that might be thought to represent the abhorrent "Justification Theory," Campbell posits the unlikely construal of Rom 1:18–3:20 largely as a "speech-in-character" representing not Paul's own position but that of an opponent whom he is attempting to demolish in argument. In relation to the Reformers, especially Luther, the overall effect is that Campbell is a kindly patron rescuing their better exegetical and theological selves from their own confusion. Campbell writes that

> the solution that I am aiming toward is deeply Protestant if not Lutheran. To put things at their simplest, only if my rereading is true is it possible to affirm coherently Paul's slogan that "God justifies the ungodly," since he means by this that God delivers the wicked from their enslavement to Sin, when they cannot deliver themselves, and thereby demonstrates his unconditional grace and love. Alternative construals of this slogan are caught by irreconcilable contradictions and theological conundrums—issues of theodicy, capacity, and so

43. Campbell, *The Deliverance of God*, 261–64, 270–76.
44. Matlock, "Zeal for Paul but Not According to Knowledge," 127.
45. The exception is Bultmann. See Campbell, *The Deliverance of God*, 292–300.

on. But in affirming the slogan in this sense we are of course being loyal to some of the central insights of Protestantism and of Luther.[46]

When the insights of the Reformers are intensified or perfected in such a manner, it is a matter of judgment as to whether their interpretations of Paul are being reflected or rejected or both.

8.4. Intensification: "Covenantal" Interpretations of Paul

The radically intensified or perfected nature of divine initiative and grace within "apocalyptic" interpretations of Paul—with its accompanying emphasis that God undertakes an invasive act of new creation in Christ—is noted by Wright. He complains that such interpretations imply that "Paul must not have a narrative, otherwise grace would no longer be grace."[47] Wright instead locates Paul's apocalyptic thought within the category of covenant and insists that Paul understood himself as an actor within a single continuous story stretching from the creation of the world and the call of Abraham forwards.[48] God entered into a covenant with Abraham's family to bless the world through that family, and what God has done in Christ is understood by Paul within that story. The people of Israel departed from their covenant obligations and ended up in exile, with even those Jews resident in the land of Israel reminded by Roman occupation that the exile continued in the sense that disobedience still estranged Israel from God and provided a barrier to blessing. Rather than such failure providing the last word, there has been a surprising and definitive new twist in the story. Through Jesus the Messiah—as Israel's representative— the covenant has been fulfilled, the curse of continuing exile broken, and the family of Abraham radically redefined so as to include the Gentiles. Yet because Messiah Jesus is Israel's representative, it remains the case that God will save the world through, and only through, Israel. In contrast to the claims of Martyn, Galatians is therefore about *"the definition of the community* as the people who are already declared to be in the right,

46. Campbell, *The Deliverance of God*, 934.

47. Wright, *Paul and the Faithfulness of God*, 467.

48. For example, Wright, *Paul and the Faithfulness of God*, 114-39. As Yinger, *The New Perspective on Paul*, 27-30, comments, Wright's version of the NPP is characterized by the setting of Paul's theology "within the larger biblical story (narrative) of God's work with Israel" (27).

declared to be part of God's single family, the true children of Abraham. That definition assumes that the sins of such people have been dealt with, but that is not Paul's theme."[49] Rather it is the theme of covenant that "forms the essential and non-negotiable context within which the writings of Paul (especially Romans and Galatians, where Abraham plays such a central role, and Romans and 1 Cor 15, where Adam plays such a central role) demand to be read."[50]

As he expounds his argument, Wright pays some attention to the relationship between his own exegesis and that of the Reformers, identifying contemporary rejection of his own position as a kind of hangover from earlier Protestant backwards projections of works-righteousness onto Second Temple Judaism:

> part of the protestant retrojection has been the idea of *a necessary break in the narrative.* Instead of the "great church" rumbling along, gathering all kinds of accumulated baggage and heresy, and insisting that everyone simply go along with it, we have the Reformers (with all the energy and breezy arrogance of the Renaissance's "new learning and new ignorance") claiming to represent a new moment, a radical discontinuity, a clean break. That vision, of the previous dark narrative and the new bright intervention, is then played out in protestant visions of individual conversion; but, more particularly, in the corporate self-awareness of a protestant church history which disclaimed continuity with its immediate past and claimed, instead, a distant continuity with much earlier periods and their texts, namely the Bible and the Fathers.[51]

Wright's statements both reflect and profoundly misunderstand the significance of the Reformers for the current discussion of continuity

---

49. Wright, *Paul and the Faithfulness of God*, 971.

50. Wright, *Paul and the Faithfulness of God*, 795.

51. Wright, *Paul and the Faithfulness of God*, 141. The origins of the stress on discontinuity in current "apocalyptic" interpretations of Paul in fact lie in Käsemann's discernment that all accounts of salvation history are vulnerable to distorted appropriation within ideologies like Nazism. See Ernst Käsemann, "Justification and Salvation History in the Epistle to the Romans," in *Perspectives on Paul* (Philadelphia: Fortress, 1971), 64: "This discovery (of the Reformation doctrine of justification) immunized us deeply against a conception of salvation history which broke in on us in secularized and political form with the Third Reich."

or discontinuity between Paul's gospel and the story of Israel. In relation to the individual, the Reformers certainly do hear in Paul's texts a radical discontinuity. The depth of human depravity does indeed mean that only a radically new beginning in conversion can grant life through the righteousness of Christ. Yet at the corporate level there can be no "clean break" for the Reformers in the sense that Wright alleges. They are as concerned as he is to assert a single divine plan to which God has been consistently faithful. This emphasis on continuity is more easily visible in a Reformed hermeneutic that emphasizes the continuing relevance of the law for Christian living and places considerable theological weight upon the category of covenant.[52] Calvin came to assert that even in the worst times God had maintained the covenant and a living church through the preservation of baptism and other vestiges of true catholicity.[53] Yet even a Lutheran hermeneutic of law and gospel does not deny such continuity but instead configures it in a dialectical manner, discerning tension between divine demand and divine promise in both Old and New Testament rather than a more straightforward progression between two eras of salvation history (see 3.2). As we have seen in his debate with Erasmus (see 1.2), Luther is insistent that "it is impossible for the Church to err, even in the smallest article."[54] This is not the assertion of someone who regards continuity as a dangerous denial of grace but rather, as he goes on to explain, that of someone convinced that the persistence throughout history of the people of God is that of a faithful remnant sustained by divine grace. What is disputed is the true identity of the people of God and the form of its survival, not the persistence of that people. In the context of sinful humanity, the persistence of the church is a fragile but miraculous testimony to a continuity of divine purpose that "typically cuts against the grain of human history and is independent of human processes of development or descent."[55]

---

52. Wright, *Paul and the Faithfulness of God*, 499, does later identify the Reformed tradition with acceptance of a single continuous divine plan but without really explaining how this is consistent with his earlier identification of all Protestant traditions with a necessary break in the narrative.

53. Diarmaid McCulloch, "Calvin: Fifth Latin Doctor of the Church?" in *Calvin and His Influence 1509-2009*, ed. Irena Backus and Philip Benedict (Oxford: Oxford University Press, 2011), 37-38.

54. *LW* 33:85 = *WA* 18:650, 3-4.

55. John M. G. Barclay, review of *Paul and the Faithfulness of God*, by N. T. Wright, *SJT* 68.2 (2015): 238. Barclay, *Paul and the Gift*, 413: "The relation of past human history

Thus, when Wright reflects negatively upon the impact of the Reformers' legacy on Pauline interpretation, he misunderstands important aspects of what they say. It is certainly true that there are vitally important points at which his own interpretation of Paul is seriously at odds with theirs: for example, the meaning of the phrase "works of the law," the construal of justification, and Wright's denial that Abraham and his family stand among the ungodly (Rom 4:5).[56] Yet none of this concerns the issue of continuity at the corporate level of the people of God. Wright's deep concern with the importance of covenant for understanding Paul mirrors and intensifies the same emphasis in the exegesis of Calvin. It is certainly true that in exegesis of texts where Paul comments on the significance of Abraham in relation to justification by faith (Rom 4, Gal 3), Wright places more emphasis on the importance of covenant than does Calvin. It is certainly also true that there are important differences in the accounts of justification offered and that Wright has been much criticized on this basis from within the Reformed tradition.[57] However, there is also now at least one scholarly monograph treating Wright's account of justification as an evolution within the Reformed tradition. Wright is in fundamental continuity with Calvin not only in asserting that justification is forensic but also that it is received through a faithful union with Christ: "the Judge rules favorably for believers who are brought into union with Christ by faith."[58] It might also be added that for all the exegetical differences in handling Paul's use of the figure of Abraham, and therefore also in the nature of justification, both Wright and Calvin strongly connect

---

is not that of the partial to the complete, or the beginning to the end; it is the relation of potential to actual, anticipated to realized, frustrated to enacted. . . . [T]he Christ-gift is both entirely *congruous* with the promise of God and wholly *incongruous* with the prior conditions of human (including Israelite) history" (his emphasis).

56. Wright, *Paul and the Faithfulness of God*, 1004.

57. See especially, John Piper, *The Future of Justification: A Response to N. T. Wright* (Wheaton: Crossway, 2007).

58. Jonathan Huggins, *Living Justification: A Historical-Theological Study of the Reformed Doctrine of Justification in the Writings of John Calvin, Jonathan Edwards, and N. T. Wright* (Eugene: Wipf and Stock, 2013), 216. Huggins's treatment of Reformed accounts of justification as a living, evolving tradition is hermeneutically sophisticated but is somewhat marred by rather uncritical acceptance of Wright's exegetical conclusions, and the apparent assumption that a context of conflict like the Reformation *necessarily* leads to exegetical distortion rather than clarification. On Wright and the Reformed tradition see also Bird, *The Saving Righteousness of God*, 183-93, who considers Wright "an interpreter from and for the reformed tradition" (184).

Paul's covenantal language with familial imagery.[59] Wright prefers the rhetorical strategy of placing his insights in contrast to what has gone before,[60] especially but not only the exegesis of the Reformers, but this represents only part of the reality of the relationship between his work and the Reformed tradition. Despite the rhetorical positioning of NPP scholarship in opposition to exegetical trajectories stemming from the Reformers, closer examination of contemporary scholarship reveals a more complex reality. Both in the work of those unambiguously committed to the NPP and in that of those seeking to move beyond it, there is exhibited not only opposition to the Reformers' exegetical conclusions but also continued dependency upon them and the intensification of some of the Reformers' key themes.

8.5. Erroneous Contrast: The Introspective Conscience

Yet what of those aspects of contemporary scholarship that stand in more straightforward opposition to exegetical trajectories stemming from the Reformers? As such exegetical trajectories are rejected, are the views of the Reformers reported accurately? And are the rejections exegetically necessary? As already noted, the work of Stendahl was of enormous significance here. He alleged the projecting back onto Paul of Luther's own

59. Huggins seems to miss this point. He also misconstrues Calvin's understanding of faith as essentially passive, failing to pay sufficient attention to the important role for Calvin played by faith in sanctification as well as in justification.

60. In his endorsement of Huggins's monograph, Wright describes his discussion alongside Calvin and Jonathan Edwards as "an alarming honor." This tendency towards contrast with the past sometimes leads Wright into absurd generalizations. See Wright, *Paul and the Faithfulness of God*, 755: "When humans are 'saved', rescued from sin and its effects and restored to their image-bearing, heart-circumcised, mind-transformed vocation, then, according to Paul, *creation itself can and will be rescued* from the bondage to decay which has come about through the human derogation of duty. As for humans themselves, they will be raised to new life as part of this larger scene, rescued from the death that was the natural entail of that sin. This is a much bigger picture than traditional western soteriology, whether catholic or protestant, liberal or conservative, has usually imagined." This can be compared but scarcely contrasted with Calvin, *Comm. Rom* 8:21, *CNTC* 8:173-4 = *OE* 13:169, 37 - 170, 5: "all innocent creatures from earth to heaven are punished for our sins. It is our fault that they struggle in corruption. . . . Paul does not mean that all creatures will be partakers of the same glory with the sons of God, but that they will share in their own manner in the better state, because God will restore the present fallen world to perfect condition at the same time as the human race."

struggles with a guilty conscience and—pointing to Paul's claim to have been blameless before his conversion with regard to righteousness under the law (Phil 3:6)—argued that "Paul was equipped with what in our eyes must be called a rather 'robust' conscience. . . . [T]here is no indication that he had any difficulty in fulfilling the law."[61] In making these points Stendahl provided the basis on which Sanders would later argue that Paul worked from solution to plight, only realizing his plight and his need for a savior once he was convinced that he had already met that savior. This in turn then helped to undermine the conviction that Paul's objection to the "works of the law" is because he regards them as futile attempts to achieve righteousness that are doomed to fail because obedience to the law is in fact impossible for fallen humanity. Paul's concern in articulating justification by faith is not to counter works-righteousness but to affirm the possibility of Gentile inclusion in the messianic community.

As we have seen, however (3.3), neither Luther nor others imagine the preconversion Paul struggling with inability to keep the law. Further, the phrase "works of the law" is not identified with the revelation of sin but rather with the kind of false confidence that one is fulfilling the law possessed by the preconversion Paul. Here the conscience errs in evaluating the self not as a sinner but as righteous and this is in fact only one of three possible relationships between the human conscience and the law. There may also be the sinner willfully disregarding the law or the person realizing his or her true position before the demand of the law and therefore in the process of being driven to Christ. The conscience is an unreliable guide and when Paul says that no one will be justified before God through the "works of the law" because "through the law comes the knowledge of sin" (Rom 3:20), he is speaking of the need for a revelation of the true human situation.[62] Perhaps precisely because they perceive the human conscience as such an inaccurate guide, the Reformers have

---

61. Stendahl, "Paul and the Introspective Conscience of the West," 80.

62. Indeed, from a historical-critical perspective the Reformers' most implausible exegetical conclusion about the law and the conscience is reached not because they assume that the preconversion Paul struggled with a guilty conscience but because they are so committed to the view that he did not. The insistence by early Protestant interpreters that Paul's reference to life apart from the law in Rom 7:9 speaks of his time as a Pharisee is clearly incorrect. Yet they reach this doubtful conclusion because they regard Paul's life as a Pharisee as characterized by a false confidence in his capacity to obey God's commands that the coming of the law exposes as an illusion when it convicts of sin.

little interest in the psychological dimensions of how the law reveals sin. Their concern is rather that it does in fact do so and that individuals are prompted to recognize their need of Christ. Melanchthon comes closest to establishing an experiential sequence in which the experience of a guilty conscience becomes a necessary prelude to faith as an intermediate stage of repentance between it and an earlier false confidence in fulfilling the law. However, both Luther and Calvin insist that repentance is only fully present in the experience of faith and not merely as its prelude.[63]

Both some of Stendahl's own points and also many of the inferences drawn from his arguments by others are therefore wrong. The Reformers' conviction that it is impossible for human beings to fulfill the law, which thereby brings condemnation, can coexist without tension both with the robust conscience of the preconversion Paul and with the notion that his theologizing about salvation moves from solution to plight. Wright is simply misleadingly incorrect when he states that "the standard assumption, since Augustine at least, and especially since Luther, was that Paul had been laboring under the problem of a guilty conscience, aware of his own inability to meet the inexorable demands of the Law, and unable to find peace with his maker—and that he discovered in the crucified Jesus the answer to all this."[64] Yet a central exegetical point remains, which is that the Reformers clearly do take Rom 3:20 and other important texts to indicate that for Paul the function of the law is to reveal sin. Is their insistence on this point itself evidence of a distorting attachment to the importance of an introspective conscience? In this regard, it is instructive to see how Paul's statement is interpreted by Wright:

> But from Paul's perspective there was no chance that anyone, however devout, would in fact keep Torah perfectly: "through the law comes the knowledge of sin." From one point of view this might be taken as a further demarcation of Israel: through the law comes the knowledge of *the sin which those pagans out there are committing*. To that extent, the law did indeed function as a fence around Israel. But for "Paul through the law comes knowledge of sin" meant, more particularly, that those who embraced Torah for themselves—i.e., the

63. On all these points, see Chester, "Paul and the Introspective Conscience of Martin Luther," 508–36.

64. Wright, *Paul and the Faithfulness of God*, 747-48. See Tomlin, "Luther and the Deliverance of God," 27-28, who doubts even that the struggle with an introspective conscience was as vital as is usually assumed to the biography of the early Luther.

343

Jewish people—were themselves under the covenantal curse which Torah pronounced on those who broke it. Moses himself, at the climax of Torah in Deuteronomy, had warned that this curse would unfailingly fall on Israel itself. "Whatever Torah says, it speaks to those who are under Torah"—in other words, to Israel.[65]

Clearly Wright reads Paul's statement as intending primarily to point out Jewish sinfulness. The statement that Jews and Gentiles alike are under sin (Rom 3:9) does indicate universal sinfulness, but from Paul's perspective Gentile sinfulness is obvious. It is Israel's sinfulness that must be demonstrated and this is the point of the previous medley of scriptural quotations (Rom 3:10–18). Whether the sharpness of this distinction between Jewish and Gentile sinfulness is true to Paul's argument or underplays the relevance to Gentiles of the statement that "through the law comes the knowledge of sin" could be debated. Even if Torah speaks primarily to Israel as those under the Torah, to what degree is Israel here representative of humanity? Yet, even if Wright is correct, nothing he says contradicts the basic exegetical point that for Paul a principal function of the law is to reveal human sinfulness. This is true for Wright even in Paul's own biography: "Torah declared that the devout Jew (his own former self) had in fact broken it—at the very moment when he was rightly clinging to it."[66] If one were to respond as if from the perspective of the Reformers, one might well at this point argue from the greater to the lesser: "If it is true that Paul here speaks of even God's holy law bringing knowledge of sin to Jews who are committed to faithful observance of Torah, how much more is it true that Gentiles who attempt to establish their own righteousness before God through any other kinds of ethical behavior will find only knowledge of sin." This of course would be unacceptable to Wright, who puts the law's revealing of sin into a very different interpretative framework, going on to speak of the sin revealed to Jews not as that of those attempting to establish righteousness through ethical behavior but as that of those treating Torah as "*a badge of privilege.*"[67]

Yet what this reveals is that the tension between his position and that of the Reformers is not actually about the knowledge of sin and the introspective conscience. Instead, it primarily concerns the interpreta-

65. Wright, *Paul and the Faithfulness of God*, 1034.
66. Wright, *Paul and the Faithfulness of God*, 1035.
67. Wright, *Paul and the Faithfulness of God*, 1034.

tion of what Paul means by the phrase the "works of the law" and its implications for Paul's perceptions of the nature of Judaism and the nature of justification by faith. The main issue is whether the Reformers are misguided in their conclusion that one of Paul's principal concerns is to contrast justification with works-righteousness. This point requires some emphasis since it is all too easy to connect the two issues by imagining that the Reformers' exegetical comments about the conscience lead directly to an insistence that an experience of guilt and self-loathing is the necessary prelude to a breakthrough to faith. Yet in fact they do not establish an unvarying sequence. The knowledge of sin is indeed ultimately necessary to faith and repentance, but the point is not "that an awareness of sin always precedes a knowledge of the gospel. . . . [A]lthough experientially at times law precedes gospel and at other times gospel precedes law, theologically they are correlative to each other: each needs the other for a true understanding."[68]

At this point the Reformers' conclusions can helpfully be brought into conversation with recent work seeking to discern Paul's expectations about the revealing of sin. In my own study, *Conversion at Corinth*, I concluded that the revelation of sin is typically backwards-looking: it is in the moment of faith and not in a prior struggle with a guilty conscience that a person's unrecognized sin is revealed. There may be for a Gentile convert "a move from a state of contentment to a state of crisis,"[69] but this crisis is also simultaneously resolved as faith brings security in Christ. For Paul himself, his persecution of the church in devotion to the law is retrospectively recognized as sinful from the perspective of faith when it would previously have been evaluated positively. My sense that Paul typically expects the knowledge of sin to be backwards-looking from the vantage point of faith is different from the Reformers' sense that this sequence is perfectly possible but that frequently the knowledge of sin may be prospective and cause a struggle with sin that precedes the receiving of the gospel. Yet this difference is one of emphasis about what is typical, not a difference about what could be regarded as possible on the basis of Paul's texts. There is nothing that could lead one to the conclusions that the Reformers expect that all will

---

68. Tomlin, "Luther and the Deliverance of God," 29–30.

69. Chester, *Conversion at Corinth*, 124. The part played for Paul in conversion by the exposure of unrecognized sin is a major theme of chapters on Gentile conversion (113–48) and Jewish conversion (149–204).

experience a struggle with a guilty conscience prior to faith, or that they include Paul in this, or that they take the experience of such struggle to be typical of Jewish engagement with the law. Their characterization of Judaism in terms of justification by works in no way depends upon any of these conclusions. Stendahl's work on the introspective conscience represents a misleading dead end for contemporary scholarship.[70] This is not because he is wrong to object to portrayals of Paul as a hero of the introspective conscience but because such portrayals are not essential to Reformation perspectives on Paul. It simply fails to follow that if Paul possessed a robust conscience, justification must be focused solely on the inclusion of the Gentiles in God's people in a way that excludes any concern with works-righteousness.

8.6. The Heart of the Matter: Judaism and Works of the Law

We are thus forced back upon debate about the nature of Second Temple Judaism, a debate in which the dice can no longer be loaded by supposing that the Reformers must be wrong because they are wrong about the conscience. Nevertheless, the basic historical question remains: is the characterization of Judaism by the Reformers in terms of righteousness by works sustainable? It seems that here there is a clear choice between such an opinion and the proposal that in view instead are those aspects of the law such as circumcision, the food laws, and Sabbath observance that serve to separate Jews from Gentiles. Dunn writes that "the boasting which Paul condemned had more to do with pride in ethnic privilege than with pride in self-achievement. . . . [S]eparateness to God (holiness) was understood to require separateness from the (other) nations as two sides of the one coin."[71] Yet even here we should note a significant point of agreement between NPP scholars and exegetical conclusions reached by the Reformers. Dunn also writes, "I have no doubt that 'works of the law' refer to what the law requires, the conduct prescribed by the Torah; whatever the law requires to be done can be described as 'doing' the law, as a work of the law."[72] Such an insistence that the term "works of the

---

70. For a statement of essentially the same conclusion but with a different focus, see Stephen Westerhom, *Justification Reconsidered* (Grand Rapids: Eerdmans, 2013), 1–22.

71. Dunn, "The New Perspective: Whence, What and Whither?," 14–16.

72. Dunn, "The New Perspective: Whence, What and Whither?," 23–24.

law" refers to all that the law requires was, of course, the indispensable exegetical basis of everything that the Reformers understood it to mean.

If one asks whether the exegesis of an NPP advocate like Dunn is here closer to that of the Reformers or those medieval and patristic interpreters who took Paul's phrase to refer exclusively to the ceremonial aspects of the law, then the answer is clear. Dunn's point is not that the Reformers are wrong in this conclusion but that they are wrong to understand obedience to the whole law in terms of self-achieved works-righteousness. Instead, Dunn argues that in any context where it matters to be obedient to all that the law requires, those items that are contentious will take on particular significance precisely as indicators of fidelity to the whole law. Therefore, reflecting on Gal 2, Dunn writes that "the issue which caused the first recorded statement of the great principle of justification by faith alone was the works of the law by which Judaism distinguished itself and kept itself separate from the (other) nations."[73] Paul's teaching on justification finds its foil not in works righteousness but instead in an insistence on separation from Gentiles that fails fully to recognize the radical breaking down of such boundaries wrought by the gift of Christ and the accompanying full inclusion of the Gentiles in God's people.

This difference about what lies in the foreground when Paul contrasts justification by faith with the "works of the law" is itself susceptible to different assessments of who is right and who is wrong depending upon the particular questions in relation to which such assessments are framed. If we ask whether the Reformers pay sufficient attention in their exegesis to Jew/Gentile relationships in the early church, then they do not emerge favorably. Dunn's complaint that "Luther's fundamental distinction between gospel and law was too completely focused on the danger of self-achieved works righteousness"[74] could be illustrated by looking directly at Luther's treatment of Gal 2 itself. There is little sign of incorporation of the boundary-defining function of the "works of the law" into his exegesis of Paul's statements about such works and justification.[75] The best that can be found elsewhere is Calvin's suggestion that Paul insightfully perceives questions of practice (that Calvin terms "cer-

73. Dunn, "The New Perspective: Whence, What and Whither?," 28.

74. Dunn, "The New Perspective: Whence, What and Whither?," 20.

75. See *LW* 26:106 = *WA* 40.1:192, 19–20. Luther's opening remarks on the dispute at Antioch (Gal 2:11–14) immediately move beyond the questions of practice at stake: "For the issue here is nothing trivial for Paul; it is the principal doctrine of Christianity."

emonial"), such as observance of the food laws, as indicative of deeper soteriological principles.[76] This line of thought arguably has the potential to prompt reflection on the difference between Paul's perception of the significance of the "works of the law" as an apostle of Christ and the perceptions of the significance of the "works of the law" held by other Jews of his time.[77] We have seen evidence that it did so in the form of the identification of the phrase the "works of the law" with those falsely confident of their obedience to the law. What it does not achieve is to do justice to the significance of issues of practice to Jewish identity, which renders suspect both in relation to Paul and to other Jews the notion of deeper soteriological principles detachable from the practices embodying them.

This neglect of the significance of Jewish practice is a serious weakness in Reformation exegesis when assessed from a contemporary perspective. Relevant at this point is the rather obvious reflection that the Reformers were not seeking an accurate portrayal of Second Temple Judaism as a goal in itself, nor did they have access to the range of sources that allows contemporary scholarship to present more nuanced accounts of Second Temple Judaism. They were primarily concerned rather with how the gospel expressed in Paul's letters spoke to issues of pressing concern to them and their contemporaries. For this reason, they emphasize Paul's exclusion of self-earned righteousness in their interpretation of all texts where he discusses justification (and many others besides) and this feeds the analogy they draw between Paul's opponents and their own. Given the overwhelming evidence that circumcision, food laws, and Sabbath-observance did serve in important ways to maintain boundaries between Jews and Gentiles, it is undeniable that in drawing attention to this the work of NPP scholars represents a welcome advance.[78]

---

76. See Calvin, *Sermons on Galatians,* 162–64 = *CO* 50:407–8 (Sermon 11).

77. In defending a position sympathetic to the Reformation tradition this distinction is emphasized by Stephen Westerholm, *Israel's Law and the Church's Faith: Paul and his Recent Interpreters* (Grand Rapids: Eerdmans, 1988), 149: "The methodological error has often been committed in the past of concluding that, since Paul contrasts grace and works and argues for salvation by grace, his opponents (and ultimately, Judaism) must have worked with the same distinction but argued for salvation by works. Clearly this distorts Judaism, which never thought that divine grace was incompatible with divine requirements."

78. On this boundary-defining function see John M. G. Barclay, *Judaism in the Mediterranean Diaspora* (Edinburgh: T&T Clark, 1996), 428–44.

Yet while this contrast between the Reformers and recent historical scholarship is valid, it too can become little more than a convenient way rhetorically to justify recent scholarship if presented in absolute terms. To discern the contemporary relevance of the gospel expressed in Paul's letters is what theological interpreters are supposed to do and, for all the differences between sixteenth- and twenty-first-century scholarly methods, NPP scholars are also engaged in this task whether it is acknowledged or not. A less prejudicial account of Second Temple Judaism arose precisely in a post-Holocaust context where it was a pressing contemporary need, and to understand Paul's objection to the "works of the law" in terms of a rejection of the exclusivity of his own ethnic tradition provides a significant theological resource for today's diverse global Christianity.[79] Recognition of this contemporary relevance should at one and the same time prompt an appreciation of NPP scholarship and cause us to ask whether it also interprets Paul's phrase in too monolithic a manner. *If it is unconvincing to understand obedience to the whole law almost exclusively in terms of self-achieved works-righteousness, is it any more convincing to understand it almost exclusively in terms of the boundary-marking function of the works performed?*

If the question is framed in this way, then the debate begins to appear less unfavorable to the Reformers. For Dunn sees Paul's polemic against "works of the law" as correcting a misunderstanding of what the law truly requires: "the 'works' which Paul warns against were, in his view, Israel's misunderstanding of what her covenant law required."[80] If this is Paul's view, it is odd that he contrasts not only the "works of the law" with faith and grace but also the law itself (e.g., Gal 3:11; Rom 6:14, 15), treating the law and its works interchangeably.[81] Paul does not respond to the insistence that Gentile converts must be circumcised by saying that this is to misunderstand the law but rather with the assertion that "if justification comes through the law, then Christ died for nothing" (Gal 2:21). Paul has already identified Christ's death as necessary to the justification of Jews as well as Gentiles (Gal 2:15–16), so his point here is

---

79. In seeking to exploit this theological resource it is essential to be aware of the danger of leaping from the frying pan of mischaracterizing Judaism as a religion of works-righteousness into the fire of implicitly mischaracterizing Judaism as a religion of misanthropic exclusivism.

80. Dunn, *Theology of Paul the Apostle*, 366.

81. Barclay, *Paul and the Gift*, 374, says of Galatians that "There is no material difference in this letter between 'works of the Law' and 'the Law.'"

not solely the chronological point that his opponents err in failing to appreciate that the ages have turned in the coming of the Messiah and the giving of the Spirit and that God's purpose is now to include the Gentiles in his people. Paul clearly also intends to say, even if such knowledge is only possessed retrospectively from the vantage point of faith in Christ, that the law never could justify since if it could have done so, the saving death of the Messiah would not have been necessary. If this is so, then Paul does not denote by the phrase the "works of the law" a misunderstanding of the law's requirements but rather his conviction that the deeds rightly understood as required by the law simply do not justify.[82]

Given this interchangeable treatment of the law and its works by Paul in relation to justification, and given the exegetical agreement between the Reformers and NPP scholars that the phrase the "works of the law" denotes all that the law requires, then the degree of emphasis upon the boundary-marking function of the law and its works in NPP scholarship becomes questionable. While accepting that the maintenance of separation between Jews and Gentiles is often what Paul has in mind when discussing the law and its works, and their inability to justify, is it always the case that this is what he intends to emphasize? Just as the Reformers too exclusively emphasized Paul's exclusion of human ethical achievement from justification because that was what served the needs of their own historical context, does some NPP scholarship too exclusively emphasize Paul's rejection of ethnocentrism for the same reason? One hint that it is too exclusive in this way emerges from NPP scholarship itself in its convincing emphasis on the remarkably all-embracing nature of the law and its defining of the Jewish way of life. Marking boundaries between Jews and Gentiles is often crucial as an expression of obedience to God's commandments, but it is the commitment to an entire way of life swathed in divine regulation that is itself peculiarly Jewish. This can be illustrated by reference to the work of none other than E. P. Sanders, who emphasizes that "Judaism's most distinctive point . . . was the extension of divine law to all the areas of life. . . . This emphasis on

---

82. The implication, of Paul's interchangeable treatment of "the works of the law" and the "law" itself, that Paul is therefore not criticizing a misunderstanding of the law is spelled out by Stephen Westerholm, *Perspectives Old and New on Paul*, 297–340. I pursue a related argument in Chester, *Conversion at Corinth*, 159–64, when pointing out that Paul's positive evaluation of his Pharisaic past (Gal 1:13–14) is most odd if he was then deeply concerned to maintain that separation of Israel from the Gentiles but now regards such separation as a misunderstanding of the law's requirements.

correct action in every sphere of life, technically called 'orthopraxy', is a hallmark of Judaism. Judaism, that is, required obedience to the law, which includes the sacrifices and offerings, but also much more."[83]

In Sanders's long discussion of observing the law of God that follows, the fact clearly emerges that practices such as circumcision, the food laws, and Sabbath observance did serve to delineate Jews from Gentiles. Yet there is also recognition of the theological significance of these practices (e.g., circumcision is a sign of Israel's election and of the covenant with Abraham; observance of the Sabbath either reflects the rest of God on the seventh day of creation or it commemorates the exodus from Egypt) and considerable emphasis on the law's mandate of love for humankind, including the Gentiles and those among their number who might specifically count as enemies of Israel. Jewish responses to Gentile society varied. "Some Diaspora Jews responded to their pagan environment, full of idolatry and sexual immorality (from their perspective), by cutting themselves off from too much contact with Gentiles. . . . Other Jews, it must be emphasized, participated in numerous aspects of pagan culture, such as the theatre and games, quite cheerfully."[84] Given such an account, we should conclude not simply that Jews could vary in very significant ways as to how much separation from Gentiles was required by obedience to the law or that there could be significant disagreement over how to practice individual commandments. We should note also that if the great Jewish distinctive is commitment to the all-embracing law itself, then the meaning of the law and its constituent commandments will be understood in various ways. A phrase like the "works of the law" may indeed refer simply to the conduct required by the Torah, but that required conduct is itself complex and multi-faceted. Neither the phrase itself nor the very wide range of mandated behaviors to which it refers are convincingly to be explained exclusively in relation to any single function or purpose: *the phrase 'works of the law' refers to the distinctive way of life of the Jewish community, but without any necessary orientation towards boundary-markers. . . .* [T]here is no need to import a reference to 'boundary markers' every time Paul uses the term 'works.'"[85] The failing of NPP scholarship on the "works of the law" is

83. E. P. Sanders, *Judaism: Practice and Belief 63 BCE–66 CE* (London: SCM; Philadelphia: Trinity Press international, 1992), 191.

84. Sanders, *Judaism: Practice and Belief*, 216.

85. Francis Watson, *Paul, Judaism, and the Gentiles: Beyond the New Perspective*, 2nd ed. (Grand Rapids: Eerdmans, 2007), 19 (his emphasis). See also Bird, *The Saving*

not its emphasis on their boundary-marking function, which is indeed significant, but rather its apparent inability to discern any other function or purpose, either in general or in the argument of Paul's texts.

This point can be illustrated by consideration of circumcision, indisputably a key component of what Paul means by the "works of the law." Just as indisputably, circumcision is of sociological significance as a boundary-marking ritual. It would be foolish, for example, to ignore the powerful barrier it erects to marriage between Jewish women and Gentile men.[86] Yet a focus on distinguishing Jews from Gentiles by no means exhausts the ways in which Jews could think about circumcision's meaning or purpose. In a recent study of Second Temple texts, Nina Livesey finds considerable variety. Circumcision "signifies allegiance to Hasmonean rule" (1 Maccabees), or it "identifies one as a son of the covenant" (*Jubilees*). In the context of martyrdom it denotes "pious sacrifice" (2 Maccabees) or the triumph of "pious reason over the passions" (4 Maccabees). In Philo circumcision is variously said to "promote health (*De specialibus legibus*), to "draw the male mind closer to God" (*Quaestiones et solutiones in Genesim* III), to be the means through which "a Jew can obtain spiritual insight" (*De migratione Abrahami*). In Josephus, circumcision denotes the true commitment of the convert King Izates to his new Jewish faith (*A.J.* 20.2-4).[87] While circumcision is "the sign of a Jew" that distinguishes Jews from Gentiles, the Jewishness that it signifies is complex and varied and therefore so too are the meanings or purposes assigned to the rite itself.

While clearly dissatisfied with Dunn's treatment of circumcision, Livesey does not herself go on to ask what the variety she has uncovered in relation to this particular commandment might imply for the meaning

---

Righteousness of God, 98: "The 'works of the law' is a metonym for the stipulations of the entire Mosaic code."

86. See Barclay, *Jews in the Mediterranean Diaspora*, 411-12.

87. Nina Livesey, *Circumcision as a Malleable Symbol*, WUNT 2.295 (Tübingen: Mohr Siebeck, 2010), 155-58. Diversity in the meaning of circumcision is not only a matter of the diverse perspectives of different authors within a single historical period but also of change over time. Shaye J. D. Cohen, *Why Aren't Jewish Women Circumcised? Gender and Covenant in Judaism* (Berkeley: University of California Press, 2005), 50-51, writes that "The surgical aspect changed; the attendant ritual changed; the meanings changed. The ritual as delineated in the Bible is at once the same as, and yet very different from, the ritual as practiced and understood by the Jews of Europe in the high Middle Ages."

of a more general phrase such as the "works of the law."[88] This ground is covered, albeit from a very different viewpoint, by Simon Gathercole, who argues that the "works of the law" are not only identity markers but also "have a functional role as a criterion for final salvation."[89] Here Gathercole disputes Sanders's characterization of Judaism in terms of a covenantal nomism that is essentially two-fold, with "getting in" determined on the basis of election and obedience to the law following simply as the means of "staying in."[90] On the basis of a wide-ranging survey of Second Temple texts, Gathercole persuasively argues that "There is very good reason to distinguish . . . between entry into the covenant, which of course is based on God's election, and final justification, salvation in the end. So, the category that is often missed is the role of works in 'getting into the world to come,' 'getting into the life of the future age,' or 'getting there.'"[91] One of the many texts to which Gathercole appeals is 4QMMT,

88. On Dunn's perspective on circumcision, see Livesey, *Circumcision as a Malleable Symbol*, 148. Livesey insists that Paul treats the issue in relation to Gentiles considering circumcision without devaluing the continued practice of circumcision by Jewish followers of Jesus. The rite itself is simply a neutral sign of Jewishness. On this basis Livesey criticizes theological interpreters who assign a negative significance to circumcision, but in the process fails to grapple with the issue that it is Paul himself who establishes a dichotomy between justification and works of the law and asserts that those who are of the works of the law are under a curse (Gal 3:10), i.e., even if he finds appropriate the continued practice of "works of the law" such as circumcision, there are senses in which Paul characterizes the law negatively even as it relates to Jews and not only with regard to attempts to apply it to Gentiles.

89. Simon J. Gathercole, *Where Is Boasting? Early Jewish Soteriology and Paul's Response in Romans 1-5* (Grand Rapids: Eerdmans, 2002), 13. Gathercole questions the NPP from a more traditional perspective whereas Livesey's sympathies are closer to the "radical new perspective." On the "radical new perspective" see above, n. 4.

90. Sanders seems to miss the implications of his own emphasis on the law as an entire way of life primarily because of his desire to establish Judaism as a religion of grace by eliminating from it all taint of works righteousness. Yet this argument itself embodies a rather Pauline judgment that grace and law are in important senses antithetical. It does not follow that because Paul made this contrast, other Second Temple Jews also did so in a similar way. See Watson, *Paul, Judaism, and the Gentiles*, 12-19. See now also the commentary offered by Barclay, *Paul and the Gift*, 151-58, who suggests that Sanders fails to distinguish between the priority of grace (that most other Second Temple Jews insisted upon in a manner similar to Paul) and the incongruity of grace (that Paul insisted upon in ways that most other Second Temple Jews did not).

91. Gathercole, *Where Is Boasting?*, 24. Watson, *Paul, Judaism, and the Gentiles*, 17, is in agreement with Gathercole: "When Paul looks to the Jewish communities of the present, what he sees is a zealous (though misguided) practice of the law that under-

a text from Qumran in which the phrase the "works of the law" is used and in which it is said that for those who keep the *halakhoth* outlined in the document (calendrical instructions and purity regulations) in the manner instructed "it will be reckoned to you as righteousness" (C31).[92]

The significance of this usage is much disputed. For Dunn, the sectarian context is crucial, with the distinctive Qumran interpretations of the law providing the "ground necessary and sufficient for the Qumran sect to 'separate' (that word again) from the rest of the people (cf. Gal 2:12)."[93] What these particular interpretations of how the law was to be followed do in demarcating the Qumran sect from other Jewish groups mirrors what the "works of the law" more generally do in demarcating Jews from Gentiles. In contrast, Gathercole draws attention to the broader framework into which the author of 4QMMT places the concern for the particular regulations stipulated in the document, referring to the works or deeds of the kings of Israel (C23) and the faithful acts of David (C25). The concern for works goes beyond that of separation. Further, the reckoning of righteousness to those who are obedient takes place eschatologically: "Then you shall rejoice at the end time when you find the essence of our words to be true" (C30). Those who are reckoned righteous will be so reckoned because they have been obedient. Gathercole has the better of this argument, for although Dunn's emphasis on the boundary-defining function of the "works of the law" in 4QMMT is indisputably valid, it also provides only an incomplete explanation of their meaning and function. The text's eschatological dimension is neglected and the result is that only the boundary-defining function of the "works of the law" is visible. Other important dimensions are simply missed.[94]

---

stands itself as, first, the visible outworking of Israel's election; second, the precondition for a righteous standing before God in the present life; and third, the way that leads to the eschatological life of the age to come (cf. Rom 9:30–10:5)."

92. For the full text, see Michael Wise, Martin Abegg Jr., and Edward Cook, *The Dead Sea Scrolls: A New Translation* (San Francisco: Harper, 1996), 358–64.

93. Dunn, "The New Perspective: Whence, What and Whither?," 15.

94. N. T. Wright, "4QMMT and Paul: Justification, 'Works,' and Eschatology," in *History and Exegesis: New Testament Essays in Honor of Dr. E. Earle Ellis for His 80th Birthday*, ed. Aang-Won (Aaron) Son (New York and London: T&T Clark, 2006), 104–32, acknowledges that Dunn does not do justice to the eschatological emphasis of 4QMMT but argues that the works described do not earn membership in God's eschatological people but instead demonstrate it. The problem with this position is that while the works required by 4QMMT certainly do demarcate God's people from the author's perspective, this is not what is emphasized in C31–32 in relation to eschatological justification: "And

We have now seen that (1) the term the "works of the law" refers generally to the conduct that the law requires, (2) that Paul's negative characterization of such works in contrast to faith is not in response to what he regards as a misunderstanding of the law, (3) that the ascription of a single meaning or purpose to the law fails adequately to reflect the complex and multi-faceted nature of the conduct required in its relation to all aspects of life, and (4) that one of the functions of works that appears regularly in Second Temple literature is that of "getting into the world to come." Given these conclusions, one might expect to find that when Paul contrasts the "works of the law" with faith in relation to justification, his primary concern will not always be the same meaning and function of these works. This is a crucial issue, since while Dunn is prepared to say that "I do not want to narrow the 'works of the law' to boundary issues,"[95] and while he also regards many Protestant formulations of justification as legitimate inferences from Paul's texts, he insists, like many other NPP scholars, that when Paul uses the phrase he is always primarily concerned with the boundary-defining function of the "works of the law." This is maintained vigorously despite the various occasions on which Paul appears explicitly to contrast the gospel he preaches with human ethical achievement. Paul contrasts working to receive wages with the nature of justification by faith as a gift (Rom 4:4–5). He argues that God's election of Jacob but not Esau before they were born, and had done anything good or bad, demonstrates that election is not by works but reflects divine freedom (Rom 9:10–13). When he lists his reasons for confidence in the flesh (Phil 3:4b–6), Paul includes his blamelessness in relation to righteousness under the law as one component of the righteousness of his own that he then goes on to contrast with righteousness by faith (Phil 3:9). For each of these texts, NPP exegetes attempt to provide alternative interpretations in which Paul speaks not of the exclusion from justification of ethical achievement but instead of the exclusion of ethnocentrism. Ultimately such debates can be pursued only through detailed exegetical argument, but none of these alternative interpretations have succeeded in establishing a consensus. NPP proposals also often

---

it will be reckoned to you as righteousness, *in that you have done what is right and good before him*, to your own benefit, and to that of Israel" (my emphasis). Against Dunn's interpretation of 4QMMT, see also the pertinent remarks of Bird, *The Saving Righteousness of God*, 96–99.

95. Dunn, "The New Perspective: Whence, What and Whither?," 28.

contrast with each other as well as with more traditional alternatives,[96] and the details of these texts are not most naturally explained in relation to ethnocentrism.

It is far from clear why these particular exegetical debates are necessary and why the texts under discussion cannot straightforwardly be read as concerned with human ethical achievement. Paul is indeed frequently concerned with the "works of the law" in their boundary-defining function and with contrasting it to the inclusion of the Gentiles in God's people through justification by faith. Yet, precisely because the law is God's law and Jews are characterized by obedience to it, this boundary is also the boundary between holiness and sinfulness (Gal 2:15). Inevitably the pinnacles of human ethical achievement all lie on the Jewish side of the boundary with Paul confident that he was himself an exemplary representative of the Jewish tradition (Gal 1:14–15; Phil 3:4–12).[97] As Stendahl puts it, Paul regards himself as having been a very successful Jew "even when he thinks about it from his Christian perspective."[98] Given Paul's realization that, despite all this, Jews as well as Greeks are under sin (Rom 3:9) and that therefore even the very best of human life partakes of sinfulness, it would be scarcely surprising if on some occasions his primary concern in contrasting justification by faith with the "works of the law" was to state clearly that justification cannot be received through human ethical achievement.

That Paul does so is not a diminution of his emphasis on the boundary-defining function of the "works of the law" and the two aspects appear side by side. The prominence of one does not eliminate the other precisely because Paul's reference is to an entire nomistic way of life. One aspect or another may be the focus in particular statements, but the wider reference is not eliminated. This is, of course, also the case in texts where the boundary-defining function of the "works of the law"

---

96. Thus, for example, Dunn "The New Perspective: Whence, What and Whither?," 47–49, argues that Rom 4:4–5 concerns only initial justification ("getting in") with Abraham as "the type of the ungodly-idolator-become-proselyte" (48) and intends to point out simply that Abraham's election did not depend upon a preexisting covenant faithfulness. In contrast, Wright, *Paul and the Faithfulness of God*, 1004, is so insistent that the focus of the chapter is solely on membership of Abraham's family as to deny that Abraham himself should be numbered among the ungodly.

97. See Chester, *Conversion at Corinth*, 153–83, for a fuller discussion of these two texts.

98. Stendahl, "Call Not Conversion," 13.

is clearly in view. This can be illustrated with reference to one of the most heavily disputed of Paul's uses of the phrase the "works of the law" in Gal 2:16. Scholarship of the NPP has rightly emphasized the relevance in the context (the crisis in Galatia over circumcision and the immediately preceding discussion of the incident at Antioch in 2:11–14) of the boundary-defining function of these works. Yet as Stephen Westerholm points out:

> Substantiating Paul's point is a verse in the Psalms that, in the Psalms, reads as follows: "Do not enter into judgment with your servant; for before you no-one living is found righteous;" Paul paraphrases: "by works of the law no flesh will be justified." Now, if Paul's point had been that circumcision and other "boundary markers" are not requirements for sitting at the table of God's people, it is not clear why he would even have thought of Psalm 143:2 let alone deemed it proof of his claim. The verse from the Psalms was the perfect one to quote, however, if he wanted to say that human beings (Jews like Peter and Paul no less than Gentiles like the Galatians) are sinners who can never be deemed righteous before God by anything they do: "before you no-one living is found righteous."[99]

The point is not that "anything they do" means that Paul's focus here is not on the boundary-marking function of the "works of the law" but instead on human ethical achievement. Rather, it is that even as the boundary-marking function is highlighted, it is as a part of the wider nomistic way of life in which recognizing and even boasting in praiseworthy and obedient behavior is appropriate.[100] Scholarship of the NPP often acknowledges this wider nomistic reference of Paul's phrase, but even as it does so glides by its implications in order to concentrate only and in every text on the boundary-defining function of the "works of the law." The Reformers were guilty of a similar error, rightly hearing in Paul a denial that justification can be received through human ethical achievement,

---

99. Westerholm, *Justification Reconsidered*, 77. In both Gal 2:16 and the LXX version of Ps 143 (142):2 the verb is an identical third person singular future indicative passive: δικαιωθήσεται. The same allusion is also found in Rom 3:20.

100. On boasting see the excellent discussion in Gathercole, *Where Is Boasting?*, 161–94. As Gathercole points out, the critique of Jewish boasting in Paul's texts comes not because all boasting is wrong but because the perception of blameless obedience to the Torah is a false one from Paul's perspective. If the boast were true, it would be valid.

but erroneously taking all his contrasts between faith and the "works of the law" to speak of this single concern.

In offering this criticism of both the NPP and the Reformers, I am not proposing that Paul operates with two different meanings of the phrase "works of the law" between which he alternates. The phrase is used consistently by Paul with a single reference to the nomistic way of life characteristic of Judaism. Yet, the social practices that make up this single way of life are multiple and complex within the unity granted to them by the fact that they all express divine requirements. When Paul denies that the "works of the law" justify, he sometimes does so in contexts where his focus is on separation from Gentiles, sometimes in contexts where his focus is on human ethical achievement, and sometimes in contexts where the two jostle together. As Barclay argues in his ground-breaking study *Paul and the Gift*, the reason for this is that Paul construes the Christ-gift as always incongruous, as always given to those who are unworthy of it. This is true of its Jewish recipients just as much as of its Gentile recipients. Paul's target is not as such either a principle of ethnic superiority or a principle of works-righteousness. Paul is not attacking the mistaken notion that divine approval of Israel depended upon separation from Gentiles or the mistaken notion that it is possible to earn salvation, but more fundamentally insisting that God's grace in Christ disregards any and every dimension of human worthiness including even observance of a nomistic way of life. The Christ-gift is not given because there is something about the recipients that makes them the fitting beneficiaries of it. "Paul has ruled out numerous qualifying criteria for divine selection: birth (natural rights of descent), status (comparative 'greatness'), and practice ('works'), all forms of symbolic capital humanly ascribed or achieved."[101] Since all are "under sin" (Rom 3:9), grace can belong to no one, and "it is because grace belongs to no-one that it goes to everyone."[102]

The error of both NPP scholarship and the Reformers is therefore to mistake the possible expressions of human worthiness in Paul's historical context as a Second Temple Jew (ethnic identity, ethical achievement) for the underlying issue that from Paul's perspective these expressions embody. Paul talks about both precisely in order to make it clear that the Christ-gift is not conditioned by any aspect of human worthiness. The Reformers' error is more pernicious in the sense that their sugges-

---

101. Barclay, *Paul and the Gift*, 531.
102. Barclay, *Paul and the Gift*, 572.

tion that Paul's contemporaries believed that through works they could establish their own righteousness before God paved the way for prejudicial accounts of Judaism as a religion of legalism.[103] Yet, at least in the process of their assault upon theologies of merit and polemic against works-righteousness, the Reformers insisted loudly and correctly that Paul's phrase the "works of the law" refers to the whole law. To return to their polemic today would be a profound mistake, but to hear their voices afresh as a much-needed corrective to dominant contemporary concerns is vital and necessary. Both the content of Paul's texts and the all-embracing nature of the law as a way of life within Judaism suggest a broader focus for the term the "works of the law" than an exclusive concern with boundary-marking will allow.[104]

8.7. Conclusions

Contemporary Pauline scholarship characteristically misunderstands its relationship with Reformation exegesis in ways that are rhetorically convenient. This allows the Reformers to serve as a dark backdrop of misinterpretation against which the light of contemporary insights can shine all the more brightly. Yet—while any sober historical account must conclude that there are very significant ways in which the Reformers are indeed in error—the reality of the relationship is far more complex and interesting than might otherwise be concluded:

1. Dominant contemporary treatments of Paul's anthropology under the rubric of apocalyptic dualism depend in significant but often unacknowledged ways upon exegetical conclusions championed by the Reformers about the meaning of key terms. Far from standing

---

103. In *On the Jews and their Lies*, published in 1543, Luther utters intentional, vicious, and completely indefensible slanders against Judaism, but he attacks Jews less on the grounds of works-righteousness than that of perceived misanthropy. See *LW* 47:121–306 = *WA* 53:412–552.

104. Relevant here also is Paul's contrasting of his gospel with Gentile culture in 1 Cor 1:26–29. No one may boast before God on the grounds of education, power, or noble birth. The Gentile context of course means that "the works of the law" are not under discussion here, but across his letters Paul sets the gospel against many and varied aspects of human worthiness. It would actually be a little odd if nowhere in his letters did he contrast it with human ethical achievement.

against the majority report of contemporary scholarship, the Reformers here provide its foundation. This should not be obscured by the fact that they were also influential in relation to previously rejected accounts of Paul's anthropology (e.g., Bultmann) that were more typically labelled "Lutheran." Although not every contemporary perspective reflects the Reformers' influence, these dominant strands in recent discussions of Paul's anthropology contrast with each other but nevertheless form a dispute *within* a trajectory of interpretation stemming from the Reformation.

2. In what has come to be known as the "apocalyptic" interpretation of Paul in contrast to those that emphasize "covenantal" or "salvation-historical" categories, the soteriological priority placed by the Reformers upon divine initiative has been intensified or perfected. Other interpretative elements or motifs, including several of great significance to the Reformers themselves, are marginalized so that divine initiative may be preserved in what is perceived to be the purest possible form. The sheer puzzlement with which the Reformers are received as interpreters of Paul in the work of Campbell provides the clearest example of this. In "covenantal" interpretations of Paul a similar pattern can be discerned. In the work of Wright the important position occupied by the category of covenant within the Reformed tradition is intensified to such an extent that other important elements in Paul (e.g., justification by faith) must be interpreted very largely in covenantal terms. Alongside other figures from the history of reception, careful attention to the exegesis of the Reformers can enable us to hear notes in Paul currently muted by our intensification or perfection of particular themes.

3. In relation to the introspective conscience, NPP scholarship typically misunderstands its relationship to Reformation exegesis, mischaracterizing this relationship as one of opposition. The Reformers often reach the same exegetical conclusions about texts relevant to discussion of the conscience as did Stendahl. Although the Reformers do expect that an awareness of sin will often experientially precede acceptance of the gospel, they do not establish this as a norm. With the possible partial exception of Melanchthon, they also do not believe that a struggle with a guilty conscience was experienced by Paul prior to his encounter on the Damascus Road with the risen Christ. Nor do they assume a struggle with a guilty conscience to be typical of Jewish engagement with the law.

4. The NPP does represent a very significant advance in its portrayal of Judaism. Former descriptions of Second Temple Judaism as a religion centrally concerned with earning righteousness were a distortion and the exegesis of the Reformers lay at the historical roots of this distortion. Their interpretation of Paul's contrasts between the law and his gospel almost exclusively in terms of self-achieved works-righteousness is unconvincing. It pays too little attention to the significance for Paul of issues of Jewish practice. Yet NPP scholarship simply perpetuates the opposite error. A theoretical acknowledgment that the phrase the "works of the law" denotes the whole complex of conduct required by the law is coupled with an actual insistence that Paul's concern is always with the boundary-defining function of such works. This boundary-defining function is indeed important, but the exclusive emphasis upon it does not do justice to the multi-faceted and all-embracing nature of the conduct required by the law. In Paul's Jewish context, righteous behavior was synonymous with a nomistic Jewish way of life and sinful behavior with a Gentile way of life. To say that justification does not result from human ethical achievement coheres with and is an inevitable consequence of saying that it does not result from Jewish ethnic identity. Paul is not always concerned with human ethical achievement, but in those texts where it does arise (e.g., Rom 4:4–5; 9:10–13; Phil 3:6) he means what he appears to say.

9 Righteousness in Christ

Towards the Reconciliation of the Perspectives

9.1. Staging the Dialog between the Sixteenth and Twenty-First Centuries

As identified at the outset of the previous chapter, the third broad area of criticism directed at the Reformers in contemporary Pauline scholarship concerns justification. Yet to explore this is no easy matter, for the current debate about justification by faith in Paul is thoroughly confused and confusing. Students of Paul are faced with a bewildering variety of opinions that make it difficult to frame alternatives, let alone decide between them. For previous generations in the twentieth century the lines of debate between Protestant and Roman Catholic were generally clear, even if sometimes simplified into justification as God declaring righteous (Protestant) versus justification as God making righteous (Roman Catholic). The complexity of the current situation stems from the way in which this earlier debate has been overlaid in recent decades by various proposals that the heart of justification is the declaration that persons are members of God's single family irrespective of ethnic identity, or that in varying degrees and ways justification should be understood as participatory, taking its force from Paul's language of union with Christ and perhaps even appropriately to be termed as *theosis* or divinization. Still, what is clear in contemporary scholarship is the widespread rejection of accounts of justification that could be characterized as a cold legal fiction in which the believer is left basically unchanged by an event that is essentially transactional or even contractual in nature. Whether or not this characterization is entirely fair, it is most often aimed at accounts that uphold the significance of the concept of imputation in justification. Despite the continued advocacy of imputation in some conservative evangelical circles,[1] the notion that on account of their faith in Christ's sin-bearing death the righteousness of Christ is transferred to believers has lost currency.

These rejected views are often directly associated with the Reformers in general or with Luther in particular. Yet as Grant Macaskill observes, "biblical scholars have all too often traded on 'received' accounts of the theology in question: how many of the studies that have casually dismissed 'Lutheranism' have actually examined the writings of Luther or the Lutheran tradition in any depth?"[2] As we have seen, these caricatures of theologies of justification in fact correspond only very partially to the views of Melanchthon, but fail to do justice to the strongly relational aspects of his approach. In regard to Luther and Calvin, they miss the mark entirely, for the accounts of justification offered by both men obviate any notion of a legal fiction or a contractual emphasis by connecting justification with participation in Christ in profoundly significant ways. And while they freely use the term "imputation" they do not intend by it a *transfer* or passing of righteousness from Christ to the believer but rather a crucial aspect of what it means to be united with Christ. Somewhat ironically, therefore, justification is an aspect of Pauline interpretation where potential might be discerned for exegetical insights drawn from the Reformers to enhance and strengthen, rather than contradict, NPP discussions of the theme.[3]

Exploring and exploiting this potential requires the careful staging of a dialog between sixteenth- and twenty-first-century interpretations. This involves attention to the specifics of interpretation. It would

---

1. See Don A. Carson, "The Vindication of Imputation: On Fields of Discourse and Semantic Fields," in *Justification: What's at Stake in the Current Debates?*, ed. Mark Husbands and Daniel J. Treier (Downers Grove, IL: InterVarsity Press, 2004), 46–78. It should be noted, however, that Carson's defense of imputation does not defend the idea of a transfer of righteousness abstracted from union with Christ and in fact explicitly rejects any notion of transfer apart from being included in Christ (72), i.e., Carson's use of the term "imputation" is rather closer to that of Luther and Calvin than it is to the uses of the term to which those who wish to reject imputation object.

2. Macaskill, *Union with Christ in the New Testament*, 4.

3. This project has already been pursued to some effect, although largely without direct attention to the exegesis of the Reformers, by Bird in *The Saving Righteousness of God*, referred to by Scot McKnight in his endorsement on the cover of the volume as "a peace plan" for "traditional reformation theology and the New Perspective."

of course be absurd simply to say, for example, that Luther and Calvin emphasize participation in relation to justification, that several contemporary interpreters do likewise, and that therefore their positions on justification are all essentially the same by virtue of all being participatory. This would ignore a whole host of significant factors: (1) Luther's and Calvin's positions are certainly not identical to each other and yet they were part of a paradigm shift that resulted in a new exegetical grammar of Pauline theology, (2) participation in Christ is itself a complex concept, capable of explanation in various and not necessarily compatible ways, (3) interpreters are always involved in complex discernments of the overall shape of Pauline theology so that how the concept of participation is related to other elements may be just as crucial as what is said about participation itself, and (4) as we have seen with "imputation," the meaning of a term may itself change over time. What is therefore needed first is a critical discernment that, even if it is not the only possible one, identifies ways in which Luther's and Calvin's particular patterns of relating justification and participation have gifts to offer to contemporary interpretation. These conclusions need then to be brought into dialog not with abstract generalizations about contemporary interpretation but with the exegetical conclusions of distinguished NPP interpreters. How could the resources offered by the Reformers serve to question or strengthen these contemporary interpretations? In selecting these contemporary interpreters, careful attention will be paid to the process of interpretation. In the first chapter of this book when exploring the hermeneutical nature and goals of a project in reception history that seeks to make available to contemporary interpreters of Paul resources from a crucial past era in that history, I argued for a mixed hermeneutic. This mixed hermeneutic employs the combined criteria of historical plausibility, canonical consistency, and contemporary theological fruitfulness. It is those contemporary interpreters in whose work, even if they do not espouse such a hermeneutic themselves, these criteria find various forms of expression that will be suitable for the purposes of dialog. It is those who are concerned to understand how the crucial theological and soteriological themes of the Pauline texts cohere, how they relate to the rest of Scripture, and their significance for today, with whom it will be fruitful to compare the insights of the Reformers.

9.2. The Gifts of Reformation Exegesis for Contemporary Pauline Theology

Earlier in this book we charted among the Reformers the development of a remarkably coherent new grammar of Pauline exegesis that structured conversation about the interpretation of the Pauline texts (Part II "Shared Convictions: The Reformers' New Pauline Exegetical Grammar"). We also explored, within the framework provided by this exegetical grammar, the rather different ways in which major figures interpret the christological focus of the Pauline texts and express this in their teaching concerning justification (Part III "Individual Perspectives: Luther, Melanchthon, and Calvin on Righteousness in Christ"). It should therefore come as no surprise that in relation to justification itself we find a similar pattern. There is no single Reformation concept or doctrine of justification, but there are shared features of early Protestant treatments of justification that provide a unified framework or structure within which differences occur. Luther and Calvin both make union with Christ central to justification whereas Melanchthon does not, but the particular textures of union with Christ in justification that Luther and Calvin discern on the basis of the Pauline texts owe much to the unified structure or interpretative framework to which they all adhere. The fact that Luther and Calvin respond so powerfully to the theme of participation in Christ as integral to justification marks them out as the more profound exegetes among the trio, but attention must also be paid to the framework they share with Melanchthon and others. It is not simply the strength of Luther's and Calvin's emphasis on union with Christ in justification that is of potential value for twenty-first century interpretation but the fact that it occurs within a shared early Protestant framework. This framework serves to structure Luther's and Calvin's accounts of union with Christ in justification and does so in ways that are distinctive and helpful in relation to contemporary accounts of union with Christ and justification by faith.

In relation to justification the framework shared across early Protestant accounts emphasizes its extrinsic nature (see 5.1). The perfect righteousness granted to the believer in justification is alien: it remains wholly and entirely that of Christ. It is received by faith through the preaching of the biblical word, with those who believe drawn out of themselves and into total reliance on the promises of God. People do not encounter God by looking inwards but instead they encounter God as the convicting power of the word turns them outwards towards Christ. The believer will experience ethical transformation, but such transformation does not form part of the basis of justification before God. It is in this relentless external emphasis, in the insistence that God encounters people in justification only outside of themselves and that the righteousness of Christ remains an alien righteousness, where the particular value resides for contemporary Pauline interpreters of early Reformation exegesis. To many this will seem a surprising claim, for an external emphasis appears to risk all the failings commonly associated with Protestant accounts of justification. Is it not when justification remains external that it becomes a legal fiction separated from the transformation that Paul so clearly expects in the lives of believers? Is it not when justification remains external that it becomes contractual, with faith filling the role of a human disposition that satisfies a divine requirement?

It is at this point that union with Christ is especially vital. The claim that the external emphasis is of particular contemporary value only holds true if union with Christ is treated as integral to justification. Melanchthon's account of justification is often unfairly derided for offering a fictional, contractual perspective, but it is precisely the failure to treat union with Christ as integral to justification that lays him open to the charge.[4] Even if he avoids these theological pitfalls himself, it is possible to see how his account could degenerate in the hands of lesser interpreters to the point where these negative characterizations are apt. In contrast, in the hands of exegetes such as Luther and Calvin, who do make union with Christ integral to justification, these dangers are averted. Justification is not a legal fiction. This is evident in Luther's conviction that, although righteousness remains alien to the believer, it is essential that the believer lives an alien life and in Calvin's insistence that, alongside justification, sanctification is one of the simultaneous twin key aspects of union with Christ. Neither is justification contractual. The focus of both Reformers is christological and not contractual. Far from holding that faith justifies because it is the right kind of religious disposition to fulfill the human side of a contract with God, both insist that faith justifies

---

4. I find the account of Melanchthon offered in Campbell, *The Deliverance of God*, 258–61, one-sided in its negative assessment and misleading in its implicit claim that Melanchthon understood Luther's thought better than Luther himself: "Melanchthon is a faithful tradent of Luther's initial insights, in certain senses greatly clarifying the position of his theological master" (261). Yet it is not for nothing that Campbell finds in Melanchthon a consistent advocate of the "Justification Theory" that he constructs as an abstract representation of error in Pauline interpretation.

because it grasps hold of Christ and unites the believer with him. This treatment of union with Christ as integral to justification prevents the emphasis of the Reformers upon the extrinsic, alien nature of the righteousness received by believers from leading into fictional or contractual accounts. When protected in this way, the external emphasis is left free to deliver considerable theological benefits.

Such theological benefits abound because the Reformers' external emphasis connects union with Christ so clearly to Paul's theology of grace. In Rom 6:7 those who have died with Christ will rise with him because in so dying they have been justified from sin.[5] Sin, which reigns in death, has as its opposing and conquering power grace that, in contrast, exercises dominion "through righteousness" (Rom 5:21). Righteousness here is clearly the gift of righteousness discussed in Rom 5:16-19,[6] and previously "we encountered the phrase διὰ δικαιοσύνης ('through righteousness') in 4:13, in reference to Abraham's descendants who would inherit the promises not through law but 'through righteousness of faith.' The phrase does not occur elsewhere in the NT."[7] In other words, the righteousness through which grace reigns certainly includes justification, which is indeed by faith, and precisely as such is to be identified with dying with Christ in baptism and not contrasted with it. Given that the argument of Romans unfolds in this manner, any adequate account of union with Christ must be placed in the context of this reign of grace. Grace is here a power and carries demands, and it is in Christ Jesus that believers are dead to sin and alive to God (Rom 6:11). Yet it is precisely in living the resurrection life of Christ and not their own lives, which have to die, that believers fulfill these demands and obligations. Their new lives are continually externally sourced, "wholly dependent on the life of Another, the One who is risen from the dead" and it cannot be otherwise given that resurrection remains a future hope and believers still have mortal bodies that will die (6:12).[8] This continuous external dependence allows grace to

---

5. English translations often here unhelpfully translate the verb δεδικαίωται as "has been set free." To be justified is indeed to be set free from the dominion of sin but the translation helps to obscure the unfolding of the argument of the letter and the connections between its themes. See 9.5 for further discussion of this problem.

6. Thomas Schreiner, *Romans*, BECNT (Grand Rapids: Baker, 1998), 296.

7. Robert Jewett, *Romans*, Hermeneia (Minneapolis: Fortress, 2007), 389.

8. John M. G. Barclay, "Under Grace: The Christ-Gift and the Construction of a Christian *Habitus*," in *Apocalyptic Paul: Cosmos and Anthropos in Romans 5-8*, ed. Beverly R. Gaventa (Waco: Baylor University Press, 2013), 65. Barclay's argument is now also

carry demands without compromising its nature as grace: "the obligation now incumbent on believers is not to 'gain' grace (or salvation), nor to win another installment of grace: there is a single χάρισμα of eternal life (6:23) which runs from Christ-event to eternity (cf. 8:32)."[9]

The placing by Paul of union with Christ in justification in the context of the reign of grace receives little attention in some of the most prominent works of NPP scholarship. For example, in Wright's *Paul and the Faithfulness of God*, the longest ever published work of Pauline theology, grace does not even appear in the subject index. In James Dunn's *Theology of Paul the Apostle* it receives only brief discussion.[10] This is not because NPP scholars are unaware of the importance of grace in the Pauline texts but it is perhaps instead due to the assumption that, since Judaism is a religion of grace, Paul's views on the topic are simply typical of his contemporaries. Yet while the aversion reflected in this assumption to anachronistic portrayals of Second Temple Judaism as devoid of grace is to be applauded, in Paul's gospel grace has particular patterns.[11] Grace is shaped differently when it is defined by how God has acted in Jesus Christ and grace is shaped differently when its reign over individuals and communities involves union with Christ in justification. In emphasizing the external nature of justification while still making union with Christ integral to justification, Luther and Calvin, in their different ways, offer to contemporary interpreters several means of explicating this distinctive nature of Pauline grace:

1. The external nature of justification explains why the union of believers with Christ does not simply deconstruct in the face of continued Christian sinfulness. It has often been observed that Paul knows full well that, living in the overlap of two ages, those to whom he writes continue to sin but that this does not lead him to doubt

---

expressed in his *Paul and the Gift* (Grand Rapids: Eerdmans, 2015), esp. 493–519, that places his treatment of Rom 5–8 in a wider context. However, "Under Grace" remains helpful for its detailed engagement with texts.

9. Barclay, "Under Grace," 73.

10. James D. G. Dunn, *The Theology of Paul the Apostle* (Grand Rapids: Eerdmans, 1998), 319–23.

11. Barclay, "Pure Grace?," 4–20, argues that Paul expresses a distinctive Jewish theology of grace that is different from other contemporary Jewish reflections upon the nature of grace. See also Barclay, *Paul and the Gift*, 565: "grace is everywhere in the theology of Second Temple Judaism, but not everywhere the same."

their ultimate acceptance by God. Even when Paul expresses the view that wrongdoers will not inherit the kingdom of God (1 Cor 6:9), he immediately describes his readers as those no longer in this position (1 Cor 6:11). Indeed, it is his eschatological confidence that as saints his readers will judge the world (1 Cor 6:2), not any fear that they will lose the opportunity to do so, that forms part of the basis for his objection to their current behavior in bringing legal cases against one another. The explanation for this confidence on Paul's part is not any thought that God will indulge sin. It is rather that, because believers are united with Christ in justification, his death and resurrection are continuously present realities that deal with sin. Because of these realities, believers are able to stand under grace (Rom 5:2). The crucifixion of the believer *with* Christ that is so central to union with Christ in justification for Paul is not to be understood apart from an equally strong emphasis on the fact that Christ's death is *for* us: "I have been crucified *with* Christ . . . who loved me and gave himself *for* me" (Gal 2:19–20).

2. That justification continues to provide believers with an alien righteousness also successfully captures an important aspect of the apocalyptic nature of Pauline theology. The invasive grace of justification is not rightly understood if justification is conceived exclusively as the crucial event that initiates the journey of the Christian life. Justification certainly is the genesis of the Christian life and that life certainly is a journey away from sin: Paul "expects that the *moral* incongruity at the start of the Christian life will be reduced over time, as the believers' slavery to righteousness draws them towards holiness ([Rom] 6:19)."[12] Yet the union with Christ involved in justification retains its dynamic character as event such that the believer is continually set free and the initial liberating event is a continuously present reality. The event of justification does not simply yield or lead to something else. Justification not only was an apocalyptic event but continues to remain an apocalyptic event. Believers do not journey away from the apocalypse of Jesus Christ but are borne along by it. God's invasive grace in Christ is the flood upon which the ark of the Christian life floats. In their accounts of union with Christ, Luther and Calvin are passionately concerned with the transformation of believers. However, this and the con-

---

12. Barclay, "Under Grace," 73.

tinuing nature of justification as event are conceptualized together. As Barclay writes of Galatians, "Without this constant present time, of gift and demand, the church becomes merely the bearer of a new tradition, playing out her part in a narrative whose turning point is long in the past. But for Paul the decisive event is always now: Will Christ be formed in you (4:19)?"[13] Because Christ has been raised from the dead, his cross is a continuously disruptive, fracturing presence.

3. The external emphasis in Luther's and Calvin's accounts of justification brings assurance of forgiveness for the sins of believers. When rightly understood, this emphasis also counters any temptation to treat grace either as a possession or as an object of consumption. Assurance is possible only and precisely because the righteousness granted is not the believer's own, and does not become the believer's own, but remains that of Christ with whom the believer is united. There is a new creation continually resourced from the life of the risen Christ, the miraculous appearance of which requires the death of the self (Rom 6:6; Gal 2:19-20). This "is not some reformation of the self, or some newly discovered technique in self-mastery; it is an ectopic phenomenon, drawing on the 'life from the dead' that began with Jesus' resurrection."[14] To grasp the permanently alien nature of new life in Christ involves rejection both of any temptation to superiority in which "the religious person sees himself as an exception to sinful human possibilities, claiming a perceivable nearness to God,"[15] and of any claim to autonomy or the capacity for the self to remake identity according to personal preferences.

4. Even as these dangers are avoided, the manner in which new creation is conceived as a miracle of divine grace unceasingly and exclusively reliant upon union with Christ in the power of the Spirit nevertheless requires a transformation in behavior without which faith is not authentic. As Luther puts it, "Paul's view is this: Faith

---

13. John M. G. Barclay, "Paul's Story: Theology as Testimony," in *Narrative Dynamics in Paul: A Critical Assessment*, ed. B.W. Longenecker (Louisville: Westminster John Knox, 2002), 146.

14. Barclay, "Under Grace," 65.

15. Eberhard Busch, *Karl Barth and the Pietists: The Young Karl Barth's Critique of Pietism and Its Response*, trans. Daniel W. Bloesch (Downers Grove, IL: InterVarsity Press, 2004), 84.

is active in love, that is, that faith justifies which expresses itself in acts."[16] Justification is by faith and not by deeds, but any notion of a passive, inactive faith is simply a contradiction in terms. Works of love either remain a constitutive part of justification (but not its basis, so Luther) or are distinguished from justification but are nevertheless intimately and inseparably connected to justification (so Calvin). Everyday practice therefore continues to be of profound significance, and is given a sociological pattern by the continuous and intensive dependence of the believer upon the crucified and risen Christ. In Luther's and Calvin's own contexts all kinds of complex relationships to power impacted their attempts to express this pattern, but at their best they perceived clearly the attack on all normal human notions of worth and worthiness inherent in being united by faith with a crucified and risen messiah. As Luther comments on Gal 5:6, "it is true faith toward God, which loves and helps one's neighbor—regardless of whether the neighbor is a servant, a master, a king, a pope, a man, a woman; one who wears purple, one who wears rags, one who eats meat, or one who eats fish."[17] This is rooted in texts like Rom 5:6–8 which speak of divine grace and of God's love for sinners, expressed in the cross of Christ. In contrast to merely human or fleshly love, divine love is oriented not towards what is good and lovable, but instead towards what is bad or evil, and gives itself in spite of the unlovable nature of its object. Thus, NPP scholarship is right to insist that simply to identify Paul's gospel as incompatible with individual attempts to earn salvation represents an intolerable narrowing and that there must be a sociological dimension to justification. It is also right to insist that this dimension cuts against all forms of ethnocentrism. What NPP scholarship is able less often to perceive is that this focus is itself also too narrow and fails to fully express the shattering impact on human values and practices of the conviction that in Christ a gracious God justifies the ungodly (Rom 4:5; 5:6).[18]

---

16. *LW* 54:74 = *WA* TR 1:199, 10–12 (no. 458).

17. *LW* 27:31 = *WA* 40.2:38, 27–31. See 7.9 for Calvin critiquing the contemptuous giving of alms and demanding that the rich be prepared to live in community with the poor.

18. On the contemporary sociological potential of justification, see especially Barclay, "Pure Grace?," 17: "If God's action in Christ is the sole source of symbolic capital, the regnant systems of worth lose their authority, and communities can be founded that sit loose to, and even contradict, the goals and values of normal society."

371

5. This has profound ecclesiological consequences. On the one hand, all of Paul's ideas are always directed towards the social practice of the church. The deep desire within contemporary scholarship to correct the excessive concern with self-understanding in existential accounts of Pauline theology is anything but misplaced. We must be deeply engaged with what we can learn about the formation of early Christian communities and the patterns of their common life. For, "what grace creates *ex nihilo* by raising humankind from the dead is not a mere empty space, an *absence*. . . . [A]n account of God's revelatory self-presence must necessarily be completed by an account of the church which is the first fruit of God's utterance . . . a community which engages in visible acts."[19] If grace is to be at all tangible, there must be the community of the church with its identifiable culture, tradition, and practices. Yet on the other hand if the church really is created by the grace of God expressed in a crucified and risen messiah, then it will live "a common life centered on a confession which subverts."[20] The church all too quickly degenerates into simply another human society if it forgets that its "being is characterized by externality: it is 'ectopic' because its 'place' is in the being and act of the communicative God of the gospel."[21] The people of God are delivered *into* fragility, instability, and exile as they attempt to instantiate in social practice the (humanly speaking) impossible task of loving all that is unlovable.

6. This external character of the being of the church, its righteousness continuously constituted solely by union with Christ in justification, points to the fact that its existence is not self-generated but depends on faith elicited by the proclaimed word of God. The church is the church of the word (not Scripture the word of the church) and all the attempts of the church to practice righteousness in a common life result from receiving "the word of faith which we proclaim" (τὸ ῥῆμα τῆς πίστεως ὃ κῆρυσσομεν, Rom 10:8). While protests against a sterile separation between theology and ethics in Pauline studies are entirely legitimate, they subvert their own aspiration to the integration of the two if the result is the neglect of Paul's emphasis on

---

19. John Webster, *Holy Scripture: A Dogmatic Sketch* (Cambridge: Cambridge University Press, 2003), 71.

20. Webster, *Holy Scripture*, 57.

21. Webster, *Holy Scripture*, 47.

proclamation. Far from regarding a focus on the distinctive social practices of early Christian communities and a focus on a theology of the faith-eliciting word of God as opposites, Pauline scholarship would be better served by treating them as correlates. Paul has no difficulty in articulating such a theology of the word (e.g., Rom 10:6–21; 1 Cor 1:17–24; Gal 3:1–5) precisely in contexts in which he cares passionately about which practices his readers adopt. Here the limitations of the Reformers' understanding of Judaism mean that they only partially hear the full import of their own theology of grace. While they certainly cannot be accused of failing to impact the social practices of the church in their own context on the basis of their theology of justification, we have seen neglect in their exegesis of the full significance for Paul of questions of Jewish practice. Yet to attempt to put that right by attending little to what the Pauline texts say about the faith-eliciting proclamation of the gospel will have results that are just as one-sided.[22]

Luther and Calvin thus provide several potentially significant resources for Pauline theology in their distinctively extrinsic account of justification and the particular contours this gives to union with Christ and vice versa. This ensures a simultaneous and equal emphasis in the economy of salvation on: 1) the complete sufficiency of divine grace and its radical disregard of normal human accounts of worth, and 2) the transformation of believers and the significance of the church. Both are essential, for if an account of justification is offered that is extrinsic without union with Christ being made central, the familiar results are legal fictions and contractual overtones. Yet if an account of justification is offered in which union with Christ is central but there is little or no extrinsic emphasis, the result is just as serious: what Luther would disparagingly term theologies of glory. What is important is not simply that Luther and Calvin emphasize union with Christ but how they do so within a coherent overall

---

22. See Philip G. Ziegler, "Some Remarks on Apocalyptic in Modern Christian Theology," in *Paul and the Apocalyptic Imagination*, ed. Ben C. Blackwell, John K. Goodrich, and Jason Matson (Minneapolis: Fortress, 2016), 199–216: "A Christian theology funded by a fresh hearing of New Testament apocalyptic will acknowledge that it is the world and not the church which is the object of divine salvation. It will thus conceive of the church as a provisional pilgrim community created by the effective announcement of the Gospel for the sake of the world. Both individually and corporately, the Christian life is chiefly to be understood as discipleship" (214).

account of what the Pauline texts have to say about union with Christ and justification by faith. Yet, of course, alongside these very strong shared elements we have also seen that each constructs a synthesis that has some important differences from that of the other and the exercise of comparing the two can also be instructive for contemporary interpretation. As identified in earlier chapters, Luther does not clearly distinguish between justification and sanctification, but treats justification as a lifelong process to which the non-meritorious works of the believer are integral (see 5.7 and 5.8). Calvin instead distinguishes quite sharply between justification and sanctification as the twin principal saving benefits received by the believer in union with Christ (see 7.2 and 7.3).

Each of these procedures has a characteristic difficulty or limitation. For Luther, the works of the believer are always spontaneous and free, deriving from a life now orientated outwards towards God and neighbor in gratitude for the complete and inexhaustible gift of new life in Christ. He is drawn always to organic metaphors for the Christian life lived well: as good trees believers simply will now bear good fruit. It is a joyful vision and not without its basis in the Pauline texts, particularly when the concept of fruit-bearing is applied to the lives of believers (Rom 6:22; 7:4; Gal 5:22; Eph. 5:9; Phil 1:11; Col. 1:10). Yet Luther struggles more in accounting for texts in which good works are discussed in terms of obligations laid upon believers by the gift of salvation. For Luther, the believer certainly has such obligations but they exist within a framework of eagerness and love and it is precisely in order to explain this "righteousness of works" that he conceives of gratuitous necessity / the necessity of unalterable condition in which the works of the believer arise more or less spontaneously (see 6.8). On Calvin's part, the distinction between justification and sanctification enables him to conceptualize the obligations that the gift of salvation brings to the believer more straightforwardly as external demands. To these demands the believer must respond and the extrinsic emphasis that believers must look only outside of themselves, so strong in relation to justification, is not so clearly applied to sanctification. The challenge faced by this procedure is whether the sharpness of Calvin's distinction between justification and sanctification is exegetically sustainable. Calvin argues that although Romans 5 "touches on the fruits and effects of the righteousness of faith,"[23] it is almost entirely concerned with continuing the explanation of justification by faith given through

23. *Comm. Rom,* "Theme of the Epistle," *CNTC* 8:7 = *OE* 13:9, 16.

discussion of the figure of Abraham in the previous chapter. In Rom 6 Paul "turns to discuss the sanctification which we obtain in Christ."[24] The difficulty, of course, is whether Paul's argument really reflects such a clear-cut distinction. Despite the prevalence of the noun "righteousness" (δικαιοσύνη) in both chapters (5:16–21; 6:13–20), a defense of Calvin can argue that a shift is signaled by the mention of "newness of life" (ἐν καινότητι ζωῆς) in 6:4 and "sanctification" (ἁγιασμός) in 6:19, 22. But, as identified in my description above of the flow of the argument of Rom 5–6, the appearance of the verb "justify" (δικαιόω) in 6:7 seems directly to identify with justification the preceding discussion of dying with Christ in baptism rather than identifying this discussion simply with the mortification of the flesh in sanctification.[25]

These comparisons helpfully establish an important question for Pauline interpreters. Luther sustains the external emphasis that we identified as so vital in Reformation accounts of justification by treating the satisfaction of the obligations of believers to God largely in organic terms. Calvin can instead treat such obligations as divine demands, to which believers must decide to respond, but then sustains the external emphasis in justification by distinguishing sharply between it and sanctification. Is there a way to maintain an appropriate external emphasis without either treating obligations to God largely in organic terms or distinguishing between justification and sanctification more definitively than is exegetically warranted? The recent work of Barclay points towards such a possibility. Drawing on ancient notions of gift, Barclay notes that gifts in the ancient world were usually understood as strongly obligating the recipients to their benefactors. Further, givers in the ancient world were expected to bestow gifts on worthy recipients able to make good use of them in fulfillment of the obligations entailed. What Paul says about the Christ-gift is culturally shocking in that God selects as recipients the unfitting, the unworthy, and the ungodly, but also culturally unexceptional in that Paul too thinks of a gift as strongly obligating. The intention of the gift is frustrated if concrete obedience in deeds does not follow. Yet, precisely because the recipients are so unfitting, it is only in utter dependence on the gift, i.e., in union with Christ, that the obligations entailed

---

24. *Comm. Rom*, "Theme of the Epistle," *CNTC* 8:7 = *OE* 13:9, 25–26.

25. For a defense of a clear distinction between justification and transformation, see Bird, *The Saving Righteousness of God*, 12–18. For the opposite view, see Michael J. Gorman, *Inhabiting the Cruciform God: Kenosis, Justification, and Theosis in Paul's Narrative Soteriology* (Grand Rapids: Eerdmans, 2009), 73–79.

can be fulfilled. The presence of such strong obligations thus in no way indicates that the Christ-gift ceases to be a gift or that believers are no longer externally dependent on this gift, which supplies in perfect form what they cannot possibly ever supply for themselves:

> The final justification / vindication of the believers is not a separate divine decision, nor a second "stage" in a multi-stage narrative with different conditions operative at different points, nor even a second focal point in an ellipse. This gift begins—shockingly—as a gift to the unworthy, the unfitting and wholly unsuitable; this is "creation out of nothing" (Rom 4:17; 1 Cor 1:28), without prior condition, and nothing that results from it (in the obedience and holiness of the believer) could ever constitute a reason or basis for this saving gift. Indeed, this is the source and origin of the very existence of the believer, everything that is thereafter the case "in Christ" is a product of this unfitting gift: in that sense the gift does not only *begin* as an unfitting gift, but *remains* as such forever, even when the "fruit of the Spirit" begins to "fit" the recipient to the giver. But this gift has a shape and a purpose, and will finally be completed (as gift) in the full transformation of fitting recipients. These will be made fully fitting only at the day of the Lord, when they will be presented "blameless" and given imperishable bodies, but God is already at work in them in this life to press them towards that "fit," a work which is also theirs at the same time as it is God's (Phil 2:15-16).[26]

Believers therefore have a responsibility to make their lives fit the gift. The greater the fit, the greater will be the commendation of the believer at the last judgment. The less there is a fit, the more the believer will experience shame. The works of the believer matter greatly, but they

---

26. John M. G. Barclay, "Believers and the 'Last Judgment' in Paul: Rethinking Grace and Recompense," in *Eschatologie = Eschatology: The Sixth Durham-Tübingen Research Symposium, Eschatology in Old Testament, Ancient Judaism and Early Christianity*, ed. Hans Joachim Eckstein, Christof Landmesser, and Hermann Lichtenberger (Tübingen: Mohr Siebeck, 2011), 195-208 (esp. 207-8). See also Barclay, *Paul and the Gift*, 569: "The transformative power of grace thus creates a fit between believers and God, which will be evident at the eschaton. Judgment 'according to works' does not entail a new and incompatible principle of soteriology: it indicates that the incongruous gift has its intended effect in embedding new standards of worth in the practice of those it transforms."

do so in making the gift fitting and not in some alternative way inconsistent with the nature of gift that reintroduces notions of merit or their equivalents as among the causes of justification. Barclay is striving towards a strong account of the obedience of the believer that integrates the works undertaken into the single and complete gift of God in Christ, but does so without thinking of these works solely in organic terms. Unconcern with obedience would signify repudiation of the gift, whereas the believer's pursuit of obedient works expresses its acceptance and the desire to remain in the "kindness of God" (Rom 11:22). In so doing, Barclay is acutely aware of the relationship between his own proposals and Reformation debates concerning similar themes.[27] The creativity of Barclay's proposals demonstrates the benefits of thinking with past interpreters about contemporary Pauline interpretation. He neither simply reproduces nor repudiates earlier figures but formulates new proposals enabled both by original research concerning the ancient world and by critical engagement with the exegesis of earlier Pauline interpreters.

9.3. Reformation Exegesis and NPP Scholarship: Richard Hays and the Faith of Jesus Christ

If Barclay provides us with an example of a sympathetic critic, in fundamental agreement with various aspects of the NPP but still in important ways finding the exegesis of Luther and Calvin valuable as a resource for contemporary interpretation, what of those who have not regarded Reformation exegesis as such a resource? An influential study that fits this category, but which nevertheless attempts to grasp the coherence of soteriological themes in the Pauline texts, their relationship to the rest of Scripture, and their significance for today, is the monograph *The Faith of Jesus Christ* by Richard Hays. The book is famous for popularizing among Pauline scholars in the English-speaking world the subjective translation ("the faithfulness of Christ") rather than the objective translation ("faith in Christ") of Paul's genitive phrase πίστις Χριστοῦ.[28] Yet for Hays him-

---

27. See Barclay, *Paul and the Gift*, 97–129, for his discussions of Luther and Calvin.

28. Those unfamiliar with the debate can grasp its essential nature by considering the following English sentence: "Robert did it for the love of Mary." It is not clear whether Robert acted because of Mary's love for him or because of his love for Mary. The ambiguity arises because the genitive phrase "the love of Mary" could be subjective (Mary's love for Robert) or objective (Robert's love for Mary). The ambiguity in Greek

self the main argument of the book is the rather wider one that "*a story about Jesus Christ is presupposed by Paul's argument in Galatians, and his theological reflection attempts to articulate the meaning of that story.*"[29] Although Paul writes within an epistolary genre, narrative is essential to his theology. In arguing this, Hays was decisively distancing himself from the work of Rudolf Bultmann and its perceived characteristic danger of stripping away all narrative elements in Paul and so turning the gospel into a message about human decision and human self-understanding in encounter with God's word. Rather, Hays argues, "we know God in no other way than as the God who has acted through the faithfulness of Jesus Christ to 'rescue us from the present evil age' (Gal 1:4)."[30] On this account, participating in Christ's faithfulness becomes the key to Pauline soteriology in general and to justification in particular: "Paul's understanding of the πίστις of Jesus is integrally related to his understanding of δικαιοσύνη."[31]

As Hays makes this wider argument, an interest in canonical consistency is expressed. He is careful to set his narrative project in the context of the wider claim of Hans Frei that "biblical criticism, especially in Germany, had gone astray by failing to grasp the narrative sense of Scripture."[32] Further, the final chapter of the book discusses the relationship between the narrative nature of Pauline theology and other early Christian traditions and writings:

> Paul was less theologically distinctive than is generally supposed—that is, his Christology and soteriology are closely in sync with Hebrews, with the Deutero-Pauline letters, and with the writings usually thought to represent "early catholicism"—and that, despite the near-total absence of synoptic Jesus tradition in Paul's letters, his story-

---

with the phrase πίστις Χριστοῦ is parallel. It could refer to Christ's own faith (subjective genitive) or to the faith of those who believe in him (objective genitive).

29. Richard B. Hays, *The Faith of Jesus Christ: The Narrative Substructure of Galatians 3:1–4:11*, 2nd ed. (Grand Rapids: Eerdmans, 2002), xxiv (his emphasis).

30. Hays, *Faith of Jesus Christ*, xxvi. In "Humanity Prior to the Revelation of Faith," in *Beyond Bultmann: Reckoning a New Testament Theology*, ed. Bruce W. Longenecker and Mikeal C. Parsons (Waco: Baylor, 2014), 61–78, Hays expresses apposite criticisms of Bultmann clearly and succinctly but is disappointingly blind to the provocative and helpful challenges that Bultmann's work poses to contemporary scholarship.

31. Hays, *Faith of Jesus Christ*, xxix.

32. Hays, *Faith of Jesus Christ*, xxv.

grounded preaching marks a point on a historical trajectory towards the composition of written gospel narratives.[33]

In identifying a narrative substructure in Galatians, Hays is therefore exposing something significant to its relationship with other texts within the New Testament canon.

Hays also communicates strong interest in contemporary theological fruitfulness: "the struggles of the church in our times are a result of losing touch with its own gospel story . . . [T]here is too much emphasis on individual faith-experience and not enough grounding of our theological discourse in the story of Jesus Christ."[34] Indeed, attractiveness of theological vision is clearly part of the substantial appeal of Hays's work and he is refreshingly self-aware about this. His theological claims are supported by grammatical arguments about the phrase πίστις Χριστοῦ, but the potential fruitfulness of the wider theological argument also helps to make his preferred translation more compelling. In particular, it enables Hays pejoratively to characterize "faith in Christ" as the "anthropological" translation option (emphasizing the salvific efficacy of the human act of faith) that stands in contrast to the "faithfulness of Christ" as the "christological" option (emphasizing the salvific efficacy of Christ's faithfulness for God's people).[35] As Hays comments, lexicographers inevitably make "*theological* judgments about the meaning of the sentences in which the word πίστις appears."[36]

These interests make Hays a particularly appropriate recent interpreter with whom to bring the exegetical insights of the Reformers into critical dialog. That the Reformers unhesitatingly adopt the objective interpretation of the phrase πίστις Χριστοῦ only increases the aptness of this procedure. Their reasons for doing so are not explored in detail in *The Faith of Jesus Christ*, but as Hays comments: "almost no attention is given to the church's long history of reading Paul, except for occasional sidelong disapproving glances at Luther."[37] Hays regards participation motifs

33. Hays, *Faith of Jesus Christ*, xliii.

34. Hays, *Faith of Jesus Christ*, lii.

35. Hays, *Faith of Jesus Christ*, 277. See Barclay, *Paul and the Gift*, 378–84 (Galatians) and 476–77 (Romans), for summary statements of the objective genitive position that dispute the characterization of the debate in terms of christological versus anthropological translation options.

36. Hays, *Faith of Jesus Christ*, xlvii.

37. Hays, *Faith of Jesus Christ*, xlvii.

in patristic theology as the resource in reception history most likely to be helpful for our understanding of participation in Paul and hopes that "the objective genitive understanding of πίστις Ἰησοῦ Χριστοῦ may be in some respects a modern, or at least post-Reformation, innovation that offers a truncated account of what the broader Christian tradition has heard in Paul's language about 'the faith of Christ.'"[38] At one level this tendency to identify Luther as a source of error simply represents the misunderstanding of the exegesis of the Reformers that is characteristic of so much NPP scholarship. For Luther, who was deeply concerned to clarify that justification does not result from human actions, implicitly to typify an exaggerated concern with the soteriological effectiveness of human decision and individual faith-experience at the expense of the story of Jesus Christ is a travesty. Yet, in Hays's defense, he has clearly read and digested an important essay by the great theologian and Luther scholar Gerhard Ebeling, entitled "Jesus and Faith."[39] Writing in the 1950s, Ebeling is not only interested in the question of Jesus' own faith but, in the course of exploring this, explicitly criticizes what he regards as the Reformers' failure to connect Christology and the doctrine of justification.[40] Melanchthon is named as the supreme instance of this, but it apparently does not occur to Ebeling to look to Luther for resources with which to address the problem he identifies. Ebeling (who was a student of Bultmann) is critical enough of the existential interpretation of the New Testament to be able to explore the issue of the faith of the historical Jesus but does not seem to question to the same degree an existential interpretation of Luther or recognize the significance of participation in Christ for Luther's thought.[41]

In Hays, we therefore have an interpreter whose work appears on the surface to be directly opposed to that of the Reformers, the differ-

38. Hays, *Faith of Jesus Christ*, lii.

39. Gerhard Ebeling, "Jesus and Faith," in *Word and Faith*, trans. J. W. Leitch (Philadelphia: Fortress, 1960), 191-246.

40. Ebeling, "Jesus and Faith," 202-3.

41. Gerhard Ebeling, *Luther: An Introduction to His Thought* (Philadelphia: Fortress, 1970), 168-74, provides a particularly telling example of this neglect of participation in Christ. Ebeling comments that Luther's "real and primary concern is not with the imparting of additional powers to human existence, but with man's becoming something radically new, with a rebirth that includes the end of the old man, and with a change in regards to man's very existence as a person" (168). He then quotes Luther on Gal 2:20 but in expositing how Luther's words are to be understood does not mention union with Christ despite the prominence of the theme in the quotation.

ence over πίστις Χριστοῦ apparently indicative of wider theological differences in the interpretation of the Pauline texts. Yet the realities of the relationship are rather more complicated. Precisely in emphasizing union with Christ, Hays can make the following statement, which, if the account I have offered of their views in this study is even remotely correct, could only be received with agreement by Luther and Calvin:

> We receive salvation insofar as we are united with Christ and belong to him. This has far-reaching implications. . . . For one thing, a participatory soteriology ensures that salvation always has an *ecclesial* character: we are not saved as solitary individuals, but we become incorporate in Christ, so that our fate is bound together not only with him but also with our brothers and sisters in him. Second, participation in Christ entails conformity to the pattern of self-sacrificial love that he embodied and enacted on our behalf (as Gal 2:19b-20 elegantly suggests).[42]

In making union with Christ central to Pauline soteriology, and in asserting its ecclesial and ethical implications, Hays is completely consistent with Reformation insights. The same is true of his desire to make union with Christ central to justification and his rejection of attempts to treat them as unrelated or to play one off against the other. Further, although the category of narrative and the part it plays in Hays's approach certainly reflects twentieth-century conceptuality, and although there are various important questions to be asked about the degree to which it is truly helpful in relation to the Pauline letters,[43] the resulting focus on the whole of God's action in Christ would also be compatible with Luther's and Calvin's convictions concerning justification. For them too, justification depends on incarnation, flowing from the life, death, and resurrection of Jesus. For it is only in becoming human that the Son of God is able to take upon himself the sins of humanity, and it is only in remaining divine that he is able to overcome both sin and death. And it is with the incarnate Son of God, human and divine, who fought and conquered sin and death, that the believer is united in justification.

---

42. Richard Hays, "Christ Died for the Ungodly: Narrative Soteriology in Paul?," *HBT* 26.2 (2004): 62.

43. See Francis Watson, "Is There a Story in These Texts?" in *Narrative Dynamics in Paul: A Critical Assessment*, ed. Bruce W. Longenecker (Louisville: Westminster John Knox, 2002), 231-39.

There is also a shared emphasis on the priority of divine initiative in salvation. Again, it is difficult to imagine Hays provoking any disagreement from Luther or Calvin when he writes that "because justification hinges upon this action of Jesus Christ, upon an event *extra nos*, it is a terrible and ironic blunder to read Paul as though his gospel made redemption contingent upon our act of deciding to dispose ourselves toward God in a particular way"[44] Yet differences arise when Hays goes on to make mutually exclusive what is more appropriately mutually implied: "The logic of the gospel story requires that the deliverance of 'those who believe' depend not upon their knowing or believing but upon the action of Jesus Christ, who faithfully discharges the commission of God."[45] This will not do since, after prioritizing divine initiative in salvation in no uncertain terms in his argument in Rom 9, Paul is perfectly able then to place considerable emphasis on the part played in salvation by believing. It is everyone who calls upon the name of the Lord, verbally confessing Christ, who will be saved (Rom 10:9-13). As Paul then goes on to ask in Rom 10:14-15:

> But how are they to call on one in whom they have not believed? And how are they to believe in one of whom they have never heard? And how are they to hear without someone to proclaim him? And how are they to proclaim him unless they are sent? As it is written, "How beautiful are the feet of those who bring good news!"

The point for Paul, of course, is that it is the God who acted in Jesus Christ who is active now in sending those who proclaim the gospel. The necessity of its proclamation and of the response of faith of those to whom it is addressed neither detracts from the finality or completeness of the deliverance provided by Christ nor compromises the priority of divine initiative. Nor will it do to respond to this challenge by contrasting proclamation with human believing,[46] for Paul here treats them as

---

44. Hays, *Faith of Jesus Christ*, 211.

45. Hays, *Faith of Jesus Christ*, 211.

46. Hays, *Faith of Jesus Christ*, 132, contrasts proclamation and believing in discussing the meaning of the phrase ἀκοῆς πίστεως in Gal 3:2-5. In *Echoes of Scripture in the Letters of Paul* (New Haven: Yale University Press, 1989), 73-83, Hays concludes in relation to the use of Deut 30:11-14 in Rom 10:5-10 that for Paul "the real meaning of Deuteronomy 30 is disclosed not in lawkeeping but in Christian preaching" (82), and argues that confessing with the mouth and believing with the heart (Rom 10:9-10) is

different necessary elements of the same process by which God grants salvation. Divine sending of those who proclaim the gospel (Rom 10:15) initiates the process, but Paul does not mean that the actions that follow (proclaiming, believing, calling upon the name of the Lord) are any less God's actions because they are performed through human beings.

Hays's apparent aversion to emphasizing human dispositions or actions is not maintained, however, when he discusses the Christian life. Participation in Christ means that Christians do not merely imitate Christ. Rather, "Christ's victory . . . has won freedom for humanity, but this freedom is neither an end in itself nor the end of the story: it is the necessary precondition that enables those who are redeemed to complete the story by carrying out their own mandate, by becoming active subjects who fulfill God's original purpose by loving one another."[47] The idea that through redemption God restores true human agency in union with Christ is unproblematic, but it then becomes all the more odd not to offer a robust account of the gift of faith in Christ as itself part of that restoration. If loving one another is a divinely granted and enabled human disposition and action, then so too is faith in Christ. Part of the problem here may be a reaching of the limits of the helpfulness of the category of narrative in explaining Paul's presentations of the gospel. The notion of those redeemed *completing the story* is not self-evidently the most satisfactory way of describing union with a crucified and risen messiah whose death is an ever-present reality subverting any smooth linear unfolding of the life of the church. If so, then consideration of Reformation accounts of the extrinsic nature of the righteousness of Christ granted to those who believe could bring greater coherence. In what ways, in Hays's account, might *the faithfulness of Christ* in which they participate be conceived of as extrinsic to believers in a parallel manner? Further, Hays's concern properly to prioritize divine initiative and undo an excessive concern with individual religious experience would be served by critical interaction with the Reformers' emphasis on the faith-eliciting proclamation of the gospel. If Hays is correct that human faith is "the mode of participation in the pattern definitively enacted in Jesus Christ: as we respond in faith, we

---

a line by line rereading of Deut 30:14, which has just been quoted in Rom 10:8a: "But what does it say? The word is near you, on your lips and in your heart" (81-82). Hays's own insights here seem to demand attention to human faith as a significant element in Pauline soteriology.

47. Hays, *Faith of Jesus Christ*, 223.

participate in an ongoing reenactment of Christ's faithfulness,"[48] then for this faith to come into being is neither merely human nor only human but an act of God.

Yet, although Hays's argument might in this way become an all the more convincing and rounded account of Pauline soteriology, this would come with a rhetorical price tag. For if faith in Christ is an act of God, then it is difficult to see why it is only the subjective genitive translation of πίστις Χριστοῦ (faithfulness of Christ) that can properly express the priority of divine initiative in salvation. Nor is it clear why only the subjective genitive translation can be appropriately christological. In Luther's and Calvin's exegesis the priority of divine initiative is expressed precisely by asserting the God-given nature of human faith in Christ (objective genitive translation of πίστις Χριστοῦ) that unites the believer with him. Far from representing an improperly anthropological focus, their translation choice expresses the properly christological nature of the human faith granted by God. Faith in Christ as expounded by Bultmann may be unduly anthropocentric, but it does not follow that faith in Christ is unduly anthropocentric in the hands of all other interpreters. Its christocentric nature as interpreted by Luther and Calvin represents a concern, just as strong as that of Hays, to hear participation in Christ as central to what Paul's texts have to say about salvation.[49]

Indeed, the Reformers' emphasis within this union with Christ on receiving his righteousness could be argued to bring into focus the christological aspects of the arguments of Romans more clearly than an emphasis on Christ's faithfulness. Not only does Paul characterize the human plight in terms of unrighteousness (e.g., 1:18, 29; 3:5), but he also characterizes the positive state resulting from the liberation of justification in terms of slavery to obedience and righteousness (e.g., 6:16, 18, 19, 20). God justifies the unrighteous ἐκ πίστεως (by faith) in order that, in Christ, they might be righteous. If one asks what attribute of Christ this union might naturally focus around for Paul, then Christ's righteousness appears a likely and appropriate answer. This does not mean that it is necessary in theological terms to drive a sharp wedge between

48. Hays, *Faith of Jesus Christ*, 211.

49. Morna D. Hooker, "Another Look at πίστις Χριστοῦ," *SJT* 69.1 (2016): 46–62, defends the subjective genitive translation but does so in a way that recognizes the appropriate emphasis to be given in interpreting Paul's letters to faith in Christ: "So were Luther and his followers wrong? They were certainly not wrong to emphasize the role of faith" (62).

Christ's righteousness and his faithfulness or between this righteousness and the faith of the believer. Irrespective of whether it also is to be interpreted as an objective or a subjective genitive, the "righteousness of God" (δικαιοσύνη θεοῦ) is not to be divorced from divine faithfulness (Rom 1:17). Yet Paul's linguistic usage remains significant. If the opening verses of Rom 6 give powerful expression to justification in the context of dying and rising with Christ (6:7), and if Paul really does conceive this union primarily in terms of sharing in Christ's faithfulness, why does this not find expression here? One might answer that participation in the faithfulness of Christ is the threshold of righteousness for the believer, the gateway that leads to it, but, if so, surely we should expect to see this discussed nowhere more than in the context of dying and rising with Christ in baptism.[50] Similarly, in the discussion of walking by the Spirit in Rom 8 participation in Christ is not discussed in terms of participation in Christ's faithfulness.

Thus, in translating the phrase πίστις Χριστοῦ there are two different christological options available, and the debate between them cannot be weighted towards the subjective genitive translation by appeal to the obvious priority and centrality of christological considerations for Paul. In the context of union with Christ, both are equally christological. This, of course, does not prove that the subjective genitive translation is wrong, but it does reveal as illusory the theological superiority claimed for it by Hays. The objective genitive translation is consistent with the same advantages. The whole debate concerning the phrase πίστις Χριστοῦ may ultimately be of less theological significance than those engaged in it assume.[51]

---

50. Hooker, "Another Look at πίστις Χριστοῦ," 57–58, correctly emphasizes the significance of participation in Christ for justification and skillfully draws out the connections between obedience, faith, and righteousness in the argument of Rom 5–6. The obedience of believers in 6:16–17 certainly should be related to Christ's obedience in Rom 5:19. However, this makes it all the more striking that Paul pictures believers as participating in Christ's righteousness and obedience but does not say that they participate in Christ's faithfulness. Hooker evades this difficulty only by reliance on the widely rejected messianic interpretation of Hab 2:4 in Rom 1:17 (see note 52 below) so that the later discussion of righteousness and obedience in Rom 5–6 becomes an expression of an emphasis on Christ's faithfulness (Christ is "the righteous one" who lives by faithfulness). Quite apart from the difficulties of this interpretation of Hab 2:4, Rom 5:1–2 clarifies that it is the faith of believers (see the immediately preceding Rom 4:24) that is connected to the argument about righteousness and obedience that will unfold in Rom 5–6.

51. The point that the same theological destination may be reached by different

9.4. Reformation Exegesis and NPP Scholarship:
Douglas Campbell and the Deliverance of God

Similar issues arise in relation to the arguments of Hays's colleague, Campbell, whose work was discussed in the previous chapter as an example of the intensification or perfecting of Paul's emphasis on divine initiative in salvation (see 8.3). Deeply concerned to develop a coherent picture of what Paul's texts say about divine deliverance, and deeply concerned with its contemporary theological fruitfulness, Campbell pits his own "rereading" of Romans against the "Justification Theory" that he constructs in order to embody what he regards as interpretations of Paul's letter with an unduly anthropological focus. His intention is to move the discussion of Pauline theology beyond old and new perspectives. Campbell pursues this project as a convinced advocate of the subjective genitive translation ("faithfulness of Christ") of πίστις Χριστοῦ and follows Hays in arguing for a messianic interpretation of Paul's use of Hab 2:4 in Rom 1:17: "the one who is righteous will live *by faith*" (ἐκ πίστεως). The one who is righteous here ("the righteous one") is taken to be Christ, and the faith spoken of is taken as the faithfulness of Christ, and, for Campbell, this suggests that the subsequent uses by Paul of the construction ἐκ πίστεως are shorthand references to the faithfulness of Christ.[52] The faith of the believer participates in the faithfulness of Christ and the

---

exegetical routes is further illustrated by the differences in how Luther and Calvin explain the christological focus of faith in Christ, Luther characteristically by the presence of Christ in faith and Calvin by the Spirit's activity in uniting the believer with Christ through faith. Hays, *Faith of Jesus Christ,* 224, unintentionally echoes Calvin by noting the Spirit's role in uniting the believer with Christ.

52. For argument in support of these positions, see Hays, *Faith of Jesus Christ,* 132-41, 170-73, and Campbell, *The Deliverance of God,* 610-16. For an example of the rejection of the idea that Paul adopts the messianic interpretation of Hab 2:4, see Jewett, *Romans,* 144-46. As Hays, "ΠΙΣΤΙΣ and Pauline Christology: What Is at Stake?" in *Pauline Theology Volume IV: Looking Back, Pressing On,* ed. E. Elizabeth Johnson and David M. Hay (Atlanta: Scholars Press, 1997), 35-60, admits, "This is one interpretative proposal in *The Faith of Jesus Christ* that has encountered much skepticism, even from critics who otherwise found the book's argument persuasive" (42). It is now revived by Joshua Jipp, *Christ Is King: Paul's Royal Ideology* (Minneapolis: Fortress, 2015), 244-57. Jipp attempts to connect the citation directly with Paul's characterization of Jesus in Rom 1:3-4 as Davidic Messiah but fails to grapple with the quite explicit indication in 1:16 that the faith under discussion is that of those of who believe the gospel. There is a similar lack of indications in the immediate context of a christological interpretation of Hab 2:4 when Paul quotes it in Gal 3:11. Here it is the faith of Abraham that has been under discussion.

great danger to be avoided is instead construing the faith of the believer as satisfying a condition set by God upon the basis of which salvation is granted. These concerns are reflected in Campbell's comments on, and repunctuation of Rom 9:27–10:31, a passage that worries him: "The apocalyptic rereading of Paul faces perhaps its most difficult challenge in this stretch of text."[53] The fear of a contractual account of justification by faith here leads Campbell to recast Paul's references to the righteousness of faith (9:30, 32) as direct references to the faithfulness of Christ on the basis of Paul's use of ἐκ πίστεως. Campbell's readers will be convinced by this only if they are first convinced that Paul's earlier use of Hab 2:4 is messianic and if they are also first convinced that ἐκ πίστεως refers back to this verse so interpreted.[54] However, Campbell then goes on, despite the absence of the ἐκ πίστεως construction, and therefore without any grammatical argument as a basis for doing so, to translate 10:8c, which is Paul's gloss on the statement of Deut 30:14 that the word is on his readers lips and in their hearts, in terms of the faithfulness of Christ: "that is, the word of the faithful one (τὸ ῥῆμα τῆς πίστεως) that we proclaim."[55] Against Campbell, the fact that the noun πίστις here refers instead to the faith-eliciting nature of the gospel is spelt out by the numerous references to human faith and its accompanying confession in the immediately following verses (10:9–10). The "word of faith" is the gospel that is preached and confessing the lordship of Jesus and believing in his resurrection is the response that it evokes in its hearers, both Jew and Greek (10:12).

Campbell's unfounded transformation of Paul's reference to the faith-eliciting nature of the gospel that he preaches into a reference to the faithfulness of Christ provides a specific example of the exegetical difficulties into which excessive fear of a contractual account of justification

---

53. Campbell, *The Deliverance of God*, 782. For his repunctuation of 9:27–10:31, see 807-9. As in his controversial and almost universally rejected treatment of Rom 1:18–3:20 (see 469-600), Campbell here relies on recasting significant portions of the text as representing the voice not of Paul but a teacher whose views he is refuting.

54. I remain unconvinced. See Chester, *Conversion at Corinth*, 179 n. 103. Although persuaded that the objective genitive translation is correct, I certainly do recognize that there is a finely balanced and complex exegetical debate in relation to the seven occurrences of the disputed genitive phrase itself (Rom 3:22, 26; Gal 2:16, 20; 3:22; Phil 3:9). What is clearly illegitimate in exegetical terms is the attempt via an unlikely interpretation of Paul's use of Hab 2:4 to extend the significance of a subjective genitive translation of these phrases so that the faithfulness of Christ becomes a central, or even the central, element in Pauline soteriology.

55. Campbell, *The Deliverance of God*, 808.

leads. Campbell does not make such a dubious move because he thinks that the rest of the passage avoids all reference to human faith, for he acknowledges clearly the strength of the emphasis: Paul "is saying that if Israel only confesses and believes in Christ, then she will be saved."[56] Yet it seems that only after there has been sufficient inoculation against the disease of a contractual reading can there safely be permitted into Paul's argument any discussion of human faith. This is not Paul's procedure, whose point, of course, is not to emphasize human faith at the expense of divine initiative or to make faith the human side of a contract to be satisfied. Rather, for Paul, Christ is near precisely in the faith-eliciting proclamation of the gospel and the human response that it evokes. The personified "righteousness by faith" that speaks in 10:6 ("the righteousness that comes from faith says") represents not the exalting of a merely human disposition but, if we follow the insights offered by Luther's and Calvin's accounts of justification, the divine gift that unites the believer with Christ and his righteousness. This is the appropriately christological result of a process of proclamation that graciously employs human agents but is also never anything less than an act of God or else is completely illegitimate. As Luther, with characteristic verve, expresses it:

> If He (God) does not send, those who preach preach falsely; and this preaching is the same as not preaching, indeed it would be better not to preach. And they who hear, hear falsely, and it would be better not to hear at all. And they who believe them believe falsely, and it would be better not to believe. And they who invoke God, invoke Him falsely, and it would be better not to invoke Him.[57]

The inevitable end result of Campbell's excessive fear of contractual accounts of justification is an inadequate account of human faith.[58] He is rightly concerned to dismiss accounts of faith in Romans 10 that are essentially propositional (a point at which he is certainly at one with the Reformers), contrasting "thin" conditional readings, in which the acceptance of a set of propositions satisfies a divine condition on the basis of which God will then justify, with his own "thick" christological and apocalyptic description. Yet, Campbell's own account of faith is actually

---

56. Campbell, *The Deliverance of God*, 817.

57. *LW* 25:413 = *WA* 56:421, 24-29.

58. On the nature of faith see Campbell, *The Deliverance of God*, 817-21.

rather "thin" in other ways. He comments that faith "ends up functioning more as a *marker* of salvation than a solitary *condition*; it is a marker of participation in the faithful and resurrected Christ, which thereby implicitly *guarantees* for the believer a future participation in the resurrection that Christ has already achieved."[59] This summary is unobjectionable as far as it goes, but it does not go very far. The description of faith in Christ as a marker of salvation does not do justice to the reality-defying nature of faith's trust in God's promises, something which Campbell earlier rightly emphasizes in his treatment of the faith of Abraham in Rom 4 (see 9.6) and which again puts him at one with the exegesis of the Reformers.[60] More importantly still, the description of faith in Christ as a marker of participation in Christ leaves a somewhat curious disconnect between justification by faith and participation in Christ. Faith marks participation in Christ and guarantees future participation in the resurrection, but how is this participation created and sustained? As we have seen, in Luther's and Calvin's exegesis the divine gift of faith is not primarily a marker of salvation, an *indication* or expression of the reality that someone is participating in Christ. Rather it is the bond by which the believer is united with Christ, the instrument employed by the Spirit to create and sustain the union. Faith actively grasps hold of Christ, the only source of saving righteousness and the one who is salvation. Campbell's characterization of faith simply as a "marker" of participation in Christ is, in this important respect, insufficiently participatory. For if faith is not in this sense the bond of union with Christ, how is there to be an account of what faith does in working through love (Gal 5:6) which is thoroughly participatory and not primarily imitative?

Campbell's description of faith as a marker is also, somewhat ironically, insufficiently apocalyptic. This can be illustrated with reference to Campbell's account of justification as "forensic-liberative," an issuing by the divine king of a command that frees a captive in the same way as a verdict releases a prisoner from jail:

> Jesus died and was resurrected and has thereby been "set free" or "released" from the evil grip of Sin. He has left the prison of fleshly captivity and been set free into resurrection life. Read in this liberative way, it (justification) speaks of *both* aspects of the journey

59. Campbell, *The Deliverance of God*, 817 (his emphasis).
60. Campbell, *The Deliverance of God*, 730–61.

of Christ—and therefore of the baptized Christian—*away from Sin*, stretching across and speaking of both his death and resurrection. It indicates where that journey began, in a captivity to Sin and Death, within an Adamic body, which is appropriately likened to life in captivity or in a prison. But it also indicates release from that captivity through a liberating event into a positive state.[61]

Justification is thus a divine event of liberation leading to a positive state in which faith is a marker of salvation. Here justification is clearly a liberating act, apocalyptic in the sense that it comes to the believer from outside as an expression of invasive divine grace and can only come in this way.

Yet while Campbell's emphasis on justification as a journey away from sin successfully captures the transformation of the believer involved and its participatory nature, it does not so successfully capture the reality that justification retains its dynamic character as event. A stronger sense is needed that the believer is continually set free under the reign of grace, which rules through righteousness (Rom 6:21). The initial liberating event is a continuously present reality, and does not simply yield or lead to some other positive state in which the primary significance of faith is as a marker.[62] As we saw when considering the particular strengths of Luther's and Calvin's exegesis (see 9.2) in both emphasizing the external nature of justification and making union with Christ integral to it, the believer does not journey away from the apocalypse of Jesus Christ but is borne along by it. Faith unites the believer to the one who died and was raised from the dead and whose death and resurrection are present realities. The transformation of the believer and the continuing nature of justification as event are therefore to be conceptualized together. Justification not only was apocalyptic but continues to remain apocalyp-

---

61. Douglas Campbell, "Rereading Paul's ΔIKAIO-Language," in *Beyond Old and New Perspectives on Paul: Reflections on the Work of Douglas Campbell*, ed. Chris Tilling (Eugene, OR: Wipf & Stock, 2014), 211-12.

62. I am not suggesting that Campbell would necessarily disagree with me about this, especially given his acknowledged indebtedness to Käsemann (who insisted on the inseparability of gift and giver so that the gift has the character of power) in the interpretation of the phrase "the righteousness of God." See Campbell, *The Deliverance of God*, 677-704. My point is rather that Campbell's apparent fear that any emphasis on human faith compromises divine initiative and introduces conditionality prevents him from fully and appropriately reflecting these themes.

tic. Whatever one's position on the πίστις Χριστοῦ debate, it should be clear that a fully participatory and apocalyptic account of human faith in Christ is a pressing need within contemporary Pauline scholarship. Such an account will not simply reproduce Luther's or Calvin's exegesis or rely solely upon them, but it would be wise to attempt it in critical dialog with them as one important resource among others.

9.5. Reformation Exegesis and NPP Scholarship: N. T. Wright and the Faithfulness of God

The work of Wright displays a deep concern with the coherence of Pauline theology, seeking to integrate all its motifs into a single synthesis and to relate this to the wider biblical narrative. As was discussed in the previous chapter, the framework by which Wright structures his synthesis provides an example of the intensification or perfecting of one particular motif or element in Pauline theology, in this instance the "covenantal" (see 8.4). Within this process of intensification there are elements of continuity with the Reformed tradition in Wright's understanding of justification. His covenantal approach holds to the forensic nature of justification and the involvement of union with Christ. Yet there are also profound differences, especially concerning the nature of what Paul intends by the vocabulary of righteousness. As Wright expresses it, "'Righteousness' denotes the status enjoyed by God's true family, now composed of both Jews and Gentiles who believe in Jesus the Messiah. . . . 'Justification,' as in the verbs of Galatians 2:16-17 . . . denotes the verdict of God himself as to who really is a member of his people."[63] For those who receive this covenant membership there is forgiveness of sins as a consequence of Christ's atoning death, and the worldwide Abrahamic family of God exists for the purpose of dealing with sin and its consequences, but the vocabulary of justification is primarily covenantal so that membership of the covenant provides the context in which forgiveness of sins takes place.[64] This covenant family is the means by which all the world might escape the clutches of sin and death and enter into life and new creation. God's initial verdict of covenant membership will be eschatologically confirmed for believers: "The present verdict gives the assurance that

---

63. N. T. Wright, *Justification* (Downers Grove, IL: InterVarsity Press, 2009), 121.
64. Wright, *Justification*, 134.

the future verdict will match it; the Spirit gives the power through which that future verdict, when given, will be seen to be in accordance with the life that the believer has then lived."[65]

Wright thus offers his own particular perspective on justification that reflects his construal of Pauline theology as a whole. He adopts the subjective genitive translation ("faithfulness of Christ") of πίστις Χριστοῦ but does not accept that Paul's use of Hab 2:4 is messianic,[66] and therefore does not make the motif of Christ's faithfulness as defining of Pauline theology in general, or of justification in particular, as does either Hays or Campbell. Wright is deeply concerned to integrate the forensic and participatory categories in Pauline theology,[67] but similarly does not make this integration the focal point of his account of that theology. It is the theme of covenant that structures his account and integrates the interpretation of Pauline texts with that of the rest of Scripture. Wright's covenantal account of justification is therefore a vital element in his overall synthesis. It has also been widely perceived as one of the points of greatest tension between his work and traditional Protestant interpretations of Paul. Whether Wright is correct in his conviction that justification is to be understood primarily as a declaration of membership in God's people is a central issue.

There are strong reasons to think that Wright is significantly misreading the discussion of justification in the Pauline texts. Yet any reasonable account of the relationship between his account of justification and those offered by Luther and Calvin must first clear away a potential misunderstanding over something about which Wright certainly is correct. He rejects as a blatant misinterpretation for which there is no basis in Paul's texts the concept of an imputed justification in which the righteousness of Christ is transferred or passed to the believer. As we have seen, whatever the situation in later Protestant interpretation, such a transfer is not proposed by the individual Reformers whose exegesis I have explored. It is not characteristic of Melanchthon, whose relational account stresses much more frequently the intercession of the resurrected Christ on the believer's behalf. Nor is it characteristic of Luther and Calvin, who do assert passionately that believers receive

65. Wright, *Justification*, 251.
66. Wright, *Paul and the Faithfulness of God*, 1470.
67. Wright, *Paul and the Faithfulness of God*, 530: "the supposed clash or conflict between two 'models of salvation' in Paul, the 'forensic' or 'juristic' on the one hand and the 'incorporative' on the other, is itself a category mistake."

Christ's righteousness but in their different ways locate that reception solely in union with Christ and not in a transfer of righteousness as if it were a substance that can be passed across the divine courtroom. There is exchange, for Christ receives the sins of the world and in return the believer receives his righteousness, but this exchange can only take place within a union of persons. If there is a transfer it is the believer who is transferred from the realm of sin and death into Christ and the reign of grace. Both Luther and Calvin freely use the term "imputation" to describe this exchange within a union, but in our contemporary context the term "imputation" usually communicates not this emphasis on union with Christ but instead a narrowly forensic account focused precisely on the kind of transfer of righteousness to which Wright correctly objects. It is, of course, possible to redefine terms, but the dominant use of the term is so deeply entrenched that it may be better simply to retire this venerable theological category.

The main issue, however, is lexical and revolves around the lack of other ancient texts using righteousness vocabulary to denote covenant membership. In his critique of Wright's account of justification, Stephen Westerholm makes the case that "'righteousness' does not mean, and by its very nature *cannot* mean, membership in a covenant. Likewise it does not mean, and by its very nature *cannot* mean, a status conveyed by the decision of a court."[68] Westerholm is here not denying the forensic nature of Paul's imagery but asserting on the basis of biblical usage that the righteous person is someone who does what he or she ought to do, that righteousness is doing what ought to be done, and that therefore when a judge justifies a person it is a declaration that this individual has done what is right and not what is wrong. If the administration of justice is not itself corrupt, the court does not confer a status but finds and declares what is the case. The Pauline paradox that God justifies the ungodly (Rom 4:5) glories in the divine capacity through Christ to draw what would

---

68. Westerholm, *Justification Reconsidered*, 63 (his emphasis). See also the excellent surveys provided by Max J. Lee, "Greek Words and Roman Meanings, Part 1: (Re)mapping Righteousness Language in Greco-Roman Discourse," in *Fire in My Soul: Essays on Pauline Soteriology and the Gospels in Honor of Seyoon Kim*, ed. Soon Bong Choi, Jin Ki Hwang, and Max J. Lee (Eugene: Wipf & Stock, 2014), 3–28, and Max J. Lee, "Greek Words and Roman Meanings, Part 2: A Prolegomenon to Paul's Use of Righteousness Language in His Letters," in *Fire in My Soul: Essays on Pauline Soteriology and the Gospels in Honor of Seyoon Kim*, ed. Soon Bong Choi, Jin Ki Hwang, and Max J. Lee (Eugene: Wipf & Stock, 2014), 29–52.

otherwise be square circles: "God can rightly declare sinners righteous when the sins that kept them from being righteous were borne by the crucified Christ: God allowed human sinfulness to spend all its force on the suffering Christ until, drained of all evil, it was 'expiated' and exists no more. Their sins done away with, there is no miscarriage of justice when erstwhile sinners are declared 'righteous.'"[69]

Westerholm's argument makes excellent sense as an account of Christ's death for us, and as an assertion that the primary concern of justification for Paul is not covenant membership but the addressing of sin (e.g., Rom 3:23-24; Rom 4:6-8; 2 Cor 5:21). However, his argument is also truncated in that he does not discuss union with Christ in relation to justification, thus failing to make the point that this factual finding in favor of sinners can only take place in Christ and missing the opportunity to provide an explanation of texts like Rom 4:25 (Christ "was raised for our justification"). This gap is ably filled by Michael Bird, who argues that "believers are incorporated into the righteousness of Christ. The matrix for understanding justification is union with Christ."[70] Bird then goes on to interpret these and other texts (including Rom 5:18-19; 1 Cor 1:30; 2 Cor 5:21; Phil 3:8-9) in terms of incorporated righteousness. Believers receive Christ's righteousness when united with him by faith, and one of the consequences of this is that union with Christ has a forensic dimension such that the common scholarly bifurcation between forensic and participatory categories in Pauline soteriology "becomes a grossly inadequate generalization."[71]

In making this argument, Bird expresses more clearly than I was able to do so an important aspect of the argument of my own earlier study *Conversion at Corinth*.[72] There I reacted against the contention of Sanders that Paul uses the verb "justify" (δικαιόω) in two sharply different senses, one forensic and concerned with the forgiveness of transgressions and the other participatory and denoting a transfer from being under the power of sin to being under the lordship of Christ. Instead I argued, particularly in relation to Rom 6:7 ("whoever has died has been justified from sin") and Phil 3:9 ("and be found in him, not having a righteousness of my own that comes from the law, but one that comes through faith in

---

69. Westerholm, *Justification Reconsidered*, 69-70.

70. Bird, *The Saving Righteousness of God*, 70. For the treatment of texts in the Pauline corpus as expressions of incorporated righteousness, see 71-85.

71. Bird, *The Saving Righteousness of God*, 86.

72. See Chester, *Conversion at Corinth*, 56-57, 172-81, 205-10, 329-36.

Christ, the righteousness from God based on faith") that Paul allows the forensic and participatory elements of his thought to interpret each other. I was particularly, and I think correctly, skeptical of Sanders's contention that the juridical meaning was normally conveyed by this vocabulary but that Paul forced it to bear a quite different participatory sense. While acknowledging that the meaning of language can be transformed through new and creative usage, I wished to insist that if such new usage is to communicate clearly, previous meanings and networks of association cannot simply be obliterated in the process. The new must relate to the old if chronic miscommunication is not to follow. I therefore saw these texts as instances of Paul bringing together the existing forensic associations of the verb with a participatory sense rather than as instances of a sharp distinction between them.

What I then failed to see was that the righteousness of Christ received by the believer who is united to him by faith is the means by which Paul accomplishes this bringing together of forensic and participatory senses. This explains how in Phil 3:9 it is both that Paul's greatest hope is to be found in Christ (united with him on the day of judgment) and that the righteousness he will then have is external and alien (not his own but from God). In relation to Paul's creative use of vocabulary it is not that he takes forensic language he has previously used in one way and then shockingly gives it a participatory sense. Rather, his forensic usage inherently has a sharply christological focus (the righteousness received by the believer in justification is that of Christ) that then lends itself to participatory expression (justification only takes place when the believer is united with Christ by faith).[73] Paul may be expanding the semantic

---

73. See also the contribution of Jipp, *Christ Is King*, 139–210, who argues that Christ's Davidic kingship (Rom 1:3-4) is the basis for Paul's teaching concerning participation in Christ, with believers sharing in the rule of Christ the King. This means that "Instead of justly enacting the verdict of condemnation and death, the Messiah rescues his people by incorporating them into his rule through destroying sin and death and sharing his righteousness with them" (271). Jipp's argument is in certain respects helpful, particularly his insistence that believers share in Christ's righteousness, but his association of Christ's righteousness and of justification exclusively with his kingship is one-sided. There is a failure to distinguish clearly between Christ's identity as a king and his reign. The resurrected Christ is at the right-hand of the Father and believers will eschatologically share in that rule, but, although having a royal identity as messiah, the earthly Jesus is not perceived by Paul as reigning. Believers also do not reign until they are resurrected. It is instructive to note that Paul's explicit uses of kingship language cluster around this eschatological sense, e.g., in Rom 5:17 believers are certainly said to

range of the vocabulary of justification by using it in participatory contexts, but this is facilitated by his strong christological focus that helps his readers to hear and understand fresh nuances of meaning. Similarly, good sense can also be made on this basis of Rom 6:7. That one who has died with Christ in baptism can be said to have been justified from sin clearly indicates that justification is something that happens in union with Christ and the perfect passive form of the verb δεδικαίωται ("has been justified") in the context of the ending of enslavement to sin (Rom 6:6) indicates that the righteousness involved in justification comes from outside. The frequent observation of commentators that the statement that the person who has died with Christ "has been justified from sin" is here equivalent to "has been set free from sin" is correct (the relationship with 6:18 is close, where it is said that believers are "set free from sin" and so "enslaved to righteousness"), but misses the point that this connection is scarcely surprising if justification involves the person united with Christ by faith receiving his righteousness. The English reader is particularly ill served by the multiple translations that obscure the point by ignoring the presence of the verb "justify" and translate Rom 6:7 as if Paul had actually written "has been set free."[74]

Thus, the combination of a strong emphasis on both union with Christ in justification and the extrinsic nature of justification that was identified earlier in the chapter as characteristic of Luther's and Calvin's exegesis helps us here to move forwards in the exegesis of specific texts.

---

reign through Christ, but the tense of the verb is future (βασιλεύσουσιν). In relation to the present Paul expects believers to experience the suffering that was first the experience of Jesus and here Christ's role is expressed in terms of slavery (e.g., Phil 2:7) and poverty (e.g., 2 Cor 8:9), not kingship. Resurrection and justification are intimately connected for Paul (Rom 4:25) and therefore sharing in Christ's rule is part of what it means to be united with Christ but the cross and justification are similarly connected (Rom 5:9) and believers must share in that also. It is the cross that is explicitly said by Paul to be a manifestation of God's righteousness (Rom 3:25) whereas Jipp emphasizes only the resurrection in this respect. Jipp argues that Paul redefines the concept of kingship in order to encompass the suffering of the cross and make it an expression of Christ's kingship. Yet the absence of explicitly royal vocabulary to signal this redefinition in relation to the cross is striking. The concept of Christ's Davidic kingship certainly coheres with the content of Paul's letters and finds occasional expression in them, but it will not bear the weight that Jipp places upon it as the conceptual basis of participation in Christ.

74. I have not made a comprehensive survey, but the most recent English translations I have found that use the verb "justify" are the American Standard Version (1901) and the Revised Version (1885).

It does so without forcing the vocabulary of justification to bear meanings sharply distinguished from its normal usage. Here all the points made against Sanders (who was, after all, at least arguing for a separate participatory sense that still involved justification as addressing sin) apply with all the more force against Wright's argument that Paul uses this vocabulary to denote covenant membership. The point that this is not what justification means emerges particularly clearly in the argument of Romans when God is first said to have put forward Jesus as a "sacrifice of atonement by his blood, effective through faith" (Rom 3:25), and then it is later said that we have been "justified by his blood" (Rom 5:9). There are many complex interpretative issues in these verses, but the connection between the blood of Christ and atonement for sin is obvious. If Christ's blood justifies, then justification primarily addresses the issue of sin, as is further suggested by the immediately preceding statement in Rom 5:8 that Christ died for us "while we were still sinners." Paul does not primarily mean that he and his readers were made members of the covenant family by Christ's blood, but rather that they were justified from sin, as he goes on to say in Romans 6:7.

Wright notes the connection between these texts, acknowledging that 5:9 indicates that "it is Jesus' sacrificial death . . . which accomplishes justification."[75] However, discerning the background to Paul's unfolding argument in Rom 3:21–4:25 as the portrait of the Servant in Isa 40–55, Wright concludes that "The divine act of dealing with sin through the sacrificial death of the faithful sin-bearing Servant is central to the passage; which means that the *forensic* account of sin, punishment, and atonement is to be located within, and only understood in relation to, the wider *covenantal* theme."[76] The problem here with Wright's argument is one of slippage. It would be a different thing to claim that Paul's use of justification vocabulary is located within, and understood in relation to, the category of covenant than to claim that justification is itself to be understood primarily as a declaration of covenant membership. Where justification is to be located, and what it is to be related to, are different (albeit connected) questions from the question of what it is. It is perfectly possible within the Reformed tradition to understand justification as primarily concerned with dealing with sin but to locate that within, and relate it to, a canonical reading strategy in which the theme of covenant car-

75. Wright, *Paul and the Faithfulness of God*, 998.
76. Wright, *Paul and the Faithfulness of God*, 1000.

ries considerable weight. In fairness, Wright is not in this passage directly discussing the meaning of justification, but the point remains that Paul's statements do not easily lend themselves to understanding justification itself as a declaration of covenant membership. While it is indisputable that Paul's statements about justification frequently occur in contexts where the corporate identity of God's people is at stake, this is because it is those justified from sin that belong to this people. The forgiveness of sins is not a benefit of family membership but that which creates the family. It is an act of creation that can be performed or commanded by no sinful human being, but only received when it is graciously bestowed by God on those united with Christ by faith.

This recognition should not lead to a downplaying of the significance of corporate themes in justification, however, but rather to their relocation and redescription. Justification takes place in Christ (Gal 2:17). It is only by dying with him that a person is justified from sin (Rom 6:3-7), and it is in Christ that Paul's readers are children of God through faith (Gal 3:26) and number among Abraham's offspring (Gal 3:29). God sent his Son to redeem those under the law that they "might receive adoption as children" (Gal 4:5). It is uncontroversial to say that these statements testify to the centrality of Christology in Paul's expressions of corporate themes in justification. Yet within what framework are they to be read? One could interpret their christological focus within Wright's covenantal framework, with Christ as Israel's representative Messiah,[77] but they

---

77. John Barclay, review of *Paul and the Faithfulness of God*, by N.T. Wright, *SJT* 68.2 (2015) 235-43 (esp. 239-40), enumerates the problematic aspects of Wright's framework: "Whatever one makes of Wright's insistence that every time Paul says 'Christos' he means us to think of Jesus' Messianic status, one may dispute several elements in the claim that he was 'Israel's representative Messiah, who summed up the life and story of the people in himself [and] brought Israel's history to its appointed if shocking and unexpected climax' (405). That Jesus 'represents' Israel and fulfils its vocation—a 'central' point that gives everything in Paul a 'tight coherence' (815-16, 823-24, 839)—is more asserted than proved. Arguments from biblical statements about David are advanced with some tentativeness (828-30), and it is admitted that there is nothing in Second Temple Judaism to support the notion that the Messiah incorporates his people (826-27). It can only be deduced from Paul himself—or from an imposition of Wright's schema onto Paul. The purported evidence does not convince: Paul is hardly speaking as a representative Israelite in Gal 2.19-20, the resurrection of Jesus is never expounded by Paul as the resurrection of Israel in nuce, while the 'casting off' of Israel in Rom 11:12, 15 has no linguistic connections with what is said of Jesus' death. That Jesus as Messiah is 'Israel in person' (842, 930), offering to God the faithfulness which Israel had failed to perform (857-58, 890), is by no means the only way to bring coherence to Pauline theology, even if it ties the knots for Wright."

can also be explained in terms of the union with Christ created through justifying faith. Faith justifies from sin because it grasps hold of Christ and receives his righteousness and, as it does so, the church, the body of Christ in the world, is created. This community is now a people, no longer defined by their previous individual identities, which were made up of the human categories of ethnicity, social status, and gender, but one in Christ Jesus (Gal 3:28) and therefore also the descendants of Abraham, who believed God's promises and was reckoned as righteous. Thus, read in terms of incorporated righteousness or righteousness in Christ, there is little difficulty in hearing and granting full weight to the corporate dimensions of Paul's statements about justification. Yet this is achieved without then leaving ourselves unable to do justice to those texts in which it is apparent that by its very nature justification addresses the issue of sin.

In his discussion of incorporated righteousness, Bird retains the term "covenantal" to designate these corporate dimensions of justification while filling it with content distinct from Wright's covenantal framework.[78] I am not convinced that this is the most helpful procedure. While the term "covenantal" appropriately captures things that are essential in any interpretation of Paul's texts—continuing divine commitment to promises to Israel, Paul's commitment to Israel's Scriptures as God's word, and the importance for Paul of both Jews and Gentiles together now constituting God's people in Christ—it does not in contemporary usage communicate very clearly the radical nature of Paul's theology of grace that informs his teaching about justification and assaults all notions of human worthiness.[79] In particular, it fails to register the implications for ecclesiology of the extrinsic nature of justification. If the Reformers were correct in their insistence that God encounters people in justification only outside of themselves and that the righteousness of Christ

---

78. Bird, *The Saving Righteousness of God*, 113–54.

79. This conclusion also stands in contrast to Macaskill, *Union with Christ*, who argues that the theme of union with Christ in the New Testament as a whole is best described as covenantal. I agree that much of the content that Macaskill gives to the term "covenantal" is significant to Paul and recognize that Paul could never have repudiated such a central scriptural concept as covenant. However, in Paul's own context covenantal terminology was so inextricably associated with interpretations of that scriptural concept incompatible with Paul's theology of grace that the concept was not a natural or effective vehicle through which for Paul to express that theology. The neglect of grace in the work of recent "covenantal" interpreters of Paul suggests that to some degree this state of affairs persists.

remains an alien righteousness, and if there are also corporate themes in justification, then the church is always also intended to be oriented outwards.

Rightly understood, justification therefore cuts against complacent communalism just as much as it does against excessively individualistic accounts of salvation. Paul's central point is not, as Wright puts it, that the people of God "has been demarcated by *pistis*" (faith),[80] but that faith is what unites this people with Christ and the love of God for sinners expressed in his death. God's people are certainly in Paul's view to be characterized by faith, and he is sharply insistent on behavioral boundaries consistent with their union with Christ, but such boundaries do not exist for the purpose of demarcation. They exist for the purpose of clear and fully embodied communication of the gospel for the sake of the world. Paul says of Christ in Rom 5:18 that "one man's act of righteousness leads to justification and life for all." I do not think that Paul here speaks of universal salvation, or implies the erasing of all human communal identities, but he does speak in a manner that positions faith not as the instrument of a newer, greater communal demarcation replacing all previous ones, but as that which relativizes and renders secondary such demarcations on the basis of God's actions in Christ. The calling of the church is to live communally in a manner that points beyond itself to these divine actions.

9.6. Romans 4: An Exegetical Test Case for Reconciling the Perspectives

Where does this discussion of Reformation perspectives in relation to distinguished recent NPP interpreters leave us as regards the reconciliation of the perspectives? Having analyzed recent NPP scholarship in light of Luther's and Calvin's insistence on the believer's reception of the alien righteousness of Christ in union with him, how does this help us in the task of interpreting the Pauline texts today? Appropriate answers to these questions can only be formed by examining actual texts, and few Pauline texts could be more suited to this purpose than Rom 4 with its discussion of the faith of Abraham, a crucial topic in both sixteenth-century and contemporary debate.[81] Which can make better sense of Paul's

---

80. Wright, *Paul and the Faithfulness of God*, 971.
81. In recent discussion see among others Campbell, *The Deliverance of God*, 730–

argument as it unfolds across 4:1–25, a solely antithetical account of the relationship between contemporary and Reformation interpretations, or an account that draws upon insights from both Reformation and contemporary scholarship?

Wright takes a largely antithetical approach, arguing that the discussion of working or not working in 4:4–5 does not stem from concern with human ethical achievement as an illegitimate basis for justification, and arguing that in 4:6–8 the apparent explanation of justification in terms of the forgiveness of sins is directed primarily to Gentiles, so that the focus of Paul's argument is covenantal rather than soteriological. In line with Wright's general understanding of justification in Paul, the righteousness received by the one who believes in Christ is covenant membership and faith is the badge of this membership. For those who receive this covenant membership there is forgiveness of sins, and the worldwide Abrahamic family exists for the purpose of dealing with sin and its consequences, but Paul's argument here is primarily about the fulfillment of God's promise to Abraham of a worldwide family. This requires a way for the ungodly Gentiles to be forgiven if they are to be included in this family, but this is a secondary concern in Rom 4. Wright makes his case by looking first at the context in Genesis of Paul's quotation from 15:6 that "Abraham believed God and it was reckoned to him as righteousness" (4:3). In particular, he suggests that 15:1 with its promise to Abraham: "your reward will be very great," is vital to Paul's argument. For in the Septuagint, the term used for reward is μισθός and this is the word (that can also mean "pay" or "wages") that Paul uses in 4:4–5 when he contrasts receiving it as a gift to receiving it as an obligation that is due to the person who has worked for it.[82]

Wright takes this as a deliberate allusion and points out that the

---

61; Andrew A. Das, "Paul and Works of Obedience in Second Temple Judaism: Romans 4:4–5 as a 'New Perspective' Case Study," *CBQ* 71.4 (2009): 795–812; Gathercole, *Where is Boasting?*, 216–51; Michael J. Gorman, "Romans: The First Christian Treatise on Theosis," in *JTI* 5.1 (2011): 13–34; Joshua Jipp, "Rereading the Story of Abraham, Isaac, and 'Us' in Romans 4," *JSNT* 32.2 (2009): 217–42; Jan Lambrecht, "Romans 4: A Critique of N. T. Wright," *JSNT* 36.2 (2013): 189–94; Francis Watson, *Paul and the Hermeneutics of Faith* (London and New York: T&T Clark, 2004), 167–269; N. T. Wright, "Paul and the Patriarch: The Role of Abraham in Romans 4," *JSNT* 35.3 (2013): 207–41.

82. From the Hebrew this phrase from Gen 15:1 can be translated into English so that the promised great reward is God himself but from the Greek this is not possible.

great reward received by Abraham is a vast family of descendants comprised of many nations (Gen 17:4; Rom 4:18). The promise of this reward is fulfilled through Isaac, whose coming forth from the "dead bodies" of the aged Abraham and Sarah will lead in Christ to a worldwide family composed both of the circumcised and the uncircumcised (4:11-12) through the actions of the God who "gives life to the dead and calls into existence the things that do not exist" (4:17). This is Paul's focus,[83] and his contrast between receiving the reward as a gift and working for it (4:4-5) is not a denial that righteousness is received in response to human obedience to Torah but simply an expression of the fact that God was not obligated to give Abraham a worldwide family of descendants but did so freely as a gift. The point of the statement that faith is credited as righteousness by the God who justifies the ungodly (4:5) is not to imply that Abraham numbered among the ungodly but to highlight God's promise to justify Abraham's ungodly (i.e., Gentile) descendants. The quotation of Ps 32 (LXX 31) in 4:7-8 is intended to refer not to Jew and Gentile alike but specifically to the Gentile need for forgiveness. Since in Wright's view righteousness here means covenant membership, when Paul speaks of circumcision as a sign and a seal of the righteousness that Abraham had by faith (4:11), he means that it was the sign of the covenant granted to him by God.

Wright's discussion is helpful in highlighting in Rom 4 the worldwide nature of the family promised to Abraham. In so doing, it addresses a significant lack in the exegesis of the Reformers and in the Protestant tradition stemming from them. Calvin will insist that when Gen 15:6 is quoted, Abraham's faith should be understood with reference to "the whole covenant of salvation and the grace of adoption which Abraham is said to have apprehended by faith."[84] However, even in Calvin's case the dynamics of Gentile inclusion are seriously neglected and the theme of covenant is not expounded in terms of Jew/Gentile relationships. The statements that God intended to make Abraham the father of all those who receive righteousness by faith, both uncircumcised and circumcised

---

83. Wright, "Paul and the Patriarch," 207-41 (esp. 225-31), seeks to reinforce his sense that Paul is focused more or less exclusively in Rom 4 on the worldwide family of Abraham by translating Rom 4:1, following Richard Hays, as "What shall we say? Have we found Abraham to be our forefather according to the flesh?" However, the more usual translation "What then shall we say that Abraham, our forefather according to the flesh, has found?" makes better sense in the context. See Barclay, *Paul and the Gift*, 483 n. 88.

84. *Comm. Rom* 4:3 = *CNTC* 8:83 = *OE* 13:80, 28-29.

(4:11–12, 17–18), are given far too little weight in the exegesis of the passage. The problem is even more exaggerated with Luther and Melanchthon. The latter simply does not discuss these verses in his exegesis of Rom 4 and Luther, in commenting on the parallel statements in Gal 3:7–8, concentrates largely on using the text to criticize Jewish boasting in physical descent from the patriarch. What matters is simply to demonstrate that righteousness is by faith rather than by any other means. In other references to Rom 4 in his works, Luther emphasizes the miraculous nature of Abraham's faith or the capacity of God to make alive (4:17), but not the purpose of the promise, i.e., Abraham's fatherhood of a family composed of both Jews and Gentiles. The positive sense, which Wright brings into the foreground, of the worldwide family itself as the blessing promised by God to Abraham is almost entirely lacking. Yet Paul clearly intends to say not only that since God justified Abraham by faith Gentiles must be justified in the same manner but, equally emphatically, that because Gentiles are justified in this same way they are children of Abraham along with Jewish believers. Paul's argument makes such Abrahamic descent a significant aspect of Christian identity, and Protestant exegesis has paid far too little attention to it.

Yet despite the fact that Wright's exegesis delivers such a necessary retrieval of an important emphasis in Paul's argument, his treatment of Rom 4 is deeply problematic. As Gathercole comments of NPP exegesis of Rom 4 in general, "reaction to Reformation thought has led merely to a different kind of one-sidedness."[85] While helpful in much of what he affirms, in the argument summarized above the denials made by Wright are exegetically implausible. Of particular concern are Wright's denial that the contrast between working and receiving a gift (4:4–5) reflects any intention on Paul's part to deny that justification is received in response to human obedience to Torah, his denial that Abraham numbers among the ungodly (4:5), and his denial that the forgiveness emphasized in 4:6–8 applies equally to Jew and Gentile alike. In relation to the first denial that Paul is refuting in 4:4–5 the idea that righteousness is received in response to human obedience, it is helpful to note the more general contrast at 6:23 between death as the wages of sin and eternal life as the gift of God. Paul uses different vocabulary in this text from 4:4–5 (ὀψώνιον for "wages" rather than μισθός) and he is certainly not in Rom 6 concerned to deny that righteousness is received in response to obedience

---

85. Gathercole, *Where Is Boasting?*, 239.

to Torah. Yet this striking contrast between wages and gift does suggest a more general opposition in the divine economy of salvation between the two than simply the thought that eternal life is not something God is obligated to provide.

More specifically, in relation to Rom 4 itself, Wright does not take sufficient account of the contrast between Paul's treatment of Abraham's justification and the widespread insistence in Second Temple literature on Abraham's obedience. Other interpretations of Gen 15:6 "are concerned to present Abraham as an exemplary figure or role model for human conduct in relation to God. . . . Apart from Paul, Jewish interpreters regard the promise motif as secondary to a story whose primary aim is to celebrate Abraham's outstanding piety and virtue."[86] For example, Philo celebrates Abraham's justifying faith as "the most perfect of virtues" (τὴν τελειοτάτην ἀρετῶν),[87] and, on the basis of Gen 26:5, which celebrates Abraham's obedience to God's commandments, regards this faith as constitutive of such obedience. The quality of Abraham's obedience was such that he himself was "a law and an unwritten statute" (νόμος αὐτὸς ὢν καὶ θεσμὸς ἄγραφος).[88]

Josephus goes so far simply as not to comment directly upon Gen 15:6 and the faith of Abraham. Instead, his discussion of the divine promise of a child and a multitude of offspring focuses upon its prompting by Abraham's virtue in renouncing the booty he has captured in his successful ambush of the invading Assyrians (Gen 14:14-24): "thou shalt not lose the rewards (μισθούς) that are thy due for such good deeds (εὐπραγίαις)."[89] Josephus interprets Abraham's immediately subsequent question to God about an heir as motivated by a sense that all such lesser rewards will be pointless if he has no child. Although Josephus does not say so directly, it would certainly be difficult to dispute that on his interpretation the prom-

86. Watson, *Paul and the Hermeneutics of Faith*, 268. See also Gathercole, *Where Is Boasting?*, 216-51. Wright's neglect of their amply documented conclusions is striking.

87. Philo, *Her.*, 91 (Colson and Whitaker, LCL).

88. Philo, *Abr.*, 276 (Colson, LCL).

89. Josephus, *A.J.* 1.183 (Thackeray, LCL). Although Gen 15:1 does not say why God promises Abraham a great reward, the Hebrew term rendered by the LXX translators as μισθός can refer to a soldier's booty (Ezek 29:19) as well as to a wage or fee more generally. Together with the military metaphor of God as a shield, this may be what prompts the connection that Josephus makes. Gordon Wenham, *Genesis 1-15*, WBC (Dallas: Word, 1987), 334, comments that "The content of this promise evokes images of Abram as a great and successful warrior enjoying the spoils of battles and alludes to his triumph in chap. 14."

ise of Isaac and of innumerable descendants is the "great reward" (Gen 15:1). Yet far from disqualifying an interpretation that regards God's promises as granted to Abraham in response to virtuous obedience, the use of the term "reward" (μισθός) here grounds it. Paul's insistence in Rom 4:4-5 that justification is not earned like wages or a reward is necessary precisely because readers of Genesis might, like Josephus, take the use of the term "reward" (μισθός) in Gen 15:1 at face value. Paul's insistence that justification by God is not earned like wages or a reward is intended to deny that Abraham was justified on account of his obedient deeds.

Wright's own argument features Phinehas, whose deeds Ps 106 (LXX 105):30-31 speaks of as reckoned to him as righteousness. Phinehas is emphasized by Wright in order on the basis of other texts that discuss Phinehas, to suggest that his being reckoned as righteous means simply that God made a covenant with him. However, correctly understood the example of Phinehas as one justified on account of his deeds only brings into sharper relief the contrast between Paul's insistence that Abraham received righteousness as a gift he had not earned and the assumption of other Second Temple interpreters that God acted in response to Abraham's obedience. Wright does not see this contrast, interpreting Phinehas' deeds exclusively in relation to Phineas' zeal for the maintenance of Israelite purity free from Gentile pollution. On this view, Paul is contrasting justification by faith specifically with zeal for the law in the context of separation from Gentiles. However, Abraham's obedience is not easily characterized in these terms and zeal expressed in separation from Gentiles cannot readily be quarantined from other aspects of obedience to the law. 1 Macc 2:52-54 says that Phinehas received a covenant of eternal priesthood because of his zeal but does so immediately after highlighting different aspects of obedience in relation to Abraham and Joseph: "Was not Abraham found faithful when tested, and it was reckoned to him as righteousness? Joseph in the time of his distress kept the commandment and became lord of Egypt." Phinehas secured divine approval because of his zeal, but this is not differentiated in its result from the other types of obedience that secured divine approval for Abraham and Joseph. When Paul contrasts the gift of justification by faith with the payment due to one who works in Rom 4:4-5, he means what he appears to say: the gratuitous nature of the justification received by Abraham demonstrates that it was not earned through obedience.

Wright's second and third denials are both necessitated by his desire to insist that, for Paul, righteousness is covenant membership and faith is its badge, issues that I have already discussed in more general terms above. Here it will be sufficient to note somewhat obvious exegetical objections to Wright's denials, beginning with the refusal to number Abraham among the ungodly. In Rom 3:9–20 Paul notes that Jew and Gentile alike are "under sin" (3:9) and then argues to the conclusion that no human being will be justified through the law (3:20), so establishing the expectation that Jew and Gentile share a common plight and a common salvation in Christ, which Paul will then go on to explicate. Unless "under sin" and "ungodly" are not parallel, then Abraham's very humanity places him in the latter category. In fact, Paul later explicitly makes the two parallel, noting in 5:6 that while we were still weak, "Christ died for the ungodly," and in 5:9 that while we were still sinners, "Christ died for us." The first person plural pronouns are here significant, since Paul begins using them in 4:23–25 when asserting that Gen 15:6 and its reckoning of righteousness was written not only for Abraham but also for "us who believe in him who raised Jesus our Lord from the dead."[90] The children of Abraham, both Jew and Gentile, believe and are reckoned righteous in the same manner as the patriarch, and all these children also number among the ungodly and the sinners for whom Christ died. How is Abraham not, according to Paul's argument, to number among the ungodly, unless a wedge is to be driven between the patriarch and his children? The whole of Paul's surrounding argument confirms precisely what we would expect from the fact that the description of God as the one who justifies the ungodly (4:5) arises as part of Paul's exposition of what Gen 15:6 means when it says that Abraham was justified through his faith: contrary to Wright, Abraham numbered among the ungodly.

Even more implausible is Wright's third denial, which is the rejection of the assumption that the quotation of Ps 32 (LXX 31) in 4:7–8 is

---

90. Stowers, *A Rereading of Romans*, argues that the indictment of 3:9 is not universal but applies to a particular time of sin (182) and that 3:20 applies particularly to Gentiles (190). He follows this implication through in his treatment of Rom 4, suggesting the significance of 4:22–25 to be that "At the last judgment, God will vindicate 'us' gentiles who share in the blessings of Abraham's heritage" (248). On Stowers's view Rom 5:1–11 then announces the reconciliation of the Gentiles, but he does not deal with the difficulty that his argument presumably requires Paul's extensive use of first person plural pronouns to include both the Gentiles and himself but not to include other Jews. There is also nothing in Rom 5:1–11 to suggest that Paul intends his statements to apply more directly to Gentiles than to Jews.

intended to refer to Jew and Gentile alike.[91] Instead of defining justification in terms of forgiveness of sins, for Wright the text quoted "gives testimony to the blessing of forgiveness to anyone who has no 'works', no outward sign of belonging to God's people."[92] Paul does not apply the text either primarily or equally to Jews, but specifically to show that Gentile sinners will also be included in God's family. This makes little sense of the psalm, which throughout is concerned with David's personal experience of sin and divine forgiveness (cf. Ps 32:5). Further, Paul explains that the quotation concerns "the blessedness of those to whom God reckons righteousness apart from works" (4:6), and it is difficult to see how David's personal experience can be explained as that of one who lacks "works" if "works" here refers primarily to boundary markers as outward signs of belonging to God's people. As Gathercole puts it, "David although circumcised, sabbatarian, and kosher, is described as without works because of his disobedience."[93] Finally, the repeated use of the noun "blessedness" (μακαρισμός) and the adjective "blessed" (μακάριος) ties together in Paul's argument precisely those things that Wright wants to keep apart. The blessedness of the person to whom God reckons righteousness apart from works (4:6) is to be equated with the blessed state of those whose sins are forgiven (4:7-8), and this blessedness is then explicitly said to be not only for the circumcised but also for the uncircumcised (4:9), i.e., Paul begins from the assumption that the blessing of righteousness apart from works understood in terms of the forgiveness of sins is a blessing that is for Jews but not for them only.

Rejecting Wright's denials is important in part because leaving his exegesis unchallenged would leave crucial aspects of Paul's argument obscured. Justification is for Paul concerned with dealing with and forgiving human sin and in 4:4-5 in particular he wishes to deny that justification can be earned by human obedience. Abraham's faith and not his obedience was the means of his justification by the one who justifies the ungodly. On all of the exegetical issues in 4:1-8 on which Wright proposes a new approach, the superiority of trajectories of interpretation deriving from the Reformers endures. Yet rejecting Wright's denials also matters for the sake of salvaging the strengths of his own interpretation. For if Wright's denials were accepted, then his

---

91. Wright, "Paul and the Patriarch," 207-41 (esp. 232-36).
92. Wright, "Paul and the Patriarch," 236.
93. Gathercole, *Where iIs Boasting?*, 247.

entirely appropriate insistence on the significance in Paul's argument of the worldwide nature of the family of both Jews and Gentiles promised to Abraham would be imperiled. Wright's defense of his particular "covenantal" account of justification puts at risk what he recovers as a major emphasis in the passage. For Paul's struggle to define and defend this worldwide family as legitimate depends upon what is true in relation to the justification of the indisputably Jewish figures of Abraham and David also being true of the justification of Gentiles and vice versa. Ungodly and sinful Gentiles can only become descendants of Abraham through the righteousness of faith that brings forgiveness and was received in the same way by Abraham and his Jewish descendants: "there is no distinction, since all have sinned and fall short of the glory of God" (3:23). If Abraham did not number among the ungodly, and if David's discussion of the blessedness of those whose sins are forgiven is not to be read in its Jewish context, then the distinction that Paul insists must be avoided is introduced. And if this distinction is introduced, then his parallel insistence is placed in jeopardy: that the faith of the uncircumcised and the faith of Abraham are to be identified with each other so that the patriarch is their father.

In his account of Rom 4, Campbell is also concerned with the paternity of Abraham and the fulfillment of the promise to the patriarch of a worldwide family, but in a rather different way from Wright. For Campbell, the granting to Abraham of a son and heir serves to illustrate the nature of justification not as covenant membership but as a liberating, apocalyptic divine act of deliverance: "it seems hard to avoid the conclusion that Isaac is God's righteous and saving act—his act of grace toward Abraham. . . . Christians are to trust in God who raised Jesus from the dead, just as Abraham trusted in a resurrecting God who conceived Isaac from sterile parents."[94] Such an "apocalyptic" understanding of justification stands for Campbell in contrast to all contractual readings. As a liberating divine act, justification is not to be understood in terms of God accepting human faith *as if* it were righteousness so that faith becomes a disposition pleasing to God that is accepted as a condition that human beings can manage to fulfill in place of the righteousness that is beyond them. "Abraham believed God, and it was reckoned to him as righteousness" cannot mean that Abraham's faith was simply viewed by God as an acceptable alternative to righteousness. Unsurprisingly, Campbell is

94. Campbell, *The Deliverance of God*, 749.

therefore not concerned to deny that Paul's contrast between working and receiving a gift (4:4-5) is aimed against the idea that human obedience is a cause of justification, or to deny that Abraham numbers among the ungodly (4:5),[95] or to deny that the forgiveness spoken of in 4:6-8 is constitutive of what Paul means by justification and applies equally to Jew and Gentile. All these elements in traditional Protestant interpretations of the passage cohere with his emphasis on the gratuitous nature of God's justifying act, and Campbell regards himself as in agreement with what he terms "the conventional reading" of 4:2-8.[96] What Campbell does want to do is to erect further barriers against what he regards as the danger of a contractual emphasis within such a conventional reading by offering his own perspective on Paul's use of Gen 15:6 and the meaning of the verb "reckon" (λογίζομαι), and by drawing attention to the reality-defying nature of Abraham's faith.

The implausibility from a normal human perspective of the promise in which Abraham trusted makes it difficult to construe such faith as a manageable condition. Abraham's faith, Campbell points out, is in Rom 4:16b-22 a faith in God's capacity to do the impossible and "bring life to Abraham's sterile, aged loins and to Sarah's equally sterile and aged womb."[97] It would be a hopeless task for Paul's Gentile readers to attempt to emulate it. Rather they have received such faith as a gift and so become children of Abraham themselves (4:16). They are not just imitating Abraham by their faith but are participating in the same narrative of divine saving action as the patriarch:

> Christians will be given δικαιοσύνη, as Abraham was, because they trust in God who raises Jesus from the dead, and v. 25 adds that Jesus himself was handed over to death and raised to life. For this analogy to hold fully, however, Abraham must trust God *concerning Isaac*, a son conceived in the face of death and thereby in a sense also resurrected. . . . Christians trust God "the Father" concerning "his Son,"

---

95. Campbell, *The Deliverance of God*, 753, seems to hint at such a denial in order to avoid any suggestion that Abraham responded with faith to a prospective revelation of his sinfulness. However, this is not a major part of Campbell's argument and the question of whether Abraham recognized himself as ungodly as a prelude to his justification should not be conflated with the question of whether he was in fact numbered among the ungodly.

96. Campbell, *The Deliverance of God*, 730.

97. Campbell, *The Deliverance of God*, 36.

dead and raised, just as Abraham trusted God concerning *his* son, conceived from the dead and thereby brought to life.[98]

The righteousness of which Paul speaks is therefore the saving and life-giving actions of divine deliverance displayed in the birth of Isaac and the resurrection of Jesus. The verb "to justify" may be a forensic image, but is "forensic-liberative . . . the trusters are being acquitted in the sense that they are being delivered or released from jail; God has liberated them through the Christ event."[99]

Campbell's insistence on this reality-defying nature of Abraham's faith is entirely valid. The problem in his argument is that he offers this emphasis as a corrective to conventional readings, and in so doing illustrates the extreme artificiality of the "Justification Theory" he considers such conventional readings to exemplify. Significantly, Campbell fails to note that the reality-defying nature of Abraham's faith is a central point of early Reformation exegesis.[100] Luther is supposedly the most significant single contributor to the excessively contractual "Justification Theory" and yet Luther is not the least concerned to construe faith as something manageable for human beings in contrast to the impossible demand of righteousness. Rather, Luther regards Abraham's faith and human reason as locked in a struggle to the death: "Faith slaughters reason and kills the beast that the whole world and all the creatures cannot kill. Thus Abraham killed it by faith in the word of God, in which offspring was promised to him from Sarah, who was barren and past child-bearing."[101] This stands in contrast to Luther's own opponents who in their insistence on an infused righteousness of works he considers "cannot strip off the thoughts of reason, which declares that righteousness is a right judgment and a right will."[102] Far from substituting the manageable requirement of faith for the impossible demand of righteousness, Luther pits the mi-

---

98. Campbell, *The Deliverance of God*, 738 (his emphasis).

99. Campbell, *The Deliverance of God*, 747. For Campbell—one of the principal advocates of the subjective genitive reading of Paul's phrase πίστις Χριστοῦ ("the faithfulness of Christ" rather than "faith in Christ")—Paul's argument in Rom 4 creates an analogy with three components: the faith of Abraham, the faith of Jesus, and the faith of the Christian.

100. See 4.3 and the important discussion in Steinmetz, "Abraham and the Reformation," 32–46.

101. *LW* 26:228 = *WA* 40.1:362, 15–17.

102. *LW* 26:233–34 = *WA* 40.1:370, 23–24.

raculous gift of faith against the rational illusion that righteousness by works is achievable.

Similarly, it is not obvious that Campbell's concern strenuously to deny that Paul considers Abraham's faith to have been regarded by God as if it were righteousness places him in tension with Reformation exegesis. Campbell argues that the use of the verb λογίζομαι indicates that righteousness is credited to Abraham according to ancient notions of credit in which a letter of credit promises to the bearer a sum that has not yet been paid. In comparison to the contemporary economy, this is more like a bank check than it is like credit. The person today to whom a check is written has a document promising payment but the money itself has not yet been paid. Thus, Paul's account of justification is here both given a strongly eschatological dimension and the key point maintained that the divine promise of righteousness is not merited: "in view of Abraham's trust God promised to do something for him in the future; a divine check was written to the patriarch that in this case had clearly not been worked for or earned."[103] Campbell goes so far as to on this basis assert that "Isaac is the δικαιοσύνη that God gifts to Abraham, having promised him earlier on."[104] There are some issues here, such as whether Paul's argument explicitly indicates this about Isaac and whether Paul's argument is so exclusively oriented towards the future, for the death and resurrection of Jesus are events that have already happened and Paul expresses a strong sense that justification is "now" (Rom 5:9). However, if we accept that Campbell is correct in this identification of Isaac with the righteous, saving act performed by God for Abraham, who or what is the righteous, saving act received by those who believe in the resurrecting God who raised Jesus (Rom 4:25)? The righteous deed of Christ leads to justification and life for all (Rom 5:18), and God has predestined believers "to be conformed to the image of his Son" (Rom 8:29). Abraham trusts God to create life from the dead for him through Isaac, and Christians trust God to raise them from the dead, yet the resurrection of believers will not be an independent event but a sharing in the resurrection of Christ (Rom 6:5). Christ is God's righteous, saving act for them, and so if it is valid to say that Isaac is the righteousness that God gifts to Abraham, then it is also valid to say that Christ is the righteousness given by God to the believer. In other words, while Campbell wishes to develop the

103. Campbell, *The Deliverance of God*, 732.
104. Campbell, *The Deliverance of God*, 749.

participatory aspects of Paul's argument in terms of Christians sharing in Christ's faithfulness, Campbell's own argument about Rom 4 points rather more towards incorporated righteousness.

Indeed, it is very difficult on the basis of incorporated righteousness to fall into the danger that Campbell is so anxious to avoid, of treating faith "as if" it were righteousness. As we might expect, for interpreters like Luther and Calvin who consider that justification involves union with Christ and the receiving of his righteousness, faith simply cannot function "as if" it were righteousness. Rather, faith justifies because it unites the believer with Christ and his actual and complete righteousness. And in Reformation exegesis more broadly, repeatedly emphasized is the nature of faith as a gift from God and the confidence placed by faith in divine grace and mercy. Melanchthon states that when Abraham believed, "he was sure he had a gracious God."[105] Similarly, Calvin says of Abraham that "the only ground of his righteousness was his trust in the goodness of God, and his daring to hope for all things from Him. . . . Faith is reckoned as righteousness not because it brings any merit from us, but because it lays hold of the goodness of God."[106] The emphasis is on the character of the divine giver of faith and not on the character of faith itself.

Nevertheless, gifts, and especially divine ones, reflect the character of the giver. This means that there are two opposite errors that must be avoided in interpreting the nature of faith. On the one side falling into the ugly ditch of treating faith as if it is a human disposition that somehow stands in the place of righteousness can be avoided by distinguishing between faith and justifying righteousness. Yet it is also necessary to re-member that it is just as possible to fall into the same ugly ditch on the opposite side by distinguishing between them so sharply that the nature of faith as a divinely gifted reality is again obscured. Although this was not what was intended, it does seem to me to become a danger in early Protestantism in the 1550s in the context of the Osiander controversy. Here the perceived danger was Osiander's error of so stressing the in-dwelling in the believer of the essential righteousness of Christ's divine nature as to minimize the part played in justification by Christ's death and resurrection. This led both Melanchthon and Calvin to distinguish faith and righteousness extremely sharply so as to highlight the extrinsic

---

105. Melanchthon, *Commentary on Romans*, 108 = CR 15:596.
106. *Comm. Rom* 4:3–4, CNTC 8:84–85 = OE 13:81, 71 – 82, 6.

christological basis of justification and its accompanying assurance of forgiveness. Melanchthon writes that when it is said that we are justified "it should be understood correlatively, that is, for the sake of the Lord Christ, not that the work, namely faith, is the merit . . . [T]he power to revitalize, pacify, and comfort the heart is not the power of faith, but of Christ himself, who through faith works, comforts, and gives his Holy Spirit in the heart."[107] For his part Calvin disputes Osiander's statement that "faith is Christ" and insists that faith is merely "a vessel" that does not have the power to justify and is simply the earthen pot that contains the golden treasure that is Christ.[108] This description of faith as an earthen pot is effective against Osiander, but it is not obvious that it sits well with Calvin's own deeply felt characterizations of faith as a work of the Holy Spirit that unites the believer with Christ.

Luther, of course, did not live long enough to need to react to Osiander. In his own context, he had countered the doctrine of faith formed by love by insisting that the righteous Christ is the form of faith, i.e., that which determines or shapes its properties and activities. This manner of insisting on the presence of Christ in faith means that Luther does not distinguish between faith and righteousness in the same sharp way that Melanchthon and Calvin were later to do. He comments on Gen 15:6 that

> faith is indeed a formal righteousness, but this does not suffice, for after faith there still remain remnants of sin in the flesh. . . . From these words, "It was imputed to him as righteousness," we conclude, therefore, that righteousness does indeed begin through faith and that through it we have the first fruits of the Spirit. But because faith is weak, it is not perfected without the imputation of God. Hence faith begins righteousness, but imputation perfects it until the day of Christ.[109]

Thus, despite all his discomfort with the notion of merit and his polemic against works-righteousness, far from treating faith as something substituting for righteousness as if it were righteousness, Luther considers that there is a sense in which it is legitimate to say that faith

---

107. *Melanchthon on Christian Doctrine*, 159 = CR 22:331.
108. *Institutes* 3.11.7 = CO 2:547–48.
109. *LW* 26:229–30 = WA 40.1:364, 12–28.

simply is righteousness. As a divine gift (not merely a human disposition) faith properly worships God by trusting in God's promises and in so doing gives glory to God (Rom 4:20). Yet since those engaged in trusting God are sinful human beings, faith is also always itself imperfect and reliant on the alien righteousness of Christ, for righteousness "is outside us, solely in the grace of God and in His imputation. In us there is nothing of the form or of the righteousness except that weak faith or the first fruits of faith by which we have begun to take hold of Christ."[110] Thus faith and righteousness are distinguished but not in a way that obscures the nature of faith either as divine gift or as human deed. Faith involves factual change in the believer, but it is not this change that is justifying but rather Christ's presence in faith.[111]

Luther thus insists on the reality of faith as righteousness but emphasizes that it is not meritorious and is incomplete and utterly dependent upon the righteousness of Christ, on whose account "God reckons imperfect righteousness as perfect righteousness."[112] In Gen 15:6, in view of Abraham's trust (his imperfect righteousness), God credits to him that perfect righteousness that will belong to believers on the day of Christ. Viewed from the perspective of the believer's behavioral righteousness, this gives a strong future dimension to the crediting that is involved in justification. The perfect righteousness that is promised will be the believer's own only eschatologically. Luther uses a different image, "We have received the first fruits of the Spirit, but not the tithes,"[113] but this manner of emphasizing what the believer will receive in the future is not in any obvious way in conflict with Campbell's interpretation of "reckoning" ($\lambda o\gamma i\zeta o\mu\alpha\iota$) in terms of ancient notions of credit in which the person to whom credit is extended is promised something for the future. Yet Luther would obviously also insist that, when viewed from a heavenly perspective, in justifying faith the alien righteousness of Christ is fully present now and is complete now. Indeed, it is upon this present alien righteousness that the forgiveness of the believer's continued sin and the fulfillment of the eschatological promise depend.[114] Once again, it

110. *LW* 26:234 = *WA* 40.1:370, 29–31.

111. On this point, see Mats Wahlberg, "Why Isn't Faith a Work? An Examination of Protestant Answers," *SJT* 68.2 (2015): 201–17.

112. *LW* 26:232 = *WA* 40.1:367, 19–20.

113. *LW* 26:230 = *WA* 40.1:364, 18.

114. Barclay, *Paul and the Gift*, 490, points out the careful pattern of similarity and difference contained in Paul's parallel between the faith of Abraham and that of

matters to insist that the initial liberating event of justification remains a continuously present reality in the life of believers and does not simply give way to something else. From either perspective, however, faith is not treated by Luther as a substitute for righteousness that becomes the means by which the human side of a contract with God is fulfilled. The weak faith of the believer is, as a work of God in a fallen human being, a real but imperfect righteousness, and this imperfect righteousness grasps hold of the perfect alien righteousness of Christ.

Having discussed Reformation perspectives on Rom 4 in dialog with Wright and Campbell, we can now identify several essential elements of any exegetically satisfying account of this vital text. Against Wright, Paul's exposition of Abraham's justifying faith in Rom 4:4–5 using a contrast between wages/rewards and gift cannot be explained away. Paul really is concerned to emphasize at this point in his argument that justification does not result from human obedience, and in the context of that concern he numbers Abraham among the ungodly. Justification is then further explained in 4:6–8 in terms of forgiveness of sin, a blessing illustrated with reference to David, Israel's greatest king. Further, the faith that justified Abraham in this way so clearly defies all human reality and reason that it makes little sense if discussed as an alternative condition on the basis of which human beings are justified when they satisfy it. What might be termed an anti-contractual tradition in the interpretation of Rom 4, whether in its Reformation form, or as presented by Campbell, finds abundant material in the text on which to base itself. Faith does not justify as a replacement for righteousness, treated by God "as if" it were righteousness. Yet this anti-contractual tradition goes astray if Paul's emphasis on justification as forgiveness is used to narrow its significance to a resolution of the guilt of transgressions alone. As Campbell rightly argues when commenting on 4:23–25, the correlation between resurrection and justification points towards justification as a liberation or deliverance in which the forgiveness of sins is a central feature but stands alongside

---

believers: "both entail faith in 'resurrection from the dead.' But this surface similarity accompanies a significant difference: in the one case, Abraham believed that God *would create something from his and Sarah's deadness*, while in the other, believers believe that God *has raised Jesus from the dead*. Is Paul content with this limited parallel, or does the believers' faith regarding Christ also, like Abraham's, concern 'life out of death' *in relation to themselves*? Later chapters will show that the parallel does indeed extend this far. . . . In fact, 4:25 already indicates that belief about Christ is self-involving, and in no sense *only* about Christ" (his emphasis).

an emphasis on the granting of life: Paul is discussing "the deliverance of humanity from a realm characterized by transgressions and death," i.e., in order to sustain a proper emphasis on the forgiveness of transgressions, it is not necessary to narrow justification to such forgiveness alone. However, this is not the only way in which such a tradition might go astray. There is also the danger of development in an exclusively individualistic direction. To neglect the fact that the fulfillment of God's promises to Abraham results in a worldwide family (Rom 4:11-12, 16-17) is, as Wright reminds us, also a distortion of Paul's argument. There is a powerful ecclesial and communal element in this argument in which the Abrahamic descent granted to believers through faith becomes a vital aspect of the identity of the people of God.

In constructing such a list of essential elements in the argument of Rom 4, I am holding together complementary features that are often instead contrasted by exegetes, and suggesting that we should regard as mutually implied elements more typically treated as alternatives. I have rejected as unwarranted and unnecessary Wright's denials of several crucial Reformation insights concerning the nature of Abraham's faith and of justification, argued that some of Campbell's best insights in his apocalyptic account of justification in Rom 4 are consistent with incorporated righteousness, and recognized that Wright is correct to assert the significance in Paul's argument of the worldwide family of Abraham. The crucial question that then remains is whether, despite the relative neglect of this familial theme in Reformation exegesis of Rom 4, incorporated righteousness can provide a basis on which to integrate an emphasis on the worldwide family of Abraham with an anti-contractual reading that denies the capacity of human obedience to justify.[115] Clearly it can only do so if the theme of union with Christ is

---

115. See the treatment of Rom 4 provided by Barclay, *Paul and the Gift*, 479-92: "Our task is to integrate Paul's dual portrayal of Abraham as both *believer* in God and *father* of a multinational family" (481, his emphasis). Barclay argues that the contrast between wages and gift (Rom 4:3) is not directed against any general soteriology of works but rather to insist on the incongruity of grace: "there was nothing in Abraham's conduct that made God's crediting of 'righteousness' a matter of congruous reward" (485). Barclay is correct that Paul does not *characterize* Judaism in terms of works-righteousness or attempts to earn salvation. However, if divine grace is itself characterized by its incongruity, then other Jewish accounts in which grace is congruous are, from Paul's perspective, in danger of construing human ethical achievement as contributing to justification. This is far from the only dimension of human worthiness that Paul portrays as disregarded by incongruous grace, but it is a significant one and it is in view in Rom 4:1-8.

powerfully present in the argument of Rom 4. As we have seen, Campbell partly recognizes this, stressing the significance for interpreting the figure of Abraham in Rom 4 of the christological material in 3:21-22, 3:27-31, and 4:24-25. Paul is not arguing that Abraham is an example of faith that Christians copy but instead that that he and they participate in the same divine saving act.[116] However, Campbell develops this largely as another safeguard against a contractual reading.

The positive significance of union with Christ for interpreting Rom 4 is explored more thoroughly by Michael Gorman, who regards Romans as a treatise on *theosis* in which 1:18-3:20 describes the loss of the righteousness and glory intended for humanity by the Creator. These good gifts are exchanged for unrighteousness and death, and the rest of Romans concerns the divine undoing of this unhappy exchange through Christ. "For Paul, the solution to the human condition of sin and death, of unrighteousness and un-glory, is new and eternal life by participation in Christ. . . . In Christ, humans begin sharing in the righteousness of God and even begin the process of sharing in God's glory. This is because God's righteousness and glory are found in Christ."[117] The unhappy exchange is undone by its joyful antidote: Christ became what we are in order that we might become what he is. This framework for reading the whole of Romans means that Gorman rejects any idea that Rom 5-8 represents a stage in the Christian life subsequent to or separate from justification. The theme of righteousness runs through the whole of Romans and, for example, "3:21-26 should be read in connection with ch. 6, which does not describe a supplement to 'justification by faith' but rather depicts justification as an experience of death and resurrection."[118]

116. Campbell, *The Deliverance of God*, 751-54.

117. Gorman, "Romans: The First Christian Treatise on Theosis," 23. In emphasizing exchange, Gorman depends on the classic articles by Morna D. Hooker, "Interchange in Christ," in *From Adam to Christ: Essays on Paul* (Cambridge: Cambridge University Press, 1990), 13-25, and Morna D. Hooker, "Interchange and Atonement," in *From Adam to Christ: Essays on Paul* (Cambridge: Cambridge University Press, 1990), 26-41. Both Hooker and Gorman recognize that in emphasizing exchange they are appropriating an interpretative tradition with a long pedigree. However, both seem more aware of patristic examples than they do of Luther, for whom exchange is of considerable importance in his accounts of justification. See also Michael J. Gorman, *Becoming the Gospel: Paul, Participation, and Mission* (Grand Rapids: Eerdmans, 2015), 261-96.

118. Gorman, "The First Christian Treatise on Theosis," 23. Although not engaging with Reformation interpreters, Gorman is clearly on this point in sharp disagreement with Calvin's conviction that the argument of Romans transitions to discussion of sancti-

Within this framework the faith of Abraham in Rom 4 is read as "an exemplum of Paul's unique participatory understanding of justification by faith as co-crucifixion and co-resurrection with Christ (4:16-17). . . . [B]ecause Abraham himself was functionally dead (4:19a)—along with his wife's womb (4:19b)—his faith was that God could bring life out of *his* death, could transform *his* deadness into life."[119] For Gorman, this stands in contrast to flat readings that emphasize that Abraham was justified by inactive trust that did not result in any fundamental change in his situation: "That he was *justified* by faith means not that he was fictitiously considered just or righteous but that he was granted the gracious gift of new life out of death, which was concretely fulfilled in the birth of a descendant."[120] In the argument of Romans, "Abraham's experience is prospectively analogous to what Paul says about all baptized believers in Rom 6: their justification by faith means a participatory experience of resurrection out of death."[121]

There are a number of problems with Gorman's development of this argument. As his reference to fictitious righteousness implies, Gorman sees the emphasis he wishes to develop as in conflict with previous exegesis and rails against what he regards as the western theological tradition's narrowing of justification to a concern with forgiveness of sins and neglect in Romans of the themes of glory, life, and immortality.[122] Yet, it would not be difficult, for example, to construct a medley of quotations from Luther's, Melanchthon's, and Calvin's comments on Rom 4 in which considerable concern with these themes is expressed. To take but one example, Calvin, as the text demands, emphasizes forgiveness in relation to justification when commenting on 4:6-8 but sees no tension between this and his comment on Rom 4:25 that Christ "is said to have been raised for our justification, because he fully restored life to us by his resurrection."[123] Further, although an emphasis on trust may not be a sufficient account of Abraham's faith, the fact that Abraham's trusting reception of the promise of Gen 15:6 bookends the chapter (4:3-5, 4:20-22) does mean that it and a participatory account of that faith are

---

fication with the start of chapter 6. Gorman's position is in this respect more compatible with Luther's refusal to draw sharp distinctions between justification and sanctification.

119. Gorman, "The First Christian Treatise on Theosis," 23.
120. Gorman, "The First Christian Treatise on Theosis," 23-24.
121. Gorman, "The First Christian Treatise on Theosis," 24.
122. Gorman, "The First Christian Treatise on Theosis," 22.
123. *Comm. Rom* 4:25, *CNTC* 8:103 = *OE* 13:100, 18-20.

scarcely to be set against each other. Finally, Gorman leaves the term *theosis* only very generally defined,[124] and this both ignores the major recent debate as to whether Luther, scarcely a marginal figure in the western theological tradition, understands justification in this way and fails to recognize that there may be other ways of giving expression to the theme of exchange in Paul's letters.

Yet, despite these problems, one of the virtues of Gorman's argument is the quite explicit connection he makes between the participatory nature of faith, which experiences resurrection out of death, and the communal dimensions of Paul's argument: "This resurrection life is actualized, not merely in the birth of Isaac, but in the subsequent reality of many descendants."[125] Gorman does not develop this further, but he does here provide a perspective on Paul's argument from which it can be seen that God's calling into existence of a worldwide family of Abraham, composed of both Jews and Gentiles, is not a circumstantial consequence of God's justifying activity in Christ. Rather, it is an expression of divine identity as one who has made Abraham the father of many nations and "who gives life to the dead and calls into existence the things that do not exist" (4:17). Thus, God's justifying activity creates the church, a family of Abraham from many nations that exists without any human basis, that is a reality only in Christ, and that is called upon to embody righteousness in its common life. In justifying the ungodly and bringing to them the blessedness of forgiveness God does something that is just as startlingly incommensurate with normal human experience as creation *ex nihilo*, the conception of Isaac, and the raising of Jesus from the dead. As Calvin puts it, "when we are called of God we arise out of nothing."[126] The people of God thus exists only because of justification, the communal life of the church as the body of Christ resting upon the union of its members with Christ created by the gift of justifying faith. "Abraham believed God and it was credited to him as righteousness," and, were it not so, there would be no Isaac and no worldwide family of Abraham. Justification does not declare a person to be a member of God's people so that sins are then

---

124. Gorman, *Becoming the Gospel*, 269, terms *theosis*, "transformative participation in the kenotic (self-emptying), cruciform character of God through Spirit-enabled conformity to the incarnate, crucified, and resurrected/glorified Christ." This definition is unobjectionable but fails to make it clear in what way the term *theosis* is more helpful than "participation in Christ" or "union with Christ."

125. Gorman, "The First Christian Treatise on Theosis," 24.

126. *Comm. Rom* 4:17, *CNTC* 8:96 = *OE* 13:93, 9.

forgiven as a consequence of that membership. Rather, in dealing with sin, justification creates a family that otherwise could not exist.

Gorman also rightly sees that the communal dimension he identifies in Rom 4 points forward to the argument of Rom 12-15, with its portrayal of communities of righteousness and glory (features which he dubs "Spirit-Enabled Christlike Godlikeness") that embody the gospel in social practice on the basis of the ongoing participation in Christ that begins at baptism. As Gorman comments, "Paul will not allow us to interpret the experience of this divine life individualistically. What will make the Roman community truly the antithesis of Rom 1-2, and a credible exemplum of what God intended for humanity, is the community's gathering together to glorify God."[127] What is not grappled with, either here or in Gorman's writing on holiness elsewhere,[128] is the continuation of sin and the frequent failure of Christian communities to establish common patterns of life that reflect the righteousness and glory spoken of by Paul. Gorman helpfully draws attention to the prominence of glory in Romans, but fails to give due weight to Paul's strongly eschatological emphasis in discussion of the theme (see Rom 8:17-21). For the church to wait for the glory to be revealed in believers (Rom 8:17b) in complacent unconcern at its failures would indeed be to reject the work of God in justification. Yet, as frail and faltering and inglorious as they may be, Christian communities which press forward in present suffering (Rom 8:17a), seeking to fit their common life to the revelation of God in Jesus Christ, remain communities of the justified.

Gorman correctly insists that righteousness must be embodied in ecclesial communities, but fails to emphasize that such communities can only be a reality because God encounters people in justification outside of themselves. The union with Christ that results in communal behavior that glorifies God is the union created in the justification of sinners, a union in which believers receive the alien righteousness of Christ that does not depend on them or their deeds but is a complete and final reality. Thus it is that the failures of God's people do not divorce them from Christ or rob them of the opportunity again and again to embody righteousness in their lives together. The one with whom they are united, his death and resurrection continuously present as sin-destroying, life-giving realities, is an inexhaustible extrinsic source of the righteousness that they are to practice socially. In justification, believers are united with Christ by faith

---

127. Gorman, "The First Christian Treatise on Theosis," 32.
128. Gorman, *Inhabiting the Cruciform God*, 105-28.

and receive his righteousness and, as they do so, the church is created and forever after sustained. Gorman's emphasis on union with Christ in the interpretation of Rom 4 therefore needs to be clarified in relation to the alien nature of the righteousness of Christ received by believers, but he does succeed in demonstrating that it is significant in Paul's argument. Union with Christ must take its place in the list of elements crucial to the exegesis of Rom 4. By bringing Wright, Campbell, and Gorman into critical dialog with the Reformers, we have clarified that list of elements: Paul's denial of the capacity of human deeds to justify, his emphasis on the worldwide family of Abraham, and his explanation that justifying faith is participatory, uniting the believer with Christ and his righteousness.

9.7. Conclusions

In this final chapter I have sought through careful critical dialog with distinguished contemporary interpreters of the Pauline letters to establish the potential for insights drawn from Reformation interpreters to inform our own attempts to interpret these texts in and for today's world. In doing so I have argued that it is Luther and Calvin, who in their different ways make union with Christ central to their accounts of justification by faith, that most repay attention. In particular, they hold this insistence on the importance of union with Christ alongside an equally emphatic conviction that the nature of justification is extrinsic and that the believer receives Christ's alien righteousness. Far from perceiving these twin emphases as in tension or need of reconciliation, both regard them as belonging together since it is when united with Christ by faith that the believer receives his righteousness. This incorporated righteousness offers an approach to interpreting Paul's statements about justification that makes sense both of texts in which it is apparent that justification directly addresses the issue of sin and texts in which justification appears to have strongly participatory or communal dimensions. I have sought to illustrate this with particular reference to Rom 4 and the faith of Abraham, arguing that incorporated righteousness helps us to hear with proper force all the major elements in Paul's argument (justification as forgiveness, the worldwide family of Abraham, and the participatory nature of faith) without subordinating and marginalizing one or more of them. Incorporated righteousness also helpfully integrates justification with two other crucial themes in the Pauline letters and clarifies their nature:

1. Grace. God's justifying activity displays complete disregard for all normal human notions of worth. No dimensions of human worthiness, even ethical or ethnic ones, can be a contributory cause of justification, which rests solely upon what God has done in Jesus Christ. Yet, far from rendering human actions or communal practices insignificant, such radical divine grace can only be understood and communicated when embodied in the community of believers. Justification creates and sustains the church, which is called to practice this grace in social life and so bear witness to the good news of God's gratuitous love in Christ for sinners. For Paul, the living together of both Jews and Gentiles as the people of God in a united worldwide family of Abraham is one of the primary features of such authentic communal embodiment of grace.

2. Faith. The apparent fear in much contemporary scholarship that an emphasis upon the significance for Paul of human faith detracts from the primacy of divine initiative in salvation is misplaced. Faith is indisputably a human action and disposition, typified by believing trust in God's promises, but it is also participatory. What is justifying about faith is not what it does as a human action and disposition but the fact that it unites the believer with Christ and his righteousness. Further, the very implausibility, from the perspective of normal human experience, of the promises in which faith believes illustrates that such faith is not something that can be summoned by an act of the human will or entered into as an autonomous human decision. Rather, human faith is a divine gift, granted by God through the proclamation of the gospel that is the divinely appointed means by which it is evoked. An emphasis upon this proclamation and the faith it elicits need not detract from, or stand in competition with, an emphasis upon the social practices of Christian communities. In reality, the former is the indispensable presupposition of the latter.

In these ways, thinking about the interpretation of the Pauline letters with the Reformers helps us to hold together theological insights that were intimately and inextricably connected for the apostle but have not been recognized as so closely connected in much recent interpretation. Pauline scholarship must cease putting asunder what was joined together by Paul and the Holy Spirit.

Medieval and Reformation Figures

Agricola, Johannes (1494-1566), early follower of Martin Luther. Their friendship came to an end as a result of the *Antinomian* controversy. Agricola maintained that the law has no continued relevance for the Christian life. Agricola relocated to Berlin, becoming court preacher to the Elector of Brandenburg.

Alesius, Alexander (1500-1565), Scottish theologian, biblical commentator, and Protestant exile, who from 1532 spent his life in Germany and England. He was resident in Wittenberg for a time, where he became close to Melanchthon. He later became rector of the University of Leipzig.

Anselm (c. 1033-1109), influential monk, theologian, and philosopher. He was Archbishop of Canterbury from 1093 until his death. He is best known for his writings on the atonement and his development of the ontological argument for the existence of God.

Aquinas, Thomas (1225-1274), Dominican theologian and biblical commentator. He adapted Aristotle's metaphysics and epistemology to Christianity. Remembered as one of the greatest Catholic theologians. The philosophical school of Thomism takes its name from him.

Biel, Gabriel (c. 1420-1495), Ockhamist theologian and philosopher. In 1484 he became the first Professor of Theology at the University of Tübingen. His views on justification, in which God covenants to grant grace to those who do what lies within them, were radically rejected by Luther.

Bray, Guy de (1522–1567), Walloon pastor and Reformed theologian, who was hanged for his beliefs. He was the author of *The Belgic Confession* (1561).

Brenz, Johannes (1499–1570), early Lutheran theologian and biblical commentator. He was won over by encountering Luther in person at the Heidelberg Disputation in 1518. He later spearheaded the Reformation in Württemberg.

Bucer, Martin (1491–1551), key figure in the Reformation in Strasbourg and one of the most influential exegetes, theologians, and church leaders in the early Reformed tradition. Bucer was also a key figure at the *Diet of Regensburg* in 1541, where an unsuccessful attempt was made to reach agreement with representatives of the Catholic church.

Budé, Guillaume (1467–1540), a French humanist scholar and correspondent of Erasmus, famed for his expertise in ancient law, monies, and measures.

Bugenhagen, Johann (1485–1558), a Pomeranian priest convinced by the writings of Luther. He moved to Wittenberg and became the pastor of St. Mary's church, combining this from 1533 with a chair in theology. Possessed of considerable organizational gifts, he was a key figure in facilitating reform across northern Germany and Scandinavia.

Bullinger, Heinrich (1504–1575), successor to Zwingli as leader of the reformation in Zurich, a position he held for over forty years. Effective in the pulpit and influential through the publication of his sermons, he was a key figure in maintaining the unity of the Reformed movement in its second generation. He was also the main author of the *Second Helvetic Confession* (published 1566).

Bure, Idelette de (d. 1549), Dutch widow of John Storder, an Anabaptist. She married John Calvin in Strasbourg in 1540 after being recommended to him by Martin Bucer. Their marriage was successful and her death a source of great grief to Calvin. They had no surviving children.

Calvin, John (1509–1564), aspiring French lawyer and humanist scholar who, after a conversion experience in the early 1530s, went into exile and became leader of the Reformation in Geneva. Through his preaching, biblical commentaries, and works of theology (especially the *Institutes of the Christian Religion*) he became the dominant intellectual force within the Reformed tradition.

Campeggio, Lorenzo (1474–1539), cardinal and papal diplomat, a key figure in the refusal to grant Henry VIII of England an annulment of his marriage to Katharine of Aragon and in Henry's subsequent excommunication.

Capito, Wolfgang (c. 1478–1541), a native of Alsace who from 1523 was a key ally of Martin Bucer in the reform of the church in Strasbourg.

Charles V (1500–1558), Holy Roman Emperor and King of Spain. Charles was a committed opponent of the Reformation but through the *Peace of Augsburg* in 1555 he ultimately had to accept the division of Germany on confessional lines.

Chemnitz, Martin (1522–1586), theologian and one of the main authors of the *Formula of Concord* (1577), he was a key figure in maintaining the unity of Lutheranism in its second generation. A student of Luther and Melanchthon at Wittenberg, his most influential works were his textbook (*Loci Theologici*) and his detailed *Examination of the Council of Trent*.

Contarini, Gasparo (1483–1542), native of Venice, cardinal, papal diplomat, humanist scholar, and theologian. An advocate of dialogue, Contarini was one of the main Catholic participants in the *Diet of Regensburg* (1541). Loyal to Rome, his views on justification nevertheless later came to be regarded as suspiciously close to those of the Reformers.

Cordatus, Conrad (1480–1546), pastor and leading figure in the Reformation in Brandenburg. He was close to Luther and a student at Wittenberg. In 1536 he initiated disputes concerning justification with Caspar Cruciger and Philip Melanchthon, whom he suspected of departing from Luther's teaching.

Cruciger, Caspar (1504–1548), professor of theology and philosophy, and pastor of the Castle Church in Wittenberg. He wrote several theological works and biblical commentaries. He was remembered as being close to Philip Melanchthon, to whom his writings have sometimes been incorrectly attributed.

Dietrich, Veit (1506–1549), pastor and reformer at Nuremberg. Dietrich also spent several years in Wittenberg. He was a trusted collaborator with Luther, acting as a kind of secretary and playing a significant role in the recording and publishing of several of Luther's works.

Erasmus, Desiderius (1466–1536), Dutch humanist of enormous significance for New Testament scholarship through his work on the Greek and Latin text (*Novum Testamentum*), the philological erudition of his *Annotations*, and the devotional impact of his *Paraphrases*. He remained loyal to the Catholic church but was viewed by many as having provided the groundwork for Luther's theology.

Gropper, Johannes (1503–1559), jurist and theologian, opponent of the Reformation in Cologne, and author of the *Enchiridion* (1538), perhaps the most important pre-Tridentine critique of the Reformers' theology. Yet as a convinced humanist and follower of Erasmus, Gropper came to be viewed with suspicion by some Catholics.

Hausman, Nicholas (1478/79–1538), follower of Luther, pastor and reformer at Zwickau in Saxony, who clashed with the "Zwickau Prophets," early advocates of a more radical form of Reformation.

Henry VIII (1491–1547), King of England. Although his personal religious views were conservative, Henry's desire to annul his marriage to Katharine of Aragon led him to break with Rome and make himself Supreme Head of the Church of England (1534), thus initiating the English Reformation.

Laski, Jan (1499–1560), Polish priest who became a friend of Erasmus and Zwingli in exile in Switzerland in the 1520s and joined the Reformed tradition. Later, he was a pastor of a church for Protestant refugees in London in the reign of Edward VI. He spent his final years in Poland, promoting reformation there.

Latomus, Jacobus (c. 1475–1544), Flemish theologian and member of the theology faculty of Leuven who questioned William Tyndale in prison and engaged in published theological disputes with him. His early treatise criticizing Luther prompted the important tract *Against Latomus* (1521).

Lee, Edward (c. 1482–1544), an early public critic of Erasmus's work on the New Testament. Lee later became Archbishop of York in 1531.

Leo X (1475–1521), pope from 1513 and member of the Medici dynasty of Florence. His bulls required Christians to believe in papal authority to issue indulgences (November of 1518), condemned errors in Luther's published works (June of 1520), and excommunicated Luther (January of 1521).

Lombard, Peter (c. 1096–1160), Italian theologian who spent his career in Paris, where he became both professor at the cathedral school of Notre Dame and later bishop. He wrote *The Four Books of Sentences*, the standard textbook of scholastic theology for the remainder of the medieval period.

Luther, Martin (1483–1546), Augustinian monk, whose rejection of the practice of indulgences led to his development of a new soteriology centered upon justification by faith and the division of western Christianity into Protestant and Catholic confessions. His significance for biblical scholarship rests principally upon his translation of the Bible into German, his Pauline commentaries (especially Galatians), and his hermeneutical principle of law and gospel.

Mary I (1516–1558), Queen of England, daughter of Henry VIII and Katharine of Aragon. Mary's reign came between those of her Protestant half-brother Edward VI (1547–1553) and half-sister Elizabeth I (1558–1603). She made an ultimately unsuccessful attempt to restore England to the Catholic Church, during which various prominent Protestants were exiled or executed.

Melanchthon, Philip (1497–1560), humanist, theologian, and biblical commentator, who was Luther's closest collaborator in the faculty at Wittenberg and stands next only to Luther in importance for the development of Lutheranism. His *Loci Communes* (1521) was the first Protestant textbook of theology. He developed a rhetorical approach to biblical commentary and was a notable educational theorist.

Montaigne, Michel de (1533–1592), French philosopher and essayist. Himself a Catholic, Montaigne was a moderating influence in religious disputes during his time as mayor of Bordeaux (1581–1585).

Ochino, Bernardino (1487–1564), Italian vicar general of the Order of Friars Minor Capuchin who fled to Geneva when summoned before the Inquisition in 1542. He spent the remainder of his life in exile in Switzerland, England, Poland, and Moravia. He was the author of numerous works, including an exposition of Romans.

Ockham, William of (c. 1287–1347), English Franciscan philosopher and theologian, the founder of Nominalism. A strong advocate of divine freedom, Ockham maintained that God's will is not subject to external or internal constraints but itself establishes right and wrong.

Oecolampadius, Johannes (1482–1531), German priest and humanist, and collaborator of both Erasmus and Zwingli, he was cathedral preacher at Basel. In the early 1520s he embraced Luther's theology and became an advocate of reform.

Osiander, Andreas (1498–1552), German priest and theologian, important as a reformer in Nuremberg in the 1520s. Later he was professor at Königsberg University. After Luther's death, he accused Melanchthon and others of distorting Luther's teaching on justification and emphasized "essential righteousness"—the presence of Christ's divine nature in the believer.

Perkins, William (1558–1602), prolific and widely influential Reformed Cambridge theologian, whose works include an exposition of Galatians.

Petrarca, Francesco (1304–1374), usually "Petrarch" in English, Italian scholar and poet, traditionally regarded as the father of the humanist tradition, who argued for the compatibility of classical culture and Christianity. He discovered lost letters of the Roman statesman Cicero.

Pighius, Albertus (1490–1542), Dutch mathematician and theologian, who was committed to the authority of the Catholic church. His own views on justification were, however, defined at Trent as outside the Catholic tradition. He wrote against Luther and Calvin on the freedom of the will, prompting Calvin's tract *The Bondage and Liberation of the Will* (1543).

Schmedenstede, Heinrich (d. 1554), student at Wittenberg, at whose licentiate examination in 1542 Luther was an active participant. He subsequently became pastor and professor at Rostock.

Scotus, Duns (1266–1308), Scottish priest, theologian, and philosopher, active at Oxford, Paris, and Cologne. Often remembered in doctrine for his advocacy of the immaculate conception of Mary and in metaphysics for his advocacy of the univocity of being.

Seripando, Girolamo (1493–1563), Italian cardinal, theologian, and Augustinian friar, he was at different times superior general of the Augustinian order and archbishop of Salerno. He was papal legate at Trent but some of his own views on justification were not adopted by the Council, being regarded by many as too amenable to Protestant teaching.

Spalatin, Georg (1484–1545), humanist, court chaplain and secretary under Frederick the Wise of Saxony, he was influential in advocating and spreading reform once he adopted Luther's views as his own in 1523. Hundreds of letters to him from Luther survive. He also translated Latin works by Luther, Melanchthon, and Erasmus into German

Steinbach, Wendelin (1454–1519), theologian and Ockhamist, student of Gabriel Biel and professor of theology at Tübingen who lectured extensively on the Pauline letters.

Tauler, Johannes (c. 1300–1361), German Dominican preacher whose mystical theology emphasized experience of God through imitation of Christ's humility.

Textor, Benedict (d. sometime after 1556), doctor of John Calvin and his wife, Idelette de Bure, in Geneva.

Tyndale, William (1494–1536), theologian and linguist, who translated the New Testament and large parts of the Old Testament into English. An advocate of reform, he was in exile from 1524 and was executed for heresy at Vilvoorde, Belgium.

Valla, Lorenzo (1407–1457), Italian priest and humanist who famously exposed the Donation of Constantine as a forgery. He also produced annotations on the New Testament.

Vermigli, Peter Martyr (1499–1562), Italian Augustinian abbot and prior, whose reading led him to adopt the Reformed faith and flee to Switzerland in 1542. He went on to be a professor both at Strasbourg and at Oxford. He lectured on biblical texts, including Romans and 1 Corinthians, and wrote extensively in defense of a Reformed doctrine of the Lord's Supper.

Zwingli, Huldrych (1484–1531), Swiss priest and humanist, who became leader of the Reformation in Zurich and whose life and teaching were crucial to the development of the Reformed tradition. He also engaged in controversy with early Swiss Anabaptists and died on the battlefield of Kappel.

Bibliography

Allen, Michael, and Jonathan A. Linebaugh, eds. *Reformation Readings of Paul.* Downers Grove, IL: InterVarsity Press, 2015.

Althaus, Paul. *The Theology of Martin Luther.* Philadelphia: Fortress, 1966.

Anonymous. "Cordatus' Controversy with Melanchthon." *Theological Quarterly* 11.4 (1907): 193–207.

Aquinas, Thomas. *Commentary on Saint Paul's Epistle to the Galatians by St. Thomas Aquinas.* Translated by Fabian R. Larcher. Albany, NY: Magi, 1966.

Athanasius. *Defense Against the Arians.* In vol. 4 of *The Nicene and Post-Nicene Fathers*, Series 2. Edited by Philip Schaff and Henry Wace. 1890–1900. 14 vols. Repr., Peabody, MA: Hendrickson, 1994.

Augustine. *Augustine's Commentary on Galatians: Introduction, Text, Translation, and Notes.* Translated by Eric A. Plumer. Oxford: Oxford University Press, 2003.

———. *The City of God against the Pagans.* Translated by R. W. Dyson. Cambridge: Cambridge University Press, 1998.

———. *Expositions of the Psalms 99–120: The Works of St. Augustine III/19.* Translated by Maria Boulding. New York: New City, 2003.

———. *Homilies on the Gospel of John 1–40: The Works of St. Augustine III/12.* Translated by Edmund P. Hill. New York: New City, 2009.

———. *Letters 156–210: The Works of St. Augustine II/3.* Translated by Roland J. Teske. New York: New City, 2004.

———. "Miscellany of Questions in Response to Simplician." In *Responses to Miscellaneous Questions: The Works of St. Augustine I/12.* Translated by Boniface Ramsey. New York: New City, 2008.

———. *Sermons 148–183: The Works of St. Augustine III/5.* Translated by Edmund P. Hill. New York: New City, 1992.

―――. "The Spirit and the Letter." In *Answer to the Pelagians: The Works of St. Augustine I/23*. Translated by Roland J. Teske. New York: New City, 1997.

Aulén, Gustav. *Christus Victor: An Historical Study of the Three Main Types of the Idea of the Atonement*. London: SPCK, 1931.

Ayres, Lewis. "Augustine." Pages 345–60 in *The Blackwell Companion to Paul*. Edited by Stephen Westerholm. Oxford: Wiley-Blackwell, 2011.

Babcock, William S. "Augustine on Sin and Moral Agency." Pages 97–113 in *The Ethics of St. Augustine*. Edited by William S. Babcock. Atlanta: Scholars Press, 1991.

Barclay, John M. G. "Believers and the 'Last Judgment' in Paul: Rethinking Grace and Recompense." Pages 195–208 in *Eschatologie = Eschatology: The Sixth Durham-Tübingen Research Symposium, Eschatology in Old Testament, Ancient Judaism and Early Christianity*. Edited by Hans Joachim Eckstein, Christof Landmesser, and Hermann Lichtenberger. Tübingen: Mohr Siebeck, 2011.

―――. "Humanity under Faith." Pages 79–100 in *Beyond Bultmann: Reckoning a New Testament Theology*. Edited by Bruce W. Longenecker and Mikeal C. Parsons. Waco: Baylor University Press, 2014.

―――. *Judaism in the Mediterranean Diaspora*. Edinburgh: T&T Clark, 1996.

―――. "Mirror-Reading a Polemical Letter: Galatians as a Test Case." Pages 367–82 in *The Galatians Debate*. Edited by Mark D. Nanos. Peabody, MA: Hendrickson, 2002.

―――. "Neither Jew nor Greek: Multiculturalism and the New Perspective on Paul." Pages 197–214 in *Ethnicity and the Bible*. Edited by Mark G. Brett. Leiden: Brill, 1996.

―――. *Obeying the Truth: Paul's Ethics in Galatians*. Edinburgh: T&T Clark, 1988.

―――. *Paul and the Gift*. Grand Rapids: Eerdmans, 2015.

―――. "Paul's Story: Theology as Testimony." Pages 133–56 in *Narrative Dynamics in Paul: A Critical Assessment*. Edited by Bruce W. Longenecker. Louisville: Westminster John Knox, 2002.

―――. "Pure Grace? Paul's Distinctive Jewish Theology of Gift." *ST* 68.1 (2014): 4–20.

―――. Review of *Paul and the Faithfulness of God*, by N. T. Wright. *SJT* 68.2 (2015): 235–43.

―――. "Under Grace: The Christ-Gift and the Construction of a Christian *Habitus*." Pages 59–76 in *Apocalyptic Paul: Cosmos and Anthropos in Romans 5–8*. Edited by Beverly R. Gaventa. Waco: Baylor University Press, 2013.

Batka, L'ubomír. "Luther's Teaching on Sin and Evil." Pages 233–53 in *The Oxford Handbook of Martin Luther's Theology*. Edited by Robert Kolb, Irene Dingel, and L'ubomír Batka. Oxford: Oxford University Press, 2014.

Bauckham, Richard. *Jesus and the God of Israel*. Grand Rapids: Eerdmans, 2008.

Bayer, Oswald. "The Being of Christ in Faith." *LQ* 10.2 (1996): 135–50.

―――. "Luther as an Interpreter of Holy Scripture." Pages 73–85 in *The Cambridge*

Companion to Martin Luther. Edited by Donald K. McKim. Cambridge: Cambridge University Press, 2003.

———. *Martin Luther's Theology: A Contemporary Interpretation.* Grand Rapids: Eerdmans, 2008.

———. *Promissio: Geschichte der reformatischen Wende in Luthers Theologie.* 2nd ed. Darmstadt: Wissenschaftliche Buchgesellschaft, 1989.

Beilby, James K., and Paul R. Eddy, eds. *Justification: Five Views.* Downers Grove, IL: InterVarsity Press, 2011.

Bernado, Aldo. *Petrarch, Scipio, and the "Africa": The Birth of Humanism's Dream.* Baltimore: Johns Hopkins, 1962.

Bielfeldt, Dennis. "Luther's Late Trinitarian Disputations." Pages 59–130 in *The Substance of the Faith: Luther's Doctrinal Theology for Today.* Edited by Dennis D. Bielfeldt, Mickey L. Mattox, and Paul R. Hinlicky. Minneapolis: Fortress, 2008.

———."Response to Sammeli Juntunen." Pages 161–66 in *Union with Christ: The New Finnish Interpretation of Luther.* Edited by Carl E. Braaten and Robert W. Jenson. Grand Rapids: Eerdmans, 1998.

Billings, J. Todd. *Calvin, Participation, and the Gift: The Activity of Believers in Union with Christ.* Oxford: Oxford University Press, 2007.

———. "The Catholic Calvin." *Pro Eccl* 20.2 (2011): 120–34.

———. "The Contemporary Reception of Luther and Calvin's Doctrine of Union with Christ: Mapping a Biblical, Catholic, and Reformational Motif." Pages 165–82 in *Calvin and Luther: The Continuing Relationship.* Edited by R. Ward Holder. Göttingen: Vandenhoeck & Ruprecht, 2013.

———. "Union with Christ and the Double Grace: Calvin's Theology and Its Early Reception." Pages 49–71 in *Calvin's Theology and Its Reception.* Edited by J. Todd Billings and I. John Hesselink. Louisville: Westminster John Knox, 2012.

Billings, J. Todd, and I. John Hesselink, eds. *Calvin's Theology and its Reception: Disputes, Developments, and New Possibilities.* Louisville: Westminster John Knox, 2012.

Bird, Michael. *The Saving Righteousness of God: Studies on Paul, Justification, and the New Perspective.* Eugene, OR: Wipf & Stock, 2007.

Blackwell, Ben C., John K. Goodrich, and Jason Matson, eds. *Paul and the Apocalyptic Imagination.* Minneapolis: Fortress, 2016.

Blankenhorn, Bernhard. "Aquinas on Paul's Flesh/Spirit Anthropology in Romans." Pages 1–30 in *Reading Romans with St. Thomas Aquinas.* Edited by Matthew Levering and Michael Dauphinais. Washington, DC: Catholic University of America Press, 2012.

Bornkamm, Karin. *Luthers Auslegungen des Galaterbriefs von 1519 bis 1531—Ein Vergleich.* Berlin: De Gruyter, 1963.

Bouillard, Henri. *Conversion et grâce chez S. Thomas d'Aquin, étude historique*. Paris: Aubier, 1944.

Boyle, Marjorie O'Rourke. *Rhetoric and Reform: Erasmus' Civil Dispute with Luther*. Cambridge: Harvard University Press, 1983.

Braaten, Carl E., and Robert W. Jenson, eds. *Union with Christ: The New Finnish Interpretation of Luther*. Grand Rapids: Eerdmans, 1998.

Braunisch, Reinhard. *Die Theologie der Rechtfertigung im "Enchiridion" (1538) des Johannes Gropper*. Münster: Aschendorffsche Westfalen, 1974.

Brecht, Martin. *Martin Luther: The Preservation of the Church 1532–1546*. Translated by James L. Schaaf. Minneapolis: Fortress, 1993.

Briskina, Anna. "An Orthodox View of Finnish Luther Research." *LQ* 22.1 (2008): 16–39.

Bucer. *The Common Places of Martin Bucer*. Translated by David F. Wright. Abingdon, Berkshire: Sutton Courtenay, 1971.

Bullinger, Heinrich. *Bullinger's Decades: The Third Decade*. Edited by Thomas Harding. The Parker Society 8. Cambridge: Cambridge University Press, 1851.

———. *Bullinger's Decades: The Fourth Decade*. Edited by Thomas Harding. The Parker Society 9. Cambridge: Cambridge University Press, 1851.

Bultmann, Rudolf. *Theology of the New Testament*. 2 vols. London: SCM, 1952.

Busch, Eberhard. "God and Humanity." Pages 224–35 in *The Calvin Handbook*. Edited by Herman J. Selderhuis. Grand Rapids: Eerdmans, 2009.

———. *Karl Barth and the Pietists: The Young Karl Barth's Critique of Pietism and Its Response*. Translated by Donald W. Bloesch. Downers Grove, IL: InterVarsity Press, 2004.

Butin, Philip W. *Revelation, Redemption, and Response: Calvin's Trinitarian Understanding of the Divine-Human Relationship*. Oxford: Oxford University Press, 1995.

Calvin, John. *Commentaries on the Twelve Minor Prophets Vol. 1: Hosea*. Translated by John Owen. Edinburgh: Calvin Translation Society, 1846.

———. *Institutes of the Christian Religion: 1541 French Edition, The First English Version*. Translated by Elsie A. McKee. Grand Rapids: Eerdmans, 2009.

———. *On the Bondage and the Liberation of the Will: A Defense of the Orthodox Doctrine of Human Choice against Pighius*. Edited by Anthony N. S. Lane. Translated by G. I. Davies. Grand Rapids: Baker, 1996.

———. *Sermons on the Epistle to the Ephesians*. Edinburgh: Banner of Truth, 1973.

———. *Sermons on the Epistle to the Galatians*. Translated by Kathy Childress. Edinburgh: Banner of Truth Trust, 1997.

Campbell, Douglas. *The Deliverance of God: An Apocalyptic Rereading of Justification in Paul*. Grand Rapids: Eerdmans, 2009.

———. *Framing Paul: An Epistolary Biography*. Grand Rapids: Eerdmans, 2014.

———. *The Quest for Paul's Gospel: A Suggested Strategy*. New York & London: Continuum, 2005.

———. "Rereading Paul's ΔIKAIO-Language." Pages 196–233 in *Beyond Old and New Perspectives on Paul: Reflections on the Work of Douglas Campbell*. Edited by Chris Tilling. Eugene, OR: Wipf & Stock, 2014.

Canlis, Julie. *Calvin's Ladder: A Spiritual Theology of Ascent and Ascension*. Grand Rapids: Eerdmans, 2010.

Carson, Don A. "The Vindication of Imputation: On Fields of Discourse and Semantic Fields." Pages 46–78 in *Justification: What's at Stake in the Current Debates?* Edited by Mark Husbands and Daniel J. Treier. Downers Grove, IL: InterVarsity Press, 2004.

Chemnitz, Martin. *Examination of the Council of Trent Vol. 1.* Translated by Fred Kramer. St. Louis: Concordia, 1971.

———. *Loci Theologici Vol. II.* Translated by Jacob A. O. Preus. St. Louis: Concordia, 1989.

Chester, Stephen J. *Conversion at Corinth: Perspectives on Conversion in Paul's Theology and the Corinthian Church*. London and New York: T&T Clark, 2003.

———. "Paul and the Introspective Conscience of Martin Luther." *BibInt* 14.5 (2006): 508–36.

———. "Romans 7 and Conversion in the Protestant Tradition." *Ex Auditu* 25 (2009): 135–71.

———. "When the Old Was New: Reformation Perspectives on Gal 2:16." *ExpTim* 119.7 (2008): 320–29.

Childs, Brevard. *The Church's Guide for Reading Paul: The Canonical Shaping of the Pauline Corpus*. Grand Rapids: Eerdmans, 2008.

———. *Introduction to the Old Testament as Scripture*. London: SCM, 1979.

———. "On Reclaiming the Bible for Christian Theology." Pages 1–17 in *Reclaiming the Bible for the Church*. Edited by Carl E. Braaten and Robert W. Jenson. Grand Rapids: Eerdmans, 1995.

Christ-von Wedel, Christine. *Erasmus of Rotterdam: Advocate of a New Christianity*. Toronto: University of Toronto Press, 2013.

Classen, Carl Joachim. *Rhetorical Criticism of the New Testament*. Tübingen: Mohr Siebeck, 2000.

Clebsch, William A. *England's Early Protestants*. New Haven: Yale University Press, 1964.

Cochrane, Arthur C., ed. *Reformed Confessions of the Sixteenth Century*. Louisville: Westminster John Knox, 2003.

Cohen, Shaye J. D. *Why Aren't Jewish Women Circumcised? Gender and Covenant in Judaism*. Berkeley: University of California Press, 2005.

Corley, Bruce. "Interpreting Paul's Conversion—Then and Now." Pages 1–17 in *The Road from Damascus: The Impact of Paul's Conversion on His Life, Thought, and Ministry*. Edited by Richard N. Longenecker. Grand Rapids: Eerdmans, 1997.

Couenhoven, Jesse. "St. Augustine's Doctrine of Original Sin." *Aug Stud* 36.2 (2005): 359–96.

Coxhead, Steven R. "John Calvin's Subordinate Doctrine of Justification by Works." *WTJ* 71 (2009): 1–19.

Cummings, Brian. *The Literary Culture of the Reformation: Grammar and Grace.* Oxford: Oxford University Press, 2002.

Das, Andrew A. "Paul and Works of Obedience in Second Temple Judaism: Romans 4:4–5 as a 'New Perspective' Case Study." *CBQ* 71.4 (2009): 795–812.

Dawson, Jane. *John Knox.* New Haven and London: Yale University Press, 2015.

Dieter, Theodor. "Luther as Late Medieval Theologian." Pages 31–48 in *The Oxford Handbook of Martin Luther's Theology.* Edited by Robert Kolb, Irene Dingel, and L'ubomír Batka. Oxford: Oxford University Press, 2014.

Dingel, Irene, Robert Kolb, Nicole Kuropka, and Timothy J. Wengert, eds. *Philip Melanchthon: Theologian in Classroom, Confession, and Controversy.* Göttingen: Vandenhoeck & Ruprecht, 2012.

Donfried, Karl P. "Justification and Last Judgment in Paul—Twenty Five Years Later." Pages 279–92 in *Paul, Thessalonica and Early Christianity.* Grand Rapids: Eerdmans, 2002.

Dunn, James D. G. "The Justice of God: A Renewed Perspective on Justification by Faith." *JTS* 43.1 (1992): 1–22.

———. "New Perspective View." Pages 176–218 in *Justification: Five Views.* Edited by James K. Beilby and Paul R. Eddy. Downers Grove, IL: InterVarsity Press, 2011.

———. "The New Perspective: Whence, What and Whither?" Pages 1–97 in *The New Perspective on Paul.* Rev. ed. Grand Rapids: Eerdmans, 2005.

———. *The Theology of Paul the Apostle.* Edinburgh: T&T Clark, 1998.

Dunn, James D. G., and Alan M. Suggate. *Justice of God: A Fresh Look at the Old Doctrine of Justification by Faith.* Carlisle: Paternoster, 1993.

Ebeling, Gerhard. "Jesus and Faith." Pages 191–246 in *Word and Faith.* Translated by James W. Leitch. Philadelphia: Fortress, 1963.

———. *Luther: An Introduction to His Thought.* Philadelphia: Fortress, 1970.

———. "On the Doctrine of the *Triplex Usus Legis* in the Theology of the Reformation." Pages 62–78 in *Word and Faith.* Translated by James W. Leitch. Philadelphia: Fortress, 1963.

Edwards, Mark. *Origen Against Plato.* Aldershot: Ashgate, 2002.

Ehrensperger, Kathy, and R. Ward Holder, eds. *Reformation Readings of Romans.* New York: T&T Clark, 2008.

Elliott, Mark. "Romans 7 in the Reformation Century." Pages 171–88 in *Reformation Readings of Romans.* Edited by Kathy Ehrensperger and R. Ward Holder. New York: T&T Clark, 2008.

Erasmus, Desiderius. *Annotations on the New Testament: Acts, Romans, I and II Corinthians: Facsimile of the Final Latin Text with All Earlier Variants.* Edited by Anne Reeve and M. A. Screech. Leiden: Brill, 1990.

———. *Erasmus' Annotations on the New Testament: Galatians to the Apocalypse: Fac-*

simile of the Final Latin Text with All Earlier Variants. Edited by Anne Reeve. Introduction by M. A. Screech. Leiden: Brill, 1993.

Evans, Gillian R. *The Language and Logic of the Bible: The Road to Reformation.* Cambridge: Cambridge University Press, 1985.

———. *The Roots of the Reformation: Tradition, Emergence, and Rupture.* Downers Grove, IL: InterVarsity Press, 2012.

Farthing, John L. *Thomas Aquinas and Gabriel Biel.* Durham, NC: Duke University Press, 1988.

Fink, David C. "Divided by Faith: The Protestant Doctrine of Justification and the Confessionalization of Biblical Exegesis." PhD diss., Duke University Graduate School, 2010.

Forde, Gerhard O. *The Captivation of the Will: Luther vs. Erasmus on Freedom and Bondage.* Grand Rapids: Eerdmans, 2005.

Fredriksen, Paula. *Augustine on Romans: Propositions from the Epistle to the Romans, Unfinished Commentary on the Epistle to the Romans.* Chico, CA: Scholars Press, 1982.

———. "Beyond the Body/Soul Dichotomy: Augustine on Paul against the Manichees and the Pelagians." *Recherches Augustiniennes* 23 (1988): 87–113.

Gadamer, Hans-Georg. *Truth and Method.* 2nd ed. New York: Crossroad, 1990.

Ganoczy, Alexandre. "Calvin als paulinischer Theologe: Ein Forschungsansatz zur Hermeneutik Calvins." Pages 39–60 in *Calvinus Theologus.* Edited by Wilhelm H. Neuser. Neukirchen-Vluyn: Neukirchener, 1976.

Garcia, Mark A. "Imputation and the Christology of Union with Christ: Calvin, Osiander, and the Contemporary Quest for a Reformed Model." *WTJ* 68 (2006): 219–51.

———. *Life in Christ: Union with Christ and Twofold Grace in Calvin's Theology.* Eugene, OR: Wipf & Stock, 2008.

Gathercole, Simon J. *Where is Boasting? Early Jewish Soteriology and Paul's Response in Romans 1–5.* Grand Rapids: Eerdmans, 2002.

Geneva Bible, The: Facsimile of the 1560 Edition. Peabody, MA: Hendrickson, 2007.

Gerrish, Brian. *Grace and Gratitude: The Eucharistic Theology of John Calvin.* Minneapolis: Fortress, 1993.

Gordon, Bruce. *Calvin.* New Haven: Yale University Press, 2009.

Gorham, George C. *Gleanings of a Few Scattered Ears.* London: Bell & Daldy, 1857.

Gorman, Michael J. *Becoming the Gospel: Paul, Participation, and Mission.* Grand Rapids: Eerdmans, 2015.

———. *Inhabiting the Cruciform God: Kenosis, Justification, and Theosis in Paul's Narrative Soteriology.* Grand Rapids: Eerdmans, 2009.

———. "Romans: The First Christian Treatise on Theosis." *JTI* 5.1 (2011): 13–34.

Grabowski, Stanislaus J. *The Church: An Introduction to the Theology of St. Augustine.* St. Louis: Herder, 1957.

Graybill, Gregory B. *Evangelical Free Will: Philipp Melanchthon's Doctrinal Journey on the Origins of Faith*. Oxford: Oxford University Press, 2010.

———. *The Honeycomb Scroll: Philipp Melanchthon at the Dawn of the Reformation*. Minneapolis: Fortress, 2015.

Greschat, Martin. *Melanchthon neben Luther: Studien zur Gestalt der Rechtfertigungslehre zwischen 1528 und 1537*. Wittenberg: Luther-Verlag, 1965.

Grondin, Jean. *Introduction to Philosophical Hermeneutics*. New Haven: Yale University Press, 1994.

Grove, Peter. "Adolf von Harnack and Karl Holl on Luther at the Origins of Modernity." Pages 106–22 in *Lutherrenaissance Past and Present*. Edited by Christine Helmer and Bo Kristian Holm. Göttingen: Vandenhoeck & Ruprecht, 2015.

Haas, Günther H. "Ethics and Church Discipline." Pages 332–44 in *The Calvin Handbook*. Edited by Herman J. Selderhuis. Grand Rapids: Eerdmans, 2009.

Hagen, Kenneth. *Luther's Approach to Scripture As Seen in His 'Commentaries' on Galatians*. Tübingen: Mohr Siebeck, 1993.

———. *A Theology of Testament in the Young Luther: The Lectures on Hebrews*. Leiden: Brill, 1974.

Hall, H. Ashley. *Philip Melanchthon and the Cappadocians: A Reception of Greek Patristic Sources in the Sixteenth Century*. Göttingen: Vandenhoeck & Ruprecht, 2014.

Hamm, Berndt. *The Early Luther: Stages in a Reformation Reorientation* (Grand Rapids: Eerdmans, 2014).

———. "How Innovative Was the Reformation?" Pages 254–72 in *The Reformation of Faith in the Context of Late Medieval Theology and Piety: Essays by Berndt Hamm*. Edited by Robert J. Bast. Leiden: Brill, 2004.

———. "How Mystical Was Luther's Faith?" Pages 190–232 in *The Early Luther: Stages in a Reformation Reorientation*. Grand Rapids: Eerdmans, 2014.

———. "Impending Doom and Imminent Grace: Luther's Early Years in the Cloister as the Beginning of His Reformation Reorientation." Pages 26–58 in *The Early Luther: Stages in a Reformation Reorientation*. Grand Rapids: Eerdmans, 2014.

———. "Justification by Faith Alone: A Profile of the Reformation Doctrine of Justification." Pages 233–57 in *The Early Luther: Stages in a Reformation Reorientation*. Grand Rapids: Eerdmans, 2014.

———. "The Place of the Reformation in the Second Christian Millennium." Pages 273–300 in *The Reformation of Faith in the Context of Late Medieval Theology and Piety: Essays by Berndt Hamm*. Edited by Robert J. Bast. Leiden: Brill, 2004.

———. "What Was the Reformation Doctrine of Justification?" Pages 179–216 in *The Reformation of Faith in the Context of Late Medieval Theology and Piety: Essays by Berndt Hamm*. Edited by Robert J. Bast. Leiden: Brill, 2004.

———. "Why Did 'Faith' Become for Luther the Central Concept of the Christian Life?" Pages 153–78 in *The Reformation of Faith in the Context of Late Medieval*

Theology and Piety: Essays by Berndt Hamm. Edited by Robert J. Bast. Leiden: Brill, 2004.

Hampson, Daphne. *Christian Contradictions: The Structures of Lutheran and Catholic Thought*. Cambridge: Cambridge University Press, 2001.

Harrison, Carol. *Rethinking Augustine's Early Theology: A Case for Continuity*. Oxford: Oxford University Press, 2006.

Hays, Richard B. "Christ Died for the Ungodly: Narrative Soteriology in Paul?" *HBT* 26.2 (2004): 48-68.

———. *Echoes of Scripture in the Letters of Paul*. New Haven: Yale University Press, 1989.

———. *The Faith of Jesus Christ: The Narrative Substructure of Galatians 3:1-4:11*. 2nd ed. Grand Rapids: Eerdmans, 2002.

———. "Humanity Prior to the Revelation of Faith." Pages 61-78 in *Beyond Bultmann: Reckoning a New Testament Theology*. Edited by Bruce W. Longenecker. Waco: Baylor, 2014.

———. "ΠΙΣΤΙΣ and Pauline Christology: What Is at Stake?" Pages 35-60 in *Pauline Theology. Volume IV: Looking Back, Pressing On*. Edited by E. Elizabeth Johnson and David M. Hay. Atlanta: Scholars Press, 1997.

Helm, Paul. *Calvin at the Centre*. Oxford: Oxford University Press, 2010.

Helmer, Christine, and Bo Kristian Holm, eds. *Lutherrenaissance Past and Present*. Göttingen: Vandenhoeck & Ruprecht, 2015.

Hesselink, I. John. *Calvin's Concept of the Law*. Allison Park, PA: Pickwick, 1992.

———. "The Revelation of God in Creation and Scripture." Pages 3-24 in *Calvin's Theology and Its Reception*. Edited by J. Todd Billings and I. John Hesselink. Louisville: Westminster John Knox, 2012.

Hindmarsh, Bruce C. *The Evangelical Conversion Narrative: Spiritual Autobiography in Early Modern England*. Oxford: Oxford University Press, 2005.

Hoffmann, Manfred. "Rhetoric and Dialectic in Erasmus's and Melanchthon's Interpretation of John's Gospel." Pages 48-78 in *Philip Melanchthon (1497-1560) and the Commentary*. Edited by Timothy J. Wengert and M. Patrick Graham. Sheffield: Academic Press, 1997.

———. *Rhetoric and Theology: The Hermeneutic of Erasmus*. Toronto: University of Toronto Press, 1994.

Holder, R. Ward, ed. *Calvin and Luther: The Continuing Relationship*. Göttingen: Vandenhoeck & Ruprecht, 2013.

———, ed. *A Companion to Paul in the Reformation*. Leiden: Brill, 2009.

———. "Introduction: Paul in the Sixteenth Century: Invitation and a Challenge." Pages 1-12 in *A Companion to Paul in the Reformation*. Edited by R. Ward Holder. Leiden: Brill, 2009.

Holl, Karl. "Die Rechtfertigungslehre in Luthers Vorlesung über den Römerbrief mit besonderer Rücksicht auf die Frage der Heilsgewißheit." Pages 111-54 in

Gesammelte Aufsätze zur Kirchengeschichte Bd. 1: Luther. Tübingen: Mohr Siebeck, 1948.

———. "Was verstand Luther unter Religion?" Pages 1–110 in *Gesammelte Aufsätze zur Kirchengeschichte. Bd. 1: Luther*. Tübingen: Mohr Siebeck, 1948.

Holm, Bo Kristian. "Resources and Dead Ends of the German *Lutherrenaissance*: Karl Holl and the Problems of Gift, Sociality, and Anti-Eudaemonism." Pages 127–43 in *Lutherrenaissance Past and Present*. Edited by Christine Helmer and Bo Kristian Holm. Göttingen: Vandenhoeck & Ruprecht, 2015.

Hooker, Morna D. "Another Look at πίστις Χριστοῦ." *SJT* 69.1 (2016): 46–62.

———. "Interchange and Atonement." Pages 26–41 in *From Adam to Christ: Essays on Paul*. Cambridge: Cambridge University Press, 1990.

———. "Interchange in Christ." Pages 13–25 in *From Adam to Christ: Essays on Paul*. Cambridge: Cambridge University Press, 1990.

Horton, Michael S. "Calvin and the Law-Gospel Hermeneutic." *Pro Eccl* 6.1 (1997): 27–42.

———. "Calvin's Theology of Union with Christ and the Double Grace: Modern Reception and Contemporary Possibilities." Pages 72–96 in *Calvin's Theology and Its Reception: Disputes, Developments, and New Possibilities*. Edited by J. Todd Billings and I. John Hesselink. Louisville: Westminster John Knox, 2012.

Huggins, Jonathan. *Living Justification: A Historical-Theological Study of the Reformed Doctrine of Justification in the Writings of John Calvin, Jonathan Edwards, and N. T. Wright*. Eugene, OR: Wipf & Stock, 2013.

Husbands, Mark, and Daniel J. Treier, eds. *Justification: What's at Stake in the Current Debates?* Downers Grove, IL: InterVarsity Press, 2004.

Jauss, Hans R. *Question and Answer: Forms of Dialogic Understanding*. Translated by Michael Hays. Minneapolis: University of Minnesota Press, 1989.

———. *Towards an Aesthetic of Reception*. Translated by Timothy Bahti. Brighton: Harvester, 1982.

Jenkins, Allan K., and Patrick Preston. *Biblical Scholarship and the Church: A Sixteenth Century Crisis of Authority*. Aldershot: Ashgate, 2007.

Jenson, Matt. *The Gravity of Sin: Augustine, Luther and Barth on homo incurvatus in se*. London and New York: T&T Clark, 2006.

Jewett, Robert. *Romans*. Hermeneia. Minneapolis: Fortress, 2007.

Jipp, Joshua. *Christ Is King: Paul's Royal Ideology*. Minneapolis: Fortress, 2015.

———. "Rereading the Story of Abraham, Isaac, and 'Us' in Romans 4." *JSNT* 32.2 (2009): 217–42.

Joest, Wilfried. *Ontologie der Person bei Luther*. Göttingen: Vandenhoeck & Ruprecht, 1967.

Johnson, Merwyn S. "Calvin's Third Use of the Law and Its Problems." Pages 33–50 in *Calviniana: Ideas and Influence of Jean Calvin*. Edited by Robert V. Schnucker. Kirksville, MO: Sixteenth Century Journal Publishers, 1988.

Josephus. Translated by Henry St. John Thackeray et al. 10 vols. LCL. Cambridge: Harvard University Press, 1926–1965.

Jüngel, Eberhard. *The Freedom of a Christian: Luther's Significance for Contemporary Theology*. Minneapolis: Augsburg, 1988.

———. *Justification: The Heart of the Christian Faith*. Edinburgh: T&T Clark, 2001.

Juntunen, Sammeli. "Luther and Metaphysics: What Is the Structure of Being according to Luther?" Pages 129–60 in *Union with Christ: The New Finnish Interpretation of Luther*. Edited by Carl E. Braaten and Robert W. Jenson. Grand Rapids: Eerdmans, 1998.

Kärkkäinen, Veli-Matti. "Deification View." Pages 219–64 in *Justification: Five Views*. Edited by James K. Beilby and Paul R. Eddy. Downers Grove, IL: InterVarsity Press, 2011.

Käsemann, Ernst. "Justification and Salvation History in the Epistle to the Romans." Pages 69–78 in *Perspectives on Paul*. Philadelphia: Fortress, 1971.

———. "On the Subject of Primitive Christian Apocalyptic." Pages 108–37 in *New Testament Questions of Today*. London: SCM, 1969.

Kim, Sun-young. *Luther on Faith and Love: Christ and the Law in the 1535 Galatians Commentary*. Minneapolis: Fortress, 2014.

Klancher, Nancy. "A Genealogy for Reception History." *BibInt* 21.1 (2013): 99–129.

Kolb, Robert. *Bound Choice, Election, and Wittenberg Theological Method*. Grand Rapids: Eerdmans, 2005.

———. *Martin Luther: Confessor of the Faith*. Oxford: Oxford University Press, 2009.

———. *Martin Luther and the Enduring Word of God: The Wittenberg School and Its Scripture-Centered Proclamation*. Grand Rapids: Baker, 2016.

———. "Melanchthon's Doctrinal Last Will and Testament: The 'Responsiones ad articulos Bavaricae inquisitionis' as His Final Confession of Faith." Pages 141–60 in *Philip Melanchthon: Theologian in Classroom, Confession, and Controversy*. Edited by Irene Dingel, Robert Kolb, Nicole Kuropka, and Timothy Wengert. Göttingen: Vandenhoeck & Ruprecht, 2012.

———. "'Not without the Satisfaction of God's Righteousness.' The Atonement and the Generation Gap between Luther and His Students." Pages 136–56 in *Archive for Reformation History Special Volume: The Reformation in Germany and Europe: Interpretation and Issues*. Edited by Hans Rudolf Guggisberg, Gottfried G. Krodel, and Hans Füglister. Heidelberg: Gütersloher Verlaghaus, 1993.

———. "Philipp Melanchthon's Reading of Romans." Pages 73–96 in *Reformation Readings of Paul*. Edited by Michael Allen and Jonathan A. Linebaugh. Downers Grove, IL: InterVarsity Press, 2015.

Kolb, Robert, and Timothy J. Wengert, eds. *The Book of Concord: The Confessions of the Evangelical Lutheran Church*. Minneapolis: Fortress, 2000.

Kolb, Robert, Irene Dingel, and L'ubomír Batka, eds. *The Oxford Handbook of Martin Luther's Theology.* Oxford: Oxford University Press, 2014.

Kroeker, Greta Grace. *Erasmus in the Footsteps of Paul: A Pauline Theologian.* Toronto: University of Toronto Press, 2011.

Lambrecht, Jan. "Romans 4: A Critique of N. T. Wright." *JSNT* 36.2 (2013): 189–94.

Lane, Anthony N. S. *Justification by Faith in Catholic-Protestant Dialogue: An Evangelical Assessment.* London and New York: T&T Clark, 2002.

———. "Twofold Righteousness: A Key to the Doctrine of Justification? Reflections on Article 5 of the Regensburg Colloquy." Pages 205–24 in *Justification: What's at Stake in Current Debates?* Edited by Mark Husbands and Daniel J. Treier. Downers Grove, IL: InterVarsity Press, 2004.

Lauster, Jörg. "Luther—Apostle of Freedom? Liberal Protestant Interpretations of Luther." Pages 127–43 in *Lutherrenaissance Past and Present.* Edited by Christine Helmer and Bo Kristian Holm. Göttingen: Vandenhoeck & Ruprecht, 2015.

Lee, Max J. "Greek Words and Roman Meanings, Part 1: (Re)mapping Righteousness Language in Greco-Roman Discourse." Pages 3–28 in *Fire in My Soul: Essays on Pauline Soteriology and the Gospels in Honor of Seyoon Kim.* Edited by Soon Bong Choi, Jin Ki Hwang, and Max J. Lee. Eugene, OR: Wipf & Stock, 2014.

———. "Greek Words and Roman Meanings, Part 2: A Prolegomenon to Paul's Use of Righteousness Language in His Letters." Pages 29–52 in *Fire in My Soul: Essays on Pauline Soteriology and the Gospels in Honor of Seyoon Kim.* Edited by Soon Bong Choi, Jin Ki Hwang, and Max J. Lee. Eugene, OR: Wipf & Stock, 2014.

Lee, Yang-ho. "Calvin on Deification: A Reply to Carl Mosser and Jonathan Slater." *SJT* 63.3 (2010): 272–84.

Leppin, Volker. "Luther's Roots in Monastic-Mystical Piety." Pages 49–61 in *The Oxford Handbook of Martin Luther's Theology.* Edited by Robert Kolb, Irene Dingel, and L'ubomír Batka. Oxford: Oxford University Press, 2014.

———. "Luther's Transformation of Medieval Thought: Continuity and Discontinuity." Pages 115–24 in *The Oxford Handbook of Martin Luther's Theology.* Edited by Robert Kolb, Irene Dingel, and L'ubomír Batka. Oxford: Oxford University Press, 2014.

———. *Martin Luther.* Darmstadt: Wissenschaftliche Buchgesellschaft, 2006.

———. "Martin Luther, Reconsidered for 2017." *LQ* 22 (2008): 373–78.

Levering, Matthew. *Paul in the Summa Theologiae.* Washington, DC: Catholic University of America Press, 2014.

Levering, Matthew, and Michael Dauphinais, eds. *Reading Romans with St. Thomas Aquinas.* Washington, DC: Catholic University of America Press, 2012.

Levy, Ian Christopher, ed. and trans. *The Letter to the Galatians: The Bible in Medieval Tradition.* Grand Rapids: Eerdmans, 2011.

Levy, Ian Christopher, Philip D. Krey, and Thomas Ryan, eds. and trans. *The Letter to the Romans: The Bible in Medieval Tradition*. Grand Rapids: Eerdmans, 2013.

Lienhard, Marc. *Luther: Witness to Jesus Christ—Stages and Themes of the Reformer's Christology*. Minneapolis: Augsburg, 1982.

Lillback, Peter. *The Binding of God: Calvin's Role in the Development of Covenant Theology*. Grand Rapids: Baker, 2001.

Livesey, Nina. *Circumcision as a Malleable Symbol*. Tübingen: Mohr Siebeck, 2010.

Loewenich, Walter von. *Wahrheit und Bekenntnis im Glauben Luthers: Dargestellt im Anschluss an Luthers grossen Katechismus*. Wiesbaden: Steiner, 1974.

Lohse, Bernhard. "Conscience and Authority in Luther." Pages 158-83 in *Luther and the Dawn of the Modern Era*. Edited by Heiko A. Oberman. Leiden: Brill, 1974.

———. *Martin Luther's Theology: Its Historical and Systematic Development*. Edinburgh: T&T Clark, 1999.

Lonergan, Bernard. *Grace and Freedom: Operative Grace in the Thought of St. Thomas Aquinas*. New York: Herder & Herder, 1971.

Longenecker, Bruce W., ed. *Beyond Bultmann: Reckoning a New Testament Theology*. Waco: Baylor University Press, 2014.

———, ed. *Narrative Dynamics in Paul: A Critical Assessment*. Louisville: Westminster John Knox, 2002.

Longenecker, Richard N. *The Epistle to the Romans*. NIGTC. Grand Rapids: Eerdmans, 2016.

———. *Introducing Romans: Critical Issues in Paul's Most Famous Letter*. Grand Rapids: Eerdmans, 2011.

Lugioyo, Brian. *Martin Bucer's Doctrine of Justification: Reformation Theology and Early Modern Irenicism*. Oxford: Oxford University Press, 2011.

Luther, Martin. *Luther's Church Postil Vol. 1: Gospels: Advent, Christmas, and Epiphany Seasons*. Translated by John Nicholas Lenker. Minneapolis: Lutherans in all Lands, 1905.

———. *Luther's Epistle Sermons Vol 1: Advent and Christmas Season*. Translated by John Nicholas Lenker. Minneapolis: Luther Press, 1908.

———. *Select Works of Martin Luther Vol. 3*. Translated by Henry Cole. London: Simpkin and Marshall, 1826.

Luz, Ulrich. *Studies in Matthew*. Grand Rapids: Eerdmans, 2005

Macaskill, Grant. Review of *The Deliverance of God*, by Douglas Campbell. *JSNT* 34.2 (2011): 150-61.

———. *Union with Christ in the New Testament*. Oxford: Oxford University Press, 2013.

Mannermaaa, Tuomo. "Why Is Luther So Fascinating?" Pages 1-20 in *Union with Christ: The New Finnish Interpretation of Luther*. Edited by Carl E. Braaten and Robert W. Jenson. Grand Rapids: Eerdmans, 1998.

———. *Christ Present in Faith: Luther's View of Justification*. Minneapolis: Fortress, 2005.

———. *Two Kinds of Love: Martin Luther's Religious World*. Minneapolis: Fortress, 2010.

Marshall, Bruce. "*Beatus vir:* Aquinas, Romans 4, and the Role of 'Reckoning' in Justification." Pages 216-37 in *Reading Romans with St. Thomas Aquinas*. Edited by Matthew Levering and Michael Dauphinais. Washington, DC: Catholic University of America Press, 2012.

Martyn, J. Louis. "Apocalyptic Antinomies." Pages 111-24 in *Theological Issues in the Letters of Paul*. Edinburgh: T&T Clark, 1997.

———. *Galatians: A New Translation with Introduction and Commentary*. New York: Doubleday, 1997.

Matlock, Barry. "Zeal for Paul but Not According to Knowledge: Douglas Campbell's War on 'Justification Theory.'" *JSNT* 34.2 (2011): 115-49.

Mattes, Mark C. Review of *Justification and Participation in Christ: The Development of the Lutheran Doctrine of Justification from Luther to the Formula of Concord*, by Olli-Pekka Vainio. *LQ* 23 (2009): 114-17.

———. *The Role of Justification in Contemporary Theology*. Grand Rapids: Eerdmans, 2004.

———. "Luther on Justification as Forensic and Effective." Pages 264-73 in *The Oxford Handbook of Martin Luther's Theology*. Edited by Robert Kolb, Irene Dingel, and L'ubomír Batka. Oxford: Oxford University Press, 2014.

McCormack, Bruce L. "What's at Stake in Current Debates over Justification? The Crisis of Protestantism in the West." Pages 81-117 in *Justification: What's at Stake in the Current Debates?* Edited by Mark Husbands and Daniel J. Treier. Downers Grove, IL: InterVarsity Press, 2004.

McCulloch, Diarmaid, "Calvin: Fifth Latin Doctor of the Church?" Pages 33-45 in *Calvin and His Influence 1509-2009*. Edited by Irena Backus and Philip Benedict. Oxford: Oxford University Press, 2011.

McGrath, Alister E. *Iustitia Dei: A History of the Christian Doctrine of Justification*. 3rd ed. Cambridge: Cambridge University Press, 2005.

———. *Luther's Theology of the Cross: Martin Luther's Theological Breakthrough*. 2nd ed. Oxford: Wiley-Blackwell, 2010.

McIntosh, James. *What Hermeneutical Issues Does the Doctrine of Perspicuity Raise: Can the Canonical Approach of B.S. Childs Assist in Answering Them?* MTh diss., Glasgow: International Christian College, 2005.

McKee, Elsie A. *John Calvin on the Diaconate and Liturgical Almsgiving*. Geneva: Droz, 1984.

Meinhold, Peter. *Luthers Sprachphilosophie*. Berlin: Lutherisches Verlagshaus, 1958.

Melanchthon, Philip. *Commentary on Romans*. Translated by Fred Kramer. St. Louis: Concordia, 1992.

———. "Loci Communes Theologici." Pages 3-152 in *Melanchthon and Bucer*. Edited by Wilhelm Pauck. Philadelphia: Westminster, 1969.

―――. *Loci Communes 1543*. Translated by Jacob A. O. Preus. St. Louis: Concordia, 1992.

―――. *Melanchthon on Christian Doctrine*. Translated by Clyde L. Manschreck. New York: Oxford University Press, 1965.

―――. *Paul's Letter to the Colossians*. Translated by D. C. Parker. Sheffield: Almond Press, 1989.

―――. *Philippi Melanchthonis Epistolae, Iudicia, Consilia, Testimonia Aliorumque ad eum Epistolae quae in Corpore Reformatorum Desiderantur*. Edited by Heinrich E. Bindseil. Halle: Gustav Schwetske, 1874.

Ménager, Daniel. "Erasmus, the Intellectuals, and the Reuchlin Affair." Pages 39–54 in *Biblical Humanism and Scholasticism in the Age of Erasmus*. Edited by Erika Rummel. Leiden: Brill, 2008.

Milbank, John. "Alternative Protestantisms." Pages 25–41 in *Radical Orthodoxy and the Reformed Tradition: Creation, Covenant, and Participation*. Edited by James K. Smith and James H. Olthuis. Grand Rapids: Baker, 2005.

Mitchell, Margaret M. *The Heavenly Trumpet: John Chrysostom and the Art of Pauline Interpretation*. HUT 40. Tübingen: Mohr Siebeck, 2000.

Mosser, Carl. "The Greatest Possible Blessing: Calvin and Deification." *SJT* 55.1 (2002): 36–57.

Muller, Richard A. *The Unaccommodated Calvin: Studies in the Foundation of a Theological Tradition*. Oxford: Oxford University Press, 2000.

―――. *Calvin and the Reformed Tradition: On the Work of Christ and the Order of Salvation*. Grand Rapids: Baker, 2012.

Müller, Gerhard. "Luther's Transformation of Medieval Thought: Discontinuity and Continuity." Pages 105–14 in *The Oxford Handbook of Martin Luther's Theology*. Edited by Robert Kolb, Irene Dingel, and L'ubomír Batka. Oxford: Oxford University Press, 2014.

Nanos, Mark D., and Magnus Zetterholm, eds. *Paul within Judaism: Restoring the First Century Context to the Apostle*. Minneapolis: Fortress, 2015.

Nestingen, James A. "Introduction: Luther and Erasmus on the Bondage of the Will." Pages 1–22 in *The Captivation of the Will: Luther vs. Erasmus on Freedom and Bondage*. Edited by Gerhard O. Forde. Grand Rapids: Eerdmans, 2005.

Neuser, Wilhelm H. "Predestination." Pages 312–23 in *The Calvin Handbook*. Edited by Herman J. Selderhuis. Grand Rapids: Eerdmans, 2009.

Oberman, Heiko A. *The Harvest of Medieval Theology*. Cambridge: Harvard University Press, 1963.

―――. "Headwaters of the Reformation." Pages 39–83 in *The Dawn of the Reformation: Essays in Late Medieval and Early Reformation Thought*. Edinburgh: T&T Clark, 1986.

―――. "*Iustitia Christi* and *Iustitia Dei*: Luther and the Scholastic Doctrines of Justification." Pages 104–25 in *The Dawn of the Reformation: Essays in Late Medieval and Early Reformation Thought*. Edinburgh: T&T Clark, 1986.

———. *Luther: Man between God and the Devil*. New York: Image, 1992.

O'Kelley, Aaron. *Did the Reformers Misread Paul? A Historical-Theological Critique of the New Perspective*. Milton Keynes: Paternoster, 2014.

Ollerton, Andrew J. "*Quasi Deificari*: Deification in the Theology of John Calvin." *WTJ* 73 (2011): 237–54.

Osiander, Andreas. *Gesamtausgabe*. Edited by Gerhard Müller and Gottfried Seebaß. 10 vols. Gütersloh: Gütersloher Verlagshaus, 1975–1997.

Ozment, Steven. *The Age of Reform 1250–1550: An Intellectual and Religious History of Late Medieval and Reformation Europe*. New Haven: Yale University Press, 1980.

Pabel, Hilmar M., and Mark Vessey, eds. *Holy Scripture Speaks: The Production and Reception of Erasmus' Paraphrases on the New Testament*. Toronto: University of Toronto Press, 2002.

Paddison, Angus. *Theological Hermeneutics and 1 Thessalonians*. Cambridge: Cambridge University Press, 2005.

Parris, David P. *Reception Theory and Biblical Hermeneutics*. Eugene, OR: Wipf & Stock, 2009.

Pattison, Bonnie L. *Poverty in the Theology of John Calvin*. Eugene, OR: Wipf & Stock, 2006.

Paulson, Steven. "Luther's Doctrine of God." Pages 187–200 in *The Oxford Handbook of Martin Luther's Theology*. Edited by Robert Kolb, Irene Dingel, and L'ubomír Batka. Oxford: Oxford University Press, 2014.

Payton, James R., Jr. *Getting the Reformation Wrong: Correcting Some Misunderstandings*. Downers Grove, IL: InterVarsity Press, 2010.

Pereira, Jairzinho Lopes. *Augustine of Hippo and Martin Luther on Original Sin and Justification of the Sinner*. Göttingen: Vandenhoeck and Ruprecht, 2012.

Pettegree, Andrew. *Brand Luther: 1517, Printing, and the Making of the Reformation*. New York: Penguin, 2015.

Peura, Simo. "Christ as Favor and Gift: The Challenge of Luther's Understanding of Justification." Pages 42–69 in *Union with Christ: The New Finnish Interpretation of Luther*. Edited by Carl E. Braaten and Robert W. Jenson. Grand Rapids: Eerdmans, 1998.

Philo. Translated by F. H. Colson and G. H. Whitaker. 12 vols. LCL. Cambridge: Harvard University Press, 1968–1981.

Pils, Holger, Stephen Ruderer, and Petra Schaffrodt, eds. *Martin Bucer (1491–1551): Bibliographie*. Gütersloh: Gütersloher Verlag, 2005.

Piper, John. *The Future of Justification: A Response to N. T. Wright*. Wheaton: Crossway, 2007.

Pitkin, Barbara. "John Calvin and the Interpretation of the Bible." Pages 341–71 in *A History of Biblical Interpretation Volume 2: The Medieval through the Reformation Periods*. Edited by Alan J. Hauser and Duane F. Watson. Grand Rapids: Eerdmans, 2009.

―――. "Nothing but Concupiscence: Calvin's Understanding of Sin and the *Via Augustini*." *CTJ* 34 (1999): 347–69.

―――. *What Pure Eyes Could See: Calvin's Doctrine of Faith in Its Exegetical Context*. Oxford: Oxford University Press, 1999.

Polybius: The Histories. Translated by W. R. Paton. 6 vols. LCL. Cambridge: Harvard University Press, 1922–1927.

Raith II, Charles. *Aquinas and Calvin on Romans: God's Justification and our Participation*. Oxford: Oxford University Press, 2014.

Rhemes New Testament, The. Rhemes: John Fogny, 1582.

Riches, John K. "Book of the Month: Commenting on Romans in Its Original Context. Review of *Romans: A Commentary* by Robert Jewett." *ExpTim* 119.1 (2007): 27–29.

―――. *Galatians through the Centuries*. Oxford: Blackwell, 2008.

―――. "Reception History as a Challenge to Biblical Theology." *JTI* 7.2 (2013): 171–85.

―――. "Why Write a Reception-Historical Commentary?" *JSNT* 29.3 (2007): 323–32.

Ricoeur, Paul. "The Model of the Text: Meaningful Action Considered as a Text." Pages 197–221 in *Hermeneutics and the Human Sciences: Essays on Language, Action and Interpretation*. Edited by John B. Thompson. Cambridge: Cambridge University Press, 1981.

Rosemann, Phillip W. *Peter Lombard*. Oxford: Oxford University Press, 2004.

Rowland, Christopher, and Jonathan Roberts. "Introduction." *JSNT* 33.2 (2010): 131–36.

Rummel, Erika. *Erasmus*. London: Continuum, 2004.

―――. *Erasmus' Annotations on the New Testament: From Philologist to Theologian*. Toronto: University of Toronto Press, 1986.

―――. *The Humanist-Scholastic Debate in the Renaissance and Reformation*. Cambridge: Harvard University Press, 1995.

Saak, Eric L. *High Way to Heaven: The Augustinian Platform between Reform and Reformation, 1292–1524*. Leiden: Brill, 2002.

Saarinen, Risto. "Finnish Luther Studies: A Story and a Program." Pages 1–26 in *Engaging Luther: A (New) Theological Assessment*. Edited by Olli-Pekka Vainio. Eugene, OR: Wipf & Stock, 2010.

―――. "Justification by Faith: The View of the Mannermaa School." Pages 254–63 in *The Oxford Handbook of Martin Luther's Theology*. Edited by Robert Kolb, Irene Dingel, and L'ubomír Batka. Oxford: Oxford University Press, 2014.

Sanders, E. P. *Judaism: Practice and Belief 63 BCE–66 CE*. London: SCM and Philadelphia: Trinity Press International, 1992.

―――. *Paul*. Oxford: Oxford University Press, 1991.

Schäfer, Rolf. "Melanchthons Hermeneutik im Römerbrief-Kommentar von 1532." *ZTK* 60 (1963): 216–35.

————. "Melanchthon's Interpretation of Romans 5.15: His Departure from the Augustinian Concept of Grace Compared to Luther's." Pages 79–104 in *Philip Melanchthon (1497–1560) and the Commentary.* Edited by Timothy J. Wengert and M. Patrick Graham. Sheffield: Academic Press, 1997.

Schaff, Philip, ed. *The Creeds of Christendom Vol. III: The Evangelical Protestant Creeds.* 6th ed. Grand Rapids: Baker, 1931.

Scheible, Heinz. "Luther and Melanchthon." *LQ* 4.3 (1990): 317–39.

Schneider, John R. "The Hermeneutics of Commentary: Origins of Melanchthon's Integration of Dialectic into Rhetoric." Pages 20–47 in *Philip Melanchthon (1497–1560) and the Commentary.* Edited by Timothy J. Wengert and M. Patrick Graham. Sheffield: Academic Press, 1997.

Schreiner, Susan. *Are You Alone Wise? The Search for Certainty in the Early Modern Era.* Oxford: Oxford University Press, 2011.

————. "Creation and Providence." Pages 267–75 in *The Calvin Handbook.* Edited by Herman J. Selderhuis. Grand Rapids: Eerdmans, 2009.

————. *The Theater of His Glory: Nature and Natural Order in the Thought of John Calvin.* Grand Rapids: Baker, 1991.

Schreiner, Thomas. *Romans.* BECNT. Grand Rapids: Baker, 1998.

Schroeder, Henry J., trans. *Canons and Decrees of the Council of Trent: Original Text with English Translation.* St. Louis: Herder, 1941.

Schwarzwäller, Klaus. "Verantwortung des Glaubens: Freiheit und Liebe nach der Dekalogauslegung Martin Luthers." Pages 133–58 in *Freiheit als Liebe bei Martin Luther/Freedom as Love in Martin Luther.* Edited by Dennis D. Bielfeldt and Klaus Schwarzwäller. Frankfurt: Peter Lang, 1995.

Seeberg, Reinhold. *Textbook of the History of Doctrines.* Translated by Charles E. Hay. Philadelphia: Lutheran Publication Society, 1905.

Seifrid, Mark. "Luther, Melanchthon, and Paul on the Question of Imputation." Pages 137–52 in *Justification: What's at Stake in the Current Debates?* Edited by Mark Husbands and Daniel J. Treier. Downers Grove, IL: InterVarsity Press, 2004.

————. "Paul, Luther, and Justification in Gal 2:15–21." *WTJ* 65 (2003): 215–30.

————. "The Text of Romans and the Theology of Melanchthon: The Preceptor of the Germans and the Apostle to the Gentiles." Pages 97–120 in *Reformation Readings of Paul.* Edited by R. Michael Allen and Jonathan A. Linebaugh. Downers Grove, IL: InterVarsity Press, 2015.

Selderhuis, Herman J., ed. *The Calvin Handbook.* Grand Rapids: Eerdmans, 2009.

————. *John Calvin: A Pilgrim's Life.* Downers Grove, IL: InterVarsity Press, 2009.

Sheppard, Gerald T. "Between Reformation and Modern Commentary: The Perception of the Scope of Biblical Books." Pages xlviii–lxxvii in William Perkins, *A Commentary on Galatians.* Edited by Gerald T. Sheppard. New York: Pilgrim Press, 1989.

Sider, Robert D. "Χάρις and Derivatives in the Biblical Scholarship of Erasmus."

Pages 242–60 in *Diakonia: Essays in Honor of Robert T. Meyer*. Edited by Thomas Halton and Joseph P. Williman. Washington, DC: Catholic University of America Press, 1986.

———. "Historical Imagination and the Representation of Paul in Erasmus' Paraphrases on the Pauline Epistles." Pages 85–109 in *Holy Scripture Speaks: The Production and Reception of Erasmus' Paraphrases on the New Testament*. Edited by Hilmar M. Pabel and Mark Vessey. Toronto: University of Toronto Press, 2002.

Siggins, Ian D. K. *Martin Luther's Doctrine of Christ*. New Haven: Yale University Press, 1970.

Skottene, Ragnar. *Grace and Gift: An Analysis of a Central Motif in Martin Luther's 'Rationis Latomianae Confutatio.'* Frankfurt: Peter Lang, 2008.

Slater, Jonathan. "Salvation as Participation in the Humanity of the Mediator: A Reply to Carl Mosser." *SJT* 58.1 (2005): 39–58.

Slencza, Notger. "Luther's Anthropology." Pages 212–32 in *The Oxford Handbook of Martin Luther's Theology*. Edited by Robert Kolb, Irene Dingel, and L'ubomír Batka. Oxford: Oxford University Press, 2014.

Smeeton, Donald D. *Lollard Themes in the Reformation Theology of William Tyndale*. Kirksville, MO: Sixteenth Century Journal Publishers, 1994.

Steinmetz, David C. "Abraham and the Reformation." Pages 32–46 in *Luther in Context*. Grand Rapids: Baker, 2002.

———. "Calvin and Patristic Exegesis." Pages 122–40 in *Calvin in Context*. Oxford: Oxford University Press, 1995.

———. "Calvin and the Divided Self of Romans 7." Pages 110–21 in *Calvin in Context*. Oxford: Oxford University Press, 1995.

———. "Luther Against Luther." Pages 1–11 in *Luther in Context*. 2nd ed. Grand Rapids: Baker, 2002.

———. "Luther Among the Anti-Thomists." Pages 47–58 in *Luther in Context*. 2nd ed. Grand Rapids: Baker, 2002.

———. "Luther and Hubmaier on the Freedom of the Human Will." Pages 59–71 in *Luther in Context*. 2nd ed. Grand Rapids: Baker, 2002.

———. *Luther and Staupitz: An Essay in the Intellectual Origins of the European Reformation*. Durham, NC: Duke University Press, 1980.

———. "Preface to the Second Edition." Page ix in *Luther in Context*. 2nd ed. Grand Rapids: Baker, 2002.

Stendahl, Krister. "Call Not Conversion." Pages 7–22 in *Paul among Jews and Gentiles*. Philadelphia: Fortress, 1976.

———. "Paul and the Introspective Conscience of the West." Pages 78–96 in *Paul among Jews and Gentiles*. Philadelphia: Fortress, 1976.

Stowers, Stanley. *A Rereading of Romans: Justice, Jews, and Gentiles*. New Haven: Yale University Press, 1994.

Strehle, Stephen. *The Catholic Roots of the Protestant Gospel*. Leiden: Brill, 1995.

Stupperich, Robert. "Die Rechtfertigungslehre bei Luther und Melanchthon 1530–1536." Pages 73–88 in *Luther and Melanchthon in the History and Theology of the Reformation*. Edited by Vilmos Vajta. Philadelphia: Muhlenberg Press, 1961.

Tait, Edwin. "The Law and Its Works in Martin Bucer's 1536 Romans Commentary." Pages 57–69 in *Reformation Readings of Romans*. Edited by Kathy Ehrensperger and R. Ward Holder. New York: T&T Clark, 2008.

TeSelle, Eugene. "Exploring the Inner Conflict: Augustine's Sermons on Romans 7 and 8." Pages 111–28 in *Engaging Augustine on Romans: Self, Context, and Theology in Interpretation*. Edited by Daniel Patte and Eugene TeSelle. Harrisburg, PA: Trinity Press International, 2002.

Theissen, Gerd. *A Theory of Primitive Christian Religion*. London: SCM, 1999.

Thiselton, Anthony C. "Reception Theory, H.R. Jauss and the Formative Power of Scripture." *SJT* 65.3 (2012): 289–308.

Thompson, Mark D. *A Sure Ground on Which to Stand: The Relation of Authority and Interpretive Method in Luther's Approach to Scripture*. Carlisle: Paternoster, 2004.

Tilling, Chris, ed. *Beyond Old and New Perspectives on Paul: Reflections on the Work of Douglas Campbell*. Eugene, OR: Wipf & Stock, 2014.

Tomlin, Graham. "Luther and the Deliverance of God." Pages 23–33 in *Beyond Old and New Perspectives on Paul: Reflections on the Work of Douglas Campbell*. Edited by Chris Tilling. Eugene, OR: Wipf & Stock, 2014.

Torrell, Jean-Pierre. *Saint Thomas Aquinas*. Translated by Robert Royal. 2 vols. Washington, DC: Catholic University of America Press, 2003.

Tracy, James D. "Erasmus among the Postmodernists." Pages 1–40 in *Erasmus' Vision of the Church*. Edited by Hilmar M. Pabel. Kirksville, MO: Sixteenth Century Journal Publishers, 1995.

———. *Erasmus of the Low Countries*. Berkeley: University of California Press, 1996.

Trigg, Jonathan D. *Baptism in the Theology of Martin Luther*. Leiden: Brill, 2001.

Trueman, Carl R. "Is the Finnish Line a New Beginning? A Critical Assessment of the Reading of Luther Offered by the Helsinki Circle." *WTJ* 65 (2003): 213–44.

———. *Luther's Legacy: Salvation and the English Reformers*. Oxford: Clarendon, 1994.

Trumper, Tim J. R. "A Fresh Exposition of Adoption I: An Outline." *Scottish Bulletin of Evangelical Theology* 23.1 (2005): 60–80.

———. "A Fresh Exposition of Adoption II: Some Implications." *Scottish Bulletin of Evangelical Theology* 23.2 (2005): 194–215.

———. "The Theological History of Adoption I: An Account." *Scottish Bulletin of Evangelical Theology* 20.1 (2002): 4–28.

———. "The Theological History of Adoption II: A Rationale." *Scottish Bulletin of Evangelical Theology* 20.2 (2002): 177–202.

Tylanda, Joseph. "Christ the Mediator: Calvin versus Stancaro." Pages 161–72 in vol. 5 of *Articles on Calvin and Calvinism*. Edited by Richard C. Gamble. 14 vols. New York: Garland, 1992.

Vainio, Olli-Pekka. *Justification and Participation in Christ: The Development of the Lutheran Doctrine of Justification from Luther to the Formula of Concord (1580)*. Leiden: Brill, 2008.

———. "Luther and Theosis: A Response to the Critics of Finnish Luther Research." *Pro Eccl* 24.4 (2015): 459–74.

Van Engen, John. "Faith as a Concept of Order." Pages 19–67 in *Belief in History: Innovative Approaches to European and American Religion*. Edited by Thomas A. Kselman. Notre Dame: University of Notre Dame Press, 1991.

Vermigli, Peter Martyr. *In Epistolam S. Pauli ad Romanos commentarii doctisimi*. Basilae: Petrum Pernam, 1558.

———. *Most Learned and Fruitful Commentaries upon the Epistle of S. Paul to the Romanes*. Translated by Sir Henry Billingsley. London: John Daye, 1568.

———. *Predestination and Justification: Two Theological Loci*. Translated and edited by Frank A. James III. The Peter Martyr Library 8. Kirksville, MO: Sixteenth Century Essays and Studies, 2003.

Volf, Miroslav. *Exclusion and Embrace: A Theological Exploration of Identity, Otherness, and Reconciliation*. Nashville: Abingdon, 1996.

Wahlberg, Mats. "Why Isn't Faith a Work? An Examination of Protestant Answers." *SJT* 68.2 (2015): 201–17.

Waldstein, Michael. "The Trinitarian, Spousal, and Ecclesial Logic of Justification." Pages 274–87 in *Reading Romans with St. Thomas Aquinas*. Edited by Matthew Levering and Michael Dauphinais. Washington, DC: Catholic University of America Press, 2012.

Wallace, Ronald S. *Calvin's Doctrine of the Christian Life*. Edinburgh: Oliver & Boyd, 1959.

Wasserman, Emma. *The Death of the Soul in Romans 7: Sin, Death, and the Law in Light of Hellenistic Moral Psychology*. Tübingen: Mohr Siebeck, 2008.

Watson, Francis. "Is There a Story in These Texts?" Pages 231–39 in *Narrative Dynamics in Paul: A Critical Assessment*. Edited by Bruce W. Longenecker. Louisville: Westminster John Knox, 2002.

———. "New Directions in Pauline Theology." *Early Christianity* 1.1 (2010): 11–14.

———. *Paul and the Hermeneutics of Faith*. London & New York: T&T Clark, 2004.

———. *Paul, Judaism, and the Gentiles: Beyond the New Perspective*. 2nd ed. Grand Rapids: Eerdmans, 2007.

———. *Text and Truth: Redefining Biblical Theology*. Edinburgh: T&T Clark, 1997.

Wawrykow, Joseph P. *God's Grace and Human Action: 'Merit' in the Theology of Thomas Aquinas*. Notre Dame: University of Notre Dame Press, 1995.

Webster, John. "Biblical Theology and the Clarity of Scripture." Pages 352–84 in *Out of Egypt: Biblical Theology and Biblical Interpretation*. Edited by Craig G.

Bartholomew, Mary Healy, Karl Möller, and Robin Parry. Carlisle: Paternoster; Grand Rapids: Eerdmans, 2004.

———. *Holy Scripture: A Dogmatic Sketch*. Cambridge: Cambridge University Press, 2003.

Weigle, Luther A., ed. *The New Testament Octapla: Eight English Versions of the New Testament in the Tyndale-King James Tradition*. New York: T. Nelson, 1962.

Wendel, François. *Calvin: Origins and Development of His Religious Thought*. Grand Rapids: Baker, 1997.

Wengert, Timothy J. *Defending Faith: Lutheran Responses to Andreas Osiander's Doctrine of Justification, 1551-1559*. Tübingen: Mohr Siebeck, 2012.

———. *Human Freedom, Christian Righteousness: Philip Melanchthon's Exegetical Dispute with Erasmus of Rotterdam*. Oxford: Oxford University Press, 1998.

———. *Law and Gospel: Philip Melanchthon's Debate with John Agricola of Eisleben over Poenitentia*. Grand Rapids: Baker, 1997.

———. "Melanchthon and Luther / Luther and Melanchthon." Pages 55-88 in *Philip Melanchthon, Speaker of the Reformation: Wittenberg's Other Reformer*. Burlington, VT: Ashgate Variorum, 2010.

———. "Philip Melanchthon and Augustine of Hippo." Pages 235-67 in *Philip Melanchthon, Speaker of the Reformation: Wittenberg's Other Reformer*. Burlington, VT: Ashgate Variorum, 2010.

———. "Philip Melanchthon and John Calvin against Andreas Osiander: Coming to Terms with Forensic Justification." Pages 63-87 in *Calvin and Luther: The Continuing Relationship*. Edited by R. Ward Holder. Göttingen: Vandenhoeck & Ruprecht, 2013.

———. "Philip Melanchthon and the Origins of the 'Three Causes' of Conversion." Pages 183-208 in *Philip Melanchthon: Theologian in Classroom, Confession, and Controversy*. Edited by Irene Dingel, Robert Kolb, Nicole Kuropka, and Timothy Wengert. Göttingen: Vandenhoeck and Ruprecht, 2012.

———. "Philip Melanchthon's Last Word to Cardinal Lorenzo Campeggio." Pages 79-103 in *Philip Melanchthon: Theologian in Classroom, Confession, and Controversy*. Edited by Irene Dingel, Robert Kolb, Nicole Kuropka, and Timothy Wengert. Göttingen: Vandenhoeck and Ruprecht, 2012.

———. "Philip Melanchthon's 1522 Annotations on Romans and the Lutheran Origins of Rhetorical Criticism." Pages 118-40 in *Biblical Interpretation in the Era of the Reformation*. Edited by Richard A. Muller and John Lee Thompson. Grand Rapids: Eerdmans, 1996.

———. "The Rhetorical Paul: Philip Melanchthon's Interpretation of the Pauline Epistles." Pages 129-64 in *A Companion to Paul in the Reformation*. Edited by R. Ward Holder. Leiden: Brill, 2009.

Wengert, Timothy J., and M. Patrick Graham, eds. *Philip Melanchthon (1497-1560) and the Commentary*. Sheffield: Academic Press, 1997.

Wenham, Gordon. *Genesis 1-15*. WBC. Dallas: Word, 1987.

Westerholm, Stephen. *Israel's Law and the Church's Faith: Paul and His Recent Interpreters*. Grand Rapids: Eerdmans, 1988.

———. *Justification Reconsidered*. Grand Rapids: Eerdmans, 2013.

———. *Perspectives Old and New on Paul: The 'Lutheran' Paul and His Critics*. Grand Rapids: Eerdmans, 2004.

Wicks, Jared. "Luther on the Person before God: Review of 'Ontologie der Person bei Luther' by Wilfried Joest." *TS* 30.2 (1969): 289–311.

Wiley, Tatha. *Original Sin: Origins, Developments, Contemporary Meanings*. New York: Paulist, 2002.

Wise, Michael, Martin Abegg Jr., and Edward Cook. *The Dead Sea Scrolls: A New Translation*. San Francisco: Harper, 1996.

Wright, David F. "Justification in Augustine." Pages 55–72 in *Justification in Perspective: Historical Developments and Contemporary Challenges*. Edited by Bruce L. McCormack. Grand Rapids: Baker, 2006.

Wright, N. T. *Justification*. Downers Grove, IL: InterVarsity Press, 2009.

———. *Paul and the Faithfulness of God*. 2 vols. Minneapolis: Fortress, 2013.

———. "Paul and the Patriarch: The Role of Abraham in Romans 4." *JSNT* 35.3 (2013): 207–41.

———. "4QMMT and Paul: Justification, 'Works,' and Eschatology." Pages 104–32 in *History and Exegesis: New Testament Essays in Honor of Dr. E. Earle Ellis for His 80th Birthday*. Edited by Aang-Won (Aaron) Son. New York and London: T&T Clark, 2006.

Yinger, Kent L. *The New Perspective on Paul*. Eugene, OR: Wipf & Stock, 2011.

Yule, George. "Luther's Understanding of Justification by Grace Alone in Terms of Catholic Christology." Pages 87–112 in *Luther: Theologian for Catholics and Protestants*. Edited by George Yule. Edinburgh: T&T Clark, 1985.

Zachman, Randall. *The Assurance of Faith: Conscience in the Theology of Martin Luther and John Calvin*. Louisville: Westminster John Knox, 2005.

———. *Image and Word in the Theology of John Calvin*. South Bend: University of Notre Dame, 2007.

Zemon Davis, Natalie. *The Gift in Sixteenth Century France*. Madison: University of Wisconsin Press, 2000.

Ziegler, Philip G. "Some Remarks on Apocalyptic in Modern Christian Theology." Pages 199–216 in *Paul and the Apocalyptic Imagination*. Edited by Ben C. Blackwell, John K. Goodrich, and Jason Matson. Minneapolis: Fortress, 2016.

Index of Authors

Index of Subjects

Abraham, 9, 16n10, 85–86, 89–90, 93–94, 119, 158–63, 168, 184–86, 227, 251, 271–72, 325, 333, 337–38, 340, 351, 356n96, 367, 375, 386n52, 389, 398–422

Adam, 155, 194–95, 226–27, 288, 338, 390

adoption, 85, 278, 302–6, 317, 398, 402

Agricola, Johannes: the antinomian controversy, 130–32, 244

anthropology, Pauline, 7, 104–14, 328–32, 359–60

antinomian controversy, 130–32, 244

Antioch, incident at, 13–20, 142–45, 347–48, 357

apocalyptic: Calvin's exegesis, 292n94, 314–15; Luther's exegesis, 176, 179–83, 187–88, 194–95, 197–98, 201, 204, 214; Luther scholarship, 4, 178–79, 201, 206, 331; Pauline scholarship (recent), 4, 7, 9, 178, 329–32, 332–37, 338n51, 359–60, 369, 373n22, 387–91, 408, 416

Apology of the Augsburg Confession, 162, 166–67, 230, 236

Aquinas, Thomas: faith, 85–87; grace, 81–84, 180; justification, 84–87, 90, 292; Luther's understanding of, 97, 100–101; nominalism, his

misinterpretation in, 90; as Pauline interpreter, 81–87; predestination, 84; Trent, the council of, 103; union with Christ/participation in Christ, 82–83; works, 84–87

assurance of salvation, 102, 133–34, 136, 160–61, 176, 188, 190–91, 233, 261, 272, 277–78, 280, 303, 317, 370, 391–92, 413

atonement, 215, 228, 232–33, 238, 245, 248–51, 274, 287, 397. *See also* sacrifice of Christ

Augustine: Antioch, the incident at, 14, 19; Calvin, his influence upon, 99–100, 296n100; the conscience, 343; faith, 70, 72–73; the flesh, 77n53; grace, 70–72, 75, 150, 258; justification, 69–71, 233, 258; law, 70–71, 75–76; Luther, his influence upon 97–101, 104–6, 107n12, 116–17, 189n41; medieval Pauline interpretation, his influence upon, 78–94, 95; as Pauline interpreter, 69–78; predestination, 72; regeneration, 100; renewal, 73; repentance, 78; the righteousness of God, 63, 69–70, 245; sin, 73–74, 76–77, 104–6, 107n12, 113–14, 113n34, 332; union

Index of Scripture and Other Ancient Texts

Index of Medieval and Reformation Texts